A BREVIATE OF PARLIAMENTARY PAPERS

Parliamentary Papers Series, by P. & G. Ford

A BREVIATE OF PARLIAMENTARY PAPERS, 1900–1916.

A BREVIATE OF PARLIAMENTARY PAPERS, 1917–1939.

SELECT LIST OF BRITISH PARLIAMENTARY PAPERS, 1833–1899.

HANSARD'S CATALOGUE AND BREVIATE OF PARLIAMENTARY PAPERS, 1696–1834.

A GUIDE TO PARLIAMENTARY PAPERS.

A Breviate of
Parliamentary Papers
1940—1954
War and Reconstruction

P. FORD

Emeritus Professor of Economics

AND

G. FORD

University of Southampton

BASIL BLACKWELL

OXFORD

1961

PRINTED IN GREAT BRITAIN FOR BLACKWELL AND MOTT LTD.
BY BILLING AND SONS LIMITED, GUILDFORD AND LONDON
AND BOUND AT THE KEMP HALL BINDERY

PREFACE

THIS volume follows the same general pattern as the two previous Breviates, and aims at making accessible the material contained in the Papers issued during the years of war and reconstruction from 1940 to 1954. In this period the far-reaching aims of Government in war and peace, new ways of preparing plans and new bodies making them, have made it necessary to include new classes of Papers. Not only Reports of formal enquiries, but White Papers, Explanatory Memoranda attached to Bills, and Papers issued by public corporations but not in the Sessional Series, or published by the Stationery Office or even listed in any other single place, have had to be reviewed, in order to render intelligible the intense intellectual effort made by the British people to understand, rehabilitate and transform their society.

We wish to thank the University of Southampton for giving us the help and facilities we needed to continue the work.

We are very grateful for the support and assistance we have been given by Miss D. M. Marshallsay, B.A., A.L.A., Librarian to The Ford Collection, particularly for her work on the citations and indexes, and by Mrs. P. Dunn and Mrs. P. Powell, who have been responsible for all the typing involved.

Our thanks are also due to the Printer for the way he has set up this volume.

CONTENTS

INTRODUCTION ix

ABBREVIATIONS xv

SUBJECT CLASSIFICATION OF PAPERS xvii

SUBJECT LIST OF PAPERS xxi

BREVIATE I

APPENDICES 502
    I. List of Memoranda on the Procedure and Privileges of the House of
    Commons by Officers of the House and others.
    II. Select List of Annual Reports, 1940–1954.

INDEXES 507
    1. Alphabetical Index of Titles.
    2. Index to Chairmen and Authors.

NOTE

This volume contains

Sessional papers from 1940 to 1954–55
Non-Parliamentary Papers from 1940 to 1954

IN certain cases papers issued after these dates are included when they are necessary to complete the account of investigations concerned within the period. For an explanation of the principles of selection readers should consult the Introduction to the *Breviate of Parliamentary Papers, 1917–39*, especially pp. xii, xiii.

INTRODUCTION

'RECONSTRUCTION', in 1918 and 1945, meant not only the adjustment of a distorted economy and its physical rehabilitation, but infusing it with new social purposes. The success with which the plans were carried through after 1945 contrast sharply with the failure and disillusionment after 1918. That failure was certainly not due to lack of well-thought-out plans, but few of them were implemented at the time, some not till after 1945, and others not at all. Even the housing programme of 300,000 houses in 1918, proposed by the Salisbury Committee as a first instalment of the proposed Homes fit for Heroes, turned into only 276,000 completed by 1923. The generous enthusiasms and all the planning, made vivid by implications in the quality of satire in Housman's *Mr. Trimblerigg*, had little to show for them. But between 1939 and 1945 there was a transformation of public attitude: some of the inhibitions on our social thinking and will were shed, and the 'White Paper' plans of the Coalition Government were partly the outcome of that release of mind.

What is the best method of investigating the problems of and formulating plans for 'Reconstruction' after war? In 1917 several experiments led to the conclusion that neither Ministers nor Government Departments harassed with the tasks of war administration could give them adequate attention, and that in any case each Department would tend to approach them in the light of its own special sphere of duties. What was wanted was a body of persons free from the distractions of war and normal departmental work, without particular executive responsibility and therefore able to give Reconstruction undivided attention, to gather proposals and to make enquiries and prepare schemes on its own initiative. Thus the Ministry of Reconstruction was established, and the membership of its many committees, set out in App. I to its first Annual Report (1918 Cd. 9231, xiii), shows what a wealth of public experience and special knowledge it was able to draw upon. Many of its Reports were notable and stimulating Papers, e.g. *Currency and Foreign Exchanges After the War, Financial Facilities, The Machinery of Government, The Acquisition and Valuation of Land for Public Purposes, Agricultural Policy, Electric Power Supply, Commercial and Industrial Policy, Adult Education.* But this form of organisation did not commend itself to everyone. The critics argued that it tended to transfer initiative from the Departments already possessing practical knowledge of the matters in hand and might even involve them in implementing plans, drawn up by others, which their experience led them to regard as inadequate or impracticable. That some Departments occasionally established committees on topics which were also being considered by the Ministry of Reconstruction, so that there were two reports on the same subject, may be regarded as no more than the confusion which arises in the strenuous circumstances of war. However, with the return to peace the Departments which would be responsible for final action resumed their responsibilities and the Ministry came to an end.

In World War II the thinking on reconstruction was differently organised. Though for a time there was a Minister without Portfolio, part of whose duties was a general care of it, no separate Ministry was created and over a wide field the initiative remained with the Departments, which drew on outside experience either through the membership of such committees as they set up or by strengthening their staffs by appointments from outside. Some of their studies were in this particular sense internal to the Departments, and the Papers resulting from this process often took a different form from those issued in 1917-18. Proposals as drafted by the Departments went through the appropriate machinery to the Cabinet and as modified by them were issued in a brief 'White Paper' giving the Government proposals, unaccompanied by formal evidence. Some of them represent the Government's final conclusions after considering a report by another body; e.g. those on *Social Insurance* and *Control of Land Use* follow the Beveridge report on *Social Insurance and Allied Services* and the Uthwatt report on *Compensation and Betterment* respectively. Others, like that on the *Distribution of Industry* derived from several years of discussion on the ways of dealing with depressed areas and from the Barlow Commission on the *Distribution of the Industrial Population*. The vital Paper on *Employment Policy*, on the other hand, was not preceded by any formal committee report, but was worked out within the governmental organisation and summed up years of discussions amongst economists and others which centred round the Keynesian theory.

Other plans had their origin with bodies or organisations a little outside the Parliamentary or Departmental system of inquiry. (*a*) In 1917-18 the Board of Trade appointed a number of committees to consider the position of various trades after the war, e.g. the electrical trades, engineering trades, iron and steel trades, the members consisting mainly of persons connected with them. But in 1945 the Government, already committed to a programme of nationalising coal, power and transport, for some of those trades which were to remain in the sphere of private enterprise set up tri-partite working parties, composed of representatives of employers, employees and the Government, to prepare plans for re-organising them to improve their efficiency and amenities.

(*b*) For some of the plans put into operation—the nationalisation of coal, transport and electricity—there is in this period neither a committee report nor a White Paper—though there was a remarkable report on coal-mining by a technical committee—because the principles and many details had already been decided by the political party organisations. There were indeed many relevant Parliamentary reports on them between 1917-21, but the proposals are found in *Labour and the New Social Order*, 1918, though their immediate origin is *Let us Face the Future*, the Labour Party programme for the 1945 election. In such cases the relevant paper is an explanatory and financial memorandum either printed with a Bill, e.g. the *Transport Bill* (1946-47, Bill 12), *The Coal Industry Nationalisation Bill* (1945-46, Bill 62), or issued separately, e.g. the *Agriculture Bill* (1946-47 Cmd. 6996).

(*c*) At a later date some of the independent, financially autonomous corporations, such as the National Coal Board and the Transport Commission, themselves began to make plans, largely independently of the Parliamentary processes, such as the *Plan for Coal*, the Fleck Report on *Organisation*, and the Transport Commission's proposals on *Canals*. Though such papers may deal with vital matters over which Parliament has some ultimate and continuing responsibility and they link up with earlier Parliamentary and Departmental enquiries, they may be published independently. Even more striking is the Guillebaud Report on *Railway Pay*, important not only for those engaged on railways, but in its repercussions on other industries; it was issued independently by the Special Joint Committee on the Machinery of Negotiation for Railway Staff.

(*d*) Finally, account has to be taken of wage awards and settlements, because of the cumulative effect of *ad hoc* decisions relating to individual industries and occupations on the labour market and their contribution to the conditions in which the full employment policy had to be carried out, as well as to the generation of an inflationary spiral which called forth a succession of White Papers.

Although in the Second World War we did not suffer the loss of life which characterised the first and many of the problems of adjustment after total war were not as novel as in 1918, in some ways the task was more difficult. It was plainly stated in the White Paper of 1947 on *Economic Considerations affecting the Relations between Employers and Employed*. As a result of the efforts of the preceding seven years we had sold half our external assets and were still meeting deficits in our balance of payments by external credits. External borrowing could not continue, we had proceeded to establish many schemes of social improvement, but had to make up arrears and improve our standards by our own efforts. This required improved productivity in British industry. Further, both during and after the war, combined efforts with Allies meant that British economic and financial policy was increasingly formulated within the framework of inter-allied and international arrangements such as *Lease-Lend, Mutual Aid*, the *Marshall Plan, Bretton Woods*, worked out by international meetings of experts and presented to Parliament for formal approval in the Papers listed in Section III. It was in this setting that the great schemes of social improvement were launched and upon the successful solution of the central problem that their practicability eventually depended.

In 1918, to meet the wild disorder of international currencies, inflation was handled on the recommendations of the Cunliffe Committee 1918–19 in the light of a view of monetary policy then current, while the difficulties which followed the return to gold after the Bradbury Committee's Report of 1925 (Cmd. 6393) have been attributed to a mixture of inappropriate monetary policy, lack of appreciation of the degree of adjustment imposed upon an over-rigid British industry and to the weakening of the gold standard by a change in London's position as an international financial centre. Whatever the final assessment of these events, our inability to find ways of putting a million unemployed into work, the bitterly contested expedients of transitional payments, means tests, the calculations of the number of man-weeks of employment created by public works, and the protests in *Road to Wigan Pier, Love on the Dole*, and *Memoirs of the Unemployed*, arose from an inadequate employment theory. The official or commonly accepted version was stated in a Memo. on *Certain Proposals Relating to Unemployment* (1928–29 Cmd. 3391, vi) and in the Balfour Committee's Reports on *Industry and Trade*, · Vol. 1, Chap. 6. The researches and vigorous debates amongst economists, centring round Keynes' *General Theory*, 1936, eventually made it possible to find a way out, set forth in the White Paper on *Employment Policy*, 1944. It was this production of a workable theory which enabled us to spend our intellectual and material resources on constructive plans, instead of using them to repair the spiritual and material wastes of unemployment by doles.

But in the theoretical model involved certain quantities—national income, savings, investment, consumption, the foreign balance—were fundamental and it was the development of the statistical techniques of the annual statements of *National Income and Expenditure* which made it possible to give the kind of estimate of these which were necessary before policy could be based on them. In the *Economic Survey* for 1947 an endeavour was made to bring this knowledge and theory together in the service of economic planning. Two sets of budgets, an 'economic budget' and 'man-power budget', were to be fitted together as its basis. Here the theory underwent some education by practice. As the war-time control of labour ended and there was more free trading and restriction-free consumption, the Surveys took on the character rather less of planning and more of forecasting, but by giving us an idea of the relationship between the size of the various components, made it possible to see the significance of *ad hoc* industrial targets and social expenditure to the economy as a whole. And they brought out the problem of inflation.

The schemes for social insurance, the national health service and legal aid exemplify the variety of pressures which changed the public attitude. In the financial and intellectual conditions of 1924, Beveridge in *Insurance for all and Everything*, had proposed a modest, unified scheme, arguing that if unemployment returned to normal the problem of complete social insurance required thought rather than money. It was an indication of the change of atmosphere that the new scheme, so much bolder and more extensive, was put forward when our resources were being drained by war. The Committee on *Social Insurance and the Allied Services* was, like that of 1904 on *Physical Deterioration*, which also made a large number of imaginative and sweeping proposals, a committee of officials, but unlike it had a chairman, Beveridge, who alone became responsible for and signed the Report. His mastery of principles and methods was such that this gathered together and summed up—as the Memos. of evidence of the National Council of Women, Trades Union Congress, P.E.P., the Liverpool Shipowners' Association exemplify—the experience of experts, practitioners, university researchers, social workers and claimants for a quarter of a century.

The proposals for a *National Health Service* (1944) were in some respects a reversal of the Act of 1911. This had provided only a low grade of medical care in minor ailments for insured persons and not others, made no provision for surgical treatment, expert services or access to hospitals. The main lines of advance had already been pointed out: a salaried medical service for Ireland, by the Vice-Regal Commission of 1906 and committees of 1913 and 1920; a complete severance of medical provision from the limitations of cash benefits by Newsholme in 1918, and in *Public Health and Insurance*, 1924; the re-organisation of the hospitals, by the consultative councils of 1920, and the abolition of the approved society system, by the Minority of the Royal Commission on *Health Insurance*, 1926. The conservatism and strongly entrenched interests which had obstructed these changes had to be swept away and some hard bargaining faced. In contrast, while the problems of social insurance and the health service had been canvassed for a considerable period, the stimulus to develop voluntary legal aid into a more extensive national service came from two immediate practical problems: the great increase in the demand for it after the personal upheaval during the war, and the decline in the number of solicitors, from 17,000 in 1939 to 7,000 in 1944, able to give it.

By 1945 Departments and Ministers had already approved and were in some degree committed to publicly announced plans. Further, the Economic Section of the War Cabinet and the Statistical Office had been developed so that whether in war or peace schemes could at least be scrutinised for mutual consistency, through the procedure described by H. Morrison in *Government and Parliament*, even if Ministers for political and other reasons decided, as they sometimes did, to ignore the advice. But tidy procedure does not always guarantee the success of a plan. However careful the preparation, new ideas, like ships, may have to face the perils of storm and to receive severe buffetings before reaching port; and some may be lost. It is illuminating to study the differences between the Beveridge Report and the two White Papers on *Social Insurance*, between the Barlow and Scott Reports and those on the *Distribution of Industry* and between the Report on *Leasehold* and the White Paper on the same topic; or to trace the evolution of the idea of 'floating value' from the reports on the *Acquisition and Valuation of Land for Public Purposes* of 1918 through the Barlow and Uthwatt Reports to the White Paper on *Land Use*.

As the period progresses the Papers begin to show after-thoughts which indicate that certain weaknesses of theory had not been fully uncovered or that the plans had not been envisaged in effective relation to one another. The easy assumption that the bigger the organisation the greater the economies to be derived from co-ordination led to ill-consequences which called forth the Fleck Report on *Organisation* in coal mining, the Herbert Committee on the *Electricity Supply Industry*, 1956, and repeated attempts to provide a flexible framework for the Transport Commission. Proposed increases in the numbers of nurses, mental health workers, midwives and medical auxiliaries competed for the same supply of recruits; while the McNair, Roseveare and Stewart Committees on the supply of teachers and youth leaders show that the total demand for recruits to this and other professions substantially exceeded the total number of available school leavers.

It took some time for the full implications of a high and stable level of employment to be realised. Beveridge, following the Government Actuary, had based the financial provisions of his plan on a possible unemployment level of $8\frac{1}{2}$ per cent and this figure re-appeared in the Financial Report on the Bill, 1946. In his *Full Employment in a Free Society*, also published in 1944, he had claimed that it could be reduced to 3 per cent. But the Paper on *Employment Policy*, 1944, pointed out the dangers of inflation which could arise from unrestrained sectional wage bargaining in these conditions (paras. 49–54) as did Beveridge (paras. 283–287) and this was the theme of successive White Papers from 1951 to 1956 whose effects, however, were temporary only. The inflationary spiral which followed did some injury to two other parts of the reconstruction programme—it eroded the real value of the standard insurance benefits, while the difficulties it caused for the housing programme are vividly recorded in a series of Papers. The Dudley Committee of 1944 assumed that steps would be taken to keep building costs down to 30 per cent above the level of 1938–39. In fact, the programme had to be carried against the continually rising costs investigated by the Girdwood Committee in 1948, 1950 and 1952, and a level of productivity substantially below that of 1938–39; while the decision to subsidise the house and not the tenant both opened the way to group pressures and resistances which raised costs, and tended to fix in the public mind rigid notions about rents. Not all the research of the technical committees or enquiries in productivity were able to eliminate the consequences of the basic failure to control the price level.

English society at the end of the half century covered by the three Breviates was very different from that at the commencement of the period. During that time we have found means, as a result of leadership from above and democratic pressure from below, of protecting the aged, the sick and the unemployed from the worst insecurities and have been opening the way to new opportunities for talents of all classes. It was possible for Masterman to write in 1909, in the *Condition of England*: 'we know little or nothing today of the great multitude of people who inhabit these islands', though this was not true as it stands even when it was written. At the other end of the scale was the wealthy, brilliant and cultivated society described in Osbert Sitwell's chapter 'Before the War' in *Great Morning*, and in the percipient account of the essential unity and way of life of the governing classes given by Prince Lichnowsky, the German Ambassador, in *My Mission to London* (1918). Sufficient comment on these changes is found in a comparison of Sitwell's account with the Report on *Houses of Outstanding Historic or Architectural Interest*, 1950, and in the fact that the reconstruction programme of 1945 was carried through by a political party drawing its main strength from working-class votes. Some of the progress was the result of the 'unguided' social forces of technical invention, enterprise, saving, alteration in the rate of growth of population and such changes in the climate of opinion as these generated. But the half century includes three special periods of exceptional intellectual effort, two successful, one unsuccessful. The reading of the Papers shows how their effectiveness varied with the manner in which the processes of investigation, formulation of theory and invention of institutions were interwoven.

ABBREVIATIONS

The following abbreviations have been used:

Committee	Cttee.
Select Committee	Sel. Cttee.
Joint Select Committee	Jt. Sel. Cttee.
Select Committee of House of Lords	Sel. Cttee. HL.
Departmental Committee	Dept. Cttee.
Inter-Departmental Committee	Inter-Dept. Cttee.
Commission	Com.
Royal Commission	R. Com.
Board	Bd.
Report	Rep.
Proceedings	Proc.
Minutes of Evidence	Mins. of ev.
Appendix	App.
Chairman	Ch.
Lord	L.
Delete	del.
Appointed	apptd.
Signed	sgd.
Ordered to be Printed	o.p.
Presented	pres.
Department of Scientific and Industrial Research	D.S.I.R.
London County Council	L.C.C.
University Grants Committee	U.G.C.

SUBJECT CLASSIFICATION OF PAPERS

PAGE

I. MACHINERY OF GOVERNMENT I
    1. The Crown I
    2. Channel Islands 2
    3. Parliament 3
    4. Ministers 24
    5. Organisation of Departments 24
    6. Civil Service 32
    7. (a) Local Government 39
       (b) Local Taxation and Financial Administration . . 47
    8. London 53

II. NATIONAL FINANCE 58

III. MONETARY AND ECONOMIC POLICY, FINANCIAL INSTITUTIONS 73

IV. AGRICULTURE AND FOOD SUPPLY 75
    1. General: Production, Supply, Output . . . 75
    2. Decontrol; Marketing in General 91
    3. Production and Marketing of Particular Products . 94
    4. Discases, Wild Animals 106
    5. Forestry 109
    6. Drainage, River Pollution, Coast Protection . . 111
    7. Fishing 115

V. TRADE AND INDUSTRY 118
    1. War-time Industrial Policy. 118
    2. Distribution of Industry and of the Industrial Population 121
    3. Trade Policy Generally, Industrial Efficiency . . 124
    4. Statistical 129
    5. Particular Industries and Trades 131
    6. Monopolies and Restrictive Practices . . . 153
    7. Company and Commercial Law and Practice . . 164
    8. Weights and Measures 167

VI. COAL, FUEL, POWER, WATER 169
    1. Fuel Generally 169
    2. Coal 172
    3. Oil and Petrol 184
    4. Electricity 184
    5. Gas 188
    6. Atomic Energy 189
    7. Water 190

VII. TRANSPORT 193
    1. Railways, Canals, before Nationalisation . . . 193
    2. The Nationalised Transport System 194

PAGE

3. Roads, Road Traffic, Ferries 200
4. Sea Transport 206
5. Air Transport 210

VIII A. Post Office, Telegraphy 217
1. Post Office 217
2. Telegraphy 218

VIII B. Broadcasting, the Press 219

IX. Inventions, Patents, Copyright 226

X. Labour 229
1. Manpower, The Supply of Labour 229
2. Employment, Wages Policy, Cost of Living . . 232
3. Industrial Relations, Disputes, Wages Councils . . 238
4. Wages and Conditions in Particular Employments
    (other than Wages Councils) 249
5. Rehabilitation, Resettlement 260
6. Employment of Women 263
7. Juveniles 266
8. Factory Regulation: Safety, Health, Hours of Work . 268
9. Migration 279
10. Professions 279

XI. Social Security 281
1. Unemployment Insurance and Assistance . . . 281
2. Social Insurance, Family Allowances 283
3. National Insurance 290
4. National Assistance 296
5. Workmen's Compensation, Industrial Injuries . . 297
6. Pensions 302

XII. Health 304
1. General: War Problems, Health Services, Hospitals . 304
    (i) War Problems 304
    (ii) Health Services 306
    (iii) Hospitals 312
2. Medical Professions 317
    (i) Medical Practitioners, Dentists, etc. . . . 317
    (ii) Nurses 324
    (iii) Other Services 330
3. Particular Problems and Diseases 333
4. Drugs, Food Purity 344

XIII A. Housing 346
1. Housing 346
2. Rents 360
3. House Management, Housing Estates . . . 360

XIII B. Town and Country Planning 366

PAGE

XIV. EDUCATION 382
    1.   General Policy, Schools 382
    2. (a) Handicapped Children, Curriculum, Examinations . 398
      (b) Particular Vocations 406
    3.   Teachers, Youth Leaders: Supply, Training, Salaries . 416
    4. (a) Universities 421
      (b) Scientific and Social Research 427
    5.   Museums, Libraries 429

XV A. POPULATION 435

XV B. SOCIAL PROBLEMS 437
    1. Evacuation of Women and Children . . . 437
    2. Child Care, Homeless Children, Adoption, the Cinema 439
    3. Charities 447
    4. Betting 449

XVI. LEGAL ADMINISTRATION, POLICE, LAW 451
    1. Legal Administration, Procedure, Legal Aid . . 451
    2. Police 465
    3. Prisons, Prisoners, Punishment, Probation . . 471
    4. Legal Problems arising out of War, War Damage . 482
    5. Law of Property, Succession 486
    6. Nationality, International Law 493
    7. Law Revision and Reform 494
    8. Marriage and Divorce 498
    9. Miscellaneous Regulatory Powers . . . 500

SUBJECT LIST OF PAPERS

I. MACHINERY OF GOVERNMENT

1. The Crown

PAGE

1952–53	Cmd. 8748	The Title of the Sovereign	1
1947–48	(18)	Civil List	1
1951–52	(224)	Civil List	1

2. Channel Islands

1946–47	Cmd. 7074	Proposed Reforms in the Channel Islands	2
1948–49	Cmd. 7805	Island of Alderney	2

3. Parliament

1947–48	Cmd. 7380	Parliament Bill, 1947	3
1942–43	Cmd. 6408	Electoral Machinery	3
1943–44	Cmd. 6534	Electoral Reform and Redistribution of Seats	4
1943–44	Cmd. 6543	—— Letters	4
1944–45	Cmd. 6581	Postal Voting for the Forces, Seamen and War Workers Abroad	4
1944–45	Cmd. 6606	Electoral Law Reform. Int. Rep.	5
1947–48	Cmd. 7286	—— Final Rep.	5
1946–47	Cmd. 7004	Electoral Registration	5
1945–54		Boundary Commissions	5
1940–41	(120)	Offices or Places of Profit under the Crown	6
1945–46	(3–1)	Elections	7
1945–46	(71–1)	Elections. 1st Rep.	7
1945–46	(92–1)	—— 2nd Rep.	7
1950	(68–1)	Election of a Member (Clergyman of the Church of Ireland)	7
1950	Cmd. 8067	Rev. James Godfrey MacManaway	8
1952–53	(200)	Clergy Disqualification	8
1945–46	(93–1)	Members' Expenses	8
1946–47	(110)	Members' Fund	8
1953–54	(72)	Members' Expenses	8
1940–41	(5)	Conduct of a Member	9
1947–48	(20)	Budget Disclosure	9
1947–48	(104)	Chairman of Ways and Means (Personal Explanation)	10
1943–44	(80)	Public Petitions	10
1951–52	(286)	Public Petitions	10
1945–46	(9–1)	Procedure. 1st Rep.	11
1945–46	(58–1)	—— 2nd Rep.	11
1945–46	(189–1)	—— 3rd Rep.	11
1947–48	(192)	Standing Orders (Revision)	12
1947–48	(191)	Hybrid Bills (Procedure in Committee)	12
1945–46	(HL. 28)	Private Bill Standing Orders	12
1952–53	(HL. 113)	Standing Orders of the House	13
1954–55	(139–1)	Private Bill Procedure	13
1944–1953		Statutory Rules and Orders, Statutory Instruments	13

PAGE

1952–53	(310–1)	Delegated Legislation	14
1951–52	(332–1)	Nationalised Industries	15
1952–53	(235)	Nationalised Industries	16
1941–1955		Privileges	16
1940–1954		Publications and Debates	21
1941–42	(64)	Disposal and Custody of Documents. 1st Rep.	21
1941–42	(113)	—— 2nd Rep.	21
1942–43	(93)	—— Rep.	22
1944–45	(98)	Library (House of Commons). Special Rep.	22
1945–46	(35, 99–1)	—— 1st, 2nd Reps.	22
1943–44	(109)	House of Commons (Rebuilding)	22
1943–44	(116–1)	Accommodation in the Palace of Westminster	23
1944–45	(64–1)	—— Rep.	23
1952–53	(309)	House of Commons Accommodation	23
1953–54	(184)	—— Rep.	23

4. Ministers

| 1948–49 | Cmd. 7616 | Allegations Reflecting on the Official Conduct of Ministers of the Crown and other Public Servants | 24 |

5. Organisation of Departments

1941–42	Cmd. 6337	Office of the Minister of Production	24
1942–43	Cmd. 6420	Proposals for the Reform of the Foreign Service	25
1946	Non-Parl.	Organisation of the Colonial Service	25
1946	Non-Parl.	Post-War Training for the Colonial Service	25
1944–45	Cmd. 6576	Higher Appointments. See *Professions*	26
1945–46	Cmd. 6923	Central Organisation for Defence	26
1947–48	Cmd. 7308	Scottish Affairs	26
1953–54	Cmd. 9212	Scottish Affairs	26
1948–49	Cmd. 7836	Home Information Services	28
1953–54	Cmd. 9138	Overseas Information Services	28
1950	Non-Parl.	Survey Staffs	28
1950–51	Cmd. 8278	Ministry of Materials	29
1951	Non-Parl.	Organisation of the Ministry of Agriculture and Fisheries	29
1952–53	Cmd. 8842	The Ministry of Pensions. Proposed Transfer of Functions	30
1952–53	Cmd. 8883	Amalgamation of the Ministry of Transport and the Ministry of Civil Aviation	30
1941–42	Cmd. 6393	Allocation to Messrs. George Wimpey and Co. Ltd., during the War, of Government Contracts in Scotland	30
1950	Cmd. 7904	Intermediaries	30
1953–54	Cmd. 9176	Disposal of Land at Crichel Down	31
1953–54	Cmd. 9220	Civil Servants	32

6. Civil Service

| 1943–44 | Cmd. 6525 | Training of Civil Servants | 32 |
| 1943–44 | Cmd. 6567 | Recruitment to Established Posts in the Civil Service during the Reconstruction Period | 32 |

			PAGE
1951	Non-Parl.	Use of the Civil Service Selection Board in the Reconstruction Competitions	33
1945–46	Cmd. 6679	The Scientific Civil Service	33
1945–46	Cmd. 6680	Administrative Class of the Civil Service	33
1945–46	Cmd. 6886	Marriage Bar in the Civil Service	34
1945–46	Cmd. 6942	Pensionability of Unestablished Civil Service	34
1948–49	Cmd. 7635	Higher Civil Service Remuneration	34
1951	Non-Parl.	Organisation, Structure and Remuneration of the Works Group of Professional Civil Servants	34
1951	Non-Parl.	Pay and Organisation of Civil Service Medical Staffs	35
1952	Non-Parl.	Organisation, Structure and Remuneration of the Professional Accountant Class in the Civil Service	35
1948–49	Cmd. 7718	Political Activities of Civil Servants	35
1952–53	Cmd. 8783	Political Activities of Civil Servants	37
1955–56	Cmd. 9715	Security	37
1953–54	Cmd. 9220	Civil Servants. See *Organisation of Departments*	38
1955–56	Cmd. 9613	Civil Service	38

7. (a) Local Government

1941–42	Cmd. 6356	Working of the Financial Provisions of the Air Raid Precautions Act, 1937, under Section 10 of that Act	39
1944–45	Cmd. 6579	Local Government in England and Wales during the Period of Reconstruction	39
1946–47	(82)	Local Government Boundary Commission	40
1947–48	(86)	—— Rep.	41
1948–49	(150)	Rep.	42
1943–1953		Scottish Local Government Law Consolidation	42
1946–47	Cmd. 7126	Expenses of Members of Local Authorities	43
1950	Cmd. 7870	Local Government Manpower	44
1951–52	Cmd. 8421	—— 2nd Rep.	44
1950	Cmd. 7951	Scottish Local Government Manpower	44
1951–52	Cmd. 8658	—— 2nd Rep.	44
1947	Non-Parl.	Publicity for Local Government. Int. Rep.	44
1950	Non-Parl.	—— Final Rep.	44
1947	Non-Parl.	Transfer of Members of the National Fire Service to Fire Brigades	45
1952–53	Cmd. 8708	Publicity and Recruitment for the Civil Defence and Allied Services	45
1953–54	Cmd. 9131	—— 2nd Rep.	46
1943–44	Cmd. 6522	Newcastle-upon-Tyne Inquiry	46

7. (b) Local Taxation and Financial Administration

1943–44	Cmd. 6526	Scottish Rating System. 1st Rep. Valuation and Rating of Hydro-Electric Undertakings in Scotland	47
1944–45	Cmd. 6595	—— Rep.	47
1944	Non-Parl.	Valuation for Rates, 1939	48
1945–46	(143)	Railways (Valuation for Rating) Bill	49
1945–46	Cmd. 6765	Water Rates and Charges	49

PAGE

1952 Non-Parl. Rating of Site Values 49
1953 Non-Parl. Operation of the Exchequer Equalisation Grants in England and Wales 50
1953–54 Cmd. 9270 Investigation into the Operation of the Exchequer Equalisation Grants to Local Authorities in England and Wales 51
1953–54 Cmd. 9244 Scottish Valuation and Rating 51
1955–56 Cmd. 9606 Valuation and Rating in Scotland 52
1953 Non-Parl. Operation of the Exchequer Equalisation Grants in Scotland 52
1953–54 (6) Equalisation Grant in Scotland. Investigation under Section 30, Local Govt. Act, 1948 52
1955 Non-Parl. Operation of the Exchequer Equalisation Grants in Scotland 52

8. London

1948 Non-Parl. Greater London Water Supplies 53
1946 Non-Parl. Railway (London Plan). Rep. 53
1948 Non-Parl. —— Final Rep. 53
1949 Non-Parl. London Plan 54
1949 Non-Parl. London Planning Administration 54
1951 Non-Parl. London Traffic Congestion 55
1953 Non-Parl. Car Parking in the Inner Area of London 56
1952–53 Cmd. 8804 Taxicab Service 56
1952–53 Cmd. 8902 London's Airports. See *Air Transport* 56
1946–47 Cmd. 7094 Regent's Park Terraces 56
1957 Non-Parl. Future of the Regent's Park Terraces 57
1946–1952 Bills relating to Particular Sites, etc. 57
1950–51 Cmd. 8277 Documents Relating to Festival Gardens Ltd. 57
1954–55 Cmd. 9467 A New Queen's Hall 58
1948 Non-Parl. Birds in London 58

II. NATIONAL FINANCE

1941–42 Cmd. 6348 Taxation of Weekly Wage Earners 58
1942–43 Cmd. 6469 New System for the Taxation of Weekly Wage Earners 59
1944–45 Cmd. 6615 Hydrocarbon Oil Duties 59
1948–49 Cmd. 7728 Taxation and Overseas Minerals 60
1950 Cmd. 7969 The Form of Government Accounts 60
1951–52 Cmd. 8453 Draft Customs and Excise Bill 61
1951–52 (137) Customs and Excise Bill 61
1950–51 Cmd. 8295 Estate Duty and Family Businesses 61
1951–52 Cmd. 8452 Purchase Tax/Utility 62
1952–53 Cmd. 8830 Purchase Tax (Valuation) 63
1952–53 Cmd. 8784 Tax-paid Stocks 64
1950–51 Cmd. 8189 Taxation of Trading Profits 65
1952–53 Cmd. 8761 Taxation of Profits and Income. 1st Rep. 66
1953–54 Cmd. 9105 —— 2nd Rep. 67
1955–56 Cmd. 9474 —— Final Rep. 68
1953–54 Cmd. 9063 Taxation Treatment of Provisions for Retirement 71
1940–1952 National Expenditure. Public Accounts 72
1951–52 Cmd. 8609 Scottish Financial and Trade Statistics 72

III. MONETARY AND ECONOMIC POLICY, FINANCIAL INSTITUTIONS

			PAGE
1941–1956		Papers on International and Home Monetary and Economic Policy Generally	73
1944–45	Cmd. 6645	Capital Issues Control	73
1945–46	Cmd. 6726	Investment (Control and Guarantees) Bill	74
1946–47	Cmd. 6954	Exchange Control Bill	74
1947–48	Cmd. 7268	Capital Investment in 1948	74
1950–51	Cmd. 8318	Control of Dividends	74
1945–46	(Bill 9)	Bank of England Bill	75
1945–46	(24)	Bank of England Bill	75

IV. AGRICULTURE AND FOOD SUPPLY

1. General: Production, Supply, Output

1942–43	Cmd. 6421	Agricultural Research in Great Britain	75
1943	Non-Parl.	Agricultural Improvement Council for England	76
1951	Non-Parl.	—— 2nd Rep.	76
1943–44	Cmd. 6498	Hill Sheep Farming in England and Wales	77
1943–44	Cmd. 6494	Hill Sheep Farming in Scotland	77
1943	Non-Parl.	Principles and Objectives of Long Term Agricultural Policy	78
1946	Non-Parl.	National Farm Survey of England and Wales (1941–43)	79
1946	Non-Parl.	Agricultural Survey of Scotland	79
1946–47	Cmd. 6996	Agriculture Bill	79
1946–47	Cmd. 7072	Post-War Contribution of British Agriculture to the Saving of Foreign Exchange	80
1947–48	Cmd. 7278	Needs of the Armed Forces for Land for Training and other Purposes	80
1948	Non-Parl.	Agricultural Valuation	80
1950	Non-Parl.	—— 2nd Rep.	81
1947	Non-Parl.	Scotland's Marginal Farms	81
1948	Non-Parl.	Scottish Farm Rents and Estate Expenditure	82
1944–45	Cmd. 6577	Land Settlement in Scotland	82
1949	Non-Parl.	Smallholdings	83
1950	Non-Parl.	Allotments	84
1950	Non-Parl.	Domestic Food Production	84
1953–54	Cmd. 9091	Crofting Conditions	85
1953–54	Cmd. 9014	Rural Wales	86
1950	Non-Parl.	Qualitative Control of Seeds	87
1951	Non-Parl.	Toxic Chemicals in Agriculture	87
1954	Non-Parl.	—— Rep. Residues in Food	88
1953	Non-Parl.	A Survey of Agricultural, Forestry, and Fishery Products in the United Kingdom and their utilisation	88
1954	Non-Parl.	Natural Resources. Rep. Use of Towns' Wastes in Agriculture	89
1944	Non-Parl.	Food Consumption Levels in the United States, Canada and the United Kingdom	89
1945–46	Cmd. 6785	World Food Shortage	90
1945–46	Cmd. 6879	—— 2nd Review.	90

1946–47   Cmd. 7030   A Plan for the Mechanised Production of   PAGE
                         Groundnuts in East and Central Africa   90
1950–51   Cmd. 8125   Future of the Overseas Food Corporation   91

2. Decontrol; Marketing in General

1945–46   Cmd. 6701   Post War Loaf   91
1947   Non-Parl.   Working of the Agricultural Marketing Acts   92
1952–53   Cmd. 8745   Decontrol of Cereals and Feeding Stuffs   93
1953–54   Cmd. 8989   Decontrol of Food and Marketing of Agricultural
                         Produce   93

3. Production and Marketing of Particular Products

1941–42   (65)   Sugar Industry Bill   94
1955–56   Cmd. 9519   Future Arrangements for the Marketing of Sugar 94
1940   Non-Parl.   Cost of Milk Distribution   94
1941–42   Cmd. 6362   Milk Policy   95
1942–43   Cmd. 6454   Measures to Improve the Quality of the Nation's
                         Milk Supply   95
1945   Non-Parl.   Freezing Point (Hortvet) Test of Milk   95
1947–48   Cmd. 7414   Milk Distribution   96
1949   Non-Parl.   Milk Services Scotland   97
1953   Non-Parl.   Quality Milk Production   98
1946   Non-Parl.   Wool Marketing   98
1947   Non-Parl.   Hops   99
1948   Non-Parl.   Co-operative Marketing of Horticultural Produce
                         in England and Wales   100
1949   Non-Parl.   Factors in the Marketing of Home-Produced
                         Apples in England and Wales   101
1950   Non-Parl.   Factors affecting the Marketing of Home-
                         Produced Tomatoes in Great Britain   101
1952   Non-Parl.   Grain Drying and Storage in Great Britain   102
1954   Non-Parl.   Costs and Efficiency of Pig Production: A
                         Comparison between England and Denmark   102
1950   Cmd. 7888   Export and Slaughter of Horses   103
1952–53   Cmd. 8925   Slaughter of Horses   103
1951   Non-Parl.   Meat Inspection   104
1953–54   Cmd. 9060   Slaughterhouses (England and Wales). Int. Rep. 105
1955–56   Cmd. 9542   —— Rep.   105
1953–54   Cmd. 9061   Slaughterhouses (Scotland). Int. Rep.   105
1954–55   Cmd. 9376   —— Rep.   106

4. Diseases, Wild Animals

1950–51   Cmd. 8266   Cruelty to Wild Animals   106
1953–54   Cmd. 9214   Foot-and-Mouth Disease   107
1953–54   Cmd. 9272   Close Seasons for Deer in Scotland   108
1954   Non-Parl.   Myxomatosis. Rep.   109
1955   Non-Parl.   —— 2nd Rep.   109

5. Forestry

1942–43   Cmd. 6447   Post-War Forest Policy   109
1943–44   Cmd. 6500   —— Supplementary Rep. Private Woodlands   110
1947–48   Cmd. 7245   New Forest   110

			PAGE
1954	Non-Parl.	Forestry. 1st Rep.	111
1955	Non-Parl.	—— 2nd Rep.	111
1949	Non-Parl.	Timber and Plywood 1949–1953. See *Trade and Industry*	111

6. Drainage, River Pollution, Coast Protection

1942–43	Cmd. 6465	Water. 3rd Rep. River Boards. See *Water*	111
1949	Non-Parl.	Prevention of River Pollution	111
1950–51	Cmd. 8111	Prevention of Pollution of Rivers and other Waters	112
1950	Cmd. 7948	Land Drainage (Scotland)	113
1953–54	Cmd. 9117	Drainage of Trade Premises	113
1951	Non-Parl.	Land Drainage in England and Wales	114
1952–53	Cmd. 8923	Coastal Flooding. Int. Rep.	115
1953–54	Cmd. 9165	—— Rep.	115

7. Fishing

1943–44	Cmd. 6503	Herring Industry	115
1946	Non-Parl.	Fisheries in Wartime, 1939-44	116
1950	Cmd. 7917	Poaching and Illegal Fishing of Salmon and Trout in Scotland	117
1953	Non-Parl.	Prevention of Pollution of the Sea by Oil	117

V. TRADE AND INDUSTRY

1. War-time Industrial Policy

1940–41	Cmd. 6258	Concentration of Production	118
1941	Non-Parl.	Retail Trade. 1st Int. Rep. Opening of New Shops and the Restriction on Categories of Goods sold in Existing Shops	118
1942	Non-Parl.	—— 2nd Int. Rep. Impact of the War on the Retail Trades in Goods other than Food	119
1943	Non-Parl.	—— 3rd Rep.	119
1941–42	Cmd. 6360	Regional Boards	119
1945	Non-Parl.	The Impact of the War on Civilian Consumption	120
1943–44	Cmd. 6564	Statistics relating to the War Effort of the United Kingdom	120

2. Distribution of Industry and of the Industrial Population

1939–40	Cmd. 6153	The Distribution of the Industrial Population	121
1943–44	Cmd. 6527	Employment Policy. See *Labour*	123
1948	Cmd. 7540	Distribution of Industry	123
1944	Non-Parl.	Welsh Reconstruction	124
1950	Cmd. 7976	Highland Development	124

3. Trade Policy Generally, Industrial Efficiency

1950	Cmd. 8048	General Agreement on Tariffs and Trade. See *Monetary and Economic Policy*	124
1952–53	Cmd. 8717	Commonwealth Economic Conference	125
1953	Non-Parl.	Bilateral Trade Negotiations	125

			PAGE
1954	Non-Parl.	Duty-Free Entry of Machinery into the United Kingdom	125
1948–49	Cmd. 7665	Industrial Productivity. 1st Rep.	126
1950	Cmd. 7991	—— 2nd Rep.	126
1946	Non-Parl.	A Central Institute of Management	127
1945–46	Cmd. 6782	Exhibitions and Fairs	127
1952–53	Cmd. 8872	Festival of Britain 1951	127
1953–54	Cmd. 9013	British Industries Fair	128
1951	Non-Parl.	Organisation and Constitution of the British Standards Institution	128
1949	Non-Parl.	Standardisation of Engineering Products	128
1937–1945		Design and the Designer in Industry	129

4. Statistical

1945–46	Cmd. 6687	Census of Production	129
1945–46	Cmd. 6764	Census of Distribution	130
1953–54	Cmd. 9276	Censuses of Production and Distribution	130
1951–52	Cmd. 8609	Scottish Financial and Trade Statistics. See *National Finance*	131

5. Particular Industries and Trades

1942	Non-Parl.	Brick Industry. 1st Rep.	131
1942	Non-Parl.	—— 2nd Rep.	131
1943	Non-Parl.	—— 3rd Rep.	132
1947	Non-Parl.	Labour Requirements in the Brick Industry	132
1943–1953		Building Studies	132
1948	Non-Parl.	Distribution of Building Materials and Components	133
1950	Non-Parl.	Building	134
1951	Non-Parl.	Productivity in House-Building. See *Housing*	135
1954	Non-Parl.	Retention Moneys on Building and Civil Engineering Contracts	135
1940–41	Cmd. 6282	Cement Production	135
1947	Non-Parl.	Cement Costs	135
1947	Non-Parl.	Welsh Slate Industry	136
1945–46	Cmd. 6748	China Clay	137
1946	Non-Parl.	Ball-Clay Industry	137
1944	Non-Parl.	Cotton Textile Mission to the United States of America	137
[1944]		Post-War Problems of the Cotton Trade	138
1946	Non-Parl.	Cotton	138
1947	Non-Parl.	Cotton Textile Machinery Industry. Int. Rep.	139
1947	Non-Parl.	—— 2nd and Final Rep.	140
1948–49	(157)	Raw Cotton Commission	140
1951–52	Cmd. 8510	Cotton Import	140
1952–53	Cmd. 8861	Cotton Import (Review)	141
1944	Non-Parl.	Tendencies to Monopoly in the Cinematograph Film Industry	141
1947–48	Cmd. 7361	British Film Institute	142
1948	Non-Parl.	Film Studio	143
1949	Non-Parl.	Film Production Costs	143
1948–49	Cmd. 7837	Distribution and Exhibition of Cinematograph Films	144

PAGE

1950   Non-Parl.   Distribution and Exhibition of Cinematograph
                            Films   146
1950–51   Cmd. 8113   Agreement between H.M's Government in the
                            U.K. and N. Ireland and the Motion
                            Picture Industry of the U.S.A.   146
1944–45   Cmd. 6615   Hydrocarbon Oil Duties. See *National Finance*   146
1951   Non-Parl.   Chemical Engineering Research   146
1945–46   Cmd. 6811   Iron and Steel Industry   147
1948–49   (Bill 1)   Iron and Steel Bill   147
1951–52   (294)   Iron and Steel Corporation of Great Britain   148
1952–53   (198)   —— Rep.   148
1951–52   Cmd. 8619   Iron and Steel Industry   148
1954–55   (49)   Development of the Iron and Steel Industry 1953
                            to 1958   149
1945–46   Cmd. 6906   Restoration Problems in the Ironstone Industry
                            in the Midlands. See *Town and Country
                            Planning*   149
1948–49   Cmd. 7732   Mineral Development   149
1952   Non-Parl.   Metals Economy   150
1950   Non-Parl.   Deterioration of Cast Iron and Spun Iron Pipes   150
1947   Non-Parl.   Motor Manufacturing Industry   150
1954   Non-Parl.   Matchwood   151
1949   Non-Parl.   Timber and Plywood 1949–1953   151
1946–1948   Working Parties on Separate Industries (17)   152

6. Monopolies and Restrictive Practices

1944   Non-Parl.   Tendencies to Monopoly in the Cinematograph
                            Film Industry. See *Particular Industries and
                            Trades*   153
1947   Non-Parl.   Cement Costs. See *Particular Industries and Trades* 153
1946   Non-Parl.   Prices of Radio Valves   153
1948   Non-Parl.   Distribution of Building Materials and Com-
                            ponents. See *Particular Industries and Trades*   154
1948–49   Cmd. 7696   Resale Price Maintenance   154
1950–51   Cmd. 8274   Resale Price Maintenance   156
1955–56   Cmd. 9504   Collective Discrimination: Exclusive Dealing,
                            Collective Boycotts, Aggregated Rebates
                            and other Discriminatory Trade Practices   156
1950–1960   Monopolies and Restrictive Practices   157
1950–51   (18)   —— Dental Goods   157
1950–51   (136)   —— Cast Iron Rainwater Goods   157
1950–51   (287)   —— Electric Lamps   157
1951–52   (209)   —— Insulated Electric Wires and Cables   158
1951–52   (296)   —— Insulin   158
1952–53   (161)   —— Supply and Export of Matches and the
                            Supply of Match-making Machinery   158
1952–53   (281)   —— Imported Timber   159
1953–54   (140)   —— Process of Calico Printing   159
1953–54   (264)   —— Buildings in the Greater London Area   160
1955–56   (56)   —— Certain Semi-Manufactures of Copper and
                            Copper-Based Alloys   160
1955–56   (133)   —— Pneumatic Tyres   160
1955–56   (222)   —— Sand and Gravel in Central Scotland   161

1955–56 (294)   —— Hard Fibre Cordage   161
1955–56 (328)   —— Certain Rubber Footwear   162
1955–56 (366)   —— Linoleum   162
1955–56 Cmd. 9504 —— Collective Discrimination   162
1956–57 (13)   —— Certain Industrial and Medical Gases   162
1956–57 (14)   —— Standard Metal Windows and Doors   163
1956–57 (15)   —— Tea   163
1956–57 (16)   —— Electronic Valves and Cathode Ray Tubes   163
1956–57 (42)   —— Electrical and Allied Machinery and Plant   164
1958–59 (267)   —— Chemical Fertilisers   164

7. Company and Commercial Law and Practice

1944–45 Cmd. 6659 Company Law Amendment   164
1953–54 Cmd. 9112 Shares of No Par Value   165
1951   Non-Parl. Inspection of Bristol Rovers Football Club
                       Limited   166
1952   Non-Parl. Investigation of Bristol Rovers Football Club
                       Limited   167
1953   Non-Parl. The Savoy Hotel Limited   167
1954   Non-Parl. The Savoy Hotel Limited and the Berkeley
                       Hotel Company Limited   167

8. Weights and Measures

1950–51 Cmd. 8219 Weights and Measures Legislation   167

VI. COAL, FUEL, POWER, WATER

1. Fuel Generally

1941–42 Cmd. 6352 Fuel Rationing   169
1945–46 Cmd. 6762 Domestic Fuel Policy   169
1948   Non-Parl. Fuel and the Future   170
1951–52 Cmd. 8647 National Policy for the Use of Fuel and Power
                       Resources   170

2. Coal

1940–41 Cmd. 6236 Coal Mines (War Levy) Scheme   172
1940–41 Cmd. 6278 Coal Mines Guaranteed Wage Levy   172
1941–42 Cmd. 6364 Coal   172
1942   Non-Parl. Coal-Mining Industry. Rep. The Immediate
                       Wages Issue   172
1942   Non-Parl. —— Supplemental Rep. Output Bonus   173
1943   Non-Parl. —— 3rd Rep. Machinery for Determining
                       Wages and Conditions of Employment   173
1943   Non-Parl. —— 4th and Final Rep.   173
1944–45 Cmd. 6617 Financial Position of the Coal Mining Industry.
                       Coal Charges Account   174
1942   Non-Parl. Recruitment of Juveniles in the Coal-Mining
                       Industry   174
1943   Non-Parl. —— Supplemental Rep.   175
1947   Non-Parl. Apprenticeship for Coal Face Workers   175
1944–45 Cmd. 6575 Scottish Coalfields   175

1944–45	Cmd. 6610	Coal Mining	176
1945–46	(Bill 62)	Coal Industry Nationalisation Bill	178
1945–46	Cmd. 6716	Coal Industry Nationalisation	178
1947–48	(174)	National Coal Board	179
1948		Coal Mining Industry. Organisation	179
1955		Organisation	179
1950		Plan for Coal	181
1956		Investing in Coal	181
1959		Revised Plan for Coal	181
1948–49	Cmd. 7637	Mining Subsidence	182
1941	Non-Parl.	Amendment of the General Regulations Governing the Use of Electricity in Mines under the Coal Mines Act, 1911	182
1942–43	Cmd. 6450	Coal Dust Explosions	183
1950	Non-Parl.	Safety in the Use of Explosives in Coal Mines	183
1954	Non-Parl.	Scottish Peat	183

3. Oil and Petrol

| 1944–45 | Cmd. 6615 | Hydrocarbon Oil Duties. See *National Finance* | 184 |
| 1947–48 | Cmd. 7372 | Evasions of Petrol Rationing | 184 |

4. Electricity

1942–43	Cmd. 6406	Hydro-Electric Development in Scotland	184
1945	Non-Parl.	Severn Barrage Scheme	185
1946–47	Cmd. 7007	Electricity Supply Areas	186
1947	Non-Parl.	Electricity	186
1947–48	Cmd. 7464	Electricity Peak Load Problem in Relation to Non-Industrial Consumers	186
1948–49	(336)	British Electricity Authority	187
[1953]		Power and Prosperity	187
1953	Non-Parl.	Economy in the Construction of Power Stations	187

5. Gas

1945–46	Cmd. 6699	The Gas Industry	188
1947–48	Cmd. 7313	Gas Supply Areas	189
1947–48	Cmd. 7424	Gas Supply Areas	189
1950–51	(69)	The Gas Council	189
1954		Fuel for the Nation. The Gas Industry's Programme	189
1953–54	Cmd. 9175	Gas and Electricity (Borrowing Powers) Bill	189

6. Atomic Energy

| 1953–54 | Cmd. 8986 | Future Organisation of the United Kingdom Atomic Energy Project | 189 |
| 1954–55 | Cmd. 9389 | A Programme of Nuclear Power | 190 |

7. Water

1942–43	Cmd. 6465	Water. 3rd Rep. River Boards	190
1943–44	Cmd. 6515	A National Water Policy	191
1945–46	Cmd. 6765	Water Rates and Charges. See *Local Taxation*	192

PAGE

1946–47   (HL. 64)   Tendring Hundred Water and Gas Bill [H.L.].   192
1948   Non-Parl.   Gathering Grounds   192
1949   Non-Parl.   Water Softening   193

VII.   TRANSPORT

1. Railways, Canals, before Nationalisation

1945–46   (143)   Railways (Valuation for Rating) Bill. See *Local*
                          Taxation   193
1947   Non-Parl.   Adjustment of the Rates, Fares and Charges of
                          the Main Line Railway Companies   193
1946, 1948   Railway (London Plan). See *London*   194
1946   Non-Parl.   Forth and Clyde Ship Canal Group   194

2. The Nationalised Transport System

1946–47   (Bill 12)   Transport Bill   194
1948–49   (235)   British Transport Commission   195
1950   Non-Parl.   Applications of the British Transport Commis-
                          sion for authorisation of additional charges
                          in respect of their Railway; Harbours,
                          Docks and Piers; and Canals and Inland
                          Waterways   196
1951–52   Cmd. 8513   Increase in Passenger Fares   197
1951–52   Cmd. 8538   Transport Policy   197
1953–54   Cmd. 9191   Railways Reorganisation Scheme   197
1953–54   (25)   Road Haulage Disposal Board   198
1955   Canals and Inland Waterways   198
1951   Electrification of Railways   199
[?1955]   The System of Electrification for British Rail-
                          ways   199
1955   Modernisation and Re-equipment of British
                          Railways   199
1955–56   Cmd. 9880   British Transport Commission. Proposals for
                          the Railways   199

3. Roads, Road Traffic, Ferries

1948   Non-Parl.   Ferries in Great Britain   200
1945   Non-Parl.   Road Safety. Int. Rep.   201
1947   Non-Parl.   —— Final Rep.   201
1949   Non-Parl.   —— Rep. Pedestrian Crossing Places (Traffic)
                          Regulations, 1941   202
1952   Non-Parl.   —— Rep. Motor Cycle Accidents   202
1952   Non-Parl.   —— Rep. Bus Accident at Gillingham   202
1954   Non-Parl.   —— Rep. Massed-Start Cycle Racing   203
1956   Non-Parl.   —— Rep. Child Cyclists   203
1957   Non-Parl.   —— Rep. Minimum Age for Motor Cyclists   203
1946   Non-Parl.   Road Accidents   204
1946   Non-Parl.   Traffic Signs   204
1949   Non-Parl.   Petrol Stations   205
1950   Non-Parl.   Precautions against Fire and Explosion in
                          Underground Car Parks   205
1953   Non-Parl.   Licensing of Road Passenger Services   205

			PAGE
1953–54	(25)	Road Haulage Disposal Board. See *The Nationalised Transport System*	206

4. Sea Transport

1939–40	Cmd. 6218	Wartime Financial Arrangements between H.M. Government and British Ship-owners	206
1941–42	Cmd. 6357	Scheme for Purchase by British Shipowners of New Vessels built on Government Account	207
1941–42	Cmd. 6373	Scheme for purchase of Merchant Vessels by Allied Governments from H.M. Government	207
1944	Non-Parl.	United Maritime Authority	207
1945	Non-Parl.	Coasting and Short Sea Trades in Europe. United Maritime Authority	207
1946	Non-Parl.	Clyde Estuary	207
1948	Non-Parl.	Turn-round of Shipping in the U.K. Ports	208
1950	Non-Parl.	Increased Mechanisation in the United Kingdom Ports	208
1952	Non-Parl.	Ports Efficiency. 1st Rep.	209
1952	Non-Parl.	—— 2nd Rep.	209
1956	Non-Parl.	—— 3rd Rep.	209
1950	Non-Parl.	Fire Prevention and Fire Fighting in Ships in Port	209
1954–55	Cmd. 9359	South Wales Ports	210
1953	Non-Parl.	Prevention of Pollution of the Sea by Oil. See *Fishing*	210

5. Air Transport

1944–45	Cmd. 6605	British Air Transport	210
1947	Non-Parl.	Flying Boat Base	211
1947	Non-Parl.	Private Flying	211
1947–48	Cmd. 7307	Tudor Aircraft. Int. Rep.	211
1947–48	Cmd. 7478	—— Final Rep.	212
1948–49	Cmd. 7564	Accident Investigation Procedure	212
1948–49	Cmd. 7705	Certification of Civil Aircraft and Approval of Equipment	213
1948–49	Cmd. 7746	Recruitment, Training and Licensing of Personnel for Civil Aviation	214
1950–51	Cmd. 8147	Landing and Taking-off of Aircraft in Bad Weather	214
1951	Non-Parl.	Helicopter	215
1952–53	Cmd. 8902	London's Airports	215
1953–54	Cmd. 9215	Proposed Development of Gatwick Airport	215

VIII A. POST OFFICE, TELEGRAPHY

1. Post Office

1951–52	Cmd. 8470	Post Office (Departmental Classes) Recognition	217

2. Telegraphy

1937–38	Cmd. 5716	Cable and Wireless Limited	218
1945–46	Cmd. 6805	Cable and Wireless Limited	218
1945–46	(147, 148)	Cable and Wireless Bill	218

VIII B.   BROADCASTING, THE PRESS

			PAGE
1945	Non-Parl.	Television	219
1945–46	Cmd. 6852	Broadcasting Policy	219
1950–51	Cmd. 8116	Broadcasting	220
1950–51	Cmd. 8291	Broadcasting	222
1951–52	Cmd. 8550	Broadcasting	223
1953–54	Cmd. 9005	Television Policy	223
1948–49	Cmd. 7700	The Press	223

IX.   INVENTIONS, PATENTS, COPYRIGHT

1944–45	Cmd. 6618	Patents and Designs Acts. 1st Int. Rep.	226
1945–46	Cmd. 6789	—— 2nd Int. Rep.	226
1946–47	Cmd. 7206	—— Final Rep.	227
1948–49	Cmd. 7586	Awards to Inventors. 1st Rep.	227
1948–49	Cmd. 7832	—— 2nd Rep.	227
1952–53	Cmd. 8743	——·3rd Rep.	227
1955–56	Cmd. 9744	—— 4th and Final Rep.	227
1951–52	Cmd. 8662	Copyright	228

X.   LABOUR

1. Manpower, The Supply of Labour

1939–40	(107)	Draft Control of Employment (Advertisements) Order	229
1940–41	Cmd. 6307	Skilled Men in the Services	229
1941–42	Cmd. 6339	—— 2nd Rep.	230
1940–41	Cmd. 6301	Calling up of Civil Servants	230
1941–42	Cmd. 6324	The Principal New Measures to be introduced by His Majesty's Government in pursuance of their Man-power Policy	230
1941–42	Cmd. 6402	Man-power in Banking and Allied Businesses, in Ordinary Insurance, and in Industrial Assurance	231
1943–44	Cmd. 6564	Statistics relating to the War Effort of the U.K.	231
1943–44	Cmd. 6548	Re-allocation of Man-power between the Armed Forces and Civilian Employment	231
1943–44	Cmd. 6568	Re-allocation of Man-power between Civilian Employments	231
1945–46	Cmd. 6743	Statement relating to Defence	232
1945–46	Cmd. 6831	Call Up to the Forces in 1947 and 1948	232
1950	Cmd. 8026	Increase in the Length of Full-time National Service with the Armed Forces	232

2. Employment, Wages Policy, Cost of Living

1940–41	Cmd. 6294	Price Stabilisation and Industrial Policy	232
1943–44	Cmd. 6527	Employment Policy	233
1946–47	Cmd. 7018	Economic Considerations affecting Relations between Employers and Workers	234
1947–48	Cmd. 7321	Personal Incomes, Costs and Prices	235
1955–56	Cmd. 9725	Economic Implications of Full Employment	235
1946–47	Cmd. 7077	Cost of Living. Int. Rep.	236

| 1950–51 | Cmd. 8328 | —— Int. Rep. | 237 |
| 1951–52 | Cmd. 8481 | —— Rep. Working of the Interim Index of Retail Prices | 237 |

3. Industrial Relations, Disputes, Wages Councils

1953	Non-Parl.	Industrial Relations Handbook	238
1941–1957		Disputes in Particular Employments	238
1954	Non-Parl.	Training of Supervisors	239
1939	Non-Parl.	Wages, Hours and Conditions in the Retail Distributive Trades	240
1947–1950		Wages Councils	241
1947	Non-Parl.	—— Retail Food Trades	241
1947	Non-Parl.	—— Retail Furnishing and Allied Trades	241
1947	Non-Parl.	—— Hairdressing Trade	242
1947	Non-Parl.	—— Retail Drapery, Outfitting and Footwear Trades	242
1947	Non-Parl.	—— Retail Bookselling, Newsagency, Stationery, Tobacco and Confectionery Trades	243
1951	Non-Parl.	—— Wholesale and Retail Bread and Flour Confectionery Distributive Trades	243
1950	Non-Parl.	—— Rubber Proofed Garment Making Industry	244
1943–44	(100)	Catering Wages Commission	244
1943–44	Cmd. 6509	—— Industrial Catering	244
1944	Non-Parl.	—— Remuneration and Conditions of Employment of Workers employed by the Crown in Catering Undertakings	245
1943–44	Cmd. 6569	—— Unlicensed Non-residential Catering Establishments	245
1944–45	Cmd. 6601	—— Licensed Residential Establishments and Licensed Restaurants	245
1944–45	Cmd. 6612	—— Licensed Non-residential Establishments	245
1945–46	Cmd. 6706	—— Unlicensed Residential Establishments	246
1945–46	Cmd. 6776	—— Catering Activities of Local Authorities	246
1946–47	Cmd. 7191	—— Canteens provided by Dock Authorities	246
1950	Cmd. 8004	—— Hotel Industry	246
1945	Non-Parl.	—— Rehabilitation of the Catering Industry	247
1946	Non-Parl.	—— Development of the Catering, Holiday and Tourist Services	247
1945	Non-Parl.	—— Staggering of Holidays	248
1946	Non-Parl.	—— Training for the Catering Industry	248
1947	Non-Parl.	—— Problems affecting the Remuneration of Catering Workers which result from the Practice of Giving Tips	248
1947	Non-Parl.	—— Alleged Overcharging for Holiday Accommodation	249
1947	Non-Parl.	—— Employment Agencies serving the Catering Industry	249

4. Wages and Conditions in Particular Employments (other than Wages Councils)

| 1947 | Non-Parl. | Amenities in the Brick Industry | 249 |
| 1943 | Non-Parl. | Training for the Building Industry | 250 |

PAGE

1942–43	Cmd. 6428	Training for the Building Industry	250
1944	Non-Parl.	Building Apprenticeship and Training Council	250
1952	Non-Parl.	—— Rep. Building. Training for Management	251
1947	Non-Parl.	Payment by Results in Building and Civil Engineering during the War	251
		Coal Mining. See *Coal, Fuel and Power*	251
1945	Non-Parl.	Cotton Spinning Industry	251
1946	Non-Parl.	—— Supplement. Mule-spinners' Wages	252
1948	Non-Parl.	Cotton Manufacturing Industry	253
1949	Non-Parl.	—— Final Rep. Pt. I	254
1949	Non-Parl.	—— Final Rep. Pts. II, III, IV	254
1946	Non-Parl.	Industrial Conditions in the Cutlery Trade	255
1943		Supply of Crews for Trawlers. (Unpublished.)	255
1945	Non-Parl.	Seamen's Welfare in Ports	256
1945	Non-Parl.	Port Transport Industry	257
1946	Non-Parl.	Port Transport Industry	257
1947	Non-Parl.	Port Transport Industry	258
1947	Non-Parl.	Port Transport Industry	259

5. Rehabilitation, Resettlement

1942–43	Cmd. 6415	Rehabilitation and Resettlement of Disabled Persons	260
1945–46	Cmd. 6719	Employment for Persons suspended from the Mining Industry on account of Silicosis and Pneumoconiosis	261
1951	Non-Parl.	Employment of Blind Persons	261
1952–53	Cmd. 8963	Employment of Older Men and Women	262

6. Employment of Women

1945–46	Cmd. 6937	Equal Pay	263
1942–43	Cmd. 6481	Domestic Help	265
1944–45	Cmd. 6650	Post-War Organisation of Private Domestic Employment	265

7. Juveniles

1942, 1943		Recruitment of Juveniles in the Coal-mining Industry. See *Coal*	266
1947	Non-Parl.	Apprenticeship for Coal Face Workers. See *Coal*	266
1945	Non-Parl.	Juvenile Employment Service	266
1948–49	Cmd. 7664	Hours of Employment of Juveniles. Rep. Pt. II. See *Factory Regulation*	267
1950	Cmd. 8005	Employment of Children as Film Actors, in Theatrical Work and in Ballet	267

8. Factory Regulation: Safety, Health, Hours of Work

1940	Non-Parl.	Lighting in Factories. 5th Rep.	268
1940–41	Cmd. 6310	Welfare Work outside the Factory and Seamen's Welfare in Port	269
1942–43	Cmd. 6411	—— Memo.	269
1945–1952		Conditions of Work in the Cotton Industry	269
1945	Non-Parl.	—— Mule Spinners' Cancer and Automatic Wiping-down Motions. Int. Rep.	269

PAGE

1952	Non-Parl.	—— Mule Spinners' Cancer. 2nd Int. Rep.	269
1946	Non-Parl.	—— (1) Sanitary accommodation, washing facilities, accommodation for clothing, medical and welfare services, decoration and vacuum cleaning. (2) Dust in card rooms. Int. Reps.	269
1952	Non-Parl.	—— Dust in card rooms. 2nd Int. Rep.	269
1947	Non-Parl.	—— Ventilation, Temperature, use of steam in Humidification, and Lighting. Int. Rep.	269
1947	Non-Parl.	—— Spacing of Machinery, Cotton Weaving. 1st Rep.	269
1946	Non-Parl.	Jute Industry	270
1945–46	Cmd. 6866	Rag Flock Acts	270
1947	Non-Parl.	Wool Textile Industry. Int. Rep. Spacing of Certain Machinery Processes subsequent to Carding	271
1949	Non-Parl.	—— Final Rep.	271
1938	Non-Parl.	Prevention of Accidents in Paper Mills. Machinery Accidents. 1st Rep.	271
1953	Non-Parl.	—— 2nd Rep.	271
1943	Non-Parl.	Tile Dust	272
1950	Non-Parl.	Draft Pottery (Health and Welfare) Special Regulations	272
1945	Non-Parl.	Safety in the Use of Power Presses	272
1944	Non-Parl.	Dust in Steel Foundries. 1st Rep.	273
1952	Non-Parl.	—— 2nd Rep.	273
1947	Non-Parl.	Conditions in Ironfoundries	273
1950	Non-Parl.	Industrial Lung Diseases of Iron and Steel Workers	274
1947	Non-Parl.	Safeguarding of Milling Machines. Int. Rep.	274
1952	Non-Parl.	—— 2nd Rep.	274
1951	Non-Parl.	Health of Welders	274
1953	Non-Parl.	Conditions in the Drop Forging Industry	274
1939–40	Cmd. 6182	Hours of Employment of Women and Young Persons in Factories during the First Five Months of the War	275
1946–47	Cmd. 7147	Double Day-Shift Working	275
1946–47	Cmd. 7105	Closing Hours of Shops. 1st Int. Rep.	276
1948–49	Cmd. 7664	—— Rep. Health, Welfare and Safety in Non-Industrial Employment, Hours of Employment of Juveniles	277
1950–51	Cmd. 8378	Night Baking	278

9. Migration

| 1944–45 | Cmd. 6658 | Migration within the British Commonwealth | 279 |
| 1953 | Non-Parl. | Child Migration to Australia | 279 |

10. Professions

1944–45	Cmd. 6576	Higher Appointments	279
		Medical and Auxiliary Professions. See *Health*	280
1950	Cmd. 8059	Qualifications of Planners. See *Town and Country Planning*	280

PAGE

1944–45   Cmd. 6611   Veterinary Practice by Unregistered Persons   280
1943–44   Cmd. 6517   Veterinary Education in Great Britain   281

XI. SOCIAL SECURITY

1. Unemployment Insurance and Assistance

1940–41   Cmd. 6247   Determination of Needs Bill   281
1941–1948   Financial Condition of the Unemployment Fund   282

2. Social Insurance, Family Allowances

1942–43   Cmd. 6404   Social Insurance and Allied Services   283
1943–44   Cmd. 6550   Social Insurance. Pt. I   288
1943–44   Cmd. 6551   —— Pt. II. Workmen's Compensation, pro-
                        posals for an Industrial Injury Insurance
                        Scheme   289
1941–42   Cmd. 6354   Family Allowances   290

3. National Insurance

1945–46   Cmd. 6729   National Insurance Bill, 1946   290
1945–46   Cmd. 6730   National Insurance Bill, 1946   291
1947   Non-Parl.   Approved Societies. Int. Rep. Absorption of
                        Staffs   291
1948   Non-Parl.   —— Final Rep. Compensation and Super-
                        annuation of Staffs   291
1948–1955   National Insurance Advisory Cttee. Reps.   292
1947–48   (165)   —— Guardians Allowances   292
1947–48   (137)   —— Insurance of Share Fishermen   292
1948–49   (262)   —— Seasonal Workers   293
1951–52   Cmd. 8558   —— Seasonal Workers   293
1951–52   Cmd. 8446   —— Maternity Benefits   293
1951–52   Cmd. 8483   —— Time Limits   294
1951–52   Cmd. 8549   —— Entertainment Industry   294
1951–52   Cmd. 8600   —— Hospital In-Patients   294
1952–53   Cmd. 8860   —— Credits for Training Courses   294
1952–53   Cmd. 8894   —— Availability Question   295
1954–55   Cmd. 9432   —— Liability for Contributions of Persons with
                        Small Incomes   295
1950   Cmd. 7955   Ministry of National Insurance   295
1950–51   Cmd. 8208   Proposed Changes in the National Insurance
                        Scheme   295
1954–55   (1)   National Insurance Act, 1946. 1st Quinquennial
                        Review   295
1954–55   Cmd. 9338   National Insurance Bill, 1954   296

4. National Assistance

1947–48   Cmd. 7248   National Assistance Bill   296
1952   Non-Parl.   Reception Centres for Persons without a Settled
                        Way of Living   297

5. Workmen's Compensation, Industrial Injuries

1944–45   Cmd. 6588   Workmen's Compensation   297

			PAGE
1944–45	Cmd. 6580	Workmen's Compensation. Alternative Remedies (Contributory Negligence). Int. Rep.	298
1944–45	Cmd. 6642	—— 2nd Int. Rep.	298
1945–46	Cmd. 6860	—— Final Rep.	298
1944–45	Cmd. 6651	National Insurance (Industrial Injuries) Bill	300
1945–46	Cmd. 6738	—— Proposed Changes in the Death Benefits	300
1950–51	(284)	National Insurance (Industrial Injuries) Act, 1946	300
1954–55	(22)	—— 1st Quinquennial Review	300
1946–47	Cmd. 7076	Assessment of Disablement due to Specified Injuries	300
1948–49	Cmd. 7557	Industrial Diseases	300
1950–1954		Industrial Injuries Advisory Council. Reps.	301
1950–51	Cmd. 8093	—— Tuberculosis, etc., in relation to Nurses	301
1951–52	Cmd. 8511	—— Time Limits	301
1952–53	Cmd. 8866	—— Pneumoconiosis	301
1954–55	Cmd. 9347	—— Raynaud's Phenomenon	302

6. Pensions

1939–40	Cmd. 6169	The Financial Provisions of the Bill relating to Contributory Pensions and Health Insurance	302
1939–40	Cmd. 6204	Old Age and Widows' Pensions Act, 1940	302
1941–1943		Determination of Needs. Memos.	302
1954	Non-Parl.	National Insurance Retirement Pensions. Reasons given for Retiring or Continuing at Work	302
1954–55	Cmd. 9333	Economic and Financial Problems of the Provision for Old Age	303

XII. HEALTH

1. General: War Problems, Health Services, Hospitals

(i) *War Problems*

1939–40	Cmd. 6234	Conditions in Air-Raid Shelters with Special Reference to Health	304
1940–41	Cmd. 6245	—— Further Recommendations	304
1940	Non-Parl.	Neuroses in War-time	304
1942	Non-Parl.	Medical Personnel (Priority). 1st Int. Rep.	305
1942	Non-Parl.	—— 2nd Int. Rep.	305
1941–42	Cmd. 6353	Mass Miniature Radiography in the Detection of Pulmonary Tuberculosis among Recruits for H.M. Forces	305
1942–43	Cmd. 6448	Voluntary Aid Detachments	305
1951	Non-Parl.	Duties of Local Authorities in Relation to (I) The Casualty Services and (II) Public Health in Time of War	306

(ii) *Health Services*

1942–43	Cmd. 6472	Post-War Hospital Problems in Scotland	306
1943–44	Cmd. 6502	A National Health Service	307
1950	(84)	Central Health Services Council	309
1943–44	Cmd. 6565	Dentistry. Int. Rep.	309

PAGE

1945–46   Cmd. 6727   —— Final Rep.   310
1943   Non-Parl.   Health and Industrial Efficiency   311
1950–51   Cmd. 8170   Industrial Health Services   311
1953   Non-Parl.   Child Health   312

(iii) *Hospitals*

1945, 1946   Hospital Surveys   312
1950   Non-Parl.   National Health Service.   Development of
                          Consultant Services   312
1952   Non-Parl.   The General Practitioner and the Hospital
                          Service   313
1952   Non-Parl.   Co-operation between Hospital, Local Authority
                          and General Practitioner Services   313
1951   Non-Parl.   Reception and Welfare of In-Patients at Hos-
                          pitals   314
1953   Non-Parl.   Reception and Welfare of In-Patients in Hos-
                          pitals   314
1954   Non-Parl.   Internal Administration of Hospitals   315
1951–52   Cmd. 8615   Proposals for a Scottish Medical Research Fund 316
1953   Non-Parl.   Clinical Research in Relation to the National
                          Health Service   316

2. Medical Professions

(i) *Medical Practitioners, Dentists, etc.*

1945–46   Cmd. 6810   Remuneration of General Practitioners   317
1947–48   Cmd. 7420   Remuneration of Consultants and Specialists   317
1948–49   Cmd. 7565   Medical Partnerships   318
1952   Non-Parl.   Distribution of Remuneration among General
                          Practitioners   318
1954   Non-Parl.   General Practice within the National Health
                          Service   319
1949   Non-Parl.   Medical Certificates   320
1950   Non-Parl.   Definition of Drugs. 1st Rep.   320
1950   Non-Parl.   —— 2nd Rep.   320
1951   Non-Parl.   —— 3rd Rep.   320
1950   Non-Parl.   Prescribing. 2nd Int. Rep.   320
1954   Non-Parl.   —— Rep.   320
1948   Non-Parl.   Differences in Dispensing Practice between
                          England and Wales and Scotland   321
1944–1946   Dentistry.   Int. and Final Reps.   See *Health
                          Services*   321
1947–48   Cmd. 7402   Remuneration of General Dental Practitioners   321
1949   Non-Parl.   Chairside Times taken in carrying out treatment
                          by General Dental Practitioners   322
1951–52   Cmd. 8531   Statutory Registration of Opticians   322
1950   Non-Parl.   Average Time taken to Test Sight by Ophthalmic
                          Medical Practitioners   323
1950   Non-Parl.   Average Time taken to Test Sight by Ophthal-
                          mic Opticians and . . . by Ophthalmic
                          Opticians and by Dispensing Opticians in
                          Fitting and Supplying Glasses. Rep. Pt. I   323
1950   Non-Parl.   —— Rep. Pt. II   323

(ii) *Nurses*   PAGE

1942–1948		Nurses Salaries	324
1945	Non-Parl.	Mental Nursing and the Nursing of the Mentally Defective	324
1945–46	Cmd. 6672	Training of Nurses for the Colonies	325
1947	Non-Parl.	Recruitment and Training of Nurses	325
1948	Non-Parl.	—— Minority Rep.	327
1954	Non-Parl.	Position of the Enrolled Assistant Nurse within the National Health Service	327
1955	Non-Parl.	The State Enrolled Assistant Nurse in the National Health Service	327
1954	Non-Parl.	Function, Status and Training of Nurse Tutors	327
1949	Non-Parl.	Midwives	328
1952	Non-Parl.	Preventive Dental Services	329
1950	Non-Parl.	New Zealand School Dental Nurses	330

(iii) *Other Services*

1947	Non-Parl.	Laboratory Services	330
1950–51	Cmd. 8188	Medical Auxiliaries	331
1950–51	Cmd. 8260	Social Workers in the Mental Health Services	331
1953	Non-Parl.	Recruitment, Training and Qualification of Sanitary Inspectors	332

3. Particular Problems and Diseases

1953	Non-Parl.	Accidents in the Home	333
1953	Non-Parl.	The Ageing Population	333
1945	Non-Parl.	Artificial Limbs	334
1950	Non-Parl.	Monocular Blindness	334
1950	Non-Parl.	The Causes of Blindness in England and Wales	335
1953	Non-Parl.	The Causes of Blindness in England 1948–1950	335
1956	Non-Parl.	The Causes of Blindness in England 1951–1954	335
1945	Non-Parl.	Congenital Deaf-Mutism in Scotland	335
1951	Non-Parl.	Special Welfare Needs of Deaf-Blind Persons	335
1954	Non-Parl.	Mortality and Morbidity during the London Fog of Dec., 1952	336
1948–49	Cmd. 7557	Industrial Diseases. See *Workmen's Compensation*	336
1943	Non-Parl.	Infant Mortality in Scotland	336
1945–46	Cmd. 6834	Scottish Lunacy and Mental Deficiency Laws	337
1944	Non-Parl.	Treatment and Rehabilitation of Miners in the Wales Region Suffering from Pneumoconiosis	338
1950	Non-Parl.	Poliomyelitis. Survey of the Outbreak in Scotland in 1947	339
1947	Non-Parl.	Work of Psychologists and Psychiatrists in the Services	339
1946	Non-Parl.	Rehabilitation	340
1945	Non-Parl.	Chronic Rheumatic Diseases	340
1941–42	Cmd. 6355	Prevalence and Control of Scabies	341
1951	Non-Parl.	Tuberculosis	341
1952	Non-Parl.	Vaccination against Smallpox	341
1943–44	Cmd. 6518	Venereal Diseases (Scotland)	342
1946	Non-Parl.	Control of Midges. Int. Rep.	342
1948	Non-Parl.	—— 2nd Rep.	342

PAGE

1954   Non-Parl.   Synthetic Detergents. Int. Rep.   343
1956   Non-Parl.   —— Rep.   343
1954   Non-Parl.   Treatment and Disposal of Sewage Sludge   343

4. Drugs, Food Purity

1942–43 Cmd. 6482   The Labelling and Advertising of Foods   344
1950   Non-Parl.   Manufactured Meat Products   344
1954   Non-Parl.   Food Standards. Rep. Antioxidants   345
1954   Non-Parl.   —— Rep. Lead   345
1945   Non-Parl.   Freezing Point (Hortvet) Test of Milk. See
                       Agriculture   345
1951   Non-Parl.   Hygiene in Catering Establishments   345
1954   Non-Parl.   Toxic Chemicals in Agriculture. Rep. Residues
                       in Food. See *Agriculture*   346

XIII A.   HOUSING

1. Housing

1944   Non-Parl.   Temporary Accommodation   346
1945–46   Cmd. 6686   Temporary Housing Programme   347
1943–44   Cmd. 6552   Distribution of New Houses in Scotland   347
1944   Non-Parl.   Planning our New Homes   348
1944   Non-Parl.   Design of Dwellings   349
1944   Non-Parl.   Rural Housing. 3rd Rep.   349
1947   Non-Parl.   —— 4th Rep. Reconditioning in Rural Areas   350
1944   Non-Parl.   Private Enterprise Housing   350
1944–45   Cmd. 6609   Housing   350
1944   Non-Parl.   Housing Manual   351
1945–46   Cmd. 6741   Provision of Houses for Owner-occupation in
                        Scotland   351
1946   Non-Parl.   Conversion of Existing Houses   352
1945–46   Cmd. 6670   Selling Price of Houses   353
1947   Non-Parl.   Modernising our Homes   353
1947   Non-Parl.   Standards of Fitness for Habitation   354
                      Building Studies. See *Trade and Industry* 354
1948   Non-Parl.   Cost of House Building. 1st Rep.   354
1950   Non-Parl.   —— 2nd Rep.   354
1952   Non-Parl.   —— 3rd Rep.   354
1948   Non-Parl.   Scottish Building Costs   355
1951   Non-Parl.   Productivity in House Building   356
1953   Non-Parl.   —— 2nd Rep.   356
1951   Non-Parl.   Design and Workmanship of Non-traditional
                        Houses   356
1950   Non-Parl.   Care and Maintenance of Fittings and Equipment
                        in the Modern House   357
1953   Non-Parl.   Increase in Cost of Maintaining Houses   357
1953   Non-Parl.   Cost of House Maintenance   357
1952   Non-Parl.   Living in Flats   357
1952   Non-Parl.   Requisitioned Properties in Use for Housing.
                        Int. Rep.   358
1953   Non-Parl.   —— 2nd Int. Rep.   358
1954   Non-Parl.   —— 3rd and Final Rep.   358

PAGE

1953–54   Cmd. 8996   Houses—The Next Step   358
1953–54   Cmd. 8997   Housing Policy Scotland   359
1950   Non-Parl.   Houses of Outstanding Historic or Architectural
                      Interest   359

2. Rents

1944–45   Cmd. 6621   Rent Control   360

3. House Management, Housing Estates

1944   Non-Parl.   Community Centres   360
1945   Non-Parl.   Housing Management. 2nd Rep. Management
                      of Municipal Housing Estates   360
1949   Non-Parl.   —— 3rd Rep. Selection of Tenants and Trans-
                      fers and Exchanges   361
1953   Non-Parl.   —— 4th Rep. Transfers, Exchanges and Rents   362
1945–46   Cmd. 6901   Housing Management in Scotland   363
1950   Non-Parl.   Choosing Council Tenants   363
1948   Non-Parl.   Appearance of Housing Estates   364
1947   Non-Parl.   Estate Development and Management in War-
                      damaged Areas   365

XIII B. TOWN AND COUNTRY PLANNING

1945–1953   Papers on Town and Country Planning   366
1939–40   Cmd. 6153   The Distribution of the Industrial Population.
                      See *Trade and Industry*   366
1940–41   Cmd. 6291   Compensation and Betterment. Int. Rep.   366
1941–42   Cmd. 6386   —— Final Rep.   367
1941–42   Cmd. 6378   Land Utilisation in Rural Areas   368
1942–43   Cmd. 6440   Utilisation of Land in Rural Areas, Scotland   369
1943–44   Cmd. 6537   The Control of Land Use   369
1946–47   Cmd. 7006   Town and Country Planning Bill, 1947   370
1945–1949   Regional Plans   371
1945–46   Cmd. 6759   New Towns. Int. Rep.   371
1945–46   Cmd. 6794   —— 2nd Int. Rep.   371
1945–46   Cmd. 6876   —— Final Rep.   372
1950   Cmd. 8059   Qualifications of Planners   373
1944–45   Cmd. 6631   National Parks. Scottish Survey   374
1944–45   Cmd. 6628   National Parks in England and Wales   374
1946–47   Cmd. 7121   National Parks (England and Wales)   375
1946–47   Cmd. 7122   Conservation of Nature in England and Wales.
                      Wild Life Conservation   376
1947–48   Cmd. 7235   National Parks and the Conservation of Nature
                      in Scotland. National Parks   377
1947–48   Cmd. 7235   —— Conservation of Nature in Scotland   378
1948–49   Cmd. 7814   —— Final Rep. Nature Reserves in Scotland   378
1946–47   Cmd. 7207   Footpaths and Access to the Countryside   378
1945–46   Cmd. 6906   Restoration Problem in the Ironstone Industry
                      in the Midlands   379
1948   Non-Parl.   Sand and Gravel. Rep. Pts. 1, 2   380
1953   Non-Parl.   —— Rep. Pt. 18   381
1953–54   Cmd. 9011   Air Pollution. Int. Rep.   381
1953–54   Cmd. 9322   —— Rep.   381

XIV. EDUCATION

1. General Policy, Schools

PAGE

1950–51	Cmd. 8244	Education 1900–1950	382
1940	Non-Parl.	Adjusting between Authorities the Expenditure Incurred by them in respect of Evacuated School Children. Rep.	382
1941	Non-Parl.	—— 2nd Rep.	382
1942–43	Cmd. 6458	Educational Reconstruction	382
1946–47	Cmd. 6973	Primary Education	384
1943	Non-Parl.	Public Schools and the General Education System. Special Rep. Abolition of Tuition Fees in Grant-Aided Secondary Schools	384
1944	Non-Parl.	—— Rep.	385
1943–44	Cmd. 6523	Principles of Government in Maintained Secondary Schools	387
1946–47	Cmd. 7005	Secondary Education	387
1949	Non-Parl.	The Future of Secondary Education in Wales	388
1948	Non-Parl.	Educational Administration in Wales	389
1954	Non-Parl.	Early Leaving	389
1943	Non-Parl.	Compulsory Day Continuation Classes	390
1951–52	Cmd. 8454	Further Education	391
1951	Non-Parl.	County Colleges in Wales	392
1947	Non-Parl.	School and Life	392
1943	Non-Parl.	Youth Service after the War	392
1945	Non-Parl.	—— 2nd Rep. Purpose and Content of the Youth Service	393
1945	Non-Parl.	Needs of Youth in these Times	393
1945	Non-Parl.	Post-War Youth Service in Wales	394
1948	Non-Parl.	Out of School	395
1944–45	Cmd. 6574	Adult Education Grants	395
1954	Non-Parl.	Organisation and Finance of Adult Education in England and Wales	396
1944–45	Cmd. 6573	Education Authority Bursaries	396
1951	Non-Parl.	Educational Endowments in Scotland	397

2. (a) Handicapped Children, Curriculum, Examinations

1950	Cmd. 7866	Pupils who are Defective in Hearing	398
1950	Cmd. 7885	Pupils who are Defective in Vision	398
1950–51	Cmd. 8211	Pupils with Physical Disabilities	399
1951–52	Cmd. 8401	Pupils with Mental or Educational Disabilities	399
1951–52	Cmd. 8426	Pupils Handicapped by Speech Disorders	400
1951–52	Cmd. 8428	Pupils who are Maladjusted because of Social Handicaps	400
1951–52	Cmd. 8432	Administration of Education for Handicapped Pupils	401
1943	Non-Parl.	Curriculum and Examinations in Secondary Schools	401
1947	Non-Parl.	Examinations in Secondary Schools. Rep.	402
1952	Non-Parl.	—— 2nd Rep.	402
1948	Non-Parl.	Art Examinations	403
1942–43	Cmd. 6426	Provision made for Religious Instruction in the Schools in Scotland	403

PAGE

1943–44	Cmd. 6495	Training for Citizenship	404
1950–51	Cmd. 8102	Visual and Aural Aids	404
1953	Non-Parl.	The Place of Welsh and English in the Schools of Wales	404
1951–52	Cmd. 8661	Welsh Language Publishing	405
1953	Non-Parl.	Music in the Schools of Wales	406
1954	Non-Parl.	Drama in the Schools of Wales	406
1956	Non-Parl.	Arts and Crafts in the Schools of Wales	406

2. (b) Particular Vocations

1942–43	Cmd. 6433	Post-War Agricultural Education in England and Wales	406
1945	Non-Parl.	Provision in Secondary Schools of Courses Preparatory to Agricultural Employment	407
1945–46	Cmd. 6728	Higher Agricultural Education in England and Wales	407
1945–46	Cmd. 6704	Agricultural Education in Scotland	408
1947	Non-Parl.	Agricultural and Horticultural Institutes	409
1949	Non-Parl.	Provision of Part-Time Instruction by Local Education Authorities for Agriculturists, Horticulturists and Domestic Producers	409
1954	Non-Parl.	Agricultural Education	409
1944–45	Cmd. 6593	Technical Education	410
1945–46	Cmd. 6786	—— Rep.	410
1945	Non-Parl.	Higher Technological Education	411
1950	Non-Parl.	Future Development of Higher Technological Education	412
1950–51	Cmd. 8357	Higher Technological Education	412
1945–46	Cmd. 6673	Training for Business Administration	412
1947	Non-Parl.	National Advisory Council on Education for Industry and Commerce	413
1947	Non-Parl.	Education for Management. Management Subjects in Technical and Commercial Colleges	413
1949	Non-Parl.	Education for Commerce	414
1952–53	Cmd. 8845	Cadet Entry into the Royal Navy	414

3. Teachers, Youth Leaders: Supply, Training, Salaries

1943–44	Cmd. 6501	Teachers. Supply, Recruitment and Training in the Period immediately following the war	416
1945–46	Cmd. 6723	Training of Teachers	416
1944	Non-Parl.	Teachers and Youth Leaders	417
1946	Non-Parl.	Recruitment and Training of Youth Leaders and Organisers	418
1949	Non-Parl.	Recruitment, Training and Conditions of Service of Youth Leaders and Community Centre Wardens	419
1949	Non-Parl.	Supply of Women Teachers	419
1950–51	Cmd. 8123	Supply of Teachers. Scotland	419
1952–53	Cmd. 8721	—— 2nd Rep.	420
1951–1954		Training and Supply of Teachers. National Advisory Council. Reps.	420

                                                                              PAGE
1951   Non-Parl.   —— Training and Supply of Teachers   420
1951   Non-Parl.   —— Recruitment and Training of Youth Leaders
                              and Community Centre Wardens   420
1953   Non-Parl.   —— Graduate Teachers of Mathematics and
                              Science   420
1954   Non-Parl.   —— Training and Supply of Teachers of Handi-
                              capped Pupils   420
1947–1959   Teachers' Salaries   421

4. (a) Universities

1935–1957   University Development   421
1945–46   Cmd. 6853   Application by the University Courts of the
                              Universities of Scotland for an Increased
                              Grant from the Education (Scotland) Fund   421
1945–46   Cmd. 6824   Scientific Man-power   422
1951–52   Cmd. 8561   Scientific Policy. 5th Ann. Rep. Scientific Man-
                              power   423
1948   Non-Parl.   University Awards   423
1944   Non-Parl.   Medical Schools   424
1949   Non-Parl.   University Education in Dundee and its Relation-
                              ship with St. Andrews University   425
1951–52   Cmd. 8514   University Education in Dundee   426
1943–44   Cmd. 6517   Veterinary Education in Great Britain.   See
                              Professions   427

4. (b) Scientific and Social Research

1943–44   Cmd. 6514   Scientific Research and Development   427
1945–46   Cmd. 6868   Provision for Social and Economic Research   427
1948   Cmd. 7537   Social and Economic Research   428
1952–53   Cmd. 8776   Arrangements for the Expenditure of Counter-
                              part Funds derived from United States
                              Economic Aid   429
1952–53   Cmd. 8918   —— Programme of Expenditure of Counter-
                              part Funds derived from United States
                              Economic Aid   429

5. Museums, Libraries

1945–46   Cmd. 6827   Functions of National Gallery and Tate Gallery
                              and, in respect of Paintings, of the Victoria
                              and Albert Museum   429
1946–47   (128)   Wellington Museum Bill [Lords]   430
1950–51   Cmd. 8229   Libraries, Museums and Art Galleries   430
1951–52   Cmd. 8604   National Museum of Antiquities of Scotland   431
1952   Non-Parl.   Export of Works of Art, etc.   432
1953–54   Cmd. 9163   Departmental Records   433
1952   Non-Parl.   Imperial Institute   434

XV A.   POPULATION

1948–49   Cmd. 7695   Population   435

XV B.   SOCIAL PROBLEMS

1. Evacuation of Women and Children

1939–40	Cmd. 6213	Reception of Children Overseas	437
1941	Non-Parl.	Conditions in Reception Areas	438
1944	Non-Parl.	Hostels for 'Difficult' Children	438

2. Child Care, Homeless Children, Adoption, the Cinema

1944–45	Cmd. 6636	The Boarding Out of Dennis and Terence O'Neill at Bank Farm, Minsterley, and the Steps taken to Supervise their Welfare	439
1945–46	Cmd. 6760	Care of Children. Int. Rep. Training in Child Care	440
1945–46	Cmd. 6922	—— Rep.	440
1945–46	Cmd. 6911	Homeless Children	442
1946	Non-Parl.	Boarding Out of Children and Young Persons	444
1953–54	Cmd. 9248	Adoption of Children	444
1950	Cmd. 7945	Children and the Cinema	445

3. Charities

1952–53	Cmd. 8710	Law and Practice relating to Charitable Trusts	447
1955–56	Cmd. 9538	Government Policy on Charitable Trusts	449

4. Betting

1950–51	Cmd. 8190	Betting, Lotteries and Gaming	449

XVI.   LEGAL ADMINISTRATION, POLICE, LAW

1. Legal Administration, Procedure, Legal Aid

1940	Non-Parl.	Law Reporting	451
1943–1947		Cases of Defective Court Procedure	452
1945–46	Cmd. 6783	Case heard by Justices of the Gilling East Division North Riding of Yorkshire	453
1943–44	Cmd. 6507	Justices' Clerks	453
1947–48	Cmd. 7463	Justices of the Peace	455
1947–1953		Inquiries into Convictions for Murder	456
1947	Non-Parl.	Witnesses Allowances Order	457
1948–49	Cmd. 7639	Depositions	457
1947–48	Cmd. 7466	County Court Procedure. 1st Int. Rep.	457
1948–49	Cmd. 7668	—— Final Rep.	458
1948–49	Cmd. 7764	Supreme Court Practice and Procedure	458
1950–51	Cmd. 8176	—— 2nd Int. Rep.	460
1951–52	Cmd. 8617	—— 3rd Int. Rep. Durham Palatine Court	460
1952–53	Cmd. 8878	—— Final Rep.	460
1953–54	Cmd. 9150	New Trials in Criminal Cases	462
1950–51	Cmd. 8364	Court of Record for the Hundred of Salford	463
1952–53	Cmd. 8955	Central Criminal Court in South Lancashire	463
1944–45	Cmd. 6641	Legal Aid and Legal Advice in England and Wales	463
1945–46	Cmd. 6925	Legal Aid and Legal Advice in Scotland	464

2. Police

PAGE

1945	Non-Parl.	Income Tax on Rent Allowances	465
1948	Non-Parl.	Police Rent and Supplementary Allowances	465
1946–47	Cmd. 7070	Police Post-War. 1st Rep. Higher Training for the Police Service in England and Wales	465
1949	Non-Parl.	—— 2nd Rep. Police Organisation, etc.	466
1949	Non-Parl.	—— 3rd Rep. Buildings, Welfare and the Incidence of Sickness	467
1949	Non-Parl.	—— 4th Rep. Standardisation of Responsibilities in the Higher Ranks of the Police Service and . . . Post-War Organisation	467
1947	Non-Parl.	Local Conditions of Service for the Police	467
1948–49	Cmd. 7674	Police Conditions of Service. Rep. Pt. I	468
1948–49	Cmd. 7831	—— Rep. Pt. II	468
1952	Non-Parl.	Police Representative Organisations and Negotiating Machinery	470
1952	Non-Parl.	—— (Scotland)	470
1953	Non-Parl.	Police Extraneous Duties	470
1953	Non-Parl.	—— (Scotland)	470
1940–41	Cmd. 6312	Police Widows' Pensions	471
1948	Non-Parl.	Special Pensions	471
1952	Non-Parl.	Police Pensions	471
1953	Non-Parl.	—— (Scotland)	471
1954–55	Cmd. 9435	Police (Scotland) Bill, 1955	471

3. Prisons, Prisoners, Punishment, Probation

1939	Non-Parl.	Psychological Treatment of Crime	471
1949	Non-Parl.	Society and the Criminal	471
1950	Cmd. 8088	Psychological Treatment at Wormwood Scrubs Prison	471
1946		Alleged Ill-treatment of Individual Prisoners	471
1945–1949		Treatment and Rehabilitation of Offenders	472
1945	Non-Parl.	—— Police Warnings	472
1947	Non-Parl.	—— Remand Homes	472
1946	Non-Parl.	—— Probation with a Condition of Residence (as it affects Children and Young Persons)	473
1947	Non-Parl.	—— Approved Schools	473
1947	Non-Parl.	—— Scottish Borstal System	473
1948	Non-Parl.	—— Psycho-Therapeutic Treatment of Certain Offenders	474
1949	Non-Parl.	—— Scottish Prison System	474
1944–45	Cmd. 6594	London County Council Remand Homes	475
1946	Non-Parl.	Approved Schools and Remand Homes. Remuneration and Conditions of Service	476
1946–47	Cmd. 7150	Conduct of Standon Farm Approved School	476
1950–51	Cmd. 8256	Punishments in Prisons, Borstal Institutions, Approved Schools and Remand Homes. Rep. Pts. I, II. Prisons and Borstal Institutions	477
1951–52	Cmd. 8429	—— Rep. Pts. III, IV. Approved Schools and Remand Homes	478
1952–53	Cmd. 8932	Capital Punishment	479
1951–52	Cmd. 8594	Broadmoor	481

1952–53   Cmd. 8879   Discharged Prisoners' Aid Societies   481
1945–1952   Papers on Policy and Practice   482

4. Legal Problems arising out of War, War Damage

1940–41   Cmd. 6313   Requisitioning and Compensation   482
1942–43   (53)   Equal Compensation   483
1939–40   Cmd. 6136   Government Compensation Scheme. Principles
                        of Assessment of Damage. 1st Rep.   483
1939–40   Cmd. 6197   —— Final Rep.   483
1941–42   Cmd. 6403   War Damage to Public Utility Undertakings   483
1943–44   Cmd. 6504   War Damaged Licensed Premises and Recon-
                        structions   484
1947   Non-Parl.   War Damage   484
1944–45   Cmd. 6591   Limitation of Actions and Bills of Exchange   484
1948–49   Cmd. 7740   Limitation of Actions   485
1951   Non-Parl.   Distribution of German Enemy Property   485

5. Law of Property, Succession

1941–1942   Compensation and Betterment.   See *Town and
                        Country Planning*   486
1942–43   Cmd. 6467   Land Transfer   486
1951–52   Cmd. 8440   Local Land Charges   486
1947–48   Cmd. 7451   Land Registration in Scotland   487
1947–48   Cmd. 7285   Tenure of Shop Premises. Scotland   487
1948–49   Cmd. 7603   Tenure of Shops and Business Premises in
                        Scotland. Int. Rep.   488
1950   Cmd. 7903   —— Final Rep.   488
1948–49   Cmd. 7706   Leasehold. Cttee. Int. Rep. Tenure and Rents of
                        Business Premises   488
1950   Cmd. 7982   —— Final Rep.   489
1952–53   Cmd. 8713   Leasehold Property in England and Wales   490
1951–52   Cmd. 8656   Scottish Leases   491
1952–53   Cmd. 8714   Leases in Scotland   491
1950–51   Cmd. 8144   Law of Succession in Scotland   491
1950–51   Cmd. 8310   Law of Intestate Succession   492

6. Nationality, International Law

1947–48   Cmd. 7326   British Nationality Bill, 1948   493
1953–54   Cmd. 9068   Private International Law. 1st Rep.   493
1951–52   Cmd. 8460   State Immunities. Rep. Diplomatic Immunity   494

7. Law Revision and Reform

1948   Cmd. 7536   Law of Defamation   494
1952–53   Cmd. 8746   Law of Civil Liability for Damage done by
                        Animals   495
1952–53   Cmd. 8809   Law Reform. 1st Rep. Statute of Frauds and
                        Section 4 of the Sale of Goods Act, 1893   496
1953–54   Cmd. 9161   —— 2nd Rep. Innkeepers' Liability for Property
                        of Travellers, Guests and Residents   497
1953–54   Cmd. 9305   —— 3rd Rep. Occupiers' Liability to Invitees,
                        Licensees and Trespassers   497

8. Marriage and Divorce

PAGE

1942–43	Cmd. 6480	Matrimonial Causes (Trial in the Provinces)	498
1945–46	Cmd. 6881	Procedure in Matrimonial Causes. 1st Int. Rep.	498
1945–46	Cmd. 6945	—— 2nd Int. Rep.	498
1946–47	Cmd. 7024	—— Final Rep.	499
1948–49	Cmd. 7566	Grants for the Development of Marriage Guidance	499

9. Miscellaneous Regulatory Powers

1945–46	Cmd. 6846	Disaster at the Bolton Wanderers' Football Ground	500
1950	Cmd. 8009	Cremation	500
1950	Cmd. 7929	Celluloid Storage	501

A Breviate of
PARLIAMENTARY PAPERS, 1940-1954

I. MACHINERY OF GOVERNMENT

1. The Crown
2. Channel Islands
3. Parliament
4. Ministers
5. Organisation of Departments
6. Civil Service
7. (a) Local Government
   (b) Local Taxation and Financial Administration
8. London

1. THE CROWN

The Title of the Sovereign

pp. 3. 1953

1952–53 *Cmd.* 8748, *xxiv*, 847
pres. Feb., 1953

'The existing form of the Royal Title is not in accord with current constitutional relations within the Commonwealth. In particular it is incorrect in its reference to Ireland and it fails to reflect the special position of the Sovereign as head of the Commonwealth. The Prime Ministers and other representatives of the Commonwealth agreed that the various forms of the Title, should, in addition to an appropriate territorial designation, have as their common element the description of the Sovereign as Queen of Her other Realms and Territories and Head of the Commonwealth.' For this country it should be 'Elizabeth the Second, by the Grace of God of the United Kingdom of Great Britain and Northern Ireland and Her other Realms and Territories Queen, Head of the Commonwealth, Defender of the Faith.'

Civil List

Sel. Cttee. Rep., proc. pp. 7. 1947

1947–48 (18) *vi*, 679
apptd. Nov., o.p. Dec., 1947

The Chancellor of the Exchequer (*Ch.*),

The Prime Minister, Anderson, Benson, Butcher, Churchill, Colman (Miss), Corlett, Davies, Eden, Foot, Greenwood, Howard, Kirkwood, Lawson, McGhee, O'Neill, Scott-Elliot, Stanley, Webb, L. Winterton.

'*To consider His Majesty's Most Gracious Message of the 18th November relating to Provision for Her Royal Highness the Princess Elizabeth and Lieutenant Philip Mountbatten, R.N., on the occasion of their marriage, and to the Civil List and other matters connected therewith.*'

In his Gracious Message His Majesty desired that provision made for Her Royal Highness and His Royal Highness the Duke of Edinburgh should not impose a burden on the people at a time of grave economic difficulties, and stated that he was willing to make available a sum of £100,000 derived from savings on the Civil List during the war. Recommended that the annuity of £15,000 at present paid to Her Royal Highness the Princess Elizabeth should be raised to £40,000 and to the Duke of Edinburgh an annuity of £10,000.

Civil List

Sel. Cttee. Rep., proc., app. pp. 32. 1952

1951–52 (224) *v*, 1
apptd. May, o.p. June, 1952

The Chancellor of the Exchequer (*Ch.*), Alport, Assheton, Attlee, Banks, Benson, Crookshank, Duncan, Edwards, Elliot, Foot, Gaitskell, Glyn, Hill (Mrs.), Hurd, O'Neill, Pearson, Stokes, Viant, Williams, Cullen (Mrs.), Grimond.

'*To consider Her Majesty's Most Gracious Message of the 19th May relating to the Civil List and other matters connected therewith.*'

The Committee followed the usual procedure of fixing the Civil List at the beginning of the reign. The duties which are performed by the Sovereign and members of the Royal Family fall into three categories: the day-to-day study of State Papers and the signature of documents, the granting of audiences to official visitors, and public functions and appearances. These burdens are formidable and are likely to remain so. There is now a great increase in official visitors and the Sovereign has direct relations, not with one government, but with several; these are certain to extend the demands made by the Commonwealth on Her Majesty and the Royal Family.

The Civil List of His Late Majesty was fixed at £410,000. The recommendations were, for Her Majesty alone, £475,000, the Duke of Edinburgh £40,000. The income of the Duke of Cornwall was based on the revenues of the Duchy of Cornwall. For younger sons £10,000 per annum at the age of 21, increased to £25,000 per annum on marriage. For daughters £6000 per annum at the age of 21, increased to £15,000 per annum on marriage; this provision to extend to Princess Margaret.

2. CHANNEL ISLANDS

Proposed Reforms in the Channel Islands

Privy Council. Cttee. Rep., apps. pp. 46.
[1947]

1946–47 *Cmd.* 7074, *x*, 203
apptd. June, 1946. *sgd.* —

J. C. Ede (*Ch.*), L. Samuel, L. Ammon, Butler, Beaumont.

'*To inquire into the proposed reforms in the constitution and procedure of the States of Jersey and of Guernsey, and into the proposed judicial reform, and advise thereon.*'

The institutions, laws and customs are held dear by a great majority of the people and are respected throughout the Commonwealth. Since the liberation from enemy occupation, public opinion has felt the need of adaptations. The issues involved in the reforms proposed by the States and Royal Courts of the Islands must be resolved in the same manner as they have been resolved in the Commonwealth. Guidance and comment is therefore in the form of recommendations which His Majesty may be pleased to consider.

The proposals of the Island authorities are in the main endorsed. A Joint Court of Appeal should be established for the whole of the Islands, subject to a right of appeal to the Judicial Committee of the Privy Council in civil cases.

Island of Alderney

Privy Council. Cttee. Rep. pp. 36.
[1949]

1948–49 *Cmd.* 7805, *xi*, 611
apptd. July, Aug., 1947. *sgd.* —

J. C. Ede (*Ch.*), L. Stansgate, Peake.

'*To enquire into the state of the Island of Alderney, with particular reference to its form of government and its relationship with the neighbouring Islands, its financial position and its economic prospects.*'

When the British military forces were withdrawn in 1940, almost the whole population was evacuated, and cattle later removed to Guernsey. The Germans occupied it, constructed defence works and the land ceased to be cultivated and many houses were destroyed.

The island should offer a reasonable standard of life, but it was not in a position to offer minimum standards of amenities comparable with those of the larger islands, and might lose its younger members. In course of time it would become derelict, 'a situation which His Majesty's Government could not possibly allow to occur.'

As a result of conferences, representatives of Alderney and Guernsey agreed that Guernsey would take over the major services, subject to Alderney's being taxed on the Guernsey scale.

3. PARLIAMENT

Parliament Bill, 1947

Conference of Party Leaders.   Statement. pp. 6.   1948

1947–48 *Cmd.* 7380, *xxii*, 1001
pres. May, 1948

In the debate on Lord Salisbury's amendment to the Government motion that the Parliament Bill be read a Second Time, the Lord Privy Seal stated that the Government was willing to enter into a conference on proposals for a reform of the House of Lords, without prejudice to either side. The Party representatives at the Conference agreed that the discussion should cover the reform of its composition and the powers to be vested in a reformed House, and that the two subjects were interdependent, so that failure to agree on one might result in no general agreement being reached.

The Party representatives would, if agreement on powers had been reached, be prepared to give consideration to the following proposals regarding the composition of the House: that the Second Chamber should be complementary and not rival to the Lower House; the reformed House should be a modification of the existing chamber and not one of a new type; a permanent majority should not be assured to any one party; heredity should not be a sole qualification for membership; the Lords of Parliament would be appointed on grounds of personal distinction and might be drawn from Hereditary Peers or Commoners created Life Peers; women should be as equally capable as men of being appointed; remuneration

should be payable, so that persons of limited means should not be excluded. Peers not Lords of Parliament should be entitled to vote and to stand for election.

No agreement was reached on the question of powers. Under the provisions of the Parliament Act, 1911, a Bill in dispute between the two Houses cannot be presented for Royal Assent unless it has been introduced in three successive sessions and unless two years have elapsed between its second reading in the Commons in the first session and its third reading in the third session. The Government representatives said that this would enable a hostile House of Lords to render ineffective the legislative programme of a fourth and fifth session of a quinquennial Parliament: but offered to extend the period of delay of one year from the second reading in the first session as proposed in the Bill, to nine months from the third reading. The Leaders of the official Opposition said that this would make the period of delay largely illusory, but that they would accept eighteen months, as halfway between the Parliament Act's two years and the Bill's one year; or twelve months from the third reading. The Liberal Party representatives regretted the breakdown of the Conference on a difference of three months. But the Government and official Opposition held that the difference between them on powers was fundamental and not related only to the period of delay.

Electoral Reform

Electoral Machinery. Rep., apps. pp. 47.
1942

1942–43 *Cmd.* 6408, *iv*, 297
S. P. Vivian (*Ch.*).

As a result of the large population movements during the war, by 1941, 5 mn. adults had moved out of the constituency in which they were resident in 1939, and would be unable to vote: in addition there were large numbers in the Services and the Merchant Navy. A large counter movement could be expected after the armistice.   Some alternative system of registration would be required to enable an election to be held at short notice. The Committee proposed a scheme of continuous registration, which included a two months' residence qualification. The information regarding those qualified by residence would be supplied through the National Register to the Electoral Registration Officers, with a special provision that an elector should not be removed from one register until he had been included in the register of another constituency. For Servicemen, a special scheme of proxy voting was proposed.

On the basis of the principles laid down by the Speaker's Conference, 1917 (*Breviate, 1900–1916*, p. 6) that each vote should as far as possible command an equal share of representation in the House, and that 70,000 should be the standard unit of population per Member, as a result of 22 years of accumulated population movements, in 1939 87 constituency electorates did not justify their representation, while 32 had so increased as to require their representation to be doubled or trebled. To prevent the accumulation of maldistribution there should be a statutory Commission to review the state of the constituencies during the normal life of every Parliament: it should include representatives of the Departments most concerned with and able to contribute to the problem, and to keep it in touch with Parliament the Speaker should be Chairman. A full normal redistribution on the basis of a new register could not be carried out in time for the first post-war General Election. The alternative would be a redistribution based on the 1939 population, by dividing or merging constituencies.

Electoral Reform and Redistribution of Seats. Letters. pp. 8. 1944. pp. 6. 1944
1943–44 *Cmd.* 6534, *Cmd.* 6543, *iii*, 213
Mr. Speaker (D. C. Brown) (*Ch.*).

The Speaker's Conference agreed that there should be a general redistribution of seats as soon as possible, abnormally large constituencies being divided and a temporary increase of the size of the House by 25 being permitted. The Permanent Rules agreed were that the size of the House should be limited to 591, excluding university seats, that there should be no reduction in the representation of Scotland, Wales, or Northern Ireland, and that boundaries were to coincide where possible with local government boundaries. There should be four Boundary Commissions, Mr. Speaker being Chairman of all four. The local government franchise was to be assimilated to the Parliamentary franchise, and both elections held on the same register. The business premises qualification, university representation, and methods of election should be retained. Proportional Representation, the Alternative Vote and votes at age 18 were all rejected.

The Second Report of the Conference agreed on a maximum for candidates' expenses of £450 basic plus 1d. per elector in Boroughs and 1½d. per elector in Counties, and on the details of permitted expenses, on increased polling facilities, especially in rural areas, and on uniform polling hours. It should be an offence to attempt to influence elections by broadcasts from outside the country. Each elector should have a polling card. The arrangements for voting by men in the Services should be extended and improved. The Conference passed resolutions disapproving of prospective or adopted candidates giving substantial donations to charitable, etc., organisations benefiting the constituency, or direct or indirect payments to party organisations designed to influence their actions in selecting candidates.

Postal Voting for the Forces, Seamen and War Workers Abroad. Rep., apps. pp. 8.
1945
1944–45 *Cmd.* 6581, *v*, 51
J. Anderson (*Ch.*).

The Conference proposed arrangements, including the aid of Air Ministry aircraft and lengthening the period between nomination and count, which would enable Service voters in most of the major areas to vote.

Electoral Law Reform. Interim Rep. pp. 15. 1945. Final Rep., apps. pp. 30. 1947

1944–45 *Cmd.* 6606, *v*, 59.   1947–48 *Cmd.* 7286, *xi*, 727

C. T. Carr (*Ch.*).

The two reports deal with the application to Scotland of the principles arrived at by the Speaker's Conference. The Interim Report deals with the use of school halls, etc., better polling facilities in rural areas and with the problem of enforcing the prohibition on election broadcasting from outside the U.K. The Final Report deals with corrupt and illegal practices and the conduct of elections. Amongst the recommendations were: to ensure secrecy, the procedure for university elections should be assimilated to postal voting, which should be the only method; and where there was equality of voting the decision should be by lot and not by the returning officer's casting vote.

Electoral Registration. Rep., apps. pp. 25. 1947

1946–47 *Cmd.* 7004, *xi*, 377

G. H. Oliver (*Ch.*).

The Parliamentary Elections (War Time Registration) Act, 1943 and 1944, provided for an *ad hoc* register based on the National Registration machinery. The Act of 1943 was intended primarily for bye-elections, and had difficulties in operation; it was doubtful if simultaneous *ad hoc* registers could be made in event of a general election. The Representation of the People Act, 1945, as amended by the Elections and Jurors Act, 1945, removed the requirement of *ad hoc* registers, and substituted an annual Register based on the voter's National Registration address. This register was less accurate than pre-war registers during the three months'

qualifying period. There should be a reversion to the use of canvass and registration forms every 6 months, based on normal place of residence. Proposals are made for postal voting in Local Government elections, and for Service, Seamen's and war workers' votes by proxy or post.

Boundary Commissions

The House of Commons (Redistribution of Seats) Act, 1944, established four Boundary Commissions. Section 2 required the Commission for England to make recommendations for immediate division of abnormally large constituencies with more than 100,000 electors: this was done in 1944–45 Cmd. 6634, iv, 79. Section 3 required each Commission to make initial proposals for redistribution on the basis of rules set out in the Third Schedule to the Act. Four reports, 1946–47 Cmd. 7231, x, 121 (Northern Ireland), 1947–48 Cmd. 7260, Cmd. 7270, xv, 791 (England and Scotland), and 1947–48 Cmd. 7274, xv, 895 (Wales) show how the Commissions dealt with the difficulties of interpreting the rules requiring local unity and that in rural constituencies, geography, size, shape and accessibility could be considered, without creating excessive disparities or variations of size.

The following papers are reports of the Commissioners on proposed individual constituences: 1947–48 Cmd. 7400, Cmd. 7425, xv, 779; 1948–49 Cmd. 7745, Cmd. 7787, xi, 721; 1950–51 Cmd. 8100, Cmd. 8151, Cmd. 8158, Cmd. 8164, (203) (231) viii, 821; 1951–52 (44) (204) viii, 475; 1952–53 (113) Cmd. 8703, vii, 535.

Section 4 of the 1944 Act required the Commission to make periodical reviews at intervals of not less than three or more than seven years. Papers 1953–54 Cmd. 9311, Cmd. 9312, Cmd. 9313, Cmd. 9314, ix, 1, and *Parliamentary Constituencies, England, Scotland and Wales*, 1953–54 Cmd. 9319, xxvi, 739 set out the results of the first periodical review.

Offices or Places of Profit under the Crown

Sel. Cttee. Rep., proc., mins. of ev., apps., index. pp. lvi, 188. 1941

1940–41 (120) *iii*, 487
apptd. March, o.p. Oct., 1941

D. Herbert (*Ch.*), Noel-Baker, Barnes, Davies, Headlam, Maclean, Mander, Maxton, McEwen, Peters, Pickthorn, Williams.

'To enquire into the law and practice governing the disqualifications for Membership of the House of Commons by reason of the holding, or the acceptance of, Offices or Places of Profit under the Crown, and to make recommendations.'

The Committee was set up following the appointment of certain M.P.s to certain offices abroad, and the debate on the House of Commons Disqualification (Temporary Revision) Bill, 1941, which revealed the 'archaic, confused and unsatisfactory conditions of the law on the subject,' of which there exists no comprehensive statement. The sources of existing law include a series of decisions by the House asserting the right to control its own composition and defining its privileges; statute law, embodied in 80 Public Acts, including the Succession to the Crown Act, 1707; and decisions of the House on individual cases from 1707 onwards.

The historical survey (paras. 9–19 and App. 2, Memo. by Sir Gilbert Campion, Clerk to the House of Commons) showed that the attitude of the Commons to the holding of offices under the Crown passed through three phases. In the 'privilege' phase (1575–1640), when it was concerned to establish its position as an independent deliberative body, it tried to insist on its claims to the physical attendance of members of the House and objected to office-holding which would prevent this. In the 'corruption' phase, which ran from 1660 to the establishment of Cabinet Government in the first half of the eighteenth century, its endeavours were directed to the exclusion of persons appointed to office as a means of increasing the influence of the Crown over Parliament. In 1714 271 members, rather more than half the House, held offices or pensions, excluding those with military or naval commissions. In the third phase of 'ministerial responsibility', it was seen that Parliamentary control required the presence of ministers, and a distinction was drawn between the holders of executive or non-political offices, e.g. civil servants, who were, and the holders of political offices, who were not excluded. The principle of the incompatibility of certain non-ministerial offices with membership of the House, and the need both to limit the total number of office-holders and for the presence of ministers to ensure Parliamentary control found expression in the Act of Succession, 1707.

Existing legislation should be repealed and a bill passed which should disqualify from membership all officers other than two excepted classes—the holders of specified political and ministerial offices, of whom only a limited maximum number, 60, should be allowed to sit, and the holders of certain non-ministerial offices, which should not disqualify. The proportion between ministers and parliamentary secretaries laid down in the Ministers of the Crown Act, 1937 should be maintained. A new development is the great increase in the number of unpaid parliamentary private secretaries; it is desirable that a convention should be established reducing or limiting their number. Pensions should not be a disqualification unless they can be terminated by the Crown otherwise than for good reason, such as misconduct. Amongst the non-political officers who should be expressly disqualified are civil servants, judges, stipendiary magistrates. No suggestion is made on the disqualification of clergy of any denomination.

During the war there have been important departures from these principles. Members have held offices which prevent attendance for long periods; the number of ministers has greatly increased and the number of paid and unpaid offices still more. But the relevant legislation was often passed hastily; the Ministers of the Crown (Emergency Appointments) Act, 1939, should be amended to limit its duration, and the emergency legislation repealed as soon as practicable after or even before the cessation of active hostilities. The House, for the removal of doubts, should come to a resolution agreeing with the conclusions of the Report.

See Memo. by Sir Gilbert Campion, App. 2, and his evidence.

Elections

Sel. Cttee.

D. Grenfell (*Ch.*).

The Committee was appointed to consider whether the elections of certain persons were invalid because at the time of election they held offices or places of profit under the Crown.

1945–46 (3–1) *vi*, 119

Rep., proc., mins. of ev., apps. pp. vi, 20. 1945

The holding of office or place of profit under the Crown disqualifies the holder from being elected, sitting or voting in the House. The actual receipt of remuneration is immaterial, provided it was payable. See Memo. and evidence by Sir Gilbert Campion, Clerk to the House. The disqualification arose out of fear that the independence of Members would be weakened by dependence on the Crown and it is still important to see that the House is not filled with persons holding office and dependent on the Executive.

Mrs. Mann and Mr. Forman were members of Rent Tribunals. The remuneration set against expenses was negligible, the work was undertaken out of public duty and not for profit and they were unaware of their disability. A statute should validate their election. The Report of the Select Committee on Offices or Places of Profit (see p. 6 above) should be adopted at the earliest opportunity.

1945–46 (71–1) *vi*, 155

First Rep., proc., mins. of ev., apps. pp. x, 50 [1946]

Mr. Harrison was a member of a Pensions Appeal Tribunal, Mrs. F. K. Corbett and Mr. Awbery part-time assessors with the Umpire on hardship cases under the National Service (Armed Forces) Act, 1939. All three were incapable of election. A statute should validate their election. Mr. J. Jones had resigned before the date of the poll. A repeal of the Succession to the Crown Act, 1707, and the clarification of the Statute law is urgent. Maintenance of the Act in its present form might discourage public service as part-time members of statutory boards. To protect candidates from inadvertence, a provision should be inserted in the statute requiring any Parliamentary candidate to sign a general declaration relinquishing or resigning from all offices and this should be effective immediately or on election.

1945–46 (92–1) *vi*, 221

Second Rep., proc., mins. of ev., apps. pp. vi, 18. [1946]

Captain Hewitson was a member of six trades boards, received only expenses and allowances and was not entitled to fees or remuneration. The offices were not places of profit and his election was not invalid.

Election of a Member (Clergyman of the Church of Ireland)

Sel. Cttee. Special Rep., proc., mins. of ev., apps. pp. x, 51. [1950]

1950 (68–1) *v*, 11

apptd. April, o.p. May, 1950

F. J. Bellenger (*Ch.*), Cocks, Donovan, Foster, Morris, Mott-Radclyffe, Oliver, Spens, Thurtle, Waterhouse.

'*To consider and report whether the election of the Reverend James Godfrey MacManaway to this Parliament as Member for Belfast, West, is void by reason of the provisions of the House of Commons (Clergy Disqualification) Act, 1801.*'

The arguments on both sides of the question are evenly balanced, and the Committee are unable to come to an unanimous conclusion. It recommends that immediate legislative action should be taken to clarify the law.

Order in Council directing that the Report of the Judicial Committee in the case of the Reverend James Godfrey MacManaway, a Member of Parliament, be communicated to the House of Commons: with reasons for such report as delivered by their Lordships. pp. 11. 1950

1950 *Cmd.* 8067, *xviii*, 415

Their Lordships advise that the Rev. J. G. MacManaway is disabled from sitting and voting in the House of Commons by reason of the fact that, having been ordained as a priest according to the use of the Church of Ireland, he has received episcopal ordination.

Clergy Disqualification

Sel. Cttee. Rep., proc., mins. of ev., apps. pp. viii, 64. 1953

1952–53 (200) *vi*, 201
apptd. Nov., 1952. *o.p. June,* 1953

R. K. Law (*Ch.*), Bing, Brooke, Clarke, Fletcher, Griffiths, Grimston, Kerr, Medlicott, Wade, Williams, Woodburn.

'*To consider whether any amendment is desirable in the law relating to the disability of certain ministers of religion from sitting and voting in the House of Commons.*'

The law makes a distinction between those ministers of religion who have been ordained by a bishop and those who have not. As a result some clergymen are and some are not debarred from standing for election. The disqualification has nothing to do with whether they are actively engaged in their ministry, and while clergymen of the Church of England can divest themselves of their religious office and become candidates, those of other churches cannot even if they have abandoned their faith. Witnesses from churches in full communion with the Church of England preferred their

clergy not to be eligible. The Roman Catholic Church preferred the ineligibility to be preserved by ecclesiastical rather than civil law, whilst churches where ministers are not episcopally ordained and are eligible expressed no wish for that freedom to sit to be taken away. No change in the law should be made at present.

Members' Expenses, Salaries and Pensions

Sel. Cttees.

apptd. Nov., 1945, *Feb.,* 1947, *Nov.,* 1953
Members' Expenses. Rep., proc., mins. of ev., apps. pp. xiv, 116. [1946]

1945–46 (93–1) *viii*, 163

T. Smith (*Ch.*).

All the evidence recommended a material increase in the remuneration of Members. Salaries should be increased to £1000 per annum, of which £500 should be an expense allowance free of tax, which should also be given to Ministers with salaries of less than £5000, to the Chairman of Ways and Means and the Deputy Chairman. In view of this, a general extension of free travel or grant of free postage, telegrams and telephones was unnecessary.

Members' Fund. Rep., proc., mins. of ev., index. pp. xvi, 51. 1947

1946–47 (110) *ix*, 145

S. P. Viant (*Ch.*).

As a result of the working of the House of Commons Members' Fund, set up as a result of the Committee on Pensions for Members (see *Breviate 1917–1939*, p. 7), the Members' contribution should be reduced from £12 to £9 per annum.

See *House of Commons Members' Fund.* Statement; 1947–48 Cmd. 7282, xii, 623.

Members' Expenses, etc. Rep., proc., mins. of ev., apps. pp. xxxiv, 85. 1954

1953–54 (72) *vii*, 217

C. Davies (*Ch.*).

The expenses necessarily entailed are

such that £1000 is insufficient, and many Members are largely or wholly dependent upon it. The payment to Members should be such as to enable men and women from all walks of life to enter this field of public service. The House should be representative of the people and not drawn from certain sections only. Few would support the idea of a House composed principally of full-time politicians, but it would be no less damaging if the Members could not give of their best because of the need to escape from financial pressure. Instead of enlarging postal, travelling and other concessions there should be a straightforward increase of salary to £1500.

Linked with the salary increase should be a non-contributory pension scheme based on a pension, payable at 65, after retirement, of £350 a year after 10 but less than 15 years' service, and £500 for longer service. Members should contribute to a new Benevolent Fund at double the existing rate, i.e. £24, to deal with cases of hardship, etc.

Conduct of a Member

Sel. Cttee. Rep., proc., mins. of ev., apps. pp. xx, 290. 1941

1940–41 (5) *ii*, 489
re-apptd. Nov., o.p. Dec., 1940

J. Gretton (*Ch.*), Benson, Cadogan, Denman, Ellis, Evans, Pethick-Lawrence, Pickthorn, Schuster, Spens.

'*To investigate the conduct and activities of Mr. Boothby in connection with the payment out of assets in this country of claims against the Government of and institutions in the Republic of Czechoslovakia: to report generally on these matters and in particular to consider and report whether the conduct of the honourable Member was contrary to the usage or derogatory to the dignity of the House or inconsistent with the standards which Parliament is entitled to expect from its Members.*'

Mr. Boothby, a Member of the House of Commons for 15 years, was a managing director of a firm of merchant bankers in the City, and interested in the affairs of Czechoslovakia. In the course of his business he had become the personal friend of Mr. Weiniger, an international financier. In April, 1939, a Committee was formed, with Mr. Boothby as chairman, representing claimants against Czechoslovak assets.

The Committee found that 'Mr. Boothby had a claim to participation to the extent of £24,000 in the realisation of Czech assets belonging to the Weiniger ladies', and that the promise to pay was given on the understanding that he would render services in return. He 'took no steps at any time to disclose to the House of Commons as a whole or to those members to whom he wrote urging particular action or to the Treasury that his private interests were in any way affected by what might be done about the Czech assets'. His conduct 'was contrary to the usage and derogatory to the dignity of the House and inconsistent with the standards which Parliament is entitled to expect from its members'.

Budget Disclosure

Sel. Cttee. Rep., proc., mins. of ev., apps. pp. xvi, 53. 1947

1947–48 (20) *vi*, 545
apptd. Nov., o.p. Dec., 1947

J. J. Lawson (*Ch.*), Anderson, Boyd-Carpenter, Donovan, Dugdale, Hale, Hicks, Manningham-Buller, Mitchison, Morris, Peake, Poole, Proctor, Silverman, Webb.

'*To inquire into all the circumstances relating to or associated with the disclosure of Budget information by Mr. Dalton, then Chancellor of the Exchequer, on Wednesday, 12th November.*'

Mr. Dalton made a premature and unpremeditated disclosure to Mr. Carvel, Lobby Correspondent of the *Star* which he had no right to make. He did not make it for premature publication and believed there was no possibility of this. In good faith Mr. Carvel made an error of judgment in disclosing the information to his newspaper in the guise of a forecast, in the mistaken belief that he was at liberty to do so. There were no movements of prices or sales which could be attributed to the leakage of news.

App. III is a Memo. by Eden, Hon. Sec. of the Parliamentary Lobby journalists, unanimously approved by a special meeting of them, on the code of conduct which they observe in their contacts with Members of the House.

Chairman of Ways and Means (Personal Explanation)

Sel. Cttee. Rep., proc., mins. of ev., apps. pp. vi, 40. [1948]

1947–48 (104) *vi*, 615
apptd. March, o.p. March, 1948

J. Westwood (*Ch.*), Fletcher, Galbraith, Keeling, Leslie, Lloyd, Morris, Thurtle, Ungoed-Thomas, Viant, Wilmot.

'*To enquire into the Statement made to the House on 22nd March by the Chairman of Ways and Means and Deputy Speaker, that he acted in his professional capacity as a solicitor against an honourable Member of this House in a matter which might have resulted in legal proceedings; and to report whether such action is consonant with the proper and impartial discharge of the duties of this office.*'

Major Milner, Chairman of Ways and Means and Deputy Speaker, acted as mediator only after his firm of solicitors, without his knowledge, had become involved in a dispute between two Members. He was not actuated by any partiality, the sole aim being to effect an amicable settlement. The Committee agreed with his statement that the Chair should not only be impartial, but give the appearance of it. It was for the House to consider whether there should be rules governing the conduct of the Deputy Speaker in his professional or business relationships with any Member of the House.

Public Petitions

Sel. Cttee. Special Rep., proc., mins. of ev., app. pp. vi, 9. 1944

1943–44 (80) *ii*, 1005
apptd. Nov., 1943. *o.p. May,* 1944

E. Campbell (*Ch.*), Acland-Troyte, Chater, Clarry, Daggar, Graham, Hambro, Horabin, Hurd, Makins, Russell, Thomas, Tinker, Viant, Wells.

'*To examine and classify the Petitions on Public Matters presented to the House, and to prepare Abstracts of the same and . . . to direct the printing in extenso of such as might appear to them to require it.*'

Most petitions are not presented by the formal procedure recognised by the rules of the House, but are deposited in a bag behind the Speaker's chair, examined by the Clerk of Public Petitions and unless irregular are entered in the Votes as presented and ordered to lie on the Table. Petitions which are found to be irregular are not recorded in the Votes or the Journals and are not referred to the Committee. Members should consult the rules and where there is any doubt as to the correct form of a petition, they should consult the Clerk of Public Petitions.

The Old Age Pensions petition was irregular because it asked for a charge on public funds, which is the King's sole right to initiate, without having received the King's recommendation. The Speaker was prepared to interpret standing orders so as to exempt from the need of the King's recommendation petitions which pray for legislation involving expenditure as distinct from paying for expenditure directly.

The Appendix contains a Memo. on Petitions prepared by Sir Gilbert Campion, Clerk to the House.

—— Sel. Cttee. Special Rep. pp. [4]. 1952

1951–52 (286) *vii*, 39
apptd. Nov., 1951. *o.p. July,* 1952

Brook, Carson, Grey, Hughes, King, Lambert, Lancaster, Legge-Bourke, Maitland, McGhee, Morrison, Pargiter, Raikes, Thornton-Kemsley, Watkins.

Appended to the Petition relating to Health Service charges presented May

1952, were columns headed donations, and at the bottom of each sheet was printed the body responsible for organising the Petition. In the past Petitions have been disallowed when extraneous matter was attached to them; to allow it might lead to abuses of the right of petitioning. In future Petitions containing such matter should not be received by the House.

Procedure

Sel. Cttee. 1st Rep., proc., mins. of ev., index. pp. xxii, 107 [1945]

1945–46 (9–1) *ix*, 23
apptd. Aug., o.p. Oct., 1945

R. Young (*Ch.*), Brown, Cocks, Cove, Crookshank, Crossman, Davies, Gaitskell, L. Hinchingbrooke, Messer, Pickthorn, Reid, Silverman, Viant, Webb, Willey, L. Winterton.

'*To consider the Procedure in the Public Business of this House and to report what alterations, if any, are desirable for the more efficient despatch of such business.*'

A scheme was originally drafted by a Committee of Ministers in the Coalition Government to meet the heavy programme of legislation which would be required in the transition from war to peace. The proposals that substantially all Bills should be referred to Standing Committees and that these should be increased in number and reduced in size were accepted. The permanent nucleus of each committee should be 20 members. The sittings should be lengthened by half an hour, the Committees being free to arrange the number of their sittings. When the Government wished to prescribe a time limit for a Committee, the guillotine motion should name the date by which the Bill should be reported. There are Memos. by the Speaker, Sir Gilbert Campion, Clerk to the House, and by Mr. P. F. Cole, the editor of the official Report.

—— Second Rep., proc., mins. of ev., app., index. pp. viii, 71. [1946]

1945–46 (58–1) *ix*, 161
o.p. Jan., 1946

The exercise of the right to put questions to Ministers is the readiest and most effective method of parliamentary control over the executive and anything which diminished its effectiveness is to be deprecated. But because Departments give a high priority to preparing their answers to them, they should be put only when other methods have failed and some action is urgently required, and time enough should be given for the preparation of the answer. The period of notice should be increased to two days, questions for oral answer should be answered in seven days. The Committee did not wish to limit further the number of questions a Member might ask. No convenient means were found of reducing the time spent on divisions.

There are Memos. by E. Fellowes, Second Clerk Assistant, who handled Questions, by the Speaker and by Clerks of the Public Bill Office.

—— Third Rep., proc., mins. of ev., app., index. pp. lxvi, 400 [1946]

1945–46 (189–1) *ix*, 305
o.p. Oct., 1946

add Fletcher, del. Gaitskell.

The Clerk of the House, Sir Gilbert Campion, was invited to prepare a comprehensive scheme for the reform of procedure, which is given in the Appendix. The proposal to relieve the House of legislative detail by delegating the report stage to re-organised standing committees and other suggestions for shortening the procedure on bills were not accepted. The means of controlling administration should be improved by re-organising the procedure in Committee of Supply in the ways specified, to make it more convenient for criticism of policy. A committee, or joint committee with the Lords, should enquire into the delegation of legislative power through statutory instruments and the procedure relating to it. In the field of finance the cumbrous procedure of Budget Resolutions and the Finance Bill has practical advantages, but the examination of expenditure should be undertaken by a single committee combining the function of the Committee of Public Accounts and the Select Committee on Estimates. The ballot is the fairest method of allocating private members' time, but suggestions are made for distributing private members' days more conveniently over the session.

There are Memos. by the Clerk to Financial Committees on the proposed Public Expenditure Committee and by Sir C. Carr on Statutory Instruments. Sir Gilbert Campion's proposals in his Memo. (pp. xliv, xlv) that the order of reference to the Select Committee on Statutory Instruments should be extended to enable it to report on the merits of an Instrument as an exercise of the powers delegated and on the grievances arising out of Instruments actually in operation are discussed in Memos. by Dr. C. K. Allen and Prof. E. C. S. Wade, who gave evidence by invitation.

Standing Orders (Revision)

Sel. Cttee. Rep., proc., app. pp. iv, 45. 1948

1947–48 (192) *ix*, 603
apptd. July, o.p. July, 1948

J. Milner (*Ch.*), Bowles, Butcher, Diamond, Fletcher, Leslie, Lucas-Tooth, MacAndrew, Mathers, Morris, Thurtle, Williams.

'*To consider and report upon the re-arrangement and re-drafting of the Standing Orders so as to bring them into conformity with existing practice.*'

Existing Standing Orders should be repealed and the revised Standing Orders, based on draft proposals by Sir Gilbert Campion, Clerk to the House, adopted. Those relating to Public Money, some of which are of considerable antiquity, and are an inadequate expression of modern practice, have been left untouched as much research and special technical know-

ledge would be involved. Attention should be given to these at a future date.

Hybrid Bills (Procedure in Committee)

Sel. Cttee. Rep., proc., mins. of ev., apps. pp. xviii, 109. [1948]

1947–48 (191) *ix*, 297
apptd. Dec., 1947. *o.p. July,* 1948

G. Benson (*Ch.*), Lennox-Boyd, Lucas-Tooth, McLeavy, Morris, Sharp, Sparks, Wells.

'*To consider the procedure in Select Committees on Public Bills to which the Standing Orders relative to Private Business apply and to report whether any, and if so what, rules should be laid down to regulate their proceedings.*'

A hybrid bill is a public bill which affects particular interests differently from other interests in the same category, so that if it were a private bill preliminary notices would have to be served on the affected parties, e.g. London Transport Bill, 1931, Bank of England Bill, 1946. All hybrid bills are referred to a select committee to enable affected parties to defend their interests and to secure proper compensation. Since the bill is a public bill, a petitioner against it should not be permitted to discuss the public policy which inspires it, the expediency of which is decided when the House has given it a second reading. He should be heard only by virtue of his *locus standi*, and should not be allowed to argue on matters which cannot give him *locus standi*, but provided his arguments do not exceed this, may traverse the principle of the bill.

Private Bill Standing Orders

Sel. Cttee. HL. Rep., proc., app. pp. vi, 97. 1945

1945–46 (HL.28) *iv*, 101
apptd. Aug., o.p. Dec., 1945

Lord Mersey (*Ch.*).

'*To revise the Standing Orders relative to Private and Provisional Order Bills.*'

All Standing Orders were examined, much redrafting, regrouping and pruning carried out, but little change in practice or procedure made. Where they are common to both Houses, the revised form approved by the Commons has been followed.

Standing Orders of the House

Sel. Cttee. HL. Rep., app. pp. 60. [1953]. Mins. of proc. pp. 14. [1953] 1952–53 (HL.113) (HL.126) *iii*, 1043 *o.p. July, Oct.,* 1953
Lord Drogheda (*Ch.*).

Presents the draft of revised Standing Orders. Standing Order No. 26, on avoiding asperity of speech in debate, 'so aptly worded that it would be a mistake to modernise, has been left in the wording of 1626: "To prevent misunderstanding, and for avoiding of offensive speeches, when matters are debating, either in the House or at Committees, it is for honour sake thought fit, and so ordered, That all personal, sharp, or taxing speeches be forborn, and whosoever answereth another man's speech shall apply his answer to the matter without wrong to the person: and as nothing offensive is to be spoken, so nothing is to be illtaken, if the party that speaks it shall presently make a fair exposition or clear denial of the words that might bear any ill-construction; and if any offence be given in that kind, as the House itself will be very sensible thereof, so it will sharply censure the offender, and give the party offended a fit reparation and a full satisfaction".'

Private Bill Procedure

Jt. Sel. Cttee. Rep., proc., mins. of ev., app. index. pp. xxxviii, 480. 1955
1954–55 (139–1) *iii*, 217
apptd. Dec., 1954. *o.p. May,* 1955
G. Hall (*Ch.*), L. Derwent, L. Hindlip, L. Merthyr, L. Faringdon, L. Belstead, L. Latham, L. Grantchester, Bowles, Erroll, Hall, Lockwood, Mitchison, Powell, Wilson.

'*To consider what alterations, if any, are desirable in the practice and the Standing Orders of the two Houses relating to private legislation, having special regard to the desirability of lessening the expense at present incurred.*'

The terms of reference followed closely those of the Committees of 1930 and 1936 (*Breviate 1917–39*, pp. 10, 12). Power should be given to the Chairman of Committees and of Ways and Means to authorise the carrying over of private bills from one session to another of the same Parliament. It should no longer be possible for a single Member to block the second reading by saying 'Object' save in the case of bills for county borough status or extension, or promoted by nationalised industries, or if a bill raises a new important principle. Unless there is a reasoned motion in the names of six Members, the Speaker should declare the bill carried. Town meetings and polls should be abolished.

Statutory Rules and Orders, Statutory Instruments

The Select Committee considers each Statutory Rule and Order to determine whether the attention of the House should be drawn to it because it imposes a charge on the public revenues, requires a payment to be made for a licence, etc., contains any provision excluding it from consideration in the Courts, makes some unusual or unexpected use of statutory powers, or requires elucidation. There are many papers each year reporting the results of the scrutiny, some calling the attention of the House to an Order on one of these grounds. Some reports or special reports make general comments. 1943–44 (113) ii, 1029, recommends that the illogically diverse periods, varying from 20 to 40 days, for which Orders must be laid before the House should be made uniform. The choice between affirmative resolution and annulment should be modified by a requirement that orders imposing taxation or modifying a statute should need affirmative resolutions. The Third Special Report 1945–

46 (186) ix, 837, welcomes the explanatory notes attached to the Orders, but deprecates any tendency which might follow to frame the instrument itself in technical language which has no meaning to ordinary citizens. The Committee hoped for a discontinuance of five-tier cumulative delegated legislation by Statute, Defence Regulation, Orders under regulation, directions made under an Order, and licences issued under directions.

In the Third Report of the Select Committee on *Procedure* (1945–46 (189–1) ix, 305) there are memos. by Sir Gilbert Campion, Sir C. Carr, and memos. by Dr. Allen and Prof. Wade on delegated legislation. See above p. 12. See also *Ministers' Powers, Breviate 1917–39*, p. 20.

Delegated Legislation

Sel. Cttee. Rep., proc., mins. of ev., apps. pp. xlii, 183. 1954

1952–53 (310–1) iv, 157

apptd. Dec., 1952. *o.p.* Oct., 1953
C. Davies (*Ch.*), Astor, Boyle, Ede, Edwards, Elliot, Erroll, Hale, Hudson, Nicholson, Powell, Wallace, Willey, Woodburn.

'*To consider in what respects the existing procedures, by which the control of this House over delegated legislation is exercised, need to be improved or supplemented and by what means this can best be achieved.*'

Delegated legislation is needed because of the pressure on Parliamentary time, the technicality of a subject, the need for flexibility and the means for dealing with emergencies. The volume of delegated legislation now exceeds that by statute. The practice is that important matters of policy and principle are dealt with in the Acts themselves, regulation-making power being limited to detailed technical and procedural matters, matters in which elasticity is desirable to enable alterations to be made in the light of changed circumstances, and those on which new statutory powers are being created and

on which the future lines of development cannot be foreseen.

While accepting that delegated legislation was necessary, the Donoughmore Committee on *Ministers' Powers* (1931–32 Cmd. 4060, xii, 341) thought that the risks of abuse demanded safeguards. Its recommendation that a Standing Committee should report on every Bill containing a proposal to confer law-making power was not adopted, but since 1944 there has been a Select Committee on Statutory Instruments, referred to as the Scrutiny Committee. This may not consider the policy or merits of any proposed Statutory Instrument, but reports on whether the attention of the House should be drawn to any Instrument because it imposes a charge, appears to make an unusual and unexpected use of the powers confirmed by statute, purports without authority to be retrospective, excludes challenge in the Courts, has been unjustifiably delayed in publication or needs elucidation.

The Statutory Instruments Act, 1946, defines Statutory Instruments, requires publication and sets out the standard procedure.

The chief forms of Parliamentary control are approval by affirmative resolution, and negative, i.e. laying with immediate effect, subject to annulment. The affirmative procedure would be preferred where there are powers to alter an Act in extent or duration, powers to impose a charge, or powers to fill in skeleton powers.

A considerable number of suggestions for altering procedure to make control more effective were rejected. The recommendations were that the existing negative procedure should continue, except that if the matter is still under discussion at 11.30 p.m., the Speaker should put the question unless he considers that there has not been adequate time for debate, in which case it could be adjourned to the next ordinary sitting day, and that the prayer for annulment should set out the reason for annulment. The Scrutiny Committee should be appointed at the beginning of each session as a matter of urgency, should include in its report any letter to a Government Department on the point in issue and the reply of the Department. The time limit of 40 days before the expiration of which an instrument may not be made or submitted to Her Majesty in Council, should commence from the day when it is available to Members in the Vote Office or if it is one to which the Committee draw the attention of the House, 10 days from its report if that is longer. At the head of the Instrument there should be printed a note stating whether it is subject to affirmative or negative procedure, or whether exempt from both processes. The recommendations of the Donoughmore Committee that the expressions 'regulation, rule, order' should not be used indiscriminately are endorsed.

Nationalised Industries

Sel. Cttee. Rep., proc., mins. of ev., apps. pp. xxvi, 140. [1952]

1951–52 (332–I) *vii*, 145
apptd. *Dec.*, 1951. *o.p. Oct.*, 1952

R. Assheton (*Ch.*), Albu, Champion, Davies, L. Hinchingbrooke, Linstead, Noel-Baker, Spens, Thornton-Kemsley, Williams (H.), Williams (R.).

'*To consider the present methods by which the House of Commons is informed of the affairs of the Nationalised Industries and to report what changes, having regard to the provisions laid down by Parliament in the relevant statutes, may be desirable in these methods.*'

In this report the Committee concentrated on Questions to Ministers on five industries nationalised since the war, as these were set up as independent corporations with the deliberate intention of freeing them from the immediate control of Government and Parliament. The practice is that Questions should relate to the public affairs with which the Ministers are officially connected, to proceedings pending in Parliament or to matters of administration for which they are responsible. Thus certain classes of Questions may not be asked about nationalised industries. As a Question is inadmissible if it repeats in substance one to which an answer has already been refused, the refusal of a Minister to answer a single Question may enlarge extensively the excluded classes of Questions. The limits are determined by the Clerk at the Table, subject to a ruling by the Speaker.

Questions about nationalised industries are limited both by statutes, which set out the matters for which the Minister is responsible, e.g. giving directions of a general character affecting national interests, and by Government policy, which has been that Ministers should not concern themselves with day-to-day administration, so that a Minister's refusal to answer Questions on it would mean that the Clerk would not put that class of Question on the Order Paper. Taking the immunity away on the first ground would involve legislation, and the power to obtain information on any point should not be used to hamper corporations, as chairmen of nationalised industries said it would. There was a strong desire to have the same power of questioning as in the case of the Post Office, which testified that this did not cause any special difficulty, but nationalised industries were not constituted as Civil Departments and detailed questions would be inappropriate. But the decision as to whether a Question was not obviously ruled out, should not be decided by the Clerks, but should appear on the Order Paper, leaving the Minister to answer or refuse to answer. As nationalisation has led to a great increase in the number of oral questions, the number permitted to a Member should be reduced from three to two.

There are Memos. by the Clerk of the House on the opportunities for and restrictions on questions about nationalised industries.

—— Rep., proc., mins. of ev., app. pp. xviii, 118. 1953

E

1952–53 (235) *vi*, 361
re-apptd. Nov., 1952. *o.p. July,* 1953

The general desire for information by Parliament and the public about the nationalised industries is not met by the voluminous reports which they publish, partly because these are so complicated and partly because information is not necessarily available on matters on which or when it is required. On the proposal that a select committee should be set up there was great diversity of opinion. H. Molson, M.P., Parliamentary Secretary to the Ministry of Works stated that in the past the House of Commons has always found it convenient when confronted with a special problem to appoint a committee so that a few Members of Parliament may give intensive study to the problem, that there may be interrogation of witnesses and investigation of papers and maps, and that in the seclusion of the committee room there may be comparative freedom from political prejudices. Such a committee would elucidate deep problems of policy and give Parliament an opportunity of taking stock. This was supported by Sir Edward Bridges and Lord Hurcomb, Chairman of the Transport Commission, who thought that it would do much to satisfy the very legitimate demands of Parliament for greater knowledge, and that if it were in the nature of a standing committee there would be continuity of personnel. Such a committee would mean that Members would have an opportunity of conveying, not by way of attack, but by way of suggestion, the points where they thought something might go wrong. The opposition to the proposal was strongly represented by Lord Reith and Herbert Morrison. They maintained that it was a negation of what Parliament did in passing a self-denying ordinance taking from itself the right of direct interference; that it would impede the working of the nationalised industries and destroy initiative in them.

The various methods by which the House can perform its functions are not adequate. A committee should be set up by Standing Order, with power to send for persons, papers and records, for the purpose of informing the House about the problems of the corporations and not of controlling their work. It should set up a tradition of conduct which will result in its being regarded as a protection of the Boards against irresponsible pressure as well as a guardian of the public interests. A permanent staff should include an officer of the status of the Controller and Auditor General.

Privileges
Cttees.
—— Rep., proc. pp. vi.   1941
1940–41 (94) *iii*, 733
C. R. Attlee (*Ch.*).

Publication in the Observer *newspaper of the 25th day of May last of an article purporting to give an account of the Debate in Secret Session on Wednesday, the 21st day of May last.*—Any disclosure or report of proceedings in secret session whether by a member or by any other person is a breach of privilege, and the publication of the article which referred to the secret session constituted a breach of privilege. But having regard to the unqualified regret expressed by the editor and the lobby correspondent's explanation that the information used was given at a Press Conference, no further action need be taken in this case.

—— Rep., proc., mins. of ev. pp. xiii,
10. [1941]
1940–41 (103) *iii*, 739
C. R. Attlee (*Ch.*).

Letters addressed to all Members of Parliament from the Highland Development League, referring to seeming irregularities in the procedure by which the Grampian Electricity Supply Order Confirmation Bill had been advanced to its present stage.—The reference to 'seeming irregularities' was in very general terms and was not specifically directed against any member or officer of the House or against the House collectively. The promotion of this Order in war time had excited considerable opposition, and it was wrong to expect all critics to be familiar with the procedure and practice of Parliament. The words in the original letter did not constitute a breach of privilege.

—— Rep. pp. 4. 1942
1941–42 (93) *iii*, 437
C. R. Attlee (*Ch.*).

Certain passages in a speech by Mr. McGovern, Member for the Burgh of Glasgow (Shettleston Division), reported in the New Leader *newspaper of 2nd May, 1942, as constituting a disclosure of proceedings in the Secret Session of the 23rd day of April last.*—If a member is free to give a general impression of what had been said a controversy might be started which would lead to revealing what had taken place. There had been a breach of the rule, but Mr. McGovern was exonerated from any intention to infringe it.

—— Rep., proc. pp. 6. 1943. Mins. of ev., app. 1943
1942 43 (109) (109) *iii*, 695
C. R. Attlee (*Ch.*).

A letter which Mr. Tom Smith, a Member of this House, had received from one of the directors of the National Marketing Company, enclosing a cheque purporting to be in payment of contingent expenses.—It is conceivable that there might be instances where the payment of expenses offends against the rule, but there are occasions when they do assist members to inform themselves on matters of Parliamentary and Public interest. The intention of one of the directors of the Marketing Company was to get the presence of Members of Parliament in Court, so as to bring pressure on a Government Department concerned to withdraw a prosecution. Whatever the Committee's opinion of this intention, it did not create a breach of privilege.

—— Rep., proc. pp. 6. 1944
1943–44 (85) *ii*, 999
C. R. Attlee (*Ch.*).

The action of the National Union of Distributive and Allied Workers in addressing a letter to Mr. Robinson, Member for the Borough of St. Helens, withdrawing financial support on the ground of his refusal to resign his seat.—The cause of the Union's dissatisfaction and their withdrawal of financial support was 'alleged neglect to deal with constituency matters and dissatisfaction with Mr. Robinson's conduct as an individual'. There had been no attempt to influence the action of the Member in the House of Commons in voting or speaking, therefore there had been no breach of privilege. (Minutes not published.)

—— Rep., proc., mins. of ev., app. pp. 6. 1945
1944–45 (63) *iii*, 613
C. R. Attlee (*Ch.*).

A letter addressed to Mr. Reakes, Member for the Borough of Wallasey, by Mr. Donald F. S. Henderson, offering in certain contingencies to donate a cheque for one hundred guineas to Mr. Reakes's local Association for their Party Funds.—On 3rd March, 1945, Mr. D. F. Henderson wrote to Mr. G. Reakes, M.P., offering 'if it would be in order' to donate 100 guineas to a local party fund if he could 'bring to a successful conclusion' some difficulty Mr. Henderson was having with the Department for Scotland. An offer of money to a member to take up a question with a Minister would be a breach of privilege within the principle laid down in a Resolution of 2nd May, 1695. There was no breach of privilege as no offer was made, the question was asked in good faith, and there was no intention to bribe.

—— Rep., proc., mins. of ev., app. pp. ix, 25 [1945]
1945–46 (31) *viii*, 511
H. Morrison (*Ch.*).

A Writ of Summons had been served upon one of the Officers of the House within its precincts.—Service of process within the precincts of the House on a day on which the House or any Committee thereof is to sit, is sitting, or has to sit will constitute a breach of privilege. 'The law of Parliament on this point had not been well defined, and no breach of privilege had been intended by any officer of the Metropolitan Police, therefore no interposition of the House is called for by any proceedings against the officers concerned.'

—— Rep. pp. 5. [1945]
1945–46 (47) *viii*, 547

A statement alleged to have been made by Mr. Granville, Member for the County of Suffolk (Eye Division), purporting to disclose the substance of part of a speech made by the Prime Minister in the course of proceedings during the Secret Session of Thursday, 23rd April, 1942.—The complaint made by Dr. MacManus was sent to Sir Brograve in the form of a report of a conversation which had taken place before a dinner at the flat of Major Mackenzie in Bruton Street. There was a conflict of evidence. The charge against Mr. Granville of having committed a breach of privilege had not been proved.

—— Rep., proc., mins. of ev., apps. pp. viii, 36. [1946]
1945–46 (181) *viii*, 553
H. Morrison (*Ch.*).

The publication of a poster which stated that 'Names of M.P.s voting for bread rationing in the Commons on Thursday will be published here as public enemies and dictators.'—This poster was displayed in the streets on the day on which the House was expected to vote. The author, Mrs. Tennant, had tried to bring improper pressure on Members, but it was so petty in scale and so insignificant in its result that 'the House would best consult its dignity by taking no further notice of the offence'.

—— Rep., proc., mins. of ev., apps. pp. x, 67. 1947
1946–47 (36) *ix*, 353
A. Greenwood (*Ch.*).

That Mr. Piratin, Member for the Borough of Stepney (Mile End Division) had been assaulted in the precincts of the House by a stranger.—Both Mr. Piratin and Mr. Lucy had used provocative and offensive language and had assaulted one another and had seriously offended the dignity of the House. In view of the full apologies offered the dignity of the House would be vindicated and safeguarded by expressing and recording its extreme displeasure.

—— Rep., proc., mins. of ev., apps. pp. xxxviii, 90 [1947]
1946–47 (118) *ix*, 431
A. Greenwood (*Ch.*).

Certain actions by the Executive Committee of the Civil Service Clerical Association which, it was submitted, were calculated improperly to influence Mr. W. J. Brown, Member for the County of Warwick (Rugby Division) in the exercise of his parliamentary duties.—As its Parliamentary Secretary, Mr. Brown held a contractual relationship with the Association. Because of certain views he had expressed he had come under criticism and the Association had sought not to influence his actions, but to sever its connection with him. It has long been recognised that where M.P.s receive financial assistance from outside there must be no control over the freedom of the Member concerned, although it is an inevitable corollary that the outside body is entitled to terminate the relationship, if it lawfully can, where it is necessary for the protection of its own interests. There had been no breach of privilege. There is a Memo. by the Clerk of the House on actions calculated to influence a Member in the exercise of his Parliamentary duties.

—— Special Rep. pp. [2]. 1947
1946–47 (137) *ix*, 559

A. Greenwood (*Ch.*).

Mr. Guy Schofield, Editor of the *Evening News*, and Mr. Stanley Dobson, Political Correspondent of the same newspaper, witnesses before the Committee, refused to answer certain questions put to them. The circumstances are reported in order that the House might take such steps as it thought proper and necessary. See qq. 353–5 in 1946–47 (142) *ix*, 713.

—— Rep., proc., mins. of ev., apps. pp. xx, 129. 1947

1946–47 (138) *ix*, 561

A. Greenwood (*Ch.*).

Publication in the World's Press News *newspaper of the 3rd day of April, 1947, of an article purporting to be written by Mr. Garry Allighan, Member for the County of Kent (Gravesend Division), containing passages reflecting on the conduct of Members of this House.*—The article was mainly directed to showing how information concerning what took place at the Parly. Labour Party meeting is obtained 'in return for consideration paid by newspapers' in the form of retaining fees, 'payment for what is produced', 'payment in kind', the 'offer of intoxicants to Members' and that 'expenses sheets of Parliamentary Reporters are full of such expenses', and 'every newspaper in the street has anything up to half a dozen M.P.s on its "contact" list'. The Committee's enquiries elicited that Mr. Allighan had himself received £30 a week from the *Evening Standard* for such information. Reflections upon Members, even where individuals are not named, brings disrepute on the body to which they belong and constitutes an affront to the dignity of the House. Proof that such a charge was true would not of necessity provide a defence, but if the publication was designed so that proved discreditable facts should be brought to an end, such high purpose would constitute a defence. The article in question had no such object.

The betrayal of information from Party meetings is a breach of confidence, but not a breach of privilege, as all such meetings do not enjoy the privileges of the House. But where information has come confidentially in his capacity as a Member, it is only as a Member that he can part with it. Payment for such information constitutes bribery and is a breach of the privileges of the House. Mr. Allighan was guilty of aggravated contempt of the House and of a gross breach of privilege. The Editor and Publisher of the *World's Press News* should be reprimanded. There is a Memo. by the Clerk of the House on *Adverse Reflections on the House* in Writings by a Member and on offers of money to Members.

—— Rep., proc., mins. of ev., app. pp. vii, 20. 1947

1946–47 (142) *ix*, 713

A. Greenwood (*Ch.*).

A Personal Statement made by Mr. Walkden, Member for the County of York, West Riding (Doncaster Division) relative to certain matters contained in the Report and Special Report which, upon the 23rd day of July last, were made from the Committee of Privileges.—Mr. Walkden stated that he gave advice to the Lobby Correspondent of the *Evening News* on what had happened at private meetings of the Labour Party and that he received the payment of £5 per week in cash. The Committee regarded the transactions of this kind in the nature of bribery and concluded that Mr. Walkden had been guilty of a breach of privilege.

An alternative draft report, supported by J. Reid and Lord Winterton (pp. vii, viii) stated that while the Committee did not accept Mr. Walkden's contention that the disclosure was legitimate and involved no breach of confidence, they did not regard it as a breach of privilege, since the meetings were not part of the proceedings of the House. Members could not by agreement to regard proceedings of such meetings as confidential, create a privilege which did not otherwise exist. This draft was rejected.

—— Rep., proc., mins. of ev., apps. pp. vi, 20. 1948

1947–48 (112) *ix*, 543

H. Morrison (*Ch.*).

Publication of certain passages in the Daily Mail *newspaper of the 6th day of March, 1948, reflecting on Members of this House.*—The general tenor of Mr. C. Brogan's broadcast and interview with the *Daily Mail* 'indicated an apprehension that in the event of a future crisis Members of Parliament now in the Labour Party, 29 in number, would reveal themselves in what he alleged to be their true colours as members of the Communist Party and would act traitorously'.

Contempts of Parliament vary greatly from grave attacks undermining the institution to vulgar and irresponsible abuse. To become involved in protractive and possibly inconclusive inquiries would be inconsistent with the dignity of the House. No action should be taken. Memo. by the Clerk of the House on *Reflections on Unnamed Members.*

—— Rep., proc. pp. iv. 1949

1948–49 (261) *x*, 307

J. C. Ede (*Ch.*).

Publication in the Daily Worker *newspaper of the 22nd day of July last of a passage purporting to give a report of the speech of a Member in the House on the 21st day of July last.*—By a resolution of 1762, any publication of reports of speeches of Members is a breach of privilege, and this was technically such a breach. The Committee compared the report given by the newspaper with the version of his speech which the Honourable Member gave to the House on 26th July and were of the opinion that the report in the *Daily Worker* called for no action by the House.

—— Rep., proc., app. pp. vii.   1951

1950–51 (149) *vii*, 25

J. C. Ede (*Ch.*).

A broadcast on Friday the 9th day of March last by the B.B.C. commenting on the subject already raised as a Matter of Privilege on Thursday, the 8th day of March last and left for the future decision of the House. Letters purporting to have been written by Mr. L. N. Tomlinson.—Contempt of the Courts by comments on judicial proceedings may be punished if they tend to obstruct the course of justice. The broadcast did not influence, alter or modify the decision of the Speaker and no breach of privilege arose. The letter complained of by Mr. Silverman contained scurrilous abuse of a general kind, but as there was no reference to him in his capacity as a Member of the House, there was no breach of privilege.

—— Rep., proc., mins. of ev. pp. viii, 12 [1951]

1950–51 (235) *vii*, 33

J. C. Ede (*Ch.*).

Speech of Lady Mellor reported in the Sutton Coldfield News *newspaper of the 16th day of June last.*—Lady Mellor had referred to a ruling of the Deputy-Speaker as being 'very deplorable', though in answers to questions she said he was always 'scrupulously fair and without bias'. Precedents showed that criticisms outside the House of the impartiality of the Chair were a breach of privilege, but in view of her answers no further action should be taken.

—— Rep., proc., mins. of ev. pp. xii, 30. [1951]

1950–51 (244) *vii*, 53

C. Davies (*Ch.*).

Two complaints that Mr. John Lewis was obstructed by the police during traffic congestion on his way to the House, and that he had been served with summonses after a motion dealing with the same subject matter had been placed on the Order Paper.—The Committee found that no obstruction or delay had been caused by the policemen and no breach of privilege had been committed. On the second matter Mr. Lewis received on 14th July a notice of intention to prosecute him for his conduct during the incident and on the 16th he tabled a motion. A Member of Parliament is not privileged from service of process, and in any case he cannot protect himself by tabling a motion. There was no breach of privilege. The privileges of the House apply to individual Members only as they are necessary in order that the House may perform its functions, and do not place them above the ordinary restraints of law which apply to fellow citizens.

—— Rep., proc., mins. of ev. pp. iv, 15. 1953

1952–53 (171) *vi*, 285

H. F. C. Crookshank (*Ch.*).

The Committee did not wish to comment on the taste of an article by a new member, Mrs. Ford, in the *Sunday Express*. While all reports of proceedings in the House without its authority are breaches of its privileges, in the normal course the House waives its privileges. As Mrs. Ford has apologised to the House and to Mrs. Braddock, no further action should be taken.

—— Rep., proc. pp. 4. 1953

1953–54 (31) *vii*, 337

H. F. C. Crookshank (*Ch.*).

The passage in the *Daily Worker* was defamatory of members in the capacity of members and was a breach of privilege, but the House should not occupy further time in considering it.

—— Rep., proc. pp. iv. 1955

1954–55 (112) *iii*, 737

H. F. C. Crookshank (*Ch.*).

The action of the Deputy Assistant Chaplain General, Salisbury Plain District, in threatening one of his subordinate chaplains with a view to influencing proceedings in Parliament.—There is no precedent for treating an attempt of one individual to influence another individual not a Member in his communications with an M.P. as a breach of privilege. But it is a right of members of the Armed Forces to communicate with Members on non-military matters free from pressure or punishment. The Committee assume that the Minister for War will take such action as is necessary to see that this right is preserved.

Publications and Debates
Sel. Cttees. Reps.

From 1940 the series of reports deal mainly with the difficulties arising from scarcity of paper and labour. In 1939–40 ((133) iii, 697) the Committee recommended that in future bound volumes of Hansard, which members were entitled to receive free, should be supplied only on payment, a decision confirmed in 1943–44 ((110) ii, 1021). Difficulties in printing debates were due to shortage of skilled reporting staff: every effort should be made to attract recruits (1946–47 (136) ix, 331). In 1952–53 ((308) vi, 305) it was proposed that Division Lists should no longer be printed as part of the Votes and Proceedings, and that the lists in Hansard should be the official lists. But Mr. Fellowes, Clerk Assistant, had pointed out in evidence that the records of the House were in two series, that as a result of the earlier refusal of the House to allow the Clerks to make a record of what was said, the Minutes were confined to what was done, including Divisions, which could not be logically separated from the rest of the Minutes. The Speaker did not accept the recommendations. In 1939–40 ((68) iii, 671) a proposal from Commander King Hall for a weekly edition of a selection from Hansard at 2d. was not approved; every effort should be made to increase sales in the existing form. The cost of producing Hansard is £30,000, sales £5,000 to £6,000 a year. But 1945–46 ((185) ix, 775) recommended a weekly edition at 1s. 6d.

Disposal and Custody of Documents

Sel. Cttee. 1st Rep. pp. 6. 1942. 2nd

Rep., proc., app. pp. 10. 1942. Rep., proc. pp. 6. 1943

1941–42 (64) (113) *iii*, 1.   1942–43 (93) *iii*, 35

apptd. Dec., 1941, re-apptd. Nov., 1942. o.p. March, Oct., 1942, June 1943

D. Herbert (*Ch.*) 1st and 2nd Reps. P. Harris (*Ch.*) Rep.

'To examine all documents and records in the custody or control of any officer of the House, to report which of these may be destroyed and which are of sufficient historical interest to justify their preservation; and to recommend methods for securing the safe custody of any classes of documents which ought to be preserved.'

The First Report names the classes of documents which could be disposed of immediately for pulping, and those which could be made available if the national need for paper became more urgent.   A Commons resolution accepted these recommendations.   The Second Report deals with original documents, stored in the Victoria Tower, which ought to be preserved, and the alterations necessary for their protection. The Third Report gives the main classes of original documents in the custody of the officers of the House.

Library (House of Commons)

Sel. Cttee. Special Rep., proc., mins. of ev., apps. pp. iv, 30.   1945. 1st and 2nd Reps., proc., mins. of ev., app., index. pp. xii, 86. [1946]

1944–45 (98) *iii*, 345. 1945–46 (35, 99–1) *viii*, 45

apptd. April, o.p. June, 1945. re-apptd. Oct., 1945. o.p. Nov., 1945, March, 1946

G. Benson (*Ch.*), Cocks, Douglas, Gruffydd, Hudson, Paton, Pickthorn, Savory, Smith.

'To inquire into the present state of the Library of the House of Commons.'

The Special Report is formal only, presenting minutes of evidence and suggesting re-appointment of the Committee. The Apps. contain Memoranda from the Librarian on the condition of the Library, where there had been no thorough reorganisation since it moved to its present accommodation in 1858. As so many of the books had been moved to the country for safety during the war, there was now an opportunity to reorganise the Library before they were brought back again. The Library was 'woefully short' of books on Finance and Political Economy, Social Science, History and Constitutional Law, the Dominions, the Colonies, the U.S.S.R. and Asiatic countries; a modern card index of subject and authors to replace the only author catalogue printed in 1910, and more assistant librarians were needed. Evidence showed that all purchase of books, binding, etc., was met by a credit of £1200 per annum with the Stationery Office. This had resulted in inconvenience and delays (1944–45 (98) qq. 69–76). Recommended that the deficiences should be filled in the contents of the library in certain subjects, that a card index should be made, that two additional assistant librarians should be appointed, that eight unused cellars should be converted into a store, that the library staff should be reorganised and their status and salaries equated with those of clerks in the Department of the Clerk of the House, and that the Librarian should be permitted to purchase all books direct from the trade. Adequate facilities should be provided outside the House to enable Members to deal with correspondence, so that the library is freed for its proper purposes of research and reading.

House of Commons (Rebuilding)

Sel. Cttee. Rep., proc., apps., plans. pp. 28.   1944. Mins. of ev., apps., index. 1944

1943–44 (109) *ii*, 591. Mins of ev., etc.; 1943–44 (109–1) *ii*, 643

apptd. Dec., 1943. o.p. Oct., 1944

Lord Winterton (*Ch.*), Agnew, Benson, De Chair, Erskine-Hill, Hannon, Harris, Hore-Belisha, Nicholson, Pethick-Lawrence, Rathbone (Miss), Shakespeare, Smith, Wedderburn, Wilmot.

'*To consider and report upon plans for the rebuilding of the House of Commons and upon such alterations as may be considered desirable while preserving all its essential features.*'

The Committee were unanimous that the sense of intimacy and almost conversational form of debate encouraged by the dimensions of the old Chamber should be maintained. The present intimate and traditional style of discussion was firmly established in the customs and affections of the nation. Features of the new chamber would include preserving the traditional dimensions, an increase in the number of Press and other Strangers' seats, improved vision from all Strangers' seats, etc.; modern lighting, ventilation and heating, and better accommodation for Members' activities. Alterations in the roof proposed would have but slight effect on the acoustics on the Floor of the House and an unobtrusive sound amplification system should be installed (see mins. of ev. p. 135). In view of the restrictions imposed by the terms of reference, competitive designs were not called for, but Sir G. G. Scott appointed as architect.

Accommodation in the Palace of Westminster

Jt. Sel. Cttee. Rep., proc., mins. of ev. pp. vii, 60. 1944. Rep., proc., mins. of ev., apps., index. pp. xxii, 92. 1945

1943–44 (116–1) *ii*, 1041. 1944–45 (64–1) *iii*, 691
apptd. June, re-appted. Dec., 1944. *o.p.* Nov., 1944, *March*, 1945

Lord Stanhope (*Ch.*), L. Normanby, L. Mersey, L. Southwood, L. Teviot, L. Ammon, L. Schuster, Anderson, Entwistle, Harvey, Mander, Raikes, Reed, Taylor.

'*To enquire into the accommodation in the Palace of Westminster, and to report thereon with such recommendations as appear to them desirable.*'

Report (116–1) is a formal report presenting mins. of ev. only.

There is a shortage of rooms in each House and practically no accommodation where a Peer or private member can hold an interview, provision for dictating and typing letters is inadequate, as are the canteen facilities for the 700 staff. Various minor suggestions are made for re-allocation of rooms, etc., but no great increase of accommodation is possible in the existing structure: this requires new building and outside accommodation.

House of Commons Accommodation, etc.

Sel. Cttee. Rep., proc., mins. of ev., apps. pp. xvi, 162. [1953]

1952–53 (309) *vi*, 23
apptd. May, o.p. Oct., 1953

R. R. Stokes (*Ch.*), Bing, Brooke, Daines, Davidson (Viscountess), Grimond, Keeling, Lee (Miss J.), McCorquodale, McLeavy, Macpherson, Pannell, Price, Williams.

'*To report on . . . the allocation of accommodation . . . the amenities necessary to enable members to carry out efficiently the services required of them; the desirability of appointing a Sessional Committee . . . the methods of appointment of the staff at all levels of employment . . .*'

No substantial improvement of accommodation can be made except by extensive building operations. A disproportionate amount of space is at the disposal of other users. Control of the Palace, at present delegated to various authorities, should be unified. A 'House' Committee is suggested.

—— Sel. Cttee. Rep., proc., mins. of ev., apps. pp. xxii, 169. 1954

1953–54 (184) *vii*, 5
re-apptd. Nov., 1953. *o.p. May*, 1954

Recommendations are made on individual desks for members, improvements in the library, kitchen, etc.

The present method of appointment and qualifications of staff for all posts should be clearly stated, on the principle that every vacancy should be available to anyone competent to fill it. The House and its committees must be properly served in all circumstances, even if this entails over-staffing at certain periods of the year. The duties of clerks of committees to aid in or draft reports under the instruction of the chairman are set out. The Commissioners of the Offices of the House of Commons should be replaced by a more representative House of Commons Commission, under the chairmanship of The Speaker, to deal with all matters of principle affecting allocation of rooms, staff, library, etc.; it should deal with the application of collective bargaining to the special circumstances of the staff of the House. A unified control of the whole Palace of Westminster is desirable.

4. MINISTERS

Allegations Reflecting on the Official Conduct of Ministers of the Crown and other Public Servants

Tribunal. Rep. pp. iv, 82. 1949. Proc., mins. of ev. 1949

1948-49 Cmd. 7616, xviii, 425. Mins. of ev., etc.; 1949 Non-Parl.
apptd. Oct., 1948. sgd. Jan., 1949
G. J. Lynskey (Ch.), Vick, Upjohn.

'For inquiring into a definite matter of urgent public importance, that is to say, whether there is any justification for allegations that payments, rewards or other considerations have been sought, offered, promised, made or received by or to Ministers of the Crown or other public servants in connection with licences or permissions required under any enactment, regulation or order or in connection with the withdrawal of any prosecution and, if so, in what circumstances the transactions took place and what persons were involved therein.'

The report discusses in detail a large number of transactions and incidents. In two cases Mr. Belcher received small gifts and hospitality, given for the purpose of securing favourable treatment from the Board of Trade, knowing the purpose for which they were made, and intervened to give assistance. But there is no evidence that he received large sums or any sum. Mr. G. Gibson, although he received only trivial gifts, assisted Mr. Stanley in the hope of material advantage. Mr. Key did not seek or receive any benefits in connection with applications to his Ministry and his actions were not influenced in any way. The other Ministers and public servants named were not offered and did not seek or receive any considerations.

The allegations that larger sums of money were being or had been paid to some Ministers and public servants were largely the result of statements by Mr. Stanley. 'We are satisfied that for his own purposes he represented to various persons that upon payment by them to him of substantial sums he could secure licences for various purposes and also assistance from different Ministries, and in particular the Board of Trade, and that he was able to do this by paying part of the money received by him to the Minister and officials who would have to deal with these matters. . . . He was, however, able to give colour to his statements because Mr. Belcher, Mr. Gibson and Mr. Key received him on apparently friendly terms and it is not therefore surprising that rumours arose and these baseless allegations of payments of large sums of money were made.'

5. ORGANISATION OF DEPARTMENTS

Office of the Minister of Production

pp. 4. 1942
1941-42 Cmd. 6337, ix, 151
pres. Feb., 1942

The Minister of Production is the War Cabinet Minister charged with the business of war production in accordance with the policy of the Minister of

Defence and the War Cabinet, except that relating to man-power and labour, which will be the responsibility of the Minister of Labour and National Service. His duties include the allocation of production capacity and raw materials, and the settlement of production priorities. The common services in the field of production and raw material and other controls will continue to be administered by the Departments at present responsible for them.

Proposals for the Reform of the Foreign Service

pp. 10. 1943

1942–43 *Cmd.* 6420, *xi*, 117

The Diplomatic Service has been criticised on the ground that it is recruited from too narrow a circle and that its members have insufficient understanding of economic and social questions. The conditions under which the Diplomatic Service grew up no longer exist unchanged: economics and finance have become interwoven with politics, and reforms are needed in its recruitment, training and organisation. There has been a lack of mobility between the Foreign Office, whose conditions are assimilated to the Home Civil Service, and the Service abroad.

The Foreign and Diplomatic, the Commercial Diplomatic and the Consular Services will be amalgamated immediately into a new Foreign Service, although posts cannot be interchanged immediately and amalgamation cannot become complete until new entrants have received the type of training needed to prepare them for all three types of post. The subordinate staff, the permanent members of which belong to the Home Civil Service, will be included in the new unified Foreign Service. Recruitment will be either by open competition followed by training abroad or, for a period of ten years, for not more than 25 per cent. of the vacancies, by selection. The question of admission of women will be considered after the war.

Organisation of the Colonial Service

pp. 12. 1946

1946 *Non-Parl. Colonial Office*

There are fifty separate self-contained administrative territories, each with its own public services. They vary greatly in size, population, resources and social development. Each has its separate budget. There must be no barrier to the appointment of a colonial candidate or locally-recruited public servant, and there must be equality of treatment irrespective of race or colour, but for some time to come many colonies will need qualified staff from outside. £1 mn. will be provided over the next ten years to give selected colonial candidates training to qualify them for the higher grades of the Colonial Service. Training after selection in a Staff College is rejected, as it would isolate them from other students. Instead £1½ mn. will be spent on post-selection training in universities. The salaries of all posts should be determined by the nature of the work, irrespective of race or domicile, and at rates for locally-recruited staff. If these are insufficient to attract or retain officers from overseas, expatriation pay should be added. The Secretary of State will continue to control the appointment of persons to the higher posts in accordance with the colonial regulations. Public Service Commissions should be established in the colonies. Appointments in the biological research services and the survey, geological and meteorological services will cover the whole Colonial empire and be controlled by the Secretary of State.

Post-War Training for the Colonial Service

Cttee. Rep., memo. pp. 46. 1946

1946 *Non-Parl. Colonial Office*
apptd. March, 1944. *sgd. Feb.,* 1945

Duke of Devonshire (*Ch.*) and four representatives from Oxford, Cambridge and London Universities, and three from the Colonial Office.

A Memo. by Sir R. Furse, Director of Recruitment for the Colonial Service, rejected the creation of a Colonial Staff College and concentration of training in one university in favour of a team of three Universities, Oxford, Cambridge and London; and proposed two courses, one to be taken by candidates selected for the Administrative Service before proceeding overseas and the other by all officers, administrative and professional, after their 'apprentice' tour of duty. The report gives the details of the courses worked out with the universities.

Higher Appointments
Rep.

1944–45 *Cmd.* 6576. See *Professions*, p. 279

Central Organisation for Defence
pp. 12. [1946]

1945–46 *Cmd.* 6923, *xx*, 155
pres. Oct., 1946

The defects of our position in 1939 were due partly to the absence of means of formulating a united defence policy for the three services, whose needs tended to be examined separately. This was not overcome by the appointment of a Minister of Defence, since his duties were limited to co-ordination, he could not take executive action, and had no jurisdiction over the apportionment of resources to the three services. A unified defence policy was achieved during the war through the assumption of executive control by the Prime Minister and Minister of Defence. How was that to be achieved in peace?

The paper rejects both the complete unification of the three services and a combined General Staff to plan without regard to sectional interests. The British principle is that the men who are responsible in the service departments for carrying out the policy approved should be brought together to formulate it in the Chiefs of Staff Committee and in the Joint Staffs.

The plan of the new organisation is that the Prime Minister will retain supreme responsibility for defence and be Chairman of the Defence Committee, which will be responsible to the Cabinet for reviewing current strategy and co-ordination. A Minister of Defence, who will be Deputy Chairman, will be responsible for the apportionment of resources between the services in accordance with strategic policy of the Defence Committee, for research and the correlation of production plans; the Chiefs of Staff Committee will be responsible for presenting strategic appreciation and military plans to the Defence Committee and the Joint Staffs system will be developed under their direction. The Service Ministers will continue to be responsible to Parliament for the administration of their services in accordance with the general policy approved by the Cabinet and within the resources allotted to them.

Scottish Affairs
Memo., app. pp. 6. 1948

1947–48 *Cmd.* 7308, *xxii*, 1071

Gives the Government proposals to improve the handling of Scottish affairs by changes in Parliamentary procedure, and convening a Scottish Economic Conference, and its reasons for rejecting a proposed Committee of Enquiry.

Scottish Affairs

R. Com. Rep., apps., index. pp. 126. 1954. Mins. of ev., 10 days, index.
    1953–54. Memos. I–IV. 1953

1953–54 *Cmd.* 9212, *xix*, 1. *Mins. of ev.,* etc.; 1953–54 *Non-Parl.*
apptd. July, 1952. *sgd. July,* 1954
Lord Balfour (*Ch.*), Gardiner, Gavin, Stephen, Chance, Muirhead, Dollan, Guillebaud, Fraser, McNaughton, Campbell, McGinniss, Stirling, Cockburn, Walker.

'*To review, with reference to the financial, economic, administrative, and other con-*

siderations involved, the arrangements for exercising the functions of Our Government in relation to Scotland and to report.'

The remit did not include the question of Parliamentary separation, but the substantial majority of those who commented on the matter were opposed to it.

Dissatisfaction with the relationship between England and Scotland has become evident because of the economic difficulties of the inter-war and post-war periods, the greater interference with individual activities as a result of the growth of regulations and controls applying to Great Britain as a whole, with ultimate authority resting in London and a sense of 'remote control', and the public's lack of knowledge of the extent to which devolution in Scottish affairs has taken place.

There is no evidence of any failure to realise the seriousness of Scottish problems of housing, health and unemployment. Rather more houses proportionately to population have been built in Scotland than in England, and the amount of factory space allocated in the Scottish Development Area is greater than in any other. It is difficult to estimate the income and expenditure and the respective contributions to and benefits from 'common services' of Scotland and England because they are parts of a unified economic system with free intercourse between them. Income per head is lower in Scotland; Scotland's share of 'local' expenditure was in excess of the revenue she contributed, and represented 51 per cent. of the revenue she contributed, as compared with 38·5 per cent. for England and Wales. The distribution of expenditure on Government contracts depends on industrial capacity (e.g. the Scottish monopoly of sandbag contracts). The principles followed in the existing contracts procedure are sound, but Departments should periodically review the distribution and take active steps to utilise latent capacity.

Scottish legislation may be dealt with either by normal procedure or by the Scottish Standing Committee of 71 Scottish M.P.s. The Committee cannot initiate legislation, but does consider Scottish estimates. The widening of devolution would have the effect of removing Scottish business from the floor of the House, which would be unacceptable, and holding the Standing Committee in Scotland would impose too much work on and inconvenience to Scottish M.P.s, who would for that time be separated from Westminster. Criticisms that not enough Parliamentary time was given to Scotland were not accepted, since the Standing Committee could have dealt with more work, but the Government did not make more use of it for various reasons, e.g. difference of views between and within the parties on proposed reforms of Scottish rating.

Legislation is given effect in Scotland either by a separate Act, by parallel provisions, by applying an English Act to Scotland by 'application' provisions, or by re-enacting an English Act in Scottish form. Where the Scottish 'application' clauses are likely to become lengthy or complicated, there should be a separate Scottish bill. As a matter of routine, each bill should specify whether it applies to Scotland. There is no adequate provision in Scotland for considering law revision: the existing informal committee should be reconstituted as a permanent body with power to consider on its own initiative any aspect of Scottish legal reform. The House of Lords should continue to be the final appellate tribunal in Scottish civil cases.

The Secretary of State for Scotland is primarily concerned with the determination of policies and issues of importance to Scotland, and is assisted by a Minister of State, and three Parliamentary Under-Secretaries. His position would be weakened by the appointment of another Scottish Minister. Since both countries are part of a unified economic system, any proposal to divide ministerial responsibility for trade, industry, shipping, etc., on national lines would need strong evidence to support it. The work of the relevant departments is reviewed. The main changes suggested are: that the heads of U.K. offices in Scotland ('Scottish Controllers') should have as much power devolved upon them as possible, their status should be improved and they should be referred to as Scottish controllers, never regional controllers; responsibility for Highway matters and for animal health should be transferred to the Secretary of State.

See *Scottish Administration*. Handbook; 1950 Non-Parl.

Home Information Services

Cttee. Rep. pp. 16. 1949

1948–49 *Cmd.* 7836, *xvii*, 249
apptd. — *sgd. July*, 1949
H. L. French (*Ch.*), Bailey, Crombie, Nicholson, Ryan.

'*To examine the cost of the Government Home Information Services, and to make recommendations as to any direction in which economies may be desirable or the organisation can be improved.*'

Departments should keep expenditure below £5,168,000, which is too high. The Central Office of Information should continue to act as a specialised common-service agency for departments. Because it has no responsibility for the policy of projects, and the cost is borne on its Vote, all requests by Departments should first be approved by their Finance Divisions.

Other recommendations concern the correct choice of media, a scrutiny of cost in money and manpower, measurement of results, avoidance of costly national press and poster advertising except where specific action from the public is being enlisted. The size of Departments' Information Staffs should be reviewed, and Press Officers retained, but they should act as channels, not barriers between Departments and the Press.

Overseas Information Services

Independent Cttee. Summary Rep. pp. 55. 1954

1953–54 *Cmd.* 9138, *xxxi*, 901
apptd. Oct., 1952. *sgd.* —
Lord Drogheda (*Ch.*), Platt, Heyworth, Feather, Stocks (Mrs. M. D.), Huxley, McLachlan.

'*To assess the value, actual and potential, of the overseas information work . . .; to advise upon the relative importance of different methods and services in different areas and circumstances and to make recommendations for future policy.*'

The Information Services must be regarded as part of the normal apparatus of diplomacy of a Great Power. More money must be spent on them and changes are required in the pattern of work. They must always aim at a definite political or commercial result and unless they do, are a waste of public money. They should be directed at the influential few and through them at the many. Propaganda is no substitute for policy: its effect is never likely to be more than marginal, but may sometimes be decisive.

The level of activity is inadequate and an increase of annual expenditure of £1,850,000 is required. The services undertake an essentially long term operation and have been damaged by short term financing. Planned expansion is required. Some economies can be made in the B.B.C. and British Council Services in Europe. Detailed recommendations are made for each of the services.

Survey Staffs

Inter-Dept. Cttee. Rep., apps. pp. 23. 1950

1950 *Non-Parl. Min. of Agric. & Fish.* (*Ordnance Survey*)
apptd. Dec., 1948. *sgd. Feb.*, 1950
G. Brown (*Ch.*), Cheetham, Hibbert, Houghton, McCandlish, Stephens, Sumner.

'*To consider the staffing of the Ordnance Survey and of all other Government Survey organisations in relation to the Ordnance Survey and to recommend how it can be regulated and co-ordinated to the best national advantage.'*

Before adopting any scheme involving mapping or survey work, departments should consult the Ordnance Survey, to see whether it is best carried out by them or by the department concerned: if the latter, staff should be seconded from the Survey, or recruited into its grades.

Recruitment to the Ordnance Survey as surveyors or draughtsmen should normally be by Civil Service Examination. Women should be eligible. Recruits to Royal Engineers units who wish to join Ordnance Survey at the end of their military engagements should pass an entrance exam similar to that for juvenile civil recruits. Regular R.E.s should be eligible for a Special Limited Competition for Ordnance Survey vacancies, and if accepted should be given civil employment at a grade which takes account of age and experience. Higher posts should be filled, partly by R.E. officers and partly by civilians (the number of R.E.s being limited to 35), by a Selection Board on the basis of the best man for the post.

Ministry of Materials

Memo., apps. pp. 11. 1951

1950–51 *Cmd.* 8278, *xxvii*, 853
pres. June, 1951

The new Minister will do everything possible to ensure adequate supplies of the materials with which he is concerned, and when they are dealt with on public account, will be responsible for their purchase and sale. The paper sets out the division between the departments of the responsibilities for matters connected with the materials. Allocation of scarce materials will be decided through existing inter-departmental arrangements.

Organisation of the Ministry of Agriculture and Fisheries

Cttee. Rep., apps., index. pp. ii, 57.
1951

1951 *Non-Parl. Min. of Agric. & Fish. apptd. Nov.,* 1949. *sgd. Feb.,* 1951

J. Ryan (*Ch.*), Bickersteth, Dunnett, Grant, Purcell, Simpson.

'To review the development of the organisation of the Ministry of Agriculture and Fisheries since 1939, with particular reference to the working of the County Agricultural Executive Committees, its decentralised activities generally and their relationship to the headquarters offices; to consider whether any changes are necessary and to make recommendations.'

Developments during the war and the post-war agricultural expansion programme had involved a six-fold increase of staff, the establishment of the Agricultural Executive Committees and of new technical services, and an expansion of local and field activities, so that the proportion of staff at headquarters fell from 60 per cent to 20 per cent in 1950.

Substantial changes in county organisation are necessary: the Minister must have a body of practical men on the County Agricultural Executive Committees to act on his behalf. Their task was now to give leadership in promoting the development and efficiency of agriculture, and to carry out the supervisory and other duties under Parts II and III of the Agriculture Act, 1947. To free them for these tasks they should be relieved of the administration of trading services and of routine work, schemes of assistance to farmers, etc., which can be done by officials. These should be run from a county office responsible to the Ministry, which should have a strong county Organisation Division under an Under-Secretary, to be the channel of communication with the county offices.

The National Agricultural Advisory Service officers should cease to be officers of the Committees and District Committees and should not be associated with their disciplinary and police work, but freed to do their technical and advisory work, under a County Agricultural Advisory officer.

The organisation of the finance

division under a Director of Accounts has not kept pace with the expansion of the Ministry's work, and should be placed under an Under-Secretary (Finance). Much local expenditure should be delegated to the county offices, and a complete internal audit set up.

Ministry of Pensions. Proposed Transfer of Functions

app. pp. 11. 1953

1952–53 *Cmd.* 8842, *xxiv*, 739
pres. May, 1953

The work of the Ministry of Pensions is declining and sooner or later the question of its retention will arise. Much of its work in the award and payment of pensions and allowances is similar to that of the Ministry of National Insurance, and will be transferred to it. There will be economies of integration, but the war pensioners will have 900 local offices available, instead of 80. The new Ministry will be called the Ministry of National Insurance and Pensions. The medical work—management of hospitals, supply of artificial limbs, etc., will be transferred to the Ministry of Health and the Department of Health for Scotland.

Amalgamation of the Ministry of Transport and the Ministry of Civil Aviation

pp. 2. 1953

1952–53 *Cmd.* 8883, *xxiv*, 751
pres. June, 1953

The main tasks of reviving civil aviation after the war have now been carried to a stage that they no longer need the undivided attention of one Minister; the balance of advantage lies in closer association with other forms of transport in a Ministry of Transport and Civil Aviation.

Allocation to Messrs. George Wimpey and Co. Ltd., during the War, of Government Contracts in Scotland

Rep., apps. pp. 26. 1942

1941–42 *Cmd.* 6393, *iv*, 287
apptd. — sgd. Aug., 1942
J. L. Clyde.

The inquiry arose out of comments in the House that an undue proportion of Government constructional contracts in Scotland placed with Wimpey & Co. had elbowed out reputable Scottish firms, who had not been invited to tender, that the firm paid higher wages and prices than others, and that they had received unreasonably high prices.

There was no evidence to justify the charges against the firm, nor was there any improper influence on the placing of contracts, which they obtained through their proved merit. The total value of their contract was £7 mn. out of £47 mn. Only in the case of certain contracts by the Office of Works and the Air Ministry was the procedure open to criticism, the method of nomination or simple selection being used only in overwhelming urgency.

Intermediaries

Cttee. Rep., apps. pp. 92. [1950]

1950 *Cmd.* 7904, *xii*, 391
apptd. Feb., sgd. Oct., 1949

E. S. Herbert (*Ch.*), Carpenter, Foot, Gater, Geddes.

'*To inquire how far persons are making a business of acting as specialists in the submission of applications for licences or permits, or otherwise as intermediaries between Government Departments and the public; and to report whether the activities of such persons are liable to give rise to abuses, and to make recommendations. The inquiry is not intended to cover the activities on behalf of their clients by members of recognised professions.*'

There is a large field within which Government Departments come into contact with many organisations, firms and individuals. Even when certain categories are omitted, over 19 mn. applications are made to Departments annually, many of them concerned with materials and permits or monetary grants and benefits. In order to handle this volume of applications some Departments have incorporated representation of industries into their administrative system, others have decentralised their organisation. In the first instance applications must be dealt with by junior officers by routine in accordance with rules aiming at equality of treatment, and they handle a wide variety of technical subjects in which they are not as expert as the applicants. By contrast, the applicant feels that his case is unique, he is used to doing business personally, and wishes to explain the technicalities.

A person who knows the ropes can aid an applicant because he knows to whom and in what form an application can be made, what grade of officer deals with it and the instruction under which he is working, how and when to move to a higher level. Large firms obtain this knowledge because of the number of their transactions and often maintain specialised staffs to deal with them. Smaller firms without these advantages, need help. Some turn to trade associations: in practice the associations sift cases before taking them up. Some may go to private intermediaries, some of whom are professional men, e.g. accountants, while there are some, not always reputable, in the 'refugee and naturalisation industry'. But they are few in number and do not occupy an important part of the field. Their activities are liable to give rise to abuse, but are not on such a scale that a general restriction on them is justified.

Departments should constantly overhaul their control system, and should consider the appointment of an officer to do this; should facilitate the access of applicants, and draft their publicity from the point of view of the outsider who has to understand it. Where Departments think that a person is acting as a private intermediary for reward, it should ask him to declare the capacity in which he is acting, and if not satisfied, inform the applicant that its further dealings will be with the applicant direct.

F

Disposal of Land at Crichel Down

Public Inquiry. Rep., apps. pp. 34. [1954]

1953–54 Cmd. 9176, xi, 203
apptd. Nov., 1953. sgd. May, 1954
A. Clark.

'To enquire into the procedure adopted (a) *in reaching the decision that land at Crichel Down should be sold to the Commissioners of Crown Lands;* (b) *in the selection of a tenant by them; and the circumstances in which those decisions were made, but excluding from the enquiry all questions of governmental policy and, in particular, any question of whether preferential treatment should have been given to any applicant on the ground of previous ownership or occupation of the land.'*

The whole of Crichel Down had been compulsorily acquired for defence purposes, in face of opposition from the owners, at a cost to the Government of £12,006. In 1949 it was transferred to the Ministry of Agriculture. The previous owners, including Lt. Commander Marten, all first class farmers, were anxious to re-purchase their holdings at a total of about £21,000 in its then condition. The Land Commission had decided to equip it as a self-contained unit, at a cost of £32,000, and to let it. This was financially unsound and in their eagerness to create a model farm the Land Commission adopted an irresponsible attitude to the expenditure of public money, and were not always as frank with the Ministry as they might have been. Eventually it was transferred to the Crown Lands for £15,000, as it stood, with an obligation to equip, and a tenancy agreement was entered into. Lt. Cmdr. Marten's offer to purchase in May 1952 was not considered by the Land Commission or passed on to the Ministry. The previous applicants, however, had been told that they would have an opportunity to tender and that it would be let by public tender. In Sept. 1953 a petition signed by persons farming a total of 167,000 acres was sent to the Ministry.

The Report goes through the whole

proceedings in detail, commenting on mistakes, errors of judgment, failure to transmit accurate information, errors in briefing the Minister, etc. There was a regrettable attitude of hostility to Lt. Cmdr. Marten, who acted perfectly properly, which seems to have been engendered by a feeling of irritation that a member of the public should have the temerity to question the decisions of a Government department. There was no suggestion of corruption or personal dishonesty, and granted the policy decision that Crichel Down should be equipped and farmed as a self-contained unit, the sale and subsequent letting could not give rise to legitimate complaint. There was a certain amount of lack of liaison between officials at the Ministry. The procedure adopted naturally gave rise to misgiving amongst farmers and landowners.

See *Report of a Committee to consider whether certain civil servants should be transferred to other duties,* 1953–54 Cmd. 9220, x, 333, which considers the case of five officers whose actions were adversely commented upon. 'In present times the interests of the private citizen are affected to a great extent by the actions of civil servants. It is the more necessary that the civil servant should bear constantly in mind that the citizen has a right to expect, not only that his affairs will be dealt with effectively and expeditiously, but also that his personal feelings, no less than his rights as an individual, will be sympathetically and fairly considered. We think that the admitted shortcomings in this respect are the main cause of such loss of public confidence as has resulted from the present case.'

Some of the deficiencies may have been due as much to the organisational relationship between the Departments as to the faults of individuals.

6. CIVIL SERVICE

Training of Civil Servants

Cttee. Rep., apps. pp. 34. 1944

1943–44 *Cmd. 6525, iii,* 119
apptd. Feb., 1943. *sgd. April,* 1944
R. Assheton (*Ch.*), Curtis (Miss M.), Day, Gardiner, Hartley, Houghton, Lee, Smith, Wood.

'*To examine the general question of the training of civil servants, including the question whether a Staff College should be established, and if so, the particular form and character which that College should take.*'

The Treasury should exercise general control over training and should appoint a Director of Education and Training. Each Department should have a training scheme, with a full-time Departmental Training Officer in large, and a part-time officer in small departments. There should be routine training for all entrants, including initial training preceding actual duty, live work in a department, background training and encouragement to obtain outside qualifications. No centralised or institutional training is needed for the clerical and little for executive and professional grades. The Committee rejects both a Civil Service College, and participation in a National Administrative Staff College with people from industry, etc., in favour of a Civil Service central organisation for training Administrative cadets. The final training should be in the hands of the Director of Education and Training. Suggestions include service as private secretary to a Minister or high official, and in the field, and not more than two years in any one branch. There should be a break in the early thirties for those likely to hold a position of high responsibility, e.g. by a period of secondment to a local authority. Selected servants should be granted sabbatical leave for approved study and research.

Recruitment to Established Posts in the Civil Service during the Reconstruction Period

Statement of Government Policy and National Whitley Council Rep. pp. 23.
1944

1943–44 *Cmd. 6567, viii,* 7
apptd. Feb., 1944. *sgd.* —

J. A. Barlow (*Ch.*), Hamilton, Sharp, Smith, Street, Waterfield, Wilson, Day, Broom, Crook, Edwards, Herbert, Houghton, Leicester, White.

The historical order of the Papers included is the reverse of that in which they are printed.

Part III. Statement by the Chancellor sets out the problem as referred to the National Whitley Council. Part II is the Council's Report. There should be 'reconstruction competitions' for those who have lost opportunities of competing for the Civil Service owing to the war, and 'normal competitions' for those who reach normal ages as recruitment is re-opened. Ex-service men should be guaranteed one-half the vacancies in the clerical, two-thirds in the executive and three-quarters in the administrative grades. A number of 'accrued vacancies', i.e. vacancies accrued during the war by wastage and permanent expansion, should be reserved for older candidates.

Part I. Statement by the Government, accepts Council's proposals.

Use of the Civil Service Selection Board in the Reconstruction Competitions

Civil Service Com. Memo., apps. pp. iv, 46. 1951

1951 *Non-Parl. Civil Service Com. sgd. Dec.,* 1950

The pre-war examinations for the administrative class produced a large proportion of recruits of high academic and personal qualities, but since there was no minimum interview mark, they enabled a minority of candidates to succeed though lacking the desired personal qualities. The increasing employment of graduates by business would place the Civil Service at a disadvantage if it insisted on a large-scale examination in addition to graduation. As candidates in 1945 differed by as much as 10 years in age and education, a full academic examination was im-

possible. After consideration of the use of modern selection techniques by the War Office Selection Boards, a Civil Service Selection Board was established to conduct 'extended interviews', in which all the evidence of past record, individual and group tests were considered. The Memo. describes the tests, the work of the team of three assessors, which included an observer and a psychologist, etc. Whether after 1957 provision should be made for entry by a choice of two methods the Commissioners express no opinion on the evidence available. But they think that the CISSB would be a valuable adjunct to any system of interviewing for the higher grades.

The Scientific Civil Service

Reorganisation and Recruitment during the Reconstruction Period. pp. 16. 1945

1945–46 *Cmd. 6679, xviii,* 733

Following a report by an informal committee appointed by the Treasury (*Ch.* Sir Alan Barlow), printed as an Annex, the Government propose to reorganise the scientific civil service. (i) To improve conditions of service, a small panel will be set up to maintain a uniform standard for promotions and advancements, and to keep the organisation under review. Secrecy restrictions should be relaxed to enable scientists to publish work of their own and to discuss it with outside persons. Scientific officers will be brought into the Federated Universities' Superannuation Scheme. (ii) Highly qualified graduates in science will be appointed at the same salary as Principals. The number of Principal Scientific officers will be increased. 'Experimental officers' will replace the Assistant class. (iii) The whole scientific civil service will in future be recruited centrally through the Civil Service Commission.

Administrative Class of the Civil Service

pp. 2. 1945

1945–46 *Cmd.* 6680, *xviii*, 731
pres. Sept., 1945

The salaries of Permanent Secretaries of major Departments are to be increased from £3000 to £3500. The three grades of Under-Secretary, Principal Assistant Secretary and Assistant Secretary are to be reduced to two, that of Principal Assistant Secretary being abolished. This will facilitate the devolution of responsibility and reduce the steps in the administrative structure.

Marriage Bar in the Civil Service

National Whitley Council. Cttee. Rep., app. pp. 24. [1946]
1945–46 *Cmd.* 6886, *x*, 871
apptd. — sgd. March, 1946

J. A. Barlow (*Ch.*), Douglas, Ince, Lidbury, Padmore, Sharp (Evelyn A.), Smith, Street, Day, Broom, Geddes, Herbert, Rowe (Winifred E.), White.

'*To examine the working of the marriage bar in the Civil Service, and the arguments for and against its retention; and to consider and report upon the implications of a removal of the bar.*'

The report makes no recommendations on the removal or retention of the bar, but reviews the working of the rule and the implications of change. The economic and social pros and cons, as well as effects on the efficiency of the service are set out. Some unions and associations wish it to be retained, others to see it removed. Its removal would have very important effects on the turnover of staff in the large routine grades, and would reduce the number of vacancies and so of promotion opportunities and prolong the period of monotonous work in the lower levels.

Pensionability of Unestablished Civil Service

National Whitley Council. Cttee. Rep., app. pp. 10. [1946]
1945–46 *Cmd.* 6942, *x*, 895
apptd. May, sgd. Oct., 1946
H. W. Smith (*Ch.*).

The Committee considered details arising out of the decision of the Chancellor that one-half the period of service after the end of 1914–18 of certain unestablished entrants and age-barred officers should count for pension.

Higher Civil Service Remuneration

Cttee. Rep., apps. pp. 14. 1949
1948–49 *Cmd.* 7635, *xii*, 703
apptd. — sgd. Sept., 1948

Lord Chorley (*Ch.*), Bain, Gibson, Hetherington, L. Layton.

'*To advise Ministers as to the general level of remuneration of the higher posts of the Civil Service—administrative, professional, scientific and technical—and on any particular principles involved.*'

The salaries, etc., of the higher posts in the Civil Service must be sufficiently attractive to secure an adequate supply of suitable recruits and the level of remuneration should reflect the long-run trend in wage-levels and in the economic condition of the country. The heaviest jobs in industry and other professions or commerce are not more exacting than those of senior civil servants. Salaries should not be determined on a purely competitive basis, but should yield a standard not markedly lower than those of comparable status in other employments: at present the top ranks in industry commonly receive double the salaries of Permanent Secretaries. The difference in their salaries and those of recently established Government sponsored employment is difficult to justify. Committees should be set up to examine the salary structure of various classes; the complement of posts in the professional and technical classes should be such that each class offers an attractive career. The possibility of contributory superannuation arrangements should be examined.

Organisation, Structure and Remuneration of the Works Group of Professional Civil Servants

Cttee. Rep., apps. pp. 28. 1951

1951 *Non-Parl. Treasury*
apptd. — sgd. Aug., 1951

T. R. Gardiner (*Ch.*), Bailey, Cronshaw, Endicott, Frank, Holmes, Howitt, Keay.

'*In accordance with the recommendations of the Committee on Higher Civil Service Remuneration (Cmd. 7635) to consider and advise on the future organisation, structure and remuneration on a common basis of the Works Groups of Professional classes.*'

Three major professional groups were involved—architects, engineers and surveyors. The general body consisted of three grades—Basic, Main and Senior; the higher grades also of three—Superintending, Directing and Senior Directing. This structure should be continued.

The question of remuneration should be approached from the point of view of staff shortages. The General Body complements are below strength in number and quality, many candidates are of mediocre quality and a substantial number of those offered appointments refuse them, the proportion of refusals being highest amongst the best candidates. Recommendations are made on salaries, devolution of work to sub-professional groups, interchange, transfer to administrative work, etc. The payment to eminent professional men in top-ranking posts of higher salaries than would be paid to a civil servant who has spent most of his career in the Service is not open to objection.

Pay and Organisation of Civil Service Medical Staffs

Cttee. Rep., apps. pp. 20. 1951

1951 *Non-Parl. Treasury*
apptd. — sgd. Aug., 1951

H. G. Howitt (*Ch.*), Bailey, Boldero, Cronshaw, Gardiner, Haward, Jameson, Topping.

'*In accordance with the Recommendations of the Committee on Higher Civil Service Remuneration (Chorley Report, Cmd. 7635) to consider and to advise on the future organisation, structure and remuneration of medical staffs employed in Government Departments.*'

Recommendations are made on salaries, interchange of staff between departments, the National Health Service and local authorities; on integrating small medical branches with larger ones in other departments. Recruiting from outside to above-basic grades should continue, and with Treasury approval, it should be open to a department to upgrade a post while retaining the same officer, if he is outstanding.

Organisation, Structure and Remuneration of the Professional Accountant Class in the Civil Service

Cttee. Rep., apps. pp. 22. 1952

1952 *Non-Parl. Treasury*
apptd. — sgd. May, 1952

T. R. Gardiner (*Ch.*), Bailey, Cronshaw, Holmes, Howitt, Morison.

'*In accordance with the recommendations of the Committee on Higher Civil Service Remuneration (Cmd. 7635) to consider and to advise on the future organisation, structure and remuneration of the Civil Service Class of Professional Accountants.*'

There are two groups of accountants —the general Service Executive Accountants, and fully qualified professional accountants, with which the report is concerned. The existing five-tier structure of the latter group should continue. Recommendations are made on salaries, pooling of staff between large and small departments, transfer to administrative and other non-professional work.

Political Activities of Civil Servants

Cttee. Rep., apps. pp. 42. 1949

1948–49 *Cmd.* 7718, *xii,* 717
apptd. April, 1948. *sgd. April,* 1949

J. C. Masterman (*Ch.*), Adam, Cadogan, Cash, Chester, Curtis (Dame M.), Hopkins, Mitchell, Stephenson, White.

'To examine the existing limitations on the political activities (both national and local) which may be undertaken by civilian Government staffs, and to make recommendations as to any changes which may be desirable in the public interest.'

Civil servants generally are disqualified from sitting in the House of Commons and must not become candidates until they have resigned, though exemption from this was granted to persons, other than those in supervisory grades, employed in establishments predominantly industrial in character. They may vote and belong to political parties, but other political activities— holding political party offices, speaking publicly or writing books on party political matters and canvassing—are restrained by departmental rules. Service on local councils is subject to the permission of the Head of each Department and is more restricted when the department is closely concerned with the regulation of local authorities. Industrial civil servants are not under these restrictions.

Since the Blanesburgh Committee, 1925, the number of civil servants subject to these rules has risen to 1,100,000, the civil service is more intimately associated with the life of individual citizens and civil servants now have considerable delegated legislative and semi-judicial and discretionary powers.

The Staff side of the Civil Service National Whitley Council wished civil servants to have an unfettered right to stand as candidates and to be free to return to the civil service whenever they wished. All restrictions on other political activities should be swept away, reliance being placed on a convention of discretion, though they should be liable to disciplinary action if by indiscretion they created an intolerable position in their department.

As many citizens as possible should play an active part in public affairs, but the maintenance of and confidence in the political impartiality of the civil service is essential. A distinction must be made between free expression of views in private and in voting, and expression in public in furtherance of a political party. Democratic government depends on confidence of the public and the Minister that notwithstanding political changes loyal and impartial service will be given. There would be harmful effects if the Minister knew and had to take account of the political views of his officials. This is especially the case with those of the administrative staffs who are the advisers of ministers. Though these form only a small proportion of the total, the departments are made up of branches and grades which work in teams, each contributing to the decisions and submissions to ministers. There are also large numbers of local offices in which even junior officials have powers of interpretation of regulations affecting individuals. Here their relation is with the public and they must be and be felt to be impartial. The view that civil servants can be trusted in the free exercise of political rights in a way not detrimental to the public interest relies too much on the continuance of that traditional civil service attitude which has been formed by decades under the present conventions. Rules are necessary to protect an officer from errors in ignorance.

A distinction should be made between those whose participation in political activities would imperil confidence and efficiency and those whose activity would involve no such risk. Those 'above the line', i.e. administrative, professional, executive, clerical and typing grades should not be permitted to be candidates nor hold office in a political party, speak, or write on party political matters or canvass. Those 'below the line'—minor, manipulative and industrial grades—should be free to become candidates without resignation, be entitled to re-instatement under certain conditions and, subject to the Official Secrets Act, be completely free in the other forms of political activity except when on duty or in uniform, etc. The recommendations would exempt a further 466,000 from restrictions.

Political Activities of Civil Servants

apps. pp. 16. [1953]

1952–53 *Cmd.* 8783, *xxii*, 915
pres. March, 1953

The Government accepted the recommendations of the Masterman Committee, but as a result of discussions with the Whitley Council agreed to add to the two categories of the 'completely free', 'restricted', a third intermediate category of 'free by permission', of persons eligible for permission to engage in all political activities other than Parliamentary candidature. The granting of permission would depend on acceptance of a code of discretion (draft on p. 13). Canvassing will be barred for all 'restricted' servants and be open to the intermediate group by permission only. As a result of these changes 62 per cent of the Service will be completely free, 22 per cent will be in the 'permissive' group and only 16 per cent completely restricted.

Security

Conference of Privy Councillors. Statement on the Findings. pp. 5. [1956]

1955–56 *Cmd.* 9715, *xxxvi*, 955

It would not be in the public interest to publish the full text of the Report, but the paper gives the substance so far as it can properly be made public.

The main security risk used to be espionage by foreign powers through professional agents, but it is now communists and other persons subject to communist influence. The communist faith overrides a man's normal loyalty to his country and induces the belief that it is justifiable to hand over secret information to the communist party or to the communist foreign power. This risk extends to sympathisers and other persons. One of the chief problems is now to identify members of the communist party and the wider body of sympathisers and thereafter to take steps to see that secret information is not handled by anyone who would betray it.

The Government will continue to base their policy on preventing persons of this nature from having access to secret information. The Conference finds nothing organically wrong or unsound about the present security arrangements, but makes certain recommendations to strengthen them. The Government will give effect to all the recommendations. In certain of the public services, e.g. foreign service, defence and the atomic energy organisation, the need for stringent security precautions is greater than elsewhere. There is a relationship between security risks and the defects of character and conduct as factors tending to make a man unreliable or expose him to blackmail or influence by foreign agents. Departments have a duty to inform themselves of serious failings such as drunkenness, drug addiction, homosexuality or any loose living which may affect reliability. While nothing could be worse than encouraging malicious gossip, it is the duty of heads of departments and supervisory officers to know their staffs and to report anything affecting security. The measures necessary will require very careful consideration. In individual cases or certain sections of the service, a serious character defect may be the determining factor in a decision to dismiss or transfer any individual. The fact that a public servant is a communist may not only bar his employment on secret duties, but in some departments have an unfavourable effect on the prospect of promotion. In deciding difficult borderline cases of persons not members of the communist party, but having communist sympathies or close association with members of the party, the practice of tilting the balance in favour of the security of the State rather than safeguarding the individual will be continued. An individual living with a wife or husband who is a communist or a sympathiser may for that reason alone have to be moved from secret work.

It is recognised that some of the measures needed for security are alien to our traditional practices, e.g. not revealing the full details of supporting evidence, refusal to employ on secret duties or even to employ at all, even though nothing may have been proved on standards acceptable in a court of law. Though distasteful in some respects, these measures are essential, but public opinion should feel that the procedures will not be exercised unreasonably. The Conference approves the Tribunal set up in 1948 to hear appeals from civil servants threatened with transfer from secret duties or dismissal. A person whose continued employment is called in question will be able to have his case considered by it and its terms should be widened to enable them to present a fuller report to the responsible Minister. No additional powers should be sought to detain suspects or to prevent them leaving the country. The Conference was in favour, if suitable arrangements could be made, of giving those engaged on secret Government contracts the same right of access to the Tribunal.

See *Disappearance of Two Former Foreign Office Officials*. Rep.; 1955–56 Cmd. 9577, xli, 191.

Civil Servants

Rep.

1953–54 *Cmd.* 9220. See *Organisation of Departments*, p. 32.

Civil Service

R. Com. Rep., apps., index. pp. viii, 239. 1955. Mins. of ev., 28 days, index. 1954–56. Apps. I, II. 1954, 1955. Memo. by H.M. Treasury and Supplement. 1954

1955–56 *Cmd.* 9613, xi, 925. *Mins. of ev., etc.;* 1954–56 *Non-Parl.*
apptd. Nov., 1953. sgd. Nov., 1955

R. E. Priestley (*Ch.*), Albermarle (Diana), Mowbray, Gray, Menzler, Williams, Burman, Cash, Hall, Jackson, Thorneycroft, Wootton (Barbara).

'*Whether any changes are desirable in the principles which should govern pay; or in the rates of pay at present in force . . . in the hours of work . . . in the superannuation scheme.*'

There should be one set of principles of pay for the whole service. The principle approved by the Tomlin Commission that pay should be sufficient to recruit men appropriate to the duties they have to perform and to retain them without loss of keenness or efficiency is not adequate, for rates of pay sufficient for this may not be fair. Recruits may be moved by motives other than pay, wastage is not a reliable test as it may be affected by changes in outside demands for particular skills, and in conditions of near-full employment and shortage of labour some other criterion is needed to modify the recruitment test. The end in view must be a civil service recognised as efficient and staffed by members whose remuneration is thought fair both by themselves and by the community; the test is fair comparison with the current remuneration of outside staffs employed on comparable work. This principle of 'fair comparison' safeguards a non-political service from political pressure and can be applied by successive Governments of different political complexions.

The service should not 'give a lead' in this matter to outside, since this would break the rule of fair comparison and raise political difficulties. The remuneration should be such as to secure for it a number of persons of the highest and a high proportion of average ability, but should not cream off ability at the expense of other important fields of national life. Due recognition of internal relativities both within and between classes is important. They should not override the primary principle, but should be used to supplement it, especially when outside comparisons will provide no more than a vertical span and a few intermediate points. They must not become rigid; changes in the relative value of different occupations in the outside world must be reflected in the services. For the higher civil service minor differences of work should not be met by minor differences of pay; the principle of broadbanding should be followed. The Commission rejected basing rates on some method of measuring average trends, which might distort relativities between civil servants and those in outside employments.

In making outside comparisons the Treasury obtains information given to it by employers in confidence and it is understandable that the staff side is not fully content with this. A distinction should be made between fact-finding on job-comparability, the pay attached to comparable jobs, etc., and subsequent negotiation. A fact-finding unit should be established as a branch of the civil service not connected with the divisions of the Treasury concerned with negotiations on pay. The Treasury and staff associations should agree on a selection of organisations in public, semi-public and private employment and other callings whose work is comparable and whose rates of pay should be taken into account. Where factors such as bonuses, payments in kind, superannuation, etc., can be quantified, this should be done in order to arrive at 'true money rates' as a basis of the civil service rate. If they cannot be quantified, they should be roughly assessed. As outside rates may exhibit considerable variations amongst themselves, any comparison with rates paid by 'good employers' should be near the median of outside true money rates.

Gross working hours (including meal times) should become 'conditioned' hours (hours to be worked before overtime is payable), regular overtime and extra duty allowances abolished; hours per fortnight should be 84 gross and 74 net in London, 88 gross and 78 net elsewhere. The basis of provincial differentiation should be a national rate with London additions. Some widening of differentials is justified.

In the light of these principles the Report makes detailed proposals for the rates of pay of the various classes and grades. The proposed rates, hours, leave and provincial differentiation

should be regarded as a comprehensive unity. A standing committee of five persons chosen to represent a cross-section of informed opinion in the country should be appointed by the Prime Minister to concern itself solely with a general oversight of the remuneration of the higher civil service. Changes in the specialist classes should not be based on parity with non-specialist classes, but on fair comparison in an economy increasingly based on scientific and technological development. For the legal class, comparison with the few salaried outside lawyers or with the earnings of private practice is not practicable: pay should be based on internal relativities.

There is an *Introductory Factual Memo. on the Civil Service*, by H.M. Treasury; 1954 Non-Parl. See *Civil Service Pay Research Unit*. 1st Ann. Rep., 1957; 1958 Non-Parl., and succeeding Ann. Reps.

7. (a) LOCAL GOVERNMENT

Working of the Financial Provisions of the Air Raid Precautions Act, 1937, under Section 10 of that Act

Investigation. Rep. pp. 4. 1942

1941–42 *Cmd. 6356, ix,* 1

Local authorities submitted that where in 1941–42 or any subsequent year, after allowing for any grant receipt, the burden left on the rates in respect of civil defence expenditure exceeded the produce of a 3d. rate, the Exchequer should bear 50 per cent of the excess. The Government proposed to make a supplementary grant (*a*) where the general rate levied was not less than the average general rate levied in the same year in the same class of area, (*b*) where the rate was at least 6d. above the 1939–40 level, (*c*) where the net local expenditure on civil defence exceeded the produce of a 6d. rate.

Local Government in England and Wales during the Period of Reconstruction

pp. 19. 1945

1944–45 *Cmd.* 6579, x, 273

I. The Future Structure.—After the war local authorities will have many new duties, in housing, education, health and physical reconstruction, and some have thought that (i) the present structure will prove inadequate for these tasks, wider areas of administration being necessary, and (ii) the reconstruction programme will place an impossible burden on local government finances. The Government have decided against any general recasting of the structure of local government, as it is not generally desired and would cause great delays. The Government will not perpetuate the war-time system of Regional Commissioners, though certain departments may maintain localised staffs, etc.; it is opposed to the creation of directly elected regional authorities and to any general centralising of essentially local services, though certain services, e.g. trunk roads, some public utility services and residual public assistance functions may be transferred to the central government. Any necessary co-ordination should be through Joint Boards and Committees.

II. Finance.—The cost of the new and expanded services will rise, but will be mitigated by direct grants, the General Exchequer (Block) Grant, and by taking over certain services previously locally administered. At the outset expenditure on education will rise from £93·8 mn. to £129 mn. and on health from £41 mn. to £92 mn., but grants will rise from £41 mn. to £71 mn. and from £$\frac{1}{2}$ mn. to £44 mn. respectively, while the Block Grant, based on a statutory formula, is fixed at 22½ per cent and can be adapted as new factors become known. Areas with special problems—those with resources diminished by evacuation, war-damaged towns and old 'poor' areas, will be dealt with by separate grants.

III. Procedure for Adjusting Local Government Areas. — The Local Government Act, 1929, checked the process of creating new and extending existing county boroughs (which had reduced the populations of the county areas affected by nearly a quarter and rateable value by a fifth), by raising the population minimum for a county borough to 75,000, abolishing the Minister's power to create new ones by Provisional Order and requiring that extension proposals not agreed should proceed by Private Act. It is expected that there will be a number of Bills for extending or creating county boroughs, while at the same time the ten-yearly reviews of county districts and parishes required by the Act will be resumed, but there is no co-ordination between the two procedures. This process will be made more orderly by the establishment of a small Local Government Boundary Commission to take it over. The Minister will have powers to give it general directions for guidance, e.g. on the minimum population and rateable value for satisfactory units, linking of country towns with the surrounding countryside, etc. Its more important decisions will be subject to confirmation by the House, but the others will be final. The problems of financial adjustment between enlarged and curtailed areas will be examined. Owing to its special problems no new county boroughs will be permitted in Middlesex. The extension of the L.C.C. area would not be opportune, but the relations between the metropolitan boroughs and the county will be studied by an authoritative body.

Local Government Boundary Commission

M. T. Eve (*Ch.*), Maude, Holmes, Rees, Webster.

—— Report for 1946, apps. pp. 20. [1947]
1946–47 (82) *xiii*, 71
sgd. March, 1947

The task of the Commission was, as far as practicable, to make all local authorities, both individually and collectively, effective and convenient units.

Unlike a tribunal, the Commission takes the initiative in collecting information and its proposals are its own.

Variations in size, population and rateable value call for drastic alterations. The product of a 1d. rate in 24 county boroughs is less than £2000 and in 29 more than £4000; in 24 counties less than £4000, in 25 above £8000, in 127 non-county boroughs less than £400, in 116 more than £800. The mere application of a formula will not improve matters, since each area has its own characteristics, patriotisms and affinities. Local authorities' proposals would increase the area of county boroughs by 266 per cent, but decrease the population and rateable value of counties by one-quarter. In Wales and East Anglia some reorganisation of the counties themselves is inevitable, the population in seven counties in the former being below the minimum of 100,000 needed before an Order can be made without substantial agreement. The proposals made to the Commission for county boroughs include: limited extensions, large extensions designed to take in surrounding areas looking to the town hall or to provide for redistributed populations, which would sometimes result in a solid block of county boroughs, and have a serious effect on county government; and a novel proposal from the Manchester 'conurbation' by which county boroughs would relinquish their status to create a new two-tier county area wholly urban in character, with county districts to preserve local interests. Most non-county boroughs are or can by extensions be made effective units of government, but others are not and cannot be made so except by union with neighbouring districts. Very small towns could be allowed to retain their charters and ceremonial rights, but should not remain units of local government. The distinction between boroughs, urban and rural districts has been steadily narrowing and is slight. All urban and rural districts should have the same functions, and be known as county districts. The principle of compensation for added burden is wrong and the opportunity given by the alterations in the block grant system to get rid of it should be taken.

—— Report for 1947, apps. pp. 62.
1948

1947–48 (86) *xiii*, 23
o.p. March, 1948

In many areas, which include the great bulk of the population, the Commission's powers and instructions do not permit it to form effective and convenient units. Functions and boundaries cannot be considered separately and it has no power to deal with functions. It therefore made no Order, but instead sets out its views and recommendations, some of which will require legislation and amendment of Principles.

The chief causes of weaknesses in local government were: disparity in size, population and resources within the main types of authority, so that systematic allocation of functions between the types is impossible; failure to keep pace with the changing pattern of urban concentration; increase of central control, partly owing to the weakness of the smaller units in all types of authorities, haphazard allocation of functions between the different types, and conflict over boundaries.

A one-tier system of local government, in which all local government services are controlled by one council is simple, intelligible and concentrates the interest of the electors. But for efficiency different services require different sizes of area and different populations, so that outside large towns two-tier government is preferable. The efficiency of a two-tier system depends on the proper allocation of functions between the two tiers and a distinction between the powers which each exercise autonomously and those which they share. The various methods for securing collaboration between the two tiers include delegation, which though valuable depends for success on mutual confidence and is less effective than autonomous provision by an authority of an appropriate size. The appropriate size of an authority depends on geography, on the need to make local administration local and for an appropriate population catchment area, while large units can attract good officers, economise in man-power, etc. Populations of 60,000 and 200,000 seem to be critical figures at which distinction of powers could be made. The increase in the range and complexity of local government services makes it necessary to interpose between all-purpose authorities and minor - purpose authorities a third type, for middle sized towns, of a most - purpose authority.

The main proposals are: (1) there should be three types of authority—new counties, new county boroughs (the most-purpose authority) and county districts. (2) The whole of England and Wales, including existing county boroughs, should be divided into new counties. Some would be existing counties, united or divided, with populations of 200,000 to 1 mn. on a two-tier basis, others large towns having populations of 200,000 to 500,000, with a one-tier system. (3) Creation of new county boroughs, with populations of 60,000 to 200,000 which, though looking to the county for certain services, would be most-purpose authorities, autonomous in education, health, etc. (4) The functions of non-county boroughs, urban and rural districts would be assimilated. (5) Establishment of machinery for the delegation of functions in two-tier counties. (6) The Commission should be empowered to deal with non-county boroughs and the bar on changes within ten years should be modified. All these proposals except the first will require legislation.

These principles, as applied in detail mean that instead of 49 existing counties there would be 47 two-tiered and 21 one-tiered new counties; instead of 80 existing county boroughs, 63 new

county boroughs. In Wales the difficulties are that over half the 2 mn. population live in Glamorgan and excluding this, the population is not much greater than that of county Durham although the area is $7\frac{1}{2}$ times as great. And there are complications of geographical conditions due to mountains, rivers, estuaries, etc. Glamorgan should be a two-tiered county, Cardiff a one-tier county. Four alternative proposals are made to unite Welsh counties to form two, three, four or five new counties.

One member of the Commission, Holmes, wished to proceed on the lines of its original instructions.

See *Local Government (Boundary Commission) Regulations*, 1945; S.R. & O. 1945, No. 1569.

—— Report for 1948, app. pp. 8. [1949]
1948–49 (150) *xvii*, 743
o.p. April, 1949

As the Minister had announced in the House that it would not be practicable to introduce comprehensive legislation on local government reconstruction in the near future, the Commission would proceed on the basis of the existing Statute law and General Principles. But in order to take no steps which would be inappropriate if the recommendations of earlier reports were acted upon, the Commission would select cases to which an Order would be appropriate both under existing law and if the law were amended.

The four alternative proposals for alternative combinations of Welsh counties had been unanimously rejected by the counties.

Scottish Local Government Law Consolidation

There are five reports and one memo.
Local Government and Public Health Consolidation (Scotland).—Cttee. Rep.; 1942–43 Cmd. 6476, Cmd. 6477, v, 35. apptd. Dec., 1937, sgd. Aug., 1939.

Ch. J. Jeffrey. The proposals involved an examination of legislation extending over more than a century, and include the repeal of 23 Acts and the partial repeal of 148 others. The aim was not to put forward an ideal code, but to reproduce existing law with such amendment as was desirable and would command general assent. Cmd. 6477 is a draft Bill.

Local Government (Scotland) Bill H.L.— Jt. Cttee. Rep.; 1946–47 (117) ix, 41. apptd. April, o.p. June, 1947. Ch. W. E. Elliot. Explanatory Memo.; 1946–47 Cmd. 7068, xix, 1307. The Bill was substantially that prepared by the Jeffrey Committee.

Scottish Local Government Law Consolidation.—Cttee. Reps.; 1952–53 Cmd. 8729, Cmd. 8751, xv, 19. 1953–54 Cmd. 8993, xvi, 555. apptd. June, 1948, sgd. Nov., 1952, —, Oct., 1953. Ch. M. G. Fisher. These reports deal with the provision of various Acts relating to public order, police, cremation, shops and a number of miscellaneous subjects.

Expenses of Members of Local Authorities

Inter-Dept. Cttee. Rep., apps. pp. 51.
1947

1946–47 *Cmd. 7126, xiii*, 91
apptd. July, 1946. *sgd. April*, 1947

Lord Lindsay (*Ch.*), Anderson, Bradbeer, Dallas, Grenfell, Murdock, Nimmo, Shiner, L. Terrington, Thurtle (Mrs. D.), Turton.

'*To consider and report on the question whether it is desirable to extend the powers of local authorities, joint boards and kindred authorities to pay, as a charge to local rates and without Exchequer assistance, travelling allowances, subsistence allowances and allowances for loss of remunerative time to their members in respect of attendance at meetings of the authorities or travelling on their business; and to make recommendations indicating by which classes of authority and under what conditions any such allowances should be payable.*'

The law and practice in the various types of authority are reviewed. It is generally accepted that local government service should be given voluntarily, without recompense or personal gain, although this might mean some sacrifice. Sacrifice should stop short of hardship and the principle of voluntary service can best be preserved by reducing the strain on individuals. Excessive sacrifice may distort the membership of local authorities by debarring suitable candidates from seeking election. The major associations of local authorities were in favour of payment of travelling expenses, subsistence and loss of remunerative time, though rural district councils favoured only travelling expenses.

Local authorities should have power to pay actual fares reasonably incurred on public transport, reasonable mileage allowances for the use of members' cars, and subsistence expenses of members absent from home, at rates not exceeding 5s. od. for 4 hours, 10s. od. for 8 hours and more, etc. Allowances for loss of remunerative time should be at a maximum rate of £1 for a full day, and 10s. od. for half a day. A prescribed form of claim should be used. It should be mandatory on local authorities to establish the three sets of payments and members should have a right to the appropriate payment. Details of the payments to each member should be published in the minutes. The authorities and meetings in respect of which claims may be made are specified.

In a Minority Report Turton argued that the voluntary character of local government work should be preserved, that 316 out of 444 rural district councils were opposed to payment for remunerative time and that 40 out of 59 county councils were satisfied with things as they stood. The combined effect of allowances was too generous, and certain councillors will draw up to £297 a year. Some councillors have attended 400 meetings a year on 200 days. Some mileage allowances are excessive.

Local Government Manpower

Cttee. 1st Rep., apps. pp. 30.   1950
1950 *Cmd.* 7870, *xiii*, 1
apptd. Jan., sgd. Dec., 1949

P. D. Proctor (*Ch.*) and 19 others.

'*To review and co-ordinate the existing arrangements for ensuring economy in the use of manpower by local authorities and by those Government Departments which are concerned with local government matters; and to examine in particular the distribution of functions between central and local government and the possibility of relaxing departmental supervision of local authority activities and delegating more responsibility to local authorities.*'

In June 1947 the Ministry of Health sent circular No. 96/47 to local authorities inviting them to review the organisation and staffing of their departments with a view to effecting economies and making the fullest practicable reduction of the numbers employed. The Associations of local authorities, in a Memo. to the Ministry, suggested that only by a substantial diminution in the detailed control of the central departments could an effective reduction be made in the size of local authorities' staffs. The Government invited the Associations to join representatives of the central departments in a comprehensive examination of the problem, and the Committee was set up. Sub-committees were appointed which investigated the administration procedures used by the Home Office, the Ministries of Health, Education, Town and Country Planning, Transport, and the procedure for grant claims and loan sanction. Many detailed recommendations are made. App. I gives the Memo. of guidance issued by the Committee to the sub-committees.

—— Second Report, apps. pp. 54. 1951
1951-52 *Cmd.* 8421, *xvi*, 495
sgd. Nov., 1951

add E. W. Playfair (*Ch.*).   del. P. D. Proctor (*Ch.*).

The efficient conduct of work by local authorities is hampered by the requirements to appoint statutory committees to perform specified duties, the lack of power of committees to delegate to sub-committees, and the requirement in many cases that estimates and liabilities in excess of £100 must be approved by the Council. There are two important Memos. on statutory committees and the need for flexibility (App. IX) and on the history and practice of delegation in counties (App. X).

Scottish Local Government Manpower

Cttee. 1st Rep., apps. pp. 28.   1950.
    2nd Rep., apps. pp. 38.   1952
1950 *Cmd.* 7951, *xiii*, 33.   1951-52 *Cmd.* 8658, *xvi*, 551
apptd. June, 1949.   *sgd. March*, 1950, *July*, 1952

D. Milne (*Ch.*) and 18 others.

This committee, like the one for England and Wales with similar terms of reference, appointed sub-committees to make detailed recommendations on improved procedures within the sphere of the Scottish Home Department, the Scottish Educational Board, the Department of Health and the Ministry of Transport and on grant claims and loan sanction.

The second rep. includes Memos. by Associations of Scottish local authorities on delegation, staff control, division between local authorities' departments.

Publicity for Local Government

Consultative Cttee.   Interim Rep. pp. 10.   1947.   Final Rep., apps. pp. 17.
    1950
1947, 1950 *Non-Parl. Min. of Health*
apptd. — *sgd.* —, *Feb.*, 1950

L. J. Edwards (*Ch.* Interim Rep.), A. Blenkinsop (*Ch.* Final Rep.).

'*To advise the Ministry and the local authorities' associations on general questions of local government publicity.*'

Publicity ought to be directed to the

mass of the population through as many agencies as are available and as persistently as possible.

Relations with the Press.—As much business as possible should be taken in open council. The Committee deprecates the practice whereby a substantial part of business is transacted at a private meeting followed by a brief public meeting in which there is no real discussion. Advance circulation of agenda and reports is approved, and there should be no embargo on advance publication or comment. The admission of the Press to committee meetings is one for the determination of the individual authority in the light of the degree of its delegation of powers to committees, but more authority should be given for the supply of information to the Press where it is not admitted.

Large authorities may need Public Relations Officers, but special Public Relations Committees are not favoured.

the Fire Services and 10,560 were appointed after the war from those already serving or from the Fighting Services. On transfer they will continue in the new Service, but without guarantee as to rank.

All whole-time members of the N.F.S. of any rank should be eligible for consideration for any appointment. This was on the assumption that promotions in the N.F.S. had been based on merit and that eventually regulations might prescribe a period of service in the lower ranks as a qualification for appointment. In order to leave the door open to exceptional cases, appointments should not be limited to men holding permanent positions. In a minority reservation, the Fire Brigades Union wished the recommendation to be without qualification, and that the local authorities should be free to make whatever adjustments in rank they desire.

Transfer of Members of the National Fire Service to Fire Brigades

Central Advisory Council. Cttee. Interim Rep., apps. pp. 12. 1947

1947 *Non-Parl. Home Office apptd. Oct., sgd. Nov.,* 1947

A. S. Hutchinson (*Ch.*), Sargood, Jones, Mowbray, Adcock, Knight, Cathcart, Hutchinson (G.), Field, Horner, Grahl.

'*To consider and make recommendations as to—*(a) *the principles on which the number of posts of each rank above Fireman in each Brigade should be settled; and* (b) *the procedure to be followed in allocating members of the National Fire Service to Fire Brigades on the Appointed Day, including the procedure for appointment to posts in the Brigade above the rank of Fireman.*'

The permanent element of the N.F.S. composed 15,609 men, of whom 13,896 were employed at fire stations and 1713 in other parts of the organisation, mostly in higher ranks. Of these 5049 men were professional members of fire brigades before the nationalisation of

Publicity and Recruitment for the Civil Defence and Allied Services

Advisory Cttee. 1st Rep., apps. pp. 16. 1952

1952–53 *Cmd.* 8708, viii, 349 *apptd. July, sgd. Nov.,* 1952

W. Mabane (*Ch.*), L. Burnham, Dunnett, Evans, de Freitas, Gerrish, Godwin (Miss B. A.), Harvey, Lee, Morrison, Parish, Prichard, Reading (Dowager Lady), Struthers, Thomas, Wheatley.

'*To consider and make recommendations with due regard to the importance of economy in public expenditure on the following questions:* (1) *What measures should be taken to improve recruitment for the Civil Defence Corps, the Auxiliary Fire Service, the Special Constabulary and the National Hospital Service Reserve.* (2) *What information and guidance should be given to the public as to the steps which they should take in the event of war.*'

The object is to create a peace-time nucleus one-third the size of expected war requirements and capable of rapid expansion. The actual strength is 358,000 or 44 per cent of this target. Recruiting fluctuates, is better in rural than in urban districts, and is unbalanced as between the various sections. The chief obstacle has been the reluctance of people recovering from a long war to think of further Civil Defence. A change in the climate of opinion is required. Civil Defence is not an emergency organisation; it must be presented as the permanent fourth arm of defence and be given appropriate status and financial support.

Recommendations include the appointment of a head of the Civil Defence Services, designation of local controllers, adequate pay for Civil Defence officers, subsistence allowances and compensation for injury.

—— Second Report, apps. pp. 18. [1954]

1953–54 *Cmd.* 9131, *x*, 315
sgd. March, 1954

add. Hayday, Pilkington. del. Evans, Lee.

Over half a million volunteers are enrolled. If in the view of the Government war were imminent, it would be a duty to inform the whole nation of the nature of the attack to be expected and the action all individuals ought to take. Publicity should include the issue of a set of detailed instructions to every householder. Such publication at the present time would be inopportune, but plans for the issue of such information should be kept in a state of preparedness.

Newcastle-upon-Tyne Inquiry

Tribunal. Rep. pp. 60. 1944

1943–44 *Cmd.* 6522, *iv*, 315
apptd. Feb., sgd. April, 1944

R. Burrows

'To *inquire into the administration by the Council of the City and County of Newcastle-upon-Tyne and of its Committees and Officers of their functions in relation to the Fire, Police and Civil Defence Services with particular reference to the disposal of fire* engine B.B.999, *the acquisition and use as a fire float of the East Coast Scottish fishing vessel called 'The Premier', and the use of personnel, food, stores and equipment intended for the aforesaid Services.'*

The matters investigated came under the jurisdiction of the Watch Committee and the Fire Service. The two responsible officers were Councillor Embleton, who at all material times had been Chairman of the Watch Committee, Superintendent of the Special Constabulary (Mounted Branch) and Mr. Crawley, who during the same period was Chief Constable and A.R.P. Controller. It follows that the Chairman of the Watch Committee as Superintendent has been the subordinate of the Chief Constable and the Chairman of the Emergency Committee as Deputy Controller has been the subordinate of the A.R.P. Controller.

In many matters investigated there had been irregularities arising from personal interest, misuse of public material and property and loss through mismanagement. 'The Fire Services of Newcastle are now in the hands of the National Fire Service, a new Controller in charge of the civil defence organisation and the canteens under the management of a professional caterer.' No evidence supported the suggestion that corruption was prevalent in the services.

Section 10 of the Local Government Staffs (War Services) Act, 1939, which permitted a person employed in civil defence to be a member of the employing authority could with advantage be repealed. The Newcastle City Council delegates the fullest authority to a number of its committees, but it is also the practice for existing Chairmen to be automatically elected; this gives him great power in relation to the executive officers, and does not check any tendency on his part to engross authority. All minutes of all committees, save for certain functions of the Watch Committee, should be circulated to all members of the council. Newcastle should adopt the Standing Order of the L.C.C. and other authorities which enables a specified number to require any matter on committee to be referred to the council. A Standing Order should state expressly that no one can make a contract, however small, binding the City, unless he has authority to do so.

7. (b) LOCAL TAXATION AND FINANCIAL ADMINISTRATION

Scottish Rating System

Cttee. 1st Rep., *Valuation and Rating of Hydro-Electric Undertakings in Scotland,* apps. pp. 23. 1944

1943–44 *Cmd.* 6526, *iv,* 129
apptd. June, 1943. *sgd. March,* 1944

J. G. McIntyre (*Ch.*), Beattie, Fraser, Imrie, Lockhart, Mathers, Morrison, Welsh.

'*To review, with reference to post-war requirements, the law and practice in Scotland in relation to* (1) *the valuation and rating of hydro-electric undertakings (with special reference to the recommendations of the Committee on Hydro-Electric Development presided over by Lord Cooper);* (2) *the effect of the existing system of rating on the provision of houses, and the question whether it is practicable and desirable to limit the maximum amount payable in respect of owners' rates;* (3) *the liability for rates in respect of empty or unused premises. . . .*'

In the case of properties not ordinarily let at a rent, the assessor must estimate rent to a hypothetical tenant. This estimate may be based on the Comparative Principle (rent of similar properties actually let), the Contractor's Principle (percentage of cost of construction) or the Revenue Principle (value of profits resulting from occupation). The third principle is applied to these undertakings, as a result of which they are heavily rated, since their capital cost of construction is high and they are more heavily rated than undertakings producing electricity by coal, the cost of which is deducted.

The purpose of hydro-electric development is to exploit a new reservoir of natural wealth and it is in the national interest that this should be encouraged. Hydro-electric undertakings should be permanently relieved either by the deduction of an additional 25 per cent from gross value or the deduction from gross revenue of a sum equal to $3\frac{1}{2}$ per cent on the capital spent on generating works in excess of £30 per kilowatt installed, or by an adjustment of the valuation of generating works in accordance with the proportion which £30 per kilowatt installed bears to actual cost of construction per kilowatt installed.

—— Report, apps. pp. 34. 1945

1944–45 *Cmd.* 6595, *v,* 465
sgd. Dec., 1944

The basic difference between the English and Scottish rating systems is that in England and Wales liability for rates is confined to occupiers and no levy is made upon owners (except in certain instances when they recover the amount levied from the occupiers) while in Scotland they are levied on owners and occupiers. In Scotland as soon as a house is completed its owner is liable for rates; as a result Scottish speculative builders tend to build only for an established market, and not as in England, in reasonable anticipation of demand. Further, the demand for owner-occupation is affected because of the risk that if the house has to be let at any time, there may be a period when rates have to be paid on an empty house. In the inter-war years proportionately less houses were privately built for sale or letting in Scotland than in England, and to this the incidence of rating contributed, though it was only one element in a complexity of causes.

The complete abolition of owner's rates and the transfer of the entire rate-burden to the occupier, as in England, would be the surest way to remove the rating deterrent to private enterprise house building for letting, but the implications of such a change are not envisaged in the terms of reference.

G

The need for homes is so urgent that a more modest and immediately practicable step of limiting the amount payable by way of owners' rates is required.

Limitation of the total amount of owners' rates on each property and restricting this to a flat maximum in all areas were rejected in favour of limiting owners' rates to the existing poundages in each area. The tendency since 1914 to share rates equally between owners and occupiers was made obligatory, unless otherwise provided, by the Act of 1929. Limitation of owners' rates on houses to existing poundages would therefore remove from owners the liability for increases of rates, which would be borne by the occupier. Recommended that the consolidated owners' rate on houses should not in future exceed the existing rate, and that there should be an additional alleviation for new houses, which for the first £60 of annual value should for 25 years be rated at 25 per cent of rates for other houses in the same rating area.

If property is unoccupied for 3 months or more, owners and occupiers should not be liable for occupiers' rates nor should there be liability for owners' rates, except that in the latter case the assessor should have power to assess any lettable property which the owner is not genuinely seeking to let.

Valuation for Rates, 1939

Dept. Cttee. Rep., apps. pp. 57.   1945
1944 *Non-Parl. Min. of Health*
apptd. July, 1938. *sgd. Aug.*, 1939

M. Fitzgerald (*Ch.*), Bond, Dixon, Griffiths, Harfield, Harvey, Hewison, Hobson, Raynes, Thomas, Westwood, Simon (Lady).

'*To consider allegations which have been made that a strict application to certain classes of property of the existing law of valuation for rating purposes would cause undue hardship, and, if these allegations are found to be justified, to report what amendment of the law is desirable.*'

The basis of valuation (Section 68 of the Rating and Valuation Act, 1925) of dwelling-houses and similar types of property, is gross value, i.e. rent at which an hereditament might reasonably be expected to let from year to year if the tenant undertook to pay all usual tenant's rates and taxes, etc., and if the landlord bore the cost of repairs and insurance, etc.

Before the 1914–18 war the valuation of dwelling-houses gave rise to little difficulty as rents were comparatively static, and since most houses were let or available for letting, the rents actually paid provided a clear guide to the gross value. Since 1918, rent restriction, improved house design, increased costs of land and building and owner-occupation aided from various sources, have all led to differences of rent levels between pre-war controlled, pre-war uncontrolled, post-war privately owned and post-war council houses which are not commensurate with the differences of size and amenity. Before 1925 the law did not require, except in London, periodic valuation, and many lists in force had operated for many years without revision. For the purposes of the valuation list made under the Act of 1925 many local authorities have taken as their basis the rents paid for pre-war controlled houses, and little or no regard has been paid to the rents paid for post-war houses or even to the rents paid for pre-war non-controlled houses. The figures contained in the returns show that while generally the gross values of pre-war controlled houses approximate closely to the actual rents, the gross values of pre-war non-controlled houses and of post-war privately owned houses are definitely lower than the rents. Local authorities will have to pay greater regard to non-controlled rents and post-war (1914–18) rents. This in general would lead to increased assessment of post-war houses. Some tenants and occupier-owners of smaller types of post-war houses would suffer hardship. The hardship would be individual, and could not be dealt with by relieving classes of houses or by modifying the definition of gross value. Assessment Committees should be empowered to give relief in individual cases of undue hardship, i.e. financial embarrassment, by temporarily reducing the operative rateable value.

There are a number of reservations, and a Minority Report by Lady Simon proposing that gross values should represent the rental appropriate to the general economic circumstances of the occupying class in the locality.

Railways (Valuation for Rating) Bill

Scl. Cttee. Proc., mins. of ev. pp. iii, 5. 1946

1945–46 (143) *ix*, 779
apptd. May, o.p. May, 1946

T. Reid (*Ch.*), Evans, Fletcher, Morrison, Poole, Walkden.

Bill as amended is reported to the House.

Water Rates and Charges

Cttee. Rep., apps. pp. 32. 1946

1945–46 *Cmd.* 6765, *xiv*, 811
apptd. July, 1944. *sgd. Nov.,* 1945

R. B. Walker (*Ch.*), Anderson, Fraser, Home, Imrie, Lockhart, McBoyle, Mackie, McNeill, Rutherford.

'*To consider the basis of valuation for the purposes of water rates and the methods of rating and charging for water supplied by statutory undertakers in Scotland and to make recommendations.*'

The great diversity in the various systems of rating is of comparative minor importance in a small area, but when the administrative unit in the future covers a much wider area of supply the difficulty of combining water authorities with different systems of rating for water will be increased unless some uniform basis can be devised for adoption in a combined area.

There should be a uniform system throughout the country and it should consist of a public water rate for the public service aspect of water supply, and a domestic water rate. The public water rate should meet the first 25 per cent of water expenditure, be levied on all subjects in the area of supply, be not less than 2d. nor more than 6d., and be equally divided between owners and occupiers. The domestic water rate should be levied on the occupier only of all subjects within 100 yards of a main and not otherwise supplied with wholesome water. Recommendations are made for shops, factories, etc.

Rating of Site Values

Cttee. Rep., apps. pp. 133. 1952

1952 *Non-Parl. Min. of Housing and Local Gov., Scottish Home Dept.*
apptd., Nov., 1947. *sgd.* —

E. Simes (*Ch.*), Darling, Eve, L. Greenhill, Hicks (Mrs. U. K.), McBoyle, L. Douglas, Walker, Waterhouse.

'*To consider and report on the practicability and desirability of meeting part of local expenditure by an additional rate on site values, having regard to the provisions of the Town and Country Planning Acts and other factors.*'

The Report reviews the findings of the many previous enquiries into the rating of site values, but the historical case for it is not relevant, as the position has been profoundly altered by the Town and Country Planning Act, 1947. The unrestricted value of land, i.e. full value as if the Act had not been passed, is not suitable as a basis because the owner of land no longer enjoys any value beyond its restricted value. Rating on the basis of unrestricted value (i.e. full value as if the Act had not been passed) would rate him on something he does not own, while dividing it between the owner on the site value as developed and the Central Land Board on the difference between that value and the unrestricted value would mean that the Land Board would have to draw from the Exchequer for the money for payment: local rates would be subsidised on a basis unrelated to local needs. Basing a rate on restricted value would produce assessments lacking essential uniformity. The only practicable basis would be existing use value in its literal meaning. This would necessarily exclude any increase in value other than an increase within existing use. If a rate on this basis were accepted, it should be on annual, not capital value and in a closely populated country like Britain, should not be optional for local authorities, but obligatory at a uniform rate. The relationship between the amount to be raised by an additional rate on site values and the present rate would be best settled by a prescribed uniform poundage throughout the country. But existing contracts between landlord and tenant as to which should pay rates should be respected. Valuation would not be easy, the alternatives being valuation as a bare site, by reference to transactions in sites, or since the sites being valued will have buildings on them, valuation by the residual method of valuing with buildings and deducting current cost of the buildings.

The argument has been that rating of site values would prevent land from being kept out of use; but on the basis of existing value any development outside existing use would be reflected in a rise of site value assessment, which would thus not encourage development. If the proportion of the total value of property attributable to site value is between 20 per cent and 30 per cent, the total site value assessments would not be more than £300 mn. and might be as low as £100 mn., so that a 2s. od. rate would yield only a small part of total rate expenditure. The main effect would be to redistribute rates between properties according to the ratio of value of site to total rateable value, to shift rates from outskirts of towns and residences with a low ratio to the inner areas and commercial properties with a high ratio. Apart from existing contracts, the owner's power to shift a site value rate to the tenant will depend on the conditions of supply and demand

for the properties. There is no evidence that there would be any advantage in other shifts of incidence between classes and properties. The impact of the Town and Country Planning Act has altered the position by enforcing the claims of the community to the fruits of development as far as they can be foreseen. An additional rate on site values is neither practicable nor desirable.

A Minority Report, by Douglas of Barloch, Walker and Waterhouse states that the arguments in favour of rating of site values are unimpaired, that it is practicable and desirable. The present rating system is a deterrent against new buildings and improvements since they increase assessments, undeveloped land makes no contribution, and existing rates are regressive. Local authorities should be required to levy a minimum rate on site values, and empowered to raise a higher one if they wished. The basis should be (annual) unrestricted site value. If restricted site value is less than the unrestricted value, the Crown should bear the rate on the difference.

Operation of the Exchequer Equalisation Grants in England and Wales

Cttee. Rep., apps. pp. 59. 1953
1953 *Non-Parl. Min. of Housing and Local Gov.*
apptd. — *sgd. May,* 1953

F. L. Edwards (*Ch.*), and 26 others.

By the formula a county or county borough is entitled to Equalisation Grants if its actual rateable value is less than its 'standard rateable value', which is national average rateable value multiplied by its weighted population. The formula has been criticised on the ground that rateable value alone is an inadequate criterion and that successive deferments of revaluation have allowed inequities to develop. Proposals to correct these, pending revaluations, by the use of indices of under-assessment or by distributing the grant wholly or partly at a flat rate per head of population, are rejected. Though there is no evidence that the existing form of grant has induced local extravagance, there should be fixed for each class of authority limits in the permissible increase of expenditure (related to average increase of expenditure of that class) which could be made without grant penalty. The weighting of the formula should be modified as specified, in respect of sparsity weighting, and to assist areas whose populations have substantially decreased or greatly increased. Equalisation payments should be replaced by direct deficiency payments. The name of the grant should be changed to Rateable Value Deficiency Grant. The recommendations have to be made on the basis that they should not increase the total grant burden on the Exchequer.

See *Investigation into the Operation of the Exchequer Equalisation Grants to Local Authorities in England and Wales;* 1953–54 Cmd. 9270, xxvi, 501.

The Government decided that there was not sufficient agreement amongst associations of local authorities to justify implementing the recommendations.

Scottish Valuation and Rating

Cttee. Rep., apps. pp. 107. 1954

1953–54 *Cmd. 9244, xviii,* 779
apptd. May, 1953. *sgd. Aug.,* 1954

J. G. McIntyre (Lord Sorn) (*Ch.*), Banks, Byrne, L. Greenhill, Mackenzie, McNiven, Pinkerton, Thomson.

'*To review the present system of valuation and rating (other than the derating of agricultural, industrial and freight transport lands and heritages) in Scotland; to consider whether any and, if so, what changes should be made in the system, and what other action would in consequence of any such changes be required; and to report.*'

Neither a local income tax, rating of site values nor a poll tax are practicable, and provided it is not overloaded, the existing system of levying rates on property should be continued, subject to certain modifications. It was not, however, designed for meeting the present financial responsibilities. The incidence of owners' rates was an important factor in hindering the building of houses to let and one cause of the disrepair of many houses; they should be abolished and rents abated in proportion. The current system of valuation on the basis of actual rent passing is not without advantages, but it assumes a free market, and has been outmoded by the Rent Restriction Acts, the growth of local authorities' housing in which rents are not fixed on an economic basis, etc., and a decision that gross valuation of municipal houses should not exceed rents fixed by the local authority. The system no longer brings it about that occupiers of similar houses have similar valuations, and the disparities are aggravated by the increased poundages. Valuations should be dissociated from actual rents and should be fair rents, i.e. rents which the properties might reasonably be expected to yield from year to year, at current, not 1939 values. Section 73 (6) of the Housing (Scotland) Act, 1950, by which the value of a local authority house for rating purposes is not to exceed the rent, should therefore be repealed, or the assessor should be expressly directed that in determining the rateable value of a rent-restricted house, no account was to be taken of the restriction in rent. The owner's rates should be abolished in the year following amending legislation, and all valuations adjusted to the new principles by a purely arithmetical calculation. This would consist of deducting from 'real' gross value under the existing law a sum representing the owner's rates component, taken at the average for the whole of Scotland in 1939, to arrive at an approximation to the gross amount which would be determined on the new principles. When all the reforms were fully implemented and valuations throughout Great Britain made on broadly the same principles, the average rateable value arrived at could properly be used as the standard for the distribution of the equalisation grant in England and

Scotland; the arithmetically adjusted ones could be so used in the interim.

Valuation and Rating in Scotland

pp. 8. 1955

1955–56 *Cmd.* 9606, *xxxvi*, 947

The Government accepts the principles of the Sorn Committee's report. Owner's rates will be abolished and rates reduced in proportion; valuation will be dissociated from actual rents and based on fair rent in a free market at current values. But the new system of valuation cannot be introduced immediately; instead of introducing it by stages as proposed by the Committee, all valuations will be frozen for five years during the process of revaluation, and all property rated on the new valuation when it is completed.

Operation of the Exchequer Equalisation Grants in Scotland

Cttee. Rep., apps. pp. 36. 1953

1953 *Non-Parl. Scottish Home Dept.* apptd. —. sgd. Aug., 1953

C. C. Cunningham (*Ch.*), and 17 others.

The Committee made an interim report, printed as App. A, on whether the addition of 25 per cent to the standard rateable value per head of population in England and Wales to give the standard rateable value used in the calculation of the Scottish grant was sufficient. Owing to their different basis, Scottish rateable values are substantially higher than in England and Wales, but until there has been a complete revaluation in the latter, no precise figure can be given. For the time being Scotland should receive the Goschen equivalent of 11/80ths of the equalisation grant payable to England and Wales.

This grant should be distributed by reference to a notional rateable value per head of weighted population. In view of the burden imposed by planned migration and new towns, the existing formula should be modified by increasing the 'weighted population' by

twice the number by which the increase of the civilian population exceeded 5 per cent. It was wrong that a local authority should be able, by fixing the rents of its own houses at a low figure, to influence the amount of its credited rateable value. In future each such house should be given a notional rateable value, which should be the average rental of all local authority houses in Scotland.

See *Equalisation Grant in Scotland. Report on Result of Investigation under Section 30*; 1953–54 (6) xvi, 541. This sets out illustrations of the effects of the existing and proposed systems. The Government accepts the proposals, subject to arrangements to safeguard local authorities against loss while the new arrangements continue in force.

Operation of the Exchequer Equalisation Grants in Scotland

Cttee. 2nd Investigation. Rep., apps. pp. 24. 1955

1955 *Non-Parl. Scottish Home Dept.* apptd. June, sgd. Oct., 1955

J. N. Browne (*Ch.*), and 16 others.

The Government declined to implement the Sorn Committee's recommendations on the arithmetical adjustment of rateable values pending revaluation, as they would not result in comparable levels of rateable values between Scotland and England and Wales. An interim basis for the equalisation grant was therefore required. In application the Goschen formula was not equitable. In 1953–54 the relevant expenditure per head of weighted population in Scotland was £8·04 as against £7·56 for England and Wales excluding London, and the residual rate burden, after grant, per head of actual population was £8·55 in Scotland and £7·18 in England and Wales excluding London. The position would be improved by a total grant equal to the difference between what expenditure and what rate burdens would be if both cost per head of weighted population (notional relevant expenditure) and rates per head of actual population (notional rate burden) were the same as in England and Wales excluding London. The Goschen formula should be used as a safeguard against unforeseen reductions. The principles of the distribution of grant should remain unaltered.

8. LONDON

Greater London Water Supplies

Dept. Cttee. Rep., apps. pp. 15. 1948

1948 Non-Parl. Min. of Health
apptd. Nov., 1946. sgd. March, 1948

R. M. Hughes (Ch.), Alban, Des Forges, Dixon, Hetherington.

'To examine the present system of water supply administration in the Greater London area; and to consider and report on the question whether changes in that system are desirable in the public interest and, if so, what should be the constitution, powers and duties of the new body or bodies in which control should be vested.'

The public water supplies of Greater London are administered by a number of autonomous water undertakings, the largest being the Metropolitan Water Board, whose area remains as it was defined in 1902 when it took over 8 water companies. The Water Act of 1945 gave the Minister powers to set up regional Joint Advisory Water Committees, but the Metropolitan Water Board contended that the water supply to Greater London needs to be planned over a wider area determined on hydrogeological grounds. They suggested an area with a population of 10,300,000 people, which included the whole or part of the areas of 177 local government authorities, and of 64 water undertakings. Most of the other water undertakings in the area were opposed to a large single authority, and preferred suitable amalgamations and four Joint Advisory Water Committees.

The potential yield of the area was about 620–680 mn. gallons a day, requirements in 1960 670 mn. gallons.

In a drought there might be a deficiency of 70 mn. gallons a day. The area must be treated as a whole and all water resources pooled. The development of one major outside source was required. The Chairman and Alban recommended a single water authority for the whole area; Des Forges, Dixon and Hetherington four joint water boards, with a central co-ordinating authority.

Railway (London Plan)

Cttee. Rep., app. pp. ii, 26. 1946.
 Final Rep. pp. iv, 8. 1948

1946 Non-Parl. Min. of War Transport
1948 Non-Parl. Min. of Transport
apptd. Feb., 1944. sgd. Jan., 1946, March, 1948

C. E. Inglis (Ch.), and 7 others.

'To investigate and report upon the technical and operational aspects of those suggestions made in the County of London Plan of 1943 which relate to the main line and suburban railway system of London, both surface and underground, bearing in mind that these suggestions are intended to contribute towards and form part of a comprehensive scheme for the re-development of the area in question. . . .'

The County of London Plan proposed amongst other works to remove the bridges and viaducts between Westminster Bridge and London Bridge, and to dispense with the need for them by two deep level loops, one of which would connect Waterloo Junction, Charing Cross, Blackfriars, Cannon Street and London Bridge. The cost of the civil engineering work only would at post-war prices be about £180 mn.

The Committee does not agree with many of the Plan's strictures on the railway system, but many of the inner areas are poorly served with railway facilities and the main line terminals are congested. It endorses electrification or the use of diesel on all railways in London, the underground system should be separated from the main line track as far as inter-running is concerned, and it is possible to project urban traffic across London in tunnels.

The proposed deep level stations for long distance main traffic are not practicable; Charing Cross and Cannon Street should not be removed until alternative facilities are provided. The volume of traffic both in journeys and passenger miles will increase.

Its own proposals are (1) to facilitate the planning of the South Bank, five lines in tunnel, two north and south lines in tunnel and a terminal station reconstruction; (2) five new routes to meet immediate traffic requirements. The removal of Blackfriars and Holborn Viaduct stations would take place in the first stage, the removal of Charing Cross and the construction of a new terminal at Waterloo Junction in the third, and the removal of Cannon Street in the fourth. The cost, excluding electrification and work outside tunnels, would be £139 mn., or £229 mn. to £232 mn. if post-war prices exceed pre-war levels by 65 per cent. The work would take 30 years.

The Final Report deals with improvements in the northern main line terminals. For goods traffic an early decision on the location of the main markets is desirable, but the adoption of the proposals for the South Bank and for the elimination of the three cross-river bridges as working principles is necessary if the detailed investigations are to be started without delay.

London Plan

Working Party. Rep., apps. pp. iv, 35. 1949

1949 *Non-Parl. Min. of Transport apptd.* — 1948. *sgd. Oct.,* 1948

British Transport Commission, C. Hurcomb (*Ch.*). Working Party, V. M. Barrington-Ward (*Ch.*).

As the British Transport Commission had entered upon its duties, which include a general responsibility for the co-ordination of transport, it appointed a Working Party to review the proposals of the Railway (London Plan) Committee. The Report of the Working Party is preceded by the observations of the Transport Commission.

The differences between the recommendations of the Committee and of the Working Party are due to two factors. (i) The Working Party proposals are governed by the consideration of urgent traffic needs. The Committee's terms of reference implied accepting the removal of the three bridges as first priority: its alternative seven routes were necessary substitutes, though the traffic value would be secondary and incommensurate with the expenditure involved. The removal of Charing Cross, Cannon St. and Blackfriars Bridges is not justified by traffic requirements. The large works needed merely to replace the first two would lead to the postponement of works for more urgent traffic needs, and they should be left over for 25 to 30 years. For the third, the new works would not be so formidable. (ii) The Working Party had later information on traffic needs and on the intended size and distribution of the population in the London region. It draws a distinction between urban service, i.e. distribution of traffic in detail in the inner area, which requires high frequency, frequent short stops and high overload capacity, and outer suburban service, which requires high speed, high seating capacity, but lower frequency. For the proposed new cross-river freight route in tunnel to replace Blackfriars Bridge, the Party prefers a route via Greenwich. The cost of the routes and works proposed, on the same basis as those of the Committee, would be £238 mn. compared with those of the Committee's proposals at existing prices of £295 mn.

London Planning Administration

Cttee. Rep., apps. pp. 21. 1949

1949 *Non-Parl. Min. of T. and C. Planning apptd. March,* 1946. *sgd. Feb.,* 1949

Majority: C. Davies (*Ch.*), Neal, Allen, Bolton, Vickers, Warren. Minority: MacColl, Pike, Robson.

'To advise on the appropriate machinery for securing concerted action in the implementation of a Regional Plan for London as a whole.'

Between 1943 and 1947 three plans have been produced for London, one by Prof. Abercrombie and Mr. Forshaw for the County of London; one by Prof. Abercrombie for Greater London and one by Dr. Holden and Prof. Holford for the City of London. These three documents comprise a plan for the Metropolitan area embracing some 10 mn. people and about 2700 square miles. The main proposals are for the re-development of the congested areas: decentralisation by the creation of new towns; some re-disposition of industry; the provision of a green belt; a radial system of roads; and a railway plan including electrification, the removal of three cross-river bridges, the re-location of main line stations and substantial development of the suburban and underground system. Carrying out the Plan would involve the integrity of the Region and there must be concerted action of the whole of it.

The majority say that planning in the Region is in the hands of 12, and development is carried out by 181 local authorities, as well as by statutory undertakers. The central Departments are ill-adapted to carry out development. A regional authority, with powers of direction, finance and supervision is needed, but as this would affect the whole of local government, a Local Government Commission should review the local administration of the whole Region. In the meantime, a Regional Advisory Committee should be established.

The minority hold that attempts by central Departments to secure concerted action would add to the acute congestion in central administration and the proposed interim advisory committee would be moribund. Instead, the Minister should exercise his powers to create a Joint Planning Board.

London Traffic Congestion

London and Home Counties Traffic Advisory Cttee. Sub-Cttee. Rep., apps. index. pp. 58. 1951

1951 Non-Parl. Min. of Transport apptd. March, 1950. sgd. Jan., 1951

A. Samuels (Ch.), Burnell, Dalton, Hole, Hollinghurst, Northcott, Welland, Young.

'To consider traffic congestion in Inner London, with particular reference to parking problems.'

'Inner London' is interpreted to include an area of $7\frac{1}{2}$ square miles. Traffic needs at present and for some years to come can be met only by (a) increasing road space, (b) reducing traffic, (c) decreasing hindrances to free flow, (d) other measures to improve flow. (a) Ten schemes of road widening and five schemes in the surrounding area should be given priority. (b) A general reduction in the volume of traffic is not only undesirable, but impracticable. No reduction in the number of buses or of taxi cabs is necessary, nor of goods vehicles, though loading and unloading may have to be prohibited during specified hours, nor of contract coaches, though waiting and setting down points may need regulation. (c) Surveys show that there is no proper parking accommodation for 40 per cent to 50 per cent of the number of vehicles parked and a substantial reduction of indiscriminate parking is essential. Multi-storey parking, underground parking and compulsory provision in new offices are recommended. Central car parks will not pay commercially and Government grants are necessary. £5 mn. spent on them will give much more benefit than the same amount spent on road improvements. There should be further restrictions on horse-drawn traffic, and experiments with parking meters. (d) More one-way streets, no waiting and unilateral waiting signs are amongst other recommendations.

Car Parking in the Inner Area of London

Working Party. Rep., app. pp. iv, 39. 1953

1953 *Non-Parl. Min. of Transport apptd. May*, 1951. *sgd. Jan.*, 1953

A. Samuels (*Ch.*), Allison-Beer, Birch (J. M.), Birch (R. W.), Botterill, Buchanan, Burnell, Chinn, Dalton, Downey, Green, Greig, Griffiths, Hole, Hollinghurst, Pollitzer, Rayfield, Ross.

'*To consider the recommendations made by the London and Home Counties Traffic Advisory Committee in their Report on* London Traffic Congestion *in regard to car parking in the inner area of London and to formulate detailed proposals.*'

The Working Party was appointed to make proposals on the recommendations of the Samuels Committee on car parking. A survey shows that in Inner London some 16,000 vehicles were parked for long periods in the streets, having nowhere to go, as accommodation off the highway was insufficient by 12,000 vehicle spaces. Within a quarter of a mile from the Grosvenor, Berkeley, Cavendish and St. James Squares at any time some 2900 cars were parked for longer than two hours.

The plan recommended consists of three interdependent elements: (i) construction of underground garages in the four squares for 1820 cars at a cost of £1½ mn. at 1951 prices, and two multi-storey garages for the remainder; all new buildings should provide parking space for those who work in or visit them; (ii) introduction of parking meters; (iii) a new and balanced system of waiting regulations.

Taxicab Service

Cttee. Rep., apps. pp. 34. 1953

1952–53 *Cmd.* 8804, *xvii*, 897 *apptd. Aug.*, 1952. *sgd. Feb.*, 1953

Lord Runciman (*Ch.*), Allen, Geddes, Kerr, Marsh (Miss J.), Smith, Waterhouse, Whitehouse.

'*To consider the effect of present economic and fiscal circumstances on the taxicab service (particularly in London) and to report what changes if any in the present system of taxation, control or organisation are desirable in the public interest.*'

The London taxicab is a specially constructed vehicle and its cost with purchase tax has risen to £1319. Most finance companies will not advance the amount of the purchase tax. The increases of fares in 1950 and 1951 were followed by a decrease of use roughly in proportion to the increase of fares, so that gross receipts varied little. The five largest proprietors are working at a loss and are not able to replace their cabs. The number of cabs licensed has fallen from 6799 in 1950 to 5437 in 1952, and the number of new licences from 960 to 132. As the one remaining cab manufacturer cannot be expected to continue for so small an output, there is a risk that there might be no effective taxicab service in London. The 58 per cent of engaged mileage is too low for economic operation and could be raised to between 60 per cent and 70 per cent without undue inconvenience to the public. Raising or lowering the fares is no solution. Limitation of numbers of cabs and drivers is rejected, as well as special rebate of petrol duty. London taxicabs should be exempt from purchase tax and the restrictions on hire purchase should be swept away. The Committee were without the operation costs of owner-drivers or small proprietors; applications for increasing the fares should be supported by uniform statistics from the trade, including a representative sample of these groups.

London's Airports

1952–53 *Cmd.* 8902. See *Air Transport* p. 215

Regent's Park Terraces

Cttee. Rep., apps. pp. 57. 1947

1946–47 *Cmd.* 7094, *xiv*, 335 *apptd. Jan.*, 1946. *sgd. Jan.*, 1947

Lord Gorell (*Ch.*), Bolton (Mrs. I. M.),

Forber, Forshaw, Maclagan, Shiels, Watson.

'*To consider the future of the Terraces adjoining Regent's Park from all aspects, architectural, town-planning and financial, and to make recommendations as to their future adaptations or replacement to meet modern requirements.*'

The Nash Terraces are of national interest and importance, and should be preserved as far as possible. Before the war they were let on leases at rents totalling £100,000, but during the war suffered damage, leases fell in or were abandoned. Unsightly additions and even vandalistic alterations of interiors had been permitted. A large number had been taken over and converted for use as Government offices.

The Committee rejected the course of demolishing and redeveloping on building leases, subject to architectural and planning control. They should be preserved as far as practicable without strict regard to the economies of prudent estate management. A minimum list for preservation is given. Preservation could be undertaken either by reconditioning in their present form, or by some conversion scheme, such as that prepared by Mr. de Soissons. They should not be used as offices, but as residences, and rents should be fixed so that the occupation of the site was not the privilege of any one income group.

In a statement preceding the report the Government expresses its sympathy with aims of preservation, their use for residences and not offices. But the diversion of labour and materials would not be justified for some years, and the use as Government offices will be terminated as soon as the supply of office accommodation permits. It notes that by the proposals tenants would occupy on a subsidised basis.

Future of the Regent's Park Terraces

Crown Estate Com. Statement. pp. 10. [1957]
1957 *Non-Parl. Crown Estate Com.*

A number of the Terraces will be definitely preserved for effective use for many years. An attempt will be made to secure the same result for all the terraces designed by Nash or his contemporary Burton, if this can be achieved without undue capital cost. While an assured future cannot be foreseen for all of them, present plans do not provide for the demolition of any terrace or the alteration of their elevation. Details of the decisions on the individual terraces are given. Mr. de Soissons is to design and supervise some conversions. Consideration will be given to experienced private developers to convert a terrace on a commercial basis. The Royal Fine Arts Commission and other bodies are co-operating.

Bills Relating to Particular Sites, etc.

Roosevelt Memorial Bill. Jt. Sel. Cttee. (Lord Halifax, *Ch.*). Rep., proc., mins. of ev.; 1945–46 (184) *ix*, 787. *Public Offices (Site) Bill.* Sel. Cttee. (T. Braddock, *Ch.*). Proc., mins. of ev.; 1946–47 (100) *ix*, 245. *Trafalgar Estates Bill.* Sel. Cttee. (G. Benson, *Ch.*). Mins. of ev.; 1947–48 (7) *ix*, 877. *Parliament Square (Improvements) Bill.* Sel. Cttee. (E. Fletcher, *Ch.*). Mins. of Speeches. Proc.; 1948–49 (290) (290–1) *x*, 269. *City of London (Guild Churches) Bill.* Sel. Cttee. (R. H. Morris, *Ch.*). Rep., proc., mins. of ev.; 1951–52 (175) *iv*, 871.

The City of London (Guild Churches) Bill enabled the Bishop of London to designate and establish certain churches as Guild Churches to serve the non-resident population. 1947-48 (7) ix contains a Memo. and evidence by L. A. Abraham, Clerk of Private Bills, on procedure on Hybrid Bills without a preamble.

Documents Relating to Festival Gardens Ltd.

pp. iv, 40. [1951]
1950–51 *Cmd.* 8277, *xxvii*, 125

The reports on the circumstances which caused the financial commitments to be greatly in excess of the amounts estimated, call attention to the organisation of the Board, lack of adequate directing personnel or delegation of executive responsibility, lack of initial planning, change in the basis of the contract, the prestige value of working to time in expansion of plans, lack of control over payroll and materials, etc., and unfavourable weather and shortage of materials, etc.

See *Festival Pleasure Gardens Bill.* Sel. Cttee. (H. N. Linstead, *Ch.*). Mins. of proc., etc.; 1951–52 (64) *vii*, 9.

A New Queen's Hall

Cttee. Rep., apps. pp. 35. 1955

1954–55 *Cmd.* 9467, *vii*, 79
apptd. Oct., 1954. *sgd. April*, 1955

L. Robbins (*Ch.*), Boult, Kettle, Tucker, Williams.

'*To advise . . . on the need for, and economic prospects of, a new hall on the Queen's Hall site.*'

On musical grounds it is desirable to replace the destroyed Queen's Hall by another large hall of good acoustic qualities, but it is doubtful if there is a potential demand which would enable it to run without subtracting from the audiences of subsidised halls already in existence. But this should not stand in the way of a commercial tender for a lease for purposes mainly musical. There is evidence of the need for a small hall. This could be met by addition to the Festival Hall or by the creation by the Government in due course of a music centre in Regent's Park.

Birds in London

Cttee. Rep., apps. pp. iv, 28. 1948

1948 *Non-Parl. Min. of Works*
apptd. April, 1947. *sgd. April*, 1948
C. Hurcomb (*Ch.*).

Makes suggestions for increasing the resident bird population, including migratory and unusual visitors, suitable tree and shrub planting, the control of vermin, and the selection of observers and reporters.

See *Bird Sanctuaries in Royal Parks.* Cttee. (L. Earle, *Ch.*). Rep.; 1922 Non-Parl. Office of Works, and Annual Reports.

II. NATIONAL FINANCE

Taxation of Weekly Wage Earners

Memo., app. pp. 16. 1942

1941–42 *Cmd.* 6348, *ix*, 493
pres. April, 1942

The wage earner is assessed to income tax half-yearly on his wages for the half-years ending 5th October and 5th April, but his total tax depends on his income for the whole year. The tax is deducted from wages by the employer, who is notified by the Collector of Taxes on the amount to be deducted. No tax is deducted until the taxpayer has been notified of the allowances due to him, the tax is an ascertained liability and the employer is bound to deduct the amount and plays no part in its determination, nor are the employee's personal circumstances disclosed. As a result of rising wages, the number of wage-earners liable to tax has in two years grown from 1 mn. to $5\frac{1}{2}$ mn.

In industries in which wages fluctuate seasonally, some of the tax due in respect of high summer earnings is deducted in part during the period of low winter earnings. As a remedy it has been proposed that the tax should be deducted each week in respect of that week's earnings; it would then be unnecessary to wait until Inland Revenue had made the assessment and the tax would never be a disproportionate part of the wages from which it is deducted. But it has not yet been found possible to devise a weekly scheme which was fair and practicable. One type of scheme involves weekly deductions, with adjustments at the end of the year. But the annual tax collected would in many cases exceed the total tax due. Persons whose wages varied between one week or season and another would be out of pocket by over-deduction, and the claims for repayment at the end of the year might affect 2 mn. or 3 mn. of the $5\frac{1}{2}$ mn. liable to tax, as well as some not liable at all. The employer would have to make the calculation and might be able to infer the employee's personal circumstances. The second type of scheme, which proposed fixed deductions with no adjustments at the end of the year, would tax those with fluctuating incomes more than those with stable ones.

The present basis of assessment must be retained, but the following improvements were proposed. (1) The tax deduction would start a month later, giving the taxpayer a month's wage free of tax and Inland Revenue an opportunity to complete assessment and notify employers promptly. (2) For seasonal employments the tax periods would be 5 months and 7 months, which would help to level out some of the difficulties. (3) The tax deduction limits would be modified to meet the cases of irregular fluctuations of wages.

New System for the Taxation of Weekly Wage Earners

app. pp. 20. 1943

1942–43 *Cmd.* 6469, *xi*, 309
pres. Sept., 1943

A new system for collecting income tax on current earnings has been devised which will automatically adjust the weekly deductions of tax to any rise or fall in wages and at the same time relate the weekly deductions to the final liability for tax on the aggregate wages of the year. The tax deducted from any earnings in any financial year will represent the liability for that year, measured by the actual earnings of that year, and the deductions week by week

will keep pace with accruing liabilities. The system will apply to all weekly wage earners whose tax is deducted in arrear.

At the end of every week there will be ascertained the total amount of tax due on the total wages paid up to date, the proportionate part of the personal reliefs due for the whole year being taken account of. The amount of tax collected in any week will be (*a*) the cumulative tax due on the aggregate wages up to and including that week, less (*b*) the tax already deducted in the previous weeks. This avoids excessive deductions of tax in the case of fluctuating earnings. When wages fall or there is unemployment, the system provides for refund forthwith by the employer equal to the excess of the tax already deducted over the cumulative tax up to the week in question.

The employer will not be involved in elaborate calculations, since each wage earner will be given a code number by Inland Revenue in accordance with the allowances and relief due to him, and the employers will be supplied with tax tables showing for each code number the appropriate tax on any given amount of wages. The Memorandum describes in detail the procedure and administrative arrangements.

Hydrocarbon Oil Duties

Cttee. Rep., app. pp. 16. 1945

1944–45 *Cmd.* 6615, *v*, 87
apptd. July, 1944. *sgd. Feb.*, 1945

A. L. Ayre (*Ch.*), Macharg, Robinson.

'*To consider and report upon*: (a) *the effect of the hydrocarbon oil duties on the supply of raw materials to, and the development of, the chemical industry in this country so far as the use of hydrocarbons and their derivatives is concerned*; (b) *the extent to which any change in those duties would affect industries engaged in the production of similar products from coal.*'

The chief sources of hydrocarbon raw materials have been the coal tar and benzole obtained as by-products from high-temperature carbonisation at gas works and coke ovens, but increasing use has also been made of raw materials from petroleum. Whilst the former are aromatic compounds and the latter largely aliphatic compounds, coal and petroleum are still primary sources of chemicals and both are necessary to the modern organic chemical industry.

Hydrocarbon oil duties were said to have prevented the development of new processes using those oils as raw materials. Certain oil companies had developed processes by the cracking of petroleum oil, but duties had been levied even where the process utilised materials which otherwise would have been waste. The indirect effect of the duty is that it enhances the price of the indigenous oils by approximately the amount of the duty.

Recommended that there should be no duty on imported hydrocarbon oil used for chemical synthesis. Manufacturers producing or using indigenous oils should receive an allowance equal to the duty payable on imported like oils. The total cost would be under £400.

Taxation and Overseas Minerals

Dept. Cttee. Rep., apps. pp. 28. 1949
1948–49 *Cmd.* 7728, *xviii*, 395
apptd. — sgd. *March*, 1949

E. St. J. Bamford (*Ch.*), Evans, Foulsham, How, Parker, Nuttall.

'*To consider whether any handicap is placed upon United Kingdom mining concerns by the absence from the United Kingdom taxation system of allowances for capital expenditure on the acquisition of overseas mineral sources or of rights to work overseas mineral deposits, whether such allowances should be introduced, and, if so, what form a scheme of allowances should take.*'

The U.K. tax system does not allow the writing off against taxable profits of capital expenditure on overseas mineral rights, whereas this may be permitted in some other countries. There is a *prima facie* presumption that, because the

U.K. rate of taxation of profits is high, a U.K. concern with no depletion allowance must be handicapped in competing for overseas rights against overseas concerns which are given such allowances. As a U.K. concern paying royalties to a foreign mineral owner is allowed to deduct these in computing taxable profits, one which acquires mineral rights by paying a lump sum should have an equal claim for relief. The depletion allowance should be based on and limited to either the cost incurred by the first U.K. resident to acquire the rights or the cost to the person receiving the allowance, whichever is lower, and should be on the same basis as allowances in respect of exploration, etc., under Part III of the Income Tax Act, 1945.

The Form of Government Accounts

Cttee. Final Rep., apps., index. pp. 88. [1950] [Interim Rep. printed as App. B.]
1950 *Cmd.* 7969, *vi*, 1
apptd. *Nov.*, 1947. sgd. *Feb.*, 1950

W. F. Crick (*Ch.*), Dalton, Fisher, Jones, Morison, Rees, Teare.

'*To examine the existing systems of accounting in Departments in the light of modern accounting practice, and to make recommendations for improvements, with particular reference to:* (a) *possible economies in manpower;* (b) *the preservation of effective control of expenditure and providing adequate information for the management of the Department;* (c) *the possibility of improving the contribution made from Government accounts to the statistical material available to the central offices of Government and the various Departments.*'

The Interim Report, proposing the institution of a Food Trading Fund, is printed as App. B.

Final Report.—The pattern of Government accounts as presented to Parliament has remained largely unchanged despite the great increase in Government financial transactions and progress in accountancy methods. Some critics have concluded that an entirely new system, based on the best commercial practice, should be installed and in particular that an income and expenditure basis should be accepted as the foundation of Government accounts. This overlooks the constitutional and statutory differences between government and private business and the fact that the tests of success are different. Although local authorities have changed from a cash to an income and expenditure basis, here also there are wide differences in principle affecting both the raising of funds and their disbursement.

Of the various possible objectives of the system of Government Accounts—accountability, informing the public, testing costs and efficiency, forming the basis of policy and providing means of monetary and economic analysis—in the democratic system 'accountability' must be paramount. By law all revenue must be paid into the Consolidated Fund, and nothing can be paid out of it except under Act of Parliament, and it must be a cash account. Cash accounts record money received and paid and only such transactions, whether they refer to goods and services or to capital transactions.

Income and expenditure accounts may include adjustments for sums not received or paid, and exclude capital items. While an income and expenditure system is necessary to business because it shows the 'true' results of a year's working, this result is not applicable to the requirements of Government accounts: it applies only to trading services. The valuation of capital assets required would involve valuing warships, tanks, dockyards not normally sold, for which there are no rational means of estimating working life. No practical advantage would be secured by an income and expenditure basis in respect of administrative services, but some arrangement of Trading Funds should be made for large and permanent trading services. These principles are applied to the various functions of Government Departments, and detailed suggestions made for

changes, including the treatment of transactions of a capital nature. Suggestions are also made for additions to various published accounts to make them more informative; and for adding to the accounting staff and recruiting senior officers with outside experience.

App. D. is a Note on the Relevance of Commercial Accounting Principles to the requirements of Government Accounts, App. A. a memo. suggesting improvements in the Annual Financial Statement.

Draft Customs and Excise Bill

Cttee. Rep. pp. 64. [1952]
1951–52 Cmd. 8453, x, 183
apptd. June, sgd. Dec., 1951

Lord Kennet (Ch.), L. Nathan, Benson, Browett, Gilmour, Glenday, Gordon, Jackson, Marking, Martin, Mundy, Parkin.

'To consider a draft Bill submitted to the Committee by the Commissioners of Customs and Excise designed to consolidate the enactments relating to the management of Customs and Excise with such amendments as are desirable for the purpose of simplifying them and bringing them into conformity with the requirements of modern practice and conditions. . . .'

The aim has been to provide a modern and simplified code and does not include more debatable reforms or innovations. The Bill is long overdue and greatly desired by all concerned. There is a Note on the clauses of the draft Bill.

See Customs and Excise Bill. Jt. Sel. Cttee. (P. Spens, Ch.). Rep., proc., mins. of ev. pp. xii, 57. 1952. 1951–52 (137) v, 203.

Estate Duty and Family Businesses

Report on statistical investigation by the Board of Inland Revenue. pp. 9.
1951
1950–51 Cmd. 8295, xiii, 1
sgd. June, 1951

An investigation made by the Board of Inland Revenue at the instance of the Colwyn Committee of 1927 to find out to what extent, on the death of an owner of a private business, the *non-trade* assets were insufficient to pay the duty so that recourse was had to trade assets, showed that in 1922, in only 0·9 per cent of the sample firms was this the case (App. XX. 1927 Cmd. 2800, xi, 371). The Committee then concluded that estate duty did not appear to be a major factor in the disintegration of private businesses. Since that date there have been increases in the scale of duty.

The present investigation related to 1948. The definitions and sampling procedure are explained. The comparable proportion of cases in which non-trade assets were insufficient was 3·9 per cent and where they were not sufficient to meet the whole of the duty, the proportion of trade assets required to pay the balance was less than 25 per cent in 60 per cent of the cases and over 50 per cent in 17 per cent of the cases. Recourse to trade assets does not necessarily mean that family businesses are broken up, as there are various ways of dealing with the situation. Of the sample, only one business was closed down, though for other reasons. Since the date of the investigation, the rates of duty have again been increased and the difficulties may be greater.

Purchase Tax/Utility

Cttee. Rep., app. pp. 39. 1952
1951–52 *Cmd.* 8452, *xviii*, 155
apptd. July, sgd. Dec., 1951

W. S. Douglas (*Ch.*), Allen (Margaret), Barber, Caves, Goodale, Heywood, Worswick.

'*To review the present system of Purchase Tax affecting those classes of goods within which Utility schemes operate (i.e. cloth, garments, footwear, household and furnishing textiles, furniture and bedding) in relation to international agreements bearing on the internal taxation of imported goods, and to the interests of the export trade, consumers and manufacturers. . . .*'

The proportion of 'utility' production to total home supplies varies from 50 per cent to over 90 per cent. Existing utility schemes provide for exemption from purchase tax and for a maximum price limit; a few have some quality control. The original utility schemes were technically necessary to make price control effective, but it was inevitable that in time of peace the range of goods included should be increased so much that their only advantage was exemption from purchase tax and that there was often no real guarantee of quality. In addition, the sudden jump from a tax-free price to tax on wholesale value of a non-utility good outside the price range meant that the consumer might be paying the whole amount of the tax, say 7s. od., for an increase of quality costing only 1s. od. Thus there was a blind spot extending at least as far as 25 per cent above top utility prices, and virtually no goods on the market at prices just above the maximum. So long as there are tax-free utility goods of high quality, the tax on non-utility goods hinders manufacturers in competition in the home market and this has an adverse effect on the maintenance of standards and the recruitment of craftsmen. This limits the home market necessary for the development of certain classes of exports. Further, although by commercial treaties and under the General Agreement on Tariffs and Trade, the United Kingdom has obligations to give 'national treatment' to imported goods in matters of internal taxation, imported goods comparable with home-produced utility goods have to pay an import duty, but are not exempted from Purchase Tax.

There are no practicable means of removing the discrimination against imported goods by permitting those of utility type to be given a utility mark which would qualify them for tax exemption. Other proposals for adjusting purchase tax as it relates to utility goods, such as an intermediate rate of tax to deal with the 'blind spot', restricting utility schemes to qualities used by the lower income groups, a flat rate purchase tax on utility and non-utility goods alike, and tax exemption by value were all rejected. The simplest way to relieve the cheaper goods of purchase tax without creating sudden disproportionate jumps in the amount of tax is to charge the tax only on the excess of value over a fixed tax-free limit (called D), deducted from the wholesale value of both utility and non-utility goods. This would remove any discrimination against imports, would preserve tax exemption of cheaper goods, the gently rising tax above the free limit would remove the 'blind spot' and many anomalies could be eliminated. If revenue is to be maintained, there is little room for reduction in the tax on the most expensive goods. The deductions should be fixed in such a way that a given proportion, not less than 50 per cent, of all classes of goods concerned should be exempt. A 'D' scheme of this kind would sever the link between purchase tax and utility status and remove such remaining guarantee of quality as their status still conferred. Consumers still desire some assurance of quality and the Board of Trade should encourage manufacturers to adopt minimum standards worked out with the British Standards Institution.

Purchase Tax (Valuation)

Cttee. Rep., apps. pp. iv, 51. 1953

1952–53 Cmd. 8830, xvi, 953

apptd. July, 1952. sgd. March, 1953

F. Grant (Ch.), Hall (Mrs. M.), Jay (Mrs. P.), Jones, Lawson, Wall.

'To examine the representations of traders as to the principle of assessing purchase tax at a common value level; and to make recommendations as to the manner in which this or any alternative principle should be applied in valuation for purchase tax, having regard to the different points in distribution at which the tax has to be levied.'

The rates of purchase tax are applied to wholesale value, except that in the case of certain classes of articles 'D allowances' are deducted from wholesale value and tax levied on the excess. The same class of goods may pass through various channels of distribution, including not only manufacturer-wholesaler-retailer, but also manufacturer direct to retailer, and manufacturer direct to consumer. The definition of purchase tax value was based on the principles that (a) the amount of tax should not vary with the stage of distribution at which it was collected, (b) that any price advantage enjoyed by large buyers should not be magnified by the tax and (c) as far as possible similar articles should carry the same tax, irrespective of the channel of distribution. The tax was based on 'open market' values, so that businesses buying from associates, etc., should not pay less than others and that goods were valued at a common level and not simply at the price of the actual chargeable purchase. It also aimed at not giving buyers of large quantities at lower prices the additional advantage of paying less tax. This means that sometimes the wholesale price for tax purposes is higher than the actual price charged. This 'uplift' to increase actual to notional wholesale price has been widely criticised.

Manufacturers of price-maintained goods, wholesale merchants and small retailers supported the present basis of valuation and opposed the abolition of uplift, while chain and department stores and manufacturers of free price goods who normally sell direct to retailers wanted it altered.

The basis of value should continue to be wholesale value, fixed by reference to the retailers' buying price, and this must be notional in many cases. Where the uplift has meant that the actual prices paid by the retailer have been increased by regarding wholesale price as that which a wholesaler would have charged, this involves the interposition of an imaginary wholesaler. Where the purchase is by a retailer direct from a manufacturer, this has the effect of applying an uplift by reference either to the saving by the seller of some dis-

H

tribution costs which would have been incurred by a wholesaler or to the quantity of goods purchased. The price paid by a retailer buying from a manufacturer ought not to be uplifted unless the retailer performs some substantial wholesale functions; any saving of costs by reduction of wholesaling functions would thus reduce the tax payable. If the actual price is reduced by reason of the quantity of goods purchased, the reduction should be disregarded. In a Minute of dissent Mrs. Hall and Mrs. Jay argue that the uplift should be abolished also where the actual price is reduced by the advantages of buying in large quantities.

Tax-paid Stocks

Cttee. Rep., apps. pp. v, 58. [1953]
1952–53 *Cmd.* 8784, *xvii*, 833
apptd. July, 1952. *sgd. Feb.*, 1953

M. Hutton (*Ch.*), Blackwell, Davies, Lawrie, Slimmings, Whittaker, Worswick.

'*To examine the position of traders holding stocks of goods on which Purchase Tax or other duties of Customs and Excise have been paid, on an alteration of those rates of tax or duty: to consider how far there is a case in principle for the payment of compensation at the expense of the Crown for loss occasioned by a reduction of tax. . . .*'

The duty element in the value of various stocks is estimated to be: tobacco, £75 mn. (£50 mn. manufacturers', £25 mn. retailers'); beer, £20 mn.; wine and spirits, £10 mn.; hydrocarbon oil, £6 mn.; other customs and excise duties, £15 mn. For stocks subject to purchase tax the amount was about £75 mn. The Exchequer does not pay a rebate on duty-paid stocks when duties are reduced, nor impose a surcharge when they are increased. The trader therefore has a risk of loss or opportunity of gain. A trader who because of **increase** of duty, sold stocks at a correspondingly higher price, would, if he wished to go on trading on the same scale, need the extra funds to buy replacement stocks

at the high price; while if because of duty reductions he sold at lower prices and made a loss, he would need less to buy replacement stocks at the lower price. Traders in goods subject to customs and excise duties in the main acquiesced in this traditional rule.

Traders dealing in purchase tax were almost unanimous that there should be some reimbursement of tax on tax-paid stocks at the time of a reduction. They held that competition between traders made it imperative to mark down prices at the time of purchase tax reduction and impossible to raise them when tax was increased. This was unjust, since the tax was intended to be a tax on the consumer and not on the retailer. There were dislocations of trade on account of anticipated changes of tax, against which 'split-delivery' systems, where practised, were not a complete protection.

In law, however, the retailer is accountable for the tax, and this is independent of the trader's success in passing tax on to others, which will depend on the strength of competition. This is true also of customs and excise duties. The effects of anticipated changes of tax in causing dislocations of trade, though they exist, had been overstated. The loss of trade to retailers as a result of the public's insistence on reduction of price forthwith must be negligible on many small articles on which the tax is no more than a few coppers, and on non-standardised goods, but more severe on standardised goods of high unit value, e.g. refrigerators.

On grounds of equity as between trader and the Crown, neither the policy of preventing gains and not compensating losses, nor one of permitting gains and compensating losses could be recommended. The choice was therefore between preventing gains and recouping losses, or the traditional policy of doing nothing to prevent gains or recouping losses. Since purchase tax is designed to influence consumption, an adequate scheme of rebates and surcharges would do this more promptly than, e.g. selling 'at pre - Budget prices'. The various schemes suggested, e.g. stock declaration schemes or stock-turn schemes, would be too complicated or not equitable. If, however, there is to be no official limitation of loss on stocks at tax reduction, there should be no official limitation on gains at tax increases.

The traditional system, which has applied to customs and excise duties should continue and should be applied also to purchase tax. No compensation should be paid to stockholders when rates of duty or tax are reduced, nor should Government action prevent a trader from selling existing duty-paid stocks at a higher price when they are increased, nor should excise duty be charged, when rates are increased, on duty or tax-paid goods. These recommendations should be regarded as a whole. Large and frequent changes of purchase tax should be avoided, changes should be made at the time of the Budget. As far as necessary, official assistance should be given to schemes of deferred delivery and of contracts deferring liability to purchase tax.

Taxation of Trading Profits

Cttee. Rep., apps., index. pp. 132. [1951]

1950-51 *Cmd.* 8189, *xx*, 1
apptd. June, 1949. *sgd. Feb.*, 1951

J. M. Tucker (*Ch.*), Carrington, Cater, Howard, Shepherd, Woodcock.

'*To enquire into the method of computing net trade profits for the purpose of charging them to Income Tax and to consider the question of the basis period to be taken in assessing the tax on the profits so ascertained; to enquire into the method of computing net profits for the purpose of charging them to Profits Tax; and to report upon any alterations of the tax law which may be desirable.*'

The Committee proceeded on the broad principles that taxable profits should be neither more nor less than true profits computed on accountancy principles, that a distinction must be drawn between expenditure incurred as part of the process of earning profits and expenditure of profits when earned, and that it was not concerned with matters which involved only questions of the incidence of the tax. Recommendations had to pay regard to the fact that a large proportion of the businesses are small ones and that since surtax rates are very progressive, to an individual owner of a business or a partnership the proper allocation of profits to particular periods is of great importance.

Basis of Assessment.—Although a majority of witnesses favoured a change from the existing system to one based on current year's profits, a review of various proposals led to the conclusion that it would be impracticable. For the existing anomalies in the treatment of partnerships, the current year basis would be the best solution, but as this was rejected other measures are recommended to alleviate the worst of them Business losses.—An owner should be allowed to carry these forward and set them against later profits without time limit. When a business incurs a large loss in its last year and the owner has no substantial income from another source against which it can be set, he should be able to carry it back to set against assessments on that business for the three preceding years. To meet the hardship which arises from the application of steeply progressive rates to fluctuating incomes, e.g. an author's income from his books, surtax should be computed as at present, but spread at the tax-payer's option by averaging over a 5-year period.

Inflation gives rise to the problem of allowances for replacement of fixed assets and stocks. Although some hold that the profits of a business cannot be properly computed unless an adjustment is made for changes in the value of money, and that an industry ought not to pay tax on profits which have to be devoted to maintaining productive capacity in real terms, a majority of accountants do not accept this view

Alternative remedies, such as revalorisation and special allowances, are rejected as neither equitable between businesses nor practicable. The rate of initial allowances should be increased, but as the rise in costs of plant, etc., varies between different industries it should take the form of a minimum initial allowance, with the provision that on the representation of any industry the authorities should be able to give a larger allowance, taking into account the cost of the plant and the importance of the industry.

Depreciation and Wasting Assets.— Income tax law should give relief in respect of wastage of assets used up or consumed in the course of business, which is distinct from fluctuations of value or capital losses incurred through extraneous circumstances having no connection with use in the business. Depreciation allowances should be given on commercial buildings, and in the case of mines, oil wells, etc., on land which has to be surrendered at the expiration of a concession and on depreciation of sites of works near mines abroad, on abortive exploration expenditure. Payments for an asset of limited life or which result in an advantage of limited duration should be written off by allowances deemed reasonable by the Commissioners.

Taxation of Profits and Income

R. Com. 1st Rep. pp. vii, 20. 1953
1952–53 *Cmd. 8761, xvii*, 805
apptd. Jan., 1951. *sgd. Feb.*, 1953

Lord Radcliffe (*Ch.*), Heyworth, Gill, Sutherland (Lucy S.), Anstey (Vera), Bullock, Carrington, Crick, Greenwood, Hicks, Kaldor, Tucker, Woodcock.

'*To inquire into the present system of taxation of profits and income, including its incidence and effects, with particular reference to the taxation of business profits and the taxation of salaries and wages . . . and to make recommendations consistent with maintaining the same total yield of the existing duties in relation to the national income.*'

Extended: '*To make recommendations bearing in mind that in the present financial situation it may be necessary to maintain the revenue from profits and income: and, in so far as they make recommendations which would on balance entail a substantial loss of revenue, to indicate an order of priority in which such recommendations should be taken into consideration.*'

The present system taxes income arising in the U.K., no matter to whom it belongs, and taxes residents in U.K., no matter where their income arises. A company is 'resident' in U.K. if its central office and management are in this country, and even though all its trading operations take place abroad, the activity of management and control establish that for tax purposes its profits are those of trade carried on in U.K. and are taxable. This has been criticised as placing British controlled concerns at a disadvantage compared with foreign competitors. 'Overseas profits' is taken to mean profits earned outside the country, or a credit balance on overseas trading, as distinct from 'overseas income', which may include rents from land, dividends from a non-resident country, interest on loans, etc. Some critics have urged that the basis of taxation should not be profits earned, but profits remitted. But there is no natural relation between the profits balance and the moneys remitted to the U.K.; the trader will be remitting money and goods to and fro for the purposes of the business, and the practical difficulties make the remittance basis undesirable.

Three improvements are recommended. While a trader who comes within the benefit of a double taxation agreement gets full credit in the U.K. for the comparable overseas taxes, where there is no agreement he gets credit to the extent of only a half the U.K. tax in the case of foreign countries and three-quarters in the case of Commonwealth countries. Unilateral relief should be granted without the present restriction as to the amount of U.K. tax against which credit may be given. The taxpayer should have the option of deducting from assessed profits such part as is unremittable on account of local legislation or executive action. The U.K. Government should be authorised to enter into agreement with other countries to give credit to its taxpayer against its tax on overseas profits for such an amount of tax as the other country certifies has been spared the taxpayer by 'Pioneer Industries Concessions'.

—— Second Report, apps. pp. x, 125.
1954
1953–54 *Cmd.* 9105, *xix*, 187
sgd. April, 1954
add Gates.

Part I. Taxation of Wages and Salaries.—Proposals have been made to integrate income tax and the social security systems. The State collects fixed flat rate weekly contributions to national insurance from 23 mn. citizens, and progressive income tax from 15 mn. (mostly included in the 23 mn.), largely also in weekly contributions. It pays fixed weekly family allowances in respect of children irrespective of means or need, and pays benefits where earnings cease or are interrupted, the amounts varying with the number of dependents. The flat rate contributions irrespective of income mean that they must be fixed at a low level suited to the lowest incomes and cannot be raised to pay for or enlarge benefits; the high marginal rates of progressive rates of income tax are a dis-incentive to effort. The chief proposals were that insurance contributions should be abolished, a proportional tax substituted for the existing income tax, personal income tax allowances abolished and replaced by regular cash allowances to every man, woman and child, and a supplementary graduated income tax imposed, starting at a lower level than surtax exemption limit, but exempting the majority of lower incomes. The merging and simplification would lead to considerable savings in administration.

A special investigation by the Social Survey (App. I.) and other evidence showed that the marginal tax rate had little influence on incentives to work, and that most wage earners are neither in the position nor know enough to increase effort and earnings on account of it. The savings of 10,000 to 15,000 in the staff of Inland Revenue would be counterbalanced by the extra 28,000 needed by the Ministry of National Insurance to pay the universal cash allowances. The need to abandon the contributory principle of insurance was also a serious objection. The proposals were therefore rejected.

Of the $15\frac{1}{2}$ mn. persons liable to tax in 1952–53, $6\frac{1}{2}$ mn. had taxable incomes of less than £600 and contributed only £50 mn. of tax revenue. Proposals to meet this by a simpler, more intelligible proportional tax on low incomes which would save administrative costs are rejected: there is more need to adjust tax details to incomes where incomes are small than where they are high. Two proposals aiming at diminishing any dis-incentive due to the marginal rate of tax by basing PAYE not cumulatively on current earnings, but on the earnings of the previous week or a standard week were also rejected.

Part II. Graduation and Differentiation.—Progressive taxation is often justified on the basis of least aggregate sacrifice, though this taken literally would mean that no tax at all should be levied on incomes below a certain figure and all incomes above it confiscated. But the practical considerations as to the effect on incentives and the temptation to tax avoidance forbid this, as well as the facts that capacity to pay depends on the source of the income, e.g. whether it is fluctuating or not, as well as its amount, and that large incomes are the source of savings. The question is one of balance, and public opinion accepts a steep gradient of progressive taxation as equitable. The Committee therefore concentrated on the structure of the scheme. The present instruments of graduation and differentiation — personal reliefs, reduced rate reliefs and graduated supertax and earned income relief are satisfactory, but modifications are needed to render them better adapted for the purpose.

The French quotient system of aggregating the incomes of all members of the family is not recommended. The aggregation of income of husband and wife should continue, but where a wife is at work her employment throws expenses on to the household that it would not otherwise have. There should be corresponding relief.

The 'slice' method of graduation is a better method of producing a gradual progression of the effective rate than the earlier system. With the standard rate at 9s., three reduced rate bands would be preferable to two. But the present personal allowance in respect of married women's earnings is excessive. Personal allowances were intended to differentiate between tax-payers at all levels of income, but they also have the effect of exempting small incomes from tax. As a result, the starting point of liability is lower than it need be. A specific minimum relief should be granted to give a graduated exemption limit for the smallest incomes. The taxable capacity of the family man as compared to one without dependents is overrated at the middle and upper income ranges from £2000 upwards. The child allowance should, within fixed limits, vary from £85 to £100 in accordance with the size of the tax-payer's income; and the starting point of surtax (now £2000) should also vary, and be £1500 for a single man and £2000 for a married man, with an allowance of £160 for each child. The upper limit of earned income relief should be raised from £2025 to £2500 and should be a half-full rate between £2000 and £3000. Other recommendations were that the housekeeper allowance given on account of widowed status without reference to the care of children should be abolished, but where a housekeeper is needed to look after young children, it should not be dependent on the housekeeper being resident.

Reservation by Woodcock, Anstey, Bullock, Kaldor.—As a result of inflation, the starting point of taxation is at a lower level than before the war, the rise in taxation is proportionately greater on the lower incomes and on the family man than one without children. The minimum earned income relief of £63 proposed by the Majority should be raised to £120, and for married persons, etc., to £120 plus 2/7th of the additional personal allowance: the basic personal allowance should be £100 for single and £200 for married persons, and the rate chargeable on the first £100 of taxable income graduated. The children's allowances are inadequate at the higher income levels and should be extended; the cost of this should be thrown not on to the general taxpayer, but on the single persons in those higher income groups. The aggregation of incomes of husband and wife should be continued, but to prevent tax avoidance, children's investment incomes should also be aggregated. The existing differentiation between earned and unearned income is inadequate.

—— Final Report, apps., index. pp. xii, 487. 1955

1955–56 Cmd. 9474, xxvii, 721
sgd. May, 1955
del. Gill.

The Report covers the whole system of income and profits taxes and makes 90 detailed recommendations, as well as giving important statements of principle on questions which are, as well as those which are not, the subject of recommendations.

Part I. The tax code contains no general definition of income, and no advantage would be derived from the attempt to define taxable income: instead the code lists five classes of taxable income. Difficult problems arise from the arrangements to allow for the cost of obtaining it.

A company is regarded as having taxable income, being liable to income tax and, if its profits exceed £2000, to profits tax also. Profits tax is first charged at $22\frac{1}{2}$ per cent and the non-distribution relief of 20 per cent on those not distributed make the rate $2\frac{1}{2}$ per cent on undistributed profits. But since the individual proprietor of a business may be assessed on the whole profits, irrespective of how much he may retain for strengthening it, leaving undistributed profits untaxed would give a preferential advantage to a corporate undertaking and give shareholders an untaxed growth of wealth. Undistributed profits should not be exempt from tax, but they have a lower taxable capacity than ordinary income.

Capital Gains.—These, if arising out of trading activities, even isolated trading transactions, are already taxed. The question is whether those resulting from a rise in the market value of assets held or sold by a person who does not regularly offer them for sale should also be taxed. Capital gains could not be treated as taxable income unless they were realised, some gains accrue over a period of years, there would have to be allowance for realised losses, and the gains on a sale of a house by an owner-occupier in order to buy another would have to be exempted. Sometimes capital gains are the result merely of trustees rearranging investments. Retained profits in a company do increase the value of the shareholders' holdings, but the whole profits of a company are subject to income tax and profits tax. There is a great range of capital gains stretching from true gains to unanticipated gains. A tax would be difficult to graduate, the administration would require an additional 500 Inland Revenue staff. There would be a loss of estate and other duties, so that the net yield might be £50 mn. ±£250 mn., though the yield might be substantial in a period of rising security values. Capital gains should not be brought into income tax, nor should there be a supplementary flat rate tax. But in deciding whether a gain is the result of a trading venture, tests of 'badges of trade', e.g. subject matter, period of ownership, frequency and number of transactions, work done, etc., should be used.

The exemption of charities from tax has been unnecessarily widened in application and a more restricted definition should be enacted.

Part II. The present arrangements for dealing with fluctuating incomes are not satisfactory. To mitigate the hardship that progressive taxation causes where incomes show marked irregularity, a fall of total income from one year to the next of at least 50 per cent should entitle to relief by averaging. Any tax on gambling would not have to be on winnings, but on profits. But setting off a loss against gains would permit a group to gamble at the expense of the State, and the tax could not be enforced.

Part III. Depreciation and Wasting Assets. Depreciation allowances based on historic cost have been criticised because in periods of rising prices they did not cover replacement costs, the difference being treated as taxable profits, and in consequence the capital of productive industry was said to be undergoing erosion. Statistical evidence did not establish this. There was controversy between those who argued that if the money consumed by wasting assets has been made good, profits have been properly computed, the trader then having to decide whether to venture more money in the new conditions, and those who held that a business deteriorates if real assets are not maintained and that the basis should be current costs. The majority rejected various schemes of revalorisation, in which tax relief did not depend on the actual level of current investment, and regarded historic costs as more certain. Capital allowances should be given for commercial buildings, etc. Surpluses on the sale of assets qualifying for capital allowance should be taxed. A depletion allowance should be given to mining concerns for the cost of acquiring mineral rights in U.K.

Stocks. The problem of rising monetary costs affects also stock replacement. Appropriating costs on the basis of First In, First Out (historical costs), means that sale proceeds are on a higher level than when the stock was bought and the profits at the end of the year are higher than can be drawn out. Although Inland Revenue argue that this is the only permissible method, no single method should be obligatory, the trader being permitted to employ any suitable method, subject to safeguards as to the effect of a change.

Overseas Profits. It is argued that taxation of overseas profits places U.K. concerns at a disadvantage with competitors, not only because the tax rate is higher than elsewhere, but because he bears a charge which is a supplement to that borne by many competitors. The Commission was divided on the approach to this problem, but proposed recognition of a special category of overseas trading corporations, the profits of which should be exempt as long as undistributed.

The differential rate of profits tax in favour of undistributed profits was intended to discourage distribution and to encourage their retention and ploughing back into productive investment. In fact, they encourage retention but not necessarily their fruitful use, which might be better obtained by distribution to shareholders to invest elsewhere. The differential rate should be abolished and total profits taxed at a suitable flat rate. Industrial and provident societies should be taxed only on the retained balance of profits, but nationalised undertakings in principle and public utilities should be taxed like other trading concerns. The dividend of a co-operative society is regarded as an expense and no profit emerges until it has been allowed for, but varying views have been held on whether the surplus thereafter should be regarded as a taxable profit. The conception of mutual trading has widened excessively; no surplus derived from trading operations should be exempt from taxation on grounds of mutuality.

Part IV deals with double taxation relief, assessment under schedules D,

A and B; Part V with administration, Parts VI and VII with tax avoidance and evasion, Part VIII with codification.

Minority Report. Woodcock, Bullock, Kaldor.—An individual's taxable capacity consists in his power to attain particular living standards, i.e. his spending power. Income thus consists of personal consumption plus net accumulation. The present legal definition of income is defective; it omits casual profits and capital gains not acquired by way of trade, outlays to obtain income are allowed for business, but not for obtaining educational training; and various concessions have eroded the tax base. A tax on personal expenditure might be more equitable than one on income, but is excluded from the terms of reference.

The most serious omission is the exemption of capital gains from taxation. The Minority do not accept the view that a rise of capital values as a result of inflation or of a fall in interest rates are not real gains increasing taxable capacity. The great bulk of capital gains are the result of rising real income, i.e. the long-run trend of rising share values, and these are not unanticipated, but are expected. The exemption is inequitable because only property-owning classes are able to obtain them and it permits large-scale tax avoidance. They do not accept Inland Revenue's estimate of net yield, placing it in the long run at £600 mn. to £800 mn. Capital gains of individuals should be subject to income tax but not surtax, of companies to a corporation profits tax. The tax should be on net realised gains, should include short-term gains, but gains on the sale of one residence of an owner-occupier should be exempt. Company profits should be subject to one tax only, a corporation profits tax on the whole of the profits, and when a capital gains tax is introduced, the distinction between distributed and undistributed profits should be abolished. A rate of $33\frac{1}{3}$ would be appropriate.

Earned income relief should be given without any upper limit under Schedule

E; the treatment of transfers of income by way of convenant should be reviewed as part of an inquiry into the system of inheritance taxes. In the interim, the amount of covenanted income recognised for surtax exemption should be limited to £500 for any one beneficiary. While agreeing with the Majority on the hampering effects on the system of taxing overseas profits, the Minority do not find their proposal practicable.

There are memos. on the *Taxation of Capital Gains*, by the Board of Inland Revenue, annexe to Minority rep., p. 425 *et seq.*; on the reform of income tax and social security payments by Lady Rhys Williams (ev. 1st day), by the Liberal Party and the Board of Inland Revenue (ev. 2nd and 3rd days). Only oral evidence in public was published; 21 days, index; 1952, 1954, 1955 Non-Parl. Complete sets of memos. were deposited in the libraries named in para. 12 of the Final Report.

Taxation Treatment of Provisions for Retirement

Cttee. Rep., app., index. pp. iv, 159. 1954

1953–54 *Cmd.* 9063, *xix*, 327
apptd. Aug., 1950. sgd. Dec., 1953

J. M. Tucker (*Ch.*), Carrington, Cater, Kinnes, Simmonds, Woodcock.

'*To review the income tax law relating to superannuation funds . . . the law governing the treatment of income tax payments made by or for individuals with a view to providing for the individual in his retirement or old age . . . to consider whether the scope of income tax relief in respect of payments of that nature should be extended . . . having regard to the fact that contributory pensions schemes . . . are not at present available to all persons holding office . . . and are not applicable to an individual carrying on a profession or business.*"

It was not possible to deal with the subject on broad lines, since matters of principle and detail are bound up together. About 6 mn. persons are subject to approved pensions funds and schemes, and because of the great variety of ways in which employers have made arrangements for their employees and in which individuals make arrangements, the law is extremely complicated. There are over 60 main recommendations.

There were four main problems.

1. Life Assurance Relief.—The existing relief should continue in its present form, except that it should be withdrawn from payments which will qualify for expenses relief and the one-sixth limit should be modified.

2. Future Retirements Benefit Schemes for Employees.—To qualify for reliefs all schemes should be submitted for approval. Approval should be automatic if they comply with 16 conditions specified, e.g. the employer must contribute at least one-third of the cost, the employee must be given a title to defined benefits which will accrue only on retirement, death or incapacity and are solely for the benefit of employees and dependents, the aggregate value of the benefits must not exceed two-thirds of the final remuneration. The general principle should be that the build-up of bona fide schemes, i.e. premiums and investment income, should be exempt and the benefits taxed. All regular contributions by employers, and employees' contributions up to 10 per cent of remuneration or £100 per annum should be exempt. Recommendations are made respecting unapproved schemes, lump sum benefits, etc., and employees' contributions to statutory schemes should rank for expenses relief.

3. Self - employed Persons, Controlling and other Directors, and Employees having no Pension Rights.— There are about 1,600,000 self-employed persons subject to income tax and the numbers in the other groups total about 9,500,000. Largely as a result of present tax rates, persons in these classes cannot afford to set aside out of current earnings sufficient to provide retirement benefits on the scale afforded to employees who are members of approved pensions schemes. Although

it might be argued that a taxpayer should not be entitled to relief in respect of savings, this has been admitted in the case of life assurance relief. A case is made out for applying to each of these classes the same basic principles as apply to the ordinary employee, subject to suitable modifications. Schemes for individuals in these classes should require approval, should provide for retirement between 65 and 70, and contributions should be given full income tax and surtax relief. Earnings and profits of these classes are defined and recommendations made regarding lump sum benefits and annuities.

4. Annuities Purchased by the Individual Himself.—It was claimed that a part of each annuity payment is a return to the purchaser of part of the capital laid out by him, the remainder being interest, and that tax should not be paid on the capital content. An examination of practice and diverse views led to the conclusion that the part of each payment representing capital, defined as actual purchase money divided by the average expectation of life at the time the annuity was purchased, should be free of tax. The investment income of the annuity funds of life assurance should not be taxed.

Cater and Woodcock made a reservation on the proposals for class 3 above.

National Expenditure. Public Accounts

For the Reports of the Select Committees on *National Expenditure* see the following volumes of Sessional Papers:

1939–40 iii. 1940–41 iii. 1941–42 iii. 1942–43 iii. 1943–44 ii. 1944–45 iii. See also 1945–46 Cmd. 6865, viii, 311.

Public Accounts.—*Epitome of the Reports from the Committees of Public Accounts 1857 to 1937*, app., index. pp. 839. 1938; 1937–38 (154) xxii, 1. *Epitome . . . 1938 to 1950*, index (1857 to 1950). pp. 260. [1952]; 1951–52 (155) xxv, 513.

Scottish Financial and Trade Statistics

Cttee. Rep., apps. pp. 92. 1952
1951–52 *Cmd*. 8609, *xii*, 377
apptd. July, 1950. *sgd.* —

Lord Catto (*Ch.*), Byrne, Crick, Erskine, Hamilton, Hardie, Imrie.

'*To consider the practicability of making a return of (i) the revenue from and Government expenditure in—(a) Scotland; and (b) the rest of the United Kingdom, and the balances of revenue available for general expenditure from Scotland and the rest of the United Kingdom respectively; (ii) Scotland's share in the imports and exports, visible and invisible, of the United Kingdom; (iii) Scotland's imports from, exports to and balance of payments with other countries, including the rest of the United Kingdom . . .*'

Revenue from Scotland must be taken to mean revenue produced for the Exchequer by the application of United Kingdom rates of tax and principles of assessment to incomes received and the dutiable goods and services consumed by residents in Scotland. A useful and valid fiscal comparison could be made between England and Scotland. One-third of the ordinary revenue could be attributed directly, and the remainder by methods sufficiently sound. 'Expenditure in Scotland' ought to be interpreted broadly as expenditure incurred for the special benefit of Scotland as distinct from other parts of the United Kingdom; four-fifths could be allocated on the basis of costs separately incurred. Details are given of the obstacles to the ascertainment of Scotland's share in the external trade of the United Kingdom and of Scotland's balance of payments. These obstacles arise from attempting to analyse component parts of a unified economy; the cost and damaging effects of interfering with the natural flow of trade and personal freedom of movement across the border in order to obtain the information would be too high a price to pay for the statistics obtained.

III. MONETARY AND ECONOMIC POLICY, FINANCIAL INSTITUTIONS

Monetary, Financial and Economic Policy Generally

The documentation of British monetary and economic policies during the years of war and of rehabilitation following it was affected by two sets of circumstances. First, these policies were closely intertwined with those of other members of the Commonwealth and of the United States. They were not therefore reasoned out in the reports of formal inquiries, but worked out confidentially by experts and presented in international discussions with other countries' representatives, the final decisions being embodied in formal international agreements, and laid before the House, for information or in the process of ratification, or announced in statements in the House. Secondly, the need to mobilise as large a proportion as possible of our resources for the war effort, and the influence of 'Keynesian' economic doctrines on the management of the economy as a whole led to the issue as Papers of statements of Government policy on wages and inflation, reasoned analyses of the state and prospects of the economy, as in the Economic Surveys, and of basic statistical data prepared in the form of social accounts.

The list following gives the titles and references of the principal papers:

1. International agreements on monetary and economic policy.—An International Clearing Union; 1942–43 Cmd. 6437, xi. Bretton Woods; 1943–44 Cmd. 6546, viii; (see also Keynes' Speech, H.L. Debates, 18th May, 1943, 23rd May, 1944, 18th Dec., 1945). Lend-Lease; 1940–41 Cmd. 6311, viii. Mutual Aid; 1941–42 Cmd. 6391, ix. 1942–43 Cmd. 6483, xi. Reciprocal Aid; 1941–42 Cmd. 6319, viii. European Economic Co-operation (Marshall Aid); 1947–48 Cmd. 7446, Cmd. 7469, xxxi. 1950 Cmd. 7862, xxiv. 1948–49 Cmd. 7572, xxxiv. General Agreement on Tariffs and Trade; 1950 Cmd. 8048, xxiv. Torquay Tariff Negotiations; 1950–51 Cmd. 8228, xxxii. European Payments Union; 1950 Cmd. 8064, xxiv. 1950–51 Cmd. 8372, xxxii.

2. The creation of other international economic agencies.—United Nations Relief and Rehabilitation Administration; 1943–44 Cmd. 6491, Cmd. 6497, Cmd. 6566, viii. Food and Agricultural Organisation; 1942–43 Cmd. 6451, Cmd. 6461, xi.

3. The control of the economy.— Economic Surveys (see Ann. Reps., p. 504). Source of War Finance, National Income and Expenditure of U.K. (see Ann. Reps., p. 504). United Kingdom Balance of Payments, 1946 and 1947, Cmd. 7324 (see Ann. Reps., p. 504).

4. Home Policy on Prices, Costs and Inflation.—Price Stabilisation and Industrial Policy; 1940–41 Cmd. 6294, viii. See p. 232. Employment Policy; 1943–44 Cmd. 6527, viii. See p. 233. Economic Considerations affecting the Relations between Employers and Workers; 1946–47 Cmd. 7018, xix. See p. 234. Personal Incomes, Costs and Prices; 1947–48 Cmd. 7321, xxii. See p. 235. Economic Implications of Full Employment; 1955–56 Cmd. 9725, xxxvi. See p. 235.

5. Civil Consumption.—Food Consumption Levels in the U.S., Canada, and U.K.; 1944 Non-Parl. See p. 89. Impact of the War on Civilian Consumption; 1945 Non-Parl. See p. 120.

6. Statistics Relating to the War Effort of the U.K.; 1943–44 Cmd. 6564, viii.

7. Defence and Re-armament.—See the Sessional Indexes for the annual statements on Defence (1945–46 onwards).

Capital Issues Control

Memo. pp. 5. 1945

1944–45 *Cmd.* 6645, *x*, 49
sgd. May, 1945

The objects of the control are to

ensure that the order of priority of capital issues is determined according to the national interest and to current Government policy on physical investment.

Consent will be given for defence purposes and normally for issues required to finance the production or sale of exports, for undertakings in Development Areas, public utilities and housing associations, development of agriculture, production of raw materials, transport, etc., and certain productive purposes. Consent will be given for issues for financing domestic distributive and retail trades, hire purchase, amalgamations, etc., only in special cases. Consent will not normally be given to finance companies, investment and unit trusts, entertainments, etc.

See *Capital Issues Control.* Special Memo.; 1947–48 Cmd. 7281, xxii, 715.

Investment (Control and Guarantees) Bill

Memo. and Draft of Order to be made under Clause 1 of the Bill. pp. 7. 1946

1945–46 *Cmd. 6726, xx,* 67
pres. Jan., 1946

The Bill aims at regulating the borrowing of money and raising money by the issue of securities, and at providing for the guarantee of loans for reconstruction and development of an industry. It is essential to plan real capital development of all kinds. To ensure that the work of the Capital Issues Committee, the Public Works Loans Board, the Finance Corporation for Industry and the Industrial and Commercial Finance Corporation is effectively linked with the operations of the Bank of England, a National Investment Council will be established, with the Chancellor of the Exchequer as chairman and the Governor of the Bank as a member.

See *Borrowing (Control and Guarantees) Act* 1946; 9 & 10 Geo. 6. c. 58.

Exchange Control Bill

Memo. pp. 5. 1946

1946–47 *Cmd. 6954, xix,* 561
pres. Nov., 1946

The Exchange Control operates under powers conferred by the Emergency Powers (Defence) Acts, and continued under the Supplies and Services (Transitional Powers) Act, 1945, and Defence (Finance) Regulations. The Regulations are not suitable for peace conditions, and the Bill re-writes the powers, dropping those not required and adding a few new provisions. Comprehensive powers are required and the Treasury will be able to supervise the whole range of foreign payments.

Capital Investment in 1948

Statement, apps. pp. 31. 1947

1947–48 *Cmd. 7268, xxii,* 683
pres. Dec., 1947

In order to increase the volume of exports in the near future, coal, steel and other materials and labour must be switched from the manufacture for the home market to manufacture for export. The size and scope of some other investment projects must therefore be reduced. The probable £1600 mn. of gross investment for 1948 will be reduced to £1420 mn., tapering off to a rate of £1320 mn. by the end of 1948. Of this £700 mn. will go to construction, £525 mn. to plant, machinery and vehicles, and £95 mn. to ship-building and miscellaneous industries. These gross figures include repair and maintenance, which will probably be about one-half the total. Appendices give the proposed allocations in detail, together with the reasons for them.

Control of Dividends

pp. 3. 1951

1950–51 *Cmd. 8318, xxi,* 255

The Government intend to introduce a bill to control dividends for three years. It will impose a limit on the gross amount which may be distributed in dividends other than fixed rate. In the case of an existing company, the annual amount which may be distributed will be, at the option of the company, the average of the last two accounting periods before 29th July, 1951, or 5 per cent on a relevant capital or £10,000. In the case of a company other than an existing company, the amount may be 7 per cent.

Bank of England Bill

Explanatory and Financial Memo. pp.
i–ii. [1945]
1945–46 (Bill 9) *i*, 183
o.p. Oct., 1945

Provides for the transfer of the existing capital stock of the Bank of England to a nominee of the Treasury, and for the issue in exchange to the holders of Bank stock an amount of Government 3 per cent stock such that the annual interest is equal to the annual gross dividend declared during the twenty years ending 31st March, 1945. The amount of Bank stock outstanding was £14,553,000, the average annual dividend 12 per cent, the Government stock to be issued in exchange £58,212,000. The Governor, Deputy Governor and directors are to be appointed by H.M. The Treasury

may from time to time give such directions to the Bank as, after consultation with the Governor, they think necessary in the public interest. The Bank, if they think it is necessary in the public interest, may request information from and make recommendations to bankers, and if authorised by the Treasury, give directions to them.

Bank of England Bill

Sel. Cttee. Proc., mins. of ev. pp. iv, 21.
1945
1945–46 (24) *v*, 737
apptd. Oct., o.p. Nov., 1945

G. Benson (*Ch.*), Crookshank, Gaitskell, Williamson, Davies, Howard.

Includes the statements of Counsel on the terms of the compulsory acquisition of the existing stock of the Bank, and the evidence of the Governor of the Bank. Bill reported without amendment.

See *Bank of England Charter;* 1945–46 Cmd. 6752, xx, 59. *Bank of England.* [1st] Rep.; 1946–47 Cmd. 7115, *x*, 105, and succeeding Ann. Reps.

IV. AGRICULTURE AND FOOD SUPPLY

1. **General: Production, Supply, Output**
2. **Decontrol; Marketing in General**
3. **Production and Marketing of Particular Products**
4. **Diseases, Wild Animals**
5. **Forestry**
6. **Drainage, Coast Protection, River Pollution**
7. **Fishing**

1. GENERAL: PRODUCTION, SUPPLY, OUTPUT

Agricultural Research in Great Britain

Cttee. of the Privy Council. Rep. pp.
100. 1943
1942–43 *Cmd.* 6421, *iv*, 95
sgd. Dec., 1942

Agricultural Research in Great Britain is largely financed and coordinated by the State through the Ministry of Agriculture and Fisheries, the Department of Agriculture for Scotland and the Agricultural Research Council. There is a vertical relationship between these three bodies, the Council assisting the Ministry or the Department either directly or through the corresponding Agricultural Improvement Councils. There is a horizontal relationship between the Agricultural Research Council, the Department of Scientific Research and the Medical Research Council. Research institutes are of three categories: those under the direct control of the Ministry, those under the direct control of the Research Council and those financed wholly or in part by the Ministry or the Scottish Department and under the general co-ordination of the Ministry or Department and the Council. The Report describes the various research institutes and the investigations in which they are engaged.

Agricultural Improvement Council for England

1st Rep. pp. 18. 1944

1943 *Non-Parl. Min. of Agric. and Fish.*

apptd. June, 1941. *sgd. June,* 1942

D. Fergusson (*Ch.*).

'To devise methods for seeing that promising results of research are applied as rapidly as possible to the problems of agriculture and are incorporated in ordinary farming practice; and to advise from time to time concerning agricultural problems which appear to require scientific investigation.'

The application of scientific research largely depends on the economic condition of the industry. In the inter-war years of prolonged economic depression, when prices were low, wages stabilised, and low farming methods were used to save labour costs, the applications of the results of research were disappointing, although large sums were spent on research, education, eradication of diseases from livestock and general improvements to the land. A further difficulty is the large number and variety of farms and of farmers, and because of differences of soil, etc., of farming systems. In England and Wales there are 300,000 farmers, horticulturalists and small holders—200,000 farming less than 100 acres—the majority not having had a high standard of general or scientific education, and being of no more than average intelligence and enterprise. The requisites are a better standard of education of the farmer, local advisory work by practical agriculturalists who know their district,

and the widespread general improvement of farming based on sound agricultural and scientific principles; and since incorporation of new methods into farming practice will depend on their economic advantage, which is normally obtainable only over a period of years, some measure of economic stability in the industry is essential. Recommendations are made for a central institute to test and advise on agricultural machinery, on re-seeding and ley farming, hill sheep farming, soil surveys, dry rot in potatoes, artificial insemination, etc.

—— Second Report. pp. iv, 26. 1950

1951 *Non-Parl.*

D. Vandepeer (*Ch.*), E. J. Salisbury (*V.-Ch.*).

The National Agricultural Advisory Service was set up in 1946 as the result of a recommendation by the Luxmoore Committee (1943, p. 406). Since the Council, which was advisory, had no technical staff to enable it to take any action to put the findings of research into practice, or to get an overall view of farmers' problems, the Service was the proper body to do this work for the Council, which was asked to advise the Minister on its organisation and work. In view of the need for continued high output, the Council's duties were enlarged to include ensuring that promising methods were incorporated with practice as rapidly as possible, advising on the problems which required scientific investigation and on raising the technical standard of farming. (See revised terms of reference, p. 2.) Increased interest owing to the wartime drive for output, the prosperity of the industry and the growth of a generation of young farmers who have benefited from agricultural education, has changed the problem from one of persuading the farmers to adopt better methods to one of getting the results of research to him in the quickest possible time. To obtain knowledge of regional problems, pilot surveys in three different areas were arranged, and experimental husbandry farms and horticultural stations established to make tests in differing soils and climates. The Report describes the work done on numerous specific problems.

Hill Sheep Farming in England and Wales

Agric. Improvement Council. Cttee. Rep., apps. pp. 40. 1944

1943–44 *Cmd.* 6498, *iii*, 455
sgd. Aug., 1943

Lord De La Warr (*Ch.*), Griffith, Lewis, Montgomerie, Robinson, Wilson, Wheldon.

'To investigate the present position of hill and upland sheep farming in England and Wales, and in the light of modern scientific knowledge, to suggest measures which might be taken to improve the condition of hill and upland grazings, the health and hardiness of sheep stocks, and systems of management.'

There are some 5 mn. acres of hill and upland in England and Wales carrying in 1939 3 to 4 mn. breeding ewes on which the greater part of lowland sheep husbandry depended, together with a considerable but indeterminate number of cattle. Following earlier adverse influences, the price collapse of 1931 caused further depression. After 1939, the reduction of lowland grazing, the priorities given to milk, wheat, poultry, etc., and three severe winters during the war made things very serious until the Hill Sheep Subsidy of 1941. The broad impression created was one of deplorable waste in human and material resources, consequent upon the speculative shifts and changes resorted to through years of price instability and economic uncertainty. To justify any expenditure on re-equipping the industry, national policy must aim at stable prices and a healthy and well-balanced industry. The majority of hill farms are small units in terms of invested capital and the size of flocks, the major operational costs being labour, rent and hire of grazing.

As forms of land use, hill sheep farming and forestry are competitive.

There should be some unified control of all hill land. For that in private ownership, rehabilitation can best be brought about by co-ordinated development, with State assistance over a period of not less than ten years, for specific measures of improvement. While a private owner looks at the needs of his estate as a whole, using land for farming or forestry as circumstances require, the State, by organising separate ownership through the Forestry Commission, tends to do the reverse. State-owned land should be owned and managed by one authority, a Statutory Body responsible to the Ministry of Agriculture, which should provide the capital equipment and service for all purposes.

The improvement of the stock-carrying capacity of hill farms will require concentration of labour and pools of machinery, the improvement and extension of intakes, further work on breeding and production of strains of grass, on soil deficiencies, bracken control, heather burning, etc. To prevent abuse, the rights and obligations of users of common lands should be clarified, and Executive Committees given powers to prevent overstocking, etc. Recommendations are made on improving the health and hardiness of the sheep, disease control, increasing the cattle population, tenure, the landlord-tenant relationship, size of units, etc., and the general social and educational amenities of the upland communities. Discussion on the problems for research should be instituted with the Agricultural Research Council.

Hill Sheep Farming. Scotland

Cttee. Rep., apps. pp. 127. 1944

1943–44 *Cmd.* 6494, *iii*, 495
apptd. Nov., 1941. *sgd. Dec.*, 1943

Lord Balfour of Burleigh (*Ch.*), Adair, Alexander, Cranston, Gallacher, Mackie (M.), Mackie (T. J.), Maitland, Murray, Wilson.

'To investigate the present position of hill and upland sheep farming in Scotland and to

report what steps should in their opinion be taken with a view to placing this branch of the Scottish farming industry on an economic basis. . . .'

Hill farming was suffering from several generations of neglect, a failure to preserve fertility, and since 1932 almost unbroken depression. Yet the industry is of supreme importance. Over 10 mn. acres of mountain and heath land carry some 2¼ mn. breeding ewes and perhaps 100,000 head of cattle of all ages. The contribution of meat and wool, the dependence of the low ground sheep flocks for breeding stocks, the contribution to the fertility of the low ground by the winter fattening of the hill stock, which allows the fullest use of grassland in winter, are all reasons for the re-establishment of hill farming on a sound economic footing.

There should be two basic objectives, the restoration of the fertility of the hills and the encouragement of the return of skilled labour by the creation of suitable conditions. Until long-term policy takes effect direct emergency subsidies should be given. The rehabilitation of farms, the restoration of the fertility of the land, improvements in health and care of stock, reconditioning of building and equipment, etc., should form the core of a long-term ordered programme applied to individual farms and estates. The State should provide not less than 60 per cent of the cost of such programmes and powers of direction should be available to the Department of Agriculture. There should be one marketing organisation to deal with all Scottish wool. Tenants should hold farms on long leases at controlled rents, and good husbandry and good estate management should be precisely defined. The State must be ready to buy hill lands on a substantial scale where there is risk of land becoming derelict. Research in veterinary service is required. Grading of stock, stable prices, marketing organisation and the amelioration of freight charges are essential. Other

recommendations include the encouragement of the single family type of holding, the provision of social and educational amenities, the classification of deer forests, and resolving points of conflict between sheep farming, afforestation, etc.

App. XXI contains the Report of the Committee on *Valuation of Sheep Stocks in Scotland*, 1934.

See *Scottish Hill Farm Research*. Cttee. Reps.; 1951, 1953 Non-Parl. Dept. of Agric., Scot. *Survey of Blackface Sheep with special Reference to their Hardiness*. J. F. Robinson. Rep.; 1953 Non-Parl. Dept. of Agric., Scot.

Principles and Objectives of Long Term Agricultural Policy

Council of Agriculture for England. Standing Cttee. Rep. pp. 16.   1943

1943 Non-Parl. Min. of Agric. and Fish. sgd. May, **1943**

Those serving on the land would work with better heart if they were assured that they were not merely engaged upon an emergency problem, but that in peace as well as war they would have the chance to earn a fair and reasonable living at all times. Long term policy should therefore include proper use and management of the land for the production of foodstuffs to satisfy nutritional needs, the maintenance of the fertility of the soil, raising the standards of rural life and increasing the rural population. Since food imports must continue, a prosperous agriculture required guaranteed prices and assured markets and the control of imports should be exercised by commodity commissions. There should be an improvement of internal marketing through marketing boards with regulatory powers. Methods of distribution should be overhauled with a view to standardising the product, minimising costs and reducing the time taken between farm and consumer. There should be a substantial increase of the livestock industry, the level of demand for whose products depended on full employment, ley farming should be developed, poultry flocks improved, and horticultural crops encouraged. Animal disease should be actively combated, and the administration of land drainage, etc., more fully integrated. The interests of cereal cash growers should be secured through international regulation of the grain trade and domestic arrangements with the brewing and distilling industry. County land improvement committees acting as agents of the Ministry of Agriculture should be appointed to supervise the proper use and management of the land. Restoration of capital equipment should be provided for from the accumulation during the war of tax-free monies. The rural standard of life should be raised through the establishment of satisfactory wage rates, the provision of better housing, electricity, piped water, etc., and more efficient agricultural education. Research and the speedy application of the findings of research to farm practice should be encouraged.

National Farm Survey of England and Wales (1941-1943)

Summary Rep., apps. pp. vi, 109. 1946
1946 Non-Parl. Min. of Agric. and Fish.

In 1940 when it was decided to launch a campaign for increased production, there was little factual information on what quantities of food our farmers were then producing, and what were the capacities for increased production. The first survey of the farms was made to assist the campaign. This extended survey covered 14 per cent of holdings of 5 acres and over, and deals with size of holdings, type of farming, tenure, rent, length of occupation, type of fertility of soil, condition of buildings, the managerial efficiency of occupiers, etc. App. I explains the sampling technique used.

Agricultural Survey of Scotland

Rep., apps. pp. 76. 1946
1946 Non-Parl. Dept. of Agric., Scot.

This survey differs from that for England and Wales in that it was concerned more with the productive capacity of the land itself. It deals with the potentialities of the land, potential yields, factors preventing maximum production, with livestock and with heath and mountain lands.

Agriculture Bill

Memo. pp. 27. 1946
1946-47 Cmd. 6996, xix, 225

The objective of the Bill is to promote a stable and efficient agriculture producing such part of the nation's food as in the national interest it is desirable to produce in the United Kingdom, at minimum prices consistently with proper remuneration and living conditions for farmers and workers and an adequate return on capital invested.

Part I aims at providing stability by means of guaranteed prices and assured markets for the major agricultural products. The Minister must hold annual and other reviews of the prospects of the industry and in the light of them fix prices and other factors by means of guaranteed prices, deficiency payments, acreage payments, etc., and the quantities of products to which these apply. Any quantitative limitations must be imposed at the same time as the price reviews. To enable farmers to plan ahead, the prices of some products must be fixed one year, of others two years ahead.

Part II aims at promoting efficiency by setting out the rules of good estate management and good husbandry which landlords and farmers should follow, providing for the supervision and direction of any owner or tenant not fulfilling his duties under them, and for his dispossession if he fails to show improvement.

Part III aims at promoting efficiency by providing for a satisfactory relationship between landlord and tenants by a comprehensive code of compensation from a tenant to a landlord for dilapidations and deterioration and from a landlord to a tenant for improvements and

I

tenant right. For landlords the basis is cost of making good; for tenants, compensation on the basis of custom is replaced by a statutory right based on the value of specified items to an incoming tenant. There are also provisions for increasing security of tenure.

Part IV aims at enabling experienced agricultural workers to become farmers on their own account, by creating and letting publicly-owned small holdings.

Part V provides for setting up an Agricultural Land Commission, Agricultural Land Tribunals and County Agricultural Executive Committees.

See *Agriculture (Scotland) Bill.* Memo; 1946–47 Cmd. 7175, xix, 253. *Annual Review and Fixing of Farm Prices;* 1950–51 Cmd. 8239, xxviii, 1, and succeeding Anns. *Agricultural Land Com.* 1st Rep.; 1948–49 (33) xi, 1, and succeeding Ann. Reps. *Agriculture Act, 1947*; 10 & 11 Geo. 6. c. 48.

Post-War Contribution of British Agriculture to the Saving of Foreign Exchange

Memo. pp. 9. 1947

1946–47 *Cmd.* 7072, *xix*, 215

The Memo. tries to estimate the savings in expenditure on imported food which might be made after the war by expanding British agriculture, and to what extent those savings might be absorbed by changes in the level of consumption. Provided capital is available for landlord and tenant, that priority is given to a farm building programme, that there is no shortage of labour, that control over the volume and type of farming operations continues, that markets are assured and prices fixed in advance, by 1950–51, home agriculture could contribute £80 mn. at pre-war prices. This would require a capital investment of not more than £250 mn., an increase of 20 per cent, and a labour force 5 to 10 per cent bigger than pre-war. Because of full employment, higher wages, social insurance, etc., increased demand would absorb the whole of the increased output, so that savings would be small. Unless home agriculture is expanded proportionately, the requirements of foreign exchange would be increased by £80 mn.

Needs of the Armed Forces for Land for Training and other Purposes

pp. 15. 1947

1947–48 *Cmd.* 7278, *xviii*, 555

The one year National Service system and six years in the Reserves means that more land will be needed for training, etc., and because of the use of live ammunition and the larger space required for manoeuvre with modern weapons, for safety reasons the public will have to be excluded from the areas. For security reasons, a reasonable proportion of the Regular Army must be retained and trained in this country. The amount of land needed is: Admiralty 20,000 acres; Royal Air Force 34,000 acres; War Office 648,000 acres.

In November 1946 the Prime Minister gave an undertaking that public local enquiries would be held when desired in cases involving the acquisition of land. The procedure is set out in Part IX.

Agricultural Valuation

Cttee. 1st Rep. pp. 14. 1948

1948 *Non-Parl. Min. of Agric. & Fish.* apptd. Aug., 1947. sgd. Jan., 1948

R. R. Ware (*Ch.*), Allam, Clark, Farnsworth, Hill, Ingram, Montgomery, Nevile, Peacock, Righton, Shearman, Watts, Weller, Whitton.

'*To advise on matters relating to agricultural valuation and in particular to make recommendations as to the provisions to be included in regulations under the Agriculture Bill prescribing the method of calculating the measure of compensation, namely the value to an incoming tenant, claimable by an outgoing tenant in respect of improvements. . . .*'

The Agriculture Act, 1947, provided a comprehensive code of compensation to landlords for dilapidations, deterioration of land, etc., based on the cost of making good, and to tenants for improvements and matters of tenant right, based on value to an incoming tenant. The items included in tenant right and the amount of compensation paid had varied considerably with local custom. The Act abolished compensation by custom, replacing it by written agreement or statutory right created by the Act, which specified the items and the measure of compensation to be paid. It also provided for an expert committee to advise on the method of calculating the value to an incoming tenant of each item. The Committee based the proposed rules for a standard method of calculation, which are given in detail, on the customs and methods most widely used and suitable for general adoption.

—— Second Report. pp. 11. 1950 1950 *Non-Parl.*
reapptd. March, 1948. sgd. May, 1950 del. Weller.

To consider 'and report: (i) The assessment of compensation for tenant-right matters other than those included in Part II of the Fourth Schedule to the Agriculture Act, 1947. (ii) The desirability of introducing some uniformity in the present customary rights of hold over and pre-entry. (iii) The desirability of reducing the existing number of customary term-days.'

It is not necessary to establish statutory rights to compensation under tenant right for osiers and underwood, farmyard manure spread or unspread, growing fruit trees (the Evesham custom), etc. But the acclimatisation (or hefting or settlement) of hill flocks has a real value for which the outgoing tenant had paid and should recover. Since this is not always included in written agreements and some outgoing tenants may lose, the right to compensation ought to be made statutory, by varying the provisions of Part II of the Fourth Schedule by Order. The amount awarded for breeding sheep should not exceed 15s. per sheep or 15 per cent of the market price, whichever is less. Customary rights of pre-entry and holdover arose because the farming year has no real end. The ingoer is allowed to begin the year in advance to prepare the land for sowing and the outgoer to remain to complete harvesting, threshing, etc. These customary rights are often commuted for cash and thus give rise to compensation on the basis of market value. Custom is not a satisfactory basis for holdover, since it is uneven between districts and does not apply to crops of recent introduction, e.g. sugar beet, when holdover is desirable. Farm tenancy agreements should make provision for holdover of such crops; legislation would be justified only if there were evidence that agreement could not be reached. There are over 30 different term days in use in various parts of the country. These should be reduced to four: 6th August, 11th October, 2nd February and 14th May.

Scotland's Marginal Farms

General Rep., apps. pp. iv, 61. 1947 1947 *Non-Parl. Dept. of Agric., Scot.*

Marginal farms are those not an economic success, including both those making a financial loss or though just profitable, where the profits were inadequate, the farmer making less than the wage of an agricultural worker plus interest on his capital. Many of these were brought back into cultivation in 1939–45, with the aid of the hill sheep subsidy, hill cattle subsidy, or marginal agricultural production grants; others were class C farms, classified as not well-managed. When the State intervenes, the price level it fixes will determine which farms are marginal. The survey attempts to determine where they are and why they are marginal. Fifty years ago they may have afforded a satisfactory standard of living, but since their output has not greatly changed, and the general standard of living has risen, they are in a relatively disadvantageous position. The survey analyses the various causes of low output—small size of farm, soil, poor buildings and equipment, character of the farmer, etc.—and the possibilities of increasing output. A map shows the distribution of the listed marginal farms.

See Regional Reports I–VI; 1947 Non-Parl.

Scottish Farm Rents and Estate Expenditure

Enquiry. Rep., apps. pp. iv, 24. 1948

1948 *Non-Parl. Dept. of Agric., Scot.*

'The enquiry was carried out in Scotland during 1946 to obtain information about (1) changes in agricultural rents and (2) the level of agricultural estate expenditure in relation to rent. This information is required both for the preparation of statistical material used at the annual price reviews and in connection with the operation of the 'full employment' policy. The rent enquiry was designed to find out not only contract rents as given in the Valuation Rolls, but also the amount of any abatements and the relation of changes in rents to tenure conditions, etc. The enquiry into estate expenditure provided a basis for the estimation of the amount of capital expended by agricultural landowners on the maintenance and improvement of their estates.'

On the estates covered by the survey, expenditure on maintenance and improvements rose from 49 per cent of 1946 rentals in 1940–41 to 1944–45, to 69 per cent in 1945–46.

Land Settlement in Scotland

Cttee. Rep., apps. pp. 82. 1945

1944–45 *Cmd.* 6577, *v*, 103
apptd. March, 1942. sgd. July, 1944

J. B. Douglas (*Ch.*), Bruce, Henderson, MacKay, MacKenzie, Dunlop.

'*To review the operation of land settlement schemes in Scotland and, in the light of the results achieved, to advise what changes in the system of tenure or of existing methods of land settlement are desirable, with particular reference to the social and economic welfare of small holders and crofters.*'

Results Achieved.—When the holdings were properly sited and suited to the type of production, the settlers were moderately prosperous and well-satisfied with their independence. Where land had been transferred from general to specialised farming, e.g. producing milk, production and population had both increased. The failure rate was low. Small holdings on the verge of large towns had not proved satisfactory, nor were part-time holdings justified except in areas suitable for rural craftsmen. The most successful type of holding was that of 50 acres or more producing milk.

Methods of Settlement.—No system should be favoured which leads to the uneconomic use of the land. The individual small holding on which the holder is a free agent to develop his own enterprise is the best type of settlement for Scottish conditions; national organised marketing is preferable to small-holders' group schemes. Land required for settlement should be purchased by the State outright. The economic size of the holdings varies with the type of production and should be reckoned on a stock-carrying basis. Holdings should be in the form of group settlement. Holders should be selected on the basis of experience and possession of private savings, preference being given to demobilised men if they have experience and as good qualifications as others and if without experience, on condition of two years' training.

In the Highlands the guiding principle should be the proper use of the land, settlement should be planned on larger lines and co-ordinated with afforestation, hydro-electric development, etc. On the basis of a survey, areas suitable for large scale co-ordinated development should be selected and the State should purchase the whole of the land within them. Inshore fishing, which was vital to coast land settlement, should be encouraged as well as milk production. In the Islands effort should be concentrated on improving existing holdings, land reclamation and improved breeding.

Tenure.—In future holdings should be let as equipped subjects and except in the case of those with proved experience, new holders should have a two or three year probationary period. The working of the holding should be subject to the rules of good husbandry and residence made a condition of succession. Tenants using holdings merely as residence or sub-letting should be removed.

A Minority Report by Dunlop criticised many of the conclusions and recommendations.

Smallholdings

Advisory Council. 1st Rep., apps. pp. vi, 61. 1949

1949 *Non-Parl. Min. of Agric. & Fish. apptd. Oct., 1947. sgd. March,* 1949

G. Brown (*Ch.*), Angell, Case, Charlton, Daniel, Davies, Dye, Foster, Gooch, Hedley, Hobhouse, Cemlyn-Jones, Mitchell, Parsons, Richmond, Spencer, Trumper.

'*To advise on the various matters arising in connection with the administration of Part IV of the Agriculture Act, 1947, relating to smallholdings and generally on questions connected with the provision, equipment and management of smallholdings in England and Wales.*'

The Agriculture Act, 1947, aims at providing smallholdings for letting so that skilled workers with agricultural experience should have opportunities to become farmers on their own account, to the extent that this can be done without detriment to the general interests of agriculture. Publicly-owned smallholdings must be made an integral part of British agriculture as fully economic units. Part IV of the Act provides that (*a*) smallholdings must be let to persons with adequate agricultural experience; (*b*) preference must be given to agricultural workers;

and (*c*) loans up to 75 per cent of the estimated working capital required may be advanced by the Government. The creation of new holdings necessarily involves some acquisition and sub-division of larger farms and will alter the balance between large and small holdings, but it should not be carried so far as to make any radical change in the structure of the industry. The purchase of some existing small farms in private ownership for letting as smallholdings may be a practicable alternative to splitting up large farms. The land should be of good quality suitable for the type of holding, e.g. dairy holdings carrying 15–20 milking cows, mixed holdings and market garden holdings. Holdings should be large enough, normally 50 acres, to provide a full-time occupation and a reasonable livelihood of £400–£500 for the tenant and his family.

A smallholder should have the benefit of advice and assistance from the Smallholdings Authority; suitable co-operative methods should be encouraged; each authority should draw up a plan within 12 months of the Act coming into force; county borough councils should not normally be constituted as Smallholdings Authorities; compulsory acquisition of land for smallholdings is justified in certain cases; model tenancy agreements should be prescribed by the Minister; applicants must have at least five years' practical experience, and should be in the age-range 25–40; and existing smallholdings should be reviewed where they are not now fulfilling their proper purpose. Applicants who are not able to finance their holdings adequately should not be accepted. The working capital for a market garden will seldom be less than £700–£800 and £2000 for a 50-acre dairy farm or mixed holding. Care should be taken to see that the tenant is not burdened with loan repayments which, with other outgoings, would be beyond the productive capacity of the holding. The net annual income below which the incomes of tenants should not be allowed to fall after paying interest and redemption charges, should be between £300 and £350 and on this basis borrowers could be allowed to incur liabilities for interest and repayment up to a maximum of £150 per annum. Loans should be repayable over periods of up to 15 years at not more than 3 per cent interest.

See *Smallholdings Centralised Services.* Land Settlement Assoc. Rep.; 1950 Non-Parl. Min. of Agric. & Fish. and succeeding Ann. Reps. *Scottish Land Court.* Report of Proceedings, 1940–49; 1950–51 Cmd. 8107, xvi, 579.
See *Agriculture Bill.* p. 79.

Allotments

Advisory Cttee. Rep., apps. pp. iii, 20. 1950

1950 Non-Parl. Min. of Agric. & Fish. apptd. May, 1948. sgd. July, 1949

G. Brown (*Ch.*), Adkinson, Berry, Darlow, Dicks, Giles, Johnson, L. O'Hagan, Robson, Seddon.

'To consider and make recommendations respecting a number of proposals which had been put forward for the amendment of allotments legislation.'

The cultivation of allotment gardens has developed from a small movement in the interests of 'the labouring population' to a spare time occupation for over 1 mn. people. Since 1947 land for allotments can be acquired at its existing use value. The National Allotments and Garden Society had submitted to the Government proposals which they considered were necessary for reform.

As a general target 4 acres per 1000 of the population, instead of the present 3·15 acres per 1000, should be reserved for allotments; planning authorities should make provision for statutory allotments and consideration should be given to the question of preserving privately owned and long established allotments already existing in a planned area; temporarily requisitioned land should be freed and suitable allotments found elsewhere; allotments on

privately owned land should be preserved, the owner having the right to require the local authority to purchase it; and local associations should apply to have their allotments reserved in plans in preparation. The rate limit of $1\frac{1}{3}$d. in the £ should be raised to $1\frac{2}{3}$d. Allotment gardens should be understood to mean any parcel of land not occupied together with a dwelling house, cultivated wholly or mainly by the owner or occupier for the production of vegetables, etc., pigs, poultry, small livestock for his and his family's use and not exceeding 40 poles in extent. To remove differences in local authorities' practice, the rent should be a 'fair' rent based on agricultural values of similar land in the district, plus the cost of adaptation and administration. Discretion should be allowed in letting to medically unfit persons, and grants should be considered for educational and recreational activity. Communal huts should be designed and they should not be rated. There should be a year's notice to quit. Local authorities should have powers to make bye-laws against trespass and damage. Group-holdings with individual plots not exceeding $\frac{1}{4}$ acre should be fostered, but they should not prejudice the provision of allotment gardens.

Domestic Food Production

Cttee. Rep., apps. pp. iii, 27.   1950
1950 Non-Parl. Min. of Agric. & Fish. apptd. Nov., 1948. sgd. Jan., 1950

G. Brown (*Ch.*), Hodgson, Jenkins (Mrs. I.), Macpherson, Wood.

'To review the present arrangements for the organisation of domestic producers of foodstuffs and to make recommendations for their future organisation and development.'

Before 1939 the organisation of allotment holders, backyard poultry keepers, etc., was left to voluntary bodies, but with the launching of the 'Dig for Victory' campaign and with the help of the National Allotments Society, the Women's Institute and the Land Settlement Association, etc., councils were established and help given to stimulate the keeping of pigs, poultry, rabbits, goats, bees and the production of vegetables and other foods. It is estimated that from 1940–45, $8\frac{1}{4}$ mn. tons of food were produced through domestic sources—the domestic egg producers probably accounted for 20–25 per cent of the total egg production.

The potentialities for increased food production for the home are immense and should be encouraged. There is some overlapping in the work of the voluntary bodies. The financial assistance is not in every case being used to the best advantage. The aim should be independent, democratically organised bodies entirely or nearly self-supporting. The recommendations include a permanent National Council for Domestic Food Production, under the Ministry, to co-ordinate the work of the various national organisations engaged in the field, and an adequate system of technical instruction and advice.

Crofting Conditions

Com. Rep., apps. pp. 100. 1954

1953–54 *Cmd.* 9091, *viii*, 231
apptd. June, 1951. *sgd. Jan.*, 1954

T. M. Taylor (*Ch.*), Cairncross, Campbell, Dow, Gunn, Mackenzie, Macleod, Robertson, Shewan, Williamson.

'*To review crofting conditions in the Highlands and Islands with special reference to the secure establishment of a small-holding population making full use of agricultural resources and deriving the maximum economic benefit therefrom; and to report.*'

Whilst the whole of the crofting community share in the general evils caused by the wasteful exploitation of the natural resources by land and sea, deforestation and soil erosion, years of neglect and improvident management, lack of employment with resulting depopulation, poor communications and the high cost of transport, the decline was attributable mostly to the failure of auxiliary industries on which crofters depended, notably fishing, coupled with the fact that men and women are no longer content with the life which was acceptable to their ancestors. In spite of the fact that in some areas improvements may come too late to arrest the decline in population, the Committee came to the unanimous conclusion that in the national interests the maintenance of these communities was desirable because they embody the intrinsic quality of a free and independent life.

Since 1884, when the Royal Commission on *Highland Crofters* reported, there has been no major transformation in the number or size of agricultural holdings in the crofting counties. Out of the total number of 23,209 holdings there are (*a*) 2300 whole-time farms rented at more than £50; (*b*) 3709 whole-time farms rented at up to £50 and (*c*) 17,200 part-time and spare-time holdings. The (*a*) and (*b*) groups represent 46·4 per cent of the crop and grassland in the crofting counties, but the vast majority are too small to provide a livelihood by themselves, and the crofters are largely dependent on non-agricultural sources of income; in many districts crofters are occupying two or more holdings each. Whilst extreme poverty has passed away and housing conditions have improved, there are many obstacles to full agricultural production. Crofts in the hands of older people no longer able to work them fully, crofts whose owners had become absorbed in other occupations, and those bought for retirement by people from other parts of the country were neglected. The amalgamation of crofts either through the inheritance provisions of the Crofting Acts or the operations of landlords did not necessarily mean that a larger workable economic unit had been formed. Improvements had been hindered by the limitations put on individual initiative through townships sharing common grazings, as there is no incentive for a crofter to improve his land when it has to be thrown open for communal grazing in the winter. Marketing is hampered by the isolated position and smallness of the productive units, and by the high cost of transport.

The capital needed for improvements is beyond the resources of crofters themselves. Already groups (*b*) and (*c*) above receive from the Live-Stock Subsidies to the Highlands some £500,000 out of a total of £651,451 and for land improvement £165,000 out of a total subsidy of £442,441. But if the process of decay is to be arrested and reversed it will require a substantial expenditure of public money.

Owing to apathy and lack of knowledge, the crofters of townships are not producing nearly as much as they could in crop, stock and pasture. Examples of great improvements showed that the advisory services of the College of Agriculture should be strengthened, and demonstration crofts worked by crofters set up.

These communities are capable of restoration and survival if proper measures are taken in time. The many detailed recommendations include: the establishment of a Crofters Commission endowed with adequate financial and executive powers; active use of land settlement powers in the crofting counties, powers should include the re-letting of crofts falling vacant, terminating absentee tenancies, dealing with aged tenants who renounce their claims, reorganising townships which have fallen into decay, the acquisition of land in reorganised townships, supervision of voluntary improvement schemes. It should examine subsidy and grant schemes, freight charges, transport services, marketing and supply. The Forestry Commission should pursue an energetic afforestation policy.

In a note of dissent Mrs. Macpherson stated that control and supervision could be real only under State ownership, and that this was not revolutionary as the State already owned one croft in ten. Public control with private ownership will not work. There is evidence that landlords, with honourable exceptions, have not wished to stimulate the crofts, and have allowed houses to fall down and land to lie fallow. Schemes for the reorganisation of decaying townships should be prepared by the Commission and crofters in consultation and in case of disagreement should be referred to the Secretary of State. The Commission should be responsible for protecting crofters' crops and crofters should be allowed to shoot in the daytime deer and other game which interfere with their crops.

See *Crofters (Scotland) Act, 1955;* 3 & 4 Eliz. 2. c. 21. *Crofters' Commission* [1st Ann.] Rep.; 1957 Non-Parl. Dept. of Agric., Scot., and succeeding Ann. Reps.

Rural Wales

pp. 15. 1953
1953–54 Cmd. 9014, *xxvi*, 867

The two Reports of the Rural Development Panel included in the Memos. of the Council of Wales and Monmouthshire give the results of an intensive survey of 13 county districts. Rural Wales is steadily losing its population. Welsh farmers experience great difficulty in getting out of the land the most of which it is capable, even of making the fullest use of the Government grants available. The only other important industry was forestry, but only 25,557 acres out of 716,593 in the survey area had been planted and more than half the 18,000 acres of private woodlands were felled, derelict, etc. The Panel proposed a subsidy of £60 mn. for rehabilitation and development.

The Government agreed with the aims to establish a stable rural economy, but did not agree that additional subsidies would bring this about, as very heavy subsidies, which exceed the sum suggested by the Panel, are already paid in rural Wales. It would not be right to give farmers in one part of U.K. higher grants than farmers on similar land in other parts. Much poor upland soil is used for dairy farming instead of livestock. It appeared that the problem was more of how the economy could be assisted to become self-supporting. More investigation is needed into whether the pattern of farming in the uplands is best suited to the character of the land, the climate and to the quality of the soil; what pattern of ownership and occupation is best suited to the types of farming; whether farmers could be assisted by a co-operative society for farm equipment and how the need for technical knowledge for upland farmers could be satisfied. Further assistance was promised for roads, sewage, water, etc., and for a more rapid policy for afforestation which would require the diversion only of poor marginal grazings. It was not proposed to transfer to a Development Corporation services normally provided by local authorities. Capital investment in housing is at a higher rate than that suggested by the Panel and the equalisation grant makes a very heavy contribution towards local government services. The local authorities will be urged to act in concert where necessary.

See *Council for Wales and Monmouthshire.* Memos.; 1950 Cmd. 8060, xix, 883. 1952–53 Cmd. 8844, xxiv, 875.

Qualitative Control of Seeds

Cttee. Rep. pp. 31. 1950

1950 Non-Parl. Min. of Agric. & Fish. apptd. Oct., 1949. sgd. Aug., 1950

F. R. Horne (*Ch.*), Brett, Croxford, Gatenby, Jenkin, Linehan, McIntosh, McMillan, Winsor.

'*To consider what action is possible under the Seeds Act or under amendments to that Act, or otherwise, to introduce practical methods of qualitative control of seeds used in the United Kingdom, whether home-produced or imported.*'

Since the Seeds Act, 1920, there have been many developments in the quality and types of seeds, standards of purity, knowledge of the spread of harmful and injurious weeds and seed-borne diseases, etc. Whilst many things can be dealt with by amended regulations, others may require statutory provision. The

recommendations include that the Seeds Act should apply to a re-grouped and extended list of seeds set out in the Report; that the present limits above which percentages of purity and germination need not be declared, should be raised and extended to cover all seeds covered by the Act; that the list of injurious seeds should be extended and the maximum permitted quantity reduced from 5 per cent to 1 per cent in the case of cereals and 2 per cent for all other seeds. There should be powers to fix minimum limits of purity and germination, to prohibit the sale of seeds proved unsuitable for use in this country and of diseased or infected seeds, and to restrict the sale of varieties which through weakness in resisting disease would menace other crops. New varieties of cereals should be submitted to tests before they are put on sale, and provision made for a register of strain names of certain kinds of crop plants. A technical committee should be established to advise the Ministry.

Toxic Chemicals in Agriculture

Working Party. Rep., app. pp. iii, 16. 1951

1951 Non-Parl. Min. of Agric. & Fish. apptd. July, 1950. sgd. Jan., 1951

S. Zuckerman (*Ch.*), Bartlett, Galley, Gimingham, Holness, Davies, Rogan, Senior, Tinsley.

'*To make recommendations for the promotion of the safety of workers in the agricultural use of substances which are toxic or harmful to human beings; and in particular to advise on the recommendations on this subject made in the Report of the Gowers Committee on Health, Safety and Welfare in Non-Industrial Employment.*'

Seven agricultural workers have died as a result of using DNC selective weed-killer in cereal crops since 1946. The new toxic substances offer the most satisfactory means yet discovered for the control of weeds and pests, but their danger to man is that they give rise to chronic toxicity following frequent or prolonged exposure. In spite of the knowledge of the dangers many men, in using the new substances, have shown an astonishing degree of carelessness about their own safety. The report recommends a complete list of protective clothing, precaution in the use of air-conditioned cabs for tractor spraying, washing facilities, maximum working periods, meals, decontamination of machinery and equipment, etc.

—— Report, *Residues in Food*, apps. pp. iii, 32. 1953

1954 *Non-Parl.*
re-apptd. May, 1951. *sgd. April,* 1953

S. Zuckerman (*Ch.*), and 20 others.

'*To investigate the possible risks from the use in agriculture of toxic substances on the agricultural product and the stored product, and, if protective measures appear desirable, to make recommendations as to their form to the Ministers concerned.*'

To protect crops, efficient agricultural practice requires the use of chemicals, practically all of which are poisonous to man and animals. Only 40 per cent of our food is grown at home and only a fraction of this is treated by toxic chemicals. There was no evidence of fatal result and the danger was limited to the possible misuse of chemicals. Regarding the 60 per cent of imported food stuffs, little is known of the methods of treatment or of the chemicals used, but no great danger was thought to exist. There was some uneasiness about the treatment of imported seasonal fruits, but the examination of samples was reassuring, though the results did not preclude the arrival of any consignment of fruit which had been excessively treated.

There should be a committee to advise the Departments on the use of toxic substances and the maximum permissible limits of residues, etc. Manufacturers and distributors should notify their intention of using new substances, and new formulations should not be used until cleared with the Departments concerned; studies should be made on the desirability of registering all firms or individuals who apply these materials by contract, etc. As analytical control will be necessary, if permitted limits are instituted, practical methods of determining micro-quantities of toxic substances should be sought. Bacterial rodenticides should be avoided. International action should be encouraged with the aim of controlling the use of certain chemical treatments of food.

A Survey of Agricultural, Forestry, and Fishery Products in the United Kingdom and their utilisation

pp. vi, 141. 1953

1953 *Non-Parl. Development Com. sgd. June,* 1951

J. P. Maxton, A. B. Stewart, F. N. Woodward.

'1. *To survey existing products and wastes of the agricultural, forestry, fishery and allied industries in the United Kingdom, and, where practicable, to formulate the main scientific and economic problems in the better utilisation of such products.* 2. *To record the present facilities for this type of research and development.*'

As a result of an informal meeting called by the Lord President's Office the Development Commission undertook to make a survey of the utilisation of agricultural products and biological materials on the farm and as food.

Of the 358 mn. tons of raw materials used by British industry in 1950, 96 mn. tons were renewable, being of biological origin and 262 mn. tons (including 216 mn. tons of coal) were non-replenishable materials.

The food industries absorbed 78 per cent of the replenishable raw materials (13·9 mn. tons imported; 55·6 mn. tons home produced), whilst the non-food industries utilised 22 per cent (13 mn. tons imported; 6·7 mn. tons home produced). The manufacturing processes based on these replenishable materials produce in an average year approximately 25 mn. tons of by-products and wastes which contain about 10·8 mn. tons of dry matter.

Out of this 10·8 mn. tons of by-product organic matter about 70 per cent is retained by or returned for use on the farm as fodder, fertiliser, bedding, etc., although it is by no means certain that all this is beneficially utilised; the remaining 3·6 mn. tons of organic matter (dry weight basis) is dumped, destroyed, allowed to rot or run to waste. In addition, there is potentially available at least a further 1·5 mn. tons of organic matter annually in the form of seaweed and bracken growing in Scotland and of residue from British inland sewage works.

As there is an enormous annual crop residue in many British colonial territories, a pilot survey in a single colonial area would be of value.

Natural Resources

Cttee. Rep., *Use of Towns' Wastes in Agriculture*, apps. pp. iv, 25. 1954

1954 *Non-Parl. D.S.I.R.*
apptd. Nov., 1950. sgd. June, 1954

S. Zuckerman (*Ch.*), Blaker, Bretherton, Dakin, Ellingham, Galley, Garner, Gray, Knox, Linstead, Mumford, Perrin, Simonsen, Slater, Todd, Wright.

'To advise on technical problems of the development, use and conservation of natural resources.'

For the purpose of discovering how far the manurial and fertilising values of wastes are or could be used to increase the output of home-grown food and feeding stuffs the Committee endeavoured to estimate (*a*) the amount of towns' wastes actually and potentially available for use, (*b*) the content of plant nutrients and humus-forming material, (*c*) the amount of compost that might be prepared, and (*d*) the contribution which these wastes are likely to make to agriculture as compared with those of the manurial and fertilising practices normally used in good husbandry.

The total annual quantity of dry solids in domestic and industrial sewage is about 1 mn. tons, of house refuse 10·5 mn. tons. The nitrogen content of unused sewage sludge, the only waste immediately available for use in agriculture, is about 5 per cent of U.K. nitrogenous fertiliser consumption. The organic matter in unused town wastes is 0·75 mn. tons a year, compared with 15·7 mn. tons added to the soil in normal farming practice, whilst there is a potential reserve of 59 mn. tons in the roots and leaves of grassland. Apart from dried digested sludge and activated sludge the potentialities of town wastes are often over-estimated.

Food Consumption Levels in the United States, Canada and the United Kingdom

Combined Food Bd. Special Jt. Cttee. Rep., apps. pp. 131. 1944

1944 *Non-Parl. Min. of Food*
apptd. May, sgd. Nov., 1943

Koenig, Maynard, Ogdon, Reynolds, Angus, Hopper, McArthur, Pett, Speers, Barter, Northam, Williams.

'*For the purpose of providing a working basis for the guidance of the Combined Food Board and of the appropriate Governmental agencies of the two Governments in the allocation of foods in short supply: to consider and compare the pre-war and present and prospective food consumption of the civilian populations of the United States and the United Kingdom; . . .*'

Following a joint statement by the President of the United States and the Prime Minister of the United Kingdom 'that in principle the entire food resources of Great Britain and the United States will be deemed to be a common pool', comparable information was required.

The Report deals mainly with the levels of food supplies moving into civilian consumption in the United States, Canada and the United Kingdom in the year 1943 and in the pre-war period (defined for the United Kingdom as 1934 to 1938, and for the United States and Canada as 1935 to 1939). Part I of the Report sets out the general problems involved in making such a study and the methods adopted for overcoming them. The comparison of consumption levels in the United States, Canada and the United Kingdom is made in Part II, Chapter 5, making the comparison in terms of nutrients and Chapter 6 in terms of the quantities of the different foods consumed.

The conclusions were that with the exception of the Canadian marginal supply of ascorbic acid, the food supply is sufficient on a restricted basis without impairing health, morale or working efficiency. The estimated per capita supplies of most nutrients is greater in the United States and Canada than in the United Kingdom. But from the point of view of acceptability to the consumer and culinary convenience, the diet in the United Kingdom is inferior to that of the U.S. and Canada. In the United States and Canada considerable economies in basic food resources would be possible with changes in the physical composition of the diet, but the substantial changes in the United Kingdom could not be carried appreciably further without apprehension as to their effects in the health and morale of the population.

See *Food Consumption Levels in the United Kingdom.* Statements; 1946-47 Cmd. 7203, xi, 779. 1948-49 Cmd. 7842, xxix, 581. *Urban Working-Class Household Diet 1940 to 1949.* National Food Survey Cttee. 1st Rep. *Domestic Food Consumption and Expenditure 1950.* National Food Survey Cttee. Ann. Rep.; 1951, 1952 Non-Parl. Min. of Food.

World Food Shortage

pp. 23. 1946. 2nd Review, apps. pp. 35. [1946]
1945-46 *Cmd.* 6785, *Cmd.* 6879, *xx*, 211

It was foreseen that there would be a shortage of fats, meat, dairy products and sugar for a considerable time after the war. There was insufficient shipping for cargoes, lack of transport for getting

fertilisers and feeding stuffs to productive channels, Argentine stocks of grain and linseed had been burned as fuel, and lack of faith in currency made many producers unwilling to sell. But the largest and least calculable cause was the series of widespread droughts. In France, Belgium, Holland and Norway the calorie intake was only 75-80 per cent of pre-war, in U.N.R.R.A. countries 70-75 per cent, in ex-enemy countries 50-60 per cent. Increased food production in the United Kingdom, though valuable, was small compared with world totals. Some of the increase in North America was taken up by increased consumption by armed forces and low income groups, or by an increased use of grain food for animal feeding stuffs. Because of the scarcity of meat in the deficit countries there was an increased demand for the grain from North America. During the war the United Kingdom was the bastion occupied by Allied armies, and food was kept to meet emergencies; after the war the United Kingdom was involved in ensuring minimum diets to liberated areas just when the inhabitants of the United Kingdom were expecting more food. The Paper reviews the position for each of the main foods and sets out the special measures adopted to meet the crisis.

The Second Review in July 1946 brings the information up to date just as the new harvest was moving into consumption.

See *Statistics and Documents Relating to the World Grain Position;* 1945-46 Cmd. 6737, xx, 271.

A Plan for the Mechanised Production of Groundnuts in East and Central Africa

app. pp. 48. 1947
1946-47 *Cmd.* 7030, *x*, 279

In March 1946 a plan for the mechanised production of groundnuts on 2½ mn. acres of land was proposed, following which a Mission was sent to make the detailed investigation, reported on in the App. In view of the world shortage of fats, which was likely to last some time, the risks of using the techniques of mechanised production in remote, undeveloped areas were not unjustified. The scheme, based on a rotation of nuts and grass leys, was agriculturally sound. As the area selected for initial development was almost uninhabited, no question of disturbing African rights arose; the land would be leased for 25 years. The revolution of agricultural technique would have a profound effect on the whole region. Ultimately control of the scheme would be transferred to the Governments of the African territories. A Government owned and financed corporation would manage the scheme. The total average cost of shelled groundnuts f.o.b. at an African port would be of the order of £17 18s., which compared favourably with fair market price of not less than £20. The cost should not exceed £23 mn.

See *Overseas Food Corporation.* 1st Ann. Rep.; 1948–49 (252) xix, 1, which gives an account of the first year's working.

Future of the Overseas Food Corporation

app. pp. 19. 1951

1950–51 *Cmd.* 8125, *xxvii*, 925
pres. Jan., 1951

The annual clearing and planting programme proved to be beyond the Corporation's capacity and its cost much more than was anticipated, so that the programme of 3½ mn. acres by 1953 was reduced to 600,000 acres by 1954. This also proved to be impracticable; the plan was further reduced, and a decision taken to abandon the idea of working in units of 30,000 acres in favour of units of 1500 to 6000 acres under intensive supervision. This changed the whole conception of the scheme, which had now to be regarded as a scheme of large scale experimental development to establish the economics of mechanised or partly mechanised

agriculture under tropical conditions. The Corporation had emphasised the importance of continuity over seven years. The cost of this would be £6 mn., a sum not very different from the one of abandoning the whole project forthwith.

See *The Future of the Overseas Food Corporation;* 1953–54 Cmd. 9158, xxvi, 721, which announces the change of the scheme to a Colonial Development and Welfare Scheme, and its transfer to a Tanganyikan Agricultural Corporation. The Overseas Food Corporation was dissolved. *Public Accounts.* Cttee. 2nd Rep.; 1950 (70) iii, 5, and *Future of the Queensland-British Food Corporation;* 1952–53 Cmd. 8760, xxiii, 393. *Future of the Overseas Food Corporation (Tanganyika Ordinance);* 1953–54 Cmd. 9198, xxvi, 731.

2. DECONTROL; MARKETING IN GENERAL

Post War Loaf

Conference. Rep., apps. pp. 24. 1945
1945–46 *Cmd.* 6701, *xii*, 163
apptd. Jan., *sgd.* Oct., 1945

H. L. French (*Ch.*), and 27 others.

'To assist Departments in advising Ministers on post-war bread and flour policy and in particular on any regulations which might have to be made with regard to flour and bread when war-time control ended.'

The only way to ensure that the whole of the nutrients are retained in flour is by 100 per cent extraction (wholemeal flour), though practical questions of palatability, digestability and consumers' preference are involved. The Government will have to decide whether to continue to regulate the nutrient quality of flour and bread, since if the extraction falls below a certain level and nothing is done to replace the lost nutrients, the health of the nation will suffer. A minimum nutrient content based on 'token' nutrients could be defined, but in application it would be difficult to know if constituents had been artificially added; home grown wheat used in country mills sometimes fell below the standard; the import of flour below standard would have to be prohibited; and the use of baking powder could destroy up to one-half the vitamin B1. The minimum standard would be secured by 80 per cent extraction, which the medical and official members of the conference held should be continued.

Various subjects for research are specified and recommendations made for further regulations on cleanliness in bakeries, the wrapping and handling of bread, etc., and the health of operatives.

Working of the Agricultural Marketing Acts

Cttee. Rep., apps. pp. iv, 96.   1947
1947 *Non-Parl. Min. of Agric. & Fish., Econ. Ser. No.* 48
apptd. Dec., 1946. *sgd. Sept.*, 1947

Lord Lucas (*Ch.*), Bell, Mayhew, Paget, Ryan.

'*To review the working of the Agricultural Marketing Acts; to consider what modifications of the provisions of those Acts for the organisation of producers are desirable in the light of experience before* 1939 *and of the developments since then in Government policy, as it affects food and agriculture; and to make recommendations.*'

The depressed state of agriculture in the inter-war years revealed the weakness of the thousands of small scattered farms in marketing their produce, and purely voluntary producers' co-operative selling organisations were unsuccessful. By the Act of 1931 membership could be made compulsory, and since Producer Boards could take complete control of the whole home-produced supply, limit the amount for sale and share the income from sales as they pleased, they had 'powers of a statutory monopoly'. As a result of the collapse of prices after 1930 the Act, which was concerned with long-run planning, did not satisfy producers, since they wanted immediate aid by raising prices and the

regulation of imports. The Act of 1933 added powers of limiting the sale of any individual producer on the basis of past sales, but limitation of imports was made contingent on the reorganisation of the home industries by marketing schemes. Once the producers had secured limitation of imports and raised prices, save in cases in which the home producer had a monopoly (milk, hops, potatoes) little was done to improve marketing other than setting up Reorganisation Commissions to prepare marketing schemes. From the middle of 1936 not a single fresh producer marketing scheme was submitted; instead, the Government set up a number of Commodity Commissions, mainly to control the disbursement of public subsidies. There is no evidence that producers' boards resulted in any fall of distribution costs. During World War II the Ministry of Food purchased the whole of home and imported supplies and to secure co-operation often paid margins for services no longer rendered. The system was not designed to secure marketing efficiency. The Report reviews in detail the operations of Marketing Boards and Commodity Commissions which led to these conclusions.

Since the war, full employment, the levelling of incomes and government policy of expanding home food production by 50 per cent by means of guaranteed prices and assured markets, have turned the buyer's market into a seller's market. Organised marketing should not in future require restriction of supplies, while improved efficiency is imperative. It is doubtful whether consumers were adequately protected in the marketing schemes, and in the new conditions the exclusion of consumers from any positive part in the operations of marketing policy would be much more serious.

Of the four alternative policies the Committee rejected: (1) A return to a free market such as existed before 1931. (2) A return to the pre-war system of the Agricultural Marketing Acts. Distributors and consumers were interested in marketing as well as producers and a monopoly given to the latter was tolerable only so long as they were suffering from a chronic excess of supplies. In the case of commodities listed in Schedule 1 of the Agriculture Act, in effect the taxpayer buys the produce at the point at which the guarantee operates, and it would be wrong to allow a sectional interest to exercise monopoly powers over public property. (3) Continuing the control by the Ministry of Food. It was unable to effect any ruthless cutting of distributive margins.

The marketing of farm produce should be managed on public utility lines by Commodity Commissions representing not a sectional interest, but the community in general. These should be established for any product for which the State has guaranteed both outlets and price, and should take over the marketing, normally by purchase at the point at which price is guaranteed, and sell to distributive agencies, though they should have reserve powers of trading if existing agencies failed to be efficient.

Producers' Boards should negotiate contracts and prices with the Commodity Commissions. Existing agricultural subsidies were so mingled with those to consumers that it was impossible to assess the cost of assistance to agriculture; the two should be separated. If the Commission were directed to sell at less than full market price, the cost would be a subsidy to the consumer, while any loss from buying at the guaranteed price and selling at market price would be a subsidy to producers.

Decontrol of Cereals and Feeding Stuffs

pp. 4. 1953

1952–53 *Cmd.* 8745, *xxiv*, 297

It was proposed to decontrol cereals and feeding stuffs at the 1953 harvest, because apart from the economy and increased efficiency which will follow, the present feeding stuffs rationing scheme has been unsatisfactory. This will involve the removal of the subsidy on flour and the restrictions on the type produced. But the subsidised national loaf will remain price controlled. A national flour of 80 per cent extraction will continue to be produced and the national loaf subsidised and price controlled. Bread made from whiter flour of lower extraction will be neither subsidised nor price controlled, but the flour will be fortified by the addition of nutrients equivalent to those lost by further extraction. The feeding stuffs subsidy will be discontinued, the effect on costs being taken into account in the Annual Review. Greatest possible freedom consistent with the balance of payments will be given to importers.

See *Annual Review and Fixing of Farm Prices;* 1950–51 Cmd. 8239, xxvii, 1 and succeeding Ann. Reps. *Guarantees for Home Grown Cereals;* 1952–53 Cmd. 8947, xxiv, 301.

Decontrol of Food and Marketing of Agricultural Produce

app. pp. 7. 1953

1953–54 Cmd. 8989, xxvi, 511

Since 1939 the shortage of food has led successive Governments to buy or to control the purchase of many of the principal foodstuffs, whether produced at home or imported. In addition marketing, distribution and selling prices have been kept under complete control. Government purchase of home-produced foods can no longer be the sole or main instrument for implementing guarantees to farmers. The policy of expanding agricultural production to 60 per cent above pre-war is reaffirmed. Since 1951 controls over a wide range of foodstuffs have been removed, and it is proposed to end rationing, allocation and price control of meat and bacon in 1954. Details are given of the proposals for dealing with wool, eggs, cereals, sugar beet, potatoes, milk, meat and bacon. Proposals for Agricultural Marketing Schemes and Producers Boards will be sympathetically considered. Full marketing powers will be restored to the Milk Marketing Board. The annual turnover of meat and bacon is £500 mn. and includes a great variety of type and quality and of consumers' demand. Individual consumers' demand cannot be studied under any rationing system as effectively as it was by individual traders. When rationing ends private trading in meat and livestock will be restored. To protect farmers there will be a twofold guarantee combining a guaranteed individual price on each transaction with a collective guarantee of a standard price to the industry as a whole.

3. PRODUCTION AND MARKETING OF PARTICULAR PRODUCTS

Sugar Industry Bill

Sel. Cttee. Rep., proc., mins. of ev. pp. iv, 12. 1942

1941–42 (65) iii, 445
apptd. Jan., o.p. March, 1942

L. Ward (*Ch.*), Mander, Smith, Stewart, Lamb, Pym, Quibell.

'*To whom the Sugar Industry Bill was committed.*'

The object of the Bill was to adapt the provisions of the Sugar Reorganisation Act, 1936, to war-time conditions in which the Ministry of Food took over the control of sugar. The minutes of evidence give a detailed account of the work of the Sugar Commission under the 1936 Act.

See *Breviate 1917–39*, pp. 133–34.

Future Arrangements for the Marketing of Sugar

pp. 4. [1955]

1955–56 Cmd. 9519, xxxvi, 967

The Government intends to terminate the present system of State trading in sugar. Both the negotiated price of sugar purchased under the Commonwealth Sugar Agreement and the guaranteed price of sugar from home-grown beet are above world prices; all sugars entering the internal market are brought to a common selling price, which is thus above world price. Return to competitive buying is possible only if there is some other averaging device which enables trade to revert to world price.

A small Sugar Board will buy the sugar under the Commonwealth Agreement at a negotiated price, but will resell it in the country of origin at current world price to refineries and others. The deficit on Commonwealth and home-produced sugar will be met by a surcharge on all sugar entering the home market, so that the consumer will pay the true average cost of home trade supplies. Traders will handle sugar on a free market and the internal price level will be linked with world prices.

Cost of Milk Distribution

Cttee. Rep., apps. pp. iv, 38. 1940

1940 Non-Parl. Min. of Food
apptd. June, sgd. Sept., 1940

Lord Perry (*Ch.*), Anderson, Bowen, Floud, Short, Stephenson.

'*To investigate the present cost of distributing milk in Great Britain (i.e. the difference between the payment received by the producer and the charge to the consumer) and to advise what steps would have to be taken in order to bring about a substantial reduction in such costs.*'

It was customary before 1939 for the cost of imports to regulate the price of liquid milk to the home consumer. As the Milk Marketing Boards had for some time prescribed minimum or fixed prices for the sale of milk both by wholesalers and retailers, the methods of milk distribution were needlessly elaborate and costly. Milk is retailed by a variety of agencies in a variety of circumstances, so that costs of distribution vary from 6d. to 1s. od. per gallon. Co-operative societies provide an adequate standard of service at a reasonable cost. An adequate measure of costs of processing and distribution is 7d. a gallon, and a net profit of 1d. per gallon would give a 20 per cent return on capital. The allowance to distributors should be 8d. a gallon throughout the country and at all seasons, and should be introduced by stages. Various methods of reducing costs are suggested, including a deposit of 3d. on the milk bottle and the restriction of milk delivery in any district to two organisations, the local co-operative society and a combination of private traders. Milk distribution should be the concern of some organisation equipped with the necessary powers.

Milk Policy

Memo. pp. 6. 1942

1941–42 Cmd. 6362, ix, 69

Marketing of milk.—In order to increase the consumption of milk, especially by women and children under cheap or free milk schemes, the producers have been guaranteed a return for milk independent of the price it realises, whether sold for liquid consumption or manufacture. Consumption has increased more in some areas than others, a redirection of supplies has been necessary, and retailers may sell only to registered customers. Contracts between individual producers and buyers are not suited to these conditions. As from 1st October, 1942, the Milk Marketing Board will be the sole purchaser of milk from producers. The Minister will purchase it from the Board and sell it to distributors and manufacturers at uniform prices, cost of transport being paid by the Minister.

Retailing. Spontaneous amalgamations of retailers due to loss of manpower will be extended by the Minister, who will require dairymen in urban districts of over 10,000 to form associations to rationalise distribution by reallocating registered customers, each dairyman to receive the same proportion of the trade as he had before the association was formed. Minorities may be compelled to participate.

Measures to Improve the Quality of the Nation's Milk Supply

apps. pp. 8. 1943

1942–43 Cmd. 6454, xi, 149

As the consumption by women and children had greatly increased, measures to maintain the quality of milk are necessary. This required a sound breeding policy, the use of better bulls, removal of diseased cows, etc., and a general grading up of the national dairy herd. The Government proposed to introduce a system of inspection covering all herds in the country. Tuberculin tested herds will continue to be inspected once every six months; accredited herds once a year where the milk is subject to heat treatment, and once every three months, as at present, where it is not treated; all other herds once a year, where the milk is treated, and twice a year where it is not treated. The Government intend to bring in legislation which will transfer to the Ministry of Agriculture and Fisheries the responsibility for supervising the conditions, buildings, etc., in which milk is produced on the farm. The Milk Testing and Advisory Scheme is to be extended. Much of the T.T. milk is not sold as such, but is bulked with ordinary milk. To encourage the producer to produce T.T. milk his premium is to be raised from $2\frac{1}{4}$d. to 4d. a gallon, and to encourage the public to consume T.T. milk it is to be offered at a price only slightly in excess of the price for ordinary milk. Closer control over the quality of the milk will be exercised by the Ministry of Food, which will encourage pasteurisation of the milk of small producers. The schemes have to be modified to meet the different conditions of Scotland and N. Ireland.

See *Mechanisation of Milk Production.* Conference. Rep.; 1946 Non-Parl. Min. of Agric. & Fish.

Freezing Point (Hortvet) Test of Milk

Scientific Advisory Cttee. Sub-Cttee. Rep., apps. pp. 19. 1946

K

1945 *Non-Parl. Dept. of Health, Scot. apptd. —. sgd. Aug.,* 1943

A. S. M. Macgregor (*Ch.*), Cockburn, Dodd, Stewart, Tocher, Wright.

'*An authoritative appraisement of the Freezing Point (Hortvet) Test from a scientific standpoint. . . .*'

The chief difficulties involved in the present presumptive standard of 8·5 per cent solids-not-fat in milk is that genuine milk may on occasion contain less than 8·5 per cent. The freezing point depression has been shown to provide the most constant of the physical properties of genuine milk and it is capable of furnishing conclusive evidence regarding the presence or absence of added water.

Milk Distribution

Cttee. Rep., apps. pp. 99. [1948]

1947–48 *Cmd.* 7414, *xiii,* 543
apptd. Oct., 1946. *sgd. Jan.,* 1948

W. D. A. Williams (*Ch.*), Charles, Cohen (Miss R.), Sainsbury, Weeks.

'*To examine the distribution of liquid milk from the point at which it leaves the farm to the point at which it is received by the consumer or the manufacturer and to advise on any changes which are necessary to ensure that clean safe milk is delivered as efficiently and cheaply as possible.*'

The changes in Governmental policy which make the current problem so different from those investigated by pre-war inquiries are (*a*) the guaranteed price and assured market under the Agriculture Act, 1947; (*b*) Government responsibility for ensuring a supply of milk free or at reduced prices under Welfare schemes; (*c*) for some years the supply will be insufficient to meet all demands, the total sold off the farms being about 1390 mn. gallons, while liquid consumption might rise to 1500 mn. gallons if unrestricted, and in addition some must be sent to manufacturing to ease balance of payments difficulties.

Clean, safe milk.—The Government has announced that it proposes to schedule areas in which only heat-treated milk may be sold to the public and that this will be gradually extended to the whole country. The ultimate objective should be heat-treatment of all liquid milk. In scheduled areas all persons handling milk until it is bottled should be regularly examined for infections. Tests of milk should be made fortnightly.

Efficiency and cheapness of distribution.—Milk travelled unnecessary distances from farm to town processor before the war because the price-fixing arrangements removed the incentive to buyers and sellers to transport milk as short a distance as possible, and this incentive was not replaced by really effective powers given to any one body to organise the flow of milk. Under the Milk Marketing Scheme buyers paid the same delivered price for milk for the same use from whatever place they bought it. During the war farm supplies were reallocated between one buyer and another—the reorganisation of haulage services saved 75,000 vehicle miles per day, i.e. one-fifth of the transport used pre-war, and 2¼ mn. gallons of petrol per year.

Competitive buying and selling before 1929 did result in milk required for liquid markets being bought as near the market as possible, milk for manufacture being drawn from outlying areas. This cannot now work because the price charged to buyers for liquid milk is higher compared with the price for manufactured products, the farmer has a guaranteed price, and wholesale and retail prices are to be constant throughout the country. Economy can be achieved only by central control of the volume of milk passing through each country depot to consuming centres and of the amount manufactured. The farmer must receive the same net return whatever use is made of his milk and wherever it is sent. Any deduction from a fixed gross price for transport charges must be uniform for any area. Milk should not pass through country depots if it can be sent more economically to the town dairies. Depots should remain in private hands, but should be paid by the Central Authority. The Central Authority should have powers to close redundant depots, to run depots which private owners cannot operate remuneratively, and to authorise the erection of new ones. The Central Authority should control transport.

The economies in the cost of distribution from town processor to consumer were demonstrated by the savings through the wartime policy of blocking and zoning of milk rounds, and further rationalisation of overlapping rounds would produce more savings. This would be completely effective only under public ownership, otherwise it would give a legal monopoly to existing distributors in any area and close the door to new entrants. As well as reducing consumers' choice, public ownership would cause a serious upheaval to a number of concerns, including co-operative societies, large combines, and some 60,000 dairymen including producer-retailers. Processing, bottling and retailing should remain in private ownership, subject to control by the Central Authority, which should have power to operate as processors or retailers. It should supply processors with their milk at a price not varying with the source of supply. Minimum retail prices, which stimulate non-price competition, should not be enforced, minimum price agreements by retailers should be prohibited, and maximum retail prices fixed. The Central Authority's selling price should be uniform and the maximum retail price should vary from area to area, or alternatively, the maximum retail price should be fixed and the price charged by the Central Authority should vary.

The Central Authority should be an independent Milk Commission. The Government should continue to fix producers' prices, subsidies and retail prices, and operate the guaranteed price system. As the Government now guarantees prices, the Milk Marketing Board has lost its main function and it would be wrong to give a Board representing only a sectional interest the powers proposed. Instead a strong distributors' voluntary association or an Industrial Development Council is desirable.

Cohen and Sainsbury accept the proposals as an immediate step, but argue that in the long run public ownership will be required. There is a note by Charles.

Milk Services Scotland

Cttee. Rep., apps. pp. 36. 1949

1949 *Non-Parl. Dept. of Agric., Scot., Dept. of Health, Scot.*

apptd. July, 1946. sgd. July, 1948

J. R. Philip (*Ch.*), Baird (May), Dunlop, Laidlaw, Nimmo, Rennie, Wingfield (Miss P. L.).

'*To review the services at present in operation in Scotland in connection with the production of milk and the quality of the supply, and to consider and report what improvements in these services are desirable and practicable.*'

The regulation of milk production and distribution dates from the Milk and Dairies (Scotland) Act, 1914, when most of the milk was produced and disposed of locally and the local authorities were made the supervisory bodies. With the steady improvement since 1914 in quantity, quality, production and distribution, etc., there has been a development of a large number of new services and an increased number of officials under the Department of Health, the Ministry of Agriculture and Fisheries and the Secretary of State for Scotland. This has not always led to a uniform policy or clearly defined responsibilities or to a uniform code of Dairy Byelaws. There is an urgent need for the expansion of milk production, particularly in the winter months.

The administrative services should be reorganised, the supervision of production being separated from the supervision of distribution. The Department of Agriculture for Scotland should be responsible for all aspects of milk production up to delivery to the first buyer, the relevant duties of Public Health authorities and the Vetinerary Service of the Ministry of Agriculture being transferred to it. It should maintain a staff of Milk Production officers. Its executive functions should be devolved upon the Agricultural Executive Committees. The Public Health authorities and the Department of Health should be responsible for supervising distribution from the stage at which milk is delivered to the first buyer. In the case of producer-retailers, the farm gate is the point at which production ends and distribution begins. An early increase in milk production depends on an increase in average yield per cow, which in turn depends on an increase in imported feeding stuffs and would be stimulated by voluntary milk recording. There should be three designated milks, Certified, Tuberculin Tested, Pasteurised. Areas free from bovine tuberculosis should be scheduled and cleared of reactors after two years.

See *Economics of Milk Production in Scotland.* Reps.; 1948, 1949 Non-Parl. Dept. of Agric., Scot.

Quality Milk Production

Working Party. Rep., apps. pp. iv, 35.
1953
1953 *Non-Parl. Min. of Agric. & Fish. apptd. May,* 1951. *sgd. Aug.,* 1952

R. Franklin (*Ch.*), Ashworth, Baber, Bannister, Capstick, Carnochan, Clifford, Davidson, Davies, Henderson, Kay, McAllan, Nield, Peacock, Semple, Vincent.

'To examine the present structure of producers' prices for milk and to advise whether it is desirable and practicable to make revisions which would promote an improvement in the composition and quality of milk sold off farms in the United Kingdom.'

The statements regarding the decline in the compositional quality of milk were proved by the evidence over the last 30 years; it was the solids-not-fat matter rather than the fats in milk which had declined most. There had been a change in the balance of friesians and shorthorns in the herds, but as the solid content of the friesian milk had increased, any decline in composition was not due to this change. Until recently poor feeding was thought to reduce the amount of milk, but it was now established that it affected quality. It was therefore a nutritional deficiency which was responsible for the decline in quality. But from a standpoint of national nutrition any slight deterioration in quality is outweighed by the increase in consumption which has taken place.

Much is being done through breed societies, advice and research, milk recording, etc., to improve the quality, but much has to be done to educate and encourage the lower grade producer. Paying the producer for milk on the basis of quality, besides calling for a considerable amount of sampling and testing, might lead to a shift from those breeds suitable for beef to breeds yielding milk of higher fat content, and was rejected. A higher price for milk with not less than 4 per cent butter fat, changing the presumptive minimum to a fixed minimum, and raising the presumptive minimum were also rejected. The average composition of milk in England and Wales is estimated to be 3·56 per cent fat and 8·70 per cent solids-not-fat. If milk slightly exceeded these levels at all times of the year there would be little to worry about. Producers and distributors should cooperate with Government Departments through the Joint Milk Quality Control Committee in an effort to improve the quality, beginning with the poorest producers. A producer who consistently sends in milk at or near the presumptive standard should be warned and advised, and if after a specified time his milk did not improve, the Milk Marketing Board should terminate his contract.

Wool Marketing

Cttee. Rep. pp. 23. 1946

1946 *Non-Parl. Min. of Agric. & Fish., Dept. of Agric., Scot. apptd. Dec., 1944. sgd. Oct., 1945*

W. E. Elliot (*Ch.*), Bowman, Henderson, Howitt.

'*To examine the pre-war arrangements for the marketing of wool by producers in Great Britain . . . , to consider whether the organisation of wool marketing after the war could be improved through the medium of a scheme under the Agricultural Marketing Acts, 1931–1933, or by any other means.*'

Before the war home-grown wool was marketed in a great variety of ways, because it came from a great variety of sheep. In Scotland marketing was simple because the clip consisted mainly of one type of wool (Scottish Blackface) and was required by one type of manufacturer. During the war all wool was requisitioned and collected by the Wool Control, and prices were maintained at levels above those of the corresponding Dominion wools. The producers are critical of pre-war marketing arrangements. They advocate a marketing board which should effect economies and provide better prices for the producer, but their main reason was that the industry would be better able to seek Government financial aid or regulation of imports. They gave no estimates of initial expense, working capital required or cost of operations. The merchants argued that the highly competitive nature of the trade ensured to the producer the market value of his wool. The manufacturers doubted whether a Board could supply the variety and efficiency of services they were used to. There was no unanimous opinion in favour of marketing schemes, although the Scottish producers were strongly in favour of a separate scheme and the Welsh producers favoured a separate scheme if one for Great Britain could not be formulated. The possible lower level of world wool prices would place a newly formed board in difficulties.

A marketing scheme was not recommended, but a Joint Wool Council should be set up to promote good understanding between producers and users, and act as spokesman for the home wool industry in the transition from a war to a peace economy.

See *Hill Sheep Farming in Scotland.* p. 77. *U.K.-Dominion Wool Disposals Ltd. (Joint Organisation); 1945–46* Cmd. 6855, xx, 709. *Plan of Reserve Prices for Wool: Origin, History and Operations of the existing Joint Organisation; 1950–51* Cmd. 8329, xxvii, 945. *Draft Scheme under the Agricultural Marketing Acts, 1931 to 1949, Regulating the Marketing of Wool; 1950* Non-Parl. Min. of Agric. and Fish.

Hops

2nd Reorganisation Com. Rep., apps. pp. iv, 48. 1947

1947 *Non-Parl. Min. of Agric. & Fish., Econ. Ser. No. 47 apptd. Dec., 1945. sgd. Feb., 1947*

Lord Piercy (*Ch.*), Elliott, Macpherson, L. Quibell, O'Sullivan.

'*To review the operation of the Hops Marketing Scheme, 1932, as amended, with special reference to: (i) the provisions relating to quotas for the sale of hops by producers registered under the Scheme, and the desirability of continuing such provisions . . . (ii) the effect upon the efficient administration of the Hops Marketing Scheme of the Agreement between the Brewers' Society and the Hops Marketing Board, dated 21st July, 1939. . . .*'

Though there is no legal restriction on their cultivation, the sale of hops is in principle a monopoly of the Hop Marketing Board. The basic quota, which should approximate to the quantity a grower will ordinarily produce, also shows the percentage of total home demand for brewers' hops which the holder is entitled to supply. The annual quota is the same percentage of the estimated demand for the season's crop, and represents the actual quantity of hops for which the holder has an assured market at prices fixed by the

Board. The holder cannot be deprived of this basic quota, though it may lapse or can be given by the Board to a succeeding occupier. But he can transfer it by nomination, so that it has a sale value, some quotas having been sold at £6 to £13 per cwt. This is an abuse. The right should never become a saleable property, but be regarded as a licence determinable without compensation.

Although the industry is a small one, its organisation is elaborate. The establishment of the Board as a single primary marketer has eliminated some functions and demonstrated possibilities of economy. The apportionment of the market by means of quotas has justified itself and the scheme should be viewed as permanent. Basic quotas should be based on the average crop from a determinate acreage on a specified farm, and should be reviewed every five years, provision being made for transfer in case of death, reissue at change of tenancy, etc. As the yield of hops is uncertain, transfers of annual quotas are reasonable, since the periodic revision would prevent any producer from lapsing into a mere seller of annual quota. Though the present holders of basic quota are substantially those who held them in 1934, since 1942 acreage has gone ahead of basic quota and the brewers fear a shortage. Additional basic quota should be issued in respect of new acreage, to bring the total up to 22,500 acres, including brewers' acres. Provision should be made for the entry of new growers.

The Agreement between the Board and the Brewers' Society, whereby the brewers agree to contract for 90 per cent of English hops and to limit the import of hops, is wholly salutary and should be renewed. Hop prices have risen far more than agricultural prices generally; and as the monopoly is created by statute, the present primitive method of arriving at average prices should be replaced by one based on actual current costs ascertained by modern methods.

The scheme for a single modern warehouse in the Borough should be considered on the basis of its being undertaken by co-operation between the Board, merchants and factors, and the parties concerned should consider ways of bringing all hop storage under a single control.

See *Hops Marketing Scheme;* 1950 Non-Parl. Min. of Agric. & Fish.

Co-operative Marketing of Horticultural Produce in England and Wales

Rep., apps. pp. iv, 68. 1948
1948 Non-Parl. Min. of Agric. & Fish., Econ. Ser. No. 49

The horticultural industry comprises a great number of small scale producers and comparatively few large growers; for example, in Middlesex 83·5 per cent of the growers have holdings under 10 acres on 13·3 per cent of the total area cultivated. The large scale growers have as a rule a highly developed system of marketing, and plan production in the light of market experience. These advantages could be obtained by small growers distant from the market only by an organisation which places a like volume under single control. While some small growers who specialise have good local connections, a large volume of produce is marketed in a haphazard manner which results in gluts and shortages. Co-operative marketing would be a great improvement, but the grower would have to sink his individuality in his co-operative, and the high individualistic nature of the majority of growers militates against this.

There are 38 co-operative organisations comprising soft fruit, vegetables, top fruit, etc., the total volume of business being nearly £3 mn. in 1946. If future initiation is left to a few producers under the spur of insistent local need, somewhat slow progress must be expected. Arrangements will have to be made so that co-operation can be developed where no spontaneous demand is at present apparent, but the inherent and local factors which influence the success of co-operatives are complex, and early investigations seem desirable in the 'export' districts, such as Cornwall, East Anglia, Lincolnshire, and parts of Kent. An analysis is made of the advantages of creating a central body with authority, experience and equipment for making surveys, for dealing with proposals for local organisation, aiding the provision of capital, etc.

Factors in the Marketing of Home-Produced Apples in England and Wales

Rep., apps. pp. iv, 68. 1949

1949 Non-Parl. Min. of Agric. & Fish., Econ. Ser. No. 50
sgd. June, 1949

The acreage of market apples in 1946 was 134,054, of which 50,234 were used for dessert and 83,820 for cooking apples. Of the average crop, about 30 per cent is dessert and 70 per cent cooking apples. There are more than 50,000 apple growers, 91 per cent of them being on holdings of less than 10 acres.

For the five years 1934–38 the average of retained imports was 304,000 tons, but from 1940–46 it was 90,000 tons. 90 per cent of the imported apples, on an acid/sugar test, would be classed as dessert apples if grown in this country, and 85 per cent were up to good standard of quality. Too few dessert and too many cooking apples are grown. Before 1939 only about one-third of the English crop reached a good standard of quality.

To meet an assumed demand of 300,000 tons of desserts and 200,000 tons of cookers the dessert acreage would have to be doubled. If imports were on a pre-war scale, this could be done within the existing total acreage by adjusting the proportion of the two. The official planting programme of 10,000 acres of desserts in the next four years would make up the loss of planting during 1941–45.

Five main areas produce most of the crop, and each could support a marketing organisation. The services of a central packing station can be economic only when there is a concentration of orchards within about seven miles. The concentration of half the crop of desserts and 60 per cent of the cookers in the hands of the 4,000 growers of Kent who do not combine for marketing means that the bulk is sent to London from 85 stations and reconsigned. The Fruit Packers' Council aimed at a continuity of supplies, a large volume under a few brand labels, standard grades and packs, regulation of the flow to selected markets, sales promotion and national organisation. But only 4 per cent of the crop was so marketed. The development of voluntary arrangements under the Agricultural Produce (Grading and Marketing) Acts therefore appears to be the most suitable for the industry. Marketing arrangements for this new 10,000 acreage of desserts should be planned before planting takes place.

See *Draft Scheme Regulating the Marketing of Apples and Pears;* 1952 Non-Parl. Min. of Agric. and Fish.

Factors affecting the Marketing of Home-Produced Tomatoes in Great Britain

Rep., apps. pp. iv, 113. 1950

1950 Non-Parl. Min. of Agric. & Fish., Econ. Ser. No. 51

The industry has been expanding for 50 years. In 1948 121,000 tons were produced from 3646 acres of glasshouses, the Lea Valley and the Worthing areas being the largest centres. The production of outdoor tomatoes, before the war limited to a few areas and comparatively few growers, with a production of 1500–2000 tons, rose during the war to an average of 23,000 tons during 1940–47. Production, prices, grading and marketing arrangements are reviewed in detail.

Home production has supplied a special part, but only part, of home demand. Winter production is not economic in this country. If the country wishes the industry to keep pace with expanding demand, the producer's desire for reasonable certainty that his costs will be covered cannot be ignored. There are 13,000 growers, a substantial proportion of them small producers. While there is no accurate way of determining how far pre-war marketing arrangements were successful in providing continuity and balance of supplies, there was long term stability of price, though there were variations between markets. That co-ordination of supplies is feasible is shown by the success of the Tomato Distribution Scheme in such concentrated areas as the Lea Valley. A corrollary to balancing home supplies is the balancing of imported supplies in the period of home production. This probably involves some form of national organisation. The proposals for a Tomato and Cucumber Board are outlined, but not analysed as they are *sub judice*.

See *Scheme Regulating the Marketing of Tomatoes and Cucumbers;* 1950 Non-Parl. Min. of Agric. and Fish.

Grain Drying and Storage in Great Britain

Working Party. Rep., apps. pp. iv, 26. 1952

1952 Non-Parl. Min. of Agric. & Fish. apptd. Jan., 1951. sgd. Jan., 1952

R. Franklin (*Ch.*), Bean, Cashmore, Causton, Falconer, Farquharson (A. E. T.), Farquharson (R.), L. Gretton, Hastie, Hoskins, Lambert, Loombe, Lord, Page, Skilton, Watkins.

'To consider the extent to which existing drying and storage facilities need to be supplemented . . . bearing in mind the high production of cereals now called for by national policy.'

The Working Party was set up because the difficulties of maintaining a smooth flow of grain in the harvests of 1949 and 1950 indicated that the facilities were not keeping pace with the increase in the amount of combined

grain coming forward. In recent years combine harvesters have been bought at the rate of 3000 a year, but few farmers are installing complete drying plants. Farmers tend to cash in as soon as possible on that part of the crop intended for sale. In 1950, 2,100,000 tons of thrashed grain was produced in ten weeks; of this about 600,000 tons remained on the farms (about half not dried) until mid-October. The flour millers, maltsters, brewers, distillers and the Ministry of Food, stored almost to their maximum capacity. Action is therefore required to increase drying and storage facilities.

Loans at reasonable rates should be offered to farmers, merchants and ultimate users for the erection of storage, drying and cleaning plant and they should be given priority for building materials, etc., for this purpose. They should also have a special rate of depreciation for income tax purpose. To give farmers an inducement to instal facilities, the seasonal price increment for holding grain from harvest to the following January should be increased. The extension of Government storage was not recommended. The national silos were for seasonal use only. There should be a Technical Panel for investigations into drying and storage problems.

See *Grain Storage, Drying and Marketing in the United States of America.* Rep. *Bulk Handling of Grain in the United States of America.* Rep. *Bulk Handling of Home-Grown Grain.* Rep.; 1952, 1953, 1954 Non-Parl. Min. of Agric. & Fish.

Costs and Efficiency of Pig Production: A Comparison between England and Denmark

Investigation. Rep., apps. pp. iv, 45. 1954

1954 Non-Parl. Min. of Agric. & Fish.

In 1953 the total pig population in Britain exceeded that of Denmark, but home produced bacon cost 60 per cent more than imported bacon. The Ministry of Food lost £25 mn. on the home product, but made £11 mn. profit on imported bacon. In Denmark one-fifth of the population is engaged in farming against one-twentieth here, there are two acres per head of the population as against two-thirds per person here. Denmark provides all her own food and exports a considerable amount, so that the Danish farmer operates in an atmosphere of severe competition. A higher proportion of labour is provided by the farmer and his wife, and there are fewer opportunities for farm labour to move into the towns. While in Denmark pig farming is uniform and intensive, here it is often a minor enterprise, and much of the expansion since 1945 suggests that pig production has been taken up by the farmer with no previous experience.

Other factors affecting the differences in price are that in Denmark 15·5 pigs per sow per year are reared to slaughter as compared with 12·2 in Britain, cereal prices are lower and the farmers mix and balance their own rations. Labour costs are lower. Eighty per cent of all milk produced in Denmark goes for butter and the skim milk feeds the pigs. National elite herds receive a subsidy and progeny testing stations test the results of elite breeding. Breeding pigs, especially boars, are sold from elite herds, farmers' co-operatives operate most of the bacon factories and they are active in the feeding-stuffs trade. Many farmers and farm workers have education at the farm institute level.

A considerable improvement is possible in pig breeding in this country. A levy of one shilling a pig for ten years would yield £250,000, which could be used for progeny testing stations.

Export and Slaughter of Horses

Dept. Cttee. Rep., apps. pp. iv, 36. 1950

1950 Cmd. 7888, xii, 9
apptd. April, sgd. Dec., 1949

Lord Rosebery (*Ch.*), Mitchell, L. Digby, Ganley, Price-White.

The Exportation of Horses Act, 1937, provided that no horse should be exported unless it was under eight years old, or in the case of a heavy draught horse worth more than £25, or of a vanner £20. This brought to an end the export of horses for slaughter, but since 1945 these values have not prevented export, as an importer pays up to £60 for a horse intended for slaughter. Export of horses should cease; they should not be sent abroad to be slaughtered in places where the British Government has no control.

Shortage of meat and the large supply of redundant horses has led to a great increase in the consumption of horse flesh in this country. In 1948 some 130,000 horses were killed, whilst the number on agricultural holdings alone declined from 1,083,000 in 1939 to 617,000 in 1949. As the present demand for working horses is not sufficient to keep up a breeding nucleus, an outlet is needed through the slaughter of horses for human consumption. But breeding for this purpose alone would be at the expense of the more economical way of producing meat by breeding cattle and sheep.

Licences for the export of a certain number of horse carcases to the Continent should be allowed to keep the trade open; the values for exported horses should be raised to £80 a draught horse, £75 for vanners, mules and jennets and £10 for asses; the slaughter for human consumption should be allowed to continue and price control removed. Breeding for slaughter should be discouraged. Detailed recommendations are made to bring the slaughter, etc., of horses under the same kind of regulations as apply to the slaughter, etc., of other animals used for human consumption. Amendments to the Transit of Animals Order are also proposed.

Slaughter of Horses

Cttee. Rep., apps. pp. 56. 1953

1952–53 *Cmd.* 8925, *xvii*, 343
apptd. Oct., 1952. *sgd.* Aug., 1953
Duke of Northumberland (*Ch.*), Alldridge, L. Digby, Grundy, Jarvis, Mitchell, Thompson.

'To consider the law and the practice thereunder relating to the slaughter of horses in slaughterhouses and knackers' yards and to recommend whether any further safeguards should be introduced to ensure the humane slaughtering of horses in this country.'

By tradition this is a separate trade and has not become integrated with the accepted business of slaughtering animals. Premises have been situated away from public gaze and are associated with Knackery. The rapid expansion of the business of slaughtering horses for food led to the suspicion that the newcomers in the trade were interested in making money without regard to the law or the humane handling of horses. People linked 'illicit trade' with 'illegal methods of slaughter'. The evidence indicated that most slaughterhouses used for the slaughter of horses were old and generally unsuited for the purpose and that the risk of cruelty arose in the main from conditions under which horses were brought to slaughter rather than from the methods of slaughter. The law relating to the methods is sound, but that relating to the physical conditions should be extended and expressed in greater detail. There are 23 recommendations, including making licences of horse slaughter houses conditional on compliance with minimum standards.

See *Slaughter of Animals (Amendment) Act, 1954;* 2 & 3 Eliz. 2. c. 59.

Meat Inspection

Inter-Dept. Cttee. Rep., apps. pp. 56.
1951
1951 *Non-Parl. Min. of Food*
apptd. May, 1949. *sgd.* Feb., 1951

G. R. Oake (*Ch.*), Barnell, Butcher, Cameron, Grace, Howat, Lethem, Menzies, Sturdee, Vigor.

The Food and Drugs Act, 1938,

empowers an officer of the local authority to examine meat sold or to be sold for human consumption, and if he thinks it unfit it is usually surrendered voluntarily. The Public Health (Meat) Regulations, 1924–48, prohibit the slaughter of any cattle, pigs, sheep or goats unless specified requirements are met, including notification of the time of slaughter, and include provisions on slaughterhouses, sale of meat, etc. Memo. 62/Foods 1922 made recommendations regarding the details of inspection of carcases, etc. In 1940 the slaughter of livestock and the distribution of meat was controlled by the Government, livestock and meat at slaughterhouses becoming Crown property. The number of slaughterhouses was reduced and responsibility for inspection was concentrated on the local authorities where these slaughterhouses functioned. This concentration made inspection easier in some places, but in others it was inadequate through lack of trained inspectors, etc. In many of the slaughterhouses the physical conditions fall far short of the minimum standards.

All animals should be inspected ante mortem at the place of slaughter, and every carcase, its organs and viscera should be examined; slaughterhouse design should provide for this; cattle should be rested before slaughter, meat not for sale should be inspected, meat inspection records should be kept as in Scotland; the operation of a system of compulsory meat inspection should be considered by the local authorities and departments concerned. Veterinary surgeons should be appointed as senior inspectors and sanitary inspectors should hold the certificate of competency to discharge the duties of an inspector of meat. Public Health Regulations should apply to horse flesh and all meat products. Registration of retail butchers' shops should be related to suitability, open stalls prohibited, covered market stalls and mobile shops registered. Regulations should cover wrappers for meat in transit, hygiene of the workers, etc.

Slaughterhouses (England and Wales)

Inter-Dept. Cttee. Interim Rep. pp. 16.
1954
1953–54 *Cmd.* 9060, *xix*, 163
apptd. Feb., sgd. Dec., 1953

R. Herbert (*Ch.*), Crawford, Engholm, Lythgoe, Summers, Twinch.

'*To prepare a plan recommending in what localities, subject to a policy of moderate concentration, slaughterhouses (other than in bacon factories) should be sited . . . and to report on the changes that may be necessary in existing legislation to secure the central regulation of siting and design of slaughter-houses.*'

Before 1939 there were in use in England and Wales some 11,500 slaughterhouses. By 1953, under the control scheme, these had been reduced to 482, of which 119 are public and 358 are privately owned slaughterhouses and 5 were built by the Government after 1950. As this number is not sufficient to provide facilities for a free marketing system, some pre-war slaughterhouses may have to be licensed in the interim period before a pro-gramme of 'moderate concentration of slaughterhouses' can become effective. Local Authorities should be responsible for ensuring that there is sufficient slaughter accommodation in their dis-trict, for licensing private slaughter-houses in the interim period, and should have powers to acquire private slaughterhouses which could provide public slaughtering facilities. Where a local authority is of the opinion that there are sufficient slaughtering facili-ties, it should have powers to revoke a licence. Compensation for redundant slaughterhouses should be on the basis of the diminution in the value of the land and buildings consequent upon the prohibition.

See *Slaughtering of Livestock.* Economic Advisory Council. Cttee. (Lord De la Warr, *Ch.*). Rep.; 1933 Non-Parl. Treasury. *Slaughterhouses Act, 1954*; 2 & 3 Eliz. 2 c. 42.

—— Report, apps. pp. 68. 1955.
1955–56 *Cmd.* 9542, *xxvii,* 653
sgd. July, 1955

Government control over marketing and slaughtering came to an end and new methods of meat trading and slaughtering through national or regional organisations made it essential that these should have accommodation and services under their own control. The Committee therefore recommended that the main purpose of securing hygiene could be obtained by leaving private traders free to provide slaughter-houses, subject to prescribed statutory standards and normal planning require-ments. This recommendation is ac-cepted. Minimum statutory standards will be prescribed and applied to new buildings, and to existing buildings at dates to be appointed. Local authori-ties will submit slaughterhouse schemes to the Minister and in the meantime applications for licences for new and modernised slaughterhouses conform-ing to the standards should be accepted.

See *Slaughterhouses.* A policy to regulate the provision of slaughter-houses in England and Wales; 1955–56 Cmd. 9761, xxxvi, 961.

——(Scotland)

Inter-Dept. Cttee. Interim Rep. pp. 8.
1954
1953–54 *Cmd.* 9061, *xix,* 179
apptd. March, 1953, *sgd. Jan.,* 1954

J. J. W. Handford (*Ch.*), Howat, Mac-Farlane, Menzies, Paterson, Whitby.

Before 1939 some 737 slaughter-houses operated in Scotland, of which 147 were provided by local authorities and 590 by private interests. In 1953 there are 88 in use, of which 86 are owned by public authorities, so that practically the whole service is provided by public slaughterhouses. Responsi-bility for providing sufficient accom-modation should be placed on local authorities. They should have power to acquire, to revoke or to refuse to grant or renew licences on grounds of redundancy subject to right of appeal and subject to compensation on closure.

—— Report, apps. pp. 48. 1955
1954–55 Cmd. 9376, vii, 465
sgd. Dec., 1954

The responsibility for securing an adequate slaughtering service should remain with local authorities, the creation of a new central authority not being justified. Scotland should be divided into slaughterhouse areas defined by county boundaries and administered by a combined county and burghal authority. Slaughterhouse schemes should be prepared by these authorities and approved by the Secretary of State. The lines on which a long term policy of moderate concentration could be effected are indicated. Other recommendations concern siting, facilities, design, improved transport of animals and meat, etc.

4. DISEASES. WILD ANIMALS

Cruelty to Wild Animals

Cttee. Rep., apps. pp. vii, 120. [1951]
1950–51 Cmd. 8266, viii, 425
apptd. June, 1949. sgd. April, 1951

J. S. Henderson (*Ch.*), Brandon, Brown, Burn-Murdock, Cripps, Medawar, Pitt (Miss F.), Pugh.

'*To enquire into practices or activities which may involve cruelty to British Wild Mammals, whether at large or in captivity, including anything occurring in the pursuit or capture of such animals for purposes of sport or food, or done to control their numbers or to destroy them. . . .*'

Two Bills, The Protection of Animals (Hunting and Coursing Prohibition) Bill and the Prohibition of Fox Hunting Bill, led to the appointment of the Committee. Some control is necessary for most wild animals if they are not to become a pest, and if the method chosen does not inflict unnecessary suffering such methods should not be considered cruel. Control by a

sporting activity should not be regarded as cruel if the degree of suffering is no greater than is caused by the use of other methods. The general law relating to cruelty is contained in the Protection of Animals Acts, 1911, 1927, and is defined as 'an act which causes unnecessary suffering'. Animal is defined as 'any domestic or captive animal' which means that, in their wild state, animals have no protection at all.

The methods used for controlling wild animals may be concerned solely with their destruction, or may combine destruction with sport, and they may, in both cases, be used to provide food. But the problem of control is that some of the most effective methods used involve suffering, although in the long run where breeding is kept in check, there may be less total cruelty. Shooting if it kills outright is one of the most humane methods of control, but this does not always happen and a great deal of suffering may be involved. Control through field sport involves no greater suffering than the alternative methods of trapping, gassing, poisoning, etc., and the Committee was satisfied that the British Field Sports Society and the controlling bodies of other individual field sports do take precautions to see that no avoidable suffering is caused. Nevertheless, there does not exist any legal protection for a wild animal.

Recommended that all wild animals should be covered by the Act, so that action could be taken against any person who causes or permits unnecessary suffering to a wild animal. But nothing should apply to the commission or omission of any act in the course of hunting, etc., or attempted destruction of any wild animal, unless such hunting, etc., were accompanied by unnecessary suffering. Hunting, etc., of any deer, fox, hare or other animal for the purpose of sport should be lawful while conducted under the approved rules of the sport; to reduce suffering, field sports organisations should amend their rules, which should be submitted to a central authority for approval. Gin traps should be banned; the design of spring traps should be approved; snares should not be used to catch deer; the British Field Sports Society should issue a pamphlet on the proper use of guns, and poisons and gassing methods should be controlled. No prohibition was recommended for hunting the fox, hare, otter and the badger, but precautions were suggested which would prevent the hunted from suffering unnecessarily. To reduce cruelty caused by deer poaching, powers of search, etc., as for game should be applied. There should also be a closed season for deer. Suggestions were also made for more humane ways of killing badgers, rabbits, stoats and weasels, rats, moles and seals.

See *Poaching of Deer (Scotland) Bill* [H.L.]; 1951-52 (Bill 94) iii, 609.

Foot-and-Mouth Disease

Dept. Cttee. Rep., apps. pp. 151. 1954
1953-54 *Cmd. 9214, xiii,* 561
apptd. Sept., 1952. *sgd. July,* 1954

E. A. Gowers (*Ch.*), Adrian, Cator, Griffith, L. Hungarton, Robertson, Semple, Woolley.

'*To review the policy and arrangements for dealing with foot-and-mouth disease in Great Britain and to advise whether any changes should be made in the light of present scientific knowledge and the technical and administrative experience gained in recent years in this and other countries.*'

The direct loss in Europe of the 1951-52 epidemic was £143 mn., but the indirect losses were probably greater. Mortality is not high but, especially in dairy cattle, there may be such serious after-effects as loss of condition and yield of milk, abortion, sterility, heart affections, loss of hooves, chronic lameness, etc. Cloven-footed animals show little resistance, an animal may have more than one attack and every diseased animal is an active producer of virus often so infectious that the disease spreads with appalling speed. It would soon become endemic in any country which did not take rigorous measures, and in this country the milk supply would be endangered. The disease is almost world wide, the comparative immunity of New Zealand, Australia, Canada, U.S.A. and Ireland being partly due to favourable geographical positions and partly to stringent regulations; over most of the rest of the world it is endemic. Although the pattern is not quite the same in each European country, epidemics show that it has been impossible to localise the disease because of its extraordinary infectivity, which remains as it was 30 years ago. In England the average number of outbreaks in 25 years was 129; the lowest number 8 in 1930, and the highest, 670 in 1942. The 1952 epidemic, with 495 outbreaks, started in Yorkshire and in Essex, and the disease moved round the coast to Devonshire reflecting a similar movement on the continent. This led to the inference that it constantly crossed the sea. The uncontrollable agents of infection which are suspected are birds and the wind; the controllable ones, for which the various Orders seemed to have been effective, are imported animals, carcases and meat. Hay and straw brought in as packing material are not allowed to come into contact with animals susceptible to the disease. Swill has not come under the Order although scraps of contaminated meat in the swill-tub have infected pigs. Persons and motor vehicles arriving from the Continent have been suspected of carrying the virus, but no disinfection methods have yet been used.

Slaughtering is still the most effective means of stamping out the disease. As no vaccine operates against all the various types of virus, the length of immunity is not certain, and some masked infection is suspected before immunity operates, or when immunity is breaking down. Any idea of making the whole cattle population immune is in the realm of fantasy.

The recommendations are concerned with detailed steps for making the present policy more effective, e.g. defining an affected area, signposting it, artificial insemination in the infected area, closing roads, restricting movements of animals, etc. Slaughter should include contact animals and these should not be salvaged for human consumption; slaughterhouse offal should not be spread on the ground; all waste food should be sterilised before being given to animals; there should be more education and more publicity about the disease. In addition to reporting suspected foot-and-mouth disease, farmers should report any illness in an infected area. Penalties for delayed reporting and compensation for slaughter are dealt with. Compensation should continue to be the market value of the animal slaughtered; there should be no compensation for consequential losses.

See *Foot-and-Mouth Disease Research*. Interim Rep.; 1952 Non-Parl. Agric. Research Council. *Foot-and-Mouth Disease Research Institute, 1937–1953*. Rep.; [?1954] The Institute, Pirbright, Surrey.

Close Seasons for Deer in Scotland

Cttee. Rep., apps. pp. 79. 1954

1953–54 *Cmd.* 9273, x, 337
apptd. July, 1952. *sgd. May, June,* 1954

R. H. Maconochie (*Ch.*), Adair, Chalmers, L. Glentanar, McBoyle, McDiarmid, Murray, Nicholson, Ritchie.

'*To consider the desirability of introducing a close season or seasons for deer in Scotland and the manner in which, and the safeguards for agricultural and other interests under which, any close season or seasons should be made effective.*'

Majority Report.—As agreement could not be reached regarding the 'close season' the Poaching of Deer Bill was delayed in Parliament pending this report. The arguments for the close season included: the red deer is the largest of our indigenous wild animals and should be preserved; the deer population is falling rapidly; they are of economic value, are economical to maintain and need no shepherding, dipping or inoculating; they have a

grazing niche in the ecology of the Highlands and complementary grazing is good for the grazings; the damage to agriculture is local, capable of local solution. Between 1939 and 1952 the number of deer in forests fell from about 130,000 to 85,000, while sheep increased from 50,000 to 141,700.

Against a close season it is argued that very great damage is done to agriculture and the close period proposed is just when most damage is done; that the value of deer is negligible compared with that of sheep and cattle. While deer stocks are lower than before 1939, they are beyond the number which the deer forests under present conditions can carry and they overflow on to the winter keep of sheep and cattle.

Colonised deer and marauding deer should be exterminated, where in the opinion of the Regional Deer Control Board there is no other remedy; there should be a statutory close season for stags from 21st October to 30th June and for hinds from 16th February to 20th October. There should be a committee to form rules for the improved management of deer, five Regional Deer Control Boards based on the main concentrations and an Advisory Committee to guide the Secretary of State on matters relating to control, preservation and protection of red deer.

Minority Report.—McDiarmid, Murray, Nicholson.

The imposition of a statutory close season should be deferred until agricultural interests have been safeguarded and there has been a considerable reduction of the deer population, and marauding and colonised deer have been exterminated. Loss of winter grazings is considerable because the marauders number not tens and twenties, but hundreds. Their competitive grazing habits are established from post-mortem examination of deers' stomachs which show that their main diet is soft green grass which they select and eat separately. Involuntary over-stocking causes risk of disease as deer are the natural reservoirs of louping ill and red water and are hosts for certain types of fluke worm, liver fluke and are susceptible to foot-and-mouth disease, etc.

Myxomatosis

Advisory Cttee. Rep., apps. pp. iv, 13. 1954. 2nd Rep., app. pp. ii, 6. 1955
1954, 1955 *Non-Parl. Min. of Agric. & Fish., Dept. of Agric., Scot.*
apptd. Nov., 1953. sgd. March, 1954. Jan., 1955

Lord Carrington (*Ch.*), and 15 others, 1st Rep. Lord St. Aldwyn (*Ch.*), and 14 others, 2nd Rep.

'*To advise on the problems arising in connection with myxomatosis in rabbits and the action that should be taken by the Government.*'

The report reviews the history of the disease. The first recorded outbreak in this country was in Kent in 1953; all attempts to isolate the infection failed and by 1954 it had spread to every county in Great Britain except Selkirk. The industry supplied 35,000–40,000 rabbits a year for medical purposes. The income of the rabbit meat and of the fur, felt and hat trades may be about £15 mn. (of which agriculture receives only £2 mn.), while the rabbits cause an estimated loss of cereals of £15 mn., of grass of £21 mn., and in damage to trees and prevention of natural regeneration of at least £2 mn.; the potential loss is four or five times the income. Attempts to restrict the spread of the disease would serve no practical purpose. Partly for humanitarian reasons, no attempt should be made to spread or introduce it into unaffected areas. The disease should be allowed to run its course. Mortality is high and every advantage should be taken to eliminate survivors before they build up in numbers. Importation of the cotton tail rabbit should be prohibited, and consideration given to the protection of the domestic rabbits. Where rabbits have been eliminated there has been a marked improvement in vegetation, but in chalk downs they will have to be replaced by cattle or sheep, otherwise coarse grass or scrub will make the land valueless.

Second Report.—No useful purpose would be served by making the deliberate spread of the disease an offence, and such a law would be difficult to enforce. The Government accepted an amendment to the Pest Bill making it an offence: two members of the Committee resigned. Further assistance should be given to occupiers in eliminating survivors.

5. FORESTRY

Post-War Forest Policy

Forestry Com. Rep., apps. pp. 114. 1943
1942–43 *Cmd.* 6447, iv, 419
sgd. Feb., 1943
R. L. Robinson (*Ch.*), Bannerman, Courthope, L. Moray, Price, Quibell, L. Radnor, Ropner, Steel, Taylor.

After the wholesale exploitation of the woodlands which began again in 1939 the Forestry Commissioners found themselves in the same position as the Acland Committee in 1918 (*Breviate 1917–39*, p. 138). Despite disturbances and checks, of the Acland proposals 88 per cent of the acquisition and 75 per cent of the planting were accomplished. A larger reserve of standing timber could have been made available by control of felling.

It is common prudence to make certain of producing at home one-third of our probable peace-time requirements. Over a period of 50 years 5 mn. acres should be devoted to effective forest, by the afforestation of 3 mn. acres of bare ground and the development of 2 mn. acres of existing woodlands which are better suited for forestry than for any other purpose. The desirable programme for the first decade, involving the maximum practicable effort would mean planting 1,100,000 acres at a cost of £41·2 mn.; a lower, intermediate programme would be 875,000 acres costing £32 mn., the deficiency being made good in subsequent decades. In the unstable condition of the last half century private plantings declined. Private woodlands within the 2 mn. acres should either be dedicated to forestry and worked on an approved plan of operations, in which case the owners should receive State assistance up to 25 per cent of net expenditure until the woods were self-supporting, or should be acquired by the State. The war-time system of felling licences should be continued until a reserve of standing timber had been built up. Proposals for guaranteed prices were impracticable. There should be one Forestry Authority for Great Britain and in view of the close relations with private owners, a Private Woodlands Committee.

—— Supplementary Report, **Private Woodlands**

apps. pp. 11. 1944
1943–44 *Cmd.* 6500, *iii*, 323
sgd. Nov., 1943

del. Moray.

The Government made it clear that it did not propose to make a decision on private woodlands until the private owners' point of view had been considered. A representative conference was called at which the main recommendation was endorsed. The importance of the private woodlands was shown by the fact that only 4 per cent to 5 per cent of the total standing utilisable timber at the beginning of the war was due to direct State planting. The scheme for dedication was approved, but as the proposed grant of 25 per cent of expenditure was felt not to meet the varied costs of different areas, the owner should have the option of a planting grant of £7 10s. od. per acre, loans and maintenance grants of 2s. 6d. per acre for 15 years. The original estimates of cost of £2 was confirmed.

See *Census of Woodlands*, 1947–49. Summary Rep.; 1951 Non-Parl. Forestry Com.

New Forest

Cttee. Rep., apps. pp. 104. 1947
1947–48 *Cmd.* 7245, *xiv*, 79
apptd. April, 1946. *sgd. May*, 1947

H. T. Baker (*Ch.*), L. Lucas, Langley-Taylor.

'*To investigate the state and condition of the New Forest and, having due regard to existing rights and interests, to recommend such measures as they consider desirable and necessary for adjusting the Forest to modern requirements.*'

To the long conflict between forestry and the commoners' interests in stock raising which still persists in some parts, has been added a third, public concern for the preservation of the open space, the forest scenery and the natural reserve. The Forest is unique and the conflict makes it imperative that there should be a body representing all three interests.

The Forest covers 27,658 acres of private and 64,707 acres of Crown lands, of which 23,783 acres are woodlands and 39,946 open heath. There are about 2004 commoners, but the common rights, of which pasture and mast are the main, run with the land. The number of cattle turned out in 1946 was 4171, though the Forest could carry up to 8000 animals. The 8708 acres still enclosed by the Services and Departments call for urgent attention.

The administration of the Forest is delegated to the Forestry Commission by the Ministry of Agriculture and Fisheries, which by the Forestry Act, 1945, has taken the place of the Crown. The ancient Court of Verderers, comprised of six members elected by the Parliamentary voters and an appointed Chairman have the duty of controlling the grazing and health of animals, removing animals not belonging to verderers, regulating common rights, etc. The property qualification for election is too exclusive, and it does not represent the three clashing interests. For purposes of local government the Forest is divided between two rural district councils, and a small portion under the Lymington Borough Council. But with the growth of urban population in districts adjacent to the Forest and the development of main roads and forest roads in general, giving access to cars, planning in the Forest as a whole becomes important. With the central idea of the preservation of the Forest in mind a conference was called in 1937 by the Chairman of the Forestry Commission and a Planning Officers Committee was formed.

The Court of Verderers should become the Council of Verderers, composed of representatives from the bodies connected with administration in the Forest. There should be a single rural district council which, together with the Borough Council of Lymington should be the planning authority. In the statutory enclosures natural regeneration and artificial regeneration in small groups should be practised in preference to large scale plantation. The effect on the landscape should be considered and conifer plantations disguised by planting of broadleaved species. To enable use to be made of unproductive land unfit for grazing but usable for forestry, the Verderers should be empowered to offer to the Forestry Commission the suspension of common rights over a maximum of 5000 acres, to be retained for a minimum of one rotation. Power should be given to make enclosures for regeneration of ancient and ornamental woods. The Forestry Commission's duties regarding wayleaves and easement drains and bridges are specified. War-time encroachments should cease. The existing Register of Claims should be replaced by an atlas showing the lands with rights of common in 1854. The Verderers should decide and control commoners' rights regarding animals. The whole Forest should be declared a nature reserve. In addition to existing camping arrangements, there should be three communal camps of not more than six acres. Road development as proposed in the Report of the Planning Officers, 1945, should be adopted.

See *Protection of the New Forest*. Cttee. Rep.; 1939 Non-Parl. Forestry Com. *New Forest Bill* [HL.]. Scl. Cttee. HL. Mins. of ev.; 1948–49 (HL.54) v, 327. *New Forest Act, 1949;* 12 & 13 Geo. 6. c. 69.

Forestry

Advisory Cttee. 1st Rep., apps. pp. 8. 1954. 2nd Rep., apps. pp. 16. 1955
1954, 1955 Non-Parl. Min. of Works apptd. April, 1954. sgd. Sept., 1954. May, 1955

W. Taylor (*Ch.*), Gardner, L. Hurcomb, Le Sueur, Macdonald, Salisbury.

'*To advise on forestry policy and on special problems of felling and planting of trees.*'

The two Reports deal with the condition of the trees in the Royal Parks and recommendations are made concerning care, protection and future plantings. Care should be taken to maintain the English landscape and the advantages of planting oaks, hornbeam, beech, ash, etc., should be observed.

Timber and Plywood, 1949-1953

1949 Non-Parl.

See *Trade and Industry*, p. 151.

6. DRAINAGE, COAST PROTECTION, RIVER POLLUTION

Water

3rd Rep., **River Boards**

1942–43 Cmd. 6465

See *Water*, p. 190.

Prevention of River Pollution

Central Advisory Water Cttee. Sub-Cttee. Rep., apps. pp. 76. 1949
1949 Non-Parl. Min. of Health apptd. June, 1946. sgd. —.

S. R. Hobday (*Ch.*), Bray, Chaston, Ellen, Johnson, Kissane, Newman, Scorer, Sims-Hilditch, Winter.

'*To investigate measures for strengthening the law regarding the prevention of pollution of rivers and streams.*'

The recommendations in the 3rd Report of the Milne Committee on *Water* (*River Boards*, see p. 190) on the concentration of powers in the hands of River Boards have been given effect in the River Boards Act, 1948. But as the River Pollution Prevention Act, 1876, is still the main provision for preventing pollution some drastic revision in its drafting, and its definitions of types of pollutions, is needed when the River Boards take over its administration.

The Act of 1876 should be repealed, and a comprehensive code embodied in a new Act, of which the provisions in the Act of 1923 relating to pollution affecting fisheries, should form a separate part. There should be a comprehensive provision making it an offence to allow offensive or injurious matter, solid or fluid, to enter a stream (a reservation relating to mine water should be retained pending technical investigation). The River Boards should prescribe minimum standards for purity, temperatures, and innocuous discolouratives by byelaws, subject to confirmation by the Minister, but before fixing such a standard, a completed survey of a stream or part of a stream should be submitted to the Minister. New openings into streams should be controlled, and tidal waters included in an Act. The River Board should be empowered to make byelaws prohibiting the washing of cloth, wool, leather or skin and to control the washing of animals in any part of a stream, to inspect vessels to see if injurious matter is passing or can pass from them; and have power to complain to the Minister if a local authority does not carry out its powers regarding its duty to cleanse earth-closets, privies, ash-pits, or cesspools in any part of their district which is liable to flooding. Recommendations for proceedings by the River Board are outlined. The Public Health Act, 1936, should be amended to empower the Minister of Health to form a united district for sewage without application from any proposed constituent authority, and to require the communication of a sewer of one authority to that of another authority at such points as he may consider reasonable. There should be an inter-departmental scientific committee to advise on tests to which standards for polluting liquids should be related and on fixing standards of temperature for controlling heated discharges.

See *Rivers* (*Prevention of Pollution*) *Act, 1951;* 14 & 15 Geo. 6. c. 64.

Prevention of Pollution of Rivers and other Waters

Scottish Water Advisory Cttee. Sub-Cttee. Rep., apps. pp. 36. 1950

1950–51 *Cmd.* 8111, *xix*, 135
apptd. Nov., 1946. *sgd. Sept.*, 1950

H. B. Lindsay (*Ch.*), Carlile, Cozens-Hardy, Duncan, Fyfe, McBoyle, Malloch, Mann, L. Mansfield, Ronald, Taylor, Young.

'*To consider any necessary amendments to the law of prevention of rivers pollution.*'

Since the development of modern methods of treatment there has been no real excuse for the pollution of rivers by sewage, but the problem of trade waste is not so simple. Apart from effluents such as those from paper mills, for which a wholly practicable means of treatment at reasonable cost has not yet been devised, pollution need be tolerated only in the case of existing industries, or where there is no alternative location and then only if the best practicable and available means of treatment have been provided. In the case of new industries the solution forms part of the planning stage. What is now required is the acceptance of the general principle that clean rivers are as necessary as clean streets and that where pollution can be avoided the law should provide a workable code administered by responsible authorities, and that where pollution is not preventable there should be unremitting scientific research. The law should be amended to bring under control certain pollutions at present exempt, to include tidal waters, to give industry the right to discharge suitable trade waste waters and effluents into local authority sewerage systems, to widen areas of administration, reduce the number of authorities, and to institute standards regulating the discharge of effluents into rivers and tidal waters. Details of areas of administration, of the composition of the new authorities, and the determination of standards of purity, etc., are outlined.

See *Rivers (Prevention of Pollution) (Scotland) Act, 1951; 14 & 15 Geo. 6. c. 66.*

Land Drainage (Scotland)

Cttee. Rep., apps. pp. 26. 1950

1950 *Cmd.* 7948, *xii*, 677
apptd. July, 1947. *sgd. Dec.,* 1949

J. F. Duncan (*Ch.*), Campbell, Graham, McGlashan, Nicholson, Robertson, Sullivan.

'*To review the operation of drainage schemes carried out in Scotland under the Agriculture Act, 1937, the Land Drainage (Scotland) Acts, the Agriculture (Miscellaneous Provisions) Acts, and emergency wartime powers; to examine the extent to which further large scale drainage work is necessary and desirable in the interests of efficient agriculture. . . .*'

Apart from one or two major drainage works surviving from monastic times, the principal drainage systems in Scotland came into being from 1750 onwards. In essentials the old systems are perfectly sound and the task of the drainage engineer is to improve them to meet modern conditions, as well as to devise new systems. Some 200,000 acres, that is about 5 per cent of the arable area, suffer from inadequate drainage, and the statutory powers have become quite unsatisfactory for carrying out any new large scale drainage work by compulsion, since there is a statutory limit to cost of £10 per acre. The

Secretary of State, acting through the Department of Agriculture, should be the one responsible drainage authority, but where drainage affects non-agricultural interests, for example, roads and railways, the Secretary of State should be empowered to bring the interests concerned together with a view to co-operation in carrying out comprehensive schemes. The Secretary of State (acting through the Dept. of Agriculture) should be empowered to prepare schemes of main arterial works. Where the cost of a scheme is not more than £20 per acre, the proprietors should pay an amount equal to the assessed betterment (provided that this does not exceed £10 per acre or half the cost of the scheme whichever is the lesser amount) and the rest should be borne by State funds. If the cost is more than £20 per acre, the tribunal of enquiry should determine the proportions to be paid by owners and the State. Legislation should provide similar arrangements for maintenance work. The new drainage code should include specific reference to minor matters such as weeds, ground game and vermin. The drainage authority should have powers to remove weirs, control new obstructions and control the fouling of streams by effluents.

Drainage of Trade Premises

Cttee. Rep., app. pp. 15. 1954

1953–54 *Cmd.* 9117, *xi*, 545
apptd. —. sgd. Jan., 1954

L. H. Watson (*Ch.*), Andrew, Banks, Black, Burns, McBoyle, McGinniss, Storrar, Young.

'*To consider on what conditions and subject to what financial arrangements industry should be entitled to discharge trade waste waters and effluents into local authority sewerage systems, and to make recommendations.*'

The Rivers (Prevention of Pollution) (Scotland) Act, 1951, provided for the setting up of Boards which might require a higher standard of purity of effluents at present being discharged into rivers, and brought the Clyde and Forth Estuaries within its scope. The new legislation may lead local authorities into additional expense in treating the contents of their sewers. Section 7 of the Rivers Pollution Act, 1876, as it affected Scotland had been left intact, but the legal position is not clear and is unsatisfactory.

As regards new and additional trade effluents, owners and occupiers of trade premises should have the right to connect to and discharge into public sewers, subject to the safeguards that the local authority should have the right to refuse substances and to make conditions on quality and quantity and to negotiate charges. As regards existing effluents, owners may have written agreements, perpetual or terminable, or consent without written agreement, some involving no charge, and the question is whether such existing rights should be over-ridden by legislation. Perpetual and terminable agreements should be open to revision on notification by either party, subject to having to show the relationship of the proposals to the requirements of the Act; when an agreement terminates the local authority should indicate its terms for renewal, consideration being given to former agreements. Where there is no formal agreement, the local authority's terms should have regard to existing practice, and how they are affected by the Act. Increase in the volume of effluents should be treated as for a new industry; change in composition should be notified and terms re-negotiated. Laundries should not be exempt, as it was thought that any charge would be small.

Land Drainage in England and Wales

Central Advisory Water Cttee. Sub-Cttee. Rep., apps. pp. xi, 100. 1951
1951 *Non-Parl. Min. of Agric. & Fish. apptd. Feb.*, 1947. *sgd.* —.

A. P. Heneage (*Ch.*), Bray, Cemlyn-Jones, Hirst, Hobday, McClean, Newman, Toye, Winter, Worth.

'*To consider proposals and make recommendations for the amendment and modernisation of the law relating to Land Drainage in England and Wales.*'

The Land Drainage Act, 1930, provided for the establishment of catchment boards for the whole watershed areas of individual rivers or groups of rivers, and for the precepting of all local authorities within the watershed areas. By 1949 there were 53 statutory catchment boards and 360 internal drainage districts. The River Boards Act, 1948, carried this a stage further by providing that the whole of England and Wales should be covered by water boards, which will take over the powers under existing legislation of catchment boards, fishing boards and pollution prevention authorities. The task of the Committee was to make proposals for the modernisation of the land drainage powers that will be exercised by river boards in succession to catchment boards. The areas of the boards vary greatly in size and strength, and owing to derating, agricultural land outside internal drainage districts does not contribute to the cost of drainage works on main rivers. Provision has to be made for capital works and maintenance of lesser watercourses not the main river of a water board and outside an internal drainage district.

The responsibility for watercourses should lie with the river boards, for drains with the internal drainage boards, and for ditches with the owners or occupiers. To enable the river boards to meet their new responsibilities, all land within their areas should contribute, in the case of hereditaments not assessed to general or drainage rates, by a drainage charge levied at a uniform rate on occupiers. The boards should have power to collect additional contributions from authorities and owners in specified circumstances. Internal drainage boards should continue to levy a uniform rate and have power to make differential rates. River boards and internal drainage boards should prepare schemes determining the watercourses and ditches respectively for which they are responsible. There are many recommendations on the powers and duties and relationship of the various boards.

Coastal Flooding

Dept. Cttee. Rep., apps. pp. 48. 1954. [Interim Rep. See App. A also printed separately; 1952–53 Cmd. 8923, xi]

1953–54 *Cmd. 9165, xiii, 511*
apptd. April, 1953. sgd. April, 1954

Lord Waverley (*Ch.*), Dobson, Fergusson, Gwyther, Inglis, Leach, Neven-Spence, Proudman, Quartermaine, L. De Ramsey, Steers, Thomas, Wrigley, Yates.

'(*i*) *to examine the causes of the recent floods and the possibilities of a recurrence in Great Britain; (ii) to consider what margin of safety for sea defences would be reasonable and practicable . . .; (iii) to consider whether any further measures should be taken. . . .*'

Interim report on the warning system, signed July, 1953, printed as App. A. The floods were caused by a combination of a fairly high tide of the ordinary type with a very high rise of sea-level, due mainly to exceptionally strong winds over the North Sea. Such a rise of the sea-level is called a surge. Most surges have not caused flooding because they have not synchronised with that of high water; even the recent flood would have been worse if the maximum surge had been nearer the time of high water, if the ordinary tide had been as high as it had been two weeks earlier and was two weeks later, or if there had been more water coming down the rivers. Studies of the phenomena need to be carried out. For the warning system tidal gauges should be fixed at Aberdeen, Leith, Tyne Entrance, Immingham, Lowestoft and Harwich. Throughout the warning season the Harbour Masters should report the water levels to the Central Forecasting Office, which should disseminate information throughout a warning period to the River Boards and the County Police Forces, who should transmit it through channels planned by local co-operative effort. The warning system should operate on the east coast between 15th September and 30th April.

Report.—This amplifies the interim report on the causes and possibility of recurrence of floods. Researches should be undertaken into certain oceanographic questions, the suitability of vegetation for use on sand and shingle, the movements of beach material, etc. The cost of complete protection against every conceivable combination of wind and tide would be prohibitive. The maximum standard of protection should be that sufficient to withstand the floods of January 1953 and should be provided where large areas of agricultural land would be endangered or industrial property and concentrated residential property of high value seriously damaged. Elsewhere the standard should be that thought sufficient before the floods. Anyone requiring a higher standard should pay for it. There are detailed recommendations on the distribution of the administrative and financial responsibilities between the various authorities. The maximum grant to River Boards and coast protection authorities should be 85 per cent, and expenditure on the maintenance of River Board's defences should be eligible for grants up to 50 per cent. Town planning powers should be used to prevent sporadic and ill-considered development near the coast.

7. FISHING

Herring Industry

Cttee. Rep., apps. pp. 39. 1944

1943–44 *Cmd. 6503, iii, 415*
apptd. Jan., 1942. sgd. Jan., 1944

W. E. Elliot (*Ch.*), Bell, Bracey, Carstairs, Edwards, Hillman, Watt.

'*To review the position of the herring industry and the problems which are likely to confront it after the war, and to report.*'

The average pre-war catch of herring

from the North Sea alone was 939,000 tons per annum, of which 239,000 represented the catch of the United Kingdom. (Cf. imports of meat from S. America 500,000 tons.)

The decline in consumption in the inter-war years and the consequent widespread distress as a result of the uneconomic takings per boat, led to the setting up of the Herring Industry Board to organise the industry and reduce the size of the fishing fleet. Between 1934 and 1938 the Scottish steam drifter fleet fell from 686 to 402 and the English fleet from 305 to 283. In 1939 most of the boats of both fleets had been built before 1921. The decline in the numbers of herring fishermen since 1913 from 9700 to 7000 in Scotland and from 6000 to 2800 in England was due more to young men not being attracted to the industry, than to fishermen being transferred to other industries. A profit-sharing system of remunerating the crew prevails both in England and in Scotland, but in spite of the efforts to reorganise the industry earnings remained low, so low in many cases that fishermen did not earn sufficient to meet their proportion of voyage expenses. Some small part of the fleet continued fishing during the war, and has been able to pay off debts, but that part which was requisitioned by the Admiralty had little margin. On the whole, funds for big capital replacement were practically non-existent. With the cessation of the war there will be a great need for all the herring that can be caught, but a close watch should be kept on the possible future contraction of the market. A long-term policy involves the study of the foreign and home markets, the utilisation of the surpluses; the scope of the fleet and boat design; research, including shoal location, curing, pickling, packing, etc.; and price control.

The Herring Industry Board should be reconstituted and should investigate the possibilities of cold storage for surpluses, develop the process of dehydration and conduct experiments with a view to improving boat and engine designs; it should have power to buy, sell and process herrings, etc., develop markets, fix prices, promote marketing schemes and administer schemes for the re-equipment of the fleet and for research. Sales by auction should continue, but should be supplemented by a system of differential minimum prices for the various purposes and markets, a proportion of the proceeds of sale being pooled. A Joint Industrial Council for the herring industry should be set up to regulate wages and conditions, etc. The constitution of the Board and the suggested sums for financing the various proposals are set out in detail in the recommendations.

See *Herring Industry Bd.* 11th Ann. Rep. App., *Reorganisation and Development of the Herring Industry;* 1946–47 Cmd. 6957, xii, 323. *Herring Industry Bd.* 1st Ann. Rep.; 1936 Non-Parl. Scottish Office, and succeeding Ann. Reps. *Herring Industry Act, 1944;* 7 & 8 Geo. 6. c. 32.

Fisheries in Wartime, 1939-1944
Rep. pp. 108. 1946

1946 Non-Parl. Min. of Agric. & Fish. sgd. Oct., 1945

In spite of the fact that some of the best fishing grounds were mined or closed, and that the best of the trawler fleet was requisitioned for the Navy, and many others lost, the average landings during the strictly war period were a little less than 30 per cent of pre-war; foreign landings brought the total up to nearly 50 per cent. The Report reviews the effect of the war on fishing, the control of fishing operations, the stocks of fish, manpower problems, scientific investigations, whaling, etc., and deals with the powers of the White Fish Commission and the Herring Industry Board, etc.

Pp. 51–52 summarise an unpublished report of an inquiry (*Chairman*, Sir Alexander Gray) into the supply of crews, methods of engagement and their terms of employment.

See *Sea Fisheries Statistical Tables,*

1945–46; 1948 Non-Parl. Min. of Agric. & Fish., and succeeding Ann. Tables. *Fisheries of Scotland, 1939–1948.* Rep.; 1948–49 Cmd. 7726, xvi, 399, and succeeding Ann. Reps. *White Fish Authority.* 1st Ann. Rep.; 1951–52 (222) xii, 559, and succeeding Ann. Reps.

Poaching and Illegal Fishing of Salmon and Trout in Scotland.

Cttee. Rep., app. pp. 30. 1950

1950 *Cmd.* 7917, *xi,* 219
apptd. Aug., 1948. *sgd. Dec.,* 1949

R. H. Maconochie (*Ch.*), Anderson, Berry, Clarke, Gibson, Ramsay, Robertson, Stansfeld, Wotherspoon

'To enquire into the prevalence of the illegal taking or killing of salmon and trout by methods which may cause serious damage to fish stocks and to make recommendations for the protection of salmon and trout against such action.'

Poaching has become a lucrative commercial proposition to highly organised gangs operating in waters remote from the towns where they have their headquarters. Some of the reasons for this are the high price of fish, the use of explosives, poisons and electrical devices; the inadequacy of penalties because of the change in money values since the passing of the 1868 Act—a gang may collect fifty fish a night, while one large salmon will pay the fine if they are caught; the use of motor transport; inadequate powers of search; the prohibitive cost of watching staffs; and the existence of 43 instead of the 104 bailiffs contemplated under the Salmon Fisheries Acts. The use of explosives, etc., is serious, because they are capable of destroying all fish life in the waters affected.

Suggestions were made on the desirability of encouraging the formation of District Boards and Angling Associations; the encouragement of the collaboration of such bodies with the police; and bringing the public to realise the gravity both of the attack on the fish life of the river and of the development of a class of poachers and dealers who make vast profits on the Black Market. Recommendations for fresh legislation include higher penalties; greater powers of search; making night poaching a criminal offence; heavy penalties for the use of explosives, etc., and the confiscation of vehicles, boats and equipment used for poaching. All packages should be conspicuously marked and records of all transactions in salmon and trout should be kept by dealers, and should be open to inspection by the police.

Prevention of Pollution of the Sea by Oil

Cttee. Rep., apps. pp. v, 50. 1953

1953 Non-Parl. Min. of Transport and Civil Aviation
apptd. Sept., 1952. *sgd. July,* 1953

P. Faulkner (*Ch.*), and 20 others.

'To consider what practical measures can be taken to prevent pollution by oil of the waters around the coasts of the United Kingdom, and to report.'

Pollution is fairly general around the coasts of England and Wales and although it is not continuous, many beaches have been so heavily contaminated as to make the nuisance intolerable. The oil spoils the beaches; destroys or injures birds; fouls boats, fishing gear, piers, quays, etc.; damages fish, shellfish and larvae. The Oil in Navigable Waters Act, 1922, prohibited the discharge of oil in territorial waters, but international action before 1939 failed because Germany, Italy and Japan did not participate.

The oils of petroleum origin are the persistent ones; their physical properties are such that they can float more or less indefinitely and drift over great distances. If the prohibited zone were 150 miles, the evil would only be mitigated. The problem is complicated by the increasing number of foreign-registered oil-carrying and oil-consuming ships coming to the United Kingdom ports or passing through our coastal waters. The problem can be solved only by the co-operation of other maritime countries. Meanwhile, the discharge of oil residues ashore presents problems, as facilities for the reception of waste oil are inadequate or non-existent although, with the exception of the U.S.A., we are better equipped than most countries. The alternative, the separation and consumption of recovered oil in ships, requires the fitting of separators.

The Government should, as soon as possible, seek international co-operation for the prohibition of the discharge of persistent oils into the sea. As an interim measure, the United Kingdom

registered ships should be prohibited from discharging persistent oils within a wide zone indicated in Chart D. Recommendations are made regarding the fitting of separators in various classes of ship, e.g. dry cargo ships, coastal tankers, deep sea tankers, etc.; and on ballast water in tanks which have contained oil, and oil from wrecks. There should be adequate reception facilities at the ports.

See *Pollution of the Sea by Oil.* International Conference. Final Act and Text of the . . . Convention; 1953–54 Cmd. 9197, xxxi, 1057. *Oil in Navigable Waters Act,* 1955; 3 & 4 Eliz. 2. c. 25.

V.   TRADE AND INDUSTRY

1. **War-time Industrial Policy**
2. **Distribution of Industry and of the Industrial Population**
3. **Trade Policy Generally, Industrial Efficiency**
4. **Statistical**
5. **Particular Industries and Trades**
6. **Monopolies and Restrictive Practices**
7. **Company and Commercial Law and Practice**
8. **Weights and Measures**

1.   WAR-TIME INDUSTRIAL POLICY

Concentration of Production

Memo. pp. 4. 1941

1940–41 *Cmd.* 6258, *viii,* 29

The President of the Board of Trade told the House on 6th March, 1941, that the Government's policy was to facilitate the fullest possible transfer of resources to war production while maintaining exports as far as practicable. As part-time working by individual firms was uneconomical in labour, raised costs and retained factory space, production must be concentrated in a reduced number of factories working full-time, while preserving the goodwill of those closed down. In order to obtain the degree of concentration required by the Board of Trade, those industries covered by the Limitation of Supplies (Miscellaneous) Order and certain industries subject to Raw Material Control, will be expected to make voluntary arrangements whereby

'nucleus' firms take over the production of other firms, on condition that these are completely closed, that they are compensated, and that their plant is kept intact and that concentration takes place where the demand for labour in the munitions industries is least severe. The Ministry of Labour will keep a record of transferred workers so that their return to their old employment will be facilitated. Nucleus firms will be given various advantages in retaining labour, supply of materials, etc.

Retail Trade

1st Interim Rep., *Opening of New Shops and the Restriction on Categories of Goods Sold in Existing Shops.* pp. 4. 1941

1941 *Non-Parl. Bd. of Trade apptd. May, sgd. Oct.,* 1941

W. C. Henderson (*Ch.*), Tate (Mavis), Palmer, Conley, Dryer, Lyle, Mathias, Florence, Hallsworth, Greenwood, Neal, Hann.

'*To examine the present problems of the retail trade in goods other than food, having*

*regard to the immediate needs of the conduct
of the war and to the position after the war.'*

As supplies of goods, labour and transport are restricted, the opening of new shops or the sale by existing shops of goods not previously sold, except where the existing numbers or facilities are clearly shown to be insufficient, can only divert supplies from existing shops and add to the numbers eventually forced out of business. The opening of new shops or sale of new categories of goods should be prohibited except under licence. A trader who has lost his premises by enemy action, etc., should be entitled to a licence as of right, provided the alternative premises are to be used for the same categories of trade as heretofore and are not more than one mile from the original premises. Suggestions are made on the composition of the local licensing authority.

See *Location of Retail Businesses Orders, 1941.* S.I. 1941 Nos. 1784 and 1933.

—— Second Interim Report, *Impact of the War on the Retail Trades in Goods Other than Food*, apps., index. pp. 40. 1942

1942 *Non-Parl.*
sgd. Jan., 1942

Of the total of 750,000 shops, over half sold food and drink, many of them other goods as well, and of the remainder many did not confine themselves to one category of goods, so that the total number of selling points for any class of goods greatly exceeded the number of shops dealing in that class of goods alone. Not much less than 40 per cent of the total retail turnover of £1200 mn. in 1939 was represented by clothing and footwear, and 20 per cent by furniture and hardware. The great exodus of population from the east, south east, south coast and greater London to the West, North and Midlands and rural areas has meant a fall of demand in evacuation and rise of demand in reception areas, so that the survival of individual retailers has depended less on their efficiency than on the chance of their location. The retail trades have also suffered reductions of supplies owing to raw material shortages, Limitation of Supplies Orders, which have fixed maximum quotas retailers might have at one-fifth to one-half of pre-war, clothing and footwear rationing, utility grades, etc. Retailers may try to 'hang on', close for the duration of the war, or arrange a voluntary 'marriage' with other firms, with a levy to assist those closing. Trade opinion was not, in the autumn of 1941, favourable to 'marriage' schemes.

—— Third Report, app., index. pp. 38. 1942

1942 *Non-Parl.*
sgd. June, 1942

The pressures referred to in the second report have continued, especially on small and medium small businesses. The proposed concentration insurance scheme is designed to help to preserve the main structure of retailing under these stresses and to preserve right of entry for those who withdraw voluntarily. Traders continuing in business should pay into a Retail Concentration Insurance Fund a compulsory levy of 1 per cent on turnover. The difficulties of a trader withdrawing either by closure or 'marriage' with another firm were his continuing contractual liabilities, mainly rent, and mortgage interest, etc., and reopening after the war. He should receive a Standard Benefit of 5 per cent on turnover in the previous 12 months during the currency of the obligations, or Special Benefit for small traders with no or only short-term contractual obligations. Withdrawing traders should be given prior rights of re-entry into the trade in which they had been operating.

See *Schemes for Ensuring Fair Shares of Supplies for Small Retailers* of Pottery, Holloware and Clothing; 1942 Non-Parl. Bd. of Trade.

Regional Boards

Cttee. Rep., apps. pp. ii, 29. 1942

1941–42 *Cmd. 6360, iv, 681*
apptd. Feb., sgd. May, 1942

W. Citrine (*Ch.*), Chance, Deer, Dukes, Elger, Eyston, Watson, Kaylor, Locock, Marks, West.

'*To examine the present constitution and functions of the Production Executive's Regional Boards and of the Central Joint Advisory Committee to the Production Executive and to make recommendations as to any changes in these matters that may appear to be necessary or desirable.*'

'Regional Boards were set up to assist the Minister of Production and the Supply Ministries to make, in a co-ordinated manner, the fullest and most efficient use of the actual or potential productive resources and manufacturing capacity of the Regions for the purpose of carrying out productive programmes whether approved or in contemplation.' They have not generally been able to do this because there was no properly articulated system of devolution of executive authority. Regional Controllers had no control over the local officers functionally responsible to their Departmental Directorates: they should be subject also to the general direction of Department's regional controllers. The Ministry of Production should appoint regional directors of production to concert the work of the Supply Departments' regional controllers in regard to machine tools, raw material, labour and premises and to deal with overloading. To ensure the effective use of engineering capacity, Regional Boards should set up District Offices to maintain capacity and load records and a 'danger list' of overloaded firms. The Central Joint Advisory Committee, which has rarely been consulted, should be replaced by a National Production Advisory Council, on which Regional Boards should be represented. In a Memo. the Minister of Production accepts the chief recommendations, but not the proposal that the Machine Tool local organisation should be merged into the Regional Organisation.

The Impact of the War on Civilian Consumption

Combined Cttee. on Non-Food Consumption Levels. Rep., apps. pp. 163.
1945

1945 *Non-Parl. Treasury*
apptd. —. sgd. —.

M. A. Copeland (*Ch.*).

The report examines the impact of the war on civilian consumption in the United Kingdom, the United States and Canada. Part II sets forth the main factors which have restricted and altered consumption. It estimates for each country the total national product, the size and use of the labour force, enlistment, imports and exports, non-war gross capital formation and how incomes were spent. Part III analyses in detail changes in different items.

In the U.K. the aggregate per head consumption valued at pre-war prices decreased by 15 to 20 per cent, in U.S.A. and Canada increased by 10 per cent to 15 per cent. In 1943–44 in U.K. and Canada half the gross national product was war product, in U.S.A. 40 to 45 per cent. In all three countries additions to the stock of non-war buildings and capital equipment ceased, but only in U.K. was there a net reduction of national wealth, i.e. in productive capacity and command over foreign resources, and that reduction was a material one. In important categories of consumption there were decreases in U.K., e.g. in foods, clothing, household soft goods, etc., and increases in U.S.A. and Canada. Consumption increased in U.S.A. and Canada and decreased in U.K. because U.K. production could not be expanded so much, and shipping limited the imports of food and materials.

There are 13 statistical apps.

Statistics relating to the War Effort of the United Kingdom

apps. pp. 64. 1944

1943–44 *Cmd. 6564, viii, 597*

See Sections II, III and IV.

2. DISTRIBUTION OF INDUSTRY AND OF THE INDUSTRIAL POPULATION

The Distribution of the Industrial Population

R. Com. Rep., apps. pp. x, 320. 1940
Mins. of ev., 29 days. 1937–39

1939–40 *Cmd.* 6153, *iv*, 263. *Mins. of ev.;*
1937–39 *Non-Parl.*
apptd. June, 1938. *sgd. Dec.*, 1939

M. Barlow (*Ch.*), Robinson, Joseph, Whyte, Cooper, Hill (Mrs. M. N.), Jones, Morris, Smith, Thomson, Abercrombie, Elvin, Hichens (Mrs. H.).

'To inquire into the causes which have influenced the present geographical distribution of the industrial population of Great Britain and the probable direction of any change in that distribution in the future; to consider what social, economic or strategical disadvantages arise from the concentration of industries or of the industrial population in large towns or in particular areas of the country; and to report what remedial measures if any should be taken in the national interest.'

The Royal Commission was appointed after the publication in 1936 of the third report of Sir Malcolm Stewart, Commissioner for Special Areas (England and Wales) in which he said that whilst the Government was 'not justified in using compulsion to dictate to industry where it *should* go, was there not good ground . . . for directing where it should *not* go.' (*Breviate 1917–1939*, p. 358.)

Between 1921 and 1937 the population of Great Britain increased by less than one-half of one per cent per annum. This increase was unevenly distributed, being in London and the Home Counties about 18 per cent and in the Midland group 11 per cent, but there was a decline of 9 per cent in Glamorgan and Monmouth and 1 per cent in Northumberland and Durham. London and the Home Counties and the Midland group contained 35 per cent of the total population, but 70 per cent of the population added during this period. The relative increase of the insured population in these counties arose from the great importance in their economies of the 23 industries whose rate of expansion was greater than the average. In the absence of decisive natural factors, such as the existence of coal or adequate water, industries tend to be situated within easy reach of the market. A large urban area, being itself a large market, attracts light industries, so that growth may be perpetuated. There is no reason to suppose that the trend to the south-east will be arrested, but it is not inevitable. The question is whether it is desirable.

Although in the nineteenth century there was a great excess of mortality in large towns as compared with rural areas, there were great improvements, so that the difference between the two was strikingly reduced. In 1931–37 the standard death rates in county boroughs in England and Wales still exceeded those of rural districts by 25 per cent, though excess had fallen from 46 per cent 20 years earlier. Many of the disadvantages of urban living were being overcome and compensated by better medical services, water supply, etc., so that there was no uniform level of mortality in towns of the same size range; some rural districts had higher death rates than some towns, and there was no evidence that there was an optimum size of towns from the point of view of health. The evils were traceable to the overcrowding of houses on sites, overcrowding of persons per room, to congestion, smoke and atmospheric pollution. Much of this had been accentuated by haphazard development; where land in the centre formerly used for residences is taken for industry, the people are housed further and further away from their work and acute traffic difficulties are caused by long and costly journeys. On the other hand, concentration at the centre of the town causes traffic congestion and a rise in site values which is often sufficient to make it more economical for some firms to seek sites in the surrounding countryside. Much has been done to remove the disadvantages of large towns, but there should be further redevelopment of congested areas, decentralisation of both industry and population and a check, as far as possible, to a further growth of London. In view of the danger of air attack the dispersal of some of London's activities, including those of some Government Departments, is a strategical necessity.

The Commission received much evidence on what had been accomplished by town and country planning and by experiments in decentralisation by means of the garden city, the satellite town and the trading estate. Some had proposed the building of a number of new towns of about 50,000. These could make a useful contribution, provided steps were taken to prevent unnecessary competition between them and that strategical considerations were given due weight. But, owing to the magnitude of finance involved, they could not proceed satisfactorily by private enterprise. Municipal authorities should be encouraged to undertake such development; they should own the land, be given the opportunity of dealing with the problems on a regional basis and assistance should be available from Government funds.

Planning is essentially on a local basis and had not been intended to influence the geographical distribution of the population between localities. Only a small part of the country is covered by approved plans, agriculture is not one of the purposes of planning set out in the Act of 1932, planning schemes could not be enforced against government departments or statutory undertakers and there is too much 'free entry' building land. Under existing provisions there are difficulties of compensating owners whose land has been decreased in value by planning out of funds created by levies on other owners for betterment. If the potential development for each piece of land is assessed separately, the total sum arrived at is likely to exceed the sum which could be claimed if the prospective development of the country as a whole were considered. One proposal was that the State, through a national development board, should acquire the development rights in all undeveloped land. A committee of experts should be appointed to examine the problem.

The experience of 'depressed' or Special Areas is valuable in showing the need for developing new industries in areas too dependent on a few basic ones vulnerable to trade depressions and for encouraging both a reasonable balance of industrial development throughout the country and diversifying industry within each region. And the adoption of a regional system would facilitate the solution of many problems.

In the past the choice of location of industry has been that of the entrepreneur and the State has not intervened to control it, but there is a large body of opinion favourable to *some* regulation, varying from negative restriction to keep industry away from certain areas to positive encouragement or direction of new industries to certain regions. The Commission concludes that many of the industrial concentrations have serious disadvantages and that definite Government action should be taken to remedy them.

Proposals.—A National Authority should be established to investigate and regulate the distribution of industry, to promote decentralisation and a dispersal from congested areas and to encourage a reasonable balance of industrial development and diversification in the different regions. It should formulate a plan, taking into account the considerations indicated above, and in particular, should have powers to regulate and to refuse to consent to the establishment of additional undertakings in London and the south-east, unless these can prove that they could not be conducted economically elsewhere. The constitution, functions and powers of the Authority are set out.

A Reservation by Jones, Thomson and Whyte argues that the problem should be dealt with by the positive action of regulating the new industrial development throughout the country rather than by restricting growth in a particular area and that Divisional or Regional Boards should be an integral part of the new organisation.

Minority Report. Abercrombie, Elvin, Hichens (Mrs. H.).—They agree with the majority on the general analysis of the problem, but say that parts of the Report do not set out vigorously enough the urgency of the problem. The core of the problem is the control of industrial location and its relationship to national planning. Far-reaching powers should be granted to a new Government department to undertake research and prepare a plan and it should be given effective control of changes of industrial distribution meanwhile. Every manufacturer desiring to build, extend or convert a factory would have to obtain a permit. The powers of the Commissioners of Special Areas should be transferred to it and made general. The new Ministry should schedule 'free' areas where industrial development is permitted and prohibited areas where it could not take place, except where it would not be economically profitable to establish it elsewhere.

Abercrombie presented a *Dissentient Memo. on Planning* in relation to the location of industry in which he pointed out the defects in existing planning procedures and discussed the need for integrating industrial control with regional and local planning.

See especially evidence on behalf of the Board of Trade, 3rd and 4th Days, and on behalf of the Ministry of Labour, 10th and 11th Days.

Employment Policy
Statement

1943–44 *Cmd.* 6527

See *Labour*, p. 233.

Distribution of Industry
Statement, apps. pp. 52. 1948

1948 *Cmd.* 7540, *ii*, 463

The pre-war Special Areas policy was concerned with the problems of depressed areas in isolation, but experience has shown that they could not be tackled unless they were related to the distribution of industry throughout the country. Following the report of the Barlow Commission on the Distribution of the Industrial Population and Chap. III of the White Paper on Employment Policy, the Distribution of Industry Act, 1945, scheduled six Development Areas, mainly compact regions in which a special danger of unemployment existed. The Act required the Board of Trade to consider at the end of three years, whether any changes should be made in the schedule.

The Board was given powers to build factories, make loans for the erection of buildings on 'industrial estates', etc., and to control all new industrial building of more than 10,000 sq. ft., later reduced to 5000 sq. ft.

All the main types of industry in the areas were affected by the high level of demand, which also facilitated the movement of new industries into them. The progress in each of the areas is reviewed. In addition, industries had been guided into areas other than Development Areas which had idle labour, and industrialists have been permitted to build in London or Birmingham only if it would have been uneconomic to transfer production elsewhere. As a result, whereas from 1932 to 1938 57 per cent of new industrial development was in London and the Midlands, in the post-war period it has been 19 per cent. It would not yet be safe to remove the whole or any parts of the Areas from the schedule.

A special danger of unemployment—the test for scheduling—implies two conditions, a persistently high average rate of unemployment and a high aggregate number of unemployed. A number of applications did not satisfy these tests, and for blitzed or holiday areas, or small pockets of unemployment the technique was not suitable. But the Mersey did and the Board of Trade proposed to add it to the schedule. The fact that the scattered population of the Highlands and Islands has declined and was declining was not of itself sufficient to bring the whole area within the ambit of the Act, but an area including Inverness, Dingwall, Invergordon and Tain, when surplus hydro-electric power will be available, should be scheduled to serve as a focal centre of industrial development.

Welsh Reconstruction

Advisory Council.   1st Interim Rep., apps. pp. 132.   1944

1944 Non-Parl.   Min. of Reconstruction apptd. June, 1942.   sgd. Dec., 1943

J. F. Rees(*Ch.*), Bevan, Davies, Griffiths, Harrison, Humphreys, Jenkin, Jones, Lewis, Merrett, Parry, Rees (Laura G.), Webber, Williams (E.), Williams (W. M.), Williams-Ellis.

'*To survey, in conformity with the general examination of reconstruction problems now being conducted by the Government, those problems of reconstruction which are of special application to Wales and Monmouthshire, and to advise on them.*'

The bitter experiences of Wales during the inter-war years and the net loss of population by migration of 430,000 people between 1921 and 1928 has made post-war planning of special significance to Wales. In 1923 16·4 per cent of the insured population were in trades of every-day demand, 53·6 per cent in industries localised by nature and 6·4 per cent in mobile, mainly light, industries. By 1942 these proportions had altered to 28·6, 24·1 and 26·9 per cent respectively. Surveys covering half the population of Wales showed that between 40 per cent and 50 per cent of all workers in new industries were in establishments which might stop or curtail activities after the war. The political and economic assumptions on which regional plans must be based are reviewed and recommendations made on post-war policy regarding the major industries, e.g. coal, steel, slate, etc., and on the retention or attraction of new industries.

See: *Wales and Monmouthshire*. Summary of Government Action; 1945–46 Cmd. 6938, xx, 763. Rep. of Government Action; 1947–48 Cmd. 7267, xvi, 573, and succeeding Ann. Reps. *Council for Wales and Monmouthshire*. Memos.; 1950 Cmd. 8060, xix, 883, includes a report on marginal land. 1952–53 Cmd. 8844, xxiv, 875, on the basis of a pilot survey, recommends a special capital expenditure of £60 mn. for Welsh rural areas, a special Welsh Development Corporation being established to apply it. See succeeding Memos. published irregularly.

Highland Development

Programme, apps. pp. iii, 34.   1950

1950 Cmd. 7976, xix, 687

Fundamentally the problem is to encourage people to live in the Highlands by making it possible to secure there, in return for reasonable efforts, proper standards of life and the means of paying for them. The action which has been taken by successive Governments has been on the whole designed to preserve rather than to construct and has been motivated by social rather than economic considerations. The present policy is to continue and extend the provision of the basic services, with special financial assistance to Highland local authorities, and to encourage the development of the principal industries of agriculture, forestry, fisheries and tourism, the exploitation of the natural resources and the growth of manufacturing industries, particularly those based on local resources.

3.   TRADE POLICY GENERALLY, INDUSTRIAL EFFICIENCY

General Agreement on Tariffs and Trade

1950 Cmd. 8048

See *Monetary and Economic Policy*, p. 73.

Commonwealth Economic Conference

Final Communique. pp. 6. 1952

1952–53 *Cmd.* 8717, *xxiii*, 387

The Commonwealth countries agreed on the following principles: (1) Internal economic policies designed to check inflation and rises in the cost of living should be steadily pursued. Although there had been a steady improvement in the balance of payments of the Sterling Area, the level of reserves was as yet too low to warrant any substantial relaxation of the restrictions on imports from outside the Area. (2) Sound economic development should be encouraged in order to increase productive capacity and competitive strength. Development should be concentrated on projects which directly or indirectly contributed to the Sterling Area's balance of payments. As the amount of savings available for investment from outside the Area was small in relation to development programmes, the countries should stimulate their own internal savings. To enable the U.K. to maintain and increase its traditional flow of capital for Commonwealth investment, it must achieve the necessary level of internal savings and surplus on overseas capital account. It will undertake to provide additional capital if the country concerned makes a sufficient contribution and uses an adequate part of its resources to improve the Sterling Area's balance of payments. It will have the co-operation of the other countries in approaching G.A.T.T. to enable the U.K. to continue the duty-free entry of Commonwealth goods notwithstanding that it might be necessary to increase duties designed to protect domestic industry and agriculture in U.K. (3) A multilateral trade and payments system should be extended over as wide an area as possible. It was important that sterling should resume its full role as a medium of trade and exchange. An integral part of this was the restoration of the convertibility of sterling, though this could be reached only by progressive stages, and adequate financial support would be needed from the International Monetary Fund.

Bilateral Trade Negotiations

Cttee. Rep. pp. 10. 1953

1953 *Non-Parl. Bd. of Trade apptd. —. sgd. July,* 1953

H. R. Mackeson (*Ch.*), Steel, Tennant, Caswell, Williams, Winterbottom, Knowles, Cohen, Stacy, Whitehouse.

'*To review current procedures for consultation with industry in connexion with bilateral trade negotiations, especially in so far as they relate to quotas or similar arrangements affecting United Kingdom exports....*'

Governments negotiate bilateral trade agreements to obtain scarce materials which they need to import and to secure satisfactory quotas for their exports; the negotiations in themselves afford some security against sudden and arbitrary action by other countries and help to preserve good political and commercial relations. Only a small proportion of our total export trade is subject to bilateral agreements.

The arrangements for consultation had been criticised because they did not allow enough time for consultation, did not keep the industries sufficiently informed, provide for close contact of industry with the foreign negotiators, or pass on particulars regarding quotas quickly enough. A committee meeting regularly should review arrangements for consultation in trade negotiations in contemplation and should advise whether it was desirable to attach representatives from trade associations to the negotiating team. Production departments should give the Board of Trade the full substance of the advice they receive from industry.

Duty-free Entry of Machinery into the United Kingdom

Cttee. Rep., apps. pp. 34. 1954

1954 *Non-Parl. Bd. of Trade apptd. March,* 1953. *sgd. March,* 1954

H. W. Smith (*Ch.*), Bird, Board,

Fiennes, Grist, Grove, Harley, Symons, Tanner.

'*To consider and report whether it is in the national interest to provide for the duty-free admission into the United Kingdom of machinery, either by classes or in individual consignments; and, in this connection, to review the provisions of Section 10 of the Finance Act, 1932, and their administration. . . .*'

The arrangements of a discretionary nature made in the recommendations of the Import Duties Advisory Committee to allow machinery not procurable in this country to come in duty free were intended to operate in a narrow field, but this extended until in 1938–39 there were 10,500 applications. The attempt to reduce these by the preparation of detailed schedules met insuperable technical difficulties. After the war the Board of Trade acted on the advice of the Ministry of Supply, but by 1951 applications had again risen to 12,000, and as there were counter-pressures by importers and British makers, the duty-free import was suspended.

As it is clear that certain machines are not, and cannot or will not be made in this country, that recorded imports of machinery represent only a small fraction of U.K. production, that when not made in this country there is no domestic maker to protect, and that British tariff policy should encourage efficiency in British industry, the Committee felt there was a *prima facie* case for some discretionary duty-free entry of machinery. The field of exemption should be restricted, but cannot be limited by schedules and must involve individual comparisons of British and foreign machinery. The duty-free entry should apply where similar machinery, as tested by suitability for the particular work for which it is required, is not procurable in this country. Applications eligible for consideration should be confined to consignments where the value to the individual user is not less than £200. The system should continue to be operated by Government departments, but a Consultative Committee containing representatives of industry should be established.

Industrial Productivity

Cttee. 1st Rep., app. pp. 31. 1949
1948–49 Cmd. 7665, xvii, 113
apptd. Dec., 1947. sgd. —.

H. Tizard (*Ch.*), Appleton, Blaker, Gibb, Griffiths, King, Neill, Nicholson, Schuster, Stanier, Tanner, Williamson, Zuckerman, Croome, Bretherton, Roxbee-Cox, Russell.

'*To advise the Lord President of the Council and the Chancellor of the Exchequer on the form and scale of research effort in the natural and social sciences which would best assist an early increase in industrial productivity and further to advise on the manner in which the results of such research can best be applied.*'

The Committee was established as a result of experience gained in the Research and Productivity Committee of the Advisory Council on Scientific Policy and it works through the four panels on technology and operational research, import-substitution, human factors affecting industrial productivity and technical information services. Before the war British productivity measured by production per man/year increased at the rate of 2 per cent per annum. Immediately after the war there was a serious set-back in many industries, but by 1948 there was a noticeable improvement. Some industries showed an increase above pre-war, but in others, including some important ones, it was undoubtedly low and although total production was higher in 1948 than 1939, this was mainly due to a decrease in unemployment and to an increase in the working population. The report reviews general questions relating to productivity, and the work of the four panels.

—— Second Report. pp. 10. 1950
1950 Cmd. 7991, xii, 57
sgd. July, 1950

Since the Committee was formed the

main responsibility for the study of problems of productivity has been placed on specialised bodies, e.g. the Anglo-American Council on Productivity, the Productivity Department of the Trades Union Congress, the British Institute of Management, the Committee on the Standardisation of Engineering Products, etc. Recommended that the Committee be disbanded. The Annex gives a list of subjects considered during 1949.

A Central Institute of Management

Cttee. Rep. pp. 15. 1946

1946 Non-Parl. Bd. of Trade
apptd. Nov., 1945. sgd. —.

C. Baillieu (*Ch.*), and 22 others.

'*To advise . . . upon the steps which should now be taken to form a central institution for all questions connected with Management, and upon its form of organisation, functions, constitution and relationship to government industry, existing institutions and interested organisations and the public.*'

Good management practice has become so essential to industrial and commercial efficiency as to require a central institute, or British Institute of Management. It should promote research into management problems, develop training and educational schemes and propaganda on good management practice, and help to create a continuous supply of good managers. It should aim at establishing itself as a professional body with defined grades of membership, and should make provision for trade associations and trade unions, etc., to interest themselves in its work. The balance of expenditure should be made up by an annual Government grant of £150,000 for the first five years. Thereafter the institute should be self-supporting.

Exhibitions and Fairs

Cttee. Rep. pp. 16. 1946

1945–46 Cmd. 6782, xii, 1
apptd. —. sgd. Dec., 1945

M

Lord Ramsden (*Ch.*), Barlow, Bennett, Duncan, Evans, Eyles, Fawcett, Goodale, Lever, Lines, Locock, McLean, Pratt, Riggall, Streat, Wilson.

'*To consider the part which Exhibitions and Fairs should play in the promotion of export trade in the post-war era, and to advise on the policy and plans to be adopted to derive the maximum advantage from such displays.*'

H.M. Government should adopt and make known to industry a comprehensive national policy in regard to exhibitions at home and abroad. There should be a British Industries Fair held annually and concentrated in one centre. The Government should be responsible for the site and the erection of permanent buildings, which should provide all the services needed by the overseas buyers. Government participation in international fairs should be undertaken only where industry intends to take part on an adequate scale and it should then be of an adequate standard. An international convention should be negotiated to ensure some regulation of the frequency of international exhibitions. A Universal International Exhibition should be held in London in 1951.

Festival of Britain, 1951

app. pp. 8. 1953

1952–53 Cmd. 8872, xxiv, 509

The Ramsden Committee's recommendation that an international exhibition should be held in 1951 to commemorate the centenary of the Great Exhibition of 1851 was not approved as it would have cost £70 mn. at 1946 prices. In its place Herbert Morrison announced proposals to the House for 'a national display illustrating the British contribution to civilisation, past, present and future in the arts, in science and technology, and in industrial design.'

There is a list of projects on which Exchequer funds were expended. The gross estimate was £11,500,000; the actual cost was £10,686,924; the estimated revenue was £2,560,000 and the actual revenue was £2,563,199. The actual total net expenditure was £8,123,725.

British Industries Fair

Exhibitions Advisory Cttee. Sub-Cttee. Rep. pp. 12. 1953

1953–54 *Cmd.* 9013, *x*, 1
apptd. April, 1952. *sgd. Sept.*, 1953

E. W. Goodale (*Ch.*), Chance, Clark, Edwards, Evans, Locock, Maclean, Missenden, Walters.

'*To review the present arrangements for the British Industries Fair. . . .*'

The British Industries Fair, which should project the best of British Industry, has been losing ground in the eyes of buyers and exhibitors. It should be held annually. The Birmingham section has a permanent home, and despite the Ramsden Committee's proposal for concentration, should remain where it is. Though the London section needs a permanent home, and the Crystal Palace site would be suitable, in present economic conditions the Government could not be recommended to erect new buildings solely for this purpose. A public corporation should take over the responsibility for the Fair from the Board of Trade, the Government guaranteeing its borrowing up to £100,000 for five years and providing £100,000 per annum for publicity.

Organisation and Constitution of the British Standards Institution

Cttee. Rep., apps. pp. 44. 1950

1951 *Non-Parl. Bd. of Trade*
apptd. June, 1949. *sgd. —.*

G. Cunliffe (*Ch.*), Duncalfe, Harries, Humphreys, Nicolle, Palmer.

'*To consider the organisation and constitution of the British Standards Institution, including its finance, in the light of the increasing importance of standardisation and the extended size and volume of work likely to fall on the B.S.I. in future. . . .*'

A standard specification is a document which prescribes measurable technical conditions of weight, dimensions, chemical tests, resistance to light, to moisture, to heat, acidity, alkalinity, insulating capacity, breaking strain and a host of other factors differing with the commodity. Standards range from simple glossaries of technical terms to large volumes. The organisation is maintained on a committee system, with some 2600 technical and drafting committees and 53 Industry Standards Committees. There are divisional councils, a general council, executive committee and a directorate.

There is a growing interest in the economic importance of standardisation and the Institute will need to be expanded. Other expanding functions are certification marking (e.g. the Kite monogram), codes of practice, the library service, the use of British standards overseas and international work. The constitution and organisation of the B.S.I. are well adapted to the work. It should remain under the control of its Council, which consists of representatives of manufacturers, users, professional bodies and Government Departments. Increased work will involve an increase in expenditure from the present £200,000 to £400,000 in five years. The maximum Government contribution should be £150,000 a year for the first five years.

Standardisation of Engineering Products

Cttee. Rep., apps. pp. 35. 1949

1949 *Non-Parl. Min. of Supply*
apptd. Nov., 1948. *sgd. Sept.,* 1949

E. Lemon (*Ch.*), Smith, Harley, Windibank.

'*To investigate . . . the methods by which manufacturers and users of engineering products determine whether any reduction in the variety of products manufactured is desirable . . .; to report whether these methods are adequate and what, if any, further measures should be taken by industry or by the Government to ensure that such simplifications as are determined are put into effect.*'

Increasing productive efficiency can be secured by specialisation, simplification or standardisation, or a combination of these processes, and action may be taken by individual firms, industries (by agreement) on national standards, and by international standards. Specialisation is within the competence of every manufacturing organisation and in conjunction with simplification is the quickest way to reduce variety, though it is easiest for the new or growing business. But simplification involves collaboration and is therefore more easily effected in industries having a compact character and in those free from traditions. The relatively high degree of specialisation and simplification in U.S. industry is a major reason for their higher industrial productive efficiency —in this country motor car components are a typical case of simplification. Standardisation in the engineering field involves (a) codes of design, manufacture, testing or use of particular products, (b) quality or performance required, (c) dimensions and tolerances. A combination of (a) and (b) in conjunction with simplification can be most effective in reducing unnecessary and wasteful variety. There is, for example, a great disparity between standardisation in the aircraft industry and the lack of it in the agricultural machinery industry.

In so far as a reduction in the variety of engineering standards can be achieved by national standards the principle that the B.S.I. should allow industry itself to be responsible for initiating standards and deciding their nature, is sound, but is not always speedy, and there are no recognised uniform methods in operation. All sections of industry should further the work of the B.S.I.; sections of industry should not determine standards unilaterally; all Government purchases should, wherever possible be to British Standards, and the B.S.I. should, through trade associations, urge industry to adopt a similar procedure; individual firms should complete standards books for their own use; appropriate sections of industry should compile a standards handbook. The B.S.I. should extend its staff.

Design and the Designer in Industry

Council for Art and Industry. Rep., apps. pp. 63. 1937

1937 Non-Parl. Bd. of Trade sgd. Dec., 1936

F. Pick (*Ch.*).

The Gorell Committee on *Art and Industry* (1932 Non-Parl. Bd. of Trade) reported that the endeavours a century earlier to train public taste by the establishment of schools of art and museums of industrial art (see *Select List of British Parliamentary Papers*, p. 91) had an effect, but the aesthetic quality of our manufactured goods was still extremely low—a further advance was needed. There was a Memo. by Roger Fry on workshops of decorative design. As a result of the Committee's recommendation in 1934 the Council for Art and Industry was established. This report discusses the functional and aesthetic aspects of design, the recruitment, training and pay of designers, the contribution of art schools and of industry. It was followed by a series of reports on particular industries: *Design in Education. Design in the Jewellery, Silversmithing and Allied Trades. Design in the Pottery Industry. The Working Class Home, its Furnishing and Equipment;* 1937 Non-Parl. Bd. of Trade. *Design and the Designer in the Dress Trade. Design and the Designer in the Light Metal Trades;* 1945 Non-Parl. The parallel Scottish Council reported on *Design in the Scottish Woollen Industry;* 1937, and on *Printing and the Allied Trades in Scotland;* 1937.

4. STATISTICAL

Census of Production

Cttee. Rep., apps. pp. 25. 1945

1945-46 Cmd. 6687, x, 481 apptd. June, sgd. Sept., 1945

G. H. Nelson (*Ch.*), Ayre, Baylay, Campion, Clay, Hallam, Leak, Lee, Pickup, Reeder, Robson, Woodcock.

'*To consider and report what additional information should be collected at future censuses of production and to recommend what amendments should be made to the Census of Production Act.*'

In assessing the need for additional information, the Committee took into account the analysis of the White Paper on *Employment Policy* (see p. 233). In order to enable a better estimation of net output to be made, separate figures should be obtained for wages and salaries, the numbers of working proprietors, for depreciation and for rent, rates and taxes, and for the cost of services performed by other firms. As fluctuations in capital investment are a prime cause of business fluctuations, questions should also be asked on fixed assets, stocks, and work in progress; and on the different categories of manufacturer's sales, and on the control of productive firms. The disclosure rule should be modified to allow responsible officers of Government departments to examine Returns in the Census Office.

Census of Distribution

Cttee. Rep., apps. pp. v, 28. [1946]
1945–46 *Cmd.* 6764, *x*, 507
apptd. June, 1945. *sgd. March,* 1946

R. V. N. Hopkins (*Ch.*), Budgett, Cadbury, Cunningham, Gale, Hann, Jones, Leak, Meade, Miller, Milloy, Neville, Quin, Reddaway, Reeves, Schuster, Stone, Wilkinson.

'*To consider whether having regard to the importance of information being made available regarding the wholesale and retail distribution of goods a regular Census of Distribution should be instituted and if so to advise on the field to be covered and generally as to the measures which should be taken in connection therewith.*'

In order to implement their employment policy the Government had to know what was happening over the whole range of industry and commerce. Lack of knowledge on the values added to goods in the course of distribution

and about the service trades widened the chances of error in calculations of national income and expenditure. Without the knowledge of how much of the total cost of distribution goes in fixed charges, such as rent and rates, how much in wages, of the gross turnover per head in different types of business and the number of units in given size groups in different areas, discussions such as those about the spread between wholesale and retail prices must be largely based on conjecture. A Census of Distribution should be taken every five years, preceded by a pilot census to determine the best method of taking a full one. Information required should include the sales by manufacturers and wholesalers through the numerous channels, by different types of retailers; the number of retail units; the amounts paid in wages and salaries, turnover, stocks, cost of goods sold, of collection and delivery, categories of goods sold, the date of the foundation of the business, etc. Recommendations are made concerning a simple schedule for small retailers, the information which should be asked of all retailers whatever their size, and of large retailers.

Censuses of Production and Distribution

Cttee. Rep., apps. pp. iv, 43. 1954
1953–54 *Cmd.* 9276, *x*, 173
apptd. May, 1953, *Feb.,* 1954. *sgd. July,* 1954

W. R. V. Smith (*Ch.*), Birch, Carter, Davison, Douglass, Jackson, Merriam, Pugh, Quincey, Shone, Stratton, Turner, Vines, Yamey.

'*To advise . . . about future policy in regard to the taking of Census of Production and Distribution and to make recommendations.*'

Following the Nelson and Hopkins Reports the Board of Trade has taken a Census of Production for each year since 1948 and one for Distribution and Other Services for 1950. As the burden of these censuses rested largely on the business community, while the extra value accrued mainly to the Government, the problem was to discover the point at which further census activity would not be worth while, and how to equalise the burden so that censuses become more readily and cheerfully accepted as a necessary part of the statistical system. The Committee reviewed the work done under the provisions of the Statistics of Trade Act, 1947, assessed the value of the information, considered costs and drew up a long-term programme which would provide essential information, reduce form-filling, and allow industry to plan ahead so as to ensure efficiency and economy. A full Census of Production should be taken in 1957 and 1961; with a sample survey, when a full census is not taken; sampling methods should be considered in a full census. A Census of Distribution should be taken every ten years with sample checks every four or five years. Other recommendations concerned methods of presentation, an increase in the number of statisticians employed, and providing research workers with special tabulations on a cost basis.

Scottish Financial and Trade Statistics

Rep.

1951–52 *Cmd.* 8609

See *National Finance*, p. 72.

5. PARTICULAR INDUSTRIES AND TRADES

Brick Industry

Cttee. 1st Rep., apps. pp. 25. 1942
1942 *Non-Parl. Min. of Works and Buildings*
apptd. Sept., sgd. Dec., 1941

O. Simmonds (*Ch.*), and 20 others.

'*To consider and report . . . on the action to be taken for increased efficiency and economy in the manufacture of bricks, and to ensure the necessary supplies of bricks for both war-time and post-war probable de-mands . . . but not to deal with questions of wages; and to advise on any immediate steps that should be taken to assist the war effort.*'

Of the 1147 brick works operating in 1938, 366 or 32 per cent had been closed by Nov. 1941. Two-thirds of the works produced less than 400,000 bricks per month, the remainder providing 75 per cent of the output; and the maximum release of labour to the forces which the industry might be called on to make under existing arrangements was 29·5 per cent. A reduction in output spread proportionately over all works would raise costs. There should be a $12\frac{1}{2}$ per cent reduction of current output by closure of specific works, or in the case of large brick works, by a reduction of productivity; and a further reduction of 4 per cent to reduce stocks. Works should make a pro rata contribution to a fund for the maintenance of closed works and there must be a more comprehensive transfer of labour. Any loss of men by call-up in excess of those transferred from closed works should be made up by using three women for every two men. There should be one standard size of common brick throughout Great Britain.

—— Second Report, apps. pp. 28. 1942
1942 *Non-Parl.*
sgd. *May*, 1942

Sales during the first quarter of 1942 were only 600 mn. bricks, but output had not been reduced as recommended, and stocks rose to 744 mn. By April 163 works had voluntarily closed or ceased production, and by Order production of building bricks required a licence. Production will exceed anticipated demand, and to reduce stocks there should be a further reduction of output by 10 per cent, obtained by closure or reduced productivity. As the reduction has borne unevenly on Fletton and non-Fletton producers, trade should be allocated on a quota system on the basis of 1941 with adjustments, with 1938 production as 'compensation datum'. To make the quota system and compensation effective, there should be statutory minimum area prices. Provision should be made for maximum prices if necessary, every works suitable for reopening after the war should be given a compensation datum expressed as a percentage of national trade in 1938, payments from a levy on those with a surplus being made to closed works and works selling below the compensation datum. A National Brick Council should be established to operate these proposals. There are three dissents.

—— Third Report, apps. pp. 52. 1943

1943 *Non-Parl.*
sgd. Oct., 1942

The Report discusses the technical aspects of the industry, and the recommendations concern the dissemination of information on improved methods, economical use of fuel and of brick oil, and education in technology. Works and regional research laboratories should be encouraged and a scheme of research financed by a small levy on sales. Bricks should be tested by uniform methods, and the British Standards Institution should prepare a standard specification for engineering bricks. The National Brick Advisory Council should, before the end of 1947, consider the post-war organisation of the industry. App. VII, *Firing of Common Bricks*, published separately; 1943 Non-Parl.

Labour Requirements in the Brick Industry

National Brick Advisory Council. Technical Cttee. 1st Rep., app. pp. 21. 1947

1947 *Non-Parl. Min. of Works*
apptd. Aug., 1942. *sgd. Sept.*, 1946

L. W. Hutson (*Ch.*), and 15 others.

'*To consider and report to the Ministry of Works and Buildings on the action to be taken for increased efficiency and economy in the manufacture of bricks, and to ensure the necessary supplies of bricks for both war-time and post-war probable demands. . . .*'

In view of the probable shortage of labour, and of the fact that owing to the raising of the statutory school-leaving age and a fall of the birth rate, the number of juveniles available for employment will be half the existing number, investigations were made into the methods of increasing the productivity of labour by reorganisation and increased mechanisation. Manual should be replaced by mechanical methods, mechanical hauling introduced to improve working conditions and prospects. The amount of heavy manual and dirty, exposed work should be reduced, the proportion of skilled workers and therefore chances of promotion should be increased. The Ministry of Works should give priority to the manufacture of brickmaking plants. The application of the methods recommended might save 6000 to 15,000 men.

Building Studies

The volume of Government building during the war and the prospect and development of large housing and other programmes after its conclusion sharpened interest not only in the productivity of the building industries and their organisation (see p. 356), but in technical matters affecting cost, economy of materials, speed of construction, etc.

The reports and memos. on the questions issued by the Ministry of Works include: *Codes of Practice* (1943, 1948, 1951), *Use of Standards in Building* (1944, 1946), *Placing and Management of Building Contracts* (1944), *Economy of Building Materials* (1952), *Building Research and Development* (1949, 1953).

Post-War Building Studies (1944– Non-Parl.) owed their origin 'to a desire expressed by professional and other institutions connected with the building and civil engineering industries to assist and support the Ministry of Works in regard to post-war plans. During the latter part of 1941 the then Minister . . . encouraged the establishment of a series of committees to investigate and report on the major problems which are likely to affect peace-time building. He also offered . . . to provide the necessary staff and organisation to co-ordinate the various inquiries . . . to secure so far as possible uniform direction and policy. . . . The committees for the most part were either appointed by a Government department or convened by a professional institution, a research association or a trade federation, as seemed most appropriate in each case.'

National Building Studies (1948– Non-Parl.) aimed at providing a convenient source of the information issued by Government departments on matters of technical interest to the building industry. The publications are of three kinds: bulletins—summaries of information on selected topics not in scientific terms, but as far as possible in the form most useful for their practical application; special reports—comprehensive surveys intended for use by industry, dealing with a particular field of work and covering research, not only in the Ministry or department concerned, but elsewhere; technical Papers—reports intended for scientific or technical readers on research carried out by the Ministry or department responsible for the paper.

For lists of both series see the *Consolidated Lists* and *Annual Catalogues of Government Publications.* Also, *Government Publications Sectional List No. 61.*

See also *District Heating.* Working Party. Interim Rep.; 1951 Non-Parl. Min. of Local Gov. and Planning. *District Heating.* Cttee. Reps. (Post-War Building Studies 31, 32); 1953 Non-Parl. Min. of Works. *District Heating as applied to Small Housing Estates.* Memo. Min. of Fuel and Power, 1946.

Distribution of Building Materials and Components

Cttee. Rep., apps. pp. 144. 1948

1948 Non-Parl. Min. of Works apptd. July, 1946. sgd. March, 1948

Lord Simon (*Ch.*), Brown, Plant, Yeabsley.

'*To examine the organisation and methods of distribution of building materials and components with particular reference to cost and efficiency. . . .*'

Before 1939 there were 80,000 firms in the building and civil engineering industry; in 1948 there were 140,000. Although this growth was largely due to the increase in the number of small firms, the general structure of the building industry is not markedly different from what it was before the war. The units vary in size from the large contractor having several thousand employees to the one-man builder who is particularly dependent on the distributor. It follows that by the nature of the building industry and the trades producing building materials and components, the distributive functions require a very highly specialised distributive apparatus. This is done by the builders' merchant who holds stocks, provides transport and financial facilities and gives technical advice and information; by manufacturers selling straight to the builder, especially the heavy materials such as bricks, sand and gravel; by selling agents of manufacturers in a monopolistic or near monopolistic position and by specialist merchants where materials need specialist services.

Restrictive arrangements have existed on a wide scale for many years, whether in formal or tacit agreements. The broad pattern is that the manufacturer undertakes to supply the merchant on advantageous terms and the merchant agrees to maintain resale prices and not to buy outside the ring. Though profitable to manufacturers and the majority of merchants, these agreements are not in the national interest. They have tended to maintain prices at a higher level, to inflate gross and net distributive margins, to deprive consumers of improvements in the efficiency of distribution and to restrict their freedom of choice. While an annual net profit of 10 per cent on capital would involve a net profit on turnover of $2\frac{1}{2}$ per cent, the Cost Enquiry showed that in 1948 actual net profits were 6·7 per cent, or 26·8 per cent on capital.

The industry has developed in such a way that it may not be possible to establish free competition, e.g. a small number of firms have emerged who have virtually a monopolistic position based on the economies of large scale production and modern techniques, and it therefore may be necessary to have some form of public control. Merchants should improve their systems of accounting, methods of stock control, layout of yards and stores, and methods of handling heavy materials. The Government should take immediate action to control distributive margins on building materials and components. A long-term measure is essential for the elimination of the restrictive practices which exist in this field, including the registration of agreements and declaring individual or types of agreements illegal. The ten Appendices contain much statistical matter concerning the channels of distribution, the various associations, operating costs, etc.

Building

Working Party. Rep., apps., index. pp. vi, 89. 1950

1950 Non-Parl. Min. of Works apptd. July, 1948. sgd. Jan., 1950

T. W. Phillips (*Ch.*), Allen, Armstrong, Beaver, Burt, Coppock, Drake, Fawcett, Kerr, McInnes, Pears, Porteous, Sandercock.

'*To inquire into the organisation and efficiency of building operations in this country, including those of the specialist and sub-contracting trades; the position of the professions in relation thereto; the arrangements for financing operations; and the types of contract in general use, and to make recommendations.*'

During 1946–47 productive efficiency in the building industry was about two-thirds of its pre-war level; by the end of 1948 it was about three-quarters. The combined effect of lower productivity, higher wage rates and higher costs

of materials was that building costs generally throughout 1948–49 were about 2½ times those of 1939. The fall in the level of productive efficiency was due to the great reduction in the labour force during the war, its rapid increase to almost pre-war level immediately afterwards, the dislocation of managements during the war, the launching of a building programme greatly in excess of existing resources, the subsequent changes in this programme, the delays and uncertainties owing to shortages and controls, the compulsory use of untried materials, and the inflationary condition of the country's economy. Most of these conditions were temporary and efficiency slowly recovered; there are, however, two new factors which affect it—full employment and planning controls.

To raise efficiency above its pre-war levels there should be co-operation in everything which helps to improve it and to extend the use of the appliances, methods and materials resulting from scientific and technical advances. Building operations should be completely planned, building research better organised and the results made widely known. For the personnel of the industry there should be training schemes for all grades; the architect's training should give him adequate knowledge of the practical aspects of building and the use of new materials and methods. Technical advice should be available from one Government department. Schemes of incentive payments, if proper conditions are observed, are essential if output is to be increased. Other recommendations include programmes for site organisation, joint production committees, safety and welfare, costing schemes, etc. The existing scheme of registration of builders was intended to ensure that those registered observed proper terms of employment and does not denote any particular degree of competence; proposals for qualitative registration are rejected. The appendices contain a Report on *Costing Systems* by Cooper Brothers and Co. Notes on the *Measurement of Productive*

Efficiency and *Full Employment* by G. C. Allen, etc.

Productivity in House-Building

Rep.

1951 *Non-Parl.* See *Housing*, p. 356

Retention Moneys on Building and Civil Engineering Contracts

Working Party. Rep., app. pp. 9. 1954
1954 *Non-Parl. Min. of Works*
apptd. June, 1952. sgd. —.

E. A. Seal (*Ch.*), Brooks, Jeffries, Strudwick, Thatcher.

'*To investigate the possibility of bonds or guarantees replacing the present system of retentions.*'

In the building and engineering industries, it is the custom for the employer to finance contracts during the progress of the work, but part of the money due is retained to provide a reserve in case the contractor defaults on his contracts or defects in the work appear. In certain classes of building and most civil engineering it is customary for the employer to expect the contractor to enter into a bond which provides payment by a bank or insurance company in event of non-performance of a contract. These bonds are used in conjunction with retention money as guarantees of good faith. The suggestion that the bond could replace the retention money was rejected, since a third party might be called to settle the kind of dispute which hitherto has been settled by good sense or arbitration between the parties concerned, and the bond premium might operate unfairly against a small builder without financial resources. Bonds and guarantees were, for main contracts, substitutes for the traditional retention moneys, but the sums retained should be the minimum necessary. Attention was drawn to Government contract conditions providing for a maximum of 5 per cent for jobs under £50,000 and 3 per cent thereafter.

Cement Production

Cttee. Rep. pp. 10. 1941
1940–41 *Cmd.* 6282, *iv*, 157
apptd. Jan., sgd. April, 1941

G. Balfour (*Ch.*), Bullock, Cook, Coppock, Deakin, Holmes, McLintock, Parker.

'*To consider and report . . . whether, bearing in mind the probable demands for cement in meeting current needs and in post-war reconstruction; and taking into consideration economic, strategic and other factors affecting the allocation of cement, new cement works should be established, existing ones extended or old plant modernised. . . .*'

The probable consumption of cement in war-time was estimated to be no more than 6 mn. tons, though the labour force available could produce $7\frac{1}{2}$ mn. tons. It was also estimated that the immediate post-war demands would not exceed the war demand, but that some 10 mn. tons could be made available; if the post-war demand should exceed this figure, additional plant could soon be provided; extensions to existing works to increase production by $1\frac{1}{2}$ mn. tons could be made in 9 to 18 months. There should be no difficulty in providing for export as soon as the demand is created. The Ministry of Works should keep in close contact with the industry and the position should be reviewed every six months.

Cement Costs

Cttee. Rep., apps. pp. 30. 1947
1947 *Non-Parl. Min. of Works*
apptd. Dec., 1945. sgd. Dec., 1946

A. Fforde (*Ch.*), De Stein, Pears.

'*To review the financial structure of the Cement Industry, and its ancillary industries, including the manufacture of cement sacks, and . . . to report upon the price structure of the industry, with particular reference to the prices charged to merchants and to the various classes of users of cement.*'

The Cement Makers' Federation embraces all manufacturers of cement in the United Kingdom and is the body which fixes prices to which they conform. At the same time there exist within the Federation nine independent financial interests, and the industry is not therefore a monopoly in the sense of being under one single financial control. The primary function of the Federation is the fixing of prices by the votes of members. The voting power of the individual firm or group varies each year by reference to the tonnage of cement delivered by each firm or group in the preceding year, though it is so arranged that the votes do not increase automatically with the increase in delivery; but to carry a resolution against the largest group nearly all the votes of the remaining members would be required. The price structure is founded on a minimum price scheme and on a quota arrangement.

The prices are minimum (in operation, fixed) delivered-to-site prices, consisting of a base price fixed at the nearest works or coastwise importing centre and a subsidised addition for transport to the distance zone from the base point. The object of the manufacturers' quota system is to secure that each firm quotes for delivery at any point a uniform price, whether or not the cement actually comes from the base point. There are penalties for deliveries above and advantages for delivery under quota, but the quota may be revised every five years. The quota system has thus eliminated price competition. There is also a system of well-defined rebates to registered merchants and others.

The profits by reference to capital employed have not been excessive. The price system is not unsound and is not intended to work against the consumer, but (1) there are wide differences of cost between producers and the Federation should review production costs to see where individual costs are high and if the retention of high cost works is essential; (2) the time has arrived when the general level of base prices at individual base points should be reviewed. When price controls are withdrawn, the Federation should submit its price schedules to an independent body appointed for the purpose. The rebates should be left to bargaining between the individual parties. There is a strong bar against the establishment of independent new businesses, but there is no evidence that the Federation has abused its position.

Welsh Slate Industry

Cttee. Rep., apps. pp. 39. 1947
1947 Non-Parl. Min. of Works apptd. May, sgd. Sept., 1946

J. F. Rees (*Ch.*), Evans, North, Schaffer, Cutts, Gould, Williams (J. G. W.), Williams (O. T.), Jones (J. H.), Jones (R. J.), Owen, Williams (R. W.).

'*To consider and report upon the organisation of the Welsh slate industry and upon measures for increasing its efficiency and making it attractive to recruits, excluding wages and conditions of employment falling within the negotiating machinery of the Industry.*'

Slate has been quarried in Wales for local use and for export for centuries. In N. Wales in 1898 production rose to a peak of 485,000 tons, employing 16,000 men, but by 1914 production had dropped to 251,000 tons, employing 8634 men. In the inter-war years there was a further fall, slates having been replaced by mass-produced roofing tiles.

As a result of restrictions on building in the Second World War, by 1945 there were only 3728 workers in the industry, the decline being due to unemployment rather than enlistment. But an expansion of the industry involves much preparatory work in removing overburden and unproductive rock, driving of headings, etc. Slate quarrying is highly localised and specialised. The numbers of men returning from the Forces are limited, and every effort should be made to induce the return of 2000 still in other industries. Such efforts should take account of the unique social background of the Welsh quarryman.

The industry is a war casualty, and as

it is basic to the economic life of the region, it should be given special facilities for rehabilitation. It must be assured of a long-term demand. Recommendations include loans on favourable terms or grants for development work, for assisting mechanisation, reopening suitable quarries, an examination of the marketing arrangements by the trade, continuation of war-time schemes for allocating orders on a quota system, penalising price cutting, improved welfare arrangements.

China Clay

Working Cttee. Rep., apps. pp. 14. 1946

1945–46 Cmd. 6748, x, 797
apptd. Dec., 1945. sgd. Jan., 1946

W. R. Jones (*Ch.*), Bennetts, Harris.

'*To enquire into the factors affecting the efficiency of the production of china-clay and to report upon the methods which should be adopted to increase production to a degree sufficient to meet the probable post-war requirements at home and abroad.*'

The total production of china clay in 1945 was 285,000 tons for the home market and 116,000 tons for export, or one-third the pre-war figure. The labour force had dropped from 3746 to 2148, the demand in 1946 would be about 750,000 tons, but the likely labour force of 2400 would produce only 410,000 tons. The short-term policy required a substantial release of men from the forces, use of prisoners of war, and drawing in labour from other districts.

There are twenty firms in the industry, seven of which belong to the China Clay Association, which has a price-fixing quota system, and there is disunity between them. The industry is technically backward, much of the work is still done by manual labour and there is a great need of mechanisation, integration of adjacent pits and steps to prevent the accumulation of waste on good china clay ground. A Working Party should be appointed to consider long-term policy.

See *China-Clay*. Working Party. Rep.; 1948 Non-Parl. Bd. of Trade.

Ball-clay Industry

Enquiry. Rep., apps. pp. 14. 1946

1946 Non-Parl. Bd. of Trade
apptd. Jan., sgd. March, 1946

W. R. Jones (*Ch.*), Scott.

'*. . . to report as soon as possible upon the steps which should be taken to increase the production of ball-clay to meet the requirements of the expanding pottery industry— including the manufacture of housing fitments. . . .*'

Ball clay includes whiteware clays used to give plasticity and bonding power for pottery, earthenware, etc., and other clays used in stoneware, etc. In 1945 39,000 tons of whiteware clays were produced, but another 40,000 tons will be needed for domestic consumption in 1946. The pre-war labour force of 800 had fallen to 446, a quarter of whom were over 60. The work was heavy and unpleasant. Labour should be introduced from other areas. There is little use of simple mechanical equipment. Ball clay exported as clay realised £3 per ton, in manufacture £120–£200 per ton. There should be export control of clays for one year. The long-term policy should include proving the national resources of ball-clay deposits and technical training.

Cotton Textile Mission to the United States of America

Rep. pp. x, 78. 1944

1944 Non-Parl. Min. of Production
sgd. July, 1944

F. Platt and six others.

With normal staffing British P.M.H. (on the basis of total output and total labour force) is less than the American by 18 to 48 per cent in spinning, 80 to 85 per cent in winding, 79 to 89 per cent in beaming and 56 to 67 per cent in weaving. British labour requirements exceed the American by 22 to 98 per cent in spinning, 387 to 571 per cent in winding. The skill of the Lancashire operative remains unsurpassed, so that the difference is one of mechanical efficiency.

Amongst the reasons for the high American P.M.H. are the use of high-drafts, high-speed and automatic machinery; better utilisation of labour, which permits supervision of a relatively large number of units or machines by an operative; bulk production with high speed and automatic machinery on the basis of three shifts each of 48 hours, whereas British mills work one shift of 48 hours and produce a wide range of products not permitting the economical use of highly productive automatic machinery. British managers are technically efficient, but conservative.

The short-term recommendations include: a higher degree of standardisation and more bulk production, improved technical equipment, a greater use of high drafting in ring and mule spinning and in cardrooms; greater economy in the use of labour; increased number of looms per man. The long-term recommendations include: planning for the maximum P.M.H.; use of high-speed and automatic machinery; a comprehensive survey of existing plant and its suitability for modernisation.

Post-War Problems of the Cotton Trade

Cotton Board. Cttee. Rep., apps. pp. 55. [1944]

[1944] *Cotton Board*
apptd. —, 1943. *sgd. Jan.*, 1944

E. R. Streat (*Ch.*).

The Committee was appointed by the Cotton Board at the request of the President of the Board of Trade.

A permanent post-war Cotton Board should be established, with powers to administer price, redundancy and excess capacity schemes, collect levies, etc. The spinning section should be of the same size as in 1939, but in weaving and finishing there was excess capacity. In the former, new looms should be in-

stalled only against equivalent scrapping; in the latter, in view of the Government pledges to them, voluntary closure of firms which were concentrated should be encouraged by compensation, together with control over new entrants. Re-equipment on a grandiose scale was not required, but there should be speedy essential re-equipment followed by steady modernisation. A proportion of the output of textile machinery should be reserved for the home market. The implementation of long-term plans for £43 mn., at 1939 prices, of new equipment would depend on the confidence in the stability of the industry. This would require power to enforce minimum price margins, subject to supervision. This stability and improved conditions would help to build up the depleted labour force.

Two apps. give the statistical calculations on which the proposals were based.

Cotton

Working Party. Rep., apps. pp. vi, 278. 1946

1946 *Non-Parl. Bd. of Trade*
apptd. Oct., 1945. *sgd. April*, 1946

G. Schuster, Griffin, Knowles, Naesmith, Roberts, Reynolds, Clegg, Hirst, Jewkes, Shaw (Anne G.), Symons, Wiggins.

'*To enquire into the various schemes and suggestions put forward for improvements of organisation, production and distribution methods and processes in the Cotton Industry, and to report as to the steps which should be adopted in the national interest to strengthen the industry and render it more stable and more capable of meeting competition in the home and foreign markets.*'

The Party rejects as an aim a moderate-sized industry relying on the home market in favour of maintaining it as a major industry making a large contribution to British exports. It disagrees with the Report of the Cotton Board on post-war problems on three points. The recommendation in favour of compulsory minimum prices overlooks the fact that weak selling is only a symptom of redundant capacity; accepting the 1939 spindleage as the basis of the industry would require a labour force of 390,000 when only 270,000 would be available; and it did not develop fully a policy of mechanical re-equipment.

A labour force of 390,000 would be required to operate on pre-war methods the spinning capacity available and the balance in weaving capacity, but in January 1946 only 225,000 were available. If these were spread over all mills evenly none could operate at more than $61\frac{1}{2}$ per cent capacity, costs would be too high and the volume of production too low for an export trade. It would be unwise to rely upon more than 250,000, better wages would be needed to attract them, so that the industry must run on a relatively small, highly paid labour force. It must have the best tools and production per man/hour must be increased. But costly equipment cannot be installed except on the basis of a double shift system. A concerted programme is necessary.

There should be a comprehensive survey of existing plant and its suitability for modernisation, of requirements and an ordered programme for the supply of machinery over the next five years at prices subject to independent scrutiny. Control prices should be raised 1d. per pound of 24's yarn, which would average 4s. 2d. per spindle and a re-equipment levy imposed on 90 per cent of this, i.e. 3s. 9d. per spindle. Mills installing new equipment would be entitled to a rebate and to apply for a grant, not normally exceeding what the firm had paid in, for installing new and modernising plant. Spinning mills should be organised into groups and a certain number, operating about 5 mn. spindles or $12\frac{1}{2}$ per cent of the total, should be taken over and immobilised, those most suitable for modernisation being held in reserve and the rest sold. The weaving industry, still carried on by family concerns, should be reorganised by a similar levy (£9 per loom) and an increase of one farthing a

yard on utility cloth. The cost of re-equipment in spinning would be £38 mn., the fund £11 mn. to £17 mn. In weaving the cost would be £29 mn., the fund £$9\frac{3}{4}$ mn. There should be an Equipment Board, not permanent, to collect the levy and disperse the proceeds and to purchase and hold a proportion of the plant. There should be a central council for the cotton industry, a central factory board run by the industry to operate a number of mills on a commercial basis for 'yardstick' purposes, and a central marketing company to supplement existing arrangements, merchants and merchant-convertors joining as shareholders.

Clegg, Hirst, Jewkes, Miss Shaw, Symons, and Wiggins in a Memo. of dissent argue that firms are generally the size compatible with maximum efficiency, and a redundancy scheme is not the way to redistribute scarce labour. What is required is selective re-equipment suited to the varying needs of each firm and if export prices were freed from control the producer would be able to finance it. The Equipment Board and a uniform levy would delay the selective process. Griffin, Knowles, Naesmith and Roberts comment on the memo. of dissent.

Cotton Textile Machinery Industry

Cttee. Interim Rep., apps. pp. 27. 1947

1947 Non-Parl. Min. of Supply apptd. —, sgd. March, 1947

R. Evershed (Ch.), Board, Green, Madden, Robinson.

'To investigate . . . matters connected with the manufacture and supply of textile machinery to the cotton industry. . . .'

The inquiry arose out of a recommendation of the Working Party on *Cotton*, 1946. Textile Machinery Makers Ltd. had come under severe criticism because as a virtual monopoly of the manufacture in this country of machinery for cotton spinning and preparatory processes, they were thought to have abused their position by deliberately over-charging so as to make profits for themselves and their proprietors. Exhaustive enquiry shows that they had not done so. The real criticism was that the Company was deficient in the personnel of its directorate and management, that the organisation of the merger was over-complex and could be simplified, that it was deficient in the matter of research and development and that it failed to comply with modern standards of integrated costing. In the case of a monopoly the remedies found in the pressure of natural economic forces might be insufficient; and the offer of a Government subsidy to mills willing to re-equip made it necessary to ensure that the use of public money did not result in undue profits. 'The public interest would best be served if we were able to report that T.M.M. had taken the several steps we felt desirable.' The Board of T.M.M. have already taken or given assurances that they will take these steps. These included an agreement that the Ministry of Supply should satisfy itself in 18 months' time that an adequate costings system was in operation and that prices on home orders should be on the basis of costs and a rate of profit agreed with the Ministry of Supply. The Report contains a history of the merger.

—— Second and Final Report. pp. 16.
1947

1947 *Non-Parl.*
sgd. June, 1947

I. Automatic looms.—The British Northrop Loom Co. Ltd. makes automatic looms exclusively and produces the greatest proportion made in the U.K. There are certain other firms who produce the automatic looms within a range of looms. The Northrop Company developed in the inter-war years in circumstances which must have meant a continuous battle against adverse trading conditions, conservatism and even prejudice. In 1929 its maximum capacity was 1500 looms per annum, in 1939 this had doubled, and

with present expansion it should reach 6000 by 1949, of which a proportion must be exported. But the 120,000 estimated by the Working Party Report as required within six years means 20,000 per annum. The only way in which this requirement could be met would be by a scheme of intensive flow production of standard types on the lines adopted during the war for munitions of war, with far-reaching Government action to provide priorities of materials, plant and personnel. In the meantime non-automatic looms should be fitted with various devices enabling weft to be automatically replenished.

II.—The supply of warping and winding machinery should be adequate to meet demand at present foreseen, provided materials are available. Temporary deficiencies should be made up by imports or by negotiating licences.

Raw Cotton Commission

[1st] Ann. Rep. and Statement of Accounts, apps. pp. 48. [1949]
1948–49 (157) *xxi*, 1
o.p. May, 1949

H. O. R. Hindley (*Ch.*).

Describes the organisation, the decision to base price policy on replacement cost, the cover scheme, etc., and gives an account of cotton control, 1939–49.
See succeeding Ann. Reps.

Cotton Import

Cttee. Rep., app. pp. 22. 1952
1951–52 *Cmd.* 8510, *ix*, 757
apptd. Dec., 1951. *sgd. March,* 1952

R. V. N. Hopkins (*Ch.*), Brooks, Butterworth, Cockcroft, Hasty, Hutchinson, Lacey, Little, Naesmith, Roberts, Schofield, Streat, Symons, Winterbottom.

'*To consider and report to the President of the Board of Trade and the Chancellor of the Duchy of Lancaster on the question how, in the current foreign exchange position, cotton can best be supplied to the United Kingdom cotton industry on the most advantageous terms as to quality and price.*'

By the Cotton (Centralised Buying) Act, 1947, the Raw Cotton Commission succeeded the Cotton Control and became the sole authority for importing, holding and distributing cotton to spinners and other users. It started with a reserve fund of £30 mn. to enable it to meet losses through falling prices. It has sold cotton at world replacement prices. For $3\frac{1}{2}$ years it enjoyed a seller's market, but in the last two years there have emerged differing cotton prices related not to intrinsic qualities, but to whether dollar or non-dollar currencies are required to pay for it.

There are two prices for similar cottons. Futures cover is essential to most of the Lancashire industry, and unless there is complete freedom of import, this cannot be provided except by the Commission's comparable facilities. Despite the exchange position the industry enjoys an adequate cover, as the Commission carries the risks on the two basic or substitute growths. Firms say they get a fair share of any cottons in short supply and that the Commission has advantages over private traders in making long-term contracts. Its disadvantages are that financing its operations requires a considerable sum from public funds; some spinners complain that they cannot exercise personal choice in the quality of yarns needed to build up individual traditions, and that in seasons of difficult supply an intermediary cannot make prompt decisions as knowledgeably as a principal.

The full free market cannot be restored in present conditions. Detailed recommendations are made which would allow every spinner to exercise an annual option to 'contract out' and to buy certain types of cotton through merchants on his own behalf. Until some form of cover not using public funds is available, the Commission should continue to provide it.

See *Cotton Import (Review)* Cttee. Rep.; 1952–53 Cmd. 8861, ix, 1, for a review of action taken, e.g. as a result of the spinners' first option, 30 per cent of the total exports of raw cotton during the current season will be on private account.

Tendencies to Monopoly in the Cinematograph Film Industry

Cinematograph Films Council. Cttee. Rep., apps. pp. 41. 1944
1944 *Non-Parl. Bd. of Trade apptd. Dec., 1943. sgd. July,* 1944
A. Palache (*Ch.*), Citrine, Plant.

To advise 'on what further practical measures, if any, are necessary to check the development of monopoly in the film industry.'

A healthy British industry can be built up on condition that independent production is safeguarded. There are some essential requirements for maintaining it. (1) Access to story material and screen writers: there are no new adverse monopolistic tendencies. (2) Maintenance of companies producing second and low-cost feature films is important for the training of technicians and actors. (3) In war conditions the decisive factor is shortage of studio space. Half the available stages are controlled by one organisation and two-thirds are linked with the three exhibition circuits. Inadequate planning of production is said to lead to wasteful use of studio space. Since no radical increase of space can be expected for some time, it should not be left with the combines to decide what share of studio space should be reserved for independent British production, and some form of control of allocation of stage space should be adopted. (4) No permanent capital of consequence is invested in production, either in the production side of the vertically integrated groups, which depend on receipts of renting organisations from exhibitors, or in independent groups, which depend on piece-meal finance of specific films by a few rich individuals. And there is no suitable specialised organisation offering financial facilities. (5) The renting organisations, whose charges of 20 per cent to 35 per cent of receipts seem high and are tending to rise, are almost invariably connected with competing producers or may have standing arrangements to distribute for an American producer. Independent producers therefore try to maintain their own expensive renting organisations. As a condition of release, renters require exhibitors to book other films. (6) Access to the screen. The majority of the 4750 cinemas are old and small: a really successful film would penetrate to not more than 2000, and the three circuits control over 1000, the majority being the better-placed ones. The survival of independent production depends on whether or not collective bookings are made by two circuits controlled by one person and by a third circuit controlled by another. The circuits have a dominating position in London. The circuits are integrated vertically with producers and distributors. The 'bars' imposed by cinemas on bookings in competitive areas are archaic and unduly restrictive. War conditions have accentuated the dominance of American films and the rental sums transferred are a heavy exchange burden. British films in U.S.A. yield slender returns. An attempt to force a way in by the exercise of monopoly power by British integrated concerns would be undesirable. The creation of a renting organisation in America to serve all British producers is recommended.

Amongst the recommendations were: legislation should prevent any further expansion of circuits and acquisitions of studio space by vertically integrated combines, except with the consent of the Board of Trade. To allay fears that control of the combines might pass into American hands, those in control of them should consider a trustee arrangement comparable to that of *The Times* or *The Economist*. The Board of Trade should control allocation of studio space between independent and integrated production, first consideration being given to medium-cost feature films. A Film Finance Corporation should be established under Government sponsorship to give financial facilities to qualified producers; it should be empowered to establish a

renting organisation and to extend its activities to overseas marketing. Conditional bookings should be prohibited, distributors compelled to treat co-operative booking organisations of independent exhibitors on the same terms as accorded to a circuit, and the Board of Trade should endeavour to secure for independent producers a reasonable proportion of screen time and for independent exhibitors a reasonable share of feature pictures. A strong British organisation should be established in the United States and the two governments should explore methods of increasing the voluntary exhibition of British films there. A tribunal should be established to arbitrate on conditions of film hire, conditional bookings, licensing changes of cinema ownership, etc., 'bars', etc.

See *Cinematograph Films Act, 1927*. Cttee. Rep. (*Ch.*, L. Moyne). *Breviate, 1917–1939*, p. 169, and *National Film Finance Corporation*. 1st Ann. Rep.; 1950 Cmd. 7927, vii, 293, and succeeding Ann. Reps.

British Film Institute

Cttee. Rep., apps. pp. 13. 1948

1947–48 *Cmd.* 7361, *x*, 151

apptd. Dec., 1947. *sgd. March*, 1948

C. J. Radcliffe (*Ch.*), Pooley, Powell (Miss D.), Robertson, Tallents, Wilson.

'To consider and report on any changes which may be desirable in the constitution and scope of the British Film Institute and the relationship which should exist between the Institute and other bodies concerned with the film as a cultural and education medium.'

In 1933, on the initiative of the British Institute for Adult Education, the British Film Institute, to be financed from a fund established under the Sunday Entertainments Act, 1932, was set up to encourage the use and development of the cinematograph as a means of entertainment and instruction. The Institute has made an attempt to develop its activities, but has been hampered by the lack of funds. Although there are now several specialised bodies at work in the field originally assigned to the Institute, it is still of public importance that there should be an independent organisation designed to encourage the development of the art of the film and to extend its use. The extensions of work recommended would require capital expenditure of £30,000 and an annual cost of £100,000; the Institute's main funds should be derived from an Exchequer grant fixed on a quinquennial basis; the Scottish Film Council should also be given additional funds for this purpose. The Board of Governors should be appointed individually by a Minister.

Film Studio

Cttee. Rep., apps. pp. 17. 1948

1948 *Non-Parl. Bd. of Trade apptd. July, sgd. Oct.,* 1948

G. H. Gater (*Ch.*), Roberts, Edwards.

'*On the assumption that an additional film studio, capable of accommodating at least two productions simultaneously, is to be erected in Great Britain and that these additional facilities or such part of them as may be deemed appropriate are to be reserved for the use of independent producers whose needs are not otherwise adequately provided for, to consider how far it is necessary or desirable that H.M. Government should own or control the management of the aforesaid studio.*'

The terms of reference assumed that additional studio space was to be erected and reserved for the use of free-lance producers. Evidence, however, showed that owing to the abolition of the renter's quota, which had reduced the flow of American capital, the losses through extravagance of production which have discouraged financial backers, and to the unsettlement in the industry resulting from the American boycott, etc., there was now no lack of studio space.

Planning in such a highly speculative industry is difficult, and would be more so in dealing with a group of highly individualistic producers. Some of the evidence was to the effect that what restricted free-lance production was finance, not lack of studio space. The Government, like any other studio-owner, would be confronted with the problem of continuous production and in the event of failure to secure it, would be faced with serious financial loss and unemployment of staff. As a remedy, it might itself be forced to undertake the production of pictures.

The Government should invite proposals from free-lance producers for the formation of a co-operative organisation which would plan an effective production programme. When satisfied that this organisation had been set up, the Government should be the owner of a studio and its management should be entrusted to a limited company. If the free-lance producers do not achieve an efficient organisation it would be hazardous for the Government to provide additional studio-space. The Appendices contain memos from the Independent Film Producers' Association and from the trade unions.

Film Production Costs

Working Party. Rep., apps. pp. 32.
1949

1949 *Non-Parl. Bd. of Trade apptd. Feb., sgd. Oct.,* 1949

G. H. Gater (*Ch.*), Boxall, Clark, Donald, Davis, Elvin, French, Haxell, Hoare, John (Miss R.), Mingaye, O'Brien, Roberts.

'*To examine ways and means of reducing production costs.*'

Representatives of the producers in the Party stated that the present economic difficulties facing the British film industry were primarily due to the relatively small proportion of gross box-office receipts which became available for British production. At no time since the substitution of sound for silent films has the industry been on a satisfactory financial basis: British film producers face the competition from a vast import of American films whose cost of production has been largely recovered in the United States, and bear heavy interest owing to the time-lag between expenditure and cinema receipts. Some of the trade unions concerned thought that efficient organisation in the whole industry would lead to the production of films on an economic basis.

Producers attribute high costs to increase in cost of materials and labour, to high studio rents, to restrictive practices and a decline of the team spirit. Studio workers, on the other hand, stress high administrative expenses, top-heavy production executive staff, high salaries of 'stars', faulty planning, extravagance in sets and properties and exaggerated standards of perfection. Extravagance and unreality is a problem of any industry concerned with entertainment and in the years immediately after the end of the war in the film industry it was allowed to go beyond 'all reasonable bounds'; the success in certain British films led to an ever-increasing disregard of cost.

The recommendations include: co-operation at a national level in preparation of production programmes; joint production and works committees; 'cost consciousness' on managerial and overhead expenses; limited basic salaries to artists and higher technicians, with later supplementary payments; the discouragement of extravagant retakes; elimination of trivial demarcation disputes; close control and supervision and inter-studio co-operation over properties, etc., and more uniformity in the preparation of film budgets. In a Note Mr. Hoare stated that when the task of putting the industry on a sound economic basis was accomplished, there remained the problem of ensuring a reasonably steady flow of production which would avoid the violent fluctuations in output with the consequent inflation of overheads. He recommended the creation of a trade body to co-ordinate a production plan.

Distribution and Exhibition of Cinematograph Films

Cttee. Rep., app. pp. 63. [1949]

1948–49 *Cmd.* 7837, *xii*, 639
apptd. Dec., 1948. *sgd. Nov.,* 1949

A. Plant (*Ch.*), Gain, Lawrie, Richardson, Smart, Sutherland (Miss Lucy S.).

'To consider, against the background of the general economic situation in the film industry, the arrangements at present in operation for the distribution of films to exhibitors and their exhibition to the public in the commercial cinemas, and to make recommendations.'

In 1948 gross box office receipts were £109 mn. and entertainments tax £39 mn. leaving £70 mn. net receipts, of which film hire accounted for £42·5 mn. making distributors' gross receipts £27·5 mn. Distributors' gross receipts on British first feature films were £10 mn. of which £7·5 mn. was received by British producers. There were 4692 licensed cinemas, with a total capacity of one seat for every ten potential patrons, each seat being taken on the average about seven times each week. The trade estimate of attendances was 28 mn. per week at an average of 1s. 6½d.—6½d. for duty and 1s. 0d. for all costs of production and distribution. In 94 per cent of the cinemas programmes were usually made up of two feature films and two short films. The law required that 20 per cent of the screen time should be given to British products; in 1948 it was 25·6 per cent, the rest being taken by foreign films.

Films are hired by exhibitors from distributors (renters), the most usual terms for a first feature film being an agreed percentage of box office receipts less entertainments tax. The renters enter into a distribution contract with the producer covering particular films for a term of years, their fee taking the form of an agreed percentage of the rental paid by exhibitors. One-third of the cinemas are in 'circuits' owned by companies, 1000 being controlled by two groups. The production of British films is usually financed by the renters, who commonly guarantee to pay up to 75 per cent of the cost within a stated time after delivery. The producer can then discount the guarantee at a bank. Established producing units usually enter into long-term arrangements with renters.

Producers and renters are concerned to secure their share of box office receipts as soon as possible and release to the largest cinemas, which have the largest proportion of higher priced seats and then to the next largest and so on. In practice this general pattern is altered by the system of barring and by the existence of circuits. To keep his hall full, when hiring a film a cinema owner usually obtains an undertaking that it will not be shown in a competing cinema simultaneously or for some time after, but the so-called competitive areas to which this practice applies are frequently too extensive and thus prevent films from being as widely shown as they might be. The cinemas which secure the first offer of a film are not necessarily those with the highest potential box office takings, for the bargaining power of the circuits, three of which own 70 per cent of the cinemas seating more than 1500 persons, is such that they can require that some of their smaller halls shall take precedence. One organisation which controlled two circuits and had a large financial interest in the production of some films, would have been able by arranging a variety of bookings for different selections of the cinemas it controls to favour its films against those in which it had little financial interest. The independent producers were not satisfied that the centralisation of control by groups actively engaged in producing feature films would be exercised impartially.

The Committee was concerned with the aggregate revenue available to meet all the costs of the industry, with its distribution between exhibitors, distributors, producers and the Exchequer, and took it to be an accepted objective of national policy that a healthy British industry for producing films should be able to maintain itself on a self-supporting basis. To achieve this end more active competition at each stage was necessary. Proposals to divorce film production and distribution from the control of cinemas and to reduce the number of cinemas under one control were rejected. To maximise box office receipts, in every competitive district the cinemas with the greatest box office potential should be enabled to bid for the first showing and the distributor should be obliged to accept the highest offer. Similar principles should be applied to subsequent releases. In certain monopoly situations it might be in the public interest that individual cinemas should be sold to independent interests. These and other measures would not lead to any great increase in aggregate revenue; this must therefore be apportioned so as to stimulate the production of good and discourage that of bad films. The unilateral agreement amongst exhibitors to pay no more than 50 per cent for the hire of any film penalises successful and subsidises unsuccessful producers. It should be replaced by a sliding scale of film hire rising as takings exceed a number of break points. The practice of some distributors of imposing conditional hire forces unwanted goods on the public and should be prohibited. The distribution of returns between distributors and producers is affected by the various causes of unequal bargaining power, including the distributor's part in financing production. The producer should be protected by separate contracts for finance and distribution, and in separate distribution contracts a distributor's charge of 15 per cent for an average film should be adequate. There should also be standard contracts. The share of total receipts taken by entertainments tax is too heavy. A permanent body whose members should be independent of trade interests, should be established to consider and report upon the adequacy of plans for reorganising exhibition and distribution, to take the initiative in eliminating undesirable trade practices, etc.

Distribution and Exhibition of Cinematograph Films

Cinematograph Films Council.   Rep. pp. 14.   1950

1950 Non-Parl.   Bd. of Trade
sgd. May, 1950

Lord Drogheda (*Ch.*), and 21 others.

'*To work out specific practical proposals, for submission to the President of the Board of Trade, to give effect to the main objectives underlying the* [*Plant*] *Report's recommendations.*'

This is a report of a committee of trade members of the Film Council. While accepting the contention that existing arrangements are too rigid and that more competition is needed, reliance on the freest possible competition is unrealistic. Competitive bidding for films is rejected, but the trade should consider more flexible arrangements for outstanding films; monopolies of cinemas should not be broken up without regard to circumstances, but there should be a procedure for investigating solo and other monopolist situations; the barring system is satisfactory, and a joint trade committee has been correcting anomalies. The proposals for a sliding scale for film hire should be considered by the trade. The proposals for maximising the return to the producer are too rigid; an independent tribunal is strongly opposed.

In a minority report Elvin rejects the proposals both of the Plant and the trade committees. He proposes a State Distribution Corporation to distribute films it wholly or partly finances, as well as those of independent producers, a Fourth Circuit of 300–400 key cinemas to be acquired from existing circuits, a return to a quota of 40 to 45 per cent of British films, and the examination by the Board of Trade of the apportionment of box office receipts.

Agreement between H.M.s Government in the U.K. and N. Ireland and the Motion Picture Industry of the U.S.A.

Memo., apps. pp. 8.   1950

1950–51 Cmd. 8113, xxxii, 291

Normal exportation of American films to Great Britain will continue and there will be no increase of British import duties on them. The agreement sets out the amounts of American film revenues for which the Treasury will afford facilities for remission in dollars.

Hydrocarbon Oil Duties

Rep.

1944–45 Cmd. 6615

See *National Finance*, p. 59.

Chemical Engineering Research

Cttee. Rep., apps. pp. iii, 36.   1951

1951 Non-Parl.   D.S.I.R.
apptd. April, 1949.   sgd. Sept., 1950

H. W. Cremer (*Ch.*), Fox, Garner, Griffiths, Herbert, Hoblyn, Inglis, Newitt, Pratt, Robson.

'*To review the needs for research in chemical engineering and the extent to which they can be met by existing facilities.*'

The research facilities in chemical engineering, though considerable, are inadequate for the purposes of the chemical and allied industries as a whole. The research needs are of two kinds, the one relating to experimental investigations designed to elucidate the mechanism of the basic operations employed in industry (e.g. drying, filtering, evaporating) and the other to the provision of practical data, based upon large-scale operation, which are required for design purposes. The first need can be met by developing the research potential in universities and technical colleges, etc., but for the second, facilities are inadequate and there appears to be no existing central organisation for work which would ensure in collaboration with manufacturers, closer integration of basic research with actual operations. There are examples of manufacturing operations which had their origin in this country, but were developed and modernised elsewhere, and now operate here under foreign licences. The tempo of industrial exploitation of scientific research requires that existing facilities for research should be supplemented by a central organisation specially adapted and created for the purpose. Every effort should be made to confer with the staffs of the present research centres, and to make available such relevant material as they are able to provide in the normal course of their activities. Special reference was made to atomic research and fuel research, etc. There is much published research information apposite to chemical engineering proper which is either unknown to potential users, or which is in obscure or unrelated form; the central organisation should collect, interpret and distribute such information.

Iron and Steel Industry

British Iron and Steel Federation and the Jt. Iron Council. Reps., apps. pp. 107. 1946

1945–46 *Cmd.* 6811, *xiii*, 429
sgd. Dec., 1945, *Feb.–March*, 1946

In a letter to the President of the Federation in May 1945 the Government said that their first aim was to secure the rapid completion of a substantial volume of modernisation and new construction, and asked the industry to submit a plan, including proposals they thought required Government support during the period of modernisation. The Government stated that they had in mind that the plan should, when agreed, constitute the basis of action for the Government and the industry.

The plan was based on an estimated home demand of 13 mn. tons and an export demand of 3 mn. tons, a total of 16 mn. tons as compared with a peak of 11·6 mn. tons in 1937. This would involve an import of $\frac{1}{2}$ mn. tons of steel, and a 55 per cent scrap usage. Home ore for basic pig iron is less costly per unit of content than quality imported ore, but requires a high capital investment and fuel consump-

tion. Technical considerations increase the desirability of locating works using quality ores on coastal sites, while cost reasons make it desirable to increase the proportion of commoner steels based on home ores. $7\frac{1}{2}$ mn. tons of imported and $12\frac{1}{2}$ mn. tons of home ores would be required. The plan envisages the construction of $4\frac{3}{4}$ mn. tons of blast furnace and 6 mn. tons of steel ingot capacity, and involves the replacement and expansion in $7\frac{1}{2}$ years of the equivalent of about 40 per cent of the capacity of the industry at a cost of £168 mn. 24 blast furnaces with a capacity of $4\frac{3}{4}$ mn. tons will replace 53 blast furnaces with a capacity of 3 mn. tons. A new strip mill will be erected in S. Wales. Broad figures are given of the probable reduction of costs as compared with those in the 20 per cent highest cost plants. The expenditure will be at the rate of £$22\frac{1}{2}$ mn. a year; the industry could provide for about half the cost from its own resources.

Iron and Steel Bill

Explanatory and Financial Memo. pp. i–v. [1948]

1948–49 (*Bill* 1) *iii*, 19
o.p. Oct., 1948

The purpose of the Bill is to bring under public ownership the main producing undertakings in certain sections of the iron and steel industry. An Iron and Steel Corporation of Great Britain will be established to hold the securities of companies owning or operating works the average annual output of which in 1946 and 1947 was not less than 50,000 tons of iron ore, or 20,000 tons of pig iron, ingot steel or hot rolled products, any company whose main activity is manufacturing motor vehicles being excluded. The holders of securities vested in the Corporation are to be compensated by the issue to them of British Iron and Steel Stock of equal value at or about the general date of transfer. This value, in the case of quoted securities, is to be deemed the average market value of the securities on certain dates, in other cases as agreed or determined by arbitration. The general duty of the Corporation is to secure that their products are available in such quantities, at such prices and are of such types, qualities and sizes as the Corporation consider best in the public interest in all respects. The Corporation may acquire or set up companies for the purpose of its authorised activities, but may not increase those activities without the Minister's consent. In carrying out capital development and reorganisation, training, education and research, the Corporation is to act in accordance with general programmes settled from time to time with the approval of the Minister. The Minister will appoint committees of consumers.

It will be a duty of the Corporation to secure that the combined revenues of the Corporation and the publicly-owned companies are, one year with another, sufficient to meet their combined outgoings on revenue account. The Corporation is empowered to create British Iron and Steel Stock, provided that the sums outstanding (otherwise than for paying compensation) and temporary loans do not exceed £350 mn. The stock issued as compensation is to be, and other stock may be, guaranteed by the Treasury. The Corporation is to maintain a reserve, the main purpose of which will be to check undue fluctuations of price.

Businesses not acquired by the Corporation may not produce more than 5000 tons without a licence from the Minister.

Iron and Steel Corporation of Great Britain

Reps. and Statements of Accounts. pp. iv, 92. 1952. pp. iv, 104. 1953
1951–52 (294) *xvi*, 1. 1952–53 (198) *xiv*, 251

Established under the Iron and Steel Act, 1949, which nationalised the iron and steel industry, the Corporation became responsible for 298 companies employing 300,000 people and re-presenting an annual turnover of about £500 mn. The Corporation acted as a holding company controlling the policy of the companies through its shareholdings in them. The Corporation ceased after the passing of the Iron and Steel Act, 1953; 1 & 2 Eliz. 2. c. 15.

See *Iron and Steel Consumers' Council*. Reps.; 1952–53 (42) (224) *xiv*, 359.

Iron and Steel Industry
pp. 6. [1952]
1951–52 *Cmd*. 8619, *xxv*, 419

The Government propose to reorganise the iron and steel industry under free enterprise with an adequate measure of public supervision.

Public Supervision.—An Iron and Steel Board of 12 members appointed by the Minister of Supply will have under its purview all the main processes specified, thus bringing the whole of the industry, both nationalised and non-nationalised, under supervision, but it will not be concerned with extraneous activities brought under the control of the Iron and Steel Board because they happened to form part of the activities of the nationalised companies. The Board will supervise the industry in order to promote an economical and adequate supply of iron and steel, and keep under review the development of productive capacity, prices, etc. It will supervise the plans of the industry and individual firms for capital development to ensure that any necessary additional capacity, etc., will be provided, and will be empowered to restrain any scheme which would prejudice the industry's economical development. The Minister of Supply, after consultation with the Board, may arrange for schemes of development which on commercial grounds no company is willing to undertake. It will have power to fix maximum prices. All producers will be deemed to have entered into a contractual obligation with the Board to observe its decisions as to prices and development.

Transfer of Ownership.—The Iron

and Steel Corporation will be dissolved and the securities of the nationalised companies transferred to a Holding and Realisation Agency consisting of persons appointed by the Treasury. In disposing of the securities transferred to them the Agency will require Treasury approval of the terms of sale and timing. In deciding the prices, it must take account of changes in physical assets, capital structure, trading prospects and market conditions; it will where practicable give priority to former shareholders. It will be able to regroup companies after consultation with the new Board. Pending disposal, companies owned by the Board will operate on the same footing as privately owned competitors.

See *Iron and Steel Board.* [1st] Ann. Rep.; 1954–55 (138) *vi*, 311, and succeeding Ann. Reps. *Iron and Steel Holding and Realisation Agency.* [1st] Rep.; 1954–55 (70) vi, 397, and succeeding Ann. Reps.

Development of the Iron and Steel Industry 1953 to 1958

Iron and Steel Board. Special Rep., apps. pp. 42. 1955

1954–55 (49) *vi*, 351

The results of the industry's first post-war development plan (Cmd. 6811, see p. 147 above) are given in App. A. At the request of the Minister in 1952, the Iron and Steel Corporation presented the Outline of a Second Development Plan, based on an estimated demand for 21 mn. tons. This was sent to the Board on its appointment and in view of changes in the probable demand for different products, etc., revised to 22½ mn. tons. As imports will fall to 100,000 tons and 400,000 tons will be available from re-usable steel, home production in 1958 should be 22 mn. tons. This involves an increase of pig iron production from 11·2 mn. tons in 1953 to 15·15 mn. tons in 1958. The total capital cost of schemes of modernisation and expansion will be £300 mn. in the five years.

Restoration Problem in the Ironstone Industry in the Midlands

Rep.

1945–46 *Cmd.* 6906

See *Town and Country Planning*, p. 379.

Mineral Development

Cttee. Rep., apps. pp. iv, 106. [1949]

1948–49 *Cmd.* 7732, *xviii*, 285

apptd. Aug., 1946. *sgd. March*, 1949

Lord Westwood (*Ch.*), Balogh, Davies, Jones, Hill, Rankine, Ritson, Robson, Thorneycroft, Willis, Yeabsley.

'*To enquire into the resources of minerals in the United Kingdom, excepting coal, oil, bedded ironstone, and substances of widespread occurrence; to consider possibilities and means of their co-ordinated, orderly, and economic development in the national interest. . . .*'

The minerals dealt with included metalliferous, such as tin, tungsten, lead, zinc, and non-metalliferous, such as barytes, witherite, fluorspar, gypsum, etc. They are restricted in distribution. A review of production and resources shows that while in some cases the reserves will last over 50 years (e.g. ball clays, salt), in others they are sufficient only for 10 to 20 years (e.g. haematite ore, barytes, witherite) or for less than 10 years (e.g. tin and wolfram concentrates). The absence of an adequate long-term policy in the past has led to piece-meal, hand-to-mouth development so that mineral reserves have been lost, mines prematurely closed and trained labour and technicians dispersed.

Mineral ownership is defined by surface boundaries which have no relation to the shape and distribution of the minerals underneath. There are innumerable examples of small mines on a deposit which should have been worked and explored as a whole. Mineral development must be positive, but the control of land use under the Town Planning Acts, 1947, is negative. The procedure for securing planning permission to work reduces the incentives of owners and operators to agree, and will hinder exploration, as will the development charge payable after July 1951. To secure unification of rights, mineral rights should be nationalised and the development value should be re-united with ownership, by transferring development value from the Central Land Board and the fee simple from existing mineral owners to a Mineral Development Commission to be set up by the Minister of Fuel and Power. It should conduct a mineral resources survey, to include low grade and marginal deposits.

Thorneycroft disagreed with the nationalisation of mineral rights and the proposed Development Commission. All minerals should be removed from the compensation and betterment provisions of the Town and Country Planning Acts; cases where separate ownership causes difficulty could be dealt with; the general level of taxation and administrative barriers should be reduced.

Metals Economy

Advisory Cttee. Rep., apps. pp. 17. 1952

1952 *Non-Parl. Min. of Supply* apptd. *Aug.*, 1951. *sgd. Sept.*, 1952

D. A. Oliver (*Ch.*), and 16 others.

'*To bring under review . . . ways of economising in the use of scarce metals in the design, specification and the manufacturing process of metal goods for both rearmament and civil purposes. . . .*'

The critical shortage of alloying and non-ferrous metals has been averted, but the need for economy remains. Economy is difficult for a manufacturer when changes of materials or designs involve capital outlay on factory changes, new working techniques, new plant in short supply, some immediate rise in costs, and consumer resistance. Some measures taken as a result of recent shortages may be retained as established practice. But as the drive may slacken with improved supplies, the Government should emphasise the continuing need for the adoption of the latest and best techniques; research should be continued and its results should be made available, as well as information regarding future supplies of the main metals and possible shortages.

Deterioration of Cast Iron and Spun Iron Pipes

Dept. Cttee. Interim Rep., apps. pp. vi, 48. 1950

1950 *Non-Parl. Min. of Health* apptd. *Dec.*, 1948. *sgd.* —

F. G. Hill (*Ch.*), Binnie, Burns, Escreet, Hudson, Key, Morgan, Pearce, Rees, Risbridger, Vernon, Wharton, Whiskin, Williams, Wood.

'*To consider the extent to which there is evidence of early deterioration of cast and spun iron pipes, the causes of any such deterioration and the measures that should be taken to prevent it.*'

In recent years attention has been focused on the subject by the necessity for replacing considerable lengths of water mains after only short periods of service. The Report brings together the results of research for the guidance of those concerned, and makes recommendations for protective and remedial measures in highly corrosive areas.

Motor Manufacturing Industry

National Advisory Council. Rep., apps. pp. 26. 1947

1947 *Non-Parl. Min. of Supply* apptd. *April*, 1946. *sgd.* —

G. W. Turner (*Ch.*), and 14 others.

The Minister of Supply told a meeting of representatives of the car industry that to meet the crisis production for the home market must be limited, allocations of materials beyond this made on the basis of export only, and that there should be a greater degree of standardisation and a reduction in the number of models. As it was impossible to provide enough steel for the 160,000 cars needed for essential home requirements and 315,000 for export, home production must be limited to 90,000 to 100,000. The Chancellor had announced the acceptance of the principle of a flat rate licence for cars, which would in any case lead to a reduction in the number of models. The report deals with questions of standardisation, taxation, the people's car, specialist producers, etc.

Matchwood

Working Party. Rep., apps., index. pp.
i, 26. 1954

1954 Non-Parl. Bd. of Trade, Min. of Materials

apptd. — 1950. sgd. —

J. J. Breslin (*Ch.*), Andren, Brown, McKechnie, Rendle, Rumney, Terrell.

'To investigate the possibility of securing from soft currency sources supplies of timber suitable for making matches.'

Before 1939 the chief sources of the supplies of matchwood were the Baltic States and Canada. During the war home supplies were made available, but these had to be supplemented by shipments of Canadian splints. Post-war supplies have come mainly from Canada, but because of the necessity to cut dollar expenditure the matches industry has been hard-pressed to find sufficient timber to keep the factories in production. The use of Colonial or other similar woods would involve replacing at heavy cost the existing semi-automatic match-making machines by separate machines for making and filling and could not be recommended. The Working Party's conclusions were that with the possible exception of *Pinus radiata* from New Zealand, none of the species of timber investigated were, in the conditions in which they stood when tested, capable of providing splints of satisfactory quality which could be used in existing match-making machinery.

Timber and Plywood 1949-1953

Government Statement and Cttee. Rep., apps. pp. 31. 1948

1949 Non-Parl. Bd. of Trade
apptd. — 1947. sgd. April, 1948

K. Price (*Ch.*), Austin, Baynes, Ford, Hoffman, Latham, Lebus, Longley, Robinson, Tomkins and representatives of the Admiralty, Colonial Office, Ministry of Health, Board of Trade, Ministry of Transport and Ministry of Works.

'To consider the probable requirements of timber (other than mining timber) and plywood in the United Kingdom during the five years' period commencing 1949, and the supplies likely to be available, and any steps which should be taken to facilitate the acquisition and distribution of such supplies, and report.'

The United Kingdom's minimum requirements in 1953 would be 1,558,000 standards of softwood, 81 mn. cub. ft. of hardwood and 627 mn. sq. ft. of plywood, as compared with 2,411,000 standards, 56 mn. cub. ft. and 640 mn. sq. ft. before the war respectively. Owing to the widespread depletion of our stocks of standing timber for the second time in one generation, home production of softwood is falling considerably, of hardwood declining, though it will remain important, while production of plywood depends on imports of logs and veneers. Imports above the 1947 level of 1,390,000 standards are unlikely. Though increased imports may be expected from West Africa, before the war nearly half our hardwood imports came from N. America. Plywood should be available in reasonable quantities. If the Soviet Union does not resume exports of softwoods, and currency difficulties reduce the supplies of softwood and hardwoods from dollar countries, supplies of both would fall below the 1947 rate. Such steps as are possible should be taken to develop soft currency timber supplies, to encourage the private development of softwood forest areas of Central America and Brazil, and to encourage the substitution of hardwoods for softwoods and the use of secondary hardwoods. In view of the circumstances the present system of buying and distributing timber will have to continue.

The Report is prefaced by a Statement by H.M. Government, which indicates that it will not be possible to import supplies sufficient to meet the requirements as estimated, since each 100,000 standards of softwood imported costs £4 mn. as compared with £1·4 mn. before the war. While plywood imports will be needed, we shall not be able to afford supplies at the estimated level. There are no soft currency softwood supplies which would yield substantial amounts, and the amounts of tropical hardwoods available will depend on consumers' willingness to use new and unfamiliar timbers.

Plans to Reorganise British Industry: Working Parties on Various Industries. See list below

At a conference of the Lancashire and Cheshire Federation of Trades Councils held at Blackpool in September 1945 the President of the Board of Trade outlined proposals for reorganising that part of British industry which remained under private enterprise. It was proposed to set up for the various industries tripartite Working Parties representative of employers, employees and the Government, for the purpose of formulating plans of action which, after the adverse effects of the war, would bring efficiency both as regards buildings, machinery, management, hours, wages and amenities. See Board of Trade Journal, 15th September, 1945. pp. 437, 438.

The Working Parties were given uniform terms of reference:

'To examine and enquire into the various schemes and suggestions put forward for improvements of organisation, production and distribution methods and processes . . . and to report as to the steps which should be adopted in the general interest to strengthen the industry and render it more suitable and more capable of meeting competition in the home and foreign markets.'

They were thus not directed to consider particular problems in the several industries, but required to examine the whole position of each of them, its raw materials, production, organisation, labour supply and relations, distribution, finance, costings, research, etc. The chief permanent value of the Reports is that they are substantial papers covering the problems of the industries, prepared by informed persons from both sides of the industry and independent experts, aided by the research resources of the Board of Trade. They make a large number of suggestions for action by individual firms or trade organisations, as well as Government departments, for dealing with the short-run and more permanent problems of each industry. For these reasons they do not lend themselves to brief summary.

On certain points a number of the Working Parties make recommendations similar in character. That their industry should set up a Design Centre is recommended by the Parties on Boots and Shoes, Lace, Furniture, Wool, Jewellery and Silver-ware, Domestic Glass-ware, Heavy Clothing, Rubber-proofed Clothing and Linoleum. Steps to ensure standards of quality or performance enforced by a legal mark, a trade practices code or an inspection centre are recommended by the Hosiery, Furniture, Boots and Shoes, Cutlery, Heavy Clothing and Rubber-proofed Clothing Parties. A rigorous enforcement and strengthening and extension of the Factory Acts to eliminate 'the slum factory' and improve conditions of sanitation and safety, etc., is called for by the Parties on Lace, Pottery, Furniture, Cutlery, Light Clothing, Heavy Clothing. Some central trade organisation financed by a levy on members for research and intelligence is recommended by the Furniture, Wool, Boots and Shoes, Hosiery, Pottery, Lace, Glass-ware, and China Clay Parties. The establishment or enlargement of a central education institute for the industry is suggested by the Pottery and Furniture

Parties. The reports generally ask for better trade statistics and those on Boots and Shoes, Lace, Hosiery, Light and Heavy Clothing and Domestic Glass-ware for the development of improved costing systems. Those on Boots and Shoes, Lace, Wool, called attention to the great differences of productivity and cost between the various units in the industry.

The analyses in the reports, as distinct from the specific recommendations, contain matters of general interest. The Boots and Shoes Report makes a detailed study of the British United Shoe Machinery Company as the sole or dominant supplier of machines, makes recommendations on the practice of tied-leasing of machinery, the charges for leasing in relation to the cost of each machine, and the pricing of spare parts. It also asked for a revision of sizes, etc., based on mass observation of feet. The Furniture Party proposed a development of a code of performance standards for essential articles and a legal mark worked out in association with B.S.I. Some Reports are concerned with the problems of transforming an old industry based on or developed from small units and craftsmen, e.g. cutlery, jewellery and silver-ware, pottery.

The problem of greatest concern to the Hosiery Party was the provision of machinery to cope with the rapid expansion of demand for women's fully-fashioned stockings. The China Clay Party suggested integration of pits, unification of mineral rights, and reduction in coastwise freights.

The Working Party Reports were published in the Non-Parliamentary series by the Board of Trade with the following titles: *Boots and Shoes; Cotton; Furniture; Hosiery; Jewellery and Silver-ware; Pottery; 1946. Cutlery; Glass-ware; Heavy Clothing; Lace; Light Clothing; Linoleum; Rubber-proofed Clothing; Wool; 1947. Carpets; China Clay; Jute; 1948.* In view of its relation to other investigations into the cotton industry, the Working Party's report on *Cotton* is dealt with on pp. 138.

The Industrial Organisation and Development Act was passed in 1947 (10 & 11 Geo. 6. c. 40) to 'provide for the establishment of development councils to exercise functions for improving or developing the service rendered to the community by industries and for other purposes in relation thereto, for making funds available for certain purposes in relation to industries for which there is no development council, for the disposal of any surplus of funds levied under emergency provision for encouragement of exports, for the making of grants to bodies established for the improvement of design, and for purposes connected therewith and consequential thereon.' A central body for their industry was suggested by the Furniture, Jewellery and Silver-ware, China Clay, Heavy and Light Clothing industries.

See Proposals for Development Councils for the following industries: *Cotton; Furniture; Hosiery and Knitwear; Jewellery and Silver-ware;* 1948. Non-Parl. Bd. of Trade. *Clothing; Wool Textile;* 1949 Non-Parl.

6. MONOPOLIES AND RESTRICTIVE PRACTICES

Tendencies to Monopoly in the Cinematograph Film Industry

Rep.

1944 *Non-Parl.* See *Particular Industries and Trades.* p. 141.

Cement Costs

Rep.

1947 *Non-Parl.*

See *Particular Industries and Trades.* p. 135.

Prices of Radio Valves

Central Price Regulation Cttee. Rep. pp. 9. 1946

1946 *Non-Parl. Bd. of Trade apptd. Nov., 1945. sgd. June, 1946*

E. H. T. Atkinson (*Ch.*), Bussé, Allen, Lyle, Newman, Ryan, Walters.

'*To make enquiries and report . . . whether the prices at present being charged for radio valves were fair prices or whether excessive prices were being maintained by reason of restrictive practices.*'

Radio valves are price-regulated goods under the provisions of the Prices of Goods Act, 1939, and except for purchase tax, prices are the same as they were in 1939. When, on Lease-Lend account, American valves were imported, it was found that they were much cheaper than English ones. British makers have favoured a dual-purpose valve with close tolerances and a high degree of performance, thus reducing the number of valves, whilst American sets are equipped with a large number of simpler types of valves with wide tolerances; the American market absorbed some 150,000,000 a year whilst annual output before the war of the less concentrated and specialised British industry was 12,500,000. American sets are designed for a short working life, while British makers supply replacement valves for old sets. Before the war 80 per cent of all valves sold were equipment valves and only 20 per cent were replacement valves retailed to the public. The British Valve Manufacturers' Association has established for replacement valves a system of price maintenance and protection of manufacturers' retail list prices by a 'stop list,' but sales of equipment valves to set makers are not subject to any agreement as to price and such intense competition exists between member firms that prices at which sales are made do not cover their factory costs. The prices fixed for replacement valves are much higher than those of equipment valves, so that the members of the public, through the retailer, subsidise the loss which the manufacturer incurs on the sale of valves to set makers. The price policy of the Association is that of a discriminating monopoly. Manufacturers admit that if there were free competition in both markets the price of valves sold would be closer together. But much of the present practice arises from the fact that cheap equipment valves put a greater number of sets in the hands of the public. If the trade stood out for a very high price for replacement valves in the years to come, users might prefer to scrap existing sets and buy new ones. The Committee concluded that, taking the profit and loss accounts of these two activities, 'the industry in the period under review has earned only a reasonable reward.'

See *Electronic Valves and Cathode Ray Tubes*, p. 163.

Distribution of Building Materials and Components
Rep.
1948 *Non-Parl.* See *Particular Industries and Trades*, p. 133.

Resale Price Maintenance
Cttee. Rep., apps., index. pp. vi, 122. [1949]
1948–49 *Cmd.* 7696, *xx*, 383
apptd. Aug., 1947. *sgd. March*, 1949

G. H. L. Jacob (*Ch.*), Brumwell, Malone, Ryan, Sharp, Smith, Yeabsley.

'*To consider the practice by which minimum wholesale and retail prices or margins for the resale of goods are fixed by producers, . . . and to report whether in the light . . . of the need for the maximum economy and efficiency in the production and distribution of goods, any measures are desirable to prevent or regulate its continuance.*'

Resale price maintenance is designed to ensure that whatever the channels of distribution through which a product has passed, it shall be sold at a price fixed by the producer in advance. It was estimated that in 1938 30 per cent of consumer's private expenditure was on goods whose prices were so fixed. Resale price maintenance is almost always associated with branded goods. As branding is implied by self-service it may be expected to extend. Branded goods, whether consumable or new durable 'technical' goods, can be identified by the consumer as the product of a particular manufacturer, whose continued sales depend on the good will of the customer.

Since pre-packing and branding have made entry to the trades easier, established specialist and independent shops support fixed prices as some guarantee of stability and protection against loss of value of stock through price cutting. A manufacturer who offers a nationally advertised product of a certain quality at a specified price range for a section of the market needs stable production, does not wish to lose customers because the retailer raises the price above the range or fails to give adequate maintenance service to durable technical goods, and must secure outlets not only through the lowest-cost, but the ordinary retailer. But the practice was criticised by some large multiple retailers who maintained that it limited their power of competing in price. The women's organisations who gave evidence were all in favour of branding goods as a guarantee of quality and a convenience and said that fixed prices for them made it easier to plan household expenditure.

Prices and margins are said to be fixed with reference to the distributor of average efficiency, but the evidence showed that expenses varied with the type and size of business, class of market and location. In the absence of price competition, excess profits of the low-cost distributors may be used either to compete in service or to subsidise articles not price-maintained. There is a tendency for the margins to become conventional, but retail prices should fall to reflect the lower costs of improved methods of distribution. The use of well-known brands as temporary loss-leaders may cause instability, adversely affect retailers who carry a wide range of stock and hinder efforts to maintain quality. Many manufacturers do not object to the use of dividends or deferred discounts to consumers so long as they are not related to individual goods, but are treated as surpluses which go into the pool from which dividends are paid. Its extension would enable new forms of distribution, e.g. self-service, to pass its savings to the public.

The individual manufacturer can enforce his resale price by persuasion, refusal of supplies, by a direct contract with the retailer which includes resale price conditions and by using selected registered agents. Refusal by a manufacturer to supply retailers who use his branded goods as a loss-leader is reasonable, but it is contrary to public interest for him to use the power to obstruct the growth of new methods of trading or to impede the distribution of competing goods by another manufacturer.

Resale prices may be collectively enforced by a trade association of manufacturers and distributors, aided by rules to prevent concealed or indirect price cutting, and a system of fines, collective stop lists and expulsions. In addition, trading may be limited to authorised dealers. Some of the trade associations are registered or certified trade unions, and this makes lawful practices in restraint of trade if deemed reasonable with reference to the objects of the association. In most cases the responsibility for determining the price and quality of the product rests with the individual manufacturer, but some monopolistic associations fix prices as well, thus eliminating price competition also between manufacturers.

The recommendations were: no action should be taken to prevent an individual producer from fixing and enforcing the resale price of his own branded goods, but Government Departments should consult with trade organisations to consider the means of ensuring that there should be adequate provision for reduction of prices where justified by lower costs of distribution; applications of sanctions which extend beyond the remedies open to an individual producer should be made illegal.

In a Note H. Smith supports the

recommendations only because they are an advance on the existing position, accepts individual price maintenance because the prohibition of loss-leaders is difficult, but regards its continuance as more harmful than the complete restoration of free competition.

Resale Price Maintenance

Statement. pp. 11. 1951

1950–51 *Cmd.* 8274, *xxvii*, 981

Resale prices may be enforced by the individual manufacturer by refusal to supply retailers who do not comply with them, or by a trade association by means of a stop list, fines, refusal to supply co-operative societies, etc. The costs of trading vary from one shop to another and these differences should be reflected in prices. Retail price maintenance eliminates this competition, leads to excessive service and slows down improvements in trading methods. The methods of enforcement involve a system of private law and punishment without appeal to the courts. The Government rejects the arguments that the public prefers fixed retail prices, that the reputation of branded goods is damaged if prices cannot be fixed, and thinks the fears that the use of branded goods as loss-leaders would be widespread and damaging are exaggerated.

The Government proposes to introduce legislation to make illegal any arrangement for collective enforcement, and any indication by an individual manufacturer of a fixed price unless it is a maximum price. This will, apart from exceptional conditions, apply throughout the whole of industry and trade.

Collective Discrimination: Exclusive Dealing, Collective Boycotts, Aggregated Rebates and other Discriminatory Trade Practices

Monopolies and Restrictive Practices Com. Rep., apps., index. pp. iv, 111. 1955

1955–56 *Cmd.* 9504, *xxiv*, 21
referred Dec., 1952. *sgd. May,* 1955

D. Cairns (*Ch.*), Allen, Birch, Gallie, Gifford, Plant, Yeabsley, Barnes, Davidson, Goodhart.

The Commission distinguished between six categories of agreements.

1. Collective discrimination by sellers, exclusive sale to or sale at preferential rates to some buyers, who do not undertake any obligations in return. These tend to produce a rigid pattern of distribution and to impede the development of new and economical methods; and if there is little independent competition, may provide higher standards of service than many consumers desire. The adverse effects are greatest if the standards of selection are arbitrary and those on the list have a hand in selecting applicants for approval. 2. Where in return favoured buyers agree to buy exclusively from the suppliers, these tend to eliminate possible competition from outside the group. 3. Agreements that individual manufacturers will enforce conditions of sale, e.g. their own resale prices. 4. Collective discrimination and enforcement of resale prices fixed either by the individual manufacturer or collectively. This places in the hands of the Associations excessive powers over individuals. Rigid price maintenance applied to a substantial proportion of goods tends to eliminate price competition between traders and leads to a waste of economic resources. 5. Exclusive buying agreements by user buyers or distributors can be used to give established traders a privileged position as against potential competitors. 6. Aggregated rebates are used as an adjunct to and tend to accentuate the more dangerous features of common prices and operate generally against the public interest. In certain exceptional circumstances they might be a feature of a common price system not itself against the public interest.

A common feature of the practices is that they impose on the parties an obligation to act in ways which in some degree restrict competition, so that their general effect is against the public interest. But they may be justified in exceptional circumstances: where the consumers are not able to judge the standard of service it is in their interests to demand, where an exclusive dealing or exclusive buying arrangement is designed to protect an industry of strategic importance or peculiarly liable to 'dumping', or where the practice is a means of enabling smaller firms to compete with large ones itself using restrictive practices.

Registration of all agreements, and prohibition by Order of any found by independent scrutiny to be against the public interest is rejected in favour of statutory prohibition of all the practices, which should be carefully defined, provision being made for exceptions on specified grounds.

Barnes, Davidson and Goodhart do not think the evidence shows that the practices are in general injurious or should be made illegal, nor that collective enforcement of prices fixed by the manufacturers individually is inconsistent with the public interest. They would prefer a registration procedure and examination of individual cases.

Monopolies and Restrictive Practices

Reports of enquiries by the Commission on Monopolies and Restrictive Practices. The Commission had to unravel the detailed facts as to monopolistic arrangements and practices, and to report on whether they did or might operate against the public interest. The following summaries indicate briefly the chief findings and recommendations.

—— *Dental Goods*, apps. pp. v, 138. [1950]

1950–51 (18) *xvii*, 149

The Amalgamated Dental Company and its subsidiaries supply nearly half the retail suppliers of dental goods. The agreements and regulations of the Association of Dental Manufacturers and Traders, which controls nine-tenths of retail supplies, provide for collective maintenance of manufacturers' prices and for exclusive dealing arrangements, for expulsion and collective boycott, and for discouraging competition between dealers. After 1935 nearly half the manufacturers' and two-thirds of the dealer applications for membership were refused. The Amalgamated Dental Group should reduce the prices of sole agency porcelain teeth. The practices of exclusive dealing and collective boycott should be prohibited by law. Two members think it would be wrong to enforce the prohibition in this industry only of practices which are widespread, but would not exempt it from a general prohibition.

—— *Cast Iron Rainwater Goods*, apps. pp. v, 132. 1951

1950–51 (136) *xvii*, 11

The Rainwater Goods Agreements between members of the British Ironfounders Association, which produces nine-tenths of the total output and members of the merchants' associations, which distribute two-thirds of the output, provide for the fixing of minimum prices and exclusive dealing. Firms not signatories are excluded from a share in the great bulk of the trade and signatory firms cannot withdraw without jeopardising their business. The minimum price agreements retard the introduction of low-cost methods. Owing to the competition of other materials and Government price control, prices are unlikely to be excessive. The trade practices should be amended to meet the objections.

—— *Electric Lamps*, apps. pp. v, 199. [1951]

1950–51 (287) *xvii*, 293

The members of the Electrical Manufacturers' Association produce about 60 per cent of the total lamp output. The Association fixes home market prices so that there can be no price variation, and provides for exclusive dealing. The members participate in a patent pool, and in an international lamp agreement by which British companies as a whole receive a percentage of the trade, which it subdivides amongst individual firms. The companies as a whole and the individual firms pay fines and receive compensation for excess and deficiency. The Association fixes the type of lamp each manufacturer may make and its price at all stages. Members cannot obtain any competitive advantage by lower prices, a new type of lamp, or new methods, and competition is limited to advertising and salesmanship. There is some advantage in the exchange of technical knowledge and there is some efficient competition. On balance the E.M.C.A. system need not be completely broken up, provided lamp components are made available to non-members, that controlled companies will not be used as fighting companies, that the sales quota system, exclusive dealing, aggregating rebates, collective sanction and stop list are ended, and that the new patent system is revised if it leads to any substantial restriction of competition.

—— *Insulated Electric Wires and Cables*, apps. pp. iv, 170. [1952]

1951–52 (209) *xvii*, 13

The Cable Makers' Association and the Covered Conductors' Association control three-quarters, and with associated and other companies four-fifths of the home cable supplies. Some types are bought mainly by large buyers: the nationalised electricity supply industry, the G.P.O., Cable and Wireless, and the Admiralty. The C.M.A. system provides for standardised products with agreed minimum standards of quality, fixed prices and ten-yearly quotas with payments for excesses or deficiencies. Orders for some types of cable are allocated amongst the firms, often without the knowledge of the purchaser, the allottee being protected by other members quoting higher prices. Authorities asking for tenders may be faced with agreed prices by tenderers. There is a wide spread of costs be-

tween members of the Association, and agreements to share business over long periods prevents low cost producers from expanding relatively. The quotas, allocations, exclusive dealing and aggregated quantity rebates should be ended. Situations where there is nearly one monopoly seller and nearly one monopoly buyer cannot be transformed into free competition. Where there is no competition, C.M.A. members should be obliged to submit costs to the B.E.A. The G.P.O. should be free to place a proportion of orders to independent producers. As a defence against extreme price cutting, C.M.A. should be allowed, on conditions, to fix minimum prices giving reasonable profits to low cost producers.

—— *Insulin*, apps. pp. iii, 38. 1952

1951–52 (296) *xvii*, 187

Insulin was developed by research workers in the University of Toronto which, to prevent the exploitation of the public and to maintain quality, took out patents. The University assigned the British patent to the British Medical Research Council, which controlled production by licensing on conditions including testing, maximum selling prices, etc. The four firms produce the whole output (one of them being responsible for over 45 per cent of home supplies) and are members of the British Insulin Manufacturers, which is not a trade association in the ordinary sense. They charge common prices, but these are amongst the lowest in the world. There is technical collaboration between the firms. The position of the firms as sole suppliers is due to their efficiency and enterprise and the arrangements operate in the public interest.

—— *Supply and Export of Matches and the Supply of Match-making Machinery*, apps., index. pp. v, 136. 1953

1952–53 (161) *xv*, 489

The British Match Corporation group, 30 per cent of whose ordinary shares are held by Swedish Match, controls 87 per cent by quantity of all matches supplied to the U.K., participates in arrangements restrictive of exports and supplies 86 per cent by value of all match-making machinery in the U.K.

The arrangements form a complete and integrated monopoly. The absence of competition has resulted in profits, prices and in some cases costs being higher than they would have been. The development of competition by independent British producers has been hampered by inability to buy Swedish machinery as a result of agreements and by the B.M.C. practice of temporarily underselling competitors in particular areas. Payments are made to Swedish Match to reduce the import of foreign supplies.

Machinery should be set up for regulating the monopoly in the public interest. The Government should fix maximum prices for matches at all stages of distribution and review them at intervals; the prices charged by B.M.C. for materials should be the same for all manufacturers; full details of changes in agreements and financial arrangements should be reported to the Board of Trade. The proposal to establish a public wholesale organisation to oppose the power of a monopoly buyer to that of the monopoly seller is not recommended. The payments to Swedish Match to refrain from supplying machinery should cease and B.M.C.'s offer to release Swedish Match from its undertaking not to make machinery in U.K. should be accepted.

—— *Imported Timber*, apps., index. pp. iv, 138. 1953

1952–53 (281) *xv*, 347

The timber trade maintains three 'Approved Lists' of agents and importers of softwood, hardwood and plywood respectively, whose members undertake to deal only with others in the lists. Entry to the lists is controlled by those already on them, the policy being to exclude both merchants who

o

buy less than certain quantities and all users. Except in the case of hardwoods, the great bulk of imported timber would have been handled in the same way if there were no approved lists. But the tendency is to make the structure of the trade more rigid and conventional, users are prevented from choosing direct purchase and the freedom of merchants to start importing or to import another class of timber is limited. With certain exceptions (the furniture and packing case trades) the users are ignorant of or indifferent to the system. There is no national price ring and there is competition between agents, importers and non-importing merchants. The agreements between traders in the lists to deal only with each other should be abrogated and not replaced by arrangements having similar effects.

See *Imported Timber*. Rep. on whether and to what extent the Recommendation of the Commission has been complied with; 1957–58 (274) xvi, 281.

—— *Process of Calico Printing*, apps., index. pp. iv, 128. 1954

1953–54 (140) *xvi*, 1027

Members of the Federation of Calico Printers print over 98 per cent of the cloth printed in U.K., and a member group, the Calico Printers' Association, prints 50 per cent. The Federation operates a price management policy supported by a minimum price list and allotments to firms of a percentage quantum of total turnover, with payments and compensation for excesses and deficiencies. These should be abolished, together with the obligation to observe uniform conditions of trading. The engraving rental scheme should not be obligatory. The sterilisation of works premises and the Print Trade Redundancy Scheme, which provide for restrictive covenants on premises, etc., when sold to prevent their use for printing, and similar restrictions on the disposal of printing plant, should be abolished.

——*Buildings in the Greater London Area*,
apps., index. pp. iv, 115. 1954

1953–54 (264) *xvi*, 907

For a building owner the primary
purpose of a system of tendering is to
enable him to compare and choose
between competitive offers, and this
depends on the tenders being genuinely
independent. Any communication of
prices between competitors or adjustment of amounts of tenders by arrangements between the builders frustrates
this purpose. Members of the London
Building Conference, who are responsible for 65 per cent of the work,
report their intention to tender, and
details of all concerns known to be
competing are circulated. Under the
Fair Price Scheme, if there are no outside tenderers, when the preliminary
prices show a wide spread, the lowest
tenderer is directed to increase his
prices by a sum (Conad) sufficient to
raise his prices to the Fair Price, other
tenderers also being required to increase
their prices so that the original order is
maintained. Where it is unnecessary to
apply Conad, members are notified of
the sum (Tenad) they must pay to
the Conference, the over-riding factor
determining it being the strength of
outside competition. Compensation is
paid to a member who has lost a contract to a non-co-operating firm solely
because of addition. This is restrictive
because the builder would have put in a
lower price if there were no such
scheme. Builders may submit a cover
price, i.e. a price fixed after consulting a
bona fide tenderer sufficiently high not to
win the contract. This restricts competition by giving the owner a false impression of competition and limits the opportunity of selecting genuine tenders.
Agreements to communicate the amount
of any proposed tenders and agreements
to adjust the amounts of proposed tenders by additions, etc., should be ended.

——*Certain Semi-Manufactures of Copper
and Copper-based Alloys*, apps., index.
pp. viii, 232. 1955

1955–56 (56) *xxiv*, 137

Over 140 concerns in the industry,
70 accounting for more than three-
quarters of the output, belong to one
or more of twelve trading associations
which regulate the trade practices of
their members. Three of these associations co-ordinate activities through the
British Non-Ferrous Metals Federation,
of which they are the only members.
Minimum prices are fixed for the home-
market, supported by collaboration on
tenders, fixing common terms for the
purchase of scrap, regulating resale
prices, fixing discriminatory prices to
groups of customers.

The average level of profits has been
comfortable, but not unreasonable, but
in view of the wide spread of costs and
profits, an important incentive to
reduce costs is removed. The minimum
prices, loyalty and aggregated rebates,
which impede access to the market by
independent producers, and international agreements regulating imports
should be abrogated. The agreements
with other groups for common minimum export prices are designed by the
Federation to maintain our traditional
share of export markets. The Commission is not prepared to say that at
present these operate against the public
interest, but they should be reviewed in
two or three years' time.

——*Pneumatic Tyres*, apps., index. pp.
v, 233. [1955]

1955–56 (133) *xxiv*, 647

Members of the Tyre Manufacturers'
Conference (1) charge the same basic
original equipment prices, and confine
the terms to vehicle manufacturers on a
list; (2) in the replacements market
maintain and enforce collectively identical consumer prices, protect them by
agreed scales of discount, etc., and
confine trade terms to registered traders
having premises and equipment with
approved standards; (3) use a common
formula for mileage contracts with
large operators, e.g. London Transport
Executive; (4) prices for remoulds are
dealt with in the same way as new tyres
in the replacement market.

The T.M.C. contend that the identical prices are not the result of an agreement binding manufacturers to charge a common price, though prices are discussed, but are the result of price leadership and that in some markets the existence of large buyers would tend to eliminate differences of price. The effect of a small number of manufacturers operating with special equipment would tend to the same end. The collective enforcement of resale price, which the report describes in detail, is necessary if quality of service is to be maintained.

Section 3 (2) of the 1948 Act recognises that there may be restriction of competition even if there is no agreement, where manufacturers conduct their business in particular ways. The discussions on prices, the system of collective enforcement, discounts on aggregate expenditure in replacement and mileage contracts, the maintenance of the tyre trade register, etc., are against the public interest. They should be brought to an end voluntarily or by Order under Section 10 of the Act. In the circumstances of the industry the only way to introduce an element of competition is to abolish both collective and individual resale price maintenance.

Four members agree that the T.M.C. arrangements and discussions facilitate identical prices and that they should be discontinued. But tyres are made from common elements and to a common safety standard, and price variation will be small. The prohibition of individual resale price maintenance in one industry alone is not justified, would disorganise the business of 27,000 traders with adequate premises and equipment. The Tyre Trade Register should not be discontinued.

—— *Sand and Gravel in Central Scotland*, apps., index. pp. iv, 109. [1956]
1955–56 (222) *xxiv*, 1005

The firms who are members of or follow the practices of the two associations concerned have a common minimum price and haulage rate system, although in an extractive industry of this kind there was a wide variation of costs amongst producers and the great weight and bulk of the product implies similar variations in transport costs. Under price competition there would be variations of price and low cost producers would have scope for price reductions. The prices are decided in a haphazard way, being based not on the costs of the most efficient members, or average costs or on a minimum or average rate of profit, but merely on general assent despite variation of cost. The system, together with central invoicing, should be discontinued. The use of selected merchants, with an exclusive buying rule and refusal of discounts, etc., to others restricts competition by dividing the trade into the part handled by approved merchants and the part handled by non-approved merchants. This should be discontinued.

—— *Hard Fibre Cordage*, apps., index. pp. v, 143. [1956]
1955–56 (294) *xxiv*, 377

The hard fibre cordage industry, 85 per cent of whose output is for the home market, comprises 22 manufacturers ranging from large public companies to small family businesses. The four sections of the hard fibre cordage industry deal with ropes for shipping, packing cords and twine for commerce and industry, binder and baler twine for agriculture and trawl twine for fishing nets. A common minimum price system is operated by the four sections, supported by arrangements governing distribution and limiting and controlling imports. A quota system outside the scope of the Federation is operated by 16 of its members through the Cordage Manufacturers Association and affects four-fifths of the total supplies of cordage in the home market. The Federation's case was that the demand is inelastic, that a common price helps to maintain quality, and that the common prices are based not on the highest cost producer, but on an average of representative costs. The industry has to deal with organised sellers of its material and organised buyers of its output.

The manufacturers are not faced with independent competition, there is no satisfactory substitute for the bulk of their products, and imports from Eire and St. Helena are brought within its price system. The level of average profits has been moderate, but price competition would stimulate efforts to reduce costs. Since price is a minor consideration with the industrial buyers, the abolition of minimum prices would not lead to a deterioration in quality. The common price system, arrangements for rebates, exclusive dealing, etc., the price control of Eire and St. Helena imports, and the C.M.A. pool and quota scheme should be ended.

—— *Certain Rubber Footwear*, apps., index. pp. vi, 107. [1956]

1955–56 (328) *xxiv*, 887

The members of the R.F.M.A. supply two-thirds of the rubber boots and between two-fifths and a half of the canvas shoes. The competition faced by members is formidable in canvas shoes and is not negligible in rubber boots. The price consultations and understandings not to negotiate special prices for large orders without notification prevent differences of cost being reflected in price and should be discontinued. Resale prices are maintained by some members individually, but there are no collective arrangements or sanctions and there is plenty of rubber footwear not price-maintained. Compulsory observance of a list of traders entitled to wholesale terms should be discontinued. The Dunlop Rubber Company does not, otherwise than as a member of the R.M.F., do anything as a result of or to preserve its monopoly which is against the public interest.

—— *Linoleum*, apps., index. pp. vi, 114. [1956]

1955–56 (366) *xxiv*, 527

Seven of the nine companies manufacturing linoleum are members of the L.M.A., and supply four-fifths of the total home trade. Common minimum prices are supported by common rates of discount to approved wholesalers, an aggregated retail turnover bonus, common terms to certain large public buyers, and standard trading practices. Sanctions include damages and expulsion from the Association, the latter also being a penalty for transferring business to a competing firm not in the Association.

Evidence from wholesalers and retailers was that common prices tended to maintain quality; the benefits of price stability outweighed the detriment to users. There are wide differences of cost, so that expansion of low cost producers may have been retarded, but export arrangements have been assisted. The common price system should be allowed to continue only if uniform costings are introduced, and prices, costs and profits are reviewed by the Government from time to time. The loyalty provisions and aggregated retail turnover bonus should be discontinued, as should the compulsory observance of the wholesalers list. Various other practices specified are not contrary to the public interest.

—— *Collective Discrimination*. See p. 156.

—— *Certain Industrial and Medical Gases*, apps. index. pp. viii, 144. [1957]

1956–57 (13) *xvii*, 1

The British Oxygen Co. has an almost complete monopoly of the supply of oxygen and dissolved acetylene. In this industry there may be substantial economies in operating as a monopoly, but there may be serious dangers in the control by a single group which has pursued a policy of restricting competition by the control over plant and equipment, taking over other producers, use of fighting companies, and incorporating exclusivity terms in contracts, and has used the position to charge prices regarded as unjustifiably high. Steps should be taken to prevent B.O.C. from charging prices which produce a higher profit on capital employed than is reasonable in the circumstances, by means of a Board of Trade periodical review. This should be lower than the 23 per cent to 25 per cent which has been aimed at. There should be no discrimination between customers in similar circumstances, charges should be based on cost and publicly known. The use of fighting companies should be ended, the exclusivity clause modified, and more research undertaken.

There was no evidence that the producers of propane had used their monopoly power to fix prices at a level yielding exceptional profit; there was competition between them and between distributors.

—— *Standard Metal Windows and Doors,* apps., index. pp. vi, 113. [1957]

1956–57 (14) *xvii,* 153

The Metal Window Association has 38 members who between them have 90 per cent of the home sales of metal windows, three of them accounting for 75 per cent. The common price system as currently operated takes account of the weighted average costs of the three largest manufacturers, costs are calculated on a reasonable level of activity with a reasonable profit addition; the costs of individual manufacturers and the differences between them are being diminished. It does not operate against the public interest. Submission of price schedules to an independent body, would be an additional safeguard. But the selective arrangements for reducing prices for particular enquiries where there is likelihood of competition includes spreading the losses between members to the extent that different members take orders at reduced prices; they should be ended. Crittall's 'monopoly' position does not operate against the public interest.

—— *Tea,* apps., index. pp. iii, 70. [1957]

1956–57 (15) *xvii,* 273

Fifty-five per cent of the tea supplied in U.K. is sold at auctions subject to uniform and obligatory conditions, the volume of tea sold is regulated by a committee representative of producers and selling brokers, and one-half the tea is sold subject to resale price maintenance. The regulation of sales was a reasonable way of organising sales of a seasonal crop, tending to even them out over the year. The uniform conditions of sale were reasonable when auctioneers were selling at auction speed and were agreed between all parties. The individual resale price maintenance did not operate against the public interest. The individual firms are in keen competition. The fluctuations in the price of tea since decontrol were not due to monopoly or restrictive practices.

—— *Electronic Valves and Cathode Ray Tubes,* apps., index. pp. vii, 194. [1957]

1956–57 (16) *xvi,* 789

There are 16 manufacturers, 6 of whom belong to the British Valve Association which controls 97 per cent of the output, one firm, Mullard, accounting for 61 per cent of the valves and 5 per cent of the tubes. At the time the Report was drafted, the Association's practices which were restrictive of competition included a common discriminatory price and discount system distinguishing between equipment valves and maintenance valves, and between categories of buyers such as chain stores, car manufacturers, and retailers; exclusive dealing agreements with equipment manufacturers, wholesalers and others, and restrictions on freedom to import. The price system was not specifically related to costs. As from 1st September, 1956, amendments to these arrangements deleted the provisions for agreements in prices, collective resale price maintenance, and the discrimination between various classes of manufacturers of domestic sets.

Individual manufacturers would still publish retail price lists and members would agree on maximum discounts.

—— *Electrical and Allied Machinery and Plant*, apps., index. pp. vi, 353. [1957] 1956–57 (42) *xvi*, 425

The Report discusses in great detail the conditions affecting turbines and allied plant and machinery, other alternators and other generators, and transformers. The Groups and I.E.A. have common price systems; the agreements providing for notification of enquiries oblige manufacturers to make disclosures which may lower the effectiveness of competition and enable each manufacturer to know when he has little competition to fear. The compensation arrangements in tendering may cause manufacturers in some circumstances to quote prices different from those they would have quoted in their absence. Both practices interfere with the normal course of tendering. Non-signatories who habitually co-operate are parties to the restrictive arrangements. The differential price arrangements for specified classes of machinery, if they are obligatory and involve listing individual buyers entitled to allowances, are also restrictive. These and other specified practices are against the public interest and should be terminated. Certain other arrangements were not objectionable.

—— *Chemical Fertilisers*, apps., index. pp. iv, 254. 1960 1958–59 (267) *xvii*, 789

The position and activities of I.C.I. in relation to nitrogenous fertilisers, of Potash Ltd. and Fisons in relation to potash and of Fisons and B.B.S. regarding basic slag, are not against the public interest. Fisons' position in superphosphates and compounds is not in itself against the public interest, but the prices have yielded profits at a high rate, and price policy should be adjusted to yield a lower level. Attlee disagreed with the system of uniform delivered prices practised in England and Wales but not in Scotland.

7. COMPANY AND COMMERCIAL LAW AND PRACTICE

Company Law Amendment

Cttee. Rep., apps. pp. 115. 1945. Mins. of ev., 26 days. 1943–45

1944–45 *Cmd.* 6659, *iv*, 793. *Mins. of ev.;* 1943–45 *Non -Parl.*

apptd. June, 1943. sgd. June, 1945

L. L. Cohen (*Ch.*), Catterns, Fforde, Gedge, Goodhart, Heyworth, Hodgson, Kettle, Mitchell, Thomson, Watson, Wilkinson, Wilmot.

'*To consider and report what major amendments are desirable in the Companies Act, 1929, and, in particular, to review the requirements prescribed in regard to the formation and affairs of companies and the safeguards afforded for investors and for the public interest.*'

The great majority of companies are honestly and conscientiously managed, but since flexibility in changing conditions means opportunities of abuse, the fullest practicable disclosure of their activities to shareholders, creditors and the general public, more effective control by shareholders over their management and the vigorous enforcement of the Acts are desirable. The report reviews the Acts in detail, embodying its recommendations in a large number of draft sections. The following lists some of its main proposals. (1) Memoranda of Association, Names.—The doctrine of ultra vires has no positive value; provisions as to companies' powers should operate solely as a contract between shareholders and directors as to the latter's powers. The Board of Trade should have unfettered power to reject misleading names. (2) Shares of no par value are not recommended. (3) Prospectuses.— With every prospectus delivered to the Registrar should be sent a copy of every material contract mentioned, a signed statement by the auditors and accountants, and the written consent of any expert to the inclusion of any part of his report. If the prospectus states that permission to deal has been or will be applied for, application must be made within two days, all moneys received paid into a separate account and returned if permission is refused. Reports by auditors in the prospectus should state the profits and losses of the five financial years preceding, the profits of businesses controlled by purchase of shares, and in the case of an issue by a holding company, the profits and losses of the company and its subsidiaries. (4) Private companies should be obliged to file accounts, but small family ones in which no other company is a beneficial owner of any shares should be exempt. (5) Nominee Shareholders.—There is a belief that shares are placed in the names of nominees for the real owners to conceal control or for dubious purposes. There are difficulties in securing complete disclosure of the real ownership. All transfers of shares should contain a declaration as to whether the transferee is owner or nominee, every beneficial owner of more than 1 per cent of the capital should file a declaration of ownership and any change therein. The Board of Trade should have power to investigate the ownership of shares where it is deemed desirable in the public interest. (6) Relations of companies and directors.—The transactions of directors in the shares, etc., of their companies, and their remuneration should be disclosed. Loans by companies and subsidiaries to directors should be illegal. (7) Accounts.—The legal requirements as to the contents of accounts are too meagre, and the professional bodies of accountants stated that their hands would be strengthened if the law prescribed the minimum amount of information in balance sheets and profit and loss accounts: recommendations are made on these points, including fixed assets and undisclosed reserves. (8) Holding and subsidiary companies.—The accounts of a holding company should include information on the financial position of the group; accounts of subsidiaries should be consolidated with and made up to the same date as those of the holding company. (9) Shareholders' Control.—The illusory nature of the control theoretically exercised by shareholders has been accentuated by the dispersion of capital amongst small shareholders. Recommendations are made regarding notice of annual meetings, rights of shareholders to introduce resolutions and have copies of statements circulated, the rights of proxies, polls, voting by nominees, etc. Resolutions for election of directors should be submitted for each director separately; directors' retiring age should be 70 unless fixed otherwise in articles. (10) The powers of the Board of Trade should be widened to enable it to appoint inspectors at the request of 200 shareholders, on its own initiative or on a resolution by the company. Its powers of prosecution and inspection of books should be strengthened and penalties increased.

Shares of No Par Value

Cttee. Rep., apps. pp. iii, 31. 1954. Mins. of ev., 9 days. 1954

1953–54 Cmd. 9112, xix, 127. Mins. of ev.; 1954 Non-Parl.
apptd. Dec., 1952. sgd. Jan., 1954

M. L. Gedge (Ch.), Adamson, Arnold-Forster, Beard, Brown, L. Harcourt, Marker, Whittaker.

'To consider whether it is desirable to amend the Companies Act, 1948, so as to permit the issue of shares of no par value; and, if so, to consider and report what amendments in the Act should be made for this purpose, having due regard to the need for safeguards for investors and for the public interest.'

An ordinary share of a company represents a defined fraction of the equity of the company, whether that share has a nominal value or is one of no par value. The Companies Act, 1948, requires that a company must have a capital divided into shares of fixed amounts, i.e. having a nominal value. But the paid-up capital at the outset might not be comparable with the real worth of the undertaking, the worth of the undertaking may decline or increase, a war may cause a revolution in price levels, so that the £ sign becomes meaningless or misleading. The value of the stake in the company grows or declines and has no relation to the paid-up capital, which is of merely historical significance. Shares of no par value avoid the misleading effect of stating a dividend as a proportion of nominal capital. With no par shares, matters analogous to bonus issues and sub-divisions would be simplified.

Trade Union Congress opposed the proposal, partly on technical grounds that money received for such shares might be used for dividend payments, but mainly on the wider grounds that the issue of such shares would create suspicion in the minds of work people that their purpose was to conceal what was happening inside public companies and to camouflage dividends. The Committee rejects these arguments.

The issue of no par ordinary shares should be permissible, but not obligatory, and the system should not be extended to fixed dividend shares. A company's share capital must be wholly in nominal value or in no par value shares, and not partly in one and partly in the other. In the case of a company having no par shares, all proceeds of an issue should be carried to a stated capital account. Transfers of reserves, etc., to stated capital account and the splitting of shares of no par value would require special resolution.

Minority Report.—W. Beard. The technical advantages of no par shares are exaggerated. The evidence shows that there is no real demand for them. The main objections are those put forward by T.U.C., that they could be used for concealing dividends and would engender suspicion in the minds of work people.

Inspection of Bristol Rovers Football Club Limited

Reps., app. pp. vii, 82. 1951

1951 Non-Parl. Bd. of Trade apptd. Aug., 1950. sgd. Dec., 1950, Jan., 1951

A. F. Ward.

Before 1932 the Bristol Rovers Football Club Ltd. had accommodated the Bristol Greyhound Racing Association Ltd. on its football ground (Eastville Stadium) but in 1932 this relationship took legal form when a lease was signed whereby the Football Company as lessors demised to the Greyhound Company rights to use the Ground with the use of stands, enclosures, etc., for a period of 21 years on payment of a premium of £5,000 and an annual rental of £600. The lessors reserved their rights to control the ground for football on specified days at specified times, but it gave the Greyhound Company, in the event of the lessors wishing to sell, the first and exclusive right to purchase the ground and premises at a fair market price.

Subsequent history shows the financial difficulties of the Football Company after the outbreak of war when football activities practically ceased; its commitments to the Greyhound Company over the sale of the ground; the acquisition of Football shares by members of the Greyhound Company; the failure of the Football Company to keep the register required by the Companies Act, and a series of situations which finally led members of the Football Company to apply to the Board of Trade for investigation under the provisions of the Companies Act, 1948.

An investigation by the Football Association (App. 6) into the affairs of the Bristol Rovers Club showed that there had been irregular payments and other breaches of the Association's rules and regulations, including the handing over of the financial administration of the club to the Bristol Greyhound Racing Association. It censured the Chairman and Directors, fined the club, declared it undesirable that the controlling interest in it should be held by the Greyhound Racing Coy., and considered that the Directors of the club should have proper control of it.

Mr. Ward the Inspector stated that the Eastville Stadium was now the undisputed property of the Greyhound Company, but that the Football Company had important rights of user. There was *effective* if not legal shareholding control of the Football Company by the Greyhound Company. The Football Company's rights as user should be clearly defined. The Greyhound Company could demonstrate their interest in football in Bristol by admitting a wider spreading of shareholding, and by appointing an independent person with legal and commercial experience 'to advise and assist in the negotiations of a supplementary licence, designed to amend errors of fact, to clear up ambiguities and to legislate specifically . . . for the methods to be adopted in all matters of financial accounting between the Companies.'

See also *Investigation under Section 172 [Companies Act, 1948] of Bristol Rovers Football Club Limited.* E. H. C. Wethered. Rep.; 1952 Non-Parl. Bd. of Trade. This gives the findings on who can control or is financially interested in the Club.

The Savoy Hotel Limited.
Investigation under Section 172 of the Companies Act, 1948. J. B. Lindon. Interim Rep. pp. 7. 1953. *The Savoy Hotel Limited and the Berkeley Hotel Company Limited.* Investigation under Section 165 (b) of the Companies Act, 1948. E. M. Holland. Rep. pp. 27.
1954
1953, 1954 *Non-Parl. Bd. of Trade* apptd. Nov., 1953, *April,* 1954. sgd. *Nov.,* 1953, *June,* 1954

The Savoy Company and its subsidiaries owned valuable hotel properties and sites, including the Savoy, Berkeley, Claridges and Simpsons-in-the-Strand. These assets were valued in the books at cost, which was con-

siderably lower than current market values. On a short run view a large immediate profit might be made by sale of the sites or their conversion to other uses. This was particularly true of the Berkeley Hotel, which had suffered a continuous decline of profits from 1945 to 1952. The directors held the view that the continuance of all of them in the hotel and restaurant business as a balanced group would in the long run be more advantageous.

In October 1953 dealings on the Stock Exchange indicated that one or more large buyers were seeking to obtain control of the Savoy Company and it later appeared that one of the groups concerned wished to secure control of the Berkeley to change its use. The Report details the steps taken by the transfer of properties to Worcester Buildings, the issue of unissued shares, etc., designed to prevent anyone obtaining control of the Savoy Company from exercising it directly or indirectly in order to sell the Berkeley or other properties or change their use. The Board believed this was for the benefit of the companies and the stockholders of the Savoy, and received clear legal advice that they were entitled to do so. Although there was an absence of clear judicial decision, 'in my opinion it was an invalid exercise of their powers to exercise them for the purpose stated.'

8. WEIGHTS AND MEASURES

Weights and Measures Legislation Cttee. Rep., apps., index. pp. iv, 147. [1951]
1950–51 *Cmd.* 8219, *xx,* 913
apptd. Oct., Dec., 1948, Feb., 1949. sgd. *Dec.,* 1950

E. H. Hodgson (*Ch.*), Bending, Boynton, Cleland, Dakin, Jacob, Jenks, Kingham, Parkes, Pearson (Rosa), Sears, Storrar, Turner (Margaret), Warwick.

'*To review the existing Weights and Measures legislation and other legislation containing provisions affecting Weights and*

Measures and the administration thereof, and to make recommendations for bringing these into line with present day requirements.'

The purposes of the Weights and Measures law are to establish a uniform system of control over all measuring and weighing equipment so that it conforms to the established units, and to protect the public against short weight and measure. The law is sound and needs no fundamental revision, but amending Acts passed to meet the changing techniques have caused anomalies and the law should be consolidated.

The two systems of measurement in the world are the imperial system used by the Commonwealth and the U.S.A., and the metric system used by most other countries. The metric system is a closely defined and universally recognised system under the guidance of an international body. The imperial system is a conglomeration of units which form a rough whole. In Great Britain there are five different systems of weight and three of capacity. The Commonwealth bases the values of the units on Imperial Standards kept in London, but the U.S.A. defines its yard and pound on the International Metre and Kilogramme. The advantage of the metric over the imperial system is that it is entirely decimal, and being coupled with the decimal system of coinage, it makes for ease in calculation. The metric system is legal in this country. The problem is whether to maintain two legal systems or to abolish the Imperial. The metric system is used by the overwhelming majority of countries, but half the world's trade is conducted in the Imperial system; on the other hand, the imperial units are more convenient than the metric and for many purposes a quantity can be stated more concisely. The balance of the evidence given was in favour of allowing full option between the two systems to continue; the final result would then be settled by proof of convenience. This, however, would accentuate the difficulties of transition and ignored the element of inertia. The Government should take steps in concert with the Commonwealth and U.S.A. to abolish the Imperial system of measurement and replace it by the metric system over a period of 20 years.

The fundamental units are those of length, mass and time; from these are derived units in terms of which measurements of all other physical quantities are made. The standards which constitute the ultimate material representations of fundamental and derived units are called 'primary' standards. This term includes e.g., the national copies of the imperial yard and pound and the international prototype metre and kilogramme. The imperial standard yard compares unfavourably in workmanship and material with the international prototype metre. There are defects in the legal definitions of the imperial and metric fundamental units used in Great Britain. Discrepancies are important where scientific accuracy is required, as with the specifications of precision instruments made in this country and the U.S.A. The ideal would be a natural constant impervious to change. No such constant has been found for the determination of mass, but certain wave-lengths of light have been shown by science to be capable of providing an absolute unit of length. Thus whether or not the metric system is adopted, the imperial yard and imperial pound should be defined, not independently, but as specific fractions of the metre and kilogramme. An Act is not a convenient vehicle for definition of derived measurements, especially in view of constant technological progress. A permanent Commission should be established to advise on all matters relating to units, standards and lawful measurement. The units of weights and measures and the physical weights and measures recommended as the only lawful ones for use in trade are given in Apps. C. and D. The apothecaries' troy and pennyweight systems should be abolished after five years and replaced by the metric system.

The chain of verification from primary standards to traders' weights and measures has inconsistencies and inadequacies and recommendations are made for the clarification and improvement of the controls.

Short weight and measure.—It should be an offence to give short weight or measure, and this should apply to all transactions at all stages of distribution. The suggestion that all articles should be sold by weight unless specifically exempted is rejected. The Act of 1926 should be amended to provide for: an extension of the definition of 'food'; a reduction in the number of imperial weights prescribed for the sale of pre-packed foods and the addition of certain metric weights; an indication of weight or measure on pre-packed goods on self-service premises; a remedy against misleading price-for-weight tickets, etc. An additional number of foods, including certain fresh fruits, and of household articles should be sold by weight only. Specified weights or measures are recommended for milk, alcoholic drinks, coal, etc. The administration and enforcement of the Weights and Measures Law should be entrusted only to those larger local authorities where the work would require at least three inspectors. Other recommendations deal with the detailed list of scheduled articles, Board of Trade supervision and control, etc.

VI. COAL, FUEL, POWER, WATER

1. **Fuel Generally**
2. **Coal**
3. **Oil and Petrol**
4. **Electricity**

5. **Gas**
6. **Atomic Energy**
7. **Water**

1. FUEL GENERALLY

Fuel Rationing

Rep. pp. 12. 1942

1941–42 *Cmd. 6352, iv, 275
apptd. March, sgd. April,* 1942

W. H. Beveridge.

'*To report on the most equitable and effective methods of restricting and rationing the consumption of fuel.*'

Fuel rationing is difficult because, unlike food rationing, it cannot be based on individual needs, but must relate to the household itself; and supplies for industry and domestic consumption are dealt with together at all stages of distribution. It must include all important fuels; must be based on a points system with interchangeable coupons; the ration must be fixed on assessment of present needs, not on a percentage of past consumption, and consumers must be registered. The temporary staff required to issue ration books would be 15,600 distributed between 1500 local offices. An average cut of 12½ per cent or one ton in eight would produce a saving of 10 mn. tons of coal a year, and if this were distributed scientifically and equitably over the whole body of consumers it should not cause serious hardship. A scheme introduced when it could be a mild one may work without disaster if later on the screw has to be tightened. Details of a rationing scheme are outlined.

Domestic Fuel Policy

Fuel and Power Advisory Council.
Rep., apps. pp. iv, 64. [1946]

1945–46 *Cmd. 6762, xii,* 187
apptd. —. *sgd. Jan.,* 1946

E. D. Simon (*Ch.*), Crowther, Greenly, Grumell, Hartley, Hinshelwood, Jewkes, Mackintosh, L. Ridley, Robinson, Summers.

'*To consider and advise on the use of fuels and the provision of heat services in domestic and similar premises . . . with special regard*

*to the efficient use of fuel resources and to the
prevention of atmospheric pollution.'*

Of the 181 mn. tons of coal produced
in Great Britain in 1938 over one-third
was used for domestic consumption.
Houses of the lower income groups are
exceedingly badly heated, and the four
million houses built in the inter-war
period, although probably larger than
houses in other countries for corresponding income groups, have a smaller
area properly warmed for comfort
during the winter than in any other
civilised country. The cooking facilities
are generally satisfactory, but the
amount of hot water used is estimated
to be on the average less than half of the
minimum amount necessary for comfort, health and cleanliness. Moreover,
as over 80 per cent of domestic heating
is provided by the open fire, a substantial proportion of coal is discharged
into the atmosphere as soot and tar and
sulphurous gases. The main objective
in framing a national policy is the provision of fuels and appliances of
qualities and at prices to enable householders to get maximum comfort with
the minimum of dirt and labour. The
Government should encourage the production of heating appliances and
multifuel appliances, and should establish minimum standards for all leading
types. New appliances falling below the
standard should be prohibited. Codes
of practice on heating and ventilation
installations should be adopted in all
new houses. Mass production of
standardised fuel appliances should be
encouraged. In subsidised houses, the
use of approved solid fuel appliances
should be a condition or made part of
the subsidy, and subsidies should be
given to encourage replacement in old
houses; central heating plants should
be accepted as the main means of
heating blocks of flats. Provided that
the main winter space and water heating
load is taken by solid fuel, and inter-
mittent heating by gas and electricity,
the domestic heating field should be left
to free competition between the various
fuels. Free competition between gas

and electricity should continue, subject
to prices being appropriately related to
costs; the influence exerted by tariffs
should be kept under examination.
Recommendations are also made on
encouraging smokeless solid domestic
fuel and on house design. The target of
domestic fuel policy should be to replace in 20 years 50 mn. tons of bituminous coal now working at 20 per cent
efficiency by smokeless solid fuel, gas or
electricity with an efficiency of not less
than 40 per cent. App. IV is a report
by an Economist's Sub-Committee on
domestic electricity tariffs.

See *Heating and Ventilation of Dwellings.*
Cttee. (*Ch.* A. C. Egerton). Rep.; 1946
Non-Parl. Min. of Works (Post-War
Building Studies, 19).

Fuel and the Future

Conference. Proc., etc. Vols. 1–3. 1948
1948 *Non-Parl. Min. of Fuel & Power*

In October 1946 the Fuel Efficiency
Committee convened the conference on
the present state of development of fuel
utilisation and its 'future trends' and
some 5000 industrialists and members
of domestic organisations attended.
The Conference was divided into the
following eight sections: the generation
of steam; steam utilisation; heat for
drying; high temperature processes;
the carbonisation and chemical industries; special industrial sessions; modern heating and the architect; the home
and its fuel services.

The proceedings are printed in three
volumes.

National Policy for the Use of Fuel and Power Resources

Cttee. Rep., apps., index. pp. v, 242.
[1952]
1951–52 *Cmd.* 8647, *xii*, 733
apptd. July, 1951. *sgd. July,* 1952

Lord Ridley (*Ch.*), Evans, Gardiner,
Gibb, Hawthorne, McIntosh (Mrs.
Marjorie), Schofield (Miss M. Ruth),
Lewis.

'In view of the growing demands for all

forms of fuel and power arising from full employment and the rearmament programme, to consider whether any further steps can be taken to promote the best use of our fuel and power resources, having regard to present and prospective requirements and in the light of technical developments.'

The supplies of coal, oil fuel, gas and electricity in the United Kingdom were not sufficient to meet in full all demands at ruling prices. At current prices there would be a domestic demand for some extra 5 mn. tons of coal a year, and an extra 10 to 15 mn. tons at competitive prices for export. This shortage was caused by the increased demand since 1938 and a slightly smaller supply than pre-war. It was possible to meet industry's coal requirements only by restricting non-industrial use and coal exports. Electricity supply capacity had increased from some 9 mn. kilowatts in 1938 to 16 mn. in 1951, but there were still periods when the peak demand exceeded generating capacity by over 1 mn. kilowatts. It had not been possible to meet the full demand because of the shortage of steel and building labour, and of the other investment resources. Gas consumption rose from about 1500 mn. therms in 1938 to 2500 mn. therms in 1951. Shortage of investment resources has prevented increase in plant, and the shortage of gas supply has been felt most in the centres of metal-using industry. The rise in annual consumption of oil fuel (excluding its use for transport) from 2 mn. tons in 1939 to 50 mn. tons in 1951 was due partly to the shortage of coal and of the Government's encouragement of its use, and partly to the consumer's growing appreciation of its technical and economic advantages over coal and coal-based fuels. There was no oil shortage. In the next ten years, by 1959–1963, the annual demand for fuel in coal or coal equivalent might rise by 21–25 mn. tons, and for oil by 6 mn. tons.

The price of coal is fundamental. Half the Committee thought that price should be based on marginal cost, half that it should be based on average cost. Seven mn. tons were produced at a loss of 15s. 0d. per ton; allowing for the fact that coal was rationed and price-controlled, the first group argued that the average price should be raised to £1 per ton above average costs. The extra cost to consumers of £200 mn. would lead to economies. The other half of the Committee thought that price should equal average cost, thus covering the Board's costs, although this meant that some coal would be sold at more and some at less than cost; marginal pricing would increase the Board's profits, decrease incentives to efficiency, lead to demands for higher wages, and stimulate an inflationary spiral.

After a review of the economic and technical considerations governing the uses of the different fuels and the appliances for domestic and non-domestic consumption, the Committee concluded that the best pattern of fuel and power use would be promoted by the consumer's exercise of free choice between competing services, provided the competition were based on prices, tariffs and terms of supply which corresponded to the relevant costs. If the market were fully competitive there would be no need for any machinery to ensure that prices did correspond to costs. But by the nature of the electricity and gas industries there can be competition only between different fuels and not between different suppliers, so that prices could be made to correspond to costs by the policy of the Boards. Coals should be classified and separately priced, and delivered prices should fully reflect the different transport costs. Electricity charges should differentiate for large consumers between costly peak and off-peak use, and practical trials made of methods of measuring and controlling peak consumption; tariffs for stand-by supplies should reflect costs of administration. Since gas production was localised and the cost of coal varied with freight costs, gas prices should reflect these local differences. Within an appropriate framework of prices and tariffs, competition between the gas and electricity industries should continue. The Minister should be assisted in his control over the price policies of nationalised fuel and power industries by a specialised Tariffs Advisory Committee, which should examine existing and alternative pricing methods. A Joint Fuel and Power Planning Board should be set up. A large number of other recommendations are made to improve domestic and industrial fuel efficiency; e.g. new standards of performance based on a room efficiency of 40 per cent with coal should be determined for solid fuel appliances, and 100 per cent purchase tax imposed on those which fall short of the standard; encouragement of high efficiency open fires, production of devices to restrict the chimney throat, of insulating material for domestic premises; house subsidies should be conditional on a standard of insulation and installation of approved appliances.

2. COAL

Coal Mines (War Levy) Scheme

Memo., app. pp. 6. 1940

1940–41 *Cmd.* 6236, *viii*, 23

As a result of the decline of exports and of transport difficulties, many coal pits have closed and others are finding it difficult to meet the extra expense of short-time working. Flat rate price increases do little to meet the differing circumstances of collieries in the same coalfield. The scheme therefore provides for (i) a levy not exceeding 6d. per ton on all coal sold in each district, and (ii) payment to any colliery from the fund so created of 3s. 6d. for every ton by which its sales in each quarter fell short of the proportion of the national sales, as supplied in the corresponding quarter of 1939.

Coal Mines Guaranteed Wage Levy

Memo., app. pp. 4. 1941

1940–41 *Cmd.* 6278, *viii*, 19

A levy of 6d. a ton on the total tonnage sold each week was to be made to meet the cost of the guaranteed week under the Essential Works (Coal Mining) Order, which provides that a guaranteed wage shall be paid to employees available for work whether there is short time by reason of enemy action, lack of transport facilities, etc.

Coal

Memo., app. pp. 12. 1942

1941–42 *Cmd.* 6364, *ix*, 19

'Owing to the expansion of war production and other wartime causes the demand for coal is still increasing, but output of coal is tending to decline.' Although the Essential Work Order had been applied, the net annual wastage in the industry was some 25,000 miners. Some 33,000 ex-miners had returned to the mines, and it was proposed to bring back another 7800 from the Services and 3500 from industry and civil defence. Coal mining is to be added to the list of priority industries and men could choose it as an alternative to military service. Recruitment is to be stimulated by improving conditions and prospects. Output could be increased by concentrating men and machines on the more productive pits and seams, by efficient use of machinery in the pits, by providing competent mining engineers to groups of pits and reducing avoidable absenteeism. The Government have decided to take full control over the operation of all coal mines and the allocation of the coal raised, etc. A National Coal Board will be established; there will also be Regional Controllers, regional boards and pit production committees. Absenteeism will be made an offence and Regional Investigation Officers appointed to deal with it. Domestic rationing, if necessary, will be based on a points scheme.

Coal-mining Industry

Bd. of Investigation. Rep., *The Immediate Wages Issue*, apps. pp. 8. 1942

1942 *Non-Parl. Min. of Labour & N.S. apptd. June, sgd. June, 1942*

Lord Greene (*Ch.*), Briggs, Chester, Forster, McNair.

'1. *To consider and to report in the first instance upon the immediate wages issue; and further,* 2. *To enquire into the present machinery and methods of determining wages and conditions of employment in the industry, and to submit recommendations for the establishment of a procedure and permanent machinery for dealing with questions of wages and conditions of employment in the industry.*'

The Board of Investigation was set up because the Government took the view that as the National Coal Board would be concerned with increased production, its work would be prejudiced if it were associated with wages questions. The Mineworkers' Federation claimed a uniform national minimum wage of 85s. a week at the age of 18 and over, 4s. per shift increase for all 18 years and over and 2s. per shift for boys, but the Mining Association thought that any increase should be partly output and partly attendance bonus.

The main recommendations were for a national minimum wage for workers over the age of 21 at the rate of 83s. a week for underground workers and 78s. for surface workers and an unconditional flat rate addition of 2s. 6d. per shift to all workers over the age of 21. There should be an addition to the wages of all workers in accordance with a sliding scale for increases of output. See details in App. III.

—— Supplemental Report, *Output Bonus.* pp. 4. 1942
1942 *Non-Parl.*
sgd. Aug., 1942

The two sides of the industry were unanimous in preferring a scheme based on district output. Whenever during an output period the output of coal in a district exceeded the standard output, the workers in that district should be entitled to a bonus payment for every complete one per cent by which the output exceeds the standard.

—— Third Report, *Machinery for Determining Wages and Conditions of Employment*, apps. pp. 16. 1943
1943 *Non-Parl.*
sgd. March, 1943

Comprehensive conciliation machinery for expeditious consideration of all questions arising out of wages and conditions of employment was urgently needed. The scheme recommended machinery for settling all questions of a national character, district machinery for purely district questions, and for a transfer from the district to the national machinery should the transfer be desirable. There should be a National Conciliation Board consisting of a Joint National Negotiating Committee composed of equal numbers of employers' and workers' representatives, and a National Tribunal of three permanent members neither engaged in the coal-mining industry nor members of either House of Parliament, except in the case of a member of the House of Lords holding judicial office.

—— Fourth and Final Rep., apps. pp. 22. 1943
1943 *Non-Parl.*
sgd. Sept., 1943
del. McNair.

The output bonus scheme devised as a wartime measure to reward workers for additional effort failed as an incentive to greater production. The Mineworkers' Federation abandoned the idea of a bonus based on a district output and supported a scheme based on pit output, which is more related to the individual efforts of workmen; the difficulties the Mining Association foresaw because of the varying conditions of production as between pits were not insurmountable. The scheme is outlined in App. II.

See *Industrial Relations Handbook*, p. 37; 1953 *Non-Parl. Min. of Labour & N.S.*

Financial Position of the Coal Mining Industry. Coal Charges Account

Memo., apps. pp. 37. 1945

1944–45 *Cmd.* 6617, *x*, 55

Following the issue of the Memo. Cmd. 6364 the Government took operational, but not direct financial, control of the industry. In association with the industry, it stabilised finances through the operation of the Coal Charges Account for pooling the costs amongst coalowners. The Coal Charges Account was designed (1) to finance part of the day-to-day operations of the colliery undertakings, and (2) to institute a partial pooling of costs increased by war conditions. The Exchequer made loans to the industry to enable it to meet the Greene Award and other wage increases. The flat rate increases of wage costs were a greater burden on some collieries than others and collieries have recovered them from the Coal Charges Account. Increases of costs due to substantial reductions of output have not been uniform between districts; and this has been met by allowing districts to draw from the Account by way of price allowances. These payments have been financed by national levies on coal, imposed by six Coal (Charges) Orders, beginning at 7d. per ton in June 1942 and rising to 12s. od. per ton in August 1944. The principle the Government has followed has been that coal prices should cover all costs of production, including costs charged to the Account, without subsidy, and should in due course liquidate the Exchequer loans made from time to time to finance the Account. Statement I shows the expenditure and income from levies, Statement II the contribution by levies and the drawings of the separate districts.

Recruitment of Juveniles in the Coal-mining Industry

Cttee. 1st Rep., apps. pp. 20. 1942

1942 *Non-Parl. Min. of Fuel & Power* apptd. *April, sgd. July,* 1942

J. Forster (*Ch.*), Bonn, Bowen, Gould, Moss.

'*Having regard to the reluctance of juvenile workers to enter the Coal-mining Industry to enquire into the opportunities for training and advancement and the general welfare of juvenile workers in the industry, including wages and conditions of work, and to make recommendations thereon.*'

The number of juvenile entrants to the coal-mining industry, which in 1934 was 30,000, by 1942 had fallen to 14,000, a figure far short of the gross wastage rate. Unless the wastage can be reduced and/or the recruitment greatly increased there will be a contraction in personnel in the near future. Since it is unlikely that the coal-mining industry will ever attract large numbers of adults from other industries it is essential that it should look to the recruitment of juveniles for the maintenance of its manpower. Some of the reasons which have checked the flow of entrants are the memory of unemployment in the inter-war years; wage levels and working conditions which do not always compare favourably with other industries; the family tie which existed when coal was hand-gotten, by which sons worked with their fathers, has broken down with machine cutting; wider choice in occupation created by increased transport facilities and in some districts a low birth rate.

Every effort must be made to increase the sense of economic security and to assure a progressive career; every entrant should be a 'trainee' and have eight weeks training at a special centre, followed by instruction under a competent workman. The scheme should be under the supervision of the Ministry of Fuel and Power and there should be close liaison with the Board of Education and local Education Authorities. Avenues for promotion should be opened through the training scheme. Youths of $18\frac{1}{2}$ should be allowed to opt for mining instead of military service. Other recommendations were made for medical and social welfare. The limitations on recruitment under the Mining

Industry Act, 1926, section 18, should lapse.

—— Supplemental Rep. pp. 2. 1943
1943 *Non-Parl.*
add McNair, del. Bonn, Moss.

There should be a national minimum wage for juveniles. While wages considerations alone would not influence recruitment to the extent desired, the establishment of such a minimum should be regarded as part of a series of improvements designed to produce a change of outlook towards entry into the industry.

See *The Ladder Plan*. National Coal Bd. Ann. Rep. p. 185; 1950 (82) vii, 337. *Policy for Youth*. N.C.B. Ann. Rep. p. 204; 1952–53 (157) viii, 365.

Apprenticeship for Coal Face Workers

Dept. Cttee. Rep., apps. pp. 18. 1947
1947 *Non-Parl. Min. of Fuel and Power*
apptd. *April*, 1946. sgd. *Feb.*, 1947

W. Foster (*Ch.*), Armstrong, Brown, Chiverton, Henshaw, Machen, Newsome, Parker, Ravenshear, Revans.

'*To consider and report on the practicability of introducing a system of apprenticeship for young entrants to be trained as face workers in coal mines.*'

Apprenticeship in its narrow sense means a formal arrangement under indenture covering a specific period of training in a skilled craft, but in the wider sense, and as used by the Ministry, it includes learnership or other forms of progressive training for a defined and appreciable period with or without a written agreement, with a view to qualifying for a skilled occupation. An indentured apprenticeship for face workers was undesirable and impracticable. The scheme envisaged two systems, one to produce a skilled coal face worker and the other a skilled tradesman. There should be a pre-apprenticeship year for all entrants, which should include six months' preliminary training required by the Coal Mines (Training) Regulations, and six months below ground, with one day a week devoted to technical and physical education. The trainee should then be offered a choice of unindentured apprenticeship for face work, or apprenticeship to a trade. Those accepted for face work would then begin a two years' apprenticeship under a training officer. The responsibility for the scheme should be at national level.

Scottish Coalfields

Cttee. Rep., apps. pp. vi, 184. 1944
1944–45 *Cmd.* 6575, iv, 477
apptd. *July*, 1942. sgd. *May*, 1944

D. K. Murray (*Ch.*), Barbour, Brown, Cameron, Duncan, Henderson, McKinlay, Mears, Pearson, Rankine, Reid, Sherriff, Tweedie.

'*To consider the present position and future prospects of coalfields in Scotland and to report—(a) what measures should be taken to enable the fullest use to be made of existing and potential resources in these coalfields; and (b) in this connection, what provision of houses and other services will be required for the welfare of the mining community.*'

The estimated reserves of coal on which Scottish coal production will mainly depend amount to nearly 8000 mn. tons. The ultimate life of the coalfields was not assessed, but in the next 50 years there would be great changes in the centres of production. It is expected that by 1974 the decline in output in the Central Coalfield would total some $6\frac{1}{2}$ mn. tons. If the coal industry is to retain the same manpower as in 1939, the pre-war output of 30 mn. tons will have to be regained, and to do this the decline in the Central Coalfield must be replaced by increased production from the existing coalfields and from three new sinkings, one in Fife, one in the Lothians and one in Ayrshire. The possible increases are ample to make up for the decline in the Central Coalfield. Past development of the coalfields has been intensely individualistic, but as proper and systematic future develop-

P

ment was now envisaged, some grouping of the numerous undertakings, as contemplated in the Coal Act, 1938, would be essential. A statutory body which might be known as the Scottish Coal Board, should be set up to secure co-ordinated developments. A greatly expanded research organisation generously subsidised by the Government is required.

The numbers of houses needed in the existing coalfield to replace the unfit ones, to remedy overcrowding and to provide for new entrants to existing collieries, is about 19,000 and the number required for miners in connection with the contemplated new sinkings is 14,000. The ideal to be aimed at is the complete elimination of the older houses, but in view of the shortages, the better houses should be reconditioned where the rows are sited away from the collieries, where services are available and where reconstruction and replanning can go hand in hand. Where possible miners should live in mixed communities away from areas of possible subsidence and in houses preferably of the cottage type. 'Tied' cottages provided by colliery companies have outgrown their usefulness and the problem of their ownership could be solved by the establishment of housing associations under the Housing (Scotland) Act, 1935. The provision of new houses is the responsibility of the local authorities.

The Report deals with the provision of public and community services, surface subsidence and the disposal of colliery refuse.

Part II of the Report gives a detailed description of the several coalfields.

Coal Mining

Technical Advisory Cttee. Rep., apps.
pp. ix, 149. 1945

1944–45 *Cmd.* 6610, *iv*, 315
apptd. Sept., 1944. *sgd. March*, 1945

C. C. Reid (*Ch.*), Crofts, Hann, Hunter, Kirkup, Nimmo, Smith.

'*To examine the present technique of coal production from coal face to wagon, and to advise what technical changes are necessary in order to bring the Industry to a state of full technical efficiency.*'

Pt. I is historical and includes a comparison between the British coal industry and those of the Ruhr, Poland, Holland and U.S.A. Before the 1914–18 war the technical conduct of the British industry followed long-established practices, local customs and traditions often bearing no relation to those prevailing in other coalfields. The ownership of the numerous separate undertakings was often widely dispersed. Development depended on the initiative and abilities of individual mining engineers being sufficient to keep the industry ahead of neighbours. There was no encouragement to visit other countries and fresh ideas and techniques spread slowly. The employees and engineers were hard workers and they produced a large amount of coal for the home and export industries, but they left a legacy of mines not easy to reconstruct for modern requirements. The miners lived in isolated communities where son followed father into the mines. Innovations which replaced labour were immediately felt where there was no alternative employment; the miner defended his traditional skill and customs against change in methods. 'Output per man shift' improved little between the wars. In 1925 it was only 88·7 per cent of the pre-war figures, but increased between 1927 and 1936 although there was a reduction of hours. In 1914–18 there was an increase in the number of mechanical cutters and conveyors which continued from 1927 to 1939 and was interrupted during the 1939–1945 war, but this did not lead to a re-examination of traditional haulage systems, which were inadequate to handle efficiently the larger output cut at the coal face.

Before the First World War the O.M.S. in Britain compared favourably with that of practically all the major coal-producing countries other than the U.S.A., but it has now fallen behind that of its principal competitors. Although natural conditions are inferior to those in U.S.A., they are comparable with those in the Ruhr and Holland. Continental industries have been able to command adequate financial resources to carry out major improvements, and the grouping of a number of mines under one ownership has facilitated closing down or merging of uneconomic ones. In Britain the industry has been in a state of perpetual financial embarrassment, the long uncertainty over the future ownership of the industry has discouraged long-term improvements and the private ownership of the mineral led to an excessive number of mines with awkward leases too small for the best mining practice, while dispersed ownership hindered grouping.

The use on the Continent of locomotive haulage on straight level roads driven through the strata, instead of the traditional haulage systems of Britain, is one of the greatest technical causes of the differences in O.M.S. Sizes and qualities of British coal are not standardised and there is no proper training of entrants. While on the Continent the existence of closely-organised industries encouraged the collective examination of problems, in Britain the long individualistic tradition has persisted and there has been strong opposition to the principle of amalgamation. Employers have neither accepted the survival of the fittest nor fully abandoned their individualism. In America, though labour relations have been disturbed, both sides have recognised the necessity for the highest productivity per man. In England mineworkers have mostly refused to recognise that in the long run wages depend on progressive productivity. Mechanisation has not been welcomed and the insistence that the number of men discharged should be kept to a minimum has been responsible for over-staffing. The notable exception to this lack of co-operation is found in some districts in the Midlands, where relations have always been good.

Part II. Chapters XII–XIX concern and make a large number of recommendations on technical questions, some of the chief being: the use of the Room and Pillar system is best for productivity, a modified Long Wall Retreating System being second; the application and development of a revolutionary new machine which not only undercuts the coal, but tears it down from the face and automatically loads it on to a conveyor. Traditional British haulage practices are wasteful and call for revolutionary changes. The adoption of locomotive haulage in new or remodelled mines will require fundamental changes in layout and the construction of new roads. No single operation offers more scope for improved efficiency, the coal handled per haulage worker being 5 tons per shift compared with 20–25 tons in Holland and 50 tons in U.S.A. Man-riding facilities should be greatly extended. Recommendations are also made on an extensive programme of level underground roads, mine ventilation, underground lighting, the use of electricity, shaft winding, a general reconstruction of surface plant, cleaning a larger proportion of coal, standardisation of coal sizes and qualities. All new and remodelled mines should be able to accommodate wagons of at least 20 tons capacity.

Chapter XX.—The use of locomotives, new machinery and other changes recommended will require a new standard of broad-based training. The practical difficulties of establishing training faces underground must be overcome. To train officials, provision should be made for mineworkers to work their way up and acquire the qualifications, and the profession of mining engineering made to attract young men from all classes of society. There should be a national scheme organised and paid for by the industry. The amalgamation of the Mining Departments of certain Universities would be an advantage.

Chapter XVI.—Unless there is co-operation between employers and employed, the value of the technical

recommendations will be greatly reduced. Managers and men should have
more contacts on matters of common
concern. The mineworker is entitled
to proper training and education,
opportunities for advancement, explanation by the management of new
methods and of development plans,
and a wage level at least equal to that
of other industries demanding an equal
degree of skill and effort, a rapid redress
of grievances, security of employment
and proper safety measures. In return,
he should give regular attendance and
a full day's work, a cessation of light-
ning strikes, while many customs, e.g.
limitation of stint, cavilling, the seniority rules, etc., are incompatible with
modern mining practice and should be
abandoned.

The limited coal resources of the
country, which are sufficient to last a
century, must be worked on a national
plan and extensive boring for new
sources undertaken. The industry
requires long-term planning on a coalfield basis rather than mine by mine;
new sinkings are required in some
districts; mines should be larger in
size. There is a strong case on technical
grounds for a five-day week of eight
hours.

The Committee concludes that the
drastic and far-reaching changes they
recommend 'cannot be carried through
by the industry organised as it is
today'. The separate undertakings
must be merged into compact units of
such sizes as would ensure the maximum
advantages of planned production, and
an Authority should be established to
ensure that this is done. A pioneering
task awaits the employers and mining
engineers, i.e. the rebuilding of the
industry on modern lines. Workmen
will have to play their part by accepting
machinery, the transfer of workers and
some reduction in the number of
unskilled men.

Coal Industry Nationalisation Bill

Explanatory and Financial Memo. pp.
i–iv. [1945]

1945–46 (*Bill* 62) *i*, 447
o.p. Dec., 1945

The purpose of the Bill is to national-
ise the coal industry, including not only
working, getting and supplying coal,
but allied activities, e.g. colliery coke-
ovens. A National Coal Board is, with
certain exceptions, to have an exclusive
right of working and getting coal and is
to make supplies available in quantities
and at prices which seem calculated to
further the public interest. The Minister
will have power to give general directions to the Board on matters affecting
the national interests, and in framing
programmes of reorganisation and development the Board will be required
to act on lines he approves. An
Industrial Coal Consumers' Council
and a Domestic Coal Consumers'
Council will be established. The classes
of assets to be transferred compulsorily
or at the option of the owners or the
Board are defined. The aggregate sum
to be paid in compensation in respect of
assets, as defined for the purpose of the
District Wages Ascertainments for regulating wages in the industry, is to be
fixed by an Arbitration Tribunal. It is
to be the amount they might have
expected to realise if the Bill had not
been passed and they had been sold by a
willing seller to a willing buyer. The
total sum will be apportioned between
districts and between owners in the
separate districts by Central and District Valuation Boards. Compensation
is to be paid in Government stock, with
revenue payments amounting to £9½
mn. for two years after vesting date.
The capital requirements of the Board
will be met by sums advanced by the
Minister, within a maximum of £150
mn. in the first five years, but it may
borrow £10 mn. temporarily. The
Miners' Welfare Commission will be
reconstituted.

Coal Industry Nationalisation

pp. 3. [1945]
1945–46 *Cmd.* 6716, *xx*, 117

The Tribunal will consist of two
Judges of the Supreme Court appointed

by the Lord Chancellor, one of whom will be Chairman, and an accountant agreed between the parties, or in default of agreement, nominated by the President of the Institute of Chartered Accountants.

It is to determine the global sum required for fair compensation to the owners, and for that purpose to ascertain the amount which the assets might be expected to realise if sold as one unit in the open market as assets of a going concern by a willing seller to a willing buyer on the basis of (*a*) the net revenue which the assets as a whole might be expected to earn in the future, if they were not transferred to public ownership, and (*b*) the number of years purchased to be applied thereto. It is not to make any allowance because acquisition is compulsory or allow any increase of value which the assets might be expected to have after transfer by reason of their being in the hands of one owner and that owner in effect the State.

See *National Coal Board*. Report and Accounts for 1951. pp. 114–15; 1951–52 (190) viii, 675, for global sum for collieries of £164,660,000. Compensation for other fixed assets, see *National Coal Board*. Report and Accounts for 1956. Vol. II. pp. 44–5; 1956–57 (176–11) ix, 555.

National Coal Board

[1st] Ann. Rep., etc. pp. iv, 31. 1948
1947–48 (174) *x*, 351

The duties of the Board as defined in the Coal Industry Nationalisation Act, 1946, are 'to work and get the coal in Great Britain; to secure the efficient development of the coal-mining industry; to supply coal without showing "undue preference" to anyone, and to regulate qualities and sizes, quantities and prices so as best to further the public interest in all respects'. This first annual report gives details of the organisation of the Board's work, the commencement of the five-day week,

the classification and standardisation of coals, etc.

See succeeding Ann. Reps.

Coal-mining Industry. Organisation

Cttee. Statement by the National Coal Board. pp. 19. [1948]
1948 *Nat. Coal Bd.*
sgd. Nov., 1948

The National Coal Board appointed a committee to look into its organisation. The committee agreed with the Board's main decisions on organisation—the grouping of collieries into 50 areas each averaging 4 mn. tons output and under an area manager, and the grouping of coalfields under 8 Divisional Boards. It rejected suggestions that the Divisional Boards should be abolished and the areas given financial autonomy, and advocated 'line and staff' organisation. The Committee's recommendations on the size of the National Board, the relation of the Divisional Chairmen to it and of the area managers to the Division, the establishment of four standing policy committees, etc., are set out, together with the Board's reasons for accepting or rejecting them.

Organisation

Advisory Cttee. Rep., apps. pp. iii, 105. 1955
1955 *Nat. Coal Bd.*
apptd. Dec., 1953. *sgd. Jan.*, 1955

A. Fleck (*Ch.*), Benson, Lawther, Merrett, Mitchell.

'*To consider the organisation of the National Coal Board and to make recommendations to the Board.*'

The main structure of the organisation and the principle of line and staff on which it is based are sound. While the Board cannot make profits in the accepted sense, there is no aspect of financial policy in which it should not pursue much the same course as would a large commercial undertaking. Coal produced in one part of the country can be sold in any other, so that the amount of coal to be produced and capital to be spent in any part must be settled by reference to the industry as a whole. The industry had been starved of capital and technical men and at nationalisation was backward in both. In some coalfields relations between management and men are unsatisfactory and the solution for this lies in better leadership within the Board's organisation and within the unions.

For this type of industry a Board with full-time members is the proper one and apart from two or three top men with general duties of leadership, every activity of the organisation should be the particular concern of at least one member of the Board. In addition to the Chairman and Deputy Chairman there should be six full-time members each with a defined field of responsibility, and four part-time members; this reorganisation should be carried out urgently. In view of the past experience of the Board, when reconstituting it, the Minister should select men who are able to work together as a team.

The system of organising specialist staff into departments at each level should be maintained. Their executive heads have not always been given the support without which they cannot carry on their task. The functional channels should be used for direction, management, advice and control and the idea that the specialists are only advisory should be brought to an end. In an undertaking which started short of experienced staff and contained many not used to what is required in a large organisation and many who have been promoted too soon, more positive direction must come from the top and control must be firmer than it is or has been. The functional heads at each level must be of higher calibre and status than their counterparts below them, this seniority must be openly acknowledged and the senior man's views in his own field should normally be accepted at the level below. The proportion of 'staff'—which number

40,000—is not too high; rather more of higher average quality are required. The Board's staff problem will not be solved without a comprehensive policy for recruitment and training; a retirement policy for staff not able to fill responsible positions satisfactorily should be actively pursued. There should be a staff department represented at all levels and an industrial relations department, but the Board should not rely as heavily as in the past on the ranks of trade union officials as a source of recruitment into responsible positions on this side of the Board's work. The Divisional organisation is correct and no changes should be made in the number and size of Areas, but a common pattern of organisation should be provided for both. There must be a clear line of command between the Area and the colliery which should pass through the Agent, who will be another level of authority.

Making the Organisation Work.— The policies and decisions of the Board are not always properly carried out in the Divisions and Areas, largely because it has not always insisted upon it. In an ordinary business there should be no question of choosing between exhortation and direction if a policy has not been carried out; disciplinary action would be taken if it were disregarded. There is confusion at all levels between decentralisation of specified powers to lower formations and a failure to enforce decisions in the name of non-interference with day-to-day management. The Board should insist on its policies being carried out, should specify the powers delegated to Divisions and the maximum scope of delegation of Areas.

Forecasts and budgets are necessary for efficient control, but forecasts based on past results are of little use for management control. The real need is for proper standards of performance for each pit, based not on past records, but on what ought to be achieved with good management. In view of the varied conditions between pits and Divisions, financial results are an unreliable yardstick for measuring efficiency.

At present the industry is without a policy for wages. The larger capital schemes should receive more scrutiny and there should be systematic arrangement for progressing capital expenditure. The system of budgetary control by standard costs is right, but should be carried out in each Area without delay. The Directive on Organisation, issued in 1953 should be withdrawn and reissued taking account of the Committee's recommendations.

Plan for Coal

The National Coal Board's Proposals. pp. 75. 1950

1950 Nat. Coal Bd.

In order to make the Plan some initial assumptions had to be made. The demand for coal was estimated to reach 230–250 mn. tons in 1961–65, of which 205–215 mn. tons would be for inland consumption and the remainder for export and bunkers. The Board adopted the principle that in the long run the prices of each main type of coal should as far as practicable cover the cost of producing and delivery to the market zones, though this principle could not be fully applied at once. Consumers will thus be paying the true cost of their consumption, and internal subsidies from one coalfield to another will be reduced to the greatest possible extent.

A survey of reserves showed that there was unlikely to be a shortage of coal underground, but that the cost of mining certain qualities of coal will be high. The Board assumed that disparities in wage levels within localities will disappear, that the differentials for different classes of work would remain unaltered, and that wages will rise only when productivity is rising, taking each coalfield separately. Prices and wages were taken as at mid-1949, and interest on new capital at $3\frac{1}{2}$ per cent. The estimates were also based on the assumption of no discoveries or technical advances. The plan assumes a gradual

shrinking of the labour force by 80,000 to 90 per cent of its existing size in 10 to 15 years, i.e. at the rate of 1 per cent per annum. (The current shrinkage rate was higher). That is, the reduced labour force would be producing 120 per cent of current output and 250 of the 950 collieries in production will be reconstructed to yield 70 per cent of total demand; between 350 and 400 pits producing 50 mn. tons may cease to operate, 90 of them being absorbed in reconstruction or concentration schemes, most being small, exhausted or uneconomical pits. The probable capital cost of the programme would be £635 mn., £530 mn. being for collieries, i.e. an average of £40 mn. a year over the 16-year period.

Investing in Coal

Progress and Prospects under the Plan for Coal. pp. 23. 1956

1956 Nat. Coal Bd.

The Plan estimated capital investment to reach £268 mn. at mid-1949 prices: the actual amount was £353 mn. or at mid-1949 prices, £248 mn. One-half of the sum came from internal sources, as compared with the estimates of three-quarters. The number of completed projects is small in relation to the work in progress—on present techniques it takes 10 years to complete a new sinking and eight to carry out a big reconstruction. As most schemes were not started till 1950, the benefit of the investment will not accrue for some years. The original estimate of a capital requirement of £635 mn. at mid-1949 prices is now revised to £1350 mn. at current prices. The labour force required, estimated in the Plan to be 618,000 in 1965, will now be 672,000. Coal output by 1965 will remain at 240 mn. tons, though 10 mn. will come from open-cast.

Revised Plan for Coal

Progress of Reconstruction and Revised Estimates of Demand and Output. pp. 23. 1959

1959 Nat. Coal Bd.

The estimated demand for coal in 1965 is now reduced to 200–215 mn. tons. The Board hopes to regain an export of 10 mn. tons by 1965. There will be 22 shifts a year less, so that the forecast of output per man-year of 342 tons requires an increase per man shift, which it is expected will be nearly reached. The estimate of the labour force required by 1965 is reduced to 587,000–626,000. Nearly the whole output will come from 550 collieries, 220 less than in 1959. Capital expenditure for 1956 to 1965 will be £175 mn. less than estimated in 'Investing in Coal'.

Mining Subsidence

Cttee. Reps., apps. pp. 39. 1949

*1948–49 Cmd. 7637, xiii, 331
apptd. Jan., 1947. sgd. Jan., 1949*

T. Turner (*Ch.*), Clegg, Daggar, Davies, Gibson, Harvey, Lucas-Tooth, Mitchell, Wright.

'*To examine the law of support and the problem of damage caused by mining subsidence in the light of the nationalisation of coal and the coal-mining industry, and to make recommendations.*'

The basic legal conception that the surface has a natural right of support from the strata necessary to preserve it intact, has been so trenched upon both by specific statutory enactments and by contractual concessions made by the owners of the surface, that there has been created a chaotic state of the law affecting specific properties and types of property. The Coal Act, 1938, transferred to the Coal Commission all mining leases and all coal not under leases, therefore finally separating the ownership of the surface from the ownership of the minerals. It gave the right to work the mineral and to let down the surface, on payment of compensation or making good damage done to the surface, but there are difficulties because of the total lack of uniformity in surface rights; in individual cases it is impossible to ascertain what they are. It is to this miscellaneous heritage that the National Coal Board has succeeded; large areas of coal have been sterilised to provide haphazard support. But because of the concentration of all coal-mines in the hands of a single national authority, there is now an opportunity for simplification which did not exist before.

The aggregate amount of damage is not great—the Coal Board estimates that compensation for all surface damage would amount to £3 mn. per annum, or 3½d. per ton of coal raised—but hardship is suffered by individuals who may lose their homes; and the occurrence of the damage is eccentric. The main recommendations are (1) all existing rights of support which are unnecessary in the national interest should be abolished, and (2) compensation, now limited to certain classes of property, should be paid for all surface damage. The Coal Board will thus be free to work coal wherever it pleases, subject only to planning control. But as the planning authority ought not to have to determine individual rights to support, a schedule of 'key points' should determine what surface properties, e.g. power stations, gasholders, ancient monuments, etc., should be granted statutory support, disputed proposals being referred to a judicial tribunal. The extra £2 mn. compensation above the £1 mn. the Coal Board would pay under the existing law should be provided by an annual Treasury grant.

See *Breviate 1917–39*, p. 224.

Amendment of the General Regulations Governing the Use of Electricity in Mines under the Coal Mines Act, 1911

Cttee. Rep., apps. pp. iv, 55. 1941

*1941 Non-Parl. Mines Dept.
apptd. Feb., 1939. sgd. Sept., 1940*

W. M. Thornton (*Ch.*), Bell, Connell, Horsley.

'*To consider, in the light of experience and*

modern practice, what amendments are required in the General Regulations governing the use of electricity below-ground and above-ground at mines under the Coal Mines Act, 1911, taking into consideration the report of the Royal Commission on Safety in Coal Mines. . . .'

The Committee did not confine itself to the aspects of the safe use of electricity in mines mentioned in the Commission's report (*Breviate 1917–1939*, p. 234). The Report deals with the duties and qualifications of electrical staff, ventilation standards, explosion hazards, fire hazards, quality of plant, maintenance, voltage limits, control of circuits, etc. App. I contains a digest of the recommendations of the Royal Commission concerning the use of chemicals, App. III the draft of proposed regulations.

Coal Dust Explosions

Safety in Mines Research Bd. Special Rep. pp. 14. 1943

1942–43 Cmd. 6450, vi, 1
apptd. —. sgd. Nov., 1942

M. Delevingne (*Ch.*).

'To review the plans and progress of its (Safety in Mines Research Board) researches . . . into the cause and prevention of coal dust explosions.'

Stone dusting 'is the only remedy in sight' for coal dust explosions, though it is not complete. The nearer the individual managers of each mine can bring his roads to the ideal, that is to a dominant superiority of stone dust over coal dust, the nearer he will have brought the mine to complete safety against coal dust explosions.

Safety in the Use of Explosives in Coal Mines

Cttee. Rep., apps. pp. 52. 1950

1950 Non-Parl. Min. of Fuel and Power
apptd. Jan., 1948. sgd. — 1950

A. M. Bryan (*Ch.*), Walsh, Joyce, Jones, Richardson.

'To consider the precautions necessary to secure safety in the use of explosives in coal mines and in particular to recommend in what way the effective exercise of these precautions can best be ensured in practice.'

Since 1935 consumption of explosives in mines has increased by 75 per cent, but the amount of coal won per unit weight of explosives was in 1949 little more than half. Managements should review their use of explosives to secure the greatest possible reduction in the number of shots. Alternative methods and the use of machines which reduce the need for explosives should be considered. The principal safety Order 1934 (S.R. & O. 1934/6) is detailed and complicated and the six later Orders have made it much more so. Yet they still do not include a number of requirements recommended by the Royal Commission on Safety in Coal Mines 1938 or take account of recent developments. Recommendations are made for a complete overhaul of the Order and for a number of related matters which cannot be dealt with appropriately by legislation.

Scottish Peat

Cttee. Rep., apps. pp. 66. 1954

1954 Non-Parl. Scottish Home Dept.
apptd. Sept., 1949. sgd. July, 1953

E. V. Appleton (*Ch.*), Anderson, Arnold, Cargill, Cassie, Jenkins, McArthur, Small, Thomson, Woodward.

'To advise on (1) a survey of Scottish peat deposits . . . and the investigation of methods of winning and handling peat; (2) a programme of research into the burning of peat in gas turbines for the production of electric power with special reference to the exploitation of this form of power by the North of Scotland Hydro-Electric Board; and (3) the commercial exploitation of Scottish peat deposits.'

In an area covering 1,625,000 acres there are some 600 mn. tons of workable peat equivalent to 500 mn. tons of coal or 20 years' coal output in Scotland, and 600 mn. tons of mosses suitable for utilisation. In terms of fuel and energy supplies these deposits may not be great in comparison with coal or with the constantly recurring resources of water and wind power, but if properly developed they can make a vital contribution. Before the war peat was used in Germany, Sweden, Denmark and Russia mainly for agricultural and horticultural purposes, but during the war they experimented in using it for power. In Russia it is used for 30 per cent of their power stations, but there is no available information of their latest designs of boilers and grates. Peat is produced in Ireland at 42s. 3d. per ton by large machines on bogs where there is a straight three miles run.

The major problem in mechanical production is drying. So much power has to be used that the net gain of fuel is either very little or non-existent. But sufficient results had been obtained to encourage the Committee to recommend that the Department of Agriculture should continue the survey of deposits; the North of Scotland Hydro-Electric Board should be invited to order a 2000 kW. closed gas turbine to be installed at Altnabreac Moss, Caithness, and used with peat fuel; the Development Fund should finance the purchase and experiment with other equipment for the future use of the Hydro-Electric Board.

persons obtain petrol otherwise than in exchange for coupons issued to them by the proper authority, and to suggest suitable remedies of any abuses which come to light.'

Whilst there was a black market in petrol, there were no 'master minds' at work organising a market on a colossal scale or large quantities of petrol by-passing the rationing scheme—the estimates given for 1947 were from 4·3 per cent of total and 10 per cent of car consumption. Evidence pointed to a multiplicity of individual transactions within the coupon system, the widespread misuse of petrol allowed for essential purposes, failure to appreciate the country's need to mitigate the dollar shortage and a general lowering of moral standards. Black market demand came from the motorist who had withdrawn the co-operation given during the war and had no hesitation in accepting petrol supplies in breach of the law. On the supply side there was an over-issue of coupons to commercial users, to whom petrol was allocated rather than rationed. Commercial should be distinguished from private petrol by colouring commercial petrol red, and by the use of two sets of pumps marked commercial and private. Penalties should include suspension of petrol and of driving licences; motorists should keep a record card.

3. OIL AND PETROL

Hydrocarbon Oil Duties

Rep.

1944–45 Cmd. 6615 See *National Finance*, p. 59.

Evasions of Petrol Rationing

Cttee. Rep., apps. pp. 24. [1948]

1947–48 Cmd. 7372, xiv, 187
apptd. Jan., sgd. March, 1948

G. R. Vick (*Ch.*), Chapman, Parker.

'To enquire into and report upon the extent to which and the methods by which

4. ELECTRICITY

Hydro-Electric Development in Scotland

Cttee. Rep., apps. pp. 38. 1942

1942–43 Cmd. 6406, iv, 677
apptd. Oct., 1941. sgd. Aug., 1942

T. M. Cooper (*Ch.*), Beaton, Cameron, L. Weir, Williamson.

'To consider (a) the practicability and desirability of further developments in the use of water power resources in Scotland for the generation of electricity, and (b) by what type of authority or body such developments, if any, should be undertaken, and under what conditions, having due regard to the general *interests of the local population and to considerations of amenity, and to report.'*

The first developments of hydro-electricity for public supply in Scotland were started by the Grampian Electricity Company, 1922, and the Clyde Valley Company, 1924, but all six northern Scottish schemes promoted since 1929 have been rejected. All major issues of policy, both national and local, have tended to become completely submerged in sectional interests. Land-owning and sporting interests have pressed their claims beyond what was justifiable and mining interests have opposed competition with coal, though coal is virtually non-existent north of Fifeshire.

The Northern Area comprises nearly two-thirds of the area of Scotland, has less than one-sixth of the population, but possesses the great bulk of the undeveloped resources for hydro-electric power. Since the Electricity Act of 1926, the grid system has covered the whole of Great Britain, with the single exception of this Northern Area. The Commissioners did prepare a scheme in 1931, but it was not proceeded with because the Grampian Company applied to develop the area. This decision has been justified by the results of the Grampian Company's developments, which involved a total capital expenditure of £6 mn. The Grampian territory includes extensive areas, notably in the region of the Cairngorms, in which there is no possibility of giving a general public supply, but it does also include areas where it can and should be given. The Northern Area calls for exceptional development policy, practice and outlook.

The policy of the Electricity Act, 1926, based on inter-connected coal-fired stations serving well-populated areas with diversity of load, is inappropriate to the Northern Area, which has no coal or large industrial concentrations. A new coal-fired station to the extreme north of the Highlands, where the demand is building up and where there is abundant

water, would be a major error. The existing electrical development has some features which the McGowan Committee thought needed revision. The acquisition and merging of all existing undertakings into a new corporation would cause dislocations without corresponding benefits. In order to increase the general supply of electricity as an integral part of the regeneration of the Highlands, there should be a new non-profit-earning public corporation, the North Scotland Hydro-Electric Board, responsible for initiating and undertaking all further generation and for supplying present undertakers.

See *Highlands and Islands of Scotland.* Cttee. (E. L. Hilleary, *Ch.*). Rep. Scottish Economic Cttee., 1938. *North of Scotland Hydro-Electric Board.* Ann. Rep., etc.; 1950 (81) x, 705, and succeeding Annual Reports.

Severn Barrage Scheme
Rep., apps. pp. 32. 1945

1945 *Non-Parl. Min. of Fuel and Power apptd. Nov., 1943. sgd. —*

A. G. Vaughan-Lee, W. T. Halcrow, S. B. Donkin.

'To review the conclusions of the Severn Barrage Committee in the light of later engineering experience and practice and of other developments, and to suggest what modifications, if any, should be made in the proposed scheme, in the programme for its execution and in the estimates of its costs.'

The Severn Barrage Cttee. of 1933 reported favourably on the technical possibilities of a barrage scheme costing £38½ mn. and capable of supplying a total of 1610 mn. units, i.e. one-thirteenth of the requirement of the whole country. Except for alterations due to the improvement of various techniques, the findings of the 1933 Committee were confirmed. The barrage scheme is practicable from an engineering point of view and can be economically justified under conditions stated in the Report. The cost, including the transmission system, would be £47 mn.; the number of men employed annually would be 4570; it would take eight years to build and it would save 985,000 tons of coal per annum in the first 15 years of operation. The total energy available at the reception centres would be 2107 mn. kilowatt hours per annum until 1970 and 2207 mn. kilowatt hours thereafter.

See *Severn Barrage*. Cttee. Rep.; 1933 Non-Parl. Treasury (reprinted 1945).

Electricity Supply Areas

Memo. pp. 4.   1947

1946–47 *Cmd.* 7007, *xix*, 555

Under the proposals of Part I of the Electricity Bill, the distribution of electricity is to be entrusted to 14 Area Boards. The division of the country into areas has been based on geographical, sociological, administrative and technical factors. Many areas have strong local and distinctive character, e.g. East Anglia, South Wales, the North East Coast. It would be a great waste to run main transmission lines north and south over the central mountainous district of Wales; North Wales and the Merseyside have interests in common and are formed into one area. The need for adequate diversity of load in the areas has been taken into account. The London area, though the largest, with between a quarter and a fifth of the population, has been kept as small as possible in order not to deprive other areas of valuable urban loads needed to balance their rural loads.

Electricity

Jt. Consultative Cttee.   Sub-Cttee. [1st] Rep. pp. 6.   1947

1947 *Non-Parl. Min. of Labour and N.S.* apptd. March, sgd. May, 1947

R. M. Gould (*Ch.*).

'To examine the measures necessary to reduce peak industrial loads on the electricity supply system, and to advise and assist Regional Boards for Industry in this matter.'

Industrial and domestic consumers are together responsible for 82 per cent of the total consumption of electrical power, although the domestic demand is concentrated more in the winter months. Risk of shedding during the summer months has been reduced by restrictions and by measures taken to transfer some of the industrial load to off-peak hours. These measures must be continued and industry must be asked to see that the peak industrial load does not exceed two-thirds of that of the corresponding period in the preceding winter. This may involve the staggering of day shifts, a proportion of night shifts, the transfer of processes involving a heavy electrical load and comparatively few workers to night work and the operation of rota schemes on a local or district basis, etc. Industries should revise working hours through negotiating machinery and any necessary modifications to the Factory Act should be suggested to the Ministry of Labour.

See succeeding Annual Reports.

Electricity Peak Load Problem in Relation to Non-Industrial Consumers

Cttee. Rep. pp. 23.   1948

1947–48 *Cmd.* 7464, *xi*, 757
apptd. Feb., sgd. May, 1948

A. G. Clow (*Ch.*), Dunsheath, Edwards, Leach, Lewin (Mrs. S. L.), Peattie, Scott, Taylor, Unwin, Wilkinson.

The peak load is the greatest call which all consumers make together at any one time. For 1947–48 the estimated difference between the capacity and the peak demand was 1,420,000 kilowatts and there would be no appreciable surplus capacity until 1951–52, when it would rise to 500,000 kilowatts. The problem was therefore one of restricting or shedding the load in the intervening years. The winter rates for domestic two-part tariffs should be higher than the summer rates and the practice of charging commercial consumers on a basis of metered maximum demand should be extended. Where central control systems already exist, there should be trials of more extended control of water heaters, of day-time tariffs for large domestic consumers, etc. The costs of installing control devices should be compared with the alternative costs of extra generating plant.

British Electricity Authority

1st Rep., etc. pp. xi, 321. [1950] 1948–49 (336) *xiv*, 645

The electricity supply industry was nationalised on 1st April, 1948; the British Electricity Authority (the Central Authority) took over the generating stations and main transmission lines. It has a general control of policy and is responsible for the generation of electricity and its supply to Area Boards for distribution. Fourteen Area Boards took over local electricity undertakings except the generating stations, buying in bulk from the Authority and selling to consumers. These arrangements exclude (*a*) the North of Scotland District and (*b*) some small non-statutory electricity supplies, amounting to a fraction of 1 per cent of the total supplies to the public. The Authority and the Boards are statutory corporations and their members are appointed by the Minister of Fuel and Power.

See succeeding Ann. Reps.

Power and Prosperity

pp. 122. [*c.* 1953]

[1953] *British Electricity Authority*

Reviews the progress of the industry. The estimated increase of demand of 54 per cent in 1959–60 over that in 1953–54 will call for a capital investment of £1442 mn., financed as to £435 mn. from internal sources and £1007 mn. from borrowing. There are details of the cross-channel cable project.

Economy in the Construction of Power Stations

Cttee. Rep., app. pp. iv, 19. 1953

1953 *Non-Parl. Min. of Fuel and Power apptd. Aug., 1952. sgd. June, 1953*

H. Beaver (*Ch.*), Benson, Every, Ewbank, Gibberd, Maunsell, Smith, Wynne-Edwards.

'*To consider in the light of present economic and supply difficulties whether any savings of materials or manpower can be introduced into the planning, designing and construction of power stations, and in particular in regard to the scarce materials, steel, timber, bricks, cement, etc.*'

The object was to secure economies and so minimise interference with the house building programme, but the impact of power station construction (£93 mn. in 1953) on the building programme was not great, as it called for only 1 per cent of the annual output of bricks, 2 per cent of cement and 1 per cent of building and civil engineering labour. It did call for 16 per cent of the constructional steel production, but this was not used in house building. The Committee's recommendations did not apply to work in hand, but to the planning of coal-fired steam power stations over ten years.

The many recommendations include: a long-term programme for selecting sites, minimising the number of sites by increasing the size of stations, reducing the great loss of time and effort in securing approval of sites. The ultimate capacity of stations should be not less than 400,000 kW. The uneconomical practice of building stations in stages with separate plans and contracts should cease and construction planned and carried through in one progressive operation. The present four years required for construction should be reduced to nearer two. Buildings and civil engineering design should be more economical and inappropriate monumental architectural treatment avoided.

See *The Construction of Power Stations.* Observations of the British Electricity Authority on the Report; [?1954]. B.E.A.

5. GAS

Gas Industry

Cttee. Rep., app. pp. [vi], 57. [1945]
1945–46 *Cmd.* 6699, *xii*, 255
apptd. June, 1944. *sgd. Nov.*, 1945

G. Heyworth (*Ch.*), Cooper, Davidson, Martin, Newitt.

'*To review the structure and organisation of the Gas Industry, to advise what changes have now become necessary in order to develop and cheapen gas supplies to all types of consumers, and to make recommendations.*'

Between 1930 and 1938 sales of gas increased by 27 per cent, the number of consumers by nearly 51 per cent. The decline in average consumption was due to the increased efficiency of appliances, loss of the lighting load to electricity, and to the increased competition of electricity in heating and cooking. But sale of industrial gas increased. Fifty-two per cent of the gas was sold by 509 independent companies, 11·2 per cent by companies controlled by 11 Holding companies, and 35·7 per cent by local authorities. One large company supplied 12 per cent, 65 undertakings 70 per cent and 762 small undertakings only 13 per cent of the total. The minimum size for technical efficiency is an output of 1·25 mn. therms; *operating* efficiency tends to increase up to a maximum of 10 mn. therms. In the urban areas of high demand there are 42 units below the minimum size and within range of larger works. In rural areas smaller works may be justified. Holding companies at their best have promoted integration and where this was not possible, helped by advice and fresh capital. But statutory undertakings have their statutory areas and Holding companies could merge or extend their operations only with their consent, or consent at a price which would diminish the benefits. Some Holding companies have done little to improve the efficiency of their subsidiaries. Municipal areas are not now always appropriate gas areas. Early legislation on price and dividend control began when gas enjoyed a monopoly for lighting, but these and subsequent restrictions have become inappropriate with the development of competition from electricity, which has had greater freedom. It is this competition rather than the restrictions, which has been the spur to efficiency, and is the more effective protection for the consumer. A solution must be found which permits the abolition of the restrictions. There must be experimentation with tariffs, which will require consumer surveys involving staff and expense beyond the means of small undertakings.

The improvement in the efficiency of new gas appliances and competition from electricity in every field, including its use in a considerable proportion of new housing, will tend to restrict consumption, whilst the demand for a higher standard of heating and the replacement of solid fuel will tend to increase it. And 10 mn. consumers live in areas to which gas could not be supplied economically. The increase in domestic and other sales might be not less than 20 per cent in the next ten years. The present process of production has defects, and successful developments of complete gasification of coal and of the use of methane would profoundly change the economy of the industry. The distribution systems of many undertakings suffer from haphazard urban development and the survival of small undertakings with their own statutory areas.

The existing structure of the industry restricts further progress: a basic change in it is the only approach that can produce effective results quickly. The undertakings should be grouped into new larger units able to compete freely with other fuel industries and with a capital structure which does not handicap them. All existing undertakings should be purchased compulsorily. There would be ten Regional Boards, which would take over the undertakings in their regions. If companies were acquired at market value and municipal undertakings on an output standard the cost would be £272 mn.; if municipal undertakings were purchased at net outstanding debt, the cost would be £203 mn. The capital of the Boards should be of the fixed interest type guaranteed by the Government. The Boards would need £30–£50 mn. in the next five years for modernisation, integration and expansion. Prices should be fixed to cover under all normal conditions all expenses, and full interest on capital, plus ¼ per cent commission in the amount guaranteed. The Boards should not attempt to accumulate reserves other than depreciation reserves.

Gas Supply Areas

Memos. pp. 4. 1948. pp. 4. 1948
1947–48 *Cmd.* 7313, *Cmd.* 7424, *xxii*, 795
sgd. Jan., June, 1948

Under the proposals of Part I of the Gas Bill, the gas industry is to be organised under 12 Area Gas Boards: S. Eastern, S. Western, N. Thames, Eastern, Southern, E. Midlands, W. Midlands, Wales, N. Western, N. Eastern, Northern, Scotland.

As in the scheme for the 14 electricity areas, the division of the country is based on geographical, sociological, administrative and technical factors, the common element being a nucleus of at least one of the great urban and industrial districts. The principles indicated by the Heyworth Committee for the delineation of the regions have been followed; they should be suitable for the organisation, command sufficient resources, any large commercial centre should lie wholly within one region, and each area should contain some units of adequate size and efficiency.

Gas Council

1st Rep., etc. pp. x, 173. [1951]
1950–51 (69) *xiii*, 695

Under the Gas Act, 1948, the gas industry passed into national ownership and 1037 undertakings were vested in the Gas Boards of 12 Areas. The Area Boards are severally responsible to the Minister; the Council, consisting of a Chairman, Deputy-Chairman and the Chairmen of the Area Boards, is responsible for the capital transactions of the industry (including the issue of compensation stock), for labour relations and for research. The total nominal capital of the companies taken over was £151,800,000. The Area Boards finances and operations, their problems of integrating tariffs and prices, etc., are reviewed.

See succeeding Ann. Reps.

Fuel for the Nation. The Gas Industry's Programme

pp. v, 78. 1954
1954 *Gas Council*

Sets out in detail the plans of the industry 1952–53 to 1959–60. Total demand is expected to increase by 16 per cent. The technical changes and integration of plants are reviewed, and details of past or projected capital expenditure given.

Gas and Electricity (Borrowing Powers) Bill

Memo. pp. 4. [1954]
1953–54 *Cmd.* 9175, *xxvi*, 671

Tables show the revised limits of borrowings required for the developments in the two industries up to March 1960. For electricity the total requirement for 1948 is £2121 mn. including £41 mn. for working capital, of which £627 mn. will come from internal sources, leaving £1494 mn. or deducting Scottish requirements, £1400 mn. to be borrowed externally. For gas the total requirement is £579 mn. of which £129 mn. will come from internal sources, leaving £450 mn. from external borrowing.

6. ATOMIC ENERGY

Future Organisation of the United Kingdom Atomic Energy Project

Memo., apps. pp. 10. 1953
1953–54 *Cmd.* 8986, *xxvi*, 319

During the 1939–45 war atomic energy was controlled by the Department of Scientific and Industrial Research. Most of our leading scientists in the field had been transferred to the United States in 1943, when it was decided that atomic bombs should be made there. After the war British industry was committed to re-conversion, so that only a Government-sponsored organisation could provide the financial and other resources which research for the development of atomic energy required. This task was entrusted to the Ministry of Supply in 1946 on the contraction of many of its war-time responsibilities. The magnitude of the investment required, the long period of development of many novel techniques and the increasing prominence of industrial uses of atomic energy call for a form of control of the project similar to that of a big industrial concern, and with closer contact and co-operation with industry.

The report of the Waverley Committee appointed in 1953 to devise a plan for transferring the responsibility for atomic energy to the most suitable form of non-Departmental organisation was not published for security reasons, but its chief recommendations are summarised in App. I. These are: there should be a Statutory Atomic Energy Corporation with an executive Board, a designated Minister with no departmental responsibilities encroaching on the field, e.g. the Lord President of the Council; a Ministerial Committee and an Official Committee representative of the Departments concerned. Its expenditure should be voted annually, but it should have more than the usual Departmental freedom to conduct its affairs, including the execution of large capital projects. An Accounting Officer should be the official head of the Department.

See *Britain's Atomic Factories;* 1954 Non-Parl. Min. of Supply. *U.K. Atomic Energy Authority.* 1st Ann. Rep.; 1955–56 (95) xi, 123, and succeeding Ann. Reps.

Programme of Nuclear Power

apps. pp. 22. 1955

1954–55 *Cmd.* 9389, *xiii,* 379

The country's growing demand for electrical energy is placing an increasing strain on its coal supplies and the search for supplementary sources of energy is urgent. During the next ten years two types of reactor may be brought into use on a commercial scale—the gas-cooled graphite moderated thermal reactor and the liquid-cooled thermal reactor. It is expected that 3000 megawatt days of heat will be extracted from every ton of fuel, i.e. the equivalent of the heat from 10,000 tons of coal. Taking a reasonable value for the plutonium produced, the cost per unit of electricity would be the same as from a coal fuel station, 6d. per unit. The provisional 10-year programme for the construction of 12 stations by 1965, would provide 1500 to 2000 megawatts, or a quarter of the new generating capacity needed. If they are used as base load stations, this would be the equivalent of 5 to 6 mn. tons of coal. The stations will be built by private industry for the electricity authority. The cost, including the initial charges of uranium and ancilliary plant, would be £300 mn. as part of the £1200 mn. total investment in new electricity stations. By 1975 the programme could be expanded to provide all the new generating capacity. A satisfactory export trade could develop.

7. WATER

Water

Central Advisory Cttee.   3rd Rep., *River Boards,* apps. pp. 73. 1943

1942–43 *Cmd.* 6465, *vi,* 707 *sgd. July,* 1943

Lord Milne (*Ch.*), Atkey, Baker, Beale, Beddington, Cemlyn-Jones, Chaston, Clarke, Cornewall-Walker, Doncaster, Heneage, Hobday, James.

The Committee was asked to consider whether it was desirable to constitute new river authorities which would be vested with the responsibility for all or some of the functions exercised by existing bodies responsible for river control. The control of rivers is divided between various interests: including Prevention of Pollution, Land Drainage, Fishing, Navigation, and Public Water Supply. The absence of any single body in each catchment area to co-ordinate these interests means that there is an overlapping of functions, a lack of uniformity of standards, and a failure to make the fullest use of available resources. That the various functions are capable of being performed satisfactorily and economically by one and the same authority is evinced by the experience of the Thames Conservators and the Lee Conservancy Board. The number of authorities should be reduced, and new River Boards be set up with general responsibility for the conservation of water resources, for planning drainage, and for meeting and safeguarding the requirements of all interests 'in due proportion to the extent of their public value'. The River Boards, which will have authority over catchment areas, either singly or in groups, should be responsible for duties now carried out by Catchment and Fishery Boards and by the bodies responsible for the administration of the River Pollution Acts. The powers of the Navigation, Port and Harbour Authorities should be transferable on application for an Order to this effect. All affected interests should be directly represented on the River Boards, County Councils and County Borough Councils having an effective majority. The Boards should be financed from levies on County Councils and County Borough Councils, based on the rateable values of the portions of their areas under the Boards' jurisdictions, and from other means of revenue such as fishery licences.

In a reservation, Cemlyn-Jones suggests that the representation of the County Councils and County Borough Councils should be not less than two-thirds of the total membership of each Board, and that the number to be appointed by each Council should be in proportion to the amount of its contribution.

National Water Policy

apps. pp. 32. 1944

1943–44 *Cmd. 6515, viii,* 717

In England and Wales 8 per cent of the public water undertakers are local authorities, the remaining 20 per cent being statutory companies. The system has some conspicuous defects. Where their powers are derived from local Acts, the Minister has no adequate powers of supervision, where they are derived from the Public Health Acts he has no power to authorise an undertaking to take water compulsorily. Public water undertakings are not obliged to supply water for non-domestic use, e.g. to industry and agriculture, which is a matter for bargaining between the parties. Many undertakings are too small for efficiency or the flexible use of water sources. The process of amalgamation should be speeded-up, if necessary by compulsion. Thirty per cent of those living in the countryside are not reached by mains. And an overhaul is necessary, because the rise of standard of living and of sanitation has greatly increased demand. In Scotland there is a multitude of small undertakings and a lack of co-operation such that competing mains may be laid along the same road or mains may pass through villages without giving off a supply.

There must be adequate control, but changes should be made only where they can be justified by increased efficiency or reduction of costs. The Minister of Health and Secretary of State for Scotland will have the duty of promoting the provision of water supply and of conserving water resources, will be responsible for the central planning of water policy, and for seeing that the needs and water resources of the different areas are properly determined with the aid of information gathered by the Inland

Q

Water Survey and other bodies. The Central Water Advisory Committee will be reconstituted. Where local needs cannot be met from local sources, but must be supplied from farther afield, there is a risk of waste and conflict between competing authorities. In England and Wales Regional Water Boards will assess the bulk needs of the regions. The Minister's powers will enable him to compel amalgamations to secure economy and efficiency; and to compel one authority to give a bulk supply to another. Undertakings will be obliged to give a supply to industry and agriculture on reasonable terms if this does not endanger domestic supplies; they will be able to take water from a stream or river compulsorily. The Bill provides for a grant of £15 mn. to England and Wales and £6¼ mn. to Scotland towards the cost of extending piped water and sewerage in rural areas. In England and Wales the special expenses rate will cease.

The principles of the Report of the Central Water Advisory Committee on River Boards are accepted.

An Appendix gives the history of public water supplies.

Water Rates and Charges
Rep.
1945–46 Cmd. 6765 See Local Taxation, p. 49.

Tendring Hundred Water and Gas Bill [H.L.]
Sel. Cttee. HL. Special Rep. pp. 3. 1947
1946–47 (HL. 64) v, 219
o.p. May, 1947

The Promoters are a public utility company. They satisfied the committee that a source of supply was urgent, that there was no real alternative source and that care had been taken to conserve the amenities of Dedham Vale and Village.

Gathering Grounds
Central Advisory Water Cttee. Sub-Cttee. Rep., apps. pp. 34. 1948

1948 Non-Parl. Min. of Health apptd. —. sgd. —.

A. P. Heneage (Ch.), Berry, Evans, Cemlyn-Jones, Elmhirst, Hibbert, Mackenzie, McClean, Porteous, L. Rea, Winter.

'To investigate the question whether the public should be allowed access to gathering grounds owned or controlled by water undertakers and the extent to which it is desirable that afforestation and agriculture should be permitted on gathering grounds.'

With the increasing invasion of the hills by the townsman in search of health and of the farmers wishing to extend food production, it is contended that restrictions on access to draining grounds could be relaxed without endangering the purity of the water. On the other hand the water undertakers who have for the past 50 years spent large sums on the acquisition of extensive tracts of gathering grounds are advised in a pamphlet issued by the Ministry of Health after the Croydon typhoid outbreak in 1937–38 to use safety precautions against pollution; for example, the dam or intake should be protected by adequate fencing. Inquiries showed a variety of practices amongst various water undertakers, ranging from complete prohibition of access by humans and cattle to the gathering grounds and reservoirs, and the banning of farming in these areas, to a complete freedom of access.

No precautionary method of ensuring pure water is infallible, so that several lines of defence should be employed; these are: elimination of potential sources of pollution of raw water, provisions for long storage, which kills the germs of typhoid, filtration and chlorination. The odds against all of them failing at the same time are very great. Afforestation permits the productive use of land, can be a barrier against the public and cattle round reservoirs and feeder streams, provides a valuable filter against silt and surface run-off in heavy rains, and acts as a sponge to even the flow from varying rainfall.

Arrangements should be made to prevent sewage contaminating reservoirs; farm-yard manure should not drain into feeder streams; the public should be generally excluded from the banks of reservoirs and no bathing should be allowed. Any fishing or boating should be under rigorous control. In some instances these restrictions should apply to feeder streams. Subject to these safeguards, the gathering grounds should be used for agriculture and afforestation and the public should have access to them.

Water Softening

Central Advisory Water Cttee. Sub-Cttee. Rep., apps. pp. 75. 1949

1949 *Non-Parl. Min. of Health apptd. —. sgd. —.*

Lord Walkden (*Ch.*), Berry, Braddock (Mrs. E. M.), Chaston, Ellen, Hibbert, Johnson, Kirk, Porteous, Winter.

To inquire 'whether it is desirable, and if so, feasible, that public water supplies should be softened in areas where there is a high degree of hardness; the effect of softening on the finances of water undertakings and the resultant cost to consumers, as compared with economies in other directions; the degree of hardness to which water softening is desirable, and the effect on trade and industrial undertakings if softened water is supplied.'

Forty-five per cent of the population receive water which is hard or very hard, and 5 per cent water which is very hard. While some large undertakers supply water which is hard, those which distribute very hard water are generally medium or small sized. No evidence was found to support a theory that either soft water or hard water was beneficial to health, but for domestic purposes, particularly washing and cooking, soft water is preferred. Hard water has a very noticeable effect on soap consumption. Industry uses water for many purposes and its requirements in relation to quality vary widely; with exceptions, central water softening would be unlikely to benefit productive industry and it would have to be decided whether, in the event of an authority softening its water, the greater proportion of the cost should fall on the domestic user who reaps the greatest benefit. If it were decided that soft water was generally desirable, and that it ought to be softened in the home, 5 mn. water softeners at current prices costing £225 mn. would be required (App. E.). Householders should be allowed to purchase these if they wish. But if a general policy of water softening is adopted, it should take place before and not after distribution. Undertakers not supplying soft water should be encouraged to do so, but those unable for any reason to see their way to providing soft water should keep in mind its desirability and plan accordingly.

VII. TRANSPORT

1. **Railways, Canals, before Nationalisation**
2. **The Nationalised Transport System**
3. **Roads, Road Traffic, Ferries**
4. **Sea Transport**
5. **Air Transport**

1. RAILWAYS, CANALS, BEFORE NATIONALISATION

Railways (Valuation for Rating) Bill
Proc.

1945–46 (143)
See *Local Taxation*, p. 49.

Adjustment of the Rates, Fares and Charges of the Main Line Railway Companies

Consultative Cttee. Rep., apps. pp. 18. 1947

1947 *Non-Parl. Min. of Transport*

apptd. May, sgd. Nov., 1946

B. Thomas, T. E. Argile, H. E. Parkes.

'*To advise . . . as to the method to be adopted in adjusting the rates, fares and charges of all or any of the Controlled Railway Companies and London Passenger Transport Boards,*' so that the net revenue should approximate to the '*fixed annual sums* (£38,633,000) *payable by H.M. Government to the controlled Railway Companies.*'

The Companies' estimates of expenditure and receipts at the level of charges for 1947 showed a balance on the net revenue account of £19,879,000 or £18,754,000 less than the fixed annual sum of £38,633,000 payable by the Government under the Agreement. The Railway Companies proposed to make good the deficiency by an increase on all railway, collection, delivery, and canal charges to 36 per cent above pre-war charges, and all dock charges, etc., and other statutory rates and dues, etc., to 60 per cent above pre-war; they pressed the Committee not to maintain the differential for merchandise traffic, which acted as a subsidy at the expense mainly of ordinary passengers, and was destructive of the railway rates structure.

The Companies' estimates of expenditure were generally accepted, but all parties thought the railway companies' estimates for receipts at the existing level of charges of £307 mn. were too low. Evidence favoured Mr. Kaldor's higher estimates of between £323 mn. and £339 mn. There was much opposition to the proposed increases of 60 per cent above the pre-war level. The Committee estimated the receipts, including those from docks, canals and other sources, at £359 mn. and adjusted the recommended increases to between 30 and 35 per cent for all services except docks and harbours. For these they agreed with the railway companies' figures of 60 per cent above the pre-war rates, except that coastal vessels' rates should be increased by only 20 per cent.

The separate report on Coastwise Shipping referred to on p. 12 of the Report was not published.

Railway (London Plan)

Reps.

1946, 1948 *Non-Parl.* See *London,* p. 53.

Forth and Clyde Ship Canal Group

Rep. pp. 12. 1946

1946 *Non-Parl. Min. of Transport*
apptd. July, 1943. *sgd. March,* 1946

H. O. Mance (*Ch.*).

'*To review the recommendations made by the Mid-Scotland Ship Canal Committee in* 1930 *and to make a confidential report on the question whether recent developments, including strategic and general economic considerations, would justify any modifications of the conclusions of the Committee.*'

After investigations (see *Breviate 1917–1939,* p. 258) the Committee concluded that the strategic advantages of the canal are not sufficiently important to influence any discussion as to construction; that there would be serious disadvantages to railways, roads and town planning; that as the industries are on the Clyde and the Forth, any industrial development on the canal would be small; the costs would be £109 mn. excluding £19 mn. interest during construction; the whole of the interest and sinking fund charges, and probably a subsidy towards maintenance, would have to be borne by public funds. It is unlikely that the benefit to shipping would exceed the cost of maintenance and working expenses. The conclusions therefore confirmed the decisions of the 1930 Committee.

2. THE NATIONALISED TRANSPORT SYSTEM

Transport Bill

Explanatory and Financial Memo. pp. i–vi. [1946]

1946–47 (*Bill* 12) *iv,* 531
o.p. Nov., 1946

The purpose of the Bill is to set up in Great Britain a publicly-owned system of inland transport (other than by air) and of port facilities. A British Transport Commission, consisting of a chairman and four members, is to be established to provide an efficient, adequate, economical and properly integrated system and to extend and improve it. The undertaking is to be conducted so that the revenue is not less than sufficient to meet charges properly chargeable to revenue, taking one year with another. To assist the Commission there will be Railway, Dock and Inland Waterways, London Passenger Transport and Hotel Executives. The Minister may give the Commission directions of a general nature in matters affecting the national interests. There will be a Central Transport Consultative Committee and such area Transport Users Consultative Committees for goods and/or passenger traffic.

Railways and canals will be transferred on 1st January, 1948, including privately-owned railway wagons requisitioned by the Minister, and after that date private railway wagons are not to be used on the Commission's railways. The Commission will take over those road haulage undertakings which were, during 1946, predominantly engaged in ordinary long-distance traffic (carriage for distances of 40 miles or upwards and operating beyond 25 miles) under A or B licences, but 'tankers', carriage of livestock, heavy indivisible loads, and household removals are excepted. After the appointed date hauliers with A and B licences may not carry beyond 25 miles from their operating centre. It will be a condition of every B and C licence that goods may not be carried beyond 40 miles from the operating centre except by permit from the Licensing Authorities, which must have regard to the effect on the business, the need for connected premises to maintain production, the additional costs of handling and packing if the licence is refused. Liaison with coastal shipping interests, which will not be subject to the Act, will be through a Coastal Shipping Advisory Committee. The Commission may direct that none of its canals may be used by anyone for carriage for hire, without licences; it may abandon unnecessary canals.

Compensation for the undertakings nationalised is to be in British Transport Stock equal to the amount of compensation. This compensation is to be based: (1) for railway and canal undertakings, the average market value of securities at six specified dates before the introduction of the Bill; (2) for road haulage undertakings, the net value of assets, plus in certain cases compensation for cessation of business and severance; (3) for local authorities' undertakings, payments to cover interest and sinking fund charges on debt; (4) for privately-owned railway wagons, values calculated by reference to age, condition, and original cost. Charges schemes must be submitted to the Transport Tribunal (which will replace the Railway Rates Tribunal and the Railway and Canal Commission) and the Commission may borrow, by stock issue, £250 mn. for capital purposes, and raise temporary loans not exceeding £25 mn.

British Transport Commission

1st Ann. Rep., etc. pp. vii, 424. [1949] 1948–49 (235) *xii*, 1

The Commission is to be a collective policy-making body, responsibility for daily operation and conduct of services being delegated to the five Executives, composed chiefly of individuals with functional responsibilities. Certain powers are reserved to the British Transport Commission, viz., promotion of and opposition to Bills, creation of stock, making of schemes under Parts IV and V of Transport Act, 1947. The Executives' power to dispose of parts of the undertaking and to borrow are limited. Directives regarding the use of delegated powers may be given by the British Transport Commission. The Executives assist in forming policy; within their organisation maximum devolution consistent with the principle and objects of unification is encouraged, and regional organisations have been established. A line of functional responsibility has been provided in the Railway Executive. Consultation with the staff is recognised as important and the growth of appropriate machinery at all levels is encouraged.

It is laid down that the integrated transport system is to be efficient, adequate and economical, and that where the Commission is providing regular goods services of different kinds between the same points, the consumer must be free to choose between them. The greatly increased use of vehicles operated by the owner to carry his own goods under C licences is of vital importance. The Commission had inherited great disparities in rail fares and charges and in road fares and charges, and in the relationship between them. Charges schemes will be a key to integration, but they cannot be completed within the prescribed two years. Private owners' railway wagons were purchased at a total cost of £43mn. By the end of 1948, the road freight transport undertakings of Carter Paterson and Pickford had been purchased, together with 246 other 'long distance' undertakings, owning over 8000 motor vehicles, as well as trailers and horse vehicles. In the London area Thomas Tilling's road haulage and passenger undertaking was purchased, as well as 16 regional bus undertakings. The gross book value of the Commission's assets, railways, road undertakings, ships, canals, docks, hotels, etc., was £1666·4 mn. The Report analyses the receipts, costs, working results and operating efficiency of the various services and the work and problems of the five Executives are reported on in detail.

See succeeding Ann. Reps.

Applications of the British Transport Commission for authorisation of additional charges in respect of their Railway; Harbours, Docks and Piers; and Canals and Inland Waterways

Transport Tribunal sitting as a Consultative Cttee. under Section 82 of the Transport Act, 1947.

Reps. pp. 30. 1950. Procs., 12 days, 1950

1950 Non-Parl. Min. of Transport. Procs.; 1950 Non-Parl. sgd. Feb., 1950

B. Thomas (Ch.), Parkes, Sewell.

Railways. — The Commission estimated that the deficit of £21 mn. in 1949 would be £30 mn. in 1950, and proposed to raise charges on freight, but not passenger traffic, to secure a $16\frac{2}{3}$ per cent increase of receipts. Railway charges were 55 per cent, while labour and material costs were 120 per cent above pre-war. The Iron and Steel Federation urged that in total Railway working expenses of upwards of £300 mn., a good deal more than £2–3 mn. ought to be realised in economies. The Comptroller of the Commission stated that as economies of some £7 mn. had been effected in 1949 and there had been a reduction in staff in that year of 27,000, they could not expect economies of a similar magnitude in 1950. If passenger fares were increased there would be a falling off of traffic as in 1947. Recommended that the additional charges specified in the Schedule should be made.

Harbours, Docks, etc.—The Commission's Docks represent 30 per cent of the port facilities of the country and deal with 40 per cent of the weight in goods imported and exported, foreign and coastwise. The estimated excess of working expenses over gross receipts for 1950 was £1 mn. and £2 mn. if the apportionment of the central charges were included. The proposals were for an increase in the existing surcharge from 25 per cent to 50 per cent on coastwise ships and goods, and from 75 per cent to 100 per cent on other dues. There was no lack of efficiency, and no additional economies were suggested which would reduce the deficit. The additional charges were recommended, but coastal vessels trading with Eire should obtain the benefit of the coasting differential.

See British Transport Commission. 3rd Ann. Rep.; 1950–51 (210) xx, 361.

Increase in Passenger Fares

Central Transport Consultative Cttee.
Rep., app. pp. 17. 1952

1951–52 *Cmd.* 8513, *xviii*, 967
referred March, sgd. April, 1952

E. Cadbury (*Ch.*), and 15 others.

'British Transport Commission (Passenger) Charges Scheme 1952.'

The objections, which came from bodies fully representative of the users, were to any increase in fares; any alteration of fare stages; the elimination of 4d., 7d. and 10d. road fares; the failure to provide 1d. fares for short distances; the abolition of shift workers' tickets; the restrictions on the issue of early morning tickets; and application of increased fares to apprentices, lower paid workers (especially women), aged and disabled persons.

The new charges scheme, involving approximately a 20 per cent increase, was based on the principle of the same charge per mile of travel for everyone in similar circumstances. Hitherto there had been a number of charges which were in a greater or lesser degree below those ordinarily made, and this meant that passengers paying the ordinary fares were subsidising those enjoying the lower ones. The Committee approved the Passenger Charges Scheme as being fair to the travelling public, but thought it had been introduced too harshly. The increase of 20 per cent brought the total increase to 86 per cent above pre-war and to 90 per cent in the London area, and compared favourably with every other service and commodity.

Transport Policy

Pp. 4. 1952

1951–52 *Cmd.* 8538, *xxv*, 821

The Transport Act, 1947, has not achieved and is not likely to achieve its avowed purpose, the integration of road and rail services has made little progress and seems unlikely to be much more than working arrangements between separate entities; even if full integration were practicable, it would result in an unwieldy machine, ill-adapted to meet promptly the varying demands of industry. Railway administration has become excessively centralised, and the Road Haulage Executive cannot give the individual and specialised services afforded by free hauliers before nationalisation. Area passenger transport schemes and schemes for harbours have roused so much opposition that there is little prospect of bringing them into force.

The Road Haulage undertaking should revert to private enterprise. It will be divided into operable units and disposed of by open tender. The units sold will be given A licences and freed from the 25-mile limit. Since the goodwill of the former business out of which the Road Haulage undertaking was formed has disappeared, the undertaking is not likely to be sold at the price it was bought, but buyers will be expected to pay for the trading rights and opportunities.

The excessive centralisation of the railways must be reduced by giving greater autonomy to areas (including Scotland). The areas will together continue as a single entity for financial and charges purposes. The Commission will be given freedom to compete by varying charges within prescribed limits. Compensation will be paid to the Commission for the losses in which these changes may involve out of the proceeds, initially £4 mn., of a levy on goods vehicles, including those of C licensees, other than small local delivery vans.

Railways Reorganisation Scheme

Pp. 22. 1954

1953–54 *Cmd.* 9191, *xxvi*, 771

The Transport Act, 1953, required the Transport Commission to submit reorganisation proposals, which were to include the setting up of area authorities. It was originally intended that the Railways Executive should run the railways. Each of its full-time members had departmental responsibilities right down the line and all of them had corporate responsibility for management; the Executive was treated as the employer of staff. The four railway groups were, by the separation of Scotland and the North East, altered to six Regions, and as these were large, Chief Regional Officers were appointed to co-ordinate the work of the departments in them. It became clear that departmental control could be transferred to the Chief Regional Officers. After the Transport Act, 1953, the Railway Executive was abolished.

In the Interim Organisation the Commission took over the primary responsibility for major policy and general direction in design, labour relations, general level of charges, policy and principles of organisation, etc., and departmental authority was transferred to the Regions. Headquarters departmental heads are not functional officers issuing orders in their own name. To secure some decentralisation within the Regions, Area Boards should be set up to deal with policy at area level, to supervise and see that the Commission's policies are implemented. They would be like the boards of the former railway companies, and would not undertake day-to-day management, which would rest with the Chief Regional Manager. The Commission would have direct contact with both. An endeavour will be made to work out regional operating costs. Neither Hotel Services, Docks nor Inland Waterways should be transferred to regional management.

Road Haulage Disposal Board

1st Rep. pp. 8. 1953. 7th (Final) Rep. pp. iv, 19. [1956]

1953–54 (25) *xix*, 843. 1955–56 (410) *xxviii*, 759

o.p. Dec., 1953, *Oct.*, 1956

Under Section 2 (9) of the Transport Act, 1953, the Board was to make a report as to the progress made in the disposal of property held by the British Transport Commission for the pur-poses of their existing road haulage undertaking.

The 7th Report (1955–56 (410)), shows that the total effective number of vehicles for sale was 35,018, of which 19,303 were in transport units or companies. Sales had to be by public tender, and persons with only small resources had to be given an opportunity of buying small units. There was no established market for this type of property and rights; some of the value consisted in the rights comprised in the Special A Licence, and even the valuation of the vehicles was a matter of opinion. A large integrated business had to be broken up into saleable units. The market was tested by experiment, by selling units of various types and sizes. There was a lack of buyers for large units and for units with premises as well as fleets. The Government decided not to dispose of vehicles required for the continuance of the Commission's trunk service network, the total number of vehicles retained for these and other reasons being 8870. The Board agreed that it was wrong to break up the integrated network of the Parcels and Smalls organisation, and following the failure to sell the meat fleet, the Minister agreed that both should be run as operating commercial concerns, and not be offered for sale for the time being.

See 2nd–6th Reps., published twice-yearly.

Canals and Inland Waterways

Board of Survey. Rep., apps. pp. 131. 1955

1955 *British Transport Com. apptd. April, sgd. Nov.*, 1954

Lord Rusholme (*Ch.*), Hodges, Brown.

Of the waterways transferred to the Commission, 1138 miles were from independent undertakings, 965 miles from railways, and 69 miles were state owned. By the end of 1948 the traffic was 10 mn. tons. Between 1948 and 1953 £1 mn. was spent on arrears of maintenance, and £500,000 on plant and equipment; traffic increased to 13 mn. tons. The report reviews the various waterways, the criticisms and suggestions. Two-thirds of the system incur a heavy loss. The transfer of the whole of the waterways to a specially constituted body would not provide a solution if that body were required to bring up the system to a commercial standard out of its own resources. Attention should be concentrated on the ways of real value as part of the transport system and on steps to relieve the Commission of the remainder. The scheme proposes to develop 336 miles of waterways, to retain 994 miles at an adequate standard, because of their traffic and because they form part of a through route. The rest have no commercial value for navigation, though some are of importance for water supply, drainage and disposal of effluents. They should be transferred to other authorities.

See *Review of Trade Harbours 1948–1950*. Docks and Inland Waterways Executive. Reps.; 1951 British Transport Com. *Breviate, 1900–1916*, p. 145. *Breviate, 1917–1939*, pp. 257, 276.

Electrification of Railways

Cttee. (C. M. Cook, *Ch.*). Rep., app. pp. xi, 94. 1951. *The System of Electrification for British Railways.* pp. 24. [?1955] 1951, [?1955], *British Transport Com.*

The 1951 Report concludes that although the direct 3000-volt system had become more attractive in recent years, it has advantages over the 1500-volt system only in areas of relatively high traffic, and certain lines have already been electrified at 1500 volts. Standard voltage should remain at 1500 volts with overhead contacts, but areas now served by third rail at 750 volts, and some adjacent areas, should continue at 750 volts. In view of its advantages in dense traffic, the fourth rail system should continue on the London Transport system and its extensions.

The later report makes a fundamental change for all future electrification other than in the third rail area,

from 1500 V. d.c. to an overhead system at 25 kV. a.c. There will be savings in capital and annual costs. There is a map.

Modernisation and Re-equipment of British Railways

Pp. 36. 1955

1955 *British Transport Com.* sgd. Dec., 1954

The plan is based on the assumption that most of it can be started in five and completed within 15 years. It will cost £1200 mn., of which one-half would be required in any case for normal maintenance on the present basis. The total is made up of £210 mn., track and signalling; replacing steam traction by electric or diesel traction, £345 mn.; replacing passenger rolling stock, stations, etc., £285 mn.; remodelling freight traffic, £365 mn.; miscellaneous, including packet ports, £35 mn. In due course the plan should attract a return of £85 mn. (present turnover, £500 mn.).

British Transport Commission. Proposals for the Railways

Statement and Memo., apps. pp. 43. [1956]

1955–56 *Cmd.* 9880, *xxxvi*, 419

The increase of freight rates and fares for which the B.T.C. had applied were reduced or deferred, on the understanding that a fresh assessment of the position would be undertaken by the Commission, and would be followed by appropriate action. The prospects of the undertaking and of the modernisation plan are reviewed on the assumption that the Commission would not be prevented from increasing its charges to cover increases of cost, would be free to operate a flexible system of charging and to determine the services to be provided, that the resources needed for modernisation would be available, and that action would be taken to give a reasonable financial target possible of achievement, but which contained no element of subsidy.

From 1948 working surpluses have been earned, but the standing financial charges were heavy. By the end of 1955 the accumulated deficit was £70 mn. and would be £120 mn. by the end of the year. If appropriate steps were not taken it might reach unmanageable proportions.

The Commission propose to meet the problem by (1) Modernisation: in passenger traffic by faster long-distance services, electrification of intense urban services in big centres of population, and by diesel or electric units on feeder or secondary lines; in freight traffic, by providing wagons with continuous brakes, better marshalling yards and larger wagons. (2) Elimination of services for which there is no public demand or which can be performed better by other transport services. (3) Increased productivity. (4) Release from certain cramping statutory obligations and greater freedom to compete in fixing fares and charges and as regards the obligation to give equality of treatment to all persons. The 1953 Act removed the obligation to give equality of treatment, but although this has been restricted by the Tribunal's decision, freight rates will be reorganised to encourage larger consignments, regular traffic and to avoid loss on short-distance traffic.

An attempt by the Commission to cover its deficit by increasing the charges by the full amount necessary or by covering it partially by increasing those which any particular traffic would bear would be unpropitious in the present state of competition. For the present restraint is the wiser policy.

Provided these measures are given time, the annual revenue of the Commission would be balanced by 1961 or 1962, and yield a surplus of £50 mn. by 1970. But these results will not accrue in the early years of modernisation. While a commercial concern may ask its shareholders to forgo dividends during this period, the Commission is financed by fixed interest capital. Some

financial plan should be adopted which while it avoids subsidy will place the railways on a sound footing during this period of reconstruction. Any relief should be strictly limited in time and amount.

The Memo. is preceded by a Government Statement. The Government agrees that the rate of investment in 1957 should be increased to about £120 mn., that for a number of years special advances will be made to the Commission up to a total of £250 mn., and that the Commission may borrow enough to pay the first three years' interest on the sums required for capital expenditure.

3. ROADS, ROAD TRAFFIC, FERRIES

Ferries in Great Britain

Cttee. Rep., apps., index. pp. 55. 1948

1948 *Non-Parl. Min. of Transport apptd. May*, 1946. *sgd. Dec.*, 1947

N. S. Beaton (*Ch.*), Barnaby, Halcrow, Mackenzie, Ritchie.

'To investigate ferry services linking trunk and classified roads in Great Britain; to make recommendations for the improvement of the equipment or operation of such services with a view to their greater efficiency and adequacy, and, with the same object, to report as to any amendment of the law governing the provision of such services that appears to be desirable.'

Rights to operate ferries have usually had their origin in a royal grant or an Act of Parliament. Older ferries originally satisfied a local need, but those which experienced the impact of increasing traffic were often owned by private individuals who had not the resources to develop their equipment. The Ferries (Acquisition by Local Authorities) Act, 1919, and the Harbours, Piers and Ferries (Scotland) Act, 1937, empowered local authorities to acquire ferries, although they were not always highway authorities. There are 44 vehicular ferries which are part of the highway system, vested either in local authorities, or railway, dock, harbour and canal authorities or 'other owners'.

All ferries connecting trunk and classified roads should be treated as highways, and should ultimately be freed from tolls. The law should be amended to provide for the vesting in the Minister of Transport of ferries intersecting trunk roads, and to allow other highway authorities to acquire them, accompanied by a legal obligation to provide and maintain an adequate service. Compensation to owners should be determined by arbitration. Expenditure incurred by highway authorities should be met in part by grants from central funds. New ferries should be constructed to enable the first vehicle on to be the first off, and special attention should be given to boarding and landing appliances. Mechanically-operated ferries of the pontoon, etc., type should be subject to the provisions of the Merchant Shipping Acts. The abandonment of ferries for which there has ceased to be a demand should be facilitated. Other recommendations deal with conditions of specific ferries.

Road Safety

Cttee. Interim Rep., index. pp. 88. 1945

1945 Non-Parl. Min. of War Transport apptd. Dec., 1943. sgd. Dec., 1944

P. Noel-Baker (*Ch.*), and 17 others.

'To consider and frame such plans as are possible for reducing accidents on the roads and for securing improvements in the conduct of road users in the interests of safety; and to review the recommendations of the Select Committee of the House of Lords on the Prevention of Road Accidents, and to advise on those which should be adopted as measures of post-war policy for the reduction of accidents.'

'There is no mystery about the cause of the great majority of road accidents. If we could raise the standard of road manners of all road users; make the roads really adequate for today and tomorrow; and ensure that the vehicles are always in a roadworthy condition, we should have solved the problem.' The Committee makes proposals under these three headings and 60 recommendations are made. For example, propaganda based on the Highway Code should be persistent and continuous, and directed to all types and ages of road users; local safety organisations should be set up; approved expenditure by local authorities should rank for grants; roadside advice should be given by police and a universal speed limit should not be imposed, etc. Bad and inadequate road conditions should be remedied. In the planning of roads there should be regard to the principles of the segregation of traffic and classes of traffic; adequate parking spaces and lay-bys should be provided and street lighting standardised and improved. Every police force should have a traffic department manned by specially trained men. Motor vehicle testing stations should be set up; there should be extensive research on vehicle lights and light dazzle. Vehicles other than pedal and solo motor cycles should carry two red rear lights and a reflector. Pedal cycles should have two efficient brakes, carry bells, have a red rear light, a red reflector and a white patch, etc.

In a reservation Mr. Nevill Whall objected to the recommendation that pedal cycles should have a red rear light.

—— Final Report, apps., index. pp. 144. 1947

1947 Non-Parl. Min. of Transport sgd. May, 1947

add G. R. Strauss (*Ch.*), del. P. Noel-Baker (*Ch.*).

A Mission should be sent to study U.S.A. and Canadian practice. Amongst the matters dealt with by 57 recommendations are the following: Road Accident Statistics.—Improvements in reporting and tabulation of statistics, maintenance of road accident maps. Road Users.—Use of adult and school-boy patrols, research into accident-proneness, siting of new licensed premises, endorsement and inspection of licences; reckless riding of cycles and failure of pedestrians to comply with traffic signals to be made offences; registration of pedal cyclists not recommended; control of traffic and investigation of accidents of equal importance to criminal investigation; training of police in traffic matters. Roads.—The Government must promote uniformity of administration of highways; siting of tram and trolley bus stops by the Traffic Commissioners; replacement of trams by vehicles of greater manoeuvrability; queue barriers and shelters at bus stopping places. Vehicles.—Compulsory indicators and stop lights on vehicles; periodical testing of vehicles and establishment of testing stations.

—— Cttee. Rep., *Pedestrian Crossing Places (Traffic) Regulations, 1941*, app. pp. 10. 1949

1949 *Non-Parl.*
sgd. Feb., 1949
J. Callaghan (*Ch.*).

'*To consider the desirability and practicability of amending the Pedestrian Crossing Places (Traffic) Regulations, 1941 (S.R. & O. No. 397).*'

The problems were: to amend the Regulations to enable them to be more readily understood and obeyed and to remove ambiguities; to help pedestrians to assess more clearly when it is safe to step on to a crossing, and drivers so to act, that pedestrians are able to exercise their rights under the Regulations with confidence and safety; and the siting of crossing places. The 17 recommendations included that the waiting of vehicles within 45 feet of the approach side of a crossing should be prohibited.

—— Cttee. Rep., *Motor Cycle Accidents*, app. pp. 15. 1952

1952 *Non-Parl.*
sgd. March, 1952
J. G. Braithwaite (*Ch.*).

'*To consider the problem of motor cycle accidents and to advise on measures for their prevention.*'

Whilst the upward trend in motor cycle casualties has been largely due to the increase in that class of traffic, the fact remains that when a motor cyclist is involved in an accident, he or his passenger is invariably a casualty. In 50 per cent of the cases the injury is serious. Statistics show that a motor cyclist is three to four times more likely to be involved in personal injury than a driver of a four-wheeled vehicle. A serious aspect of the problem is the fact that 50 per cent of the casualties were in the 19–27 age group.

As skidding is one of the chief causes of accidents, special consideration should be given to road surfaces known to be dangerous to motor cyclists. In 34 per cent of the head to tail collisions during the hours of darkness, a motor cycle struck the rear of another vehicle; this calls for improved rear lighting on vehicles. Straying dogs cause a large percentage of accidents. If a motor cyclist hits a dog he is usually thrown from his machine; steps should be taken to control such dogs on the highways. Other recommendations deal with safety devices, crash helmets, goggles, etc. Special restriction of the speed of motor cycles should not be imposed.

—— Cttee. Rep., *Bus Accident at Gillingham*. pp. 4. 1952

1952 *Non-Parl.*
sgd. June, 1952
J. G. Braithwaite (*Ch.*).

'*To consider the accident which occurred at Gillingham on 4th December, 1951, when an omnibus ran into a marching column of Royal Marine Cadets in Dock Road, and to make such recommendations as seemed to us to be desirable.*'

There were three main features of the accident; the inadequacy of the street lighting, the lack of proper safeguards for the marching cadets and the failure of the omnibus driver to use his headlights. As street lighting throughout the country is of great importance to road safety it should receive special attention, especially in poorly-lighted roads with a record of night accidents, and if necessary lighting authorities should be given assistance from central funds. Where uniformed bodies march in the carriage-way they should have lookouts carrying a white light at the front of the column and a red light at the rear. Drivers should be advised to use properly adjusted dipped headlights in badly lighted roads, and local authorities should be encouraged to provide reflector studs in these roads.

—— Cttee. Rep., *Massed-Start Cycle Racing*, apps. pp. 12. 1954

1954 *Non-Parl.*
sgd. Jan., 1954

H. Molson (*Ch.*).

'*To examine the problem of massed-start cycle racing from the road safety point of view.*'

The National Cyclists' Union, because of danger, had banned road, as distinct from track racing to its members. Until 1942 road racing was limited to time-heats in which groups of cyclists start at timed intervals and race against the clock with other teams. The popularity of massed-start events on the Continent led to a breakaway from the N.C.U. and a British League of Racing Cyclists was formed. Despite the opposition of the N.C.U. and the criticisms of the Road Safety Committee, 1944, massed racing continued to grow and in 1952 the N.C.U. itself organised such racing and for 1953 the B.L.R.C. planned 700 events, apart from those organised locally.

The police officers overwhelmingly agree that massed-start cycle racing causes not only inconvenience, but actual danger. It leads to bodies of cyclists five or six abreast travelling at high speeds; traffic lights and standards of road conduct have been ignored and commercially promoted races led to congregations of vehicles. For a period of two years massed street racing should be allowed on condition that the events should be begun and completed before 9 a.m., major road junctions and right-hand turns should

be avoided and there should be no racing in built-up areas. At the end of two years, if substantial inconvenience and danger still remains, the sport should be prohibited.

—— Cttee. Rep., *Child Cyclists*, app. pp. 14. 1956

1956 *Non-Parl.*
sgd. Feb., 1956

H. Molson (*Ch.*).

'*To examine the problem of accidents to child cyclists with a view to making recommendations on measures for their prevention.*'

In 1954, 10,715 child cyclists under 15 years of age were casualties in road accidents, of whom 105 were killed and 2100 seriously injured. This number, it was estimated, may increase by 50 per cent within the next 10 years unless additional remedial measures are introduced. Recommended that considerable financial support should be provided by the Government and by cycling interests for a major effort directed towards the reduction of accidents to children, which should include a large expansion of voluntary schemes for training and testing child cyclists, regular inspection of children's cycles, better cycle tracks and better edges to roads; parents and road users should be made aware of their responsibilities to child cyclists, etc.

—— Cttee. Rep., *Minimum Age for Motor Cyclists*, apps. pp. 22. 1957

1957 *Non-Parl.*
sgd. July, 1957

G. R. H. Nugent (*Ch.*).

'*To consider the existing minimum age for riding a motor cycle.*'

There is no conclusive evidence to support the view that riders of the age of 16 or 17 are subject to a higher accident rate than riders of 18 or 19; the rate per rider is highest between the ages of 18 and 25. But the most dangerous feature is that a 16-year-old, without any previous experience, can ride the largest type of motor cycle, especially as the increase in the casualty rate and the seriousness of casualties occurs with the increase in the size and power of the machine.

The minimum age limit should be 15 years for riding the smaller types of machines (mopeds) and 17 years for motor cycles of over 250 c.c. Mopeds should retain their existing characteristics with a maximum speed of 25 m.p.h. A licence for a moped should be restricted to that type of machine, a motor cycle licence should cover a moped but not a three-wheeler. The minimum age for driving a three-wheeler classed as a motor cycle should be 16; and a person passing a test on a non-reversible three-wheeler should not be granted a licence for a motor cycle or moped.

Road Accidents

Rep., apps. pp. 79.   1946
1946 Non-Parl. Min. of Transport apptd. May, 1944. sgd. Aug., 1945
J. H. Jones.

'*To estimate, in terms of the National Income, the cost to the community of road accidents and traffic congestion.*'

The cost of road accidents includes the cost of human injuries, the cost of damage to and loss of use of vehicles, and the cost of other damage, e.g. to walls, animals, etc. As there is no complete record of all accidents or of the cost of recorded accidents, two independent methods of investigation were used: random sampling of road accidents in the files of the War Department Claims Commission, Police reports and the Special Report on *Road Accidents, 1936–37* (1938 Non-Parl. Min. of Transport) and the insurance method, based on insurance premiums and the numbers of registered vehicles. The estimated annual cost to the community during 1935–38 at the prices and incomes then prevailing was £60 mn., 1·33 per cent of the total National Income. At current (1945) prices the cost would be £100 mn. Nine-tenths of the total cost represented human injury, one-tenth damage to vehicles and pro-

perty.   Accidents involving serious injury often cost the community more than death and were five times as frequent. The net economic gain to the community of a reduction of accidents is the contribution to the National Income made by those who would otherwise have been fatally injured or incapacitated.   Prof. Jones and Sir Percy Harvey thought that it was not possible to suggest any reliable method of assessing the annual monetary loss due to traffic congestion.

See Final Report of the Committee on *Road Safety* (1947 Non-Parl. Min. of Transport), para. 9.

Traffic Signs

Dept. Cttee. Rep., apps., index. pp. vi, 114. 1946
1946 Non-Parl. Min. of War Transport apptd. Feb., 1943. sgd. Nov., 1944
F. C. Cook (*Ch.*), Corrin, Dudley, Finch, Foley, Gregory, Hefford, Holdsworth, Hunter, Lintern, Lunn, Morren, Munro, Perrin, Tripp, Whitelegge.

'*To consider the system of road traffic signs and other cognate means of controlling traffic on roads, and to make recommendations.*'

Traffic signs must be so designed and sited as to attract, both by day and night, the attention of the persons for whom they are intended; their significance must be clear at a glance; they must be so sited that sufficient time is allowed for road users to adapt their course of action to the indication given, and they must, as far as possible, be erected on a uniform system.   The system retained or adopted on the recommendations of the 1933 Committee (*Breviate 1917–1939*, p. 271) had in its main aspects proved satisfactory in practice. The present recommendations suggested only those modifications of or additions to existing practice, which experience, changing traffic conditions, or technical progress have shown to be desirable for greater safety and convenience of road users.   The

Report makes over 40 recommendations.

Petrol Stations

Technical Cttee. Rep., apps., index. pp. 52. 1949

1949 Non-Parl. Min. of Transport apptd. Feb., 1947. sgd. Dec., 1949

Lord Waleran (*Ch.*), and 14 others.

Discusses the technical considerations which should govern the number and distribution of petrol stations. They should be classified into three grades, for each of which a minimum standard of equipment and service is suggested, as well as standards for guidance on the desirable frequency and spacing of petrol stations in rural areas based on vehicle use, mileage, etc.

Precautions against Fire and Explosion in Underground Car Parks

Jt. Cttee. Sub-Cttee. Rep., apps., index. pp. 35. 1950 (Post-War Building Study No. 28)

1950 Non-Parl. Min. of Works apptd. — 1946. sgd. June, 1948

C. R. Woods (*Ch.*), and 18 others.

'*To consider the fire and explosion hazards in underground car parks and to make recommendations to secure the necessary degree of protection.*'

Contains a technical statement as to the design, construction and equipment, etc., of car parks and gives guidance on their operation.

Licensing of Road Passenger Services

Cttee. Rep., apps. pp. iv, 114. 1953

1953 Non-Parl. Min. of Transport and Civil Aviation apptd. Aug., 1952. sgd. Nov., 1953

G. A. Thesiger (*Ch.*), Lyne, Matthews, Reid, Speight, Tiffin, Williamson.

'*In the light of present-day conditions to enquire into the operation of the provisions of the Road Traffic Act, 1930, relating to the licensing of public road passenger services and to make recommendations.*'

The uncontrolled development of road passenger transport and the effects of unrestricted competition led to the Road Traffic Act, 1930, which set up Licensing Authorities in Traffic Areas to license services by public service vehicles for stage carriage and express carriage, having regard to existing facilities, routes, the elimination of unnecessary services and the co-ordination of all forms of passenger transport, including rail transport. The licence conditions could include the fixing of fares, so that these were reasonable and did not give rise to wasteful competition. Trams and trolley-buses, and contract services (i.e. services in which separate fares are not paid or are used for private parties) were excluded from the system.

The three main problems were: the relation between the Licensing Authorities and the Transport Commission, which had acquired a number of major road passenger undertakings; the question of the method of appeal against the Licensing Authority's decision; and the position of contract carriages operating under a road service licence, yet able to carry passengers at separate fares.

The Transport Commission's control has not materially affected the services under the licensing system. In so far as the Commission's companies have a monopoly or near monopoly, in particular areas, of services not competing with the railway services, they are in a similar position to an independent company with a monopoly. But in so far as the Commission's companies operate services in competition with the railways and there is no independent operator, the control previously operated by the Licensing Authority has largely passed to the Commission.

The problem on appeals was whether they should continue to go to the Minister, as provided in the 1930 Act for road passenger services, or to an independent Tribunal, as provided in 1933 in respect of Goods Vehicles. The criticisms of the existing procedure were that it led to undue delay, that no reasons or inadequate or insufficiently published reasons were given, and that quasi-judicial functions ought to be performed by a tribunal. But the Minister's decisions were largely determined by policy based on a consideration of what is desirable in the public interest and were seldom concerned with findings as to past fact or with the interpretation of the law. Appeals should continue to go to the Minister, but some attention should be given to the processes involved, a Bulletin of Selected Decisions should be issued periodically, and consideration be given to a provision that appeals should be heard and reported to the Minister by persons appointed by him after consultation with the Lord Chancellor or the Lord Advocate.

Stage or express carriages carry passengers who pay separate fares and require a road service licence. They include local and long-distance bus and coach services, which are licensed to maintain regular services over specified routes. Contract carriages are vehicles hired as a whole and not by payment of separate fares, and require no such licence. But as there were many uses for which a privately hired coach was appropriate, but which would involve the payment of separate fares, the Act of 1930 departed from the simple distinction of payment of separate fares or hire as a whole, and created categories of 'private parties' and 'special reasons', not easy to define, on which there could be separate fares, but which would require no road service licence. The operators of licensed services complained that these special provisions were abused and that their sphere was often encroached on by expanding journeys on contract. The Committee were not convinced that licensed road services were damaged by private hire, or that private hire should be excluded for the benefit of holders of road service licences. There should be a new form of licence to authorise the operation of contract carriages.

The licensing system as a whole had worked well. The Committee rejected proposals that the Licensing Authority's control over local authorities' services in their own area should be abolished or weakened, on the ground that the Licensing Authority must co-ordinate all services. The procedure for consent by the Licensing Authority to a local authority's services outside its area, e.g. to one of its housing estates outside its boundary, should be abolished and the control of fares put on the same basis as for other operators' services.

One member, Mr. Lyne, recommended the transfer of appeals to a tribunal similar to the Road and Rail Tribunal.

Road Haulage Disposal Board

1st Rep.

1953–54 (25) See *The Nationalised Transport System*, p. 198.

4. SEA TRANSPORT

War-time Financial Arrangements between H.M. Government and British Shipowners

Memo., apps. pp. 19. 1940

1939–40 *Cmd.* 6218, *vii*, 417

In addition to a number of British ships requisitioned from time to time for naval and military purposes, it became necessary in 1939 to requisition a number of ships to carry supplies of iron ore and cereals and in 1940 to requisition all ships on the United Kingdom or colonial register which were engaged in the deep sea liner and tramp trades. The Memo. sets out the charter party conditions and the rates of hire, which were to cover running expenses, current depreciation and reasonable return on capital, but not past depreciation, or provision for a fund for replacement. For liners the allowance of 5 per cent for depreciation and 5 per cent for return is worked out for each ship, but for tramps is based on a 'basic vessel' of fair average value and not worked out separately for each ship. Requisitioned liners are returned to the owners to be run in accordance with normal practice, but on Government account. Under the tonnage replacement scheme if a ship is lost, the pre-war value of the ship will be paid in cash, the 'increased value' credited to the owner and paid when the ship is replaced.

Scheme for Purchase by British Shipowners of New Vessels built on Government Account

Memo., app. pp. 4.   1942

1941–42 *Cmd.* 6357, *v*, 683

British owners who had lost shipping since the outbreak of war will, under the conditions set out, be able to purchase, with deferred delivery, new tonnage built or to be built during the war on Government account. The price will be cost of construction less depreciation. The vessels will be operated during the war on behalf of the Minister of War Transport, the owner to whom the vessel is allotted being appointed manager.

Scheme for Purchase of Merchant Vessels by Allied Governments from H.M. Government

Memo. pp. 2.   1942

1941–42 *Cmd.* 6373, *v*, 687

The scheme was to enable Allied Governments who had made their merchant vessels available to the Minister of War Transport, to replace in some measure tonnage lost, to purchase a proportion of new vessels built by H.M. Government in the United Kingdom and second-hand vessels purchased by H.M. Government from foreign flags. One-third of the tonnage offered is second-hand. The price paid will be, for new vessels the cost, for the second-hand vessels the cost in dollars to H.M. Government.

United Maritime Authority

Planning Cttee.   Rep., apps. pp. 24.
1944

1944 *Non-Parl. Min. of War Transport* sgd. Oct., 1944

R

W. G. Weston (*Ch.*).

For the continuance of co-ordinated control of merchant shipping the contracting governments accept common responsibility for the provision of shipping for all tasks necessary for the completion of the war in Europe, the Far East and for the supplying of all liberated areas, etc. The appendices set out the procedure for programming and allocation of dry tonnage, for handling tabled requirements, formulation of programmes, estimating tonnage available, determining the allocation of tonnage to particular countries and of particular ships; the determination of freight rates; the allocation of tanker tonnage. Different machinery is required for vessels engaged in the coastal and short sea trades.

See *Coasting and Short Sea Trades in Europe. United Maritime Authority* (1945 Non-Parl. Min. of War Transport), which describes the machinery of an Area Committee sitting in London, to make block allocations of coasting and short sea tonnage to three Zone Committees, which should allocate and control tonnage allocated to them.

Clyde Estuary

Cttee. Rep., apps. pp. 59. 1945

1946 *Non-Parl. Min. of War Transport apptd. Aug., 1944. sgd. July, 1945*

T. M. Cooper (*Ch.*), Letch, Taylor.

'*To enquire into the present arrangements for the provision and administration of navigational facilities and of docks and harbours of the River and Firth of Clyde and the lochs leading from them, and to report what modifications, if any, in those arrangements are desirable for the promotion of the trade of the estuary and the public interest.*'

The present administrative position in the Clyde estuary is the end-product of a long series of independent enterprises, initiated in the course of the last 200 years, during which the centre of gravity has shifted up the river from the Ayrshire coast, first to the Port of Glasgow and then to Glasgow itself.

Ninety-three per cent of the overseas trade of the six ports goes through Glasgow, and there is no pronounced reversal of the up-stream tendency. Proposals for a super-authority over the entire water down to Campbeltown and Stranraer are rejected. Continued administration by separate undertakings is not compatible with efficiency. Unification is required. Existing authorities in the River and Upper Estuary should be replaced by a single new authority— the Clyde Port Authority—exercising full powers within the area above Cumbrae Head and with limited powers in the lower estuary. It should acquire the assets and assume the liabilities of some existing undertakings, and maintain and develop the potentialities of the river and the estuary and collaborate with authorities concerned with the development, etc., of the industrial hinterland. The proposals for the composition of the new authority, and area, etc., are given in detail.

Turn-round of Shipping in the U.K. Ports

Working Party. Rep. pp. 36. 1948

1948 *Non-Parl. Min. of Transport apptd. Sept., 1947. sgd. May, 1948*

W. G. Weston *(Ch.)*, and nine others.

There have been delays of turn-round on account of unrepaired war damage, loss of warehouses, shortage of barges, bolster and hopper wagons and modern cranes. Traffic should be routed through more ports, many operations could be mechanised, but some employers are reluctant to invest in appliances as restrictions on manning, etc., may not make it profitable. More flexibility by overtime and transfer is desirable. The tally system is not efficient and there should be a training scheme.

Increased Mechanisation in the United Kingdom Ports

Working Party. Rep., app. pp. 16. 1950

1950 *Non-Parl. Min. of Transport apptd. Nov., 1948. sgd. Feb., 1950*

P. E. Millbourn *(Ch.)*, Ansell, Bird, James, Nicholson, Sibley, Canney.

'To make a comprehensive review of the possibilities of increased mechanisation in the ports of the United Kingdom, with special attention to the handling of timber imports; to make a study of the use of mechanical handling equipment in foreign ports; and to make recommendations in respect of the possibilities of increased mechanisation in the ports of the United Kingdom, including the extent to which the provision of such increased mechanisation will be beneficial to port operations by obtaining a speedier turnround of shipping, by the more expeditious handling of goods through the ports, and by the more economic use of the labour force.'

Certain ports are well equipped with mechanical aid, but this is exceptional and in many manhandling of cargo is still the principal method. Where the quays, transit sheds and warehouses are old in construction, they do not lend themselves to the use of modern mechanical handling. The workpeople's representatives revealed ready and frank appreciation of the need for mechanisation, but they felt that any financial advantages resulting from it should be shared between workpeople and employers. 'We have found little evidence that they appreciate the further point that the increased use of machinery is required, not for the financial gain to the employers or employees, but rather to see that an economy is made which will eventually affect the nation and the consumer by a reduction of freight rates and lower handling charges.' They also feared redundancy. The employers, on the other hand, wanted a reduction in labour costs by revised manning scales to justify the capital expenditure on equipment.

No large-scale development in the use of mechanical handling equipment is likely to take place until the problem of its use is settled on a national basis by both sides of the industry, and the fear of labour redundancy is removed.

In future planning and development of port facilities there is need for consultation to engender co-operation between port authorities, shipowners and workpeople. The National Joint Council should take steps to secure the full implementation of the principles of Clause 10 (Mechanical Appliances) of the 1931 National Agreement. A national survey should be made of the effect on the labour force of mechanisation, in order to judge the extent to which the men's fear of redundancy is a real factor. If there is a displacement of labour, allowances should be given to elderly dockers who are prepared to retire. If this and normal wastage does not provide for any redundancy, recruitment to the industry should be restricted. A study should be made of equipment used in the major ports of the U.S. and Canada.

Ports Efficiency

Cttee. 1st and 2nd Reps., apps. pp. 15. 1952. 3rd Rep., apps. pp. 19. 1956
1952, 1956 Non-Parl. Min. of Transport apptd. March, sgd. —, Aug., 1952, April, 1956

Lord Llewellin (Ch.), 1st and 2nd Reps. E. H. Murrant (Ch.), 3rd Rep.

'To investigate the working of the ports of the United Kingdom and in particular the ports of London and Liverpool, and to secure the co-operation of all the interests concerned, including shipping and inland transport authorities, in ensuring a quicker flow through the ports of inward and outward cargo; and to report from time to time.'

The major obstacle to improving the flow of goods through the ports was the difficulty of securing steel supplies, particularly for war damage repairs. The first report recommended a special allocation of steel for repairs and reconstruction, and gave a list of works which would make 23 more berths available in two years. Other factors causing congestion were that bigger ships were being used and this restricted them to berths at the main ports; ships carrying export cargoes were being more fully loaded; exports had increased in volume; export licensing caused delays at the Customs; the loss of flexibility in the arrival of imports caused by bulk buying and selling arrangements, which were an inheritance of the war, and the growth of road transport at docks built on a basis of rail feeder services. There had not been a cushion of reserve capacity needed for sudden and seasonal increases of traffic. Until the major ports have built up to a margin of capacity they are liable to have periods of serious congestion.

The 3rd Report deals with delays to road vehicles carrying goods to and from the docks. The delays occur when more traffic arrives than the sheds or labour force can handle, or the ship can receive. Shed accommodation should be increased; and regulatory schemes for staggering arrivals and smoothing out unnecessary peaks introduced.

Fire Prevention and Fire Fighting in Ships in Port

Working Party. Rep., apps. pp. 28. 1950
1950 Non-Parl. Min. of Transport apptd. — 1948. sgd. Nov., 1949

D. O'Neill (Ch.), Coombs, Daniel, Humphreys, Jarvie, Jeffers, Lees, Ombler, Pringriff, Pollitt, Riach, Skillern, Smith, Spriddell, Wilson.

'To consider and make recommendations for circulation to all interests concerned on the fire-prevention and fire-fighting arrangements to be observed in connection with ships in dock and harbour areas and in ship-building and repair yards.'

Since the war, in addition to numerous small fires, serious ones have occurred in ships in port undergoing repair, which have resulted in their becoming constructional total losses. The major causes of the fires during the years 1946–48 were burning and welding apparatus, smoking and matches, stove and stove flues, electric wires and cable, etc. Detailed recommendations are made for reducing risks from these causes, e.g. smoking should be pro-hibited except at meal times in places where there is no appreciable risk. Clearly defined instructions and their strict observance, coupled with an efficient patrolling system would pre-vent many fires. Except in the case of ships under construction, the res-ponsibility for fire prevention and initial fire fighting rests with the ship-owner, unless he delegates it, in which case there should be a clear, preferably written agreement in precise terms, so that there is no doubt as to who is res-ponsible for decisions. The dangers to stability through the intake of large quantities of water are so great that the decision to stop pumping to prevent capsizing or to move the ship away must rest with the dock and harbour author-ity. Precautions against capsizing, the steps to make full use of shore water, etc., are set out. There must be efficiency and good will on the part of managements and men.

South Wales Ports
Council for Wales and Monmouthshire.
Rep., apps. pp. 26. 1955
1954–55 Cmd. 9359, vii, 565
referred May, sgd. Nov., 1954

In 1935 the total traffic was 24½ mn. tons, 3·9 mn. tons being inward and 20·6 mn. tons outward, mainly coal. But in 1953 the balance was altered to 10 mn. tons of inward and 11·8 mn. tons of outward traffic, the main loss being coal exports. The ports fared unevenly, Swansea's traffic increasing by 91 per cent, that of Cardiff and Barry decreasing by 52 per cent and 56 per cent respectively. The new industries introduced into the hinterland had not made any large impact on general cargoes, which remained relatively small. Various remedies for this are explored, including a railway charges scheme on a uniform basis.

Prevention of Pollution of the Sea by Oil
Rep.
1953 *Non-Parl.* See *Fishing,* p. 117.

5. AIR TRANSPORT
British Air Transport
Paper. pp. 10. 1945
1944–45 Cmd. 6605, *vii,* 421

The Paper outlines the Government's policy for the development of British civil air transport and the operation of routes for the carriage of passengers, freight and mails. The requisites of the organisation are: units large enough to operate economically; each unit must have an efficient organisation covering every area served by its air lines to enable it to handle passengers, freight and mail, and facilities for co-operation with other forms of transport wherever this can promote air travel. Provision must be made for economical use and maintenance of aircraft; there must be co-operation between users and manu-facturers in deciding types of aircraft to be used; the organisation should pro-vide training for crews of Common-wealth and foreign countries, and should be able to supply these countries where required, with technical and operational staff. Unlimited competition would mean that competition would be concentrated on the lucrative routes, while those which were commercially unprofitable but essential in the public interest would be neglected. The undertakings will be granted a sufficient proportion of remunerative routes, to-gether with exclusive rights to them, in return for an obligation to run non-remunerative services as part of their systems. A field of development will be left open to competition and charter aircraft left unrestricted. Three Cor-porations were decided upon: (1) the Commonwealth Air Routes, together with the trans-Atlantic service to the United States and the services to China and the Far East; (2) European routes and the internal services of the United Kingdom and (3) South American route.

See *International Air Transport.* Memo.; 1943–44 Cmd. 6561, v, 447. *British Air Services;* 1945–46 Cmd. 6712, xv, 645.

Flying Boat Base

Cttee. Rep., apps. pp. 16. 1947

*1947 Non-Parl. Min. of Civil Aviation
apptd. May, sgd. July, 1946*

Lord Pakenham (*Ch.*), Gouge, Slatter,
Thornton.

'*To review the proposals received for the
establishment of a permanent base for civil
flying boat operations in the United Kingdom,
and, before 30th June, 1946, to make
recommendations to the Minister of Civil
Aviation as to the site offering the best
advantages in the light of all available
operational, civil engineering, cost and other
relevant data.*'

The three general considerations in
selecting a site were, the economies
which would be made by the use of
large flying boats; their principal use
would be on long haul routes, and
terminal facilities should be as adequate
as for land planes. The sites chosen for
investigation were the Brambles shoal
in the Solent; Langstone Harbour, between Portsmouth and Hayling Island,
and Cliffe between Gravesend and the
Medway. The Southampton site was
placed third because it was tidal, Cliffe
had an advantage because it was 32
miles from Piccadilly whilst Langstone
was 68 miles. But from the point of
view of meteorology, preliminary
capital cost estimates, reclamation of
land, maintenance cost and amenities,
etc., Langstone proved to be better than
Cliffe. Both sites were suitable but
Langstone Harbour was the best.

The Report is preceded by a Memo.
stating that because of problems of
defence, the cost and difficulty of
moving existing technical installations,
the Government had decided against
Langstone Harbour.

Private Flying

Advisory Cttee.   Preliminary Rep.,
apps. pp. ii, 61. 1947

*1947 Non-Parl. Min. of Civil Aviation
apptd. Jan., sgd. July, 1947*

W. Straight (*Ch.*), Bowden, Clark,
Douglas (Mrs. A. C.), Hardingham,

Harvey, Kinghorn, Lamplugh, Mahony, Preston, St. Barbe.

'*To advise the Minister of Civil Aviation
on the development of private flying (including
gliding) and to report to him from time to
time on questions relating thereto.*'

A vigorous national aviation movement, covering model flying, gliding
and powered-aircraft flying is of fundamental importance to the well-being of
the British aircraft industry. Without
State assistance most of the light aero-
plane clubs will be forced to close
down, club flying charges are too high.
Gliding is an integral part of aviation
training and should be given immediate
assistance.

Recommendations include: a subsidy
rising to £900,000 per annum to
approved flying clubs to enable them to
reduce charges to £1 an hour; the
creation of new flying clubs to bring the
number up to a network of 100; assistance to gliding clubs of not more than
£490,000 spread over five years; help
to cover prototypes of light trainer
airplanes and free loans to help the production of 1000 aircraft and of gliders;
a plan for 100 aerodromes.

Tudor Aircraft

Cttee. Interim Rep. and Government
Observations, apps. pp. 35. 1948

*1947–48 Cmd. 7307, xvi, 505
apptd. Sept., sgd. Dec., 1947*

C. L. Courtney (*Ch.*), Mould, Taylor,
Wansbrough.

'*To enquire into the development and production of Tudor aircraft for the British
Airways Corporations and to report their
findings to the Minister of Supply.*'

In the autumn of 1943 the discussion
between A. V. Roe and Co. Ltd. and
Canadian interests resulted in the proposal, to meet the post-war situation, of
converting the Lancaster IV bomber
for civil use on this route. This was
accepted as a stop-gap arrangement and
the conversion became known as the
Tudor I. In the adaptation a number of
aerodynamic faults had to be rectified,

and modifications, not regarded as numerically excessive, were asked for by the B.O.A.C. But the failure of the B.O.A.C. to co-ordinate their demands led to friction with the management and loss of enthusiasm by the workpeople. The B.O.A.C. would have preferred to operate proven United States types, but although they had accepted the policy to 'fly British', they failed to steer a middle course between technical perfection and speedy production: this was due principally to inadequate direction of the technical staff of their Project Branch.

Recommended that a service between Montreal and London be begun as early as possible with a Tudor I; that they should be considered for other Empire and South American routes. In view of the relatively short life to be expected of the Tudor I, they should be used on an annual hire basis.

In a Note giving their observations on the Report, the Government states that the criticisms made of B.O.A.C's internal organisation and their relation with the constructors relates to the period when the Corporation was on a war-time basis, or in transition to a peace-time basis. Changes have been made and the present organisation is more satisfactory than that disclosed in the Report.

—— Final Report, apps. pp. 22. [1948]
1947–48 *Cmd.* 7478, *xvi*, 541
sgd. *June*, 1948

del. Wansbrough.

Tudor II is a derivative of Tudor I. The latter was intended to be a long-range aircraft with a necessarily restricted payload, the former was to be suitable for medium ranges with a greater payload. In December 1944, the Imperial Air Conference accepted the principle of parallel operation on the trunk routes between the U.K. and Australia and between the U.K. and South Africa. Following the decision, at the request of B.O.A.C., the Ministry of Supply ordered 79 Tudor IIs and

this order remained in force until October 1946. During this period doubts arose as to its suitability and delays in production influenced the Dominions. In 1946 the Australian company took an option on four Constellations and the South African Airways proposed to use Skymasters. The B.O.A.C. recommended a reduction in the order for Tudor IIs to 50, and since February 1947 little production work took place partly because of the B.O.A.C's uncertainty regarding its ultimate acceptance, and partly because it was influenced by the awaited test trials of Tudor I.

The contending views regarding the future of Tudor II were that its production had fallen behind schedule and most of its advantages had vanished; that it would be a deplorable waste of effort to cancel the contract as 26 have been manufactured, and that the deficit on the Empire services over the next five years was likely to be the same whether the Tudor II order is cancelled or not, since the cost of operating it was balanced by the cost of cancellation. It was difficult to justify its use on routes east of Calcutta and south of Nairobi. A decision on its future should take into account that it might be improved for satisfactory operation over Empire routes, that waste of effort and materials would be avoided, and that it would provide an insurance against delay in introducing later types.

Accident Investigation Procedure

Minister's Memo. and National Civil Aviation Consultative Council, Cttee. Rep., apps. pp. 46. 1948
1948–49 *Cmd.* 7564, *xi*, 183
apptd. *Aug.*, 1947. sgd. *Feb.*, 1948

C. M. Newton (*Ch.*), Mayo, Nicholl, Purchase, Shawcross.

'*To enquire into the procedure governing investigations into accidents to civil aircraft in the United Kingdom and to British civil aircraft abroad and to make recommendations.*'

The procedure for investigation laid

down in the 1922 Regulations provided for a private, informal technical investigation and, if the Minister thought it desirable, for a public, formal judicial inquiry by a Court. Few Courts were appointed and Inspector's reports were not published. The decision after the Shelmerdine report of 1945 (not published) that Inspector's reports would be published in full did not create the necessary confidence in the industry and the public, and the Minister undertook that in certain circumstances the Inspector's investigation would take place in public. This procedure was unfair to all concerned: the Inspector was called upon, without legal assistance, to preside over a Court attended by counsel, evidence was not and could not be taken on oath, counsel for interested parties could not call witnesses nor cross-examine witnesses called by the Inspector, and hearsay evidence was admitted in the presence of the Press. Such inquiries should be discontinued. The persons conducting the initial investigation, composing the tribunal, or deciding the form of inquiry should be completely independent and not connected with any body interested in the outcome. This includes the Minister, since he controls the three airline corporations, and is responsible for the provision of aerodromes and ground organisation. Although the Inspector has independence he should not be an official of the Ministry. There should be a Civil Accident Board, with a legally qualified Chairman and 11 members, and six legally qualified Commissioners of Civil Air Accidents, who should inquire into every accident; interested parties should be entitled to appear or be represented, to call evidence and cross-examine witnesses. Evidence should be on oath and hearsay evidence excluded. The Chief Inspector and his staff should be transferred to the Board.

In a Memo. the Minister rejects the proposal for a Board, as it would impinge upon his responsibilities, and the proposed procedure would be cumbersome and costly. As an alternative, the Inspector's investigations will be held in private, and if there is a conflict of evidence, interested parties may be allowed to cross-examine witnesses. There will be more Courts of Investigation. Reports of both Inspectors and Courts will be published except in specified circumstances.

Certification of Civil Aircraft and Approval of Equipment

Cttee. Rep., apps. pp. v, 15. 1949
1948–49 *Cmd.* 7705, xi, 537
apptd. Sept., 1947. *sgd. June*, 1948

W. Helmore (*Ch.*), Wilcock, Bennett, Beswick, Bovenschen, Brotherton, Bulman, Farren, Gordon-Smith, Lamplugh, L. Lucas, Stack, Stanley, Westall.

'To consider . . . the conditions of a procedure for the certification of civil aircraft and the approval of navigational and other equipment, whether airborne or on the ground, employed in their construction, operation and maintenance.'

Airworthiness was defined as safety from the point of view of the structure, handling qualities and performance of an aircraft, when used on appropriate duties by competent operators. Before a new type of aircraft is certified for the carriage of fare-paying passengers, its performance should have been ascertained to be adequate for safety in the operating conditions it may reasonably be expected to encounter in service. The present trials should be supplemented by extended flight performance trials and by intensive endurance flights. Supervision should remain with the Certifying Authority, but constructors should participate in the trials and operators be brought in at the proper stage. The annual deficit for the Certifying Authority should be met out of public funds. A new Certifying Authority should be established, retaining the title Air Registration Board. It should be responsible to the Ministry of Civil Aviation, but be as independent as possible in its technical and administrative functions. Procedure for the certification of equipment should remain substantially unchanged.

The Minister's Memo. states that most of the recommendations were accepted in principle, but those referring to the organisation and financial structure of the Air Registration Board were under examination.

Recruitment, Training and Licensing of Personnel for Civil Aviation

Cttee. Rep., apps. pp. vi, 36. 1949

1948-49 *Cmd. 7746, xi, 559*
apptd. Sept., 1947. sgd. June, 1948

C. A. B. Wilcock (*Ch.*), Helmore, Brackley, Crowe, Gamage, Hockey, James (J. W. G.), James (R. L.), L. Milverton, Pulbrook, Robinson, Thomas.

'(*i*) *To review the present arrangements (including the procedure for medical examination) for the issue of personnel licences in Civil Aviation . . .; (ii) to consider . . . the steps which should be taken to ensure that an adequate flow of aircrew and ground personnel of the different essential categories will be available . . .; (iii) to compare the standards required of aircrew and ground personnel for Service and Civil Aviation purposes and to make recommendations with a view to enabling competent personnel of all categories to be available for Civil Aviation from Service sources . . .; (iv) to consider and make recommendations with regard to the education, recruitment and training of personnel recruited from sources other than the Services. . . .'*

Detailed estimates are given in App. E. of the numbers of eight categories of trained personnel directly connected with flying operations which will be required during the years 1948-1957, of the numbers of ex-R.A.F. who will enter, and the balance of civil entrants required. No special measures will be needed to attract and train the required number, except in the case of pilots, though there should be an apprenticeship scheme for maintenance engineers, and facilities for obtaining civil licences whilst they are in the services, and a liaison committee to pre-select air crew.

From 1951 onwards 225 pilots per annum will be required from non-R.A.F. sources, and since training is expensive, there will be a serious shortage unless there is a State Scholarship Scheme, which will cost from £110,000 to £135,000.

In a Memo. the Minister accepts most of the recommendations in principle, but takes the view that there may be no lack of pilots, and therefore rejects the proposed State aid for training civil pilots and aiding professional pilots to obtain new licence qualifications. In the interim, holders of B licences who require further licences will be able to take the test for half fees.

Landing and Taking-off of Aircraft in Bad Weather

Inquiry. Rep., apps. pp. 20. [1951]

1950-51 *Cmd. 8147, viii, 405*
apptd. —. sgd. Jan., 1951

Lord Brabazon.

'*To examine the relative responsibilities of the captain of an aircraft, the operator and the aerodome authority in deciding whether an aircraft can safely land at, or take-off from, an aerodrome in bad weather conditions.*'

The development and use of both airborne and ground aids to facilitate the navigation of aircraft has meant that the dangers of en route flight in instrument conditions are no longer critical, but no equipment or combination of equipments is yet available which meets the requirements of safe instrument landing. Similar considerations apply to instrument take-off.

In no circumstance should an aerodrome be closed against emergency; where there is temporary obstruction on the runway the aerodrome authority should inform the pilots; pilots should be informed if the aerodrome authority cannot provide safety and rescue services; arrangements should be made for the measurement of 'runway visual range' at aerodromes in the U.K. when visibility falls below one nautical mile; there should be a runway lighting system by day in bad visibility. In the present system there is a lack of relationship between the information reported, and that which the pilot desires to know, which varies with the approach. The Report states the terms in which the weather minima should be stated for various methods of approach. Operators should continue to be responsible for the establishment of minima, but these should be subject to State approval.

Helicopter

Inter-Dept. Cttee. 1st Rep., apps. pp. iv, 28. 1951

1951 *Non-Parl. Min. of Civil Aviation apptd. Aug.,* 1948. *sgd. Oct.,* 1950

G. Cribbett (*Ch.*), Cumming, Downey, Gordon, Liptrot, Locke, Mann, Masefield, Rowe, Shenstone, Walmsley, Wilson, Yates.

'*To consider in relation to present and likely future development of the helicopter:* (a) *The prospects of its future commercial use on internal air services in the United Kingdom and other fields of potential use, and the effect on air services (including aerodrome) requirements.* (b) *The related programmes of development of the helicopter and experimental work on equipment required to achieve the necessary regularity for successful commercial operation.*'

The manufacture of helicopters in this country for transport use is still in an early stage, but on the basis of information given from four firms concerned with their manufacture, it was thought that helicopters of the 10–12 passenger type would be available by 1954 and that thereafter they would become increasingly important in the pattern of our transport system. These will be followed by a more suitable 20-passenger machine operated between the centres of towns. They will offer a high degree of public convenience and time-saving advantages over all other forms of transport between distances of 50 to 300 miles. They can be operated commercially at rates competitive with fixed-wing aircraft travel and there will be economy in ground organisation and ground space requirements. It was estimated that a fleet of 50 helicopters of the 20+ passenger type could be absorbed progressively on our internal transport services and that this number may increase over a period of a few years. Requirements which a helicopter must satisfy are given as guidance to the designers.

London's Airports

app. pp. 8. 1953

1952–53 *Cmd.* 8902, *xxiv*, 729

Because of the growing traffic at the London airports—there were 109,000 landings or take-offs of civil aircraft at London's airports in 1947—a simplified pattern of air traffic is essential and it is proposed to reduce the seven airports in the London area, London airport, Northolt, Blackbushe, Bovingdon, Croydon, Gatwick and Stansted, to three—London airport, Gatwick and Blackbushe with Stansted held in reserve. Ninety per cent of the London traffic uses London airport and Northolt, but these are only five miles apart and for reasons of safety civil flying from Northolt must soon cease. London airport will take the bulk of the traffic, but two others, one as the main alternate, will be required for traffic in bad weather and for seasonal traffic.

All airports and likely sites within a 50-mile radius of London have been considered for the main alternate, and Gatwick alone meets substantially all the requirements, including good visibility when London airport is bad. H.M. Government accordingly propose to develop it as the main alternative airport, at a capital cost in the first seven years of £6 mn. The steps taken to meet the objections that Gatwick is too close to the Crawley New Town, and too close to the railway, and to deal with the criticisms of the proposed diversion of the Brighton road are outlined.

Proposed Development of Gatwick Airport

Inquiry. Rep., apps. pp. 64. 1954

1953–54 *Cmd. 9215, viii, 565*
apptd. Jan., sgd. June, 1954

C. Campbell.

'To hear and report on local objections to
the proposed development of Gatwick as a
major airport.'

Some of the vigorously expressed
objections arose from the fact that in
1946, 1947 and 1949 the Ministry of
Civil Aviation had given assurances
that Gatwick would not be developed
as a major airport, that it was after it
had informed the Ministry of Town and
Country Planning to that effect in 1946
that Crawley New Town was authorised,
and that on the strength of the assurances individuals and firms had undertaken developments which would now
be adversely affected. Surrey County
Council said that the Ministry had
ignored the procedure of consultation
between the Ministry and local authorities laid down by the Department itself
and it 'properly resented the failure to
take them into early consultation, and
being withheld confidences accorded to
Crawley Development Corporation.'
The objectors were hampered because
the terms of reference of the inquiry
specifically excluded them from making
any proposals as to how the need for an
alternative to London Airport might be
met elsewhere. Crawley New Town
Development Corporation had vigorously opposed any such proposals from
the start, and though still adhering to
their view that it was bad planning, did
not appear as objectors because it had
been impressed upon them that the
development was essential in the
national interest. And the cost of the
plans, estimated in Cmd. 8902 at £6
mn. was now given as £10 mn.

The Ministry admitted its change of
mind, and argued that though Gatwick
was not ideal, it was the only site which
met the requirements, in that it should
be in the south-east traffic area, with
weather good when it was bad at
London Airport, and near a main line.

The Ministry's meteorological expert
was of the opinion that there was no
substantial difference in weather conditions at several places that might be
regarded as possible sites for a diver-
sionary airport, and for that purpose the
choice of site should be made on other
than meteorological grounds. The
weather at Gatwick was rather better
than that at London airport in winter
and rather worse in the summer.

The objectors said that the breach of
solemn assurance alone should be
sufficient to condemn the proposal.
Experts on behalf of the Surrey County
Council argued that the statistics on
which the favourable view of weather
conditions at Gatwick was based were
derived from day-to-day records over a
limited period and that there were no
night observations, that Gatwick was at
the bottom of a saucer of fairly heavy
clay nine miles square, with a high water
table and liable to flooding, that the
rainfall was 30 per cent higher than at
London airport, and that in consequence
it was liable to radiation fog. A rural
area would be completely transformed
and it was bad planning to place the
noise of the airport so near to 75,000
people.

Mr. Campbell thought that the evidence showed that the site was meteoro-
logically suitable, but in view of the
conflict of experts the evidence on the
matter should be considered by the
Minister's technical advisers. The transformation of the area would mean a
drastic alteration in the Authority's
planning intentions. All the area will
be affected by noise, some part of it
substantially, the change of Government policy will inflict hardship, which
should be mitigated as far as possible,
ex gratia payments being made where
necessary.

The site was suitable, but whether it
was most suitable, the limitation of the
enquiry make it impossible to express
an opinion.

See *Gatwick Airport;* 1953–54 Cmd.
9296, xxvi, 519.

VIII A.   POST OFFICE, TELEGRAPHY

1. Post Office

2. Telegraphy

1.   POST OFFICE

Post Office (Departmental Classes) Recognition

Cttee. Rep., apps. pp. 24. 1952

1951–52 *Cmd. 8470, xviii*, 1

apptd. Feb., 1951. sgd. Jan., 1952

Lord Terrington (*Ch.*), Boyd, Evans, Farrar, Hancock (Florence).

'*To examine the question of recognition of organisations representing Post Office departmental classes of staff, having regard particularly to the formation of new Staff Associations within the field of existing recognised Associations, and to advise the Postmaster General on* (1) *General recognition policy with regard to Post Office classes, and* (2) *Outstanding claims for recognition.*'

There are 31 recognised unions in the Post Office catering for some 186 departmental grades and in some instances two of them represent the same grade. This atmosphere of competing trade unionism is inimical to the long-term interests both of the staff and the Department. In December 1946 the Postmaster General informed the Union of Post Office Workers that requests for recognition would be considered if they came from an association with a membership of 40 per cent of the organised staff of the grade or grade concerned, and recognition if granted would be for an initial period of three years. The question of withdrawal of recognition would arise if membership fell below 33½ per cent. This 'Listowel' formula was now thought to be a distinct encouragement to seccessionist groups among established trade unions, rendering trade union discipline extremely difficult. Facilities should not be placed at the disposal of unrecognised associations to help them to organise, nor should local recognition be re-introduced as a preliminary to national recognition (e.g. it would be undesirable for unions not recognised nationally to discuss locally matters arising from agreements with nationally recognised unions). The unrecognised unions said that as recognised unions had obtained unsatisfactory results, they were justified in seeking separate recognition under established rules. But the proper outlet for dissatisfaction was within the trade unions themselves and not in the building-up of a breakaway union. Cases may arise where it can be shown that the existing union has failed or is unable to look after the interests of the grade concerned (e.g. because of the nature of the employment). One union said that the ideal was one union for all grades, but there was no general desire for this; federation of major grades seemed more realistic.

The Listowel formula should be withdrawn and no other percentage formula introduced. It was undesirable to have more than one union representing one grade or group of grades, and in the absence of progress towards amalgamation of the unions concerned within twelve months, cases of dual recognition should be reviewed. A union claiming recognition should prove to the Postmaster General that the existing union was unable to look after the interests of the grade concerned, that it was itself financially stable, and so organised that it could serve the members better than the existing organisation. The number of unions should be reduced by grouping and amalgamation. The Departments should consult with recognised unions with a view to indicating groups of related trades for recognition purposes, and at an early stage should use its good offices to heal breaches. No recognition should be granted on the basis of sex.

In the light of these principles it was

recommended that recognition should be refused for all the claims except one, but that it should not be withdrawn from four existing cases involved in dual recognition, where the unions concerned should consider amalgamation.

2. TELEGRAPHY
Cable and Wireless Limited

Proposed Changes in the Arrangements between H.M. Government and Cable and Wireless Ltd., and of a Reduction in Empire Cable and Wireless Rates

Statement. pp. 6. 1938

1937–38 *Cmd.* 5716, *xxi*, 823

The reorganised Company which followed the 1928 Imperial Wireless and Cable Conference (*Breviate 1917–1939*, p. 300) had not been able to earn the expected revenue and was not able to reduce the telegraph tariffs; and it had to meet foreign competition of new direct wireless services on Empire routes. The relationship between Cable and Wireless Ltd., and the Governments of the Commonwealth was reviewed. The new arrangements provided for the Beam Wireless stations, leased from the Post Office for a rental of £250,000 per annum and 12 per cent of surplus profits, to be transferred to the Company in return for a transfer to the Government of 2,600,000 £1 shares in the Company out of a total capital of £30 mn. The Standard Revenue, fixed in 1928 at £1,865,000 or 6 per cent on capital, half the net revenue above which had to be used in reduction of rates and development of services, was to be reduced to £1,200,000 or 4 per cent on capital. The Commonwealth Governments in general reaffirmed their policy of according the system of Cable and Wireless Ltd. their support and co-operation. As part of these arrangements the Company agreed to an immediate and substantial reduction in Commonwealth telegraph rates, a maximum rate of 1s. 3d. a word being introduced.

Cable and Wireless Ltd.

Proposed Transfer to Public Ownership. pp. 8. [1946]

1945–46 *Cmd.* 6805, *xx*, 109

The war (1939) brought new problems and an increased volume of traffic. Contrary to the 1928 and 1938 policy, new direct wireless circuits were opened between the United States and some of the Dominions and some of the Colonies. This led to a Commonwealth Telecommunications Conference which was unanimously in favour of a fundamental change in the Commonwealth system. Private shareholders should be eliminated from the overseas telecommunication services of U.K., the Dominions and India, by purchase by the respective Governments of the shares in the companies; organisation should be uniform in the various countries and a Commonwealth Communications Board should replace the Commonwealth Communications Council. This Board should formulate joint policy, including rates; co-ordinate and develop wireless and cable systems and co-ordinate telecommunication matters affecting the defence of the Commonwealth, etc. The U.K. Government proposed to introduce legislation to acquire the shares of the Cable and Wireless Ltd. (apart from the 2,600,000 £1 shares it already owns) and to provide for payment of compensation to the shareholders.

Cable and Wireless Bill

Sel. Cttee. Special Rep., proc., mins. of ev. pp. v, 114. [1946]

1945–46 (147. 148) *v*, 785
apptd. May, o.p. June, 1946

G. Benson (*Ch.*), Anderson, Donovan, Manningham - Buller, Macpherson, Shepherd.

The Bill is one for transferring to public ownership the share capital of Cable and Wireless Ltd. The share capital consists of 30 mn. £1 shares of which 2,600,000 are already held by the

Treasury. In his evidence Mr. Capewell gives a history of the company. The Chairman was directed to report the Bill as amended. The Committee agreed to report to the House that adequate protection for officers and servants of the company whose position may be prejudiced by the provisions of the Bill, be given by such means as the House may think fit.

VIII B. BROADCASTING, THE PRESS

Television

Cttee. Rep., apps. pp. 25. 1945

1945 *Non-Parl. Privy Council Office apptd. Sept.,* 1943. *sgd. Dec.,* 1944

Lord Hankey (*Ch.*), Angwin, Appleton, Ashbridge, Birchall, Haley, Harvey.

'To prepare plans for the reinstatement and development of the television service after the war with special consideration of: (a) the preparation of a plan for the provision of a service to at any rate the larger centres of population within a reasonable period after the war; (b) the provision to be made for research and development; (c) the guidance to be given to manufacturers, with a view especially to the development of the export trade.'

On the recommendations of the Selsdon Committee (*Breviate 1917–1939,* p. 302) the first public service of high definitive television was inaugurated by the B.B.C's station at Alexandra Palace in 1936, and an Advisory Committee was set up. This Committee envisaged the development of a new industry in the manufacture of television apparatus and urged the courageous development of the science in order to put makers in a strong position in the export trade. Before these proposals had been completed, the television station was closed in 1939 for military reasons.

The Minister responsible to Parliament for sound broadcasting should be responsible for television; the B.B.C. should operate the service and an advisory committee should be set up. The London service should be re-established and a service should be extended to the provinces. Collaboration between the B.B.C. and the cinema industry should lead to mutually beneficial results. Research should be co-ordinated and manufacturers should be encouraged to pool their patents. Industry will be responsible for the development of the export market, but it should keep in close touch with the advisory committee as the normal channel of communication to the Minister. The desirability of adopting common international standards should be kept in mind. The service should be self-supporting as soon as possible and a licence for domestic viewers should be introduced at an additional fee of £1 per year.

Broadcasting Policy

Statement, apps. pp. 27. 1946

1945–46 *Cmd.* 6852, *xx,* 81

The existing Charter and Licence of the B.B.C., which expires in 1946, ran under normal conditions for only two and a half years before the war broke out in 1939. The Government have decided, without the usual committee of enquiry, to renew the Charter for a period of five years in order to span the period of transition and to enable technical developments to reach a point at which their bearing on future broadcasting in the country can be more clearly seen. Regional devolution will take place in order to develop the spirit of emulation in the regions. The Postmaster General will be responsible to Parliament for the Broadcasting Vote, but the Lord President will answer questions on major broadcasting policy. An obligation will be laid on the B.B.C. to broadcast a daily account of the proceedings of Parliament; the maintenance of an impartial balance between parties in political broadcasting must be the responsibility of the Corporation. While retaining independence in staff matters, the B.B.C. should pay due regard to Civil Service conditions and to the security of employment offered. Steps will be taken to ensure that there exists adequate machinery for negotiation and consultation between the Governors and the staff, with provision for arbitration. A third programme will be introduced and sponsored broadcasts prohibited. Overseas services will be developed and television reopened. The war-time method of financing by grant-in-aid will cease, and the pre-war system of giving it an adequate revenue out of licences revenue restored. The charge for sound licences has been raised and a new sound and television licence of £2 issued.

Broadcasting

Cttee. Rep., apps. pp. vii, 327. [1951] App. H. Memoranda. [1951]

1950–51 *Cmd.* 8116, *Cmd.* 8117, *ix*, 1 *apptd.* — 1949. *sgd. Dec.*, 1950

Lord Beveridge (*Ch.*), Binns, Crawford, L. Elgin, Lloyd George (Lady Megan), Oakeshott, Reeves, Stedeford, Stocks (Mrs. M. D.), Taylor, Lloyd.

'*To consider the constitution, control, finance and other general aspects of the sound and television broadcasting services of the United Kingdom (excluding those aspects of the overseas services for which the B.B.C. are not responsible) and to advise on the conditions under which these services and wire broadcasting should be conducted after the 31st December, 1951.*'

A review of the evidence received leads to the fundamental question— whether broadcasting, if it is to continue as an effective service, must be a monopoly. In contrast to the position at the date of the Crawford Committee (*Breviate 1917–1939*, p. 301), whose verdict in 1926 in favour of a monopoly was in accord with a strikingly unanimous stream of evidence, there was now a substantial body of opinion challenging it. Some saw danger in excessive power over men's thoughts being concentrated in a single organisa-

tion and proposed three or more fully competitive organisations; others were critical of the size of the organisation and wanted several corporations separated functionally; national minority groups asked for Welsh and Scottish corporations. Employees, writers and performers desired to have more than one market for what they offer. The Committee accepted the contention of the B.B.C. that if broadcasting is to have social purpose, competition should not be allowed to become a degrading competition for numbers of listeners, but not their assumption that the only alternative to this is monopoly, or that good as it was, past achievement justified a continuance on existing lines. It rejected proposals for several corporations, because one charter can ensure the right measure of functional and regional devolution, and because the enforcement of impartiality, fair treatment of minorities and regard to outside opinion would be easier with one than with several corporations. Broadcasting, including television and overseas services, should continue as a monopoly.

Any suggestion that broadcasting should become financially dependent on sponsoring is rejected, since it would put control ultimately in the hands of people whose interest is not in broadcasting, but the sale of goods and services or the propagation of particular ideas. Nor should the cost of broadcasting be met out of general taxation, although it might be £500,000 cheaper, but as hitherto from licences, as this increases the independence of the Corporation.

From this fundamental decision to continue the B.B.C. as a monopoly, important consequences follow. More autonomy should be given to the national regions of Scotland, Wales and Northern Ireland by the establishment of separate commissions for each area, each with a Home Service programme and large delegated powers. With the development of V.H.F., the licensing of local stations, run by voluntary bodies, universities, etc., by the B.B.C. or the

Postmaster General should be considered.

While broadcasting is a public service with a social purpose, not the sale of a popular commodity, and programmes should be devised not to meet, but to ante-date the popular vote, there are dangers that a body free from competition will be led in constructing its programmes to use performers already known to it ('innocent nepotism') and will be out of touch with its audiences. There should be a recognised channel through which comment and criticism can come from outside sources. Audience research should be developed and absorbed into a Public Representation Service, set up as an essential part of the structure of broadcasting.

Where there is only one body through which broadcasting can take place, the difficulty of religious broadcasting is in determining which bodies claiming to be religious should be invited to broadcast. The selection, generally confined to those within the main stream of historic Christianity, implies taking a broad view of Christian values, that the appeal must be to those outside as well as those inside the churches, and that the preachers selected will not attack controversially positions held by other churches. Those who, however earnest their purpose, do not accept the religious basis of morality can scarcely be provided for in religious broadcasts, but should have opportunities provided for them by the Talks Department. Very small religious minorities and other bodies 'with a message' might be given an opportunity to put their views at some time in a 'Hyde Park of the Air'. The problem of allowing a fair field for controversy and for minorities has been handled by the B.B.C. with a considerable degree of success. Free use of the microphone for discussion of questions of the day, however controversial the speakers, is of great importance, but controversy on the air should have rules as definite as controversy in Parliament; a committee of advisers should assist in drafting the rules. Simultaneous broadcasting of Parliamentary Debates would harm the debates, but the prohibition of broadcasting on a topic within 14 days of its being debated in either House is objectionable. There is no reason why the British democracy should not hear a broadcast debate when it is most topical, i.e. when the matter is before Parliament. There should be more political broadcasting during and between elections.

On television the Committee accept the main contention of the B.B.C. that sound and television broadcasting should remain 'under one authority', for both are services to the home, and the same aims and standards should apply to them. But there are differences between the two in the range and variety of a technical staff required and in the selection of performers. Within the framework of the B.B.C. the television service should be given greater autonomy, its Director being given the fullest possible authority over staff, performers, finance, etc. Sound and television should each stand on their own feet financially.

The position of the B.B.C. in relation to its staff and performers is in some ways exceptional. Because it must in all its work maintain its position of impartiality, it has placed on every member of its staff a prohibition on entering into political controversy, giving lectures, speeches, publishing books, etc., without permission. But the prohibition covers too wide a field both in relation to the staff affected and their activities; the regulation should be revised. For the same reason, it recognises the Staff Association, but will not negotiate with any external trade union. The T.U.C. argues that this infringes the rights of collective bargaining, the Staff Association claims that it is independent and that the position could be best served by a single comprehensive 'industrial' union for the broadcasting industry. The B.B.C. should be prepared to recognise any union which contains not less than 40 per cent of its class, if it does not have a closed shop and if it will co-operate with any other union with members in that class. The difficulties with associations of performers, e.g. musicians, who impose restrictions, e.g. on the number of repeat performances, the number of hours of broadcasting of records, and with theatrical managements, who restrict the appearance of artists under contract with them, and with those who control sporting events, should be dealt with by joint consultation. Some of these restrictions are ill-judged and harmful to public needs.

The B.B.C. Charter should be renewed without time limit, but subject to a quinquennial review by a small independent committee, and its annual reports should contain more financial and other details. The B.B.C's percentage of licence revenue, which should not be changed without adequate notice, should be 100 per cent for the first five years, and it should be empowered to borrow up to £10 mn. for capital expenditure.

One hundred recommendations are made for carrying out the principles of the report.

Minority Report by Selwyn Lloyd.— Disagrees with the continuance of the B.B.C. as a monopoly, because of its size and unwieldiness, because it may hinder development, is a monopolistic employer, and would have excessive power. He supports the majority's proposed safeguards, but regards competition as the only effective one. The charge that competition would degrade standards is exaggerated and in any case standards must be maintained by free choice; nor need sponsoring by advertisers degrade them, provided that (1) there was one public service system, part of whose function was to cater for minorities, (2) there was one controlling body which could make rules limiting or prohibiting advertisement of certain goods, prohibiting the interruption of an item at other than recognised intervals, regulating the time allowed for advertisement, etc. There should be a Commission for Broadcasting to licence stations, allot frequencies, and make rules on political controversy and advertising; the B.B.C. should continue on the Home and Regional wavelengths; two independent national commercial companies and local stations should be licensed, and a separate commercial television corporation licensed to accept sponsored items. If these proposals are not acceptable, there should be a separate television public corporation and a separate corporation to develop local broadcasting.

Broadcasting

Memo. on the Rep. of the Broadcasting Cttee., 1949. pp. 12. [1951]

1950–51 *Cmd*. 8291, *xxvii*, 19

The paper sets out the Government's decisions on the recommendations of the Beveridge Committee. It agrees that the B.B.C. should continue to be responsible for all broadcasting in the U.K., that there should be no commercial advertising or sponsored programmes without consent of the P.M.G., and that it should continue to have independence in programme making and administration. The Charter will be renewed, not indefinitely, but for 15 years in the first instance, with periodical reviews. The B.B.C. must delegate powers to the three national regions of Scotland, Wales and N. Ireland, and there should be 'national' Governors on the Board of Governors. There will not be a Minister for Broadcasting.

The B.B.C. will receive 85 per cent of licence revenue, not 100 per cent, and will be empowered to borrow £10 mn. It will be as independent in television as in sound broadcasting, but no decision will be made on public showing in cinemas, etc., until various interests have been consulted. V.H.F. should be developed, and the Television Advisory Committee asked to advise on methods of introducing it. Decision on whether the B.B.C. should operate relay exchanges in areas of poor reception is deferred pending development in V.H.F., in the meantime relay exchanges will be left for a period to private enterprise.

It will be a duty of the B.B.C. to keep its work under constant and effective review from without. The B.B.C. should adopt a policy of effective devolution to the Director of Television.

See *Television*. Advisory Cttee. (C. Daniel, *Ch.*). 1st, 2nd Reps.; 1953, 1954 Non-Parl. Post Office.

Broadcasting

Memo. on the Rep. of the Broadcasting Cttee., 1949. pp. 10. 1952

1951–52 *Cmd.* 8550, *xxv*, 25

The new Government proposes some arrangements alternative to those recommended by the Broadcasting Committee. Provision should be made for an element of competition in the expanding field of television, when calls on capital resources make it feasible, and for a controlling body to prevent abuses, regulate stations, etc. The new stations would not be allowed to engage in political or religious broadcasting. The B.B.C. must have first claim on resources to enable it to develop television and introduce V.H.F. It will be required to give Scotland, Wales, N. Ireland (which should have national councils) and the English regions a reasonable measure of independence and to provide for discussions with representative staff organisations. The term of its Charter should be ten years, and the Governors appointed not by the Government of the day, but by a special committee. The financial arrangements will be broadly as set out in Cmd. 8291.

See *New Charter of Incorporation granted to the B.B.C.;* 1951–52 Cmd. 8605, xxv, 67. *Licence and Agreement . . . between H.M. Postmaster General and the B.B.C.;* 1951–52 Cmd. 8579, xxv, 35.

Television Policy

Memo. pp. 7. 1953

1953–54 *Cmd.* 9005, *xxvi*, 339

The B.B.C. will continue to be the main instrument of broadcasting and the authorised extension of its activities will bring 90 per cent of the population within the range of the television programmes. The new development of television will take place on three bands apart from that used by the B.B.C. Within Band III only two or three channels will be available, but although local stations of limited range and power need not interfere with one another, a series of local independent stations would find it too expensive to maintain quality programmes. The standards of commercial programmes will not be threatened by sponsoring, which the Government have decided against; the responsibility for them will rest with the operators, not the advertisers. A public corporation will own and operate the transmitting stations, and will hire its facilities to privately-financed companies which will provide programmes and receive revenue for advertisements. In view of the control by a public corporation, the ban on political and religious broadcasting could be withdrawn after a period of practical experience, subject to their control on the plan already adopted for the B.B.C.; it would not be allowed to broadcast its own views. The Treasury would make an initial advance of capital to the corporation.

See *Television Act, 1954; 2 & 3 Eliz. 2. c. 55. Licence granted . . . by H.M. Postmaster General to the Independent Television Authority;* 1954–55 Cmd. 9451, xiii, 187. *Independent Television Authority.* [1st] Ann. Rep.; 1955–56 (123) xi, 735, and succeeding Ann. Reps.

The Press

R. Com. Rep., apps., index. pp. v, 363. [1949]. Mins. of ev., 38 days. 1947: 1948. Index. 1949. Memos., pts. 1–5. 1947, 1948

1948–49 *Cmd.* 7700, *xx*, 1
apptd. April, 1947. *sgd. June,* 1949

W. D. Ross (*Ch.*), Aubrey, Beaton, Bowman, Carter (Lady Violet Bonham), Ensor, Hull, Middleton, Owen, Robinson, Sharp, Vickers, Waters, Wootton (Barbara), Young.

s

'With the object of furthering the free expression of opinion through the Press and the greatest practicable accuracy in the presentation of news, to inquire into the control, management and ownership of the newspaper and periodical Press and the news agencies, including the financial structure and the monopolistic tendencies in control, and to make recommendations thereon.'

The circulation of newspapers, pegged in 1947–48 on account of the shortage of newsprint, totalled $15\frac{1}{2}$ mn. for national and $2\frac{3}{4}$ mn. for provincial morning dailies, $3\frac{1}{2}$ mn. for national and $6\frac{3}{4}$ mn. for provincial evening papers, and $23\frac{1}{4}$ mn. for Sunday papers. Of the national morning dailies no two are in the same ownership; the ownership of the national, provincial and local newspapers is mainly in the hands of five 'chains'. The concentration in the country as a whole does not approach monopoly, but there are pockets of local monopoly in the sense that there is only one local daily, or if more than one, that they are in one ownership. The predominant form of ownership is the joint stock company, but in some cases the majority of shares are in the hands of one person, or members of the same family, and in a few others the property is owned by a specially created trust.

Owing to the great expense of producing newspapers, those who direct these hazardous enterprises must control the general conduct of the paper, and the line it must take on political issues. This does not mean giving detailed instructions on how particular items of news shall be treated, and since a paper must preserve its character if it is to retain its readers, arbitrary exercise of power would defeat its own ends.

The present degree of concentration is not so great as to prejudice the free expression of opinion or the accurate presentation of news. Newspaper chains have highly developed common services and are not in themselves undesirable, but it would be possible for the chief proprietor to ensure that all the papers in a chain expressed a common view. They are undesirable if they are so large and so few that they reduce the number of diverse views reaching the public. In existing circumstances some local monopoly is inevitable; it may be harmful because a paper without competitors could by selection and presentation determine what people read, influence their opinions and fall into a low standard of accuracy.

The Press should satisfy two requirements. (1) While the selection of news may be affected by the newspaper's political opinions, the news should be reported truthfully and without excessive bias. A number of the quality papers do meet this demand, but all popular papers fall short of the best, either through excessive political partisanship or distorted ideas of news values. The Commission appointed a team of research workers to examine the contents of the Press and its treatment of a number of selected public topics (Appendix VII). This made it clear that political bias may show itself by a colouring of the news even when the detailed facts are accurate, by misstatements of fact and differences of view about the news value of particular items. There are obvious deficiencies in Parliamentary reporting, including the absence of straight accounts of debates, over-emphasis on incidents, and exclusion of one side. Because its news comes from a wide variety of sources and fallible eye-witnesses and through various channels, the chances of error are very great. But the desire in mass circulation papers to make arresting stories (which have some value in arousing readers' interest) can lead to misleading deductions from inadequate facts, triviality and sensationalism and over-emphasis on eye-appeal and fragmentation in lay-out. Almost half the revenue of newspapers is drawn from advertisement. Attempts by individual advertisers to influence a newspaper appear to be infrequent and unsuccessful, nor is there evidence of concerted pressure, but a newspaper not very strong financially is subject to the temptation to avoid taking a line adverse to advertisers' interests, unless by doing so it could increase its interest to the public. So long as newspapers are sold at less than cost, a supplementary income is needed and income from the performance of recognised commercial service is one of the least harmful. There was no evidence of a widespread use of blacklists of persons who were not to be mentioned either because of a personal whim of a proprietor or for political reasons, though there were sometimes bans, presumably precautionary, on persons who had brought libel actions against a paper.

(2) The number and variety of papers should be sufficient for all important points of view to be presented in terms of the varying taste and opinions of the chief groups of the population. The Press as a whole does provide a sufficient number, but it should cater for a greater variety of intellectual levels. There is too great a gap between the quality Press and the popular Press which appeals to the lowest common denominator in taste and interest. Something more serious than the popular, and more varied and easy to read than the quality papers is required.

While the Press provides cheaply a mass of information and entertainment for which there is a wide demand, acknowledges a high standard and is jealous of its independence, with few exceptions it has failed to provide the public with adequate material for sound political judgement.

Proposals and recommendations.— Proposals to reduce commercial motives by State-owned newspapers, by replacing joint stock ownership with Government licensed corporations and by limiting the size of circulation all involve an unwarrantable interference with the freedom of the individual to start or to buy any paper he likes. Limiting profits would restrict the starting of new papers and increase the power of the existing large ones. Ownership by a Trust, especially one which safeguards the independence and character of a paper, is to be welcomed,

but it cannot remove commercial motives finally, since a Trust must have power to remove an editor who persisted in a policy which made it impossible for a newspaper to pay its way. Of the suggestions made to assist independent newspapers to survive or new ones to start, a public corporation to print newspapers does not touch the root of the problem, which is running costs, and limiting the advertising revenue of large newspapers would not necessarily divert it to smaller ones who have too little. The voluntary prohibition of non-journalistic forms of competition should be continued indefinitely. It is not possible to specify in advance a statutory limit to the size of chains, but the Monopolies Commission should have power to investigate local newspaper monopoly. Chain papers should be required to disclose on the front page their membership of a chain. Compulsory disclosure of persons owning or controlling newspapers is not practicable, but the Board of Trade should have powers to investigate in any case of doubt.

Freedom and accuracy can best be provided by the Press itself. The Press should establish a General Council of at least 25 members representing proprietors, editors and other journalists, one-fifth being lay members, including a chairman chosen by the Lord Chief Justice and the Lord President of Court of Session. The present education and methods of training of journalists are not adequate to enable them to deal with the increasing complexity of events and background which must be reported and interpreted. The Council should take steps to improve them and the status of the profession. It should consider complaints about the conduct of the Press, censure undesirable journalistic conduct and build up a code with the highest professional standards.

There are reservations by Waters and Ensor.

Mins. of ev., 38 days; 1947–48, xiv, 323. 1947–48, xv, 1. Index; 1948–49 Cmd. 7690, xx, 371. Memoranda of ev., 5 parts; 1947–48 Non-Parl.

IX. INVENTIONS, PATENTS, COPYRIGHT

Patents and Designs Acts

Dept. Cttee.   1st Interim Rep. pp. 6.
1945

1944–45 *Cmd.* 6618, *v*, 421
apptd. April, 1944. *sgd. March*, 1945

K. R. Swan (*Ch.*), Gill, Mould, Peter, Pye, Robinson (Joan), Saunders, Underwood, Venning, Woodcock.

'To consider . . . what changes are desirable in the Patents and Designs Acts, and in the practice of the Patent Office and the Courts in relation to matters arising therefrom . . . and to submit an interim report or reports on—(a) the initiation, conduct and determination of legal proceedings arising under or out of the Patents and Designs Acts, including the constitution of the appropriate tribunals; and (b) the provisions of these Acts for the prevention of the abuse of monopoly rights; and to suggest any amendments . . . which would encourage the use of inventions and the progress of industry and trade.'

The procedure under which applications are made for the extension of term of patents in cases where the patentee as such has suffered loss or damage as a result of the war, is needlessly involved and prohibitive in cost. Jurisdiction should be given to the Comptroller, so that a patentee may apply at his option to the Comptroller or to the Court, with right to appeal from a decision of the Comptroller. The procedure suggested would be inexpensive. The Rules Committee of the Supreme Court should be invited to modify the Rules referring to the advertisement.

—— Second Interim Report, apps. pp. 38. 1946

1945–46 *Cmd.* 6789, *xiv*, 155
sgd. Feb., 1946

The theory upon which the system is based and to which all European countries (except the Soviet Union) and many non-European countries subscribe, is that the opportunity to obtain exclusive rights in an invention stimulates technical progress, encourages invention, induces the inventor to disclose his discoveries, offers a reward for the development stage and provides inducement to invest capital in new lines of production. The Soviet system of awards to inventors is bound up with their economic system and has little relevance to one in which technical progress depends mainly on private initiative. The present system was favoured by the Committee, but improvements were necessary.

A patentee may have his patent endorsed 'licence of right', by which he invites its use by anyone on terms agreed, or in default, settled by the Comptroller. But patents, being monopolies, can be used restrictively and in ways contrary to the public interest. Such abuses are the failure to work it in the U.K. on a commercial scale without adequate reason or because the patentee is importing the article, refusing to grant a licence to use it except on terms which prejudice the establishment of a new industry when it is desirable in the public interest that it should be granted, or failure to meet demand for the article in adequate measure or on reasonable terms. In such cases the Comptroller may grant a compulsory licence of right on suitable terms. But legal decisions have narrowed down the protective clauses so that 'demand' need not include a potential demand for a cheaper model, have defined the 'public interest' as including not only that of the public, but of the interests of the patentees, and defined a new industry so widely that one can rarely be said to be founded.

The compulsory indorsement of all patents 'licence of right', proposed as a remedy, would reduce a patent to a right to receive royalties, which might in some cases not be an adequate inducement to research, might discourage disclosure of inventions, or be inadequate to induce capital investment. This proposal is rejected in favour of an extension of compulsory licensing to cases where, although there is no legal abuse of patent rights, a more extended use of the invention could be made to meet potential or unfulfilled demands, where a new field of manufacture could be opened up, or where the export market is insufficiently supplied. The Comptroller should have power to refuse applications which lack subject matter, i.e. inventive merit, both because even an invalid patent may act as a deterrent to research and because firms are tempted to patent trivial improvements in order to obtain an unjustifiable extension of the period of protection.

Two judges with technical or scientific qualifications should be appointed to hear all patent actions, scientific assistants should be available to judges, and experts allowed to explain the meaning of a patent specification as a whole.

—— Final Report, apps. pp. 84. 1947

1946–47 *Cmd.* 7206, *xiii*, 457

sgd. July, 1947

del. Woodcock.

The principles and proposals set out in the second report, together with suggestions for dealing with inconsistencies, etc., involve changes to the law over a wide range. These are given in detail. Provision should be made for apportioning the benefit of a patent between an employer and an employee-inventor where no written contract exists and neither is exclusively entitled to it. The emergency powers of the Crown to use particular inventions during the war should be made permanently available. Patents made in the service of the State or with public money should be vested in a suitably organised central body, for exploitation. The definition of design for purposes of registration should be amended. To distinguish between industrial designs and literary copyright, printed matter of a literary or artistic character should be protected under the Copyright Act. Works of sculpture should be excluded from registration as designs, and the owner of a copyright in an artistic work should retain his remedies under the Copyright Act after he has agreed to its reproduction as a registered design.

Awards to Inventors

R. Com. 1st Rep., apps. pp. ix, 21. 1948. 2nd Rep., apps. pp. 11. 1949. 3rd Rep., apps. pp. 14. 1953. Fourth and Final Rep., apps. pp. 20. 1956

1948–49 *Cmd.* 7586, *Cmd.* 7832, *xvii*, 345. 1952–53 *Cmd.* 8743, *vii*, 505. 1955–56 *Cmd.* 9744, *xi*, 353

apptd. May, 1946, *March*, 1947. *sgd. Dec.*, 1948, *Nov.*, 1949, *Jan.*, 1953, *April*, 1956

L. L. Cohen (*Ch.*).

'*To deal with claims in respect of the user of inventions, designs, drawings or processes on behalf of the Crown.*'

The Patents and Designs Act, 1907, as amended by subsequent Acts, states that 'a patent shall have to all intents the like effect as against His Majesty the King as it has against a subject.'

The Commission were in substantial agreement with the general principles enunciated by the 1919 Commission (*Breviate 1917–1939*, p. 304) and that the basis of assessment should be a fair royalty between a willing licensor and a willing licensee, though it is not always easy to settle the amount of the royalty, e.g. in commercial practice royalties bear some relation to prospective sale price, but this may not arise in use by the Crown. The four reports set out the principles on which decisions were based. Claims made because an invention was communicated to a Department, but where the Department was already using a similar one, and by contractors for an addition to contract price for use of their patent, where the addition was not contemplated at the time the contract was made, were rejected. An employee of a firm holding a contract with the Crown should claim against the firm, not the Crown. But an award was made where the firm had waived its rights in favour of the inventor. An inventor in Crown service might be debarred from obtaining a patent, but could claim as *ex-gratia* payment. In assessing the sum, regard was paid to the utility of the invention and the status of the applicant. An invention might be brilliant or developed in the face of official neglect. Awards were made to Whittle in respect of jet propulsion, to Bailey in respect of the Bailey bridge, and to Robertson-Watt and his team for work on radar. An award was made for theoretical calculations which formed the basis of an invention.

Copyright

Cttee. Rep., apps. pp. ii, 130. [1952]

1951–52 *Cmd.* 8662, *ix*, 573
apptd. April, 1951. *sgd. July*, 1952

H. S. Gregory (*Ch.*), Allibone, Blake, Cooke, Godwin (B. Anne), Hugh-Jones, Lamb, James.

'*To consider and report whether any, and if so what, changes are desirable in the law relating to copyright in literary, dramatic, musical and artistic works with particular regard to technical developments and to the revised International Convention for the Protection of Literary and Artistic Works signed at Brussels in June, 1948. . . .*'

The Copyright Act, 1911, followed and embodied the general provisions of the original Berne Convention of 1886, and of the revised texts since that date. But the Brussels Convention, 1948, has not been ratified by the United Kingdom: if this is done, some changes will be required in the 1911 Act. The U.S. is not an adherent to the Convention and copyright of a work in the English language can be secured in the U.S. only if the type is set up there. But a U.S. author enjoys protection in the member countries of the Berne Union. International copyright is being considered under the auspices of U.N.E.S. C.O., and a bridge may be built there between the Berne and the Pan-America Unions, although the standards of protection to be considered are not of such high standard as the rights in intellectual property laid down at the Berne Convention.

The Copyright Act, 1911, gives copyright for the life of the author or 50 years after his death. The Committee rejected perpetual copyright, advocated by Dr. Marie Stopes, and the shorter period of 25–50 years after first publication proposed by Prof. Plant. Although only an exceptional book or musical composition remains in demand for 25 years, publishers need the longer period to balance unsuccessful with successful ventures. The Brussels Convention should be ratified.

The provisions permitting the reproduction of extracts for study, review, etc., without infringement should be extended to include other works necessary for the purpose of review, etc. Statutory rules should be issued setting out the conditions under which specified librarians could supply for study purposes one copy of extracts from periodicals beyond the normal scope at not less than cost price, and to make one copy of an out-of-print book. Deposit libraries should receive one copy of works first published in microfilm. MSS. could be copied if not less than 100 years old. Makers of gramophone records should have copyright in their records for 25 years. Copyright in a film should belong to the maker, should subsist in the film itself, and should last 25 years. The owner of a copyright has the sole right to authorise broadcasting, and a broadcasting authority the right to prevent the copying of its programmes. Copyright should not include the right to prevent the recording of sporting and other spectacles.

A right against copying should not be extended to include the personal interpretation of music, etc., by artists, or the promoters of sporting events, etc. The right of performers to prevent the reproduction of their performance should be extended to clandestine broadcasting. But the copyright owners have the right to grant and have granted licences for public performance subject to a scale of fees for every kind of performance; performances of music have been restricted to protect the employment of live musicians. The exercise of these rights, by collecting societies of a monopolistic or quasi-monopolistic character, or a broadcasting authority, disputes relating to their fees, etc., should be subject to review by an independent tribunal. A new 'per-forming right' should be given to the broadcasting authority in respect of television programmes. Artistic copyright should subsist in all original artistic works, irrespective of the intention of the author, and should give protection against copying, and with qualifications, reproduction in any other material.

X. LABOUR

1. Manpower, The Supply of Labour
2. Employment, Wages Policy, Cost of Living
3. Industrial Relations, Disputes, Wages Councils
4. Wages and Conditions in Particular Employments (other than Wages Councils)

5. Rehabilitation, Resettlement
6. Employment of Women
7. Juveniles
8. Factory Regulation: Safety, Health, Hours of Work
9. Migration
10. Professions

1. MANPOWER, THE SUPPLY OF LABOUR

Draft Control of Employment (Advertisements) Order

Cttee. Rep., app. pp. 8. 1940
1939–40 (107) *iv*, 33
apptd. Feb., sgd. March, 1940

W. T. Davies (*Ch.*), Kerridge, Parker, Holloway, Mitchell, Hutton, Coppock, Fawcett, Sandercock, Stephenson, Pugh.

The building industry and civil engineering contracting are to an increasing extent working directly for the Government or on construction connected with the war effort, and often in areas far removed from the sources of labour supply. The organisation of the Ministry of Labour and National Service working in collaboration with the trade unions provides machinery which should be adequate for securing the necessary labour. Indiscriminate advertising by employers can only add to the difficulty of its recruitment and tends to confuse the working of agreements about wages and conditions.

Skilled Men in the Services

Cttee. Interim Rep. pp. 7. 1941
1940–41 *Cmd.* 6307, *iv*, 473
apptd. June, sgd. July, 1941

W. H. Beveridge (*Ch.*), Bailey, Little, Simpson.

'To examine in consultation with the three Service Departments, the use now made in the Royal Navy, the Army and the Royal Air Force of skilled men and to advise in the light of the operational and maintenance commitments of the three Services. . . .'

Since the outbreak of the war carefully planned arrangements have been made to reserve men possessing scarce skill, either for civilian employment or for suitable service trades in the Armed Forces, and each of the Service Departments makes a systematic search for such men with a view to transferring them to skilled work. This does not mean that skilled men are working continuously on work requiring their skill, as there is a certain amount of unavoidable standing by for emergency, but in order to throw light on the extent of avoidable waste, associations of employers and employees have been invited to report alleged waste of skill in the Services. In view of the military programmes, a further substantial withdrawal of skilled men from civilian employment is required and should be met by dilution in civilian employment. The use of men of military age on clerical and other light work requiring less physical strength than education and ability, which could be done by older men and by women should continue only where these are not available.

—— Second Report, apps. pp. 74. 1942
1941–42 *Cmd.* 6339, *iv*, 713
sgd. Oct., 1941

The enquiries, based partly on interviews of men in the Forces whose skill was said by employers or trade unions to be insufficiently used, shows that the steps taken in the Services to re-muster skill and to search for talent have been less complete than might have been hoped. There was a reservoir of skill and initiative which could be diverted to the maintenance and repair of war machines, thus lessening the demands on industry for men for this work. The skilled man-power is being used with economy and effect in the Navy except in the case of naval reservists, not yet in the Army, and not yet wholly in the Air Force. The training schemes in the three Services are good, though there have been less new developments in the Navy than in the other two Services. Ten per cent of the demands of the Navy up to March 1942 should be met by a better use of some of the reservists, though substantial additional numbers will be needed. The unused reservoir of skill in the Army is such that its requirements, and even more, can be met from the Army itself, and whilst this is so there is no case for supplying skilled men from outside. The proportion of men now needed in the Air Force has not yet been worked out. But with every economy, more engineers must be withdrawn from civilian industry.

In a Memorandum the War Office replies that the Army cannot be fitted into the mould of civil industry, that it does not operate from central workshops, or from elaborately organised bases like the R.A.F., but that its skilled tradesmen must be distributed in small units right up to the forward fighting formations.

Calling up of Civil Servants

Cttee. Interim Rep., apps. pp. 6. 1941
1940–41 *Cmd.* 6301, *iv*, 181
apptd. —. *sgd. July*, 1941

Lord Kennet (*Ch.*), Addison, Bowen.

'To *consider what further withdrawals of men of military age to the Defence Services can be made either from National Government or from such related branches of administration as may be referred to them and to advise how, by the substitution of older men or of women or otherwise, such withdrawals can be effected so as to cause as little interference as possible to essential services.*'

After the last war normal recruitment did not start for ten years, and took place from ex-service men, so that the Service contains an abnormally large proportion of men 40–late 50, and a low proportion in the 30–40 group, which contains many of the best men with experience. 9500 have been transferred to the more hardly pressed departments. The age of reservation should be raised to 30 for the administrative and executive grades, to 35 for the clerical grades, and existing deferments cancelled three months from the date of announcement. Arrangements for new or prolonged deferments, use of university women graduates, etc., are outlined.

The Principal New Measures to be introduced by His Majesty's Government in pursuance of their Man-power Policy

Memo. pp. 4. 1941
1941–42 *Cmd.* 6324, *ix*, 65

'The main object of the National

Service (No. 2) Bill is to declare that a liability rests on all persons of either sex who are for the time being in Great Britain to undertake some form of National Service whether in the armed forces, in civil defence, in industry or otherwise.' The age limit is raised from 41 to 51, it is contemplated that men over 40 should be posted only for static and sedentary duties. (The system of block reservation must in general be replaced gradually by a system of individual deferments, though this will not apply to certain classes of men covered by the existing Schedule of Reserved Occupations.) Boys and girls between the ages of 16 and 18 will be required to register.

Man-power in Banking and Allied Businesses, in Ordinary Insurance, and in Industrial Assurance

Cttee. Rep. pp. 23. 1942

1941–42 *Cmd.* 6402, *iv*, 565
apptd. —. *sgd. Oct.,* 1942

Lord Kennet (*Ch.*), Branson, Burleigh, Cunliffe, Davies, Garrett, Lever, Pole, Witt, Wood.

'To ascertain and report what practical measures, whether by way of some form of concentration or otherwise, can still be taken to secure the greatest possible release of man-power in the sphere of banking, including investment trusts, finance and discount houses, and stock exchange businesses, in ordinary insurance business, and in industrial assurance.'

Three panels were formed for the three kinds of business, each of which submitted a report. Points which were common to all three were that 46 hours weekly (excluding meal breaks) should be taken as a standard, and full use should be made of part-time workers, especially of non-mobile women for clerical work. Banks have released 55 per cent of their male staff, and further releases depend on amalgamation of separate units, modification of methods of work, reduction of services and the use of cheques by business. Changes are proposed for trustee savings banks

which would release 20 per cent of those deferred. The number of men in insurance has fallen by 21,000 and a further 2500 await call. Reduction of staff used to seek new business, the prohibition of transfers and consultation between the offices and unions should enable further releases to be made.

Statistics Relating to the War Effort of the U.K.

apps. pp. 64. 1944

1943–44 *Cmd.* 6564, *viii*, 597

Includes statistics showing the mobilisation of man-power and redistribution of the labour force between industries.

Re - allocation of Man - power between the Armed Forces and Civilian Employment. pp. 4. 1944

Re - allocation of Man - power between Civilian Employments.

pp. 10. 1944

1943–44 *Cmd.* 6548, *Cmd.* 6568, *viii*, 289

Cmd. 6548.—In any interim period between the defeat of Germany and the defeat of Japan the problem will be one not of demobilisation, but of re-allocation between the Forces and industry. Until the requirements are known the precise level at which the Forces must be maintained cannot be determined precisely. Compulsory recruitment must continue in order to relieve men who have served for long periods. Release will be on the basis of age and length of service, two months of service being counted as equivalent to one year of age (Class A), but to provide for urgent work on reconstruction a limited number (Class B) will be selected as belonging to occupational classes specified by the Ministry of Labour, mainly for house building. The leave and reinstatement rights of each class are specified.

Cmd. 6568.—Any interim period will be one of severe adjustment between civilian employments: production of munitions must continue and priority be given to the export trade, house building and production of necessities. The demand for civilian labour will exceed the total available and the determination of its distribution on the basis of an annual man-power budget will continue. All persons will be regarded as available. The inflow of man-power released from the Forces and on balance from munitions industries will make possible the release of some who wish to go home or leave their war jobs. Class K (women with household responsibilities or wishing to join released husbands, women over 60 and men over 65) will be able to retire or leave their jobs irrespective of the work on which they are engaged, as will women over 50 unless there are strong reasons to the contrary. Those who have worked away from home for more than three years may also be released for transfer to other work of national importance. Of the surplus of labour arising from redundancy in war industries, of those in Class A, men 18 to 27 will be called up. Class B, those needed for priority vacancies, those who have worked away from home for more than one or less than three years, and others as determined by industrial agreements, will be able to transfer to other employers. The registration of young men and women will continue. Those released from the Forces on industrial grounds (Class B releases) will be directed to the work for which they are released, but if they leave it will be recalled to the Forces.

The power of direction of labour under Defence Reg. 58A, the Essential Work Order and the Control of Employment (Directed Persons) Order must be retained, but as far as possible redistribution will take place on a voluntary basis, reliance being placed on the powers in the Control of Engagement Order.

National Defence and Man-power

Statement relating to Defence; 1945–46 Cmd. 6743, xx, 147. The target was, by December 1945, to demobilise 1½ mn.

of the 5,100,000 men and women in the armed forces, retaining the principle of age and length of service, and to reduce civilian workers on war production to 1,400,000. A review of military commitments led to the conclusion that the total strength of the three Services should be 1 mn. by 31st December, 1946. The sums required for armed services and supplies in 1946 would be £1100 mn., with £500 mn. for terminal costs.

The following papers on National Service: 1945–46 Cmd. 6831, xv, 887, and 1950 Cmd. 8026, xvi, 575, and the annual Statements on Defence (see Sessional Indexes) give information on the call-up to the Services, length of service, numbers in the Forces or engaged on defence production, etc.

2. EMPLOYMENT, WAGES POLICY, COST OF LIVING

Price Stabilisation and Industrial Policy

Statement. pp. 4. 1941
1940–41 *Cmd.* 6294, *viii*, 311

There is evidence that the Government policy of stabilising prices in order to prevent the evils of inflation is not well understood. Owing to shipping difficulties and diversion of man-power and factory space to war production, there must be a reduction in the consumption of goods which in peace time were regarded as necessaries. Increases of wages and other incomes would not make more goods available, but raise prices, lead to demands for increased wages and start an inflation impossible to check after it had reached a certain point. It was estimated that in 1942 people would have incomes, after allowing for taxation and saving, of £500 mn. in excess of the value of goods available. To prevent the rise in prices and keep the cost of living index stable there had been more direct taxation, rationing, and price control.

The Government had followed the traditional policy of leaving wages negotiations to voluntary organisations and wage tribunals. It is the duty of both sides of industry to consider all possible means of preventing the rise of costs by improvement in the efficiency of production. There may be proper grounds for adjusting wages for comparatively low paid workers or to take account of changes in the method or volume of production. Increases of wages will defeat their own objects unless they are so regulated that prices can be kept under control.

Employment Policy

Statement, apps. pp. 31. 1944

1943–44 *Cmd.* 6527, *viii*, 119

The level of employment and standard of living do not depend only on conditions at home. As a result of two world wars we shall have to pay for our imports of food and raw materials by a greatly expanded volume of exports. This requires prosperity in overseas markets and international collaboration to promote trade, stability of exchange rates and to check swings in world commodity prices, as well as to help countries with temporary balance of payments difficulties. A Mutual Aid Agreement has been made with America, and the recommendations of the United Nations on food and agriculture accepted. The main responsibility must rest on the initiative and flexibility of industry, especially of export industries. Taxation policy will be adjusted to promote research and aid the modernisation of plant.

Since 80 per cent of employment in manufacturing is on government account, the transition from war to peace involves a switch of demand and the transfer of man-power to civilian production. The three dangers are (a) that patches of unemployment may develop, (b) that demand may outrun supply and cause inflation and (c) that civilian production may concentrate on the wrong things from the national point of view. To meet the first, steps will be taken to ensure that labour and capacity no longer needed for munitions production shall be released for civilian goods of high priority and that releases of premises and material are co-ordinated in advance. To meet the second, prices must be kept stable by continued rationing and price control and by stable costs, helped by subsidies to prevent temporary and considerable rises in the cost of living; by encouraging saving, and by controlling the flow and direction of investment. To meet the third, priorities must be enforced by licences, by control of raw materials and in some degree of labour.

To check the development of localised unemployment in particular industries and areas, the Government will aim at securing a balanced distribution of labour and industry (a) by influencing the location of industries in such a way as to diversify the industrial composition of areas vulnerable to unemployment, (b) by removing obstacles to the transfer of workers, and (c) by providing training facilities to fit workers from declining industries for jobs in expanding ones. The Government will steer new factory development into 'development areas' most requiring industrial diversification, and a regional organisation of the departments concerned will be established. Retraining schemes for resettling ex-Service men and women and released war workers will be continued as a permanent measure to assist necessary transfers, and trainees allowances will be separated from unemployment benefit. To assist mobility, a substantial proportion of houses built after the war will be let at rents within the means of the average worker.

The general conditions of a high and stable level of employment are that total expenditure on goods and services must be prevented from falling to a level where general unemployment appears, that the level of prices and wages must be kept stable, and that workers must be sufficiently mobile. The Government are prepared to accept a new responsibility, that of taking action at the earliest stage to arrest a threatened slump. Of the constituents of total expenditure—private consumption expenditure, public expenditure on current services, public investment expenditure, private investment expenditure and the foreign balance, the last two are subject to the greatest variations and are the most difficult to control. Public investment must be planned to off-set fluctuations in private investment and the decline of consumers' expenditure which follows a fall of private investment must be checked and reversed. Stability of wages and of prices are inextricably connected, and joint efforts of the Government, employers and organised labour will be necessary to prevent rises of cost in production and distribution.

Private capital expenditure can be influenced by variation of interest rates, through a concerted monetary policy. But since low interest rates are not always effective in encouraging investment during depression, monetary policy will be supplemented by encouraging private enterprise to plan its capital expenditure, and within certain practical limits, by expanding Government capital expenditure when private investment is declining. To alleviate any variations in consumption expenditure, when unemployment falls below an estimated average level social insurance contributions could be raised, thus reducing the purchasing power in the community, and could be reduced when unemployment rises above the average level, thus increasing the purchasing power left in the hands of the community. The Government could also vary its own purchases to act as a corrective.

None of the main proposals involves deliberate planning for a deficit on the National Budget in years of sub-normal trading, but the Chancellor need not follow a rigid policy of balancing the Budget each year regardless of the state of trade. The dead-weight war debt should be reduced steadily, but to provide for defence and reconstruction there must be some increase in public indebtedness. Although when money income is rising total debt can increase considerably without increasing the proportionate burden of interest, and the interest payments are to be regarded as a transfer between individuals and not a real burden on the community as a whole, high taxation is a drag on the effort and enterprise of the taxpayer. The Government will have both to pursue a policy of budgetary equilibrium in order to maintain confidence and to maintain the national income.

The whole of the measures proposed have never yet been systematically applied by any government, and unsuspected obstacles will emerge in practice. A small central qualified staff will be established to measure and analyse economic trends and submit appreciations of them to Ministers. More exact information on current economic movements will be required. The annual White Paper on National Income will be developed and parallel studies of man-power made by the Ministry of Labour. The debates on the Budget will provide an opportunity for Parliament to review the economic health of the country and to approve the strategy for maintaining employment.

Appendix II is a memo. on a scheme to influence consumption by varying automatically the rate of social insurance contributions, reducing them when unemployment was above the average level, thus leaving more purchasing power in the hands of consumers. An example is given to show that £100 mn. a year injected into the system might reduce the fall in aggregate demand by one-quarter.

Economic Considerations affecting Relations between Employers and Workers

Statement, app. pp. 9. 1947
1946–47 *Cmd.* 7018, *xix*, 1195

G. A. Isaacs, Minister of Labour.

The reconstituted National Joint Advisory Council, consisting of 17 representatives of employers and workers, requested that a statement should be issued on the economic state of the country, inflation, balance of payments, etc., so that management and workers should appreciate the new conditions and that increase of production need not be hindered by fears of unemployment.

As a result of the efforts of the last seven years, we have distorted our economic system, sold half our external assets and are still meeting deficits in our balance by external credits. External borrowing cannot continue and we have proceeded to establish many schemes of social improvements. We must make up arrears and improve our standards by our own efforts and this requires improved productivity of British industry.

There is more work to do than there are people to do it. Since 1939 the working population has increased (November 1946) by 574,000. But those in the Forces, munitions production, public service, professional services, entertainment, sport, increased by 815,000, so that the balance in other industries had fallen by 241,000. At least 560,000 more will be needed for the export industries alone, while there will be a loss of 370,000 boys and girls through the raising of the school leaving age. The shortage of labour is unevenly spread over industries. Exports will have to be increased in volume by 75 per cent, and since this involves an increase in our share of the world's export trade, it cannot be achieved if costs and prices rise in relation to world prices. The total income of all sections of the community, after paying income tax, is £7000 mn. a year, but the value of available goods and services only £6000 mn. The increase of production can be obtained only by full employment and by raising output per head without prejudice to earnings.

Personal Incomes, Costs and Prices

Statement. pp. 4. 1948
1947–48 *Cmd.* 7321, *xxii*, 1007

The nation's economic welfare depends largely on our ability to make and sell exports, and this would be more difficult if costs of production and therefore prices rose in relation to world prices. The Government has taken steps to check inflation by high taxation on personal incomes and distributed profits, by P.A.Y.E. and indirect taxation. But the danger of inflation will be accentuated by the drive to achieve a balance of payments, which will reduce the volume of goods in the home market. There should be no further increase in the general level of incomes without at least a corresponding increase in the volume of production. The customary relationships between wages and salaries in different occupations have no necessary relevance to modern conditions. They should be such as to encourage the movement of labour to where it is most needed, and not, as they still do in some cases, tempt it in a contrary direction.

The following considerations should guide those concerned in settling personal incomes. It is not desirable that the Government should interfere directly with the income of individuals save by direct taxation; it is essential that there should be strict adherence to the terms of collective agreements, and that individual employers should not, by departing from them, start competitive bargaining. Until more goods are on the home market, there is no justification for any general increase in individual money incomes, but there may be cases where increases may be necessary in an under-manned industry. Each increase must be justified on its merits in the national interest and not on the basis of maintaining a former relativity between different occupations and industries.

Economic Implications of Full Employment

app. pp. 13. [1956]
1955–56 *Cmd.* 9725, *xxxvi*, 565

Full employment has brought with it one problem for which no satisfactory solution has yet been found, that of continually rising prices. Unemployment, which was 10 per cent before the war, since 1946 has rarely exceeded 2 per cent, for most of the period has been under 2 per cent and is now about 1 per cent. Prices of final output have risen by 50 per cent, most of the rise being due to import prices and our own cost of production, and it is the latter which is responsible for by far the largest part. There is a continuing tendency for prices to rise as incomes increase faster than output.

Between 1938 and 1948, while prices of consumers' goods and services roughly doubled, wages and salaries rather more than doubled, and the dividends of non-nationalised companies rose by a tenth. Between 1948 and 1955 consumers' prices rose by one-third, wages, salaries and dividends by nearly two-thirds. The upward pressure of rising money incomes will produce strains which may prevent full economic growth, and even threaten employment. An adequate volume of exports will depend on the basic factor of prices, which must be fully competitive. West Germany's share of world trade, 7 per cent in 1950, has doubled, but our own share has dropped by 25 to 20 per cent. And a disproportionate rise in costs and prices, by undermining confidence in the stability in the value of money, may weaken people's willingness to save.

The Government must ensure high and steady demand, but it is then open to workers to demand wage and salary increases and for employers to grant them and pass them on to consumers, as well as to maintain profit margins. If these conditions are exploited by trade unions and business men, price stability and full employment become incompatible. The solution lies in introducing new methods and in avoiding restrictive practices not appropriate to present conditions. Firms should try to pass on gains in productivity in lower prices and to expand profits, not by maintaining high profit margins, but by increasing turnover. The counterpart of realism in relation to prices is realism in relation to personal incomes.

The satisfactory operation of the system of free negotiation of wages by collective bargaining and of freedom in fixing of dividends depends upon everyone being aware of and accepting their full implications.

Cost of Living

Advisory Cttee. Interim Rep., apps. pp. 9. 1947

1946–47 Cmd. 7077, x, 683
apptd. Aug., 1946. sgd. March, 1947

R. M. Gould (Ch.), Allen, Cromwell, Hallsworth, Hough, Cazalet-Keir (Mrs. T.), Leggett, Mathias, Stone, Tomkinson (Miss D. S.), Ainsworth, Anderson, Andrew, Handford, Stafford.

'To advise on the basis of the official cost-of-living index figure and on matters connected therewith . . . whether any revision in the basis of the figure is practicable and desirable in present conditions, and, if so, the revision that might be made.'

An inquiry was made in 1937–38 for the purpose of getting information on which to base a revision. This would have been made but for the outbreak of war in 1939. The main change compared with 1914 was a reduction in the proportion spent on food and a considerable increase in the proportion spent on other items. Information since that date confirms the popular view that the alteration in consumption habits has made the official index out of date, and that the entire conception of an index purporting to measure the changes in the cost of maintaining an unchanging standard of living of a section of the community may be inappropriate and misleading. The main alternative is an index which measures the movement of retail prices 'weighted' on a basis which is kept continuously up to date, but weighting based on the present abnormal conditions of spending would be inappropriate as a basis for any lengthy period. As an interim measure there should be a new index showing monthly changes of retail prices, weighted according to the patterns of consumption disclosed by the 1937–38 inquiry; a technical committee should be set up first to prepare an immediate scheme, and then to collect information for the preparation of a more permanent scheme.

See *Weekly Expenditure of Working Class Households.* Labour Gazette. Dec. 1940, Jan., Feb., 1941. Reprinted. Parts I, II, III. 1941 Non-Parl. Min. of Labour and N.S.

—— Interim Report. pp. ii, 7.   1951
1950–51 *Cmd.* 8328, *xi*, 1
sgd. June, 1951

R. M. Gould (*Ch.*), Allen, Badger, Cazalet-Keir (Mrs. T.), Evans, Hough, Leggett, Mathias, Ramsbottom, Stone, Tomkinson (Miss D. S.), Allen, Compton, Fearn, Fowler, Saunders, Stafford.

'To consider whether . . . conditions of spending could now be considered sufficiently stable to justify the holding of a new full-scale budget enquiry to provide information for an up-to-date weighting basis for a new index.'

The Interim Index (1947) was based on the goods and services purchased in 1937–38 according to family budgets then collected. The index starts from the cost of purchasing the quantities at the base date (mid-June 1947) and shows, at monthly intervals, the percentage changes as compared with June 1947 in the total cost of purchasing these quantities. The proportionate allocations of expenditure represented by these pre-war quantities at the prices current in June 1947 are used to combine into one 'all items' index the price changes of individual items; they form the 'weighting' basis of the index. Recent big increases in wholesale prices and other changes have brought it under criticism as failing to register the full upward movement of retail prices and because the 'weights' were based on a pre-war pattern of 'working-class' consumption. The National Federation of Professional Workers suggested that a separate index should be compiled for professional, clerical, technical, adminis-

trative and supervisory workers, or that an index should be compiled for salaried as distinct from wage earners.

No index designed to reflect average experience of a substantial number of households can measure with precision the changes of prices paid by individuals or small groups, and it was doubted whether a special index for salaried workers would be a better instrument for many of those workers. There should be a new budget enquiry to provide information regarding the pattern of expenditure and one index related to the earnings of the head of those households falling approximately within the limits of £150 to £1000— the precise limit to be determined when the budgets are analysed. Consideration was being given to the modifications which can be made to the 1947 index until a new one can be instituted, based on the results of the new budget enquiry.

—— Report, *Working of the Interim Index of Retail Prices*, apps. pp. iv, 48.
1952
1951–52 *Cmd.* 8481, *ix*, 707
sgd. Jan., 1952

The Technical Committee reported that the use of pre-war weights in computing the index had not resulted in any tendency for the index figure to understate the rise in retail prices since 1947. If the index had been based on a post-war pattern of consumption the figures might have been slightly lower, but it understates other rises, e.g. rents, so that various factors have tended to offset one another. This, however, is purely fortuitous, and could not be expected to continue indefinitely if the index is computed on its present basis. Pending the results of a budget inquiry, it was proposed to reweight a temporary index on estimates of the 1950 pattern of consumption derived from, for example, the White Paper on *National Expenditure.* The Technical Committee's report, given in full, includes an examination of the statistical problems of dealing with rent and rates, quality and seasonal changes, and forced substitutions.

See *Enquiry into Household Expenditure 1953–54*; 1957 Non-Parl. Min. of Labour and N.S. *Urban Working Class Household Diet 1940 to 1949*. National Food Survey Cttee. 1st Rep. *Domestic Food Consumption and Expenditure, 1950*. National Food Survey Cttee. [1st] Ann. Rep.; 1951, 1952 Non-Parl. Min. of Food.

3. INDUSTRIAL RELATIONS, DISPUTES, WAGES COUNCILS

Industrial Relations Handbook

Pp. v, 284. 1953

1953 *Non-Parl. Min. of Labour and N.S.*

Gives an account of the organisation of employers and workers, collective bargaining and negotiating machinery, conciliation and arbitration machinery, statutory regulation of wages.

See *Joint Consultation, Training within Industry, Works Information and Personnel Management*. Conference. Rep.; 1948 Non-Parl. Min. of Labour and N.S. *Human Relations in Industry*. Conference. Rep.; 1952 Non-Parl. Jt. Cttee. 1st Rep.; 1954 Non-Parl. D.S.I.R., Medical Research Council.

Disputes in Particular Employments

During this period many hundreds of papers were issued dealing with wages and disputes in particular employments. Some of these report the results of enquiries into major industrial disputes referred to the Industrial Court by the Minister because of the failure of the parties to agree; some deal with disputes referred or reported to the National Arbitration Tribunal set up during the war when strikes were prohibited; while others give the decisions of the Industrial Disputes Tribunal which replaced it when the prohibition of strikes was withdrawn, on issues and disputes reported to the Minister. The papers may be reports of the enquiry, setting out the case and

the conclusions, and may include the minutes of evidence taken. Many of them give a brief statement of the case presented by each side, followed without comment or reasons by the formal terms of an award on a wage claim or on the interpretation of a collective agreement in its application to a particular workman, firm or employing authority. Though these may be important to a particular individual, class or trade, most of them do not involve any principle of general significance. Others again, though directly concerned with particular trades only, comment on or give recommendations about the conventions or technique of collective bargaining which one or both parties have failed to observe.

Examples of cases in which matters other than hours of work were involved:

(1) Conditions connected with the wage bargain.—Claims to increase of wages of roadmen established, of building trade workers, not established. (Industrial Disputes Tribunal, Nos. 343, 385, 1953.) Claims of radio operators on fishing vessels part established, part not established. (Industrial Court, No. 2437, 1953.) Upgrading of a local authority for wage purposes. (Industrial Disputes Tribunal, No. 442, 1953.) Wages of certain road transport workers not fair compared with those covered by Road Transport Wages Act. (Industrial Courts Nos. 2221, 1949; 2443, 1953.) Award in favour of employers that workers should operate a modified costing system. (Industrial Court, No. 355, 1953); award in favour of union that the company should complete an incentive scheme. (National Arbitration Tribunal, No. 1459, 1950); absence of any production incentive. (National Arbitration Tribunal, No. 1182, 1948); award in favour of union which asked for replacement of small group piece rates to group piece rates. (Industrial Court, No. 2472, 1953.) Claim for further holidays with pay not established. (National Arbitration Tribunal, No. 1561, 1950.) Dismissal of a worker justified. (Industrial Court, No 2223, 1949; National Arbitration Tribunal,

No. 1489, 1950.) Employers held not to be violating the House of Commons Fair Wages Resolution, 1946, or preventing men from being trade unionists. (Industrial Court, No. 2481, 1953.)

(2) Interpretation of collective agreements.—No alteration of circumstances had occurred to justify employers terminating an agreement (Industrial Court, No. 2475, 1953); a union's interpretation of an agreement that they were at liberty to approach individual employers to secure more favourable terms than those agreed confirmed. (Industrial Court, No. 2431, 1953.)

(3) The machinery of collective bargaining.—Unions should be recognised 1940-41 Cmd. 6284, Cmd. 6300, iv; 1943-44 Cmd. 6493, iv; 1951-52 Cmd. 8607, xv. Differences between unions on negotiating rights; 1946-47 Cmd. 7097, xiv; 1947-48 (47) x; 1949 N-P. (Railway Shopmen); 1950-51 Cmd. 8232, xvi. Extension of arrangements to a whole industry; 1943-44 Cmd. 6499, iv. For conditions of union recognition, see also *Post Office (Departmental Classes) Recognition*, p. 217, and *Broadcasting* (1950-51 Cmd. 8116), p. 220.

(4) Breaches of the conventions of collective negotiation.—Calling a meeting and stoppage before the proper procedure had been gone through (1952-53 Cmd. 8839, xiii); going back on an agreement ratified (1954-55 Cmd. 9352, Cmd. 9372, v); a union insisting that employers accept the principle of an increase before negotiations, leaving the 'remainder' open to negotiation (1952-53 Cmd. 8968, xiii; 1954-55 Cmd. 9372, v); calling a 'guerilla strike' on the side of one of the employers or the employers negotiating side ('it is fundamental that people who take part in negotiations representing their sides should do so in the knowledge that their personal position will not be prejudiced') (Cmd. 8968); workshop meetings in working hours are called because men will not stay for a meeting after working hours, as they live so far from the works (Cmd. 8968). Of 40,000 members affected by a dispute, at 17

mass meetings, 2617 attended and voted. Employers' breach of practice. 1953-54 Cmd. 9093, xv; 1955-56 Cmd. 9843, xxi; Unions' breach of practice. 1954-55 Cmd. 9439, v; Failure to observe agreed procedure. 1952-53 Cmd. 8968, xiii; 1956-57 Cmnd. 105, xiv.

(5) Use of conciliation or joint machinery and joint machinery for maintenance of discipline and elimination of absenteeism should be considered (Industrial Court, No. 2274, 1950); two unions should negotiate to settle their differences (National Arbitration Tribunal, No. 1541, 1950).

(6) Unco-ordinated wage demands. 1955-56 Cmd. 9717, Cmd. 9843, xxi; 1943-44 Cmd. 6499, iv; 1952-53 Cmd. 8931, xiii; 1954-55 Cmd. 9439, v.

(7) Unofficial strikes, shop stewards' activities. 1945 Non-Parl. (Docks); 1948-49 Cmd. 7851, xxix; 1950-51 Cmd. 8236, Cmd. 8375, xvi; 1956-57 Cmnd. 131, xiv. Strike unconstitutional. 1952-53 Cmd. 8839, xiii. Union ballot unsatisfactory. 1947-48 Cmd. 7266, xvi.

Location of papers.—Most are listed in the annual *Consolidated Lists* (now *Catalogues of Government Publications*), under the heading 'Ministry of Labour', but many important ones, e.g. reports of Inquiries under the Industrial Courts Act and of certain specially appointed committees, are in the Sessional Papers as Commands or occasionally House Papers. The report of the Guillebaud Railway Pay Committee is not in the Sessional Papers nor listed in the *Catalogues of Government Publications*, but is published by the Special Jt. Cttee. on Machinery of Negotiation for Railway Staff (1960).

Training of Supervisors

Cttee. Rep., apps. pp. 56. 1954
1954 *Non-Parl. Min. of Labour and N.S.*
apptd. Feb., 1953. sgd. May, 1954
P. H. St. J. Wilson (*Ch.*), Amphlett, Bower, Bramley, Burness, Eastman, Fletcher, Frisby, Livock, Morgan, Ogden, Perkins, Towy-Evans (Miss), Warne.

'*To review the present facilities for and*

T

methods of training of Foremen (particularly in the light of the report of the team organised by the Anglo-American Council on Productivity), the extent of their use, and the possibility of evaluating their effectiveness; and to report to the Minister.'

A supervisor is broadly defined as 'a person in constant control of a definite section of the labour force in an undertaking, exercising it either directly or through subordinates and responsible for this to a higher level of management'. Many firms provide training, though they are a small proportion of the whole. The Report reviews the schemes, particularly in relation to the age at which training is given, the content of the course, the part played by the firm's own instructing staff, technical colleges, trade unions and voluntary bodies, the Ministry of Labour Training Within Industry scheme, etc.

The Anglo-American Council on Productivity team report on Training of Supervisors suggested, in relation to the status of British supervisors, that they should be regarded as responsible members of the management team, that there should be greater delegation of authority down to the supervisor level; that the line of executive authority down to the supervisor should be maintained as the chief channel of communication in both directions. The size of the supervisor's group should be limited to one which he can effectively control and influence. However excellent a course of training, a supervisor who returns from his training and has no co-operation from the management may become discontented and frustrated.

Employers' organisations and the boards of the nationalised industries should consider active participation in the field; individual firms should make one member of the management responsible for studying the needs of the firm in relation to the effectiveness of the training available; higher managements should re-examine the status of their supervisors in relation to the management team; training should be planned to cover the whole management personnel. Training College courses should be more related to day to day needs, and the Colleges should take the initiative in approaching local industry with a view to discovering needs and obtaining co-operation. Voluntary associations should extend their experiments and the Ministry of Labour should develop the T.W.I. scheme.

Wages, Hours and Conditions in the Retail Distributive Trades

Conference. Rep., apps. pp. 8. 1939

1939 Non-Parl. Min. of Labour sgd. Feb., 1939

In 1936 discussions initiated by the Ministry of Labour on conditions in the distributive trades led to the Retail Distributive Trades Conference. The report proposed that trade committees should be set up, the Minister being empowered to fix recommended rates, etc., by Order. There should be a National Retail Distributive Trades Council to define the areas of wage proposals, to co-ordinate recommendations on hours of work, wage scales, etc. A Special Committee should be appointed from the members of the Conference to consider the possible grouping of trades between which there was a relationship. The employers added that the machinery should be set up in all sections of the trades simultaneously, and the wages, etc., become operative at an agreed date. The unions wanted the arrangements made speedily and applied to as many sections as practicable.

After the war broke out, it was the expectation that the Conditions of Employment and National Arbitration Order would enable the agreements of Joint Industrial Councils to be enforced, and six such councils were set up. Applications for wages councils were made by the J.I.C.s for the Retail Food Trades, Retail Furnishing and Allied Trades, Retail Drapery, etc. Trades, and the Hairdressing Trades.

Wages Councils

The Wages Councils Act, 1945, besides converting existing Trades Boards into Wages Councils, made provision for the establishment of new Councils. The Minister can appoint a Commission of Inquiry to consider whether a Wages Council should be established either on his own initiative, or on application jointly by an employers' and workers' organisation, or by a Joint Industrial Council. The inquiries below were initiated by one or other of these processes.

—— Retail Food Trades, apps. pp. 39. 1947

1947 Non-Parl. Min. of Labour and N.S. apptd. Nov., 1945. sgd. Feb., 1947

G. G. Honeyman (Ch.), Bussey, Chell, Hanbury, Hancock (Miss F. M.), Holbein, Williams (Mrs. G.).

The inquiry covered persons other than craftsmen and productive workers in the retail trades in grocery and provisions, cooked meats, fish and game; fruit, vegetables and flowers; and off-licence liquors.

These inquiries into related retail trades showed that one of the difficulties was the lack of any generally accepted definition of the separate trades, since many shops carry on more than one trade, while some departmental stores are aggregations of shops of many kinds. On some matters there were joint hearings by the Commissioners for the retail food, drapery, etc. and furnishing trades. (i) Persons employed in the retail sale of ice-cream should be included within the scope of the wages council dealing with the sale of tobacco and confectionery. Workers in dairy shops which trade mainly in provisions or bread and flour confectionery should be covered by the wages councils for the relevant trade. The retail meat trade has little in common with the other trades and requires skill, and both sides prefer regulation by Joint Industrial Council. It should not be included. (ii) The claim of the Transport and General Workers' Union that as transport workers in the retail trades moved freely from one trade to another, their wages should be standardised by a separate wages council for all such workers was rejected in favour of including them in the wages council for the trade in which they worked. This applied also to warehouse workers. Drivers and salesmen of aerated waters should be included in the wages council for that trade. App. I gives the definition of the food trades and of the workers to be covered by the wages council, and the definition of retail furnishing and allied trades, drapery, outfitting and footwear trades, retail bookselling and stationery trades, and newsagency, tobacco and confectionery trades.

Wage regulation by voluntary agreement was not fully effective in the retail distributive trades because only 10 per cent of the workers were in unions; because in addition to multiple and departmental stores there were large numbers of small retail businesses in competition with the larger businesses which complied with wage agreements. Low wages and long hours were common in the retail trades because the work requires little preliminary training or skill, is found attractive by married women, boys and girls and persons of less than average physical strength and involves contact with the public. After the war the rates of wages might fall below a reasonable level and the machinery of the Joint Industrial Council will not be adequate: a wages council should be established. Separate wages councils are proposed for Scotland, and set out in App. II. There should be a Central Co-ordinating Committee for the wages councils in the four groups of retail trades.

See Draft Order for the Establishment of a Wages Council for the Retail Food Trades (Scotland). Com. Rep.; 1948 Non-Parl.

—— Retail Furnishing and Allied Trades, apps. pp. 19. 1947

1947 Non-Parl.

apptd. Nov., 1945. sgd. Feb., 1947

add Allen, Evans. del. Bussey, Hancock (Miss F. M.).

The definition of the trades, given on p. 3, includes not only furniture, but ironmongery, sports goods, radio, etc., apparatus, cycles, oils and paints. The number of shops was about 110,000, but the estimate of 250,000 workers was rather high. The employers' side of the Joint Industrial Council represented more than half the employers, employing well over half the workers, and much more than half the turnover. Though there was a fair union membership in multiple shops, not more than 10 per cent of all workers were in unions. The Joint Industrial Council's agreement carried little weight with unorganised employers, and a high degree of organisation on the workers' side was unlikely within a reasonable time. A wages council should be established for the whole of Great Britain. There was adequate voluntary machinery covering radio service engineers, who should be excluded, but 'mixed' workers should be included in respect of the time they spent as shop assistants.

See *Draft Order for the Establishment of a Wages Council for the Retail Furnishing and Allied Trades (Great Britain)*. Com. Rep.; 1948 Non-Parl.

—— *Hairdressing Trade*, apps. pp. 12. 1947

1947 *Non-Parl.*
apptd. Nov., 1945. sgd. Feb., 1947
add Hancock (Miss F. M.), Holmes. del. Allen, Evans.

There are 40,000 hairdressing establishments with 100,000 operatives, not more than one-tenth of whom are in trade unions. One-third of the employers are members of one or other of the organisations represented on the Joint Industrial Council. The businesses are small, and as employers and employees work side by side, union intervention is difficult. As the J.I.C. represents only a minority on each side, recourse to the machinery of the Conditions of Employment and National Arbitration Order would be of little avail since it could not be proved that the organisations were representative of a substantial proportion of employers and workers. The fact that wages are at or above the level fixed by the Council is due to shortage of labour and other conditions peculiar to a time of war. If this shortage is not permanent, and the supply of labour improves, the fact that the hairdressing trade is easy to enter, requires little capital and that it does not take long to acquire a modicum of skill, together with a possible decline in demand on the women's side when war employment ends, means that there will be a return to pre-war conditions. A wages council should be established. Hairdressers in hotels, including railway hotels, should be included, since they pass to and from other hairdressing establishments. Beauty culture, unless it is a minor part of a hairdressing saloon, chiropody, and wig-making unless part of a hairdressing establishment, should be excluded.

—— *Retail Drapery, Outfitting and Footwear Trades*, apps. pp. 15. 1947

1947 *Non-Parl.*
apptd. Nov., 1945. sgd. Feb., 1947
add Allen, Bussey. del. Hancock (Miss F. M.), Holmes.

There were 60,000 establishments employing 275,000 workers. The Joint Industrial Council represented less than 50 per cent of the employers and not more than 10 per cent of the workers. In the easier conditions of the supply of labour after the war the Council's agreements may not be complied with, and a wages council should be established. Although in Scotland a third of the establishments covering one-half the workers were represented, the council should cover the whole of Great Britain. The sale of leather and travel goods should be covered by the Furnishing and Allied Trades Council, of ladies' handbags by the Drapery, etc., Trade Council.

See *Draft Order for the Establishment of a Wages Council for the Retail Drapery, Outfitting and Footwear Trades (Great Britain)*. Com. Rep.; 1948 Non-Parl.

—— *Retail Bookselling, Newsagency, Stationery, Tobacco and Confectionery Trades*, apps. pp. 27. 1947
1947 *Non-Parl.*
apptd. *April*, 1946. sgd. *Feb.*, 1947
add Conley, Holmes.   del. Allen, Bussey.

On the Joint Industrial Council the employers' associations in the bookselling and newsagency trades represented more, those in the other trades less, than half the employers. The trade union membership in the five trades was scattered and uneven, small or negligible.   The Council had great difficulty in enforcing its agreements on unorganised employers, as it was held that an award by the National Arbitration Tribunal could not be enforced on them without taking employers individually to Court; the retail tobacconists withdrew from the Council, as well as the retail confectioners, both for this reason and because the grouping of the trade with the others might mean that booksellers would agree to wages confectioners could not pay. The machinery of the Joint Industrial Council was inadequate. All the employers' organisations were willing to accept statutory regulation, but not a grouping of the five trades under one wages council. The booksellers were in favour of statutory regulation in order to enforce rates on unorganised firms, the retail newsagents and stationers felt more allied to retail tobacconists and confectioners and wished the five trades to be regrouped; the retail confectioners felt that the grouping into five trades would cause difficulties to recur and preferred to be grouped with tobacconists and newsagents, but in view of the abnormal conditions in their trade wanted no trades council at the time, or if one were established, one not including bookselling. There should be one wages council for bookselling and stationery trades, and one for the newsagents, tobacco and confectionery trades: in Scotland, one for all five trades. Street sellers of newspapers may be either 'pointsmen' employed to sell one newspaper only and paid a retaining fee plus profits on sales, but subject to control as to their pitch and the number of editions they were required to sell, or a many times greater number of independent self-employed sellers dealing in any newspaper they chose. Although the employers object that in such circumstances statutory regulation was inappropriate, this was no reason for failing to protect those who were employed, who should be included.

—— *Wholesale and Retail Bread and Flour Confectionery Distributive Trades*, app. pp. 16.   1950
1951 *Non-Parl.*
apptd. *June*, 1949. sgd. *Aug.*, 1950
H. S. Kirkaldy (*Ch.*), Beard, Caffyn, Jack, Jackson, Spackman, Williams (Mrs. G.).

About 100,000 workers are involved, the majority being retail workers, most of them women. Not more than 15 per cent are in trade unions, two-thirds being employees of co-operative societies. There are a number of employers' organisations, the degree of organisation varying from 60 per cent to 90 per cent.   There are wage agreements covering co-operative societies, but nothing adequate outside them. Workers in wholesale distribution, mainly transport workers driving C licence vehicles, are adequately covered by the road transport arrangements, and should be excluded. There is no adequate voluntary machinery for dealing with those employed in retailing, and as there are a large number of small shops where young girls are employed as assistants, a wages council should be established, with a separate council for Scotland. Proposals to deal with the problem by extending the Bakery Wages Council and the Retail Food Trades Council were rejected; workers included in the scope of any catering wages council should be excluded. The Central Co-ordinating Committee should be extended to include the Wages Council for these trades: it should deal with anomalies which might arise through the exclusion of mixed shops.

See *Draft Order for the Establishment of a Wages Council for the Retail Bread and Flour Confectionery Trade (England and Wales)*. Com. Rep.; 1952 *Non-Parl.*

—— *Rubber Proofed Garment Making Industry,* app. pp. 15. 1950

1950 *Non-Parl.*
apptd. Dec., 1948. sgd. Sept., 1949
V. R. Aronson (*Ch.*), Coatman (Mrs. T.), Goldsmith, Holbein, Smith, Willis, Wolstencroft.

There is no joint industrial council or similar body: there are three trade associations and three trade unions, but only the two bodies named in the terms of reference have negotiated rates and conditions. In 1946, a strike arising out of a dispute between them resulted in an agreement which included a provision that both parties would join in an application for a wages council, but during the inquiry they said they had agreed under constraint, and that existing machinery for maintaining remuneration was adequate. The National Union of Tailors and Garment Workers, however, maintained that this trade does not differ from other garment making sufficiently to warrant adding yet another to the twelve wages councils already existing in the clothing industry; it should be brought within the scope of existing councils. This course the Commission recommended.

See *Rubber Proofed Clothing*. Working Party. Rep.; 1947 Non-Parl. Bd. of Trade.

Catering Wages Commission

1st Ann. Rep., apps. pp. 15. 1944
1943–44 (100) *iii*, 25
H. Shawcross (*Ch.*), Greenwood, Hich-
ens (Hermione), Knox, Powell, Robinson (Madeleine J.), Thomson.

'*To inquire into (i) the existing methods of regulating the remuneration and conditions of employment of workers to whom the Act applies and into any other matter affecting the remuneration and conditions of employment, health or welfare of such workers; (ii) means for meeting the requirements of the public, including in particular the requirements of visitors from overseas, and for developing the tourist traffic; and (iii) to make . . . recommendations. . . .*'

For the purposes of the Catering Wages Act, 1943, the catering trade includes hotels, boarding houses, tea shops, fish and chip shops, the catering departments of educational institutions, industrial canteens, etc. There was no statistical record of the number of undertakings, and because the definition of the catering trade used in the Act was different from that of the Ministry of Labour, there were no adequate statistics of the numbers employed. The Commission was unanimous that joint regulation of wages and conditions was necessary, but as there was no adequate machinery of a voluntary kind, much time had to be spent in grouping the various sections of the industry for wages board purposes.

The reports following led to the establishment of Wages Boards.

—— *Industrial Catering*. Rep., apps. pp. 8. 1944

1943–44 *Cmd.* 6509, *iii*, 1
sgd. Jan., 1944

Industrial canteens were run either as part of various industries which undertook their own catering as an ancillary activity, or by outside agencies as a distinctive industry serving a variety of other industries. In the former there was no adequate machinery for wage regulation and some highly organised industries were opposed to bringing catering workers within their own negotiating machinery, while the Joint Industrial Council represented only a part of the latter. Industrial catering should be regarded as a distinctive industry and not as an activity of the various industries which it serves. A wages board should be established.

—— *Remuneration and Conditions of Employment of Workers Employed by the Crown in Catering Undertakings.* Rep., app. pp. 9. 1944

1944 *Non-Parl. Min. of Labour and N.S. sgd. July,* 1944

The Catering Wages Act applies to civilian workers employed by or on behalf of the Crown in connection with any industrial undertaking. Some 14,349 canteen workers employed by Government departments, 63 per cent in connection with industrial undertakings, are covered by existing joint machinery, and if the informal agreements between the Ministry of Supply (7500 workers), are reviewed to cover all questions within the scope of a wages board, and formal agreements concluded by the Admiralty and the Mint, Crown workers should be excluded from any board. Where there are no agreements because the numbers employed are small or the workers unorganised, arrangements should be made which secure that no canteen workers should be employed by the Crown under less favourable conditions than those agreed for comparable grades of workers in similar Crown establishments.

—— *Unlicensed Non-Residential Catering Establishments.* Rep., apps. pp. 14. 1944

1943–44 *Cmd.* 6569, *iii,* 9 *sgd. Nov.,* 1944

Although there was 'a Catering Industry', the Commission rejected a suggestion that there should be one wages board to cover the whole of it. Such a board would become unwieldy if the 40 parent employers' associations, affiliated bodies and the many unorganised employers were given representation, while the task of drawing up a schedule of wage rates for the many classes of workers would be formidable.

Recommended, a board to cover establishments which were unlicensed and did not provide accommodation for guests or lodgers, i.e. cafés and tea-shops, restaurants, milk bars, snack bars, etc. These had substantial common interest. App. V. gives the number of establishments of different kinds (63,000) and the number of workers concerned (over 244,000).

—— *Licensed Residential Establishments and Licensed Restaurants.* Rep., apps. pp. 12. 1945

1944–45 *Cmd.* 6601, *iv,* 163 *sgd. Jan.,* 1945

The Hotels and Restaurants Association, which represented licensed establishments, maintained that their business was different from that of unlicensed establishments in the class of patrons, the types of workers employed, the hours of work and of service. A wages board should be established to cover them and licensed restaurants. Catering in public houses should be excluded, since a separate board covering the latter was proposed, unless they used four or more bedrooms for visitors or had a dining room which was their main business, when they should be included. Hotels' ancillary activities, such as bookstalls, hairdressing, etc., should be included, as well as railway companies' restaurants and refreshment rooms. The number of establishments covered was between 8000 and 10,000, employing at least 95,000 workers.

—— *Licensed Non-Residential Establishments.* Rep., apps. pp. 10. 1945

1944–45 *Cmd.* 6612, *iv,* 175 *sgd. Feb.,* 1945

There should be a Board to cover both public houses and non-residential registered clubs. It would cover about 60,000 to 70,000 public houses and at least 10,000 clubs. Recommendations are made on the question of the representation of managers and of tenants. A Scottish claim that there was adequate voluntary machinery was rejected.

—— *Unlicensed Residential Establishments.*
Rep., apps. pp. 8. 1945
1945–46 *Cmd.* 6706, *x*, 311
sgd. Jan., 1945

There should be a separate board for unlicensed residential establishments and boarding houses. Licensed hotels regarded their business as distinct from that of unlicensed hotels, which took the opposite view. So long as this difference of opinion existed, they should be covered by separate boards. Private houses letting rooms for visitors competed with boarding houses, and should be included if four or more bedrooms were used for the purpose. About 6,000 unlicensed hotels, and 70,000 boarding houses, probably employing at least 100,000 workers would be covered.

—— *Catering Activities of Local Authorities.* Rep., apps. pp. 12. 1946
1945–46 *Cmd.* 6776, *x*, 299
sgd. Dec., 1945

The report on Industrial Canteens (Cmd. 6509) took the view that catering was a distinctive industry and not an ancillary activity of the various industries with which they were associated. This applied also to local authorities' canteens; and British and Civic Restaurants, etc., competed with private establishments. They should therefore be dealt with by the respective wages boards, as set out in para. 2 of the Report, although sections of the various groups of workers affected were covered by voluntary joint machinery.

—— *Canteens Provided by Dock Authorities.* Rep., app. pp. 4. [1947]
1946–47 *Cmd.* 7191, *x*, 199
sgd. July, 1947

The Port of London Authority stated that while canteens provided for their own employees were within the scope of the Industrial Canteens board, those for other workers were not, but might be under one of two other boards, according to whether they were licensed or not. Canteens provided for dock workers should be exclusively within the scope of one wages board, that for Industrial and Staff Canteens.

—— *Hotel Industry.* Rep., apps. pp. 47 + apps. [1950]
1950 *Cmd.* 8004, *vi*, 531
sgd. July, 1950

The Commission was directed to enquire into the difficulties which had arisen through operation of the Act in the hotel industry. A full account is given of the proceedings of the 'Licensed' and 'Unlicensed' Boards, the representation on each side on each Board, and the way in which the independent members had voted on motions from the employers' and workers' sides. Four years' work of the 'Unlicensed' Board have been wasted. Difficulties have arisen relating to spread over, work on customary holidays, rest days, holidays, tips, etc. Except in a few large towns, the workers were largely unorganised. The employers said that the full-time trade union representatives had not worked in the industry and had made proposals they would not have done if they had.

The hotel is a 'domestic' industry without parallel and included a diversity of establishments, large and small, catering for all classes of the community. On the employers' side the needs of the smaller establishments have been overshadowed by those of the large luxury units—often the former had not even been consulted. The necessary flexibility, both in normal and at holiday times, could not be attained by the less expensive seasonal and rural hotels without crippling costs which restricted service, while the charges were as high as were practicable. The grades and rates were too numerous and were impracticable in the smaller establishments. The failure to take tips into account when fixing minimum rates had caused dissension between tippable and non-tippable staff.

The Board for unlicensed hotels should be abolished and one board established for both licensed and un-licensed hotels, with the aid of three Committees drawn from persons actively engaged in the hotel industry and not either employers' or workers' representatives on the Board. It should make appropriate proposals for 'large London establishments', 'large Provincial establishments', and 'small establishments wherever situated.' A joint national committee should investigate the problem of tipping. Pending the setting up of one board, in the interests of the immediate needs of the public, the Licensed Board should consider various amendments to the spread over, night duty, and holiday provisions, reducing the number of grades of workers and allowing composite grades in smaller establishments. Foreign experience shows that a completely satisfactory structure of wages flexible enough to take account of the varying conditions in the industry, can best be built up gradually by voluntary collective agreement.

—— *Rehabilitation of the Catering Industry.* Rep., apps. pp. 48. 1945

1945 *Non-Parl.*
sgd. Nov., 1944

The reduction of holiday accommodation owing to requisitioning, war damage and evacuation problems is very considerable. For example, one resort on the South East Coast had functioning only 11 out of 52 hotels and 100 out of 1000 boarding and apartment houses. It is only by giving immediate attention to the restoration of facilities that there is hope of meeting the demand for post-war holidays.

A de-requisitioning committee should be set up to determine the general order of release; where the properties are not released, market rents should be paid, and when released, rents should be paid during a reasonable period of restoration. Cost of works payments for war damage should be paid to hotels and boarding houses which would otherwise qualify only for value payments, if it is in the public interest that pre-war

standards of accommodation should be restored. Where local authorities receive interest-free advances, repayments should take into consideration the provision of adequate amenities and essential services in seaside resorts, and the sum repayable each year should not exceed the product of a penny rate. The removal of defence works, etc., should proceed with all possible speed. Catering establishments should have the first option on the pool of requisitioned and other furniture, and the allocation of part of manufacturing capacity should be considered. Other recommendations dealt with the financing of training schemes for ex-service men; the use of hostels and camps, making sea and road transport available, etc. The Commission proposes, for further discussion, the establishment of a national corporation, financed by a sleeper levy, and a levy per establishment, to make advances for rehabilitation and to classify and grade establishments, and to develop the catering industry.

—— *Development of the Catering, Holiday and Tourist Services.* Rep., apps. pp. 56. 1946

1946 *Non-Parl.*
sgd. Sept., 1945
del. H. Shawcross (*Ch.*).

The scheme for a rehabilitation fund financed by a sleeper levy and an establishment levy, outlined in the report on Rehabilitation of the Catering Industry, had not received sufficient support from the Industry, and the Commission therefore withheld any recommendation.

In order to develop the catering, holiday and tourist services there is need for a new national organisation representative of all interests, including the public interest. The Committee of this 'National Travel, Holiday and Catering Board' should be composed of representatives of a Catering Development Association, a Travel Association, with two independent members and a paid whole-time chairman. The finance for the Travel Association would be derived from voluntary subscriptions of the interests concerned, with matching Government grants, and for the Catering Development Association from a statutory contribution of 10s. per annum from public catering establishments. Suggestions were made for more attention to be given to traditional English cooking; research and experiments in design; amenities, furnishing, service and reception in hotels, classification of hotels, development of holiday camps, the provision of guide books, local information sheets, national parks and forest, etc.

—— *Staggering of Holidays.* Rep., apps. pp. 24. 1945

1945 *Non-Parl.*
sgd. Aug., 1945

Staggering holidays over a longer period of the year has become increasingly important since, with the introduction of holidays with pay, there are likely to be 30 mn. people—double the number for 1937—who want to find holiday accommodation. The conventional end of July–August period has become established through the necessity of closing down factories completely, the attraction of August bank holiday week, school holidays, the belief that August weather is the best, and the feeling that holiday attractions are usually best in August. This concentration in such a short period has resulted in peak prices, insufficient accommodation, and the need for the provision of many extra services. Para. 7 gives figures of the seasonal variation in the use of accommodation.

The aim should be to lengthen the spread-over period, but this could not be brought about by compulsory staggering because holidays are so much a matter of private life, tradition and custom. Staggering by towns, however, is the common experience in Scotland and Lancashire and certain parts of Yorkshire, and experiments in Leicester and Northampton have proved successful. In these places the difficul-

ties regarding the bank holiday, school holidays and school examinations have been coped with. But a town holiday week can in the main take place only in self-contained, substantially industrial areas. It would not be practicable where the majority of the people live in the town and work outside it, or in the larger cities. There is no general solution for these places, but something can be done to draw people away from the peak period by making things more flexible. Encouragement should be given to the alteration of school examination dates and holidays, staggering by groups of industries or firms, or by particular areas. An organisation of the interests concerned and of the appropriate Government departments should be set up to promote staggering.

—— *Training for the Catering Industry.* Rep., apps. pp. 12. 1946

1946 *Non-Parl.*
sgd. Oct., 1945

For dealing with the long-term training schemes necessary to raise the catering industry to a higher level of efficiency, the existing facilities were meagre and unco-ordinated. The immediate need was for basic training, which should not be specialised, should be given within the existing framework of technical education, and should take 3–6 months full-time or three years part-time. Examinations should be based on the common syllabus of the City and Guilds of London Institute. If necessary, local authorities should acquire a catering establishment suitable for training purposes: where there is a shortage of teachers they should be lent or seconded from the industry. A national superstructure for higher training could be built only after there had been some experience of basic training.

—— *Problems affecting the Remuneration of Catering Workers which result from the Practice of Giving Tips.* Rep., app. pp. 4. 1947

1947 *Non-Parl.*
sgd. June, 1947

add R. M. Hughes (*Ch.*), Grant. del. Knox.

Tipping can never be wholly eliminated though it would be better both for the employees and the public if it could be. The amounts received vary so widely that a general assessment of their cash value cannot be made, and they should be disregarded by the Wages Boards in assessing statutory minimum rates of wages.

—— *Alleged Overcharging for Holiday Accommodation.* Rep., apps. pp. 10. 1947

1947 *Non-Parl.*
sgd. July, 1947
add Rosc.

The complaint that there had been widespread overcharging was not substantiated generally. A social survey and information provided by local authorities and trade associations showed that $33\frac{1}{3}$ to 50 per cent increase was common, though the most general increase was between 50 per cent and 75 per cent, but these were not out of proportion to the general rise of prices or the costs of redecoration after long periods of requisition or closure. There had, however, been some over-charging by newcomers who had bought hotels at inflated prices, and by some boarding houses, owing to insufficient accommodation. This could be remedied by the provision of accommodation on a non-profit-making basis in hostels and camps erected for war-time purposes, as well as free use by the public of official local guides, etc.

—— *Employment Agencies serving the Catering Industry.* Rep., app. pp. 11. 1947

1947 *Non-Parl.*
sgd. July, 1947

The agencies provide a specialised service which the Ministry is not yet able to provide, but there are some abuses, which include the practice of charging the whole of a substantial engagement fee to the worker. Legislation should require all catering employment agencies to register with the county or county borough council, and employers to pay at least half the engagement fee.

—— *Abolition of Commission*

'On 30th May [1959], when the *Terms and Conditions of Employment Act, 1959* (7 & 8 Eliz. 2. c. 26) came into operation, the Catering Wages Act was repealed, the Catering Wages Com. was abolished, and the hotel and catering industry was brought under the more flexible provisions of the Wages Councils Acts. The four Catering Wages Boards were converted into Wages Councils, provision being made to avoid interrupting the statutory protection of the workers.' *Ministry of Labour.* Ann. Rep., 1959, p. 75; 1959–60 Cmnd. 1059.

4. WAGES AND CONDITIONS IN PARTICULAR EMPLOYMENTS (OTHER THAN WAGES COUNCILS)

Amenities in the Brick Industry

Cttee. Rep. pp. 13. 1947
1947 *Non-Parl. Min. of Works apptd. March, sgd. Aug.,* 1946

A. W. Garrett (*Ch.*), Barlow, Bullock, Coote, Gill, Hayday, Hutson, Pearmaine, Rowe, Sutton.

'To *consider and report upon measures that might be taken to make the Brick Industry more attractive to recruits, excluding wages and terms of employment falling within the negotiating machinery of the Industry.*'

The industry covers a wide range of works varying from brickfields in remote rural areas away from town drainage, water supply, etc., in which the conditions of work approximate to those of agriculture, to large mechanised works with amenities comparable to the best in many other industries. The majority employ less than 50 workers. There was little evidence that the brick workers were failing to return after release from the Forces, or failing to work up to their past records, though in some districts, where brick workers went to other industries during the war, they are not returning in great numbers. Some new labour had left because the handling of bricks calls for the use of new muscles which makes the work painful in the first few days.

This is a skilled industry which must be made better for the old worker and attractive for new ones, especially youths who are virile and strong. Mechanisation of plant should be encouraged; adequate shelter near kilns and claypits should be provided, as well as sanitary and other amenities covered in the main by the Factory Acts.

See *The Brick Industry*, p. 131.

Training for the Building Industry

Central Council for Works and Buildings. Education Cttee. Rep., apps. pp. 56. 1943

1943 *Non-Parl. Min. of Works and Planning*

apptd. — 1941. sgd. Nov., 1942

E. D. Simon (*Ch.*), and 35 others.

In 1938 the number of insured workers in the building industry was 1,050,000, the total number of craftsmen being 527,000. Estimates made by the Council and by G. D. H. Cole for the Nuffield College Social Reconstruction Survey showed that to meet a post-war building programme, 1,400,000 building trade workers will be required in the first three years, of whom the recognised proportion of numbers of craftsmen would be 700,000. To provide for this expansion and to meet the post-war deficiency of 275,000 skilled men, proposals are made to train in each half-year for $2\frac{1}{2}$ to 3 years, 50,000 men capable of developing into skilled craftsmen. Special training schemes must be organised and in order to attract the right kind of recruit there should be an authoritative pronouncement of intention to maintain a long-

term building programme, and a statutory guaranteed week for the whole industry. A Building Apprenticeship and Training Council should be set up to observe and advise on all matters concerning recruitment, education and training.

—— Government Statement. pp. 6. 1943

1942–43 *Cmd.* 6428, xi, 1

The Apprenticeship and Training Council for the Building Industry was set up to devote early attention to a review of existing apprenticeship schemes; to define minimum standards to which approved schemes should conform; to maintain a register of such apprentices and to issue certificates on completion of training, to maintain publicity designed to stimulate interest in building as a career, and to consider practical methods of encouraging employers and apprentices to participate in approved schemes.

Building Apprenticeship and Training Council

1st Rep., apps. pp. 25. 1944

1944 *Non-Parl. Min. of Works* sgd. Dec., 1943

M. T. Eve (*Ch.*), and 57 others.

'*To observe and advise on all matters concerning the recruitment, education and training of young persons for craftsmanship and management in the building industry and to encourage the development of apprenticeship schemes on a comprehensive basis.*'

On the assumption that the building industry will require 500,000 craftsmen, up to 20,000 apprentices will be needed for normal wastage. This would give 100,000 on a basis of a 5-year apprenticeship. In the inter-war years the total number of entrants in all crafts never reached the agreed limit of the proportion of apprentices to craftsmen.

The apprenticeship agreement should be in writing and be an enforceable contract at law; there should be four parties to it—the apprentice, the guardian, the employer and one other party, i.e. a public apprenticeship body with wide powers of supervision. Since a great deal of immediate post-war work will be such that it will not increase the craft knowledge of apprentices beyond a limited stage, in selecting them, preference should be given to boys who have taken junior pre-employment education for building, and up to the age of at least 18 they should be required by their agreements to attend a technical course. The minimum period of apprenticeship should be five years beginning at the age of 15. All apprentices should be enrolled by the Council on a Register of Apprentices.

See 2nd Rep.; 1945. 3rd Rep.; 1947. 4th Rep.; 1949. Final Rep.; 1957. *Building Apprenticeship. Recruitment and Training.* Rep.; 1949. *Recruitment of Masons.* Rep.; 1949 Non-Parl.

—— Special Report, *Building. Training for Management,* apps. pp. iv, 12. 1952

1952 Non-Parl.

sgd. Feb., 1952

G. Gater (*Ch.*).

Most universities except Manchester, 'show no inclination to establish building degree courses'. On the other hand, national diploma courses at technical colleges have greatly increased since the war, and a number of general courses in foremanship have been established, but those offering training for management have not been successful. The present facilities should be given widest publicity and employers should encourage all employees to pursue technical training.

Payment by Results in Building and Civil Engineering during the War

Rep., apps. pp. 20. 1947

1947 Non-Parl. Min. of Works

Before the 1939–1945 war the Working Rule Agreement of the Civil Engineering Construction Conciliation Board provided for the payment of bonuses in addition to time rates. No general scheme of bonuses was in operation, any such payment applying to individual sites only. In the building industry there was no official system of payment by results. In 1941 the Government came to the conclusion that the building programme, on a time-rate basis, was not proceeding as rapidly as the military situation demanded, and by the Essential Work (Building and Civil Engineering) Order, introduced an obligatory system of payment by results. A bonus was paid when output exceeded a fixed target, and was additional to the hourly rates of pay. The system was not applied to 3000 agricultural cottages or to permanent housing, as this would interfere with industrial arrangements when the emergency was over, and the scheme ceased in March 1945. The Report gives details of the application of the scheme to many different operations, and its effect on output, cost, quality and earnings. The average output was 34 per cent above the basic output.

See *Payment by Results.* Memo. 3rd ed. *Notes for Guidance on the Application of the System;* 1944 Non-Parl. Min. of Works.

Coal Mining

See *Coal, Fuel and Power.*

Cotton Spinning Industry

Com. Rep., apps. pp. 51. 1945

1945 Non-Parl. Min. of Labour and N.S.

apptd. Aug., sgd. Oct., 1945

R. Evershed (*Ch.*), Barnes, Butterworth, Gregson, Knowles, Lindley, Littlewood, Quill, Robertson, Roberts (A.), Roberts (W.), Schofield, Whitworth.

'*To review wages arrangements and methods of organisation of work in the cotton spinning industry, and to make recommendations.*'

If the cotton spinning industry is to play its part in the national economy, conditions of work and the wage structure will have to be made reasonably attractive in order to recruit the necessary labour force. Once an industry has lost favour among those who are or would normally be engaged in it, attention is drawn to all its disagreeable features—heat, dust, noise and the insufficient provision of lavatories, rest rooms, changing facilities and other amenities. Where operatives have struggled for better conditions and have suffered so much unemployment there is a feeling of past injustice and future insecurity.

Amenities should conform to modern standards; the representatives of both sides of the industry should establish standards of spinning conditions, and establish rapid procedure, in event of complaint, for rectifying any failure. Where new machinery or organisation is introduced there should be joint consultation in the conduct and supervision of all necessary trials and experiments. Welfare Councils should be established with a view to promoting confidence and co-operation. For juveniles there should be uniform wage for age scales, systematic training and apprenticeship schemes. Five general principles should be applied in wage arrangements. (i) There should be one single or uniform code of wage ascertainment for each section of the industry. (ii) All percentage bonus or flat rate additions should be absorbed into a '1945 wage rate'. (iii) Time rates of so much per hour should be fixed. This should constitute the basic wage for piece workers and an operative of average ability should expect to earn 20 per cent more. Where greater production by the operative is attributable to new methods, etc., some part of the increase should belong to the business installing the improvement and go in reduction of its costs of production. (iv) The industry should be organised on the basis of providing an increase in opportunities for adult male labour, save where by reason of lightness, etc., the operations are particularly adapted to female or child labour. (v) Skilled workers should be relieved of all un-skilled work, which should be done by ancillary labour. There are many recommendations on the details of work, status, pay, etc., of operatives on different processes. The Commission criticises (para. 77) the mule spinning lists as complex and inequitable, and recommends the drawing up of a single list.

In a note Butterworth and Lindley feared that a scaling-up of wage rates might put mule spinners above the wage levels payable to skilled workers in other industries, and endanger the competitive power of the coarse and medium spinning mills as against ring spinning. App. IV (pp. 2), 1946 Non-Parl. was published separately.

—— *Supplement, Mule-Spinners' Wages.* Rep. by the Chairman, app. pp. 20. 1946

1946 Non-Parl.

Following the main Report, agreement was reached upon wage-scales, except those for mule spinners. The six lists in operation, the Ashton, Hyde, Preston, Blackburn, Bolton and Oldham lists (the two latter covering 80–90 per cent of the mule operatives) embody different principles of computation and yield different earnings for the same kind of work carried on under different conditions. The weighted average level of wages in Bolton is about 10s. 6d. above Oldham, and the share of absentee's wages of 16s. 0d. is about the same in both—but when the length of mule is taken into consideration the differences in wage levels are nearer 20s. A fair figure for the general wage level should be based on mule lengths of 1051–1100 and derived from the Bolton figures, and with adjustments for compensation for share of absentees' wages and slow running would £7 0s. 0d. The time rate minimum should be £5 12s. 0d. so that the average worker would earn 25 per cent more. Figures are given for other mule lengths. This would mean some sacrifice from those operatives whose wages are relatively high, but the anomalies of the unjustifiably low rates paid to other mule gate operatives would be removed in the general scheme of wage revisions.

The Appendix gives the results of the Census of Mule Spinners' Earnings.

Cotton Manufacturing Industry

Com. Interim Rep., apps. pp. 63. 1948

1948 *Non-Parl. Min. of Labour and N.S. apptd. Nov.*, 1946. *sgd. Feb.*, 1948

R. M. Hughes (*Ch.*), Bell, Brown, Clegg, Cockcroft, Earnshaw, Fielding, Hepworth, Leadbetter, Lee, Naesmith, Pennington, Proctor.

'To review the wages arrangements and methods of organisation of work in the cotton manufacturing industry.'

The enquiry was set up to implement recommendation 19 of the Working Party on *Cotton*, 1946, and extended to all occupations which were regarded as part of the cotton manufacturing industry. Winding and beaming common to weaving and spinning were included because the majority of the operatives concerned were in the weavers' trade union. There were 119,000 people concerned; 13 per cent prepare the yarn for the loom, 70 per cent weave, including overlooking, 10 per cent are in inspection and warehousing and 7 per cent are in administrative and other occupations. As the need for a greater output is urgent, attention was given first to methods of work and payment of weavers on non-automatic looms, where the present methods hamper all attempts to increase production and where in its search for alternative methods the industry has reached an impasse.

The Uniform List of Prices, which forms the basis for the existing wage calculation, originated in 1892 and was based on the number of picks (the number of threads the shuttle throws across the warp) to a piece of cloth of a given size and fineness. Compensation for extra time and skill for deviations from the standard are set out in 83 clauses in the List, many lengthy and complicated. But the variations in the time and effort required by the weaver in dealing with the breaks (which depend on the various qualities of yarn), or with the extra shuttles required where lengths of yarn are short, are not covered. The List is thus fundamentally unsound, because it ignores the two factors which chiefly determine the effort required from the weaver. The weaving wage cost per unit remains the same, however efficient or inefficient may be the methods of production in the shed. The List provides little reward for efficient management and inadequate penalties for inefficient management.

The first need was for 're-deployment', that is for reorganisation of methods of work and payment, in order to secure the best use of skill, to create incentive and to make effective use of equipment. The weaver should be relieved of sweeping, cleaning, oiling, carrying and should have emergency help for 'smashes'; wages should be related to effort by a measurement of a weaver's work load; 'four looms per weaver' is traditional, leads to under-employment, and should be abandoned. The wages system must offer a special increment which increases with the number of looms per weaver. There must be proper work load measurement. Equipment should be improved by the introduction of the automatic shuttle and the use of the pick counter, which is the only accurate method of calculating a weaver's output and the efficiency of the loom. Various possible systems of payment are examined in detail. Wages should be based on the work of the weaver, which includes weft work, warp work, and rest, supervision and ancillary duties. Weft work can be fairly computed in terms of shuttle changes, warp work in terms of repair of warp breaks, and these can be related to the speed of the loom and the number of picks, and the time taken for the various processes. The Commission suggested a basic minimum wage and a piece-work rate on this basis (see the Appendix) which would have the effect of bettering the standards of the lower paid weavers and allowed for greater increases where weavers worked more looms. The overall effect would be to measure efficiency and to pay wages for effort made; the wages system and redeployment recommended should make it possible to increase production by 20 per cent on the same labour force. The new system should be tried over a large volunteer field of the industry.

—— Final Report, apps. Pt. I. pp. 24. 1949

1949 *Non-Parl.*
sgd. March, 1949

add Wright, del. Bell.

As the employers and workers had not agreed to apply the scheme even in a limited field, the Commission conducted a 'notional trial'. Information was collected from a number of firms willing to participate as to what earnings would have been if the new wage calculations had been used. This experiment was limited by the fact that the firms were not fully representative, and that it was based on static conditions, without the redeployment and free play of incentive which are essential. As foreseen, in these conditions the new system led to substantial increases in earnings of some, and decreases in the earnings of other weavers. Where there is also redeployment the majority of weavers will earn substantially more. A large percentage of weavers were under-occupied, especially the rayon weavers. To weave rayon cloths on four looms was antiquated and uneconomical. 'This under-employment of rayon weavers is almost as ludicrous as large-scale unemployment would be.'

—— Final Report, apps. Pts. II, III, IV. pp. 87. 1949

1949 *Non-Parl.*
sgd. June, 1949

Pt. II. A loom overlooker is an expert weaver who sets and adjusts loom mechanism, brings the new warp, lifts it into the back of the loom and 'gaits it up' for weaving to continue, as well as giving advice and assistance to the weavers on his set of looms. He is usually paid either a 50 per cent starting wage and 50 per cent poundage, the poundage being based on the earnings of all the weavers in each overlooker's section, or the fixed standing wage which is negotiated in each shed separately and is the form favoured by the Association of Loom Overlookers. This has gained acceptance because of the shortage of overlookers. He should be given an incentive to go all out for greater efficiency. Where the Commission's system of payment for weavers is operating, overlookers should be paid a base wage and a bonus calculated on the difference between starting efficiency and the running efficiency of his set of looms; they should be relieved of any duties which can be performed by unskilled and semi-skilled operatives and redeployed accordingly.

As automatic weaving is still in process of developing its technique, firms must be free to develop systems of payment best suited to methods of work, but the principles of reward in proportion to skill and effort as measured by a scientific assessment of work applies in the same way as to the ordinary weaver. There should be a minimum time rate irrespective of output, plus a negotiated target wage, piece rates being fixed to give a competent weaver not less than the target.

Pt. III applies the principles of the Interim Report to the weaving of canvas and duck cloths, hard waste, quilt, etc., and also to tape sizing, twisting and drawing, etc.

Pt. IV. Juvenile recruitment to the industry is affected by the raising of the school leaving age, the diminished flow of school leavers because of the lower birth rate, the part-time educational schemes for the 15 to 18 age group and the competition for school leavers from other industries. Only 20 per cent of the school leavers in the 13 weaving towns enter this industry in spite of the fact that it is desperately short of boy entrants. Although it offers prospects of good jobs, it fails to offer adequate training for and promotion to them. The present inadequate system of possible apprenticeship at 19 should be replaced by a properly organised and progressive scheme of apprenticeship commencing at school leaving age.

If manufacturers used the most efficient methods of doing work including, where necessary, the introduction of modern equipment, and the wage structure was related to each unit of output, the increase in productivity per man hour would go beyond any targets which have so far been suggested.

The Appendix contains a report on the cotton industry in Sweden, Switzerland and Holland. In Sweden trade unions assist in the application of wages according to work loads arrived at by time study methods, encourage the introduction of modern machinery, but protect the 'fair share' of the workers arising from increased production.

Industrial Conditions in the Cutlery Trade

Cutlery Wages Council. Rep., apps. pp. 19. 1946

1946 Non-Parl. Min. of Labour and N.S.

A. N. Shimmin (Ch.).

'That the Trade Board' (now the Wages Council) 'should enquire and report upon "the poor-environmental conditions under which a good deal of the work in the trade is carried on." '

The investigation was made at the request of the Ministry of Labour who thought that the poor conditions had arisen both from the nature of the processes and the type of premises used, particularly by small contractors. The work of grinding and sand buffing in the shops are still very dirty processes, depending for improvement on the degree of reorganisation and mechanisation which it is possible to introduce. The sanitary, etc., provisions of the Factory Act, 1937, could be imple-

mented only under schemes of rebuilding. The possibility might be considered of accommodating small occupiers in groups of workshops with common facilities, under a scheme of rebuilding in conjunction with Sheffield Corporation.

The Cutlery industry is carried on in three types of factories (1) where the firm occupies the whole premises, (2) the tenement factory with a common source of power, (3) the tenement factory with tenants providing their own source of power. There is a tendency for (2) to be transformed into (3) and this transfers the responsibility for the Factory Acts from the owner of the building to the tenants. Of the 313 factories, only 36 were completely satisfactory, and 44 should be demolished immediately.

The preponderance of the small establishments unable to provide reasonable standards constitutes the central problem, but there is no legislative power to deal with a 'slum' factory as the 'slum' dwelling-house is dealt with; and there would be the problem of alternative accommodation, which in turn would be affected by Sheffield's replanning and development schemes. Firms should not be rehoused on a preferential or subsidised basis, but should pay economic rents. Small masters should provide satisfactory accommodation themselves or they should pool their resources to provide for the purpose.

The local authority and the Factory Department should have powers to declare and demolish factories unfit for human habitation; the Factories Act, 1937, should be applied in full; there should be special regulations for the provision of amenities for health and welfare; both sides of the industry should discuss replanning, the provision of a Trading Estate, etc., with the Corporation and minimum standards should be required of newcomers to the industry.

Supply of Crews for Trawlers

Cttee. Rep.

U

Unpublished
apptd. Nov., 1942. pres. March, 1943

A. Gray (*Ch.*), Twomey, Thomson.

'*To enquire into the supply of crews for trawlers, the methods of their engagement, and the terms of their employment. . . .*'

Report not published, but communicated to owner's associations and men's unions. It recommended that there should be a special register of trawler hands, with a central corporation to finance local schemes, a reserve pool of men, and joint machinery for regulating wages and conditions. For summary see *Fisheries in War Time*, pp. 51–52; 1946 Non-Parl. Min. of Agric. & Fish.

Seamen's Welfare in Ports

Cttee. Rep., apps. pp. 52. 1945
1945 *Non-Parl. Min. of Labour & N.S.*
apptd. Nov., 1943. sgd. Nov., 1944

H. G. White (*Ch.*), Booth, Hickson, Jarman, Snedden, Tennant, Witty.

'*Having regard to the Government's acceptance of the Recommendation of the International Labour Conference concerning the promotion of seamen's welfare in ports, to consider the activities and functions respectively of the Government, the Shipping Industry and the Voluntary Organisations in the establishment and maintenance of hotels, hostels, clubs, recreational facilities and other amenities for Merchant Seamen in ports in Great Britain. . . .*'

The total number of seamen employed in sea-going vessels registered in the United Kingdom at one time and another during 1938 was over 190,000. Of these 140,000 were of United Kingdom origin, 45,000 Indian, Chinese and Colonial; 25,000 were on leave or temporarily out of employment, etc. Before 1939 the majority of seamen signed on for one voyage, and were paid off at the end of the return voyage. Their length of stay ashore depended on their own inclination or the employment available. But under the Essential Work Order, the Merchant Navy Reserve Pool system was set up and British seamen discharged on arrival in the United Kingdom entered the Pool, after taking the leave they had earned, and remained on Pool pay until allocated to a ship.

Before 1940 seamen's welfare was carried on by voluntary societies. An important stage in co-ordination of effort was reached in 1938, when the Government adopted Recommendation No. 48 (given in App. II) of the International Labour Conference. In the summer of 1940 France and the Low Countries were over-run by the Germans, and as a result additional welfare facilities were needed in the ports to deal with the increased numbers of seamen, ship-wrecked survivors, and foreign seamen whose homeland was in control of the enemy. A Seamen's Welfare Board, composed of representatives of the industry, the Government and voluntary societies, was set up to advise on the co-ordination and finance of welfare work. Port Welfare Committees were established and Seamen's Welfare Officers appointed by the Ministry of Labour. This co-ordination resulted in rising standards of accommodation and recreation, while the Ministry of Labour and National Service established new types of residential clubs (Merchant Navy Houses) and of non-residential clubs (Merchant Navy Clubs) revolutionary in design and outlook, including bedrooms, facilities for admitting wives and women friends, licensed and dining facilities, etc. The cost to the Exchequer of the clubs was £273,000, apart from some additional provision made by the Ministry of Transport and the Colonial Office, while the expenditure of voluntary societies rose from £285,000 in 1938 to an average of £700,000 during the four war years. There is some redundancy and overlapping between voluntary societies and there have been cases of extravagance, in some instances funds having been collected in excess of the requirements for which the appeals were made.

Largely in line with evidence given by the National Maritime Board, the

Committee concluded that a statutory Merchant Navy Board, representative of shipowners and seafarers, should take over the co-ordination, provision and management of the residential and non-residential clubs, prescribe standards of accommodation, facilities and prices for all clubs, including those run by voluntary organisations, and close redundant or unsatisfactory hostels, clubs, etc. The expenses of the Board should be met by a levy of not more than 6d. per week per head shared equally between employers and seafarers, and Port or Regional Welfare Committees, Welfare Officers, and a Joint Advisory Council including representatives of voluntary organisations appointed. Voluntary organisations should be required to register with the Merchant Navy Board, and prohibited from making public appeals for money without its approval.

See *Welfare Work outside the Factory and Seamen's Welfare in Port*, p. 269.

Port Transport Industry

Cttee. Rep. pp. 5. 1945

1945 *Non-Parl. Min. of Labour & N.S. apptd. Nov., sgd. Dec.*, 1945

R. Evershed (*Ch.*), Hepworth, Little, Macdonald, Rees.

'*To consider, in the light of the circumstances, and on the basis of the proposals contained in the Schedule hereto, the outstanding difference in regard to the national minimum wage and the piece-workers' minimum guarantee in the Port Transport Industry, and to make recommendations, including a recommendation as to the date from which any increase shall operate.*'

The trade unions claimed an increase of the national minimum wage from 16s. to 25s., which should be on a daily instead of a half daily basis. For the unions Mr. Deakin and Mr. Donovan said that as the 74,000 dockers registered in the Dock Labour Schemes could not expect more than four days' full-time employment a week, the daily minimum asked for was not excessive. The employers (i) were willing to make

an offer on the condition that both sides undertook to expedite the preparation of permanent decasualisation schemes, and if no agreement were reached, to report to the Minister for him to prepare one; (ii) said that the claim affected only one-tenth of their workers, that the casual character of the industry had already been modified, and that high piece-work earnings were encouraged, etc., and that under-employment in the past was due to the excessive numbers of men available.

The labour force required to be available at the docks must be such that men cannot expect full employment every day, and the minimum wage is the basis of the entire wage structure of the industry. On the assumption that existing schemes of registration and payments for attending for any turn when no work was available continued, the national minimum should be 19s. per day, on a half daily basis, and piece workers should receive the same minimum guarantee.

Port Transport Industry

Inquiry held under para. 1 (4) of the Schedule to the Dock Workers (Regulation of Employment) Act, 1946.

Rep. pp. 16. 1946

1946 *Non-Parl. Min. of Labour & N.S. apptd. Sept., sgd. Nov.*, 1946

J. Forster.

The enquiry was held because the National Joint Council had failed to agree on a scheme for decasualisation. Voluntary registration schemes, which began in Liverpool in 1912 had a varied history and despite the efforts of the MacLean Committees, progress was slow (see Min. of Labour Gazette, April 1924, p. 119, and July 1924, pp. 236–7, and *Port Labour*, Non-Parl. 1931). Between 1931 and 1939 the National Standing Advisory Committee revived old and established new Joint Registration schemes in all the principal ports, except Aberdeen and Glasgow. The employers' obligations were limited to giving priority to registered men, the workers' obligations to attending for normal calls; there was no guaranteed wage and in each port the size of the register was controlled by a joint committee. The exigencies of war led to compulsory registration in 1940, and in 1941 to the Ministry of War Transport decasualisation schemes in Clyde and Merseyside ports, and in other ports to Ministry of Labour schemes administered by the National Dock Labour Corporation. These schemes included a guaranteed weekly wage financed by a levy on port employers based on dockers' earnings, dockers being required to attend all normal and other calls and to be liable to transfer to other suitable work in the port or to other ports. The Dock Workers (Regulation of Employment) Act, 1946, provided for the temporary continuance of these schemes and for the preparation of permanent ones.

The employers proposed that each port authority should, within a national framework of conditions, determine the size of the register, and by a levy on wages and/or on goods, provide the funds for a guaranteed minimum wage, common arrangements being made to assist any authority unable to carry out its obligations. They opposed joint administration, as schemes had broken down in practice because the workers' side had opposed the removal of names of any workers on the register before 1939, and there was therefore no agreement on maintaining a labour force sufficient, but no more than sufficient, to meet the needs of the industry. The guaranteed rate should be a minimum fall back rate against which would be set all wages earned.

The workers' side proposed a national joint body charged with the duty of determining, on a national basis, the size of the dock labour force, and the levy on wages to meet decasualisation costs. With regard to the guarantee, they proposed payment of attendance money in respect of each normal turn when work was not available, and an overriding weekly guaranteed wage less than the equivalent of 11 turns, at the ordinary time rate, but considerably higher than what was at present being paid; only attendance money and wages paid in respect of work performed during the 11 turns should count against the weekly guarantee. This claim bore some similarity to the scheme in operation.

There should be a national joint body, such as the National Dock Labour Corporation, working through local (or area) boards. The local boards should keep port registers, the determination of the size of the register being vested in the central body in consultation with the local boards. The rapid reduction of the register, where reduction is deemed necessary by the central board, is imperative. Labour should be made mobile by provisions to transfer it to distant ports when required. The recommendations should be applied to those ports already covered by schemes. The guaranteed wage should be a weekly fall back sum, against which should be set all earnings during the week. This sum should be sufficient for minimum needs, but not high enough to be a temptation to rely upon it rather than upon actual employment. Dockers should have a right of appeal against removal from the register, but not where such removal was pursuant to a direction to reduce the register.

Port Transport Industry

Inquiry held under Para. 5 of the Schedule to the Dock Workers (Regulation of Employment) Act, 1946. Rep., apps. pp. 36. 1947

1947 Non-Parl. Min. of Labour & N.S. apptd. April, sgd. May, 1947

J. Cameron.

The objections fell into two main groups, those relating to the scope of the scheme and those directed to its structure.

Scope.—The proposal of the workers that the Minister should have power to include or exclude ports would be *ultra vires* and the proposal of both sides that the National Board should be empowered to vary the classes or descriptions of the dock work and workers at individual ports was not accepted, as there was no power for internal amendments provided by Parliament. Both sides asked for power to alter the grouping of the ports, since it was fortuitous and based on circumstances connected with the recent war. This was accepted, provided it was *intra vires*. The employers' objection to the inclusion of many small ports was rejected; since the purpose of the scheme is to group ports and to give the power to transfer labour, it was proper to regard certain small ports as units of the larger whole.

Objections were raised to the inclusion of: (*a*) certain weekly workers not engaged in dock work as usually understood. The clause should be deleted, but no definition of weekly worker which would apply to all ports was possible, and there should be local agreement and decision; (*b*) those with special, non-interchangeable skill, such as coal trimmers and riggers; but they could be called on to do dock work, flexibility of function being necessary, and they should be included; (*c*) timber trade regular workers in saw mills should be excluded, those engaged in loading or unloading cargo included; (*d*) workers in cold stores, whose work was regular, skilled, and concerned merchandise not imported as well as cargo. The Smithfield group would have been excluded but for the fact that their premises are requisitioned and used by the Ministry of Food for cargo storage.

Structure.—The Scottish Transport and General Workers' Union and the Watermen, Lightermen, Tugmen and Bargemen's Union proposed that the National Dock Labour Board should (*a*) limit recruitment under the specific condition that all men recruited to the register are members of the appropriate trade union or appropriate body representing the dock workers and (*b*) the reduction of the register should be effected only by stopping recruitment until the necessary reduction had taken place by natural wastage. This would be clumsy, slow and inefficient, and should not be given effect; and determination of issues of trade union membership has no proper place in a statutory scheme. Members of local appeal tribunals should not be members of the local board, but appointed from persons nominated by the local joint committee.

Port Transport Industry

Cttee. Rep. pp. 3. 1947

1947 *Non-Parl. Min. of Labour & N.S. apptd. May, sgd. June,* 1947

H. J. W. Hetherington (*Ch.*), Aronson, Bussey, Davies, Mathias.

'*To consider the amount and basis of calculation of a guaranteed payment under a scheme proposed to be made . . . by virtue of the provisions of the Dock Workers' (Regulation of Employment) Act,* 1946, *to be made to dock workers to whom the scheme applies who are available for work in respect of periods during which employment or full employment is not available for such dock workers. . . .*'

The employers' side proposed a guaranteed fall-back minimum weekly wage of £4. The workpeople asked that the guaranteed payment should consist of a payment of 6s. in respect of attendance at each of the 11 normal calls when the worker is not engaged, together with a weekly minimum wage of £4 16s. od. against which should count earnings in the normal working hours only, and payments in respect of Attendance Money. The three issues to be determined were: (*a*) whether or not the element of Attendance Money should be retained; (*b*) the amount of the guaranteed fall-back weekly payment; (*c*) what earnings, if any, should be set against this guarantee. Findings.—Attendance Money should be 5s. at each of the 11 normal turns; the guaranteed weekly payment should be £4 7s. 6d. against which should be set all payments and earnings except for work on Saturday afternoon.

5. REHABILITATION, RESETTLEMENT

Rehabilitation and Resettlement of Disabled Persons

Inter-Dept. Cttee. Rep., app. pp. 51. 1943

1942–43 *Cmd. 6415, vi*, 67
apptd. Dec., 1941. *sgd. Nov.*, 1942

G. Tomlinson (*Ch.*), Bannatyne, Smith, Dobbie, Frankau, Hale, Hamilton (Mrs. M. A.), Neville, Parker, Prideaux, Wiles.

'(a) *To make proposals for introduction at the earliest possible date of a scheme for the rehabilitation and training for employment of disabled persons not provided for by the Interim Scheme;* (b) *To consider and make recommendations for introduction as soon as possible after the war of a comprehensive scheme for* (i) *the rehabilitation and training of, and* (ii) *securing satisfactory employment for, disabled persons of all categories;* (c) *To consider and make recommendations as to the manner in which the scheme proposed for introduction after the war should be financed.*'

An Interim Report (10th March, 1942, unpublished) recommended that the training provisions of the interim scheme inaugurated in 1941 should be extended to all occupations likely to provide satisfactory employment during the war, that the facilities for employment under sheltered conditions available in voluntary undertakings should be brought into use with the aid of a grant, preference being given to service and civilian war casualties, and that artificial limbs should be issued free to enable persons to enter or resume work of importance to the war effort.

The only satisfactory form of resettlement for a disabled person is employment he can take and keep on his merits in competition with other workers. In a large industrial community there is such a great number of varied occupations that granted proper assessment and classification, ordinary employment is practicable for a majority of the disabled; but a minority will need sheltered employment.

Though disablement is popularly associated with visible physical injury, disablement from other causes may be more difficult to deal with because fitness is impaired and a substantial period of medical supervision may be needed, and because it is often wrongly assumed that a medical case whose handicap is not obvious is capable of returning to a pre-disablement job.

For rehabilitation in the strictly medical sense continuity of treatment is essential. The process should begin as soon as a patient's condition permits, but before restoration in the medical sense is achieved the services of the social and industrial expert are required to assist in deciding what kind of occupation is best suited to the patient's restored capacity. This means the fullest co-operation between the Departments concerned.

The scheme should be open to all disabled persons, whatever the nature or cause of disablement. Medical rehabilitation should be provided in the hospitals and at clinics; reconditioning and vocational training should be provided by the Ministry of Labour and National Service, at special centres and voluntary institutions. There should be training facilities at university and higher professional level, and the present schemes at training centres, technical colleges, etc., should be extended.

To aid resettlement, legislation should provide for the employment of a percentage quota of disabled persons in different industries, for prohibiting, in scheduled occupations, the employment without licence of non-disabled persons, and for setting up a register of disabled persons. Local committees should be set up in association with the Labour Exchanges, the King's Roll should be terminated, and those still in receipt of a disability pension should be entitled to registration under the new schemes. Other recommendations include: powers for training the blind to be obligatory; training in lip reading;

provision of hearing aids; provision to allow a person to set up in business; a follow-up service; a survey of occupations suited to particular disablements; a joint committee to supervise the scheme.

See *Rehabilitation and Resettlement of Disabled Persons*. Standing Cttee. Reps.; 1946, 1949 Non-Parl. Min. of Labour & N.S. *Training, Rehabilitation and Resettlement*. Sel. Cttee. on *Estimates*. 4th Rep., mins. of ev., etc.; 1951–52 (162) v, 381.

Employment in South Wales for Persons Suspended from the Mining Industry on Account of Silicosis and Pneumoconiosis

Working Party. Summary of the Results and Recommendations, apps. pp. 6. [1946]
1945–46 *Cmd*. 6719, xx, 205

D. R. Grenfell (*Ch.*), and 10 others.

A limited number of cases who require sheltered employment are the concern of the Disabled Persons Employment Corporation Ltd. The vast majority are capable of work in any light industry which does not involve work in dust or fumes, or heavy lifting. While these would have no difficulty in getting work if there were full employment, some of the areas most affected are remote and therefore places for which it is difficult to find new industries. New factories totalling $\frac{1}{4}$ mn. sq. ft. should be built by the Government in areas containing large numbers of disabled unemployed, occupation carrying with it the condition that a minimum of 50 per cent of those employed should be disabled persons, in return for a reduction of rent of 50 per cent.

Employment of Blind Persons

Working Party. Rep., apps. pp. iv, 72. 1951
1951 *Non-Parl. Min. of Labour & N.S. apptd. June*, 1948. *sgd. Oct.*, 1950

W. Taylor (*Ch.*), Adams (Miss W. L.), Anderson, Askew, Eagar, Smith, Webster, Wilson.

'*To investigate the facilities existing for the employment of blind persons in industry and in public and other services and to make recommendations for their development.*'

Of the 87,000 registered blind persons in Great Britain, 36,400 are between 16 to 65. Of these 11,000 are in employment or undergoing training, a further 3000 are capable of taking up employment if given the opportunity, and when the newly blind are brought into employment, the total will be nearly 17,000.

Full-time education is compulsory up to 16 and the majority receive residential training up to the age of 20. A newly-blinded person can receive home or residential rehabilitation. The training for various occupations under the Disabled Persons (Employment) Act, 1944, includes the services of a training officer who gives instruction on the employers' premises, and there is a special course in light engineering at the Government Training Centre, Letchworth. Specialist placing services organised by the local authorities and voluntary bodies, and working in conjunction with the Disablement Resettlement Service have been most successful.

Amongst the forms of employment in which the blind have proved successful are shorthand-typing, telephony, piano tuning and some factory employment; the administrative grade of the civil service, as solicitors, in the Church, teaching physiotherapy, home teaching, music, shopkeeping, poultry farming, gardening and the public services. A comprehensive specialist placing service, run by local authorities either directly or by arrangement with voluntary agencies, should be available in every area. The Committee was not happy about the opportunities for promotion, and urged employers to recognise ability.

For rehabilitating those becoming blind in adult life there should be an extension of the home teaching service, and institutional accommodation would be required for 800–1000 persons a year. As training and rehabilitation are available without delay in cases of blindness in the Services, it is less difficult to find employment for them.

Education in residential centres until the age of 21 was primarily intended to prepare young persons for sheltered employment in special workshops for the blind or home workers' schemes. If in the future they are to take advantage of the opportunities in a wide field of open employment, the necessary provision for general education, vocational guidance, basic occupational training and training in social development will involve radical alterations in content, method and the duration of training. A 'pilot' establishment should be created to study the needs of the adolescent. The provision of guide dogs has helped many people and the increased provision is welcomed, but a dog is not essential before a blind person can go to work.

See Circular 8/52; 1952 Non-Parl. Min. of Health.

Employment of Older Men and Women

National Advisory Cttee. 1st Rep., apps.
pp. 62. 1953

1952–53 *Cmd.* 8963, *xi*, 1
apptd. March, 1952. *sgd. Sept.*, 1953

H. Watkinson (*Ch.*), and 27 others.

'*To advise and assist the Minister of Labour and National Service in promoting the employment of older men and women.*'

'Older' does not mean aged, but applies to all whose employment is affected by age. The reasons for the acceptance of the policy that greater employment of older persons should be encouraged are the changing age structure of the community, the increasing length of life and the present and future man-power needs of the country. At the beginning of the century there were roughly 10 people per 100 over the minimum pensionable age, in 1953 there were 20 and in less than a genera-tion there will be 30, and by 1962 it is estimated that the men aged 18 to 40 will be fewer by some 300,000.

The economic consequences are that an increase in current production will be necessary for the maintenance of retired persons, especially as they will tend to expect a high standard of living. The changing age structure of the population must be matched by similar change in the age structure of the working population, so that the skill and experience of older people will have to be used. While there is great variation in their capacity to work, the majority of persons who give efficient service at 60 can work until 70, and the continuance in the rhythm and routine and the feeling of usefulness, may hold at bay the effect of ageing. There is no medical support for a fixed age of retirement. While the older worker may feel the strain of increased speed, in many jobs requiring accuracy, regularity and conscientiousness he may be at a positive advantage. He can also be most adaptable and trainable for a new job. The variations in the proportions of older workers in comparable industries suggests that factors other than suitability are operating. The traditional attitude of 'too old at 40' is still found, salary scales based on age have a deterrent effect, and in all fields of employment there is a tendency towards retirement at the minimum pensionable ages. There should be more opportunities for older women in such important womens' employments as retail distribution and clerical work. In professional and managerial work unemployment or early retirement means a great waste of ability and training. The test for engagement should be capacity not age, and the retirement policy recommended is that all men and women employed in industry, commerce, the professions or elsewhere who can give effective service, either in their normal work or any alternative work which their employer can make available, should be given the opportunity, without regard to age, to continue at work if they so wish.

See Circular No. 69/54; 1954 Non-Parl. Min. of Housing and Local Gov. *Employment of Older Men and Women*. National Advisory Cttee. 2nd Rep.; 1955–56 Cmd. 9628, xvii, 17. *Economic and Financial Problems of the Provision for Old Age*. Cttee. Rep. p. 303.

6. EMPLOYMENT OF WOMEN

Equal Pay

R. Com. Rep., apps. pp. xi, 220. [1946]. Mins. of ev., 15 days, apps. I–XIX. 1945–46

1945–46 *Cmd. 6937, xi, 651. Mins. of ev.,* etc.; 1945–46 *Non-Parl.* apptd. Oct., 1944. sgd. Oct., 1946

C. Asquith (*Ch.*), Limerick (Lady), Ridley, Loughlin (Dame A.), Robertson, Brown, Robinson, Vaughan (Janet), Nettlefold.

'To examine the existing relationship between the remuneration of men and women in the public services, in industry and in other fields of employment; to consider the social, economic and financial implications of the claim of equal pay for equal work; and to report.'

'Equal pay for equal work' is an ambiguous phrase, but was taken to mean 'raising the women's rate to whatever is, at the relevant time, the male level of remuneration.'

Part I. Factual.—The aim of the investigation was to determine, in those fields of employment in which both men and women were employed, the size of the 'overlap' areas in which they were employed interchangeably, how far in those areas women's work was equal to that of men, and to what extent they were paid less than men's rates.

In the non-industrial civil service 119,000 persons, 17 per cent of whom were women, were in an overlap area, and the Treasury fixed men's rates on the basis of 'fair relativity' with outside employments, combined with a rule that the women's maximum should be not less than 80 per cent that of men. In teaching the work done by men and women is 'equal', being parallel in one-sex schools and equivalent in mixed schools. 15,000 men and 35,000 women were in the area of full interchangeability and women's pay was 80 per cent that of men. In private industry and commerce comparisons were difficult because even within identically named occupations, occasions for differences between the work of the sexes were unlimited. Where work is done at time rates the strict overlap is small. Where it is at identical piece rates, men's earnings are often higher; where women's piece rates are lower than men's, they may be regulated by collective agreement and the difference be accounted for by 'supervision'; there may be some difference in the kind of work performed or the different piece rates may be fixed with reference to separate time rates for the two sexes which more than reflect the difference of productivity. Amongst shop assistants the work of men and women is indistinguishable, and there is an overlap in clerical work of a not very skilled kind; women's rates were 60 to 70 per cent and 60 to 80 per cent those of men respectively.

Part II. Implications of the claim for equal pay for equal work.—The effect of introducing equal pay for equal work into this structure would depend partly on the causes of these differences of pay. The Treasury principle that pay differences are based on fair relativity with outside occupations and the Stephen Committee's view that the differences in pay of men and women teachers were needed to secure the right numbers of each both indicate that the causes lie outside these particular occupations. While 'custom' and 'tradition' may have some force in perpetuating the differences, it does not follow that they are always without rational foundation. The general demand for women's labour is depressed (i) by legal prohibitions on their employment and hours of work; (ii) by 'natural factors' such as lower physical strength, which exclude them from some occupations (though they are often superior in finger dexterity) a greater sickness rate, and lower output in some industries; and because work is an incidental part of their career, in their shorter working life skill is not acquired to the same degree; (iii) by conventions on what are women's jobs, which give rise to restrictions, embodied in collective agreements or understandings under pressure from male employees and designed to prevent an occupation from passing into the hands of women. These factors tend to establish a general women's weekly wage rate on a lower level, but the overlap areas tend to be established at points at which the relative efficiencies of men and women are proportionate to their relative weekly wage rates as determined by supply and demand. But in certain of these the gap in rates is greater than the gap in efficiency.

The consequences of introducing equal pay in all fields of common employment.—The average woman would not be affected because she is not in an employment or her work is not work which men also do; the change would disturb the balance between those employed in and those employed outside the overlap areas. There would be beneficial effects on the happiness of women in the higher grades of teaching and the civil service where discontent is intense and it would remove from men the fear of undercutting. Raising women's standard of nutrition would favourably affect their health. Equality of income would not mean equality of standards if the liability to support others were unequal. While most married men have families to support and many women have not, they may have other dependents. On balance it would seem that equal pay would add a majority of women to the 'easy' cases and leave the married men with children relatively worse off.

Consequences of introducing equal pay into particular employments.— Equal pay in the civil service would cost £5 mn. to £10 mn. per annum, would not affect recruitment or increase the proportion of women employed, except in the administrative grades, or discourage the recruitment of men unless the common rates fell below those paid outside to men of the quality required. In the teaching profession it would cost £16½ mn. Equal pay would encourage more women of better quality to enter teaching but might, if the authorities were unwilling to raise the common rate to a level to compete with relevant outside men's employment, discourage the recruitment of men. In private industry and commerce the effect would depend on how broadly the principle was applied. If broadly, the British Employers' Federation, the Atkin Committee and some economists, such as Cannan, argue that men would tend to be replaced by women, while the T.U.C. stated that unions would dispense with the demarcation of men's and women's work only if the threat of undercutting were removed. But the policy of full employment has intensified the demand for women's labour and removed some of the possible adverse consequences of a higher wage for it; it should diminish men's resistance to the extension of women's work, though it would not entirely remove their fear of unemployment and displacement. If equal piece rates were instituted in overlap areas where men and women are differently paid for identical work, either men or women might be displaced according to circumstances. There is some danger that a more detailed grading of jobs and payment of equal rates irrespective of sex might lead to a segregation of women in the lower paid jobs. The alternative to a policy of equal pay is not necessarily the absence of a policy regarding the status and wages of women. A high level of employment has done much to break down the resistances to the extension of women's work and valuable results can be obtained by State intervention and organised collective bargaining.

It has been argued that the Treasury's principle of fair relativity stands in the way of its giving a lead to industry in adopting equal pay. But while in the field of public services equal pay might increase the opportunities for the employment of women and raise their wages, if extended to the very different field of private industry it might do the reverse, though it might give an upward pull to the wages of women in comparable private employment.

In a Memo. of dissent Dame A. Loughlin, Dr. J. Vaughan and Miss Nettlefold stated that 'to account for the lower wages of women in terms of supply and demand, it is not sufficient to show that there are more jobs to which men are better suited than women, than jobs to which women are better suited. It is necessary to show that there are more than three times as many jobs to which men are better suited than women.' Lower efficiency, used in its widest sense was not proven by evidence. 'The main cause of the low earnings of women is their exclusion from a number of trades in which they would be efficient workers (given opportunity and training) combined with weak trade union organisation.' The enforcement of an equal rate for the job for both sexes would lead to some reshuffling between jobs so that distribution between them was more suited to individual efficiency and would increase productivity.

There are Memos. by the Treasury, Apps. I and II, and by a number of economists (Apps. IX and X); T.U.C. evidence, 13th Day.

Domestic Help

Cttee. Rep. pp. 9. 1943

1942–43 *Cmd. 6481, iv,* 271
apptd. July, sgd. Oct., 1943

H. J. W. Hetherington (*Ch.*), Darbyshire, Elliott (Miss D.).

'*To make recommendations as to minimum rates of wages and conditions of employment which should be recognised for the purpose of any special arrangements which may be instituted for meeting the needs of hospitals, establishments for the care of young children and of sick, aged or disabled persons, the school meals service and similar organisations, for domestic help.*'

The immediate concern of the Minister was the supply of female domestic labour to hospitals and allied services and to the school meal service. It was possible to select certain basic classes of work common to hospitals and institutions and to classify female domestic workers into five categories: cooks, assistant cooks, special maids (matrons' and doctors' maids, senior house maids, etc.), general maids (wardmaids, kitchenmaids, etc.), cleaners. Emoluments (board, residence, etc.) should be assessed at £70. Domestic service for school meals is not analogous to domestic service in hospitals and should be treated separately. The replacement of the 13 wage agreements by more uniform arrangements covering the whole country should be considered. For mental institutions and local authorities' hospitals existing agreements should be recognised. For other hospitals, the Committee rejected both differential rates based on size and zoning, and recommended minimum cash wages of £100 p.a. for resident and £3 5s. od. a week for non-resident cooks, with proportionate rates for other grades. The basic wage should be for 96 hours per fortnight.

See *Min. of Labour & National Service.* Rep., 1939–46. p. 96; 1946–47 Cmd. 7225, xii, 439.

Post-War Organisation of Private Domestic Employment

Rep., apps. pp. 26. 1945

1944–45 *Cmd.* 6650, *v,* 1
sgd. July, 1944

Markham (Miss V.), Hancock (Miss F.).

'*To review the various schemes for the post-war organisation of private domestic employment which had been received by the Ministry of Labour and National Service and to make recommendations as to future plans after consultation with appropriate individuals and associations.*'

The war of 1939–45 and the over-riding claims of war industry swept away the whole structure of domestic service and there is now widespread distress and agitation due to the absence of household help.   Before the war domestic service was increasingly un-popular: it was unregulated, there was an immense variety of conditions of work and in no other work did so much depend on a personal relationship. Further, it came to be regarded as inferior, and the freedom after the factory and shop had closed came to be valued more than the comforts of a good domestic situation.   Improved status and better organisation must go hand in hand.   Conditions of employ-ment are very much the same as when the Wood Committee reported in 1923 on the *Supply of Female Domestic Servants*. The recommendations then made re-garding status and training are still relevant, but little progress has been made because no organisation was created to give effect to them.

A National Institute of House-workers should be established to supply to approved households competent domestic workers either trained in local centres by the Institute or of whose efficiency it was satisfied, and to make regulations for minimum wage rates and conditions to which the employers must conform.   Resident and part-time daily workers should be employees of the individual household, 'supply workers' going to more than one household the employees of the Insti-tute.   The minimum period of employ-ment should be four hours and workers should undertake to be available for not less than 24 hours a week.   An indepen-dent committee should settle standard wages and conditions.   All other work, except training, should be self-support-ing.   Recommendations concerned cer-tificates, advanced specialised training, training for housewives, etc.   It should be the duty of local authorities to extend Home Help schemes and to recruit trained workers for them, and also to supervise registry offices.

See Min. of Labour and National

Service Ann. Reps. for accounts of the National Institute of Houseworkers set up in 1946, and *Civil Appropriation Accounts*. p. 259; 1948–49 (319) xxviii, 1, for the grant to the Institute of £300,000.

7. JUVENILES

Recruitment of Juveniles in the Coal Mining Industry
Reps.

1942, 1943 *Non-Parl.* See *Coal*, p. 174.

Apprenticeship for Coal Face Workers
Rep.

1947 *Non-Parl.* See *Coal*, p. 175.

Juvenile Employment Service
Cttee. Rep., apps. pp. 63. 1945

1945 *Non-Parl. Min. of Labour & N.S. apptd. Jan., sgd. Sept.*, 1945

G. H. Ince (*Ch.*), Aitken, Arbuckle, Baylay, Bray, Chester, Elger, Frizell, Hancock (Miss F.), Innes, Kay, Malone, McIntosh, Marchand, Taylor, Williams, Woodhead.

'*To consider the measures necessary to establish a comprehensive Juvenile Employ-ment Service on the basis of the Memorandum circulated with the Minister of Labour's/ Secretary of State's letter of 20th/24th October, 1944, and to make suggestions for a practicable scheme.*'

The juvenile employment system, administered in some parts of the country by the Ministry of Labour and in others by the local education authori-ties, lacks the degree of co-ordination necessary for the national and compre-hensive service required for a policy of maintaining full employment and in-dustrial efficiency.   The Memorandum suggested that a date should be fixed by which education authorities should declare whether they wish to exercise or continue to exercise powers, under Section 81 of the Unemployment

Insurance Act, 1935; that the new service would be administered by a joint service of the Ministry of Labour and Ministry of Education and the Secretary of State for Scotland, but the Ministry of Labour would continue to be responsible to Parliament, and the cost would continue to be borne on its Vote. Centrally the service would be administered by a Juvenile Employment Service staffed from the three Departments, while the local machinery would be as at present.

There was unanimity on the Committee that a dual system could never be wholly satisfactory and that the work throughout the country should be done by one organisation, but no agreement could be reached as to which Department should do it (paras. 140–143). The recommendations therefore assumed the continuance of the two systems in the local areas, but a central executive staffed from all three departments must be able to give instructions to both and should be responsible to the Ministry of Labour.

The weaknesses of the present scheme are that no juvenile has had to make use of it; many employers fail to take advantage of it, and the service does not have full knowledge of vacancies, etc. Uncertainty as to which authority will operate the scheme leads to a lack of long-term thinking and a lack of the continuity needed for getting results. Every pupil should be given vocational guidance before leaving school, and every school should be required by statute to register every school-leaver with the Service, which should be able to require the attendance, for interview with a specially trained officer, of any person so registered. The school should pass over to the Service some form of school record, which should be treated as a highly confidential document. Research should be carried out on job-analysis so that the Service had detailed information about various occupations and the methods of training. A central clearing-house system should be maintained at the highest possible level of efficiency. Information about industry

and the professions should be part of normal teaching in schools and pamphlets giving preliminary information should be given to boys and girls. Jobs should be reviewed regularly and those found unfit for juveniles should be prohibited. It was not found desirable to recommend the institution of any system of compulsory control of engagements for juveniles.

See *Recruitment and Training for the Youth Employment Service.* Cttee. Rep.; 1951 Non-Parl. Min. of Labour & N.S. See also Reps. of National, London and regional Youth Employment Councils; 1933–1954 Non-Parl. *Juvenile Employment.* Enquiry (L. Chelmsford, *Ch.*). Rep.; 1922 Non-Parl. *Breviate 1917–39.* pp. 342, 343.

Hours of Employment of Juveniles.
Rep. Pt. II.

1948–49 *Cmd.* 7664. See p. 278.

Employment of Children as Film Actors, in Theatrical Work and in Ballet

Dept. Cttee. Rep., apps., index. pp. v, 119. 1950

1950 *Cmd.* 8005, *vii*, 43
apptd. May, 1948. sgd. June, 1950

D. L. Bateson (*Ch.*), Havelock-Allan, Casson, Frizell, Lilliman, Manvell, Sharpe (Bertha E. A.), Wainwright (Mrs. E. E.).

'*To consider under what safeguards as to health, welfare and education the employment of children as film actors could properly be allowed, and to review the existing provisions governing the employment of children in theatrical work and in ballet.*'

Legislation for the protection of children appearing in entertainments (chiefly in the theatre) has been mainly concerned with regulating the minimum age, hours of work, conditions of employment and school attendance or other education, by a system of licensing, but the law makes no special provision for children employed as film actors, in broadcasting or on television, or for those children who work in more than one branch of entertainment. Some simple administrative system is required which would apply to all types of entertainment. In 1945–48 5753 children were licensed to do theatrical work, less than 8 per cent having individual parts, the rest performing in troupes. In the evidence little reference was made to the function of the child on the stage, and it was necessary to ask why employment of children in the theatre should be isolated from the whole field of children's employment, especially as it had been accepted, in principle, that the period of general education should continue until a child is 16 years of age. In other occupations child labour is used as a substitute for adult labour. 'Troupe work' in the theatre which does not require a child to portray a child's part is analogous to ordinary employment and there is no reason why the age should be lower than for other employment. On the other hand there are a number of plays which cannot be presented at all without a child, or in which the substitution of an older person precludes a satisfactory presentation. The local authority should be able, subject to suitable safeguards, to license a child of any age in a play where artistic presentation requires it. The justification for the employment of children in films is said to be that they are needed in the representation of the normal family, in documentaries and for films for children's film shows. The effect on the child taking part in a film unsuitable for children was not thought dangerous as the child takes part in separate shots and does not know the whole sequences, but even where he does, illusion is destroyed, as he talks and laughs with the other actors, and sees the mechanics of film technique in operation. There was general agreement that no child under 15 or 16 years of age should become a regular member of a ballet company, and no special opportunities beyond those allowed for the theatre was necessary. Neither the employment

provisions, nor those relating to appearances in entertainments apply to broadcasting and television provided the child is not under 12 and the public is not admitted; they should be brought under the safeguards of a licensing system.

Safeguards for the welfare of children employed in entertainments should be uniform throughout the whole field, and there should be a system of licensing of all children under 16 for particular engagements and for limited periods. Leave of absence from school should not be permitted unless a teacher is provided. Performances in the theatre should be limited to four, or during holidays eight a week or eight per week where there is a teacher, or work on films to five days a week. The total amount of work should be limited to 40 days per year, not more than 20 of which might be for television. Health and welfare should be under the supervision of the School Medical Officer and a matron. Local education authorities should be responsible for licensing children between the ages of 13–16, the central authority for licensing those under 13 years of age, children coming from or going abroad and those taking part in television. Local authorities should see that licences are enforced and the central authority should have rights of entry and inspection.

8.　FACTORY REGULATION: SAFETY, HEALTH, HOURS OF WORK

Lighting in Factories

Dept. Cttee.　5th Rep., apps. pp. 14.
1940

1940 *Non-Parl. Min. of Labour & N.S.*
D. R. Wilson (*Ch.*), Baylay, Dow, Hancock, Parsons, Scholes, Thomson, Walsh, Weston.

'*To review, in the light of existing knowledge and practice, the recommendations made in the Reports presented in* 1915, 1921 *and* 1922 *by the Departmental Committee on Lighting in Factories and Workshops as to the conditions necessary to secure adequate and suitable illumination in such works . . . and to advise as to standards of sufficient and suitable lighting proper to be prescribed by regulations under Section 5 (2) of the Factories Act, 1937.'*

The improvised and permanent methods of black-out used as a result of the Lighting (Restriction) Order led to the reduction of natural light and difficulties of ventilation, while the prevalence of night work and overtime increased the proportion of the yearly hours of employment spent in artificial light from 10–15 per cent to 50 per cent or more. Such conditions justify a higher standard of lighting than previously recommended. In interior work-places illumination should be raised from 1 foot-candle at floor level to 6 foot-candles at 3 feet above floor level. Other recommendations include the use of light colour in interior walls, partitions, etc., prevention of glare, avoidance of shadow, and the use of natural light even in small quantities, etc. As there may be a shortage of equipment, the new standard must not be pressed in factories not engaged in work of primary importance, provided the old standards were complied with.

For Reports 1–4 see *Breviate 1917–1939.* pp. 312–313.

Welfare Work outside the Factory and Seamen's Welfare in Port

Memo., apps. pp. 15. 1941. [Memo.], app. pp. 12. 1942

1940–41 *Cmd.* 6310, *vii*, 371. 1942–43 *Cmd.* 6411, *xi*, 421

In June 1940 to develop welfare facilities for war workers outside the factories, the Ministry of Labour set up a department comprising the Factory Department and Inspectorate, transferred from the Home Office, and a new Welfare Department. A board was appointed to advise the Minister and also a Central Consultative Committee of Voluntary Organisations. The department was responsible for the work arising from the transfer of thousands of workers from their homes to the centres of war production, including problems of accommodation, transport, feeding, freeing mothers for war work, shopping, care of children, recreation, etc. The Seamen's Welfare Board was appointed in 1940 and was concerned with safety provision at certain docks, additional hostel accommodation, etc.

See *Seamen's Welfare in Ports.* p. 256. *Factories.* Chief Inspector. Ann. Rep. Chap. I; 1940–41 Cmd. 6316, *iv*, 331.

Conditions of Work in the Cotton Industry

Jt. Advisory Cttee.
Non-Parl. Min. of Labour & N.S. apptd. Nov., 1944

G. P. Barnett (*Ch.*), T. P. Threlkeld (*Ch.*), and other members representing the industry.

'To consider post-war plans for improving the conditions of work in both cotton spinning mills and weaving sheds' and 'to consider and advise on practical methods of implementing the Factories Act, 1937.'

The Committee set up four sub-committees, whose reports were issued separately.

Mule Spinners' Cancer and Automatic Wiping-down Motions. Interim Rep.; 1945. *Mule Spinners' Cancer.* 2nd Interim Rep.; 1952. (1) *Sanitary Accommodation, Washing Facilities, Accommodation for Clothing, Medical and Welfare Services, Decoration and Vacuum Cleaning.* (2) *Dust in Card Rooms.* Interim Reps.; 1946. *Dust in Card Rooms.* 2nd, 3rd, 4th Interim Reps.; 1952, 1957, 1960. *Ventilation, Temperature, Use of Steam in Humidification, and Lighting.* Interim Rep.; 1947. *Spacing of Machinery, Cotton Weaving.* 1st Rep.; 1947.

Amongst the conclusions and recommendations were: the most certain methods of preventing the onset of spinner's cancer are to use only non-cancer-producing oil for lubrication, i.e. 'technical white' oils; all mule spinners should be examined periodically; taking meals at workplaces should be prohibited. No mill was equipped to provide an answer to card room dust; to prevent excesses of temperature and humidity modern air conditioning plant should be installed and minimum temperatures raised.

See *Cotton Weaving Factories. Fencing of Machinery, First Aid and other Safeguards.* Agreement; 1949 Non-Parl. Min. of Labour & N.S.

Jute Industry

Factory Advisory Cttee. Final Rep., apps. pp. 55. 1946. (Interim Rep. App. B.)

1946 *Non-Parl. Min. of Labour & N.S. apptd. Nov., 1944. sgd. May, 1946*

F. W. Hunt (*Ch.*), Anderson, Chrystal, Ferguson, Laird, Lindsay, Lyon, Mac-Beth, Spence (Miss J.), Valentine.

'*To enquire into and report on the most effective methods of implementing certain requirements of the Factories Act, 1937, in the Jute Industry, and other cognate problems. . . .*'

As a result of representations to jute manufacturers in September 1944, by Sir Wilfrid Garrett, then Chief Inspector of Factories, a Joint Advisory Committee was set up. As a number of firms were initiating plans for extensive re-equipment and modernisation, prior attention was given to the spacing of machinery so as to lessen the risks of fire and accidents and avoid fatigue due to the unnecessary manhandling of materials, etc. The recommendations for new and for existing factories are set out in the Interim Rep., printed as App. B (p. 49). Recommendations are made in the Final Report on each problem set out in the terms of reference; those on cleanliness of factories, medical supervision, personnel management, seats for workers for operations which can be done sitting, and the training of new entrants were left to voluntary effort; progress should be reviewed periodically.

Rag Flock Acts

Inter-Dept. Cttee. Rep., apps. pp. iv, 36. [1946]

1945–46 *Cmd.* 6866, *xiv*, 589 *apptd. June, 1938. sgd. April, 1946*

Lord Merthyr (*Ch.*), Allerton, Armer, Cadbury, Clark, Fairholme, Grove, Jeffrey, Martin, Monier-Williams.

'*To consider whether the Rag Flock Acts, 1911 and 1928, and the Regulations made thereunder are adequate to secure proper cleanliness of rag flock used for the manufacture of upholstery, bedding and other household furniture in Great Britain . . . and whether all or any of the provisions applicable to rag flock should be applied to materials other than rag flock. . . .*'

The Rag Flock Acts and the provisions of Section 136 of the Public Health (London) Act, 1936, are neither adequate nor effective, administration is not uniform, and there is an entire absence of legislative control over other types of filling materials or of fillings in manufactured articles. Because of the difficulties of administering the Acts, unscrupulous manufacturers have sold large quantities of unclean rags. Inspection is limited to entry to those premises where there is reason to believe an offence is being committed. Identification is often difficult as it is sometimes impossible for an expert to determine whether a particular sample is rag flock within the definition of the Act because all evidence as to the nature of materials used has been destroyed in the disintegrating process. As the Acts apply to flocks sold as a commodity, local authorities have been powerless to take proceedings in cases where dirty rag flock is present in finished articles, e.g. in bedding and upholstery.

The statutory definition of 'flock manufacture from rags' should be extended, premises should be registered and subject to periodic inspection. The Fenton test under investigation by the British Standards Institution is the best available test for rag flock and animal fibres generally and should be incorporated in the regulations. Descriptive labels should be attached to articles with filling, covering and linings on upholstery should be controlled, and stuffed toys should be required to comply with the standards for cleanliness.

Wool Textile Industry

Jt. Factory Advisory Cttee. Interim Rep., *Spacing of certain machinery: processes subsequent to carding*, app. pp. 7. 1947
1947 Non-Parl. Min. of Labour & N.S. apptd. June, 1945. sgd. Nov., 1946

N. H. Jones (*Ch.*), and 20 others.

'*To enquire into and report on the most effective methods of compliance with certain requirements of the Factories Act, 1937, and other related problems in the Wool Textile Industry. . . .*'

In the rapid expansion of the wool textile industry during the latter part of last century machinery was not spaced to allow for general safety and ease of work, and with certain exceptions there are no statutory requirements nor has there been any previous co-ordinated approach concerning these machines. Fatigue and strain are caused by the manipulation of heavy warp beams in narrow spaces. Recommendations are set out in the form of tables showing the space required for the installation of plant in new buildings and for new or reorganised installations in existing rooms.

Second Interim Report not published.

—— Final Report, apps. pp. 57. 1949
*1949 Non-Parl.
sgd. Feb., 1948*

Although the wool textile industry is not dirty, oil grease and fibre can create very unpleasant conditions unless there is care, and uneven surfaces of walls and floors afford lodgement for dirt. In some factories oil seeps through the ceilings, making it impossible to clean them and floors are often covered with a compact accumulation of dirt, grease and fibre, sometimes an inch thick.

w

Inadequate heating, ventilation and lighting exist in many factories, and many power driven machines are still unfenced. The proportion of accidents due to machinery for five recent years was 36 per cent in wool textiles as against 18 per cent for all industry.

Most of the specific recommendations are simply the application of the general requirements of the Factory Acts and are well within the capabilities of a progressive firm. But the 'high hopes attached to the Agreements of 1913 and 1936 were not altogether realised in practice'. Except for scheduling gill boxes and cards as dangerous machines for the purposes of training young persons, and the extension of Regulations dealing with the lifting of weights, the voluntary method was to be given another trial; the position should be reviewed at the end of five years. A joint standing committee should be set up to watch progress and give general advice on machinery, etc., and review, at intervals, the accidents occurring in the industry.

Prevention of Accidents in Paper Mills. Machinery Accidents

Jt. Standing Cttee. 1st Rep. pp. 27. 1938. 2nd Rep., apps. pp. 54. 1952
*1938 Non-Parl. Home Office. 1953 Non-Parl. Min. of Labour & N.S.
apptd. —. sgd. Aug., 1937, July, 1952*

H. Topham (*Ch.*). H. A. Hepburn (*Ch.*).

'*To study the incidence and cause of accidents in Paper Mills and suggest methods of prevention.*'

'For many years it has been the aim of the Factory Department to secure agreements with the employers and the operatives, both as to the methods of compliance with the Factory Acts and the observance of certain practices outside the scope of the Acts. These agreements do not supersede the requirements of the Acts . . . but form a basis, derived from experience, for enforcement. . . .' Following a conference in October 1935 of both sides of the industry, a Standing Joint Committee was set up with the terms of reference above. The agreed rules were embodied in an agreement, 1937, printed and explained in the First Report. Some involved a substantial reconstruction of machines, which could not be completed before the outbreak of war. Much of this had now been overtaken, but the statistics of accidents and developments in the industry called for some revision of rules. The new agreed rules replace the old as from 1st August, 1952. The difficulties of obtaining labour had in some instances resulted in young persons not receiving the degree of training and supervision which would otherwise have been the case.

Tile Dust

Cttee. Rep. pp. 19. 1943

1943 *Non-Parl. Min. of Labour & N.S. apptd. —. sgd. Dec.,* 1942

A. W. Garrett (*Ch.*), Campbell, Cooper, Corn, Hewitt, Hollins, Jones, Price.

'*To consider methods of suppression and removal of dust containing silica in the tile making and the electrical porcelain fittings sections of the pottery industry.*'

There are still certain processes which give rise to serious risk of silicosis, particularly in the manufacture of tiles and other articles which are produced by pressure from finely ground material containing free silica in the form of ground flint. Detailed recommendations were made for all processes where there was danger of dust inhalation. Although war had broken out, the Committee realised that after the last war new works and appliances were rushed up without due thought for health, and wished its recommendations to be available before new works or alterations were carried out. For example, clay should not be dried to below moisture content finally required; breaking of clay by hand should be prohibited; pan grinding should be used; sieves should be completely boxed and provided with exhaust draught and the hopper type of ark made compulsory. The employment of women in tile dust grinding and carrying should be prohibited, etc.

Draft Pottery (Health and Welfare) Special Regulations

Inquiry. Rep., apps. pp. 30. 1950

1950 *Non-Parl. Min. of Labour & N.S. apptd. June, sgd. Nov.,* 1949

E. Sachs.

(I) The most substantial questions raised related to the weights women might lift and carry. The weight a woman might carry on her own should be reduced from the proposed 50 lbs. to 30 lbs., and if acting with other persons, from the proposed 100 lbs. to 50 lbs. The height limit beyond which women should not stack saggars should be 4 feet 6 inches. The proposed mid-day scraping of floors of potters' shops, which might do more harm by raising dust, should be altered to the removal of clay scraps from gangways. (II) Because of the possible danger of silicosis in the stoneware industry, it should come within the scope of the new Regulations, but the position should be reviewed when the degree of risk has been more fully assessed. The rigidity of regulations regarding protective clothing, and on the cleaning of shelves should be relaxed and District Inspectors should be empowered to certify the degree of protection and cleaning necessary in appropriate cases.

Safety in the Use of Power Presses

Cttee. Rep., apps. pp. 32. 1945

1945 *Non-Parl. Min. of Labour & N.S. apptd. Feb.,* 1940. *sgd. Nov.,* 1944

H. R. Rogers (*Ch.*), and 29 others.

The numbers of distressing accidents which have occurred since the great increase in the use of power presses were considered by the National Safety Congress in May 1930 and led to the appointment of a Committee on safety in the use of power presses. Three sub-committees were appointed to deal with Press Design (Press Makers), Tool Design (Tool Users) and Guard Design, and recommendations were made for safety devices for new and for existing presses. There should be a complete periodical inspection of power presses and a joint standing committee should be appointed to examine all designs.

A Joint Standing Committee was set up with a technical sub-committee representative of the makers of mechanical presses and of guards, for the purpose of examining new devices or considering technical problems involved. The following Reports have been published in the Non-Parliamentary series by the Ministry of Labour: First Report of Proceedings of the Committee with Apps. on *Interlock Guards; 1950. Fencing of Press Brakes; 1952. Fencing of Hydraulic Presses; 1952.* Second Report of Proceedings of the Committee with Apps. on *Fencing of Heavy Mechanical Presses; 1953.*

See *Safety of Heavy Power Presses. Bending Brakes.* Jt. Standing Cttee. (H. R. Rogers, *Ch.*). Rep.; 1945. Final Rep.; 1949 Non-Parl.

Dust in Steel Foundries

Cttee. 1st Rep., apps. pp. 23. 1944. 2nd Rep., apps. pp. 83. 1951

1944, 1952 *Non-Parl. Min. of Labour & N.S.*
apptd. — 1943. sgd. March, 1944, March, 1951

H. E. Chasteney (*Ch.*), and 10 others, 1st Rep. H. A. Hepburn (*Ch.*), and nine others, 2nd Rep.

'*To consider methods of preventing the production or the inhalation of Dust and the possibility of reducing the use of materials containing Free Silica in Steel Foundries.*'

First Report.—The number of cases of silicosis amongst dressers and fettlers of steel castings and sandblasters has been increasing. The risk can be reduced in three ways. (*a*) By using substitutes for materials containing free silica. Moulding compositions, parting powders and paint containing free silica should be prohibited, though no substitutes had yet been found for the 1,500,000 tons of moulding sands used each year. (*b*) By protective measures designed to reduce the amount of dust produced or to prevent its inhalation. These include use of blasting enclosures, ventilating plant, protective helmets, etc. No person under 18 should be employed in blasting, or in draining or maintaining blasting apparatus, or within 20 feet of it if the abrasive is propelled by compressed air or steam.

Second Report.—Describes the progress of research into the technical questions involved.

See *Draft Blasting (Castings and other Articles) Special Regulations 1949.* V. R. Aronson. Rep.; 1949 Non-Parl. Min. of Labour & N.S.

Conditions in Ironfoundries

Jt. Advisory Cttee. Rep. pp. 34. 1947
1947 *Non-Parl. Min. of Labour & N.S.* apptd. Aug., 1945. sgd. —

H. E. Chasteney (*Ch.*), Bennett, Broadbent, Deas, Gardner, Gardom, Gould, Gresty, Happold, Harrison, Logan, McLaughlin, McCullogh, Martin, Morton, Pearce, Wallace, Wigglesworth.

'*To advise the Chief Inspector of Factories on the most effective methods of implementing certain requirements of the Factories Act, 1937, and on other cognate problems in ironfoundries. . . .*'

There are in Great Britain about 2000 ironfoundries differing in size and methods of production. Some are new and highly mechanised, whilst others, especially the smaller jobbing foundries, have not changed appreciably during the last 50 years and many of them suffer from being housed in poor premises built in the days when too little attention was given to working conditions.

Ironfoundries should come under the general requirement of the Factory Act that every factory should be kept clean. This involves weekly cleaning of floors and benches and periodic cleaning, washing and the painting of walls, ceilings, etc. Tidy and orderly conditions avoiding obstruction and congestion should be obtained by orderly storage of materials, etc., in suitable areas, racks and bins, and the use of vacuum methods for removing dust, etc. Temperatures should not be less than 50° F after a lapse of one hour from commencing work, but open coal or coke fires should not be used for this purpose. The Factories (Standards of Lighting) Regulations should be adopted and washing facilities including baths, and accommodation for clothing should be provided. Recommendations are made for reducing the smoke and fumes in ladle drying and heating, mould drying, from mould and core stoves, core bonds, etc., and for the removal of dust. A summary is added of the main points to be observed in planning new foundries.

Industrial Lung Diseases of Iron and Steel Workers

pp. xiv, 282. 1950
1950 Non-Parl. Min. of Labour & N.S.

During 1930 both the Factory Department and the Silicosis and Asbestos Medical Board noticed an increasing number of cases of silicosis amongst fettlers of steel castings, and an investigation made in 1943 of the workers in one steel foundry revealed a high incidence of severe lung trouble. The present one concerned 3059 workers in 19 foundries, together with an analysis of the records of lung diseases of 64 foundry workers, and dust surveys in three foundries.

Safeguarding of Milling Machines

Technical Advisory Cttee. Interim Rep., apps. pp. 43. 1947. 2nd Rep., app. pp. 36. 1951
1947, 1952 Non-Parl. Min. of Labour & N.S.
apptd. — 1945. sgd. *April*, 1947, *March*, 1951

G. P. Barnett (*Ch.*), and 10 others.
H. A. Hepburn (*Ch.*), and 10 others.

'*To examine the whole problem of safeguarding milling machines and advise the Chief Inspector on such measures as were considered necessary and practicable for the prevention of accidents on them.*'

The more extensive use of milling machines as a result of technical developments in design and performance has led to a considerable increase in the numbers of accidents. A large variety of types of machines are used, but the majority of accidents occurred on the widely used machines engaged on repetitive work. The report is mainly concerned with safeguards for this type of machine.

In the Second Report further information is given regarding safeguards for such machines, as well as recommendations for ensuring higher standards of safety in connection with all kinds of milling processes.

Health of Welders

Rep., index. pp. 84. 1951
1951 Non-Parl. Min. of Labour & N.S.
A. T. Doig, L. N. Duguid.

In recent years there has been a great increase in welding and the process has undergone much development and modification. The occupation carries certain definite risks to health, but there is no specific 'welders' disease', and occupational dermatitis is not a serious cause of disability. There is no increased mortality or morbidity rate, but as the main risk is from fumes, the recommendations were concerned with an adequate standard of ventilation for the various processes. Exhaust ventilation should be provided where the fumes are particularly poisonous or irritating.

Conditions in the Drop Forging Industry

Cttee. Rep., apps. pp. 33. 1953
1953 Non-Parl. Min. of Labour & N.S.
apptd. *June*, 1951. sgd. *April*, 1953

R. Bramley-Harker (*Ch.*), Beard, Beech, Crowder, Edwards, Mawson, Perry,

Profitt, Purchase, Vaughan, Stuart-Todd.

'To consider the working conditions in the Drop Forging Industry in respect of the Safety, Health and Welfare of persons employed and to draw up an Agreement specifying the minimum standards for compliance with the requirements of the Factories Act, 1937 and 1948, together with recommendations in respect of any associated matters.'

Where new forges are being built they should conform to standards of size, design, materials, floors, etc., set out in App. I A. Much is required to bring the majority of existing forges up to modern standards. Detailed recommendations are made for lighting, cleanliness, safety measures to prevent accidents, mechanical lifting and handling techniques, welfare and sanitation, etc., which, in the opinion of the Committee can be made effective even in those buildings 'difficult and adverse to the well-being of the industry'. Trade practices and prejudices which have retarded the progress of the industry should be overcome by co-operation and joint consultation.

Hours of Employment of Women and Young Persons in Factories during the First Five Months of the War

Rep. pp. 15. 1940

1939–40 Cmd. 6182, iv, 225
sgd. Feb., 1940

During the first six months of the 1914–18 war, the Factory Acts, which allowed a maximum of 60 working hours a week, were extended to allow 65 for women and 67½ for boys over 16 years of age. But whilst this was advantageous to production for short periods, it soon produced lassitude in the workers, and adversely affected output. The Health of Munition Workers Committee (Breviate 1900–1916, p. 198) reported against it and hours were reduced for women to the limits set by the Factory Acts, though boys over 16 were allowed to work 65 hours by

day and 63 by night. As a result of this experience, the ill-effects were widely recognised, and in many industries hours were reduced by collective agreement to 48. The Factory Act, 1937, fixed 48 hours as the normal maximum working week for women and young persons.

In 1939, after temporary extensions of hours to meet immediate difficulties, no extensions were permitted except through the Factory Inspectors and the Home Office, and maximum hours were reduced to 57 for women and young persons over 16, though 54 hours or less became common. To increase production, systems of two day-shifts of eight hours and of three 8-hour shifts in 24 hours were permitted, with the proviso that there should be weekly or fortnightly alterations of shifts, and that mess room facilities were adequate. There were in operation 133 Orders allowing male young persons under 16 to work 44–48 hours a week.

It is the policy of the Government, while authorising where necessary hours not permissible in peace time, not to authorise hours which in the light of experience and scientific investigation would be detrimental to health and efficient production.

Double Day-Shift Working

Cttee. Rep., apps. pp. 50. 1947

1946–47 Cmd. 7147, xiii, 1
apptd. March, 1945. sgd. Jan., 1947

J. L. Brierly (Ch.), Elliott (Miss D. M.), Johnson, Kydd (Miss J. A.), Naesmith, Pheazey, Pilcher, Ryle.

'To enquire into the economic need for and the social consequences of the double day-shift system in manufacturing industry and the changes in the existing law that would be necessary to facilitate its wider adoption, and to make recommendations.'

In the double day-shift system production continues over a very long working day by two shifts of workpeople, each working only a normal and relatively short number of hours. The Employment of Women and Young Persons

Act, 1936, following the recommendations of the Delevingne Committee,
1935, put on a permanent basis the
procedure of applications for granting
authorisations to operate a two-shift
system. In the inter-war years authorisations were granted only on a very
limited scale, and it rarely became a
permanent feature mainly because
between 1921–39 'there was no strong
economic incentive to increase output'.
Although during the 1939–45 war
authorisations increased, they were
small in number compared with emergency authorisations for extended day
work: in 1944 there were 7820 shift
orders and 20,000 extended day work
orders.

The system has been found advantageous for meeting sudden and urgent
demands, seasonal pressures, rapid
changes of fashion and the more
temporary post-war situations, but it
has to be considered as a more permanent feature of industrial organisation
because of the relation between increasing capital charges and output and
the developments affecting the reduction of the hours of work in industry.
The Cotton Spinners' and Manufacturers' Association maintained that
because of its high cost an automatic
loom would have to run two shifts to
make it a commercial proposition.

Provided that social and educational
amenities and welfare schemes are
organised so that shift workers can
benefit by them, there is no detriment
to health and no social inconveniences
which are not outweighed by the
reduction in working hours per week
for each worker which a shift system
makes economically possible. To protect the worker against the shift-system
being introduced arbitrarily the Act
provides that the workers concerned
should first be informed and allowed a
ballot and no authorisation was allowed
unless the Minister approved. This had
proved a deterrent to its introduction
because employers did not care to risk
an unfavourable ballot, especially as
workers tend to be suspicious of
innovation.

No change in the law was recommended for male young persons or for
authorisations in respect of individual
factories or departments for women
and young persons; double day-shift
should be prohibited for young persons
under 18; working hours should fall
between 7 a.m. and 11 p.m. instead of
the present hours of 6 a.m. to 10 p.m.
and normally there should be no
Saturday work. A favourable majority
of the workpeople actually voting
should be required before an application for authorisation is allowed. In
Reservations, Johnson, Pheazey and
Pitcher stated that the ballot was an unsatisfactory proceeding not found necessary in any other country, and retarded
the introduction of the shift system;
they preferred the use of the normal
negotiating machinery. They quoted
the conclusion in Paper No. 6 of the
Industrial Health Research Board that
'the most potent factor in producing a
preference for day or shift work was
habit'. The recommendation to reduce
the hours would make the shifts uneconomical: work should be allowed
between 6 a.m. and 11 p.m. with no
Saturday work.

Closing Hours of Shops

Cttee. 1st Interim Rep., apps. pp. 39.
1947

1946–47 Cmd. 7105, xiv, 421
apptd. Jan., 1946. sgd. Jan., 1947

E. A. Gowers (Ch.), Bacon (Miss A.),
Campbell (Mrs. E.), Catlow, Duthie,
Illingworth, Jackson, Nathan (Lady E.),
Nugent, Plowman, Shinnie, Storrar,
Symington, Wootton (Mrs. B.).

'(1) To enquire into the provisions of the
Shops Acts relating to closing hours (general
or local) and to report as soon as possible
whether any alterations are desirable. (2) To
enquire into and make recommendations as to
extending, strengthening or modifying: (a)
The statutory provisions relating to the
health, welfare and safety of employed
persons at places of employment other than
those regulated under the Factories or Mines
and Quarries Acts, and (b) The statutory

regulation of the hours of employment of young persons. . . .'

This report deals with the first of the questions in the Committee's terms of reference. The second and third are dealt with in the separately titled papers following.

Various acts have provided that, with exceptions, shops should be closed one half day every week, closed not later than 8.0 or on one night 9.0 in the evening, and on Sundays. The original stimulus for early closing came as much from shopkeepers wishing to protect themselves from one another as from those concerned with the welfare of shop assistants. Though the Acts have been of the greatest benefit in protecting shop assistants from excessive hours, this method has reached its limit and the working week must be dealt with in a different way. The public must have reasonable shopping facilities. Opinion was now practically unanimous that 8.0 p.m. and 9.0 p.m. were unnecessarily late, but the attitude that shops should be closed at the earliest hour not intolerably inconvenient to the public, which should be educated to shop earlier, was not now appropriate when so many women worked until 5.30 p.m. A social survey showed that 80 per cent of the women who shop needed to do so after 6.15 p.m., and that closing at 7.0 p.m. would satisfy the vast majority of the public. The law allows for the sale of many articles after closing hours, but with the vast increase in 'mixed' shops it has become unworkable. Such a shop may sell any article until 8.0 p.m., sweets and newly cooked provisions until 9.30 p.m., and the new cooked provisions after 9.30 p.m. But sweets may be sold in theatres in the evening.

Amongst the recommendations were that 7.0 p.m. should be substituted for 8.0 p.m. as the general closing hour and 8.0 p.m. for 9.0 p.m. for the late day, with powers to local authorities to fix one hour earlier for the whole or part of their area; the provision for the sale of sweets and tobacco in shops at later hours should be repealed. The existing exemption in favour of newly cooked food commonly bought for the evening meal should be repealed and there should be substituted a prescribed list of specific articles of food drawn up from time to time by the Home Office. The power for the local authority to fix any day as half-day closing should be withdrawn and two alternative days allowed, one of them being a Saturday. No exemptions from half-day closing should be allowed and the half-holiday should begin at 1 o'clock. The exemptions are reduced and correlated.

—— *Health, Welfare and Safety in Non-Industrial Employment, Hours of Employment of Juveniles.* Cttee. Rep., apps., index. pp. 115. [1949]

1948–49 Cmd. 7664, xv, 727
sgd. March, 1949

add Low, del. Bacon (Miss A.), Catlow, Duthie, Symington.

Part I. Health, Welfare and Safety in Non-Industrial Employment. There was a wide variety of occupations not regulated by the Factory Acts, and many detailed recommendations were made on sanitary accommodation, ventilation, washing facilities, etc. Amongst them were the following: (1) In shops and offices (which accounted for 80 per cent of employees other than those in industrial and domestic work) there should be a minimum space of 400 cubic feet per person in every room in which employees worked; the use of underground rooms should be restricted, a period of grace being allowed for alterations. (2) Hotels, catering.—Some of the recommendations made for shops, and certain clauses of the Factory Acts should be adopted. (3) Indoor and outdoor entertainment. Minimum standards should be prescribed, but as most existing theatres were on restricted sites, they should be applied in full only to new buildings. (4) Railways.—Though nationalised, some statutory standards were necessary. (5) Road Transport.—For local road transport, no recommendations, for local passenger transport, those made for shops and offices should apply at terminal points where more than six persons are employed. (6) As in agriculture two-thirds of the units were small and the employees work at a distance from their head-quarters, both the requirements and the problems of enforcement were different: limited recommendations on cleanliness, fencing of machinery, etc. (7) Fishing and shipping. Gaps in the Merchant Shipping Acts should be studied by the departments concerned. (8) In domes-tic work enforcement of standard statutory regulations would be im-possible; the department should draw up a voluntary code of conditions.

Part II. Hours of Employment of Juveniles. Some 600,000 or 35 per cent of employed juveniles were engaged in unregulated employments. All juveniles needed the same degree of protection, and while no evidence was given that the hours actually worked were exces-sive, there were both a great lack of uniformity and many anomalies in the codes for regulated trades, and the law was unnecessarily complex: the hours of an usherette or lift boy in a theatre were regulated, but not those of boys and girls selling ice-cream or confec-tionery. Trade Union Congress ad-vocated a statutory maximum of 40 hours for those of 16 and over and 30 hours for those under 16. Juveniles were indispensable in many industries, but the Committee recommended a uniform maximum of 45 hours, on a wide field, including regulated in-dustries, and this would not cause undue dislocation. But these restric-tions could not be applied to agricul-ture, forestry, fishing, shipping, private domestic service or outworking and were unsuitable for building. Recom-mendations were also made on the maximum working day, spells of work, night intervals, etc., street trading; and the prohibition of unsuitable occupa-tions. As a result of these recom-mendations, only about 7½ per cent of employed juveniles would remain out-side regulation.

Recommendations are also made on the responsibilities of various depart-ments for enforcement.

Night Baking

Cttee. Rep., apps. pp. viii, 84. [1951]
1950–51 *Cmd.* 8378, *xviii,* 1
apptd. Sept., 1950. *sgd. Aug.,* 1951

J. F. Rees (*Ch.*), Bullock, Falconer, Marchand, Sutherland (Miss M. E.).

'*To consider the desirability of abolishing or limiting the practice of night baking now prevalent in the Bread Baking and Flour Confectionery Industry, to report on the economic and social consequences and to make recommendations.*'

The Report reviews the many earlier enquiries and the continuous pressure of unions for the prohibition of night baking. An Act of 1938 which limited it, was to come into force unless a trade board was established, but did not do so because a board was set up, though without power to prohibit night baking. In Scotland agreements between the unions and the employers made after the war limited operatives' night work to 25 weeks in the year.

In England and Wales only a third of the operatives were in the union, in Scotland the overwhelming majority. In England, out of nearly 17,000 bakeries employing 110,000 to 120,000 operatives, night work took place in under 6000, employing 27,000 opera-tives at night, of whom 14,000–17,000 were on continuous night work. A restriction of night baking would not affect the majority of bakeries, but these employed less than half the number of operatives. Men on continuous night work would suffer some loss of earn-ings. Night baking was not detrimental to health, was not a serious deterrent to recruiting, but had serious social dis-advantages. Abolition would work inequitably amongst employers, smaller bakeries not being seriously affected, medium-sized ones suffering some un-economic running of plant, while three-shift plants would suffer a grave loss of production which could be made up only by extensions. While 60 per cent of housewives wanted new bread, a large proportion of them did not use it the same day. But some co-operative societies which turned over to day working when their competitors had not, had suffered substantial losses of trade. Total abolition would mean some rise in price of bread, but a limitation involving a system of alternating shifts would not.

The Committee recommended that every bakery should be required *either* to employ no person on night baking between 10.0 p.m. and 5.0 a.m. *or* to employ no person between 6.0 a.m. and 6.0 p.m. for more than half the weeks worked in a calendar year. In Scotland little supervision would be needed for enforcement, as the industry was well organised, but in England some official supervision would be necessary.

See *Breviate 1917–1939*, p. 325.

9. MIGRATION

Migration within the British Commonwealth

Statement. pp. 5. 1945
1944–45 *Cmd. 6658, x*, 293

The Government's attitude towards Imperial oversea settlement and the interchange of population between one part of the British Commonwealth and the others is expressed by the Oversea Settlement Board 'that no merely theoretical calculations as to the future consequences of such movements ought to stand in the way of migration of individuals'. The discussions with Dominion representatives on the general question of assisted migration after the war resulted in a similar scheme to that in operation between 1919 and 1922. The United Kingdom Government would provide free transport for ex-service men and women to the port of disembarkation overseas, while the Dominion Government would provide certain facilities in its own country. Statements are made by the Dominion Governments on their attitudes to the present position.

See *Oversea Migration Board*. 1st Ann. Rep.; 1953–54 Cmd. 9261, xviii, 1 and succeeding Ann. Reps.

Child Migration to Australia

Rep., apps. pp. iv, 49. 1953
1953 *Non-Parl. Home Office*
sgd. June, 1952

J. Moss.

In the course of a private visit to Australia Mr. Moss made some enquiries into the conditions of Homes where children emigrating from Great Britain are received. The scheme is intended primarily for children deprived of normal home life, and migration is arranged by a number of voluntary philanthropic and religious societies. Between 1947 and 1951, 2118 British children had been received at some 42 approved institutions in Australia, but local authorities are reluctant to send children for which they are responsible. The interests of the child migrants are thoroughly safeguarded. Recommendations are made for the keeping of case histories, inspection of institutions, etc. Owing to the difficulties of fitting into a different school system, no school child should be over 12 years on reaching Australia.

10. PROFESSIONS

Higher Appointments

Cttee. Rep., apps. pp. 62. 1945
1944–45 *Cmd. 6576, iv*, 253
apptd. July, 1943. *sgd. May*, 1944

Lord Hankey (*Ch.*), Barton, Bourdillon, Davis, Dobson, Duncan, Fyfe, Hamilton (Mrs. M.), Jones, Lowery, McLean, Mitchell, Plumer (Eleanor), Tewson, Thirkill, Thomson.

'To consider and report upon the arrangements which should be made to facilitate the employment after the end of hostilities of men and women qualified to undertake responsible

work in the professions or elsewhere, with particular reference to (a) the organisation, premises and staff of the Appointments Department of the Ministry of Labour and National Service; (b) the arrangements which should be made for co-operation between the Appointments Department and other organisations and institutions (including professional, industrial and commercial organisations) and Universities, at home and abroad.'

The Committee was appointed by the Minister when it was proposed to centre in the Appointments Department the arrangements for assisting persons with qualifications for the Higher posts in professions, industry and commerce during the period of resettlement. The present Appointments Department is the result of the Central Register (1938) which was formed to provide a list of persons with high professional, etc., qualifications, for the use of the Departments, though it was used also by industry. The Supplementary List (December, 1939), was used to find appropriate employment for persons with professional and technical qualifications. It operated at 16 offices throughout the country, and worked in close co-operation with the Central Register. During the war such persons were required to register and the Central Register thus became responsible for the control and distribution of them. The Central Register worked well for those in the first group, but as there were more people than jobs in the second group, the Appointments Department was created to meet the difficulty.

Recommendations are made with a view to making the Appointments Department serve as the basis for providing a State service for dealing with higher appointments within the framework of the Ministry of Labour. Higher appointments could not be dealt with by the employment exchanges because of the wide differences in qualifications, etc., required and the wider area needed for the high appointments. There should be regional Appointments Offices; the persons dealt with should be just above the level of foreman and clerk; particulars of vacancies should be circulated; an applicant should be allowed to register at more than one Office; scientists, etc., should be dealt with centrally. Other recommendations outline the detailed working of the scheme.

Medical and Auxiliary Professions

See *Health*. p. 317.

Qualifications of Planners

Rep.

1950 *Cmd.* 8059. See *Town and Country Planning*. p. 373.

Veterinary Practice by Unregistered Persons

Cttee. Rep., app. pp. 16.   1945

1944–45 *Cmd.* 6611, *v*, 577
apptd. July, 1944. *sgd. March*, 1945

J. R. Chancellor (*Ch.*), Brown, Cabot, Chalker, Dukes, Gray, Hobbs, Holmes (C. M.), Holmes (W. F.), Jackson, Kershaw, Simpson.

'To enquire into the extent and effect of veterinary practice in Great Britain by persons who are not registered veterinary surgeons and to make recommendations as to any measures which may be desirable to limit or regulate such practice.'

The law governing veterinary practice prohibits the use of the title Veterinary Surgeon, and does not allow the recovery in Court of fees, etc., by any person unless he is qualified and registered. But it does not prevent unregistered persons practising from a 'Canine Surgery', 'Veterinary Hospital', 'Animal Dispensary', etc. Not all the work of the voluntary bodies is in the hands of qualified surgeons: the work of the People's Dispensary for Sick Animals, with an annual income of £130,000, is carried out by the society's 198 technical officers, who are trained sufficiently for first aid work, but not for diagnosis and the treatment of disease. There are in practice about 2000 qualified and about 800 unqualified practitioners, two-thirds of whom are in small animal urban and one-third in general agricultural practice. The unqualified practitioner has held his own fairly well on the farm, where the work has been the curing of disease or the treatment of individual animals, but for preventive measures, and the control of disease a wide scientific knowledge and a high standard of professional attainment is essential.

Unregistered persons should be prohibited from practising except for first-aid treatment in emergency, the destruction of an animal by painless methods, or the performance of castration or certain minor operations. Persons of good character who have practised for seven years should be registered and use the title 'Registered Animal Practitioner', and they should have the right to sue for fees, and have facilities for obtaining drugs.

Veterinary Education in Great Britain

Cttee. 2nd Rep., apps. pp. 35. 1944

1943–44 Cmd. 6517, iv, 639
apptd. Nov., 1938. sgd. Feb., 1944

T. Loveday (*Ch.*), Barcroft, Burgess, Kershaw, Smith, Wooldridge.

'*To review the facilities available for veterinary education in Great Britain in relation to the probable future demand for qualified veterinary surgeons and . . . to make recommendations as to the provision which should be made from public funds in the five years 1937–42 in aid of the maintenance expenses of institutions providing veterinary education.*'

The estimated loss due to preventable animal disease was some £30 mn.; the intention of the Government to maintain a well-balanced agriculture and the appreciation by the public that the vet is the physician of the farm, will lead to an increased demand for veterinary services. The First Report, 1938 (see *Breviate, 1917–39*, p. 495) estimated the annual demand at 150; the present estimate is 220 annually for ten years, with a possible reduction later to 150 thereafter. This could be made possible by expanding the four existing schools: London, Edinburgh, Glasgow and Liverpool, with two new schools located at Cambridge and Bristol. The universities should undertake the responsibility for the training, and their degrees should be registrable. Recommendations are made for the revised functions of the Royal College of Veterinary Surgeons, training, research, and the provision of bursaries for students. There should be a special inquiry on unqualified practice. The proposals would involve a capital expenditure of £2 mn. and a recurrent expenditure of about £210,000 a year.

XI. SOCIAL SECURITY

1. Unemployment Insurance and Assistance
2. Social Insurance, Family Allowances
3. National Insurance
4. National Assistance
5. Workmen's Compensation, Industrial Injuries
6. Pensions

1. UNEMPLOYMENT INSURANCE AND ASSISTANCE

Determination of Needs Bill

Assistance Bd. Memo. pp. 6. 1941
1940–41 Cmd. 6247, v, 841

The Bill abolishes the existing requirement that the resources of all members of a household are taken into account when assessing the allowance or supplementary pension to be given to an applicant living as a member of the household, and substitutes rules designed to ensure that regard is paid to the advantages a member of a household has in comparison with an applicant who lives alone. The resources of members of the household other than the applicant, husband and wife of applicant and any member of the household dependent on him are not to be regarded as his resources. If the householder is the applicant, his resources are deemed to include contributions from non-dependent members, e.g. sons and daughters. Draft regulations propose to fix the contribution at 7s. a week for an adult man. If an applicant without dependents is living in the household of his parents and their income exceeds a specified sum, his needs are not to be reckoned as including the need of making any contribution to his board and lodging and other household expenses.

See *Determination of Needs Act, 1941*; 4 & 5 Geo. 6. c. 11. *Draft Unemployment Assistance . . . Regulations.* Memo.; 1946–47 Cmd. 6959, xv, 473.

Financial Condition of the Unemployment Fund

Unemployment Insurance Statutory Cttee. Reps.

1940–41 (65) *v*, 825
1941–42 (73) *v*, 735
1942–43 (72) *vii*, 723
1943–44 (60) *v*, 731
1944–45 (58) *vii*, 591
1945–46 (112) *xvi*, 589
1946–47 (66) *xv*, 487
1947–48 (106) *xvi*, 563

1940–41 (65). The Act of 1940 raised contributions, increased benefits and extended the scheme to include non-manual workers earning up to £420. Income exceeded expectations by nearly £34 mn. so that the net balance of the Fund was £54½ mn. The decline of unemployment led to a decrease of £15 mn. in benefit expenditure, but a continuing expenditure of £26 mn. on benefit in a year of war activity was high enough to be surprising.

The British Employers Federation represented that in view of the size of the balance which would be built up during a period of low unemployment, benefits should not be increased, but contributions reduced. Trade Union Congress asked for the abolition of the waiting period on the continuity rule, a revision of anomalies regulations, and increased benefits, on the ground that if the Government prevented mass unemployment, increased reserves would not be necessary. But even in a year of unsatisfied demand for labour £26 mn. was spent on benefits in addition to £16 mn. on unemployment assistance; what the Government could accomplish was not certain, and the Fund was the first line of defence. Part of the balance should be applied to reduction of debt, there should be inquiries into waiting time and the anomalies regulations, and in the meantime the waiting time and continuity rules could be modified in favour of persons put out of work by direct enemy action. In 1941–42 (73) the Committee reported that the balance had risen to £80 mn. and might be expected to double if the war continued, but again rejected proposals to reduce contributions or increase benefits because the level of unemployment after the war, whether controllable or not, was at present unpredictable. For this reason it was arguable that Section 59 (2) which empowered the Committee to recommend changes in contributions and benefits by procedure not involving legislation, should be suspended. The Minister took steps to modify this. The report 1943–44 (60) recording that expenditure on benefit fell from £52 mn. in 1938, to £27 mn. in 1940, £9 mn. in 1941 and nearly £4 mn. in 1942, comments on how slow full industrial mobilisation is and that even in full employment there are intervals of not working due to changes of programmes and methods, etc. The report 1945–46 (112) states that although as the war has ended, and demobilisation proceeds and the production of munitions ceases, some increase of unemployment might be expected, there was no danger of a general trade depression. There would be an excess demand longer than there was after the first world war, but there might still be some rise of unemployment during this period owing to a revival of seasonal variations, to technological changes, to personal misfits of demobilised men, and some structural unemployment in industries and localities engaged on war production.

Under the Unemployment Insurance Act, 1935, the Statutory Committee was required to report annually: 15 reports have been published on the Unemployment Fund (General Account) and 12 on the Agricultural Account. As the Unemployment Fund was absorbed into the National Insurance Funds under the 1946 Act, these reports ceased.

See *Breviate 1917–39*, p. 383 for preceding Ann. Reports.

2. SOCIAL INSURANCE, FAMILY ALLOWANCES

Social Insurance and Allied Services

Inter-Dept. Cttee. Rep., apps. pp. 299. 1942. App. G., Memos. 1942

1942–43 *Cmd.* 6404, *Cmd.* 6405, *vi*, 119 *apptd. June*, 1941. *sgd. Nov.*, 1942

W. H. Beveridge (*Ch.*), Bannatyne, Blundun, Cox (Miss M. S.), Epps, Farrell, Hale, Hamilton (Mrs. M. A.), McKenzie, Ritson (Miss M.), White.

'*To undertake, with special reference to the inter-relation of the schemes, a survey of the existing national schemes of social insurance and allied services, including workmen's compensation, and to make recommendations.*'

The Report is made by the Chairman alone, as the other members of the Committee were civil servants representing their departments as advisers and assessors and were not to be associated in any way with views and recommendations on policy.

Part I summarises the Report, giving provisional rates of benefits and contributions and lists 23 principal changes involved. Part II gives the reasons for

these 23 changes which include the supersession of approved societies and of the existing scheme of workmen's compensation. Part III deals with three special problems, Part IV with the Social Security budget. Part V again takes up the social insurance plan as a whole in more detail, setting out the six insurance classes proposed, the various benefits and contribution conditions and the place of national assistance. Part VI discusses the three assumptions of social policy on which the plan was based—children's allowances, health service and the maintenance of employment. Parts I, II and V—Principal Changes and the Plan of Social Security.—The existing schemes of social insurance and allied services operated through disconnected bodies proceeding on different principles leave gaps and give rise to anomalies. Many persons working on their own account are poorer and more in need of State help than the employed who are included; though there is no real difference between the income needs of the sick and of the unemployed, they get different rates of benefit under different contribution conditions; and there are four different means tests. Administration is needlessly complex and wasteful. In the inter-war years social surveys revealed that the two major causes of want were loss of earning power and failure to relate earning-power to the size of the family. Britain has ample income to abolish want by a double redistribution of income through social insurance and family allowances.

The Plan is one of insurance, giving in return for contributions, benefits up to subsistence level as a right and without means tests. It is based on three assumptions: that there will be (*a*) family allowances, (*b*) a national health and rehabilitation service, and (*c*) maintenance of employment. It is a comprehensive scheme for insurance covering all citizens without upper income limit, embodying six principles: a flat rate subsistence benefit; a flat rate of contributions; unification of administrative responsibility; adequate benefit to provide in all normal cases a minimum income which will continue indefinitely as long as the need continues; comprehensiveness, i.e. it will cover all risks so general and uniform that social insurance can be justified; classification, i.e. while covering all citizens irrespective of their means, the scheme takes account of the different circumstances of the different sections of the community, e.g. employed, self-employed, housewives, etc.

The population will be grouped into six insurance classes, four of working age, one below and one above: I—employees; II—others gainfully employed; III—housewives; IV—others of working age; V—those below working age and VI—retired. Benefits and contributions will be appropriate to each class. All classes will be covered for comprehensive medical treatment and funeral expenses. Class I, II and IV will pay a single social security contribution, the employer also contributing in Class I. Class I will receive benefit for unemployment and disability, retirement pension, medical treatment and funeral expenses. Class II will receive all these except unemployment benefit and disability benefit for the first 13 weeks. Class IV will receive all except unemployment benefit and disability benefit. But as a substitute for unemployment benefit, those in classes other than I will receive training benefit to assist them to find new jobs. Class III, housewives, now recognised as a distinct insurance class, will receive a maternity grant, provision for widowhood and separation and retirement pensions by virtue of their husband's contributions, while housewives undertaking paid work will receive maternity benefit for 13 weeks to enable them to give up working before and after childbirth. Married women who earn should have an option of entering Classes I or II as appropriate, getting sickness and unemployment benefit in their own right though at a lower rate.

Unemployment benefit and disability benefit will be at full rate indefinitely,

subject in the case of the former, instead of a means test, to a requirement of attendance at a work or training centre after a limited period of unemployment, and in the case of the latter, to strengthened behaviour conditions. The rates of benefit based on minimum subsistence standards and allowing for a 25 per cent increase in the cost of living in view of the possible changes in the price level are fixed provisionally at 40s. for a couple, 24s. for a single person and 8s. for a child. This includes a margin for inefficient expenditure. Pensions will be paid to those who cease to be gainfully occupied at age 65 for men and 60 for women. The permanent, inadequate widows' pensions now granted to widows of working age without dependents will be replaced by temporary benefit 50 per cent higher than unemployment benefit; there will be a guardian's benefit if there are dependent children.

Death is not provided for in the existing State scheme and voluntary insurance against it is needlessly expensive, 7s. 6d. out of every £1 being absorbed in expenses as compared with administrative costs of 10 per cent of unemployment insurance and 2½ per cent of the amount paid in contributory pensions. There should be a funeral grant of £20, which would cost 1·8 pence per week for an adult man and 1·1 pence for an adult woman. That industrial assurance is pushed by sellers to a point beyond the interest of the buyers is shown by the high proportions of low incomes spent upon it and by the fact that each year two-thirds of the policies lapse, are surrendered for cash or reduced. Large sums continue to be paid in dividends on capital which has not been and need not be increased. A public statutory Industrial Assurance Board should take over all life assurance business for sums under £300.

The existing scheme of workmen's compensation for accidents and industrial disease is slow and legalistic in administration. It does not ensure maintenance of necessary income, permits lump sum settlements and because it is based on the liability of the employer, has failed to provide a rehabilitation service. And though the needs of an injured man are the same whether the accidents take place in the street or the factory, in the former case benefit is related to needs, while workmen's compensation is related to earnings. But partly because of the history of workmen's compensation, on balance the reasons for distinguishing accidents in employment from other causes of injury outweigh those for uniformity. Workmen's compensation should be superseded by and absorbed into social insurance subject to (i), flat rate benefits up to 13 weeks, but benefits (industrial pension) related to earnings up to a maximum of £3 thereafter; (ii), a levy, additional to ordinary contributions, on industries scheduled as dangerous.

Although the scheme is designed to guarantee subsistence income in all normal cases, national assistance will be available to meet needs not covered by insurance. These will include temporarily a considerable number of cases in the period before pensions reach subsistence level, and those who slip through the meshes, e.g. those failing to fulfil benefit conditions, people with abnormal needs in diet or care, some deserted or separated wives. Assistance must meet needs up to subsistence level, but must be less than insurance benefit, otherwise insured persons get nothing for their contributions. Assistance will be subject to a unified means test. The State should encourage voluntary insurance to provide benefits beyond subsistence level and to cover risks not uniform enough to call for compulsory insurance.

The social insurance system must be unified. There should be one contribution on one document for all benefits. The scheme should be administered by a Ministry of Social Security. The existing special schemes for agriculture, banking and insurance should be amalgamated with the general scheme, and excepted occupations, e.g. the civil service, police and domestic indoor service should now be included. Public Assis-

tance other than treatment and institutional services should be transferred to the Ministry, as well as the responsibilities for maintaining blind persons and for framing schemes with local authorities and voluntary agencies for their welfare. The Unemployment Insurance Statutory Committee should be replaced by a Social Insurance Statutory Committee with similar, but extended powers. The present system of Approved Societies, whether Friendly Societies, Trade Unions or branches of Industrial Life Offices should be superseded. There are about 6600 of them, varying in membership of a few hundreds to several millions; insured persons are continually liable to change their place of residence, and unless they belong to one of the larger agencies, they have no assurance of any personal contact or treatment. After the quinquennial valuations, each society may use its surplus for additional benefits, which vary greatly between the societies. They therefore give unequal benefits for equal contributions.

Part III. Special Problems.—1. Benefit rates and the problem of rent. Because rent varies between different parts of the country and between families of different sizes and cannot be reduced during interruptions of earnings, there is a case for varying benefits with the actual rent in each case, but owing to the difficulties of principle and administration, this is provisionally rejected and a rent of 10s. for a family is assumed. The problem should be further studied. 2. The Aged. The problem is how to guarantee the aged against want by a pension as of right, while giving maximum encouragement to voluntary saving and preventing the national burden from becoming intolerable. Pension should be at the same flat rate as unemployment benefit, should be conditional on retirement and to encourage those able to work to do so should be increased for each year of employment after the qualifying age. In 1931, 1 in 10 of the population were of pensionable age, in 1961 it will be 1 in 6. Many of the persons are not in want. Provision for old age requires contributions over a long period, but of those at or near pensionable age in the near future, many will not have contributed at all or will have contributed for an inadequate period. These pensions will therefore be introduced gradually over a transition period, till in about 20 years they rise to full rates. 3. Alternative Remedies. Some of the needs for the maintenance of income may arise from accidents, divorce or separation in which the person in need has a legal claim against another person. This alternative remedy should not prevent an insured person from getting whatever benefits he would be entitled to if there were no such remedy. But he should not have the same need met twice over or get from both sources more than he would get from one alone. The question of whether the injured person's claim should be reduced by the amount of the benefit or whether he should refund the benefit to the social insurance fund, and whether he or the Ministry should take legal action on the claim needs a special inquiry by a technically qualified committee.

Part IV. The Social Security Budget. —Assuming the scheme starts on 1st July, 1944, the cost to be met from the social insurance fund will rise from £367 mn. in 1945 to £553 mn. in 1965, when contributive pensions have risen to their full rate. The remaining £330 mn. in 1945 and £305 mn. in 1965 will be the cost of national assistance, children's allowances and the health services. Payment for benefits out of general taxation or the proceeds of a specific tax would mean payment according to means, whereas payment by equal contributions is based on the value of benefits and not on capacity to pay. Payment through taxation is rejected in favour of insurance contributions, because the growth of industrial assurance and hospital contributory schemes and other evidence show that this is acceptable to the British people; because contributions irrespective of means are the strongest grounds for

repudiating a means test, and because the insured persons realise that they cannot get more than certain benefits for certain contributions. It also enables benefits to be arranged for different insurance classes according to their different needs. The case for an employer's contribution is not so strong, except for workmen's compensation, because it is a tax on the giving of employment. But his contribution should be regarded as an addition to wages and as a proper part of the cost of production, that of maintaining the necessary labour force when it is working and when it is standing idle.

The joint contributions of employers and insured persons in Class I are designed to provide two-thirds of the cost of unemployment benefit, five-sixths of the cost of disability benefit, retirement pensions and maternity benefit; the whole cost of funeral benefit and five-sixths of the cost of other benefits, including widows' and guardians' pensions, and a contribution to the cost of the health service. The contributions in Classes II and IV, where there is no employer, are the equivalent of the employer's and insured person's share. The State will bear the remainder of the cost. The contribution of an adult man will be 4s. 3d. a week. This is within the capacity of the lower paid workers without trenching on their resources for subsistence since, allowing for a 25 per cent increase of cost, large numbers are already paying 6s. 4d. for voluntary insurance premiums, medical treatment and compulsory insurance. At the outset the insured persons' share of the total cost will be 28 per cent, but will decline to 22 per cent in 1965.

Part VI. Social Insurance and Social Policy.—i. Assumption A. Children's Allowances.—Sometimes want is due to the fact that wages are insufficient to meet the needs of large families and it is dangerous to allow unemployment benefit, which includes payment for dependents, to exceed earnings. Provision should be therefore made out of taxation for children's allowances in respect of all children except the first and for all children during the interruptions to earnings. The allowance, which should average 8s. per child, should be graduated according to age.

ii. Assumption B. A Health Service.— Medical treatment should be separated from cash benefits, include hospital and specialist treatment and rehabilitation under the supervision of the Health Departments. It is a logical corollary of high disability benefits that the State should take steps to reduce the number of cases for which benefit is needed. It should be a free service and there is a case for including a payment towards the cost in the Social Insurance contribution; but as this comes from the entire population, the scope of private medical practice may be greatly restricted. It is reasonable that the insured person who is receiving disability benefits designed to cover food, etc., requirements should make some payment towards his maintenance, 'hotel expenses', when he is in hospital.

iii. Assumption C. Maintenance of Employment.—A satisfactory Social Insurance Scheme assumes the maintenance of employment and the prevention of mass unemployment. The Social Security Budget assumes that industries already subject to insurance unemployment will average 10 per cent and that over the whole body of Class I it will average 8½ per cent. The proposals to make unemployment benefit after a period conditional on attendance at a work or training centre and the test of unemployment by the offer of work, both break down if there is mass unemployment, which in any case would increase the cost of benefits and reduce the income available to bear the cost. The State should use its powers to secure for all a reasonable chance of productive employment.

Abolition of want is a practicable aim. The rise in prosperity and wages in the last 30 or 40 years diminished want, but did not reduce it to insignificance. What is required is a redistribution of income as between times of earning and of not earning, and times of heavy and of light or no family responsibilities. Social insurance and children's allowances are the means of securing this redistribution.

Appendix A, the report of the Government Actuary, explains the basis of the calculations by which the actuarial contributions and the estimates of the income and expenditure of the social security budget were arrived at. Appendix D reviews the problem of industrial assurance, the companies and societies involved, expense ratios, the proportion of lapses, dividends, the results of earlier enquiries and proposals for reform.

Evidence.—In the abnormal conditions of war, publication of the information presented to the Committee was limited to a selection of *Memoranda from Organisations*, issued separately as App. G., which dealt either with questions of general interest or with major issues of policy. The proposals of four bodies, Trade Union Congress, the Parliamentary Committee of the Co-operative Congress, the Shipping Federation and the Liverpool Shipowners' Federation, and the National Council of Women all had some common features. These were: an inclusive scheme covering all major risks and applying to all gainfully occupied persons irrespective of income, with a standard flat rate benefit and flat rate inclusive contribution; a comprehensive free health service; assistance for persons not entitled to benefit on a personal means test; and unification under one Ministry. All proposed to accept the abolition of approved societies.

P.E.P. and the Fabian Society accept some of these principles, but propose that the insurance principle should be dropped in favour of financing out of general taxation or by a social security tax. T.U.C. and the Co-operative Parliamentary Committee proposed that the costs should be borne 25 per cent by the insured persons, 25 per cent by the employer and 50 per cent by the State, whilst the Shipping Federation and the Liverpool Shipowners suggested one-third by the State, except possibly for pensions, and one-third each by the employers and by the insured persons. On workmen's compensation, the Co-operative Parliamentary Committee and the Fabian Society argued that employer's liability should continue and that compensation should not be included in the social security scheme, the Shipping Federation and the Liverpool Shipowners and the National Council of Women that it should be absorbed into the main scheme, and better rehabilitation services provided.

Social Insurance

Government proposals. Part I, apps. pp. 64. 1944

1943-44 *Cmd. 6550, viii, 463*

Sir William Beveridge's report on Social Insurance and Allied Services (1942-43 Cmd. 6404) assumed that there would be schemes for a health service, for avoiding mass unemployment and for family allowances. Government plans for the first two were published in Cmd. 6502 and Cmd. 6527, 1944.

Extreme poverty affected households of two kinds—those in which the breadwinner was ill, out of work or past working age, and those where the number of children overstrained household resources. There must therefore be increased rates of unemployment and sickness benefit and of retirement pensions and family allowances. With the exception of family allowances and national assistance, which will be met wholly from the proceeds of taxation, the Government have adhered to the principle that freedom from want must be achieved, in the first instance, by social insurance and that benefits must be earned by contributions. Contributions will cover only 69 per cent of the costs at the outset, and some 50 per cent twenty years later. The rest will have to come out of taxation. The compulsory insurance scheme will be widened to extend the range and amount of benefits, and to cover the entire population without exclusions based upon difference of status, function or wealth. At present there are many people outside the scope of national insurance whose need of its benefits is as great as that of many of the insured population, and without this universality it would not be possible adequately to maintain the cover needed during various normal changes from one insurance class to another. No attempt is made to vary contributions with earnings, as the principle adopted has been that of equal benefits for equal contributions. Subsistence as a basis of benefits is rejected, since a high level of benefits means a high level of contributions. The objective is a rate of benefits which provides reasonable insurance against want, and the maximum contribution should be what the great body of contributors can be properly asked to bear. There remains the individual's opportunity to achieve for himself a standard of comfort and amenity which it is no part of a compulsory scheme of social insurance to provide.

The population is classified into six classes, differing in the benefits they need and the contributions they must make to receive them: (i) employees; (ii) others gainfully employed; (iii) housewives; (iv) other persons of working age not gainfully employed; (v) children below working age; and (vi) persons retired and above working age. Large numbers not hitherto covered by insurance, will be included, e.g. those earning more than £420 a year. The paper sets out in detail the contributions of each class, the amounts of various benefits and qualifying conditions, e.g. there will be a standard rate of sickness and unemployment benefit of 40s. a week for a married man with a wife not gainfully occupied. To avoid duplication of benefits, not more than one benefit or pension will be paid to an individual at any one time. The responsibilities of the public assistance authorities for cash payments will be transferred entirely to the Assistance Board. National Assistance will be available to all on proof of need. The Beveridge recommendation that sickness and unemployment benefit should be unlimited in duration subject to behaviour and training conditions respectively, are rejected as impracticable. Family allowances will be at the rate of 5s. od. for every child after the first, will be made out in the name of the father, though the wife will be entitled to draw them. Whereas in 1945 there will be 16 pensioners to every 100 contributors, by 1975 there will be 31. The Beveridge proposal to meet the situation by starting pensions at a low rate rising to 40s. od. in 20 years is rejected in favour of an immediate rate of 35s. od.

The administration of the comprehensive scheme will be unified under a Minister of Social Insurance, aided by local offices. For reasons set out in App. II it is not practicable to retain Approved Societies either as administrative agents or in a scheme providing equal benefits for equal contributions as independent financial units.

In App. I the Government Actuary reports on the finance of the proposals. Expenditure in 1945 would be £650 mn. as compared with £411 mn. under existing services.

—— Pt. II. *Workmen's Compensation, proposals for an Industrial Injury Insurance Scheme,* app. pp. 31. 1944

1943–44 *Cmd.* 6551, *viii,* 527

The Government endorses generally the criticisms of the existing scheme of workmen's compensation made in the Beveridge Report (see p. 284). The principle of placing liability on the individual employer has meant that insurance premiums are heaviest in the most hazardous industries, but they have not in practice induced these employers to take more safety precautions. Risks between industries should be pooled, as in unemployment insurance. The Government accepts the Beveridge Report's proposals that the new scheme should be comprehensive, applying to all persons under contract without income limits, that the cost should be borne by a central fund maintained by contributions from employees, employers and the State; that

claims should be determined by administrative rather than legal procedure, i.e. by a local pensions office, subject to rights of appeal to an Industrial Injury Insurance Commission; that the scheme should be administered by the social insurance authority; that commutation of weekly payments for lump sums should cease, and that provision for medical treatment and rehabilitation should be provided by the national services. The Beveridge Report suggested that there was a case for compensation for loss of earnings at a flat rate, whether the causes were unemployment, sickness or injury, but that for historical reasons and because many important industries are also specially dangerous, there was a case for special benefits for industrial casualties.

The Government rejects four 'Beveridge' proposals: (1) the limitation of special benefit for industrial disability to 13 weeks; (2) the proposal to relate industrial pensions for long-term disability to earnings, both because it contravenes the principle of uniform benefits for uniform contributions and because average weekly earnings over a period might not represent normal earnings and might lead to other inequities. Instead, industrial pensions will be based on the degree of disability, assessed by a Medical Board. (3) A lump-sum grant in fatal cases; instead, allowances are proposed. (4) The imposition of a special levy on hazardous industries, since it is unlikely to achieve the result arrived at.

The Government accepts the Beveridge proposals that a committee should be set up to consider alternative remedies, the relation between claims to security benefit and claims for damages for injuries caused by negligence, etc. (See p. 286.)

The paper sets out in detail the proposals for implementing these principles. The cost, excluding administrative cost, of the old scheme of workmen's compensation, was about £10 mn. a year, of the Beveridge proposals would be about £15 mn., and of the Government's proposals about £20 mn.

See *Social Insurance. Including Industrial Injury Insurance.* Guide to Government's Plan; 1944 Non-Parl. Min. of Reconstruction.

Family Allowances

Memo. pp. 11. 1942

1941–42 *Cmd.* 6354, *ix*, 51

Chancellor of the Exchequer.

Proposals for family allowances form part of a bigger problem of whether additional State care for children should take the form of direct provision in kind or cash payments to parents. It is argued that family allowances should lessen the risk of malnutrition and prevent inflationary movements by assisting large families rather than by increasing wages all round; would encourage parents to have children and give a cash allowance to those not getting relief by way of income tax. Others have felt that they would adversely affect collective bargaining and that the money would be better used on social services affecting children. The cost of a non-contributory scheme could be limited by confining allowances to families of limited means by an income test or other methods, none of which are free from objection, while a contributory scheme would have to be restricted to those on whom it was practicable to enforce contributions. There would have to be some adjustment with other payments made in respect of children, e.g. unemployment benefit allowances for children. Whether these allowances were paid to the mother or the father, there would be no means of ensuring that the money was properly spent; this could be done only by direct provision in kind. On the basis of a flat rate of 5s. 0d. per week for children under 15 or receiving full-time education, the net annual cost of a non-contributory scheme would be £125 mn. if all children were included, £55 mn. if the first were excluded, and £22 mn. if the first two were excluded. For a contributory scheme in respect of children of parents in insurable employ-ment, the contributions per employed person if allowances were paid to all children including the first, would be 2s. 8d. per week.

See *Family Allowances Act, 1945;* 8 & 9 Geo. 6 c. 41. *Family Allowances and National Insurance Bill.* Memo.; 1951–52 Cmd. 8517, xxv, 283. *Financial Provisions.* Rep.; 1951–52 Cmd. 8518, xii, 369.

3. NATIONAL INSURANCE

National Insurance Bill 1946

Summary of the Main Provisions of the National Insurance Scheme, apps. pp. 11. [1946]

1945–46 *Cmd.* 6729, *xvi*, 549

The Bill provides for a unified and comprehensive scheme of National Insurance, which will eventually cover practically everyone in Great Britain, and will give the following benefits: Sickness Benefit, Unemployment Benefit, Maternity Benefits (Maternity Grant, Maternity Allowance, Attendance Allowance), Widow's Benefits (Widow's Allowance, Widowed Mother's Allowance (referred to in Cmd. 6550 as Guardian's Benefit), Widow's Pension), Guardian's Allowance (referred to in Cmd. 6550 as Orphan's Allowance), Retirement Pension, Death Grant.

The paper sets out in detail the rates of benefit, contribution conditions, etc., and indicates where these differ (usually by way of increase) from the proposals in 1943–44 Cmd. 6550. A Ministry of National Insurance will be created, and to it the administration of sickness and maternity benefit will be transferred from Approved Societies. Two new Funds will be established: the National Insurance Fund, to which will be handed all the assets of the existing unemployment, health and pension schemes, and £100 mn. from the National Insurance Fund. The remaining assets of the latter will be the National Insurance (Reserve) Fund. Quinquennial reports from the Government Actuary will be followed by a ministerial review of benefit rates.

There will be power to raise or lower contributions in accordance with fluctuations in the general level of employment.

See *Employment Policy*. App. II; 1943–44 Cmd. 6527, viii, 119. *National Insurance Act, 1946;* 9 & 10 Geo. 6. c. 67.

National Insurance Bill, 1946

Rep. by the Government Actuary on the Financial Provisions, app. pp. 32. [1946]

1945–46 *Cmd. 6730, xiii,* 249
sgd. Jan., 1946

P. N. Harvey.

Presents estimates of the actuarial contributions, i.e. the amounts which the individuals who are employed, self-employed or unemployed would have to pay on an average to provide the benefits to which each of these classes is entitled, the future expenditure on benefits, the income from contributions and the resulting amount which must be paid from the Exchequer to ensure solvency. Since long-term benefits are of importance, in view of the downward trend of interest rates and Government policy, a rate of compound interest of $2\frac{3}{4}$ per cent has been assumed; and the estimates of the contributions required to meet the cost of unemployment benefit assume a rate of unemployment of $8\frac{1}{2}$ per cent. The estimates of the various classes into which the scheme divides the population were difficult because 15 years had elapsed since the last census and the war had caused many changes in social and occupational status. The outstanding feature is the size of the expenditure on retirement pensions, which will rise from £238 mn. (53 per cent of the total) in 1948 to £501 mn. (67 per cent of the total) in 1978. The cost of the scheme to the Exchequer was estimated to rise from £175 mn. in 1948 to £243 mn. in 1958 and £367 mn. in 1968. The

assumptions on which the estimates are based are explained in detail in an Appendix. 'These are unlikely to be fully borne out in actual experience.'

See *National Insurance Act, 1946.* Government Actuary. 1st Interim Rep.; 1950–51 (103) xvi, 285, and succeeding Ann. Reps.

Approved Societies

Staffing Advisory Cttee. Interim Rep., *Absorption of Staffs,* apps. pp. 30. 1947. Final Rep., *Compensation and Superannuation of Staffs,* apps. pp. 28. 1948

1947, 1948 *Non-Parl. Min. of Nat. Insurance*

apptd. Nov., 1945.   sgd. Feb., 1947, June, 1948

A. G. Lee (*Ch.*), Interim Rep.   C. G. Izard (*Ch.*), Final Rep.

'To advise on the absorption by the Ministry of the staff of Approved Societies and the compensation of those not absorbed or who otherwise suffer loss as a consequence of the transfer.'

The task of fitting into the Civil Service the widely different systems of pay and conditions of service of some thousands of approved societies arose from the decision of the Government to administer the new scheme of National Insurance direct instead of through the agency of the approved societies. Those having first claim to permanent employment with the Ministry were some 10,000 permanent staff of the societies who worked wholly or for more than 50 per cent of their time on national health insurance. Transferred staffs should come within the Civil Service pattern of classes and grades and be placed in them by the Civil Service Commissioners. Recommendations are made as to starting rates to prevent inequalities between those from different societies and between transferred staffs and civil servants, on superannuation, and on compensation for those not employed. Recent and abnormal increases in approved societies' pay made to get a better starting rate or secure more compensation should be discounted.

National Insurance Act, 1946
Advisory Cttee.

The National Insurance Act provides for the setting up of an independent National Insurance Advisory Committee. All regulations under the Act, other than those concerning certain transitional matters and reciprocal arrangements with Northern Ireland, must be submitted in draft to the Committee before being made or laid before Parliament. The Committee may be regarded as continuing in a wider field the functions of the Unemployment Insurance Statutory Committee. It secures that the mass of delegated legislation receives full consideration by an independent body, which has a duty to make known to the public the contents of the regulations, and considers the views of persons affected by them and brings them to the notice of Parliament. The Reports on draft regulations follow somewhat the same procedure as for factory regulations. See list of publications in the Ann. Rep. (1950 Cmd. 7955, xii, 205). The Minister may also refer to the Committee for consideration and advice such questions relating to the operation of the Act as he thinks fit.

—— Guardians Allowances
Rep. pp. 7. 1948
1947–48 (165) *xiii*, 877
o.p. June, 1948

W. Spens (*Ch.*).

Where a child's parents are divorced and neither has remarried, the allowance should be payable on the death of the first of them to die, provided that at the date of that death the other parent had not the child in his custody, and was under no obligation for maintenance imposed by court order. Where both parents had remarried, the allowance should not be payable unless, or until, in addition to the satisfaction of the above conditions, the death had occurred of any spouse, in whose family the child was included on the death of the natural parent. The allowance should be payable on the death of one parent if he (she) had the sole custody of the child and the surviving parent was not reasonably traceable.

—— Insurance of Share Fishermen
Rep. pp. 12. 1948
1947–48 (137) *xiii*, 941
o.p. May, 1948

Share fishermen have hitherto been excluded from unemployment insurance because they are not under contract of service, or if employed, are remunerated wholly by a share in the profits. These fishermen could be regarded as substantially in the position of an employed person where they are not the owner or part-owner of the boat, and where they are mainly engaged in fishing. If working-owners of boats were excluded there would be a strong feeling of injustice. The vessel may be owned by all or some members of the crew, proceeds less expenses being divided between owners in proportion to their share, to net owners and to labour, all members of the crew including skipper and part-owners getting the same amount for their labour. A distinction would create the employer-employee relationship which has developed only in deep-sea fishing, where there is a capital venture of some magnitude with a reasonable certainty of return. The inshore fishing industry is so dependent on individual effort that there is a very unusual degree of social equality and of identity of interests between all members of the crews—owners and non-owners alike. To preserve this solidarity all these fishermen should come under the unemployment insurance scheme. There are certain qualifications to the recommendations to fit the variety of circumstances, e.g. they should apply only to persons who follow share-fishing as a main means of livelihood; owners of boats without a crew should be excluded.

—— *Seasonal Workers*

Rep., app. pp. 14. [1949]

1948–49 (262) *xviii*, 629

o.p. Oct., 1949

The Act implies that unemployment benefit is intended only for the unemployed person who is genuinely in the 'field of employment'. The fact that a seasonal worker registers at the local exchange in his off-seasons does not necessarily show that he is in the field of employment. He should show that he has registered in the current and preceding off-seasons, and that he can reasonably expect to obtain employment during a substantial part of the off-season.

—— *Seasonal Workers*

Rep., apps. pp. 25. 1952

1951–52 *Cmd.* 8558, *xv*, 1083

sgd. May, 1952

Representations had been received relating to the position of agricultural workers, fishermen, disabled persons and from organisations representing the catering trade and holiday resorts. It was amongst this group of industries that the greater incidence of claims for benefit occurred, and amongst married women in particular, a large number of whom were not really available for work in the off-season. To be available, they must be ready to accept employment whenever it is offered on suitable terms, and must not restrict the kind of work they will do to work which cannot reasonably be expected to become available. The Regulations worked satisfactorily except in the case of the definition of seasonal worker and the off-season. A seasonal worker is defined as a person who is normally employed in a seasonal occupation or who regularly restricts his occupation to the same parts of the year and whose off-season is determined from the pattern of his seasonal employment (previously it was determined for a whole class of workers in a particular seasonal industry or particular area). This leaves very wide discretion to the adjudicating authorities in determining the merits of individual cases.

Periods amounting to seven weeks in aggregate should be ignored in determining whether or not a person is a seasonal worker; an individual period of less than one week in which a person is not employed should be disregarded in determining his off-season; work in different seasonal occupations should be aggregated for the purpose of determining the on-season. The phrase 'seasonal worker' should relate to employment which is seasonal in consequence of factors which are inherent in the nature of conditions of the industry concerned, which results in reduced opportunities of employment at similar points in successive years.

—— *Maternity Benefits*

Rep., apps. pp. 40. 1952

1951–52 *Cmd.* 8446, *xv*, 1021

sgd. Nov., 1951

The problem was one of reshuffling the available funds in order to get a more equitable distribution of them. The 1946 Act provided a Maternity Grant of £4 for each child for the general expenses of confinement, an Attendance Allowance of £1 a week for four weeks following confinement, to help pay for domestic help providing the woman does no paid work, and a Maternity Allowance of £1 16s. od. a week for 13 weeks for an insured worker, to act as an inducement to women to give up gainful employment for a time before and after confinement—the two latter payments could not be claimed together. This special allowance is, however, paid to many women who do not need an inducement to leave work, and who do not intend to return to work. Married women can choose not to pay contributions, in which case they cannot claim for unemployment or sickness, but they can qualify for Maternity Allowance. If these women were not allowed credits, the funds would be restricted to those who contributed and for whom the funds were primarily designed.

The Maternity Grant should be called the Pre-Natal Grant. The Attendance Grant should be replaced by a Maternity Grant of £6 when the confinement is at home and £3 when it is in hospital. The qualifying conditions for a Maternity Allowance of £1 6s. od. a week for 18 weeks, beginning in the 11th week before confinement should be 45 contributions, of which 26 should be actually paid in the previous year.

See *Proposed Changes in National Insurance Maternity Benefits*. Memo.; 1952–53 Cmd. 8795, xxiv, 797.

—— Time Limits
Rep., app. pp. 20. 1952
1951–52 *Cmd.* 8483, *xv*, 1113
sgd. Feb., 1952

Time limits for claiming benefit are necessary to protect the insurance fund against stale and doubtful claims, and to secure economy in administration. There is an escape clause whereby the time limit can be extended in the case where a person shows 'a good cause' for delay, but in the light of precedents set by previous decisions of the statutory authorities this has proved unduly restrictive. As no satisfactory method of general relaxation could be found, easements were recommended on the time limit for claiming attendance allowance after confinement, death grant and retrospective payments, while notice of retirement in the case of dependent wives of retirement pensioners should be discontinued.

—— Entertainment Industry
Rep., apps. pp. 21. 1952
1951–52 *Cmd.* 8549, *xv*, 1145
sgd. March, 1952

An artiste employed under contract of service in Class 1 of the insurance scheme is covered by the employer for all benefits and when unemployed is credited for the weeks he receives unemployment benefit. A self-employed artiste, i.e. under contract for services, is in Class 2 and must pay the whole contribution for benefits except the unemployment benefit, and if unemployed must continue stamping his own card. This particularly affects variety artistes performing individual turns, who have frequent periods of unemployment. There was conflict between the evidence offered by the employers and employees' organisations as to the degree of control exercised over variety artistes under contract for services, but it was not established that it approximated to a contract of service. It was not recommended that the variety artiste should be transferred by regulation to Class 1: this applies also to concert artistes, band leaders, circus artistes, etc.

—— Hospital In-Patients
Rep. pp. 14. 1952
1951–52 *Cmd.* 8600, *xv*, 1167
sgd. June, 1952

The public services should not make double provision for the same contingency, and since a patient in hospital receives free maintenance, the insurance benefit, which also includes maintenance, should be reduced, having regard to his saving in expenses and a reasonable amount for personal needs in hospital. There has been a rise in the cost of living, and the reductions should be increased at the same time as the standard rates of benefit are increased.

—— Credits for Training Courses
Rep. pp. 12. [1953]
1952–53 *Cmd.* 8860, *xiv*, 185
sgd. Feb., 1953

Students and unpaid apprentices on full-time educational courses are exempted from contributions up to 18, but receive no credits thereafter, while persons pursuing approved full-time vocational training after a period of employment or self-employment may be exempted from contributions and awarded credits. The distinction between educational and vocational courses is not clear cut. In fairness to those who have contributed, credits cannot, without substantial reason, be given to those who have not. Training credits should be awarded if the trainee is a claimant for unemployment benefit or credits; if the training course is likely to improve his prospects of employment and if the trainee satisfies the 104 contribution test (unless this is waived by the Minister). Training credits should be restricted to one year. Provision for upgrading, and for late payment is made for those who do not qualify for the above credits.

—— *Availability Question*

Rep., apps. pp. 24. 1953

1952–53 *Cmd.* 8894, *xiv*, 149
sgd. April, 1953

Since 1935 a claimant must be 'available for work'. A person is not available, if he so restricts the work he will accept that there is no reasonable prospect of obtaining it. There are some persons receiving benefit indefinitely who offer themselves for abnormally limited periods of work. The regulations should state expressly that a day shall not be a day of unemployment in respect of any claimant if the restrictions he imposes as to the nature, locality and hours of work take away reasonable prospects of employment, unless these are adversely affected only by temporary industrial conditions. Where the employment normally carried on ceases, the claimant should be given reasonable time in which to make adjustments. An occupation should be treated as subsidiary if it is consistent with the full-time employment of a claimant, or with the full-time employment for which the claimant is registered. Permitted earnings of a subsidiary occupation should be increased from 3s. 4d. to 6s. 8d. a day.

—— *Liability for Contributions of Persons with Small Incomes*

Rep., apps. pp. 21. 1955

1954–55 *Cmd.* 9432, *vi*, 281
sgd. Jan., 1955

The Act excepts from contribution insured persons with incomes not exceeding £104 a year. About 200,000 persons are excepted; 90 per cent are non-employed persons and three-quarters are women. The limit should be raised to £156 a year; family and orphans allowances, guardians' allowances, etc., should be disregarded.

Ministry of National Insurance

Rep. for the period Nov., 1944–July, 1949, apps. pp. viii, 120. [1950]

1950 *Cmd.* 7955, *xii*, 205
sgd. Feb., 1950

The Ministry of National Insurance was set up in 1944. The Report describes the creation of the administrative network for the collection of contributions and the payment of cash benefits in connection with birth, childhood, orphanhood, unemployment, sickness, industrial injury, industrial disease, widowhood, old age, death. The Appendices give statistics relating to the scheme and a list of Acts, Orders, Regulations, etc.

See succeeding Ann. Reps.

Proposed Changes in the National Insurance Scheme

Memo. pp. 4. 1951

1950–51 *Cmd.* 8208, *xxvii*, 911

The changes proposed included: an increase of retirement pensions and of the increments obtained by continuing at work, a rise in the earnings limits, and opportunity for pensioners to return to work and requalify; and increase of widowed mother's and of dependent children's allowances.

See *National Insurance Bill, 1951. Financial Provisions.* Rep.; 1950–51 Cmd. 8212, xvi, 315.

National Insurance Act, 1946

Government Actuary. Rep. on 1st Quinquennial Review, apps. pp. iii, 60. 1954

1954–55 (1) *vi*, 137
o.p. Nov., 1954

Total income up to March 1954 was £3000 mn. of which £2200 mn. came from contributions, £600 mn. from the Exchequer, and £200 mn. from interest on invested funds. £1600 mn. was spent on pensions, £500 mn. on sickness and unemployment benefits, £400 mn. on other benefits and administration, leaving £500 mn. to increase the balance.

The balance in the Insurance Fund was £340 mn. and in the Reserve Fund, £1070 mn.

National Insurance Bill, 1954

Memo. and Rep. by Minister of Pensions and N.I., apps. pp. 8. [1954]

1954–55 *Cmd.* 9338, *vi*, 243

Proposed to increase standard weekly benefits to 40s. od. for a single person and 65s. od. for a married couple, and industrial injuries benefit to 55s. od. for a single and 76s. od. for a married person. Contributions would be increased, and the Exchequer contribution continue to be one-seventh of the total contribution.

See *National Insurance Bill, 1954.* Rep. by the Government Actuary on the Financial Provisions; 1954–55 Cmd. 9332, vi, 235.

4. NATIONAL ASSISTANCE

National Assistance Bill

Summary. pp. 12. 1947

1947–48 *Cmd.* 7248, *xxii*, 989

The object of the Bill is to repeal the Poor Law and to create entirely new services founded on modern conceptions of welfare.

A. A unified service of National Assistance, to provide for those whose needs are not met by National Insurance, etc., will replace Unemployment Assistance and Supplementary Pensions now paid by the Assistance Board, Poor

Relief, Blind Domiciliary Relief, Outdoor Relief, and Tuberculosis Allowances now managed by the local authorities. The service will be the responsibility of the central government, exercised through a National Assistance Board, thus replacing all local responsibility for the relief of destitution. The standards of assistance will be expressed in scales which leave room for discretion in the individual case. The general principles on which needs will be determined (though with some variations in actual amounts) follow those in the *Determination of Needs Act, 1941.* The needs and resources of husband and wife will be considered jointly, the resources of other adult members of the household not being taken into account, though appropriate contributions to rent and overhead expenses will be assumed. The rules for disregarding certain forms of income, which now differ in the various schemes, will be unified, and graduated sums of 'unprotected' capital will also be ignored until it exceeds £400. The liability to maintain relatives which now rests on a wide range of persons will be restricted: a man (woman) being liable to maintain only his wife (husband) and children under 16. The responsibility for vagrants will be transferred to the Board.

B. The local authorities will have the duty of providing residential accommodation to be available for persons who need care because of age, infirmity, etc., irrespective of their means. Standard charges will be fixed, but the amount paid by the resident will depend on his means.

The Bill will achieve the final breakup of the Poor Law by making financial provisions in the form of National Assistance to those whose needs are not met from any other source. It provides residential accommodation for those who require care and attention in this way, although this will be a local government function, with some Exchequer assistance. See *National Assistance Act, 1948;* 11 & 12 Geo. 6. c. 29.

National Assistance (Determination of Need) Amendment Regulations. Memos.; 1950 Cmd. 7936, xix, 859. 1950–51 Cmd. 8280, xxvii, 907. 1951–52 Cmd. 8507, xxv, 509.

Reception Centres for Persons without a Settled Way of Living

National Assistance Bd. Rep., apps. pp. 23. 1952
1952 *Non-Parl. Min. of Nat. Insurance sgd. June,* 1952

While there were 7000 casuals at the outbreak of war, during the war there were very few, because the younger and able-bodied ones went into the Forces or industry, and those who remained were generally accommodated in institutions. They reappeared after the war —the highest figure being an average of 2617 a night accommodated in reception centres in February 1949. Today there are only few tramps of the traditional kind, most being young and fit enough to maintain themselves in employment: 1216 were capable of heavy labour. Many suffer from unhappy or unwise upbringing or misfortune, weakness of character, indiscipline, etc.; some wander about the country, mainly by lifts in lorries— seldom on foot—but many keep to one place. London and a few other large towns account for about half the total number. About a quarter of the total said they lived an unsettled life because they could not find accommodation. Some wandered because of family disagreements, or were turned out for drunkenness or disability, etc.

The National Assistance Act, 1948, still required local authorities to provide accommodation in 'reception centres', but because the casual problem had almost ceased to be one of wanderers on foot, casual wards at intervals of about 15 miles were out of date, and centres were closed down. There now remain 91 centres in England and Wales and 42 in Scotland, the number of busy centres being small, only 24 averaging more than 20 casuals a night. Though casuals are now the Board's responsi-

bility many local authorities act as the Board's agents, but there are marked inconsistencies of standards of administration and discipline. Whether the centre is in premises vested in the local authorities or in premises vested in the hospital authorities there is the difficulty of the cost of running it as a self-contained unit. The new centre at Teston opened to replace two centres in hospitals averaged 10 casuals a night, at an average cost of about £3 per week per casual. The wages bill alone of this centre is nearly £30 a week.

The question of agency administration is largely one of economy; at present there cannot be heavy capital expenditure on centres; those dealing with small numbers are too expensive to run as self-contained units, but where the centre causes embarrassment to the hospital authorities attempts will be made to provide accommodation.

5. WORKMEN'S COMPENSATION, INDUSTRIAL INJURIES

Workmen's Compensation

R. Com. Rep. pp. 7. 1945. Mins. of ev., 35 days. 1939–40
1944–45 *Cmd.* 6588, *vi,* 779. *Mins. of ev.;* 1939–40 *Non-Parl.*
apptd. Dec., 1938. *sgd. Dec.,* 1944

H. J. W. Hetherington (*Ch.*), Stewart, Bannatyne, Hackforth, Sadd, Boyd, Cauty, Drysdale (Miss G.), Isaacs, Lawther, Lillie, Smyth, Williams, Woolley, Wootton (Barbara).

Public sittings began on 23rd February, 1939, and continued till 21st June, 1940. It was decided to suspend the work of the Commission because, owing to the extremely grave state of the war, the British Employers Confederation could not undertake the preparation of evidence. Later, the Beveridge Report of 1942 contained a recommendation for the abolition of a separate scheme of workmen's compensation based upon the legal liability of the individual employer, and the integration of this service into the general system of social security. The Commission decided that the study of the matter had passed beyond the stage at which any further report would serve a useful purpose.

The 35 days of minutes of evidence, published in 11 separate parts, contain the memos. and the evidence of the various government departments and the opinion of widely representative bodies and individuals in contact with the problems arising from the administering of the Acts. The Home Office memo. (Paper No. 1) gives the historical sketch of the Acts, including the development of the principles of 'contributory negligence', *'volente non fit injuria'* (the workman expressly or by implication undertook the work at his own risk) and the doctrine of 'common employment'. Sir Walter Citrine presented the Memo. of the Trade Union Congress (Paper No. 13 and 13A) and discussed the Bills promoted by Congress. W. Quin and W. Elgar represented the Scottish T.U.C.

Workmen's Compensation. Alternative Remedies (Contributory Negligence)

Dept. Cttee. Interim Rep. pp. 7. 1945. 2nd Interim Rep. pp. 8. 1945

1944–45 *Cmd.* 6580, *Cmd.* 6642, vi, 763 apptd. *July,* 1944. sgd. *Dec.,* 1944, *May* 1945

W. Monckton (*Ch.*), Allen, Bannatyne, Beney, Boyd, Buckland, Craig, Davies, Goodhart, Isaacs, Napier, Warren.

Abbreviated terms: To consider (a) *how far the recovery of damages or compensation should affect or be affected by provisions under any social insurance scheme;* (b) *whether any alteration is desirable in the law governing the liability of employers independently of the Workmen's Compensation Acts;* (c) *the recovery in whole or in part of the cost of reconditioning and vocational training in cases of disablement involving employers or third parties.*

The two Reports deal with paragraph (*b*) of the terms of reference. The effect of the Lord Chancellor's Bill, drafted on the recommendations of the Law Revision Committee on the Law of Contributory Negligence, is to abolish the Common Law rule that a plaintiff suffering loss through his own fault and that of the defendant must bear the whole of the loss and be without remedy against the defendant, and to substitute a new rule under which the plaintiff's loss would be divided between him and the defendant according to the degree in which each was at fault. The Committee was asked for its views on whether provision should be made for action by workmen against employers, but was reluctant to express any views until it had heard evidence from organisations of workmen and employers, in the meantime recommending exclusion of such actions, but not actions against other persons than their employers. These did not represent its views after it had heard evidence, and the 2nd Interim Report recommended that actions by workmen against employers and by employers against workmen should not be excluded from the Bill, and that the amended law should be applied immediately to this. The workman should not have the right to claim compensation after he had received judgment for damages.

—— *Final Report,* apps. pp. iv, 72. 1946 1945–46 *Cmd.* 6860, xiii, 281 sgd. *March,* 1946

add Fawcett, del. Isaacs.

Sir William Beveridge in his Report (Cmd. 6404) stated that 'the possible existence of an alternative remedy should not prevent an injured person from getting forthwith whatever Social Security benefits he would be entitled to claim if he had no such remedy' and that 'an injured person should not have the same need met twice over'; he should not 'get more from two sources than he would have got from one alone'. The problem therefore under the National Insurance Bills, was whether the rights of action in the cases of personal injury due to the wrongful act for which damages would at present be recoverable should be preserved, and if so, whether the right to damages (or compensation) should affect the right to benefits, or whether the right to benefits should affect the right to damages (or compensation). Under existing law the court estimates the sums required to compensate the injured person fully for his pain and suffering, his disablement and every other head of loss which can reasonably be attributed to his injury, and awards that sum by way of damages which represents a 'fair compensation' for injury. If then the injured person were given benefits in addition to full damages he would recover in most cases substantially more than 'fair compensation'.

The doctrine of common employment provides that a master is not responsible for any harm done by one of his servants to a fellow servant engaged in common employment with him, and is based on the false premise that a workman has accepted the risk of his fellow servant's misconduct. This doctrine has been subject to exceptions and limitations and is so difficult to apply in practice that it gives rise to expensive litigation. To abolish the doctrine would place more responsibility on employers, but the burden will not be an unfair one and abolition will protect those persons least able to protect themselves.

The Committee recommended that where the injury is not connected with employment, the right of action for damages should be retained; where it arises out of employment, the workmen's right of action against their employers should be retained, and should not be limited to cases where the cause of injury is the serious misconduct or gross negligence of the employer; the doctrine of common employment should be abolished. In both employment and non-employment cases, the injured person or his dependents should not be allowed to recover in damages or benefits more than the maximum he could receive from either source alone; he should not be required to elect between damages and benefit, but should be allowed to receive both, but in assessing damages the court should take into account in diminution of damages the amount of benefits already received and the estimated value of future benefits. The cost of reconditioning and vocational training should not, in cases involving employers or third parties, be recoverable by the authority from the defendant.

In a reservation W. P. Allen and F. Fawcett disagreed with Sir William Beveridge's statement that 'an injured person should not have the same need met twice over'. In many instances the effect of an injury can never be met by a monetary payment. The damages awarded are as reasonable compensation and not for restoring the injured person to his former position. The damages awarded may or may not meet the need; it is unlikely that a workman who has suffered loss of £300 per annum in wages and whose expectation of life is 30 years would be awarded £7400, which is the annuity value of such an income. If a contributor is insured against certain hazards, he is entitled to receive the benefit of the insurance. By the proposal to modify damages, the benefits for which he has paid would be virtually handed over to the wrongdoer. Recovery of damages should have no regard whatsoever to the amount of benefit which a person is entitled to receive. F. W. Beney felt that this proposal would mean that the wrongdoer would be relieved wholly or partly of his wrongdoing at the expense of the Fund, and that the estimation of future benefits (taking into account possible marriage, children, etc.) would be largely guess-work. Instead, the Fund should have power to modify benefits. J. S. Boyd and Guy de G. Warren argued that the British Employers' Federation did not ask for the complete abolition of the common law rights of workmen, but that the employer's responsibilities should be limited to cases where he was morally and in fact to blame. The historical trend of workmen's compensation legislation has been to provide insurance against accident and away from common law remedies. The abolition of 'common employment' would make the employer responsible for the negligence of every individual in his employment. 'It re-echoes the centuries-old argument that if the person really to blame cannot pay, the legal responsibility should be saddled on someone who, however personally blameless, can do so.'

National Insurance (Industrial Injuries) Bill

Memo. pp. 12. 1945. *Proposed Changes in the Death Benefits.* Memo., app. pp. 12. [1946]. *National Insurance (Industrial Injuries) Act, 1946.* Government Actuary. 1st Interim Rep. pp. 8. 1951. Government Actuary. Rep. on 1st Quinquennial Review. pp. iii, 28. 1955
1944–45 *Cmd.* 6651, *vii*, 603. 1945–46 *Cmd.* 6738, *xvi*, 561. 1950–51 (284) *xvi*, 323. 1954–55 (22) *vi*, 203

The Memos. give the principal changes which have been made in the original proposals set out in Pt. II of the paper in *Social Insurance*—chiefly in relation to a scaling-up and easing conditions of benefits and allowances. Accidents arising in the course of employment will be deemed, in the absence of evidence to the contrary, also to have arisen out of that employment. The report outlines the provisions of the Act and the Liabilities in the first year. See succeeding Ann. Reps. See also *Workmen's Compensation (Supplementation) Bill.* Memo.; 1950–51 *Cmd.* 8150, xxvii, 1045.

Assessment of Disablement due to Specified Injuries

Inter-Dept. Cttee. Rep., app. pp. 19. 1947
1946–47 *Cmd.* 7076, *x*, 693
apptd. March, sgd. Dec., 1946

E. Hancock (*Ch.*), Allen, Boyd, Eyre-Brook, Fleming, Griffiths, Gordon-Taylor, Merewether, Ward (Miss G.), Webb.

'*To examine the schedule of assessment of disablement due to specified injuries which is appended to the various war-pensions instruments with reference to its application both to cases covered by those instruments and to cases covered by the National Insurances (Industrial Injuries) Scheme . . with a view to the adoption of a common schedule. . . .*'

Assessment for war pensions is made without reference to the earning capacity of the person in his disabled condition in his own or other specific trade or occupation or to individual factors or extraneous circumstances. For industrial injury assessment takes no account of particular circumstances other than age, sex, physical and mental condition. In both cases the assessment is not of failure of capacity to follow any specific occupation, but of capacity to exercise the functions of a normally occupied life, and is expressed in percentages which are multiples of ten and five. It was practicable to make different assessments for specified injuries for the young, old people and women which the industrial injuries scheme will bring within its scope, except, e.g. in the case of facial injuries to women, where the scheduled description allows discretion. The Appendix gives the proposed schedules of assessments.

Industrial Diseases

Dept. Cttee. Rep., app. pp. 15. 1948
1948–49 *Cmd.* 7557, *xvii*, 97
apptd. March, 1947. sgd. Oct., 1948

E. T. Dale (*Ch.*), Bannatyne, Dale (C. R.), Hewitt, Jones, Lane, Merewether, Piper, Stillwell, Winner (Miss A. L.).

'*To review, in the light of modern industrial conditions, the policy adopted in scheduling diseases as industrial diseases under the Workmen's Compensation Acts, and to advise as to the principles which should govern the selection of diseases for insurance under the National Insurance (Industrial Injuries) Act. . . .*'

Under the Workmen's Compensation Act, 1906, six diseases were listed in a schedule to the Act, and a workman was entitled to compensation if he could prove that he had suffered from one of them as a result of his employment during the twelve months preceding his disablement. By 1948 forty-four diseases had been added to the list. Before a disease was scheduled it had to be proved that it incapacitated a person for longer than three days and that it was a disease common in a particular trade, but rare outside it. These tests, devised when the liability to pay compensation rested on the employer, were no longer appropriate for the National Insurance (Industrial Injuries) Act, 1946. Suggestions were made to the Committee that benefits under the Act should be payable in respect of every disease which can be shown to be due to employment, in the same way as payments are made in respect of injury by accident, but the Committee ruled that the terms of reference related specifically to 'principles of selection of diseases'.

The 1946 Act provides that 'a disease or injury may be prescribed . . . in relation to any insured persons, if the Minister is satisfied that it ought to be treated as a risk of their occupations and not as a risk common to all persons'. The Committee noted the necessity of a dividing line between the application of the National Health Insurance Act and the National Insurance (Industrial Injuries) Act. The primary consideration should be 'whether a disease is specific to the occupations of the persons concerned, or if it is not so specific, whether the occupations of those persons cause special exposure to risk of disease, such risk being inherent in the conditions under which the occupations are carried on'. The satisfactory working of the disease provisions of the Act will depend largely on the valuable system of presumptions that prescribed disease is due to employment unless the contrary is proved. Proposals are made for a Standing Committee to consider and keep under review the schedule of prescribed diseases.

Industrial Injuries Advisory Council

The National Insurance (Industrial Injuries) Act, 1946, provides for the setting-up of an independent Advisory Council to advise the Minister on proposals for regulations under the Act, etc. A special sub-committee of the Council considers questions as to prescribing diseases under the Act. It has issued the following reports:

—— *Tuberculosis and other Communicable Diseases in Relation to Nurses and other Health Workers.* Sub-Cttee. Rep., app. pp. 20. 1950

1950–51 *Cmd.* 8093, *xvi*, 371 *sgd. Aug.,* 1950

A. W. Garrett (*Ch.*).

There was a high incidence of tuberculosis amongst nurses, and other health workers who had close and frequent contact with the infection were also exposed to risk of infection. Evidence suggested that the attribution could not be established with reasonable certainty, but could be reasonably presumed.

Tuberculosis infection might be prescribed under the Act, the period of prescription to begin six weeks after the claimant's entry into such employment and end two years after the date on which the claimant ceased to be engaged in the employment.

—— *Time Limits.* Rep. pp. 12. 1952

1951–52 *Cmd.* 8511, *xv*, 1133 *sgd. March,* 1952

Easements in the time limits for claiming benefits were suggested for hospital in-patients, claimants for dependents' increases, claims for main disablement benefit, etc.

—— *Pneumoconiosis.* Rep., apps. pp. 24. 1953

1952–53 *Cmd.* 8866, *xiv*, 227 *sgd. June,* 1953

For the purpose of the Industrial Injuries Act pneumoconiosis is prescribed in relation to a single schedule of occupations. Doctors on the Pneumoconiosis Medical Panels are free to make their diagnosis in the light of medical knowledge, and as this has worked satisfactorily the Committee recommended that there should be no change in the legal definition of the disease. Benefits should be paid. A claimant from unscheduled occupations should be eligible, but should discharge the onus of establishing that his disease is due to his insurable employment since 5th July, 1948. Further occupations should be added to the schedule when they are shown 'beyond reasonable doubt' to carry the risk of the disease.

—— *Raynaud's Phenomenon.* Rep., app. pp. 16. 1954

1954–55 Cmd. 9347, *vi*, 265
sgd. Nov., 1954

Raynaud's Phenomenon ('white fingers', 'dead hands') may be of constitutional origin, occurs widely in the population and the precipitating factor in an attack is exposure to cold. But it can also be caused by the use of high-frequency vibratory tools, etc. While it would be possible to distinguish between occupational and non-occupational cases if the occupational cover were duly restricted, it would be difficult to distinguish between vibratory tools and processes which do and a large number which do not give rise to it, diagnosis is not easy, and in the majority of cases the disablement is trivial. Its prescription under the Industrial Injuries Act is therefore not recommended. Dale disagrees, and thinks it should be prescribed.

6. PENSIONS

Contributory Old Age and Widows Pensions

There are a number of papers on the improvements in pensions which pre-

ceded and were superseded by the proposals of the Beveridge Report, the papers on Social Insurance, and the National Insurance Act, 1946. These are the report of the Government Actuary on *The Financial Provisions of the Bill relating to Contributory Pensions and Health Insurance;* 1939–40 Cmd. 6169, v, 125, which estimated the capital value of the added benefits as £260 mn., the present value of additional contributions as £100 mn., and the Exchequer liability as £160 mn.; Memo. on *Old Age and Widows' Pensions Act, 1940;* 1939–40 Cmd. 6204, x, 119, which provided for the payment of supplementary pensions to those persons other than blind persons who could prove need. See also: *Determination of Needs.* Memos.; 1940–41 Cmd. 6265, v, 847. 1941–42 Cmd. 6375, v, 759. 1942–43 Cmd. 6464, vii, 733. 1943–44 Cmd. 6490, viii, 439.

For the proposals in the Beveridge Report and the Government White Paper, see pp. 285, 289.

National Insurance Retirement Pensions. Reasons given for Retiring or Continuing at Work

Enquiry. Rep., apps. pp. vi, 136. 1954
1954 *Non-Parl. Min. of Pensions & N.I.*

Of the 12,009 men in the sample reaching minimum pension age of 65, nearly 40 per cent took their retirement pension and 60 per cent continued at work. At age 67 the proportions are reversed: for every four men continuing at work six have retired. Of those continuing at work 45 per cent did so for financial reasons, 25 per cent because they felt fit enough, 20 per cent preferred to work, and half of them said that the prospect of extra leisure put them against giving up work, and 1 in 100 said nothing would be likely to make him leave work. Those who retired gave three main reasons for it: the employer's action (compulsory retirement, often in connection with a superannuation scheme or discharge), 28 per cent; ill-health, including heaviness and strain of work, 28 per cent;

chronic sickness, 25 per cent; and wish for rest or leisure, nearly 7 per cent. Of those who retired because of employer's action, three out of every four said they would have been willing to go on working at their old job and most said they were willing to adapt themselves to other types of work.

The enquiry was more limited for women, covering only those who were insured on their own account, of whom a quarter had given up work five years previously. The main reasons given for retirement at 60 were sickness and strain, 45 per cent; family reasons, 13 per cent; discharge by employer, 7 per cent. Of those staying at work, 54 per cent did so for financial reasons and 29 per cent preferred to work.

Economic and Financial Problems of the Provision for Old Age

Cttee. Rep., apps. pp. iii, 120. 1954
1954–55 *Cmd. 9333, vi,* 589
apptd. July, 1953. *sgd. Nov.,* 1954

T. W. Phillips (*Ch.*), Bartlett, Cairncross, Gunlake, Honey, Imrie, McAndrews, Menzler, Ross, Vaughan (Dr. Janet).

'*To review the economic and financial problems involved in providing for old age, having regard to the prospective increase in the numbers of the aged, and to make recommendations.*'

The number of people of pensionable age, now 7 mn. or 2 in 15 of the population, in 1979 will be 9½ mn. or 3 in 15. The economic problem of providing for them arises out of the need to accumulate or to free resources for the purpose, the financial problem out of the need to transfer purchasing power to them. Though there are wide variations between individuals, an average of 40 per cent of their income is from retirement and other pensions. The annual outlay on pensions, including occupational pensions, is about £500 mn. plus £50 mn. in National Assistance, or 4 per cent of the national income; in 1979 it will be 6 per cent of the national income at that date.

Pensions expenditure at existing rates will rise two-and-a-half times as fast as the numbers of the elderly and the deficit to be met by the Exchequer to £430 mn. Because contributions to retirement pensions are based on rates appropriate to an entrant aged 16 who will pay for 45 to 50 years, whilst the Act of 1946 brought all of pensionable age within the scheme, though they had not done so, contributions to present pensions cover only one-twentieth of what would be the cost of purchasing them on commercial terms.

Building up a fund against future liabilities for retirement pensions would earmark too large a proportion of the national finances. The accumulation of capital assets should be facilitated. Progressive rise of productivity would be the most important factor in easing the burden, but it would have to be tapped by taxation and contributions. Financing by pay-as-you-go, i.e. fixing contributions in each five years to pay for the expenditure in those years, and varying contributions according to income, are rejected in favour of retaining contributions based on age 16 entry, one-seventh being paid by the Exchequer. Pensions should be universal. In view of the medical evidence and the increasing number of elderly persons who work, after five years the minimum pensionable age should be raised by one year and ultimately to 68 for men and 65 for women. The retirement and earnings rule should be retained, but increments which can be earned should not be improved. A contributive scheme cannot provide enough pensions to enable everyone to live without other means. Changes in the level of pensions should be related to changes in the cost of living, in the numbers resorting to national assistance, etc.

Occupational schemes, now covering 8 mn. people, are socially desirable. They are funded, but the funds are unlikely to be too large for the economy to absorb and they make a contribution to future cost. Part of the cost is borne by tax reliefs. The granting of these reliefs should be made conditional on the combined superannuation and retirement pension not exceeding two-thirds of the final salary and on the minimum pension age not being lower than those from National Insurance. Rights to pension on change of employment should be preserved.

In a reservation Cairncross recommended that the earnings of increments should cease, that the retirement condition and earnings rule should be withdrawn and pensions paid as a right to all above the minimum age; no contributions should be payable for part-time workers over the pensionable ages. Bartlett and McAndrews object to raising the minimum pension age in order to decrease the financial burden, which could be done best by extending employment. In some occupations continuance of work is neither desirable nor possible. Vaughan recommends a restoration of parity between the pension ages for men and women when the minimum age is reached.

XII. HEALTH

1. General: War Problems, Health Services, Hospitals
   (i) War Problems
   (ii) Health Services
   (iii) Hospitals
2. Medical Professions

   (i) Medical Practitioners, Dentists, etc.
   (ii) Nurses
   (iii) Other Services
3. Particular Problems and Diseases
4. Drugs, Food Purity

1. GENERAL: WAR PROBLEMS, HEALTH SERVICES, HOSPITALS

(i) War Problems

Conditions in Air-Raid Shelters with Special Reference to Health

Cttee. Recommendations and Statements of Government Action. pp. 7. 1940. Further Recommendations, etc. pp. 5. 1940

1939–40 *Cmd.* 6234, *iv*, 1. 1940–41 *Cmd.* 6245, *iv*, 151

apptd. Sept., 1940. *pres. Nov., Dec.,* 1940

Lord Horder (*Ch.*), Atkinson (Mrs. C.), Deedes, Rouse, Stock.

To enquire 'into the conditions of air-raid shelters used for sleeping purposes, with particular reference to health.'

Publicity was needed to urge the use of small shelters, e.g. the Anderson shelter, etc., and so effect the utmost degree of dispersal from the communal shelters. In the communal shelters there should be proper lighting, bunking for infants, allocation to specified residents, etc. A re-survey should be made of basements, railway arches, etc. Shelters in factories not used at night should be requisitioned for public use during the hours of closure, and the possibility of using the tube system for shelters examined. Further recommendations concerned the evacuation of children, the creation of a warden service, sanitary arrangements, shelter inspection, first-aid points and medical posts, e.g. beds and bunks should be allotted to the medical aid post at the rate of two beds and three three-tiered bunks for every 500 persons in the larger shelters, etc.

Further recommendations deal with tuberculosis cases frequenting shelters, louse and bug infestation, insecticides, chemicals in latrines, masks for reducing risks by droplet infection, prophylactic measures against infections and smoking. Details are given of steps taken to implement the recommendations.

Neuroses in War-time

Memo. pp. 8. 1940

1940 *Non-Parl. Min. of Pensions*

During the 1914–18 war the occurrence of large numbers of neuroses engendered by fear, exhaustion, physical and mental strain, or lack of sleep, caught both the Services and medical profession unprepared. Neuroses were popularly called 'shell shock' and it was an excellent term to explain a condition which could not easily be understood. It soon became obvious that nervous disorders arising during the war differed in no material way from those well known in civil life. Most of these neuroses occur either in the form of anxiety state or hysteria, but it is important that the cases of concussion should be differentiated. The immediate treatment of patients is extremely important; if they are neglected the morale of the population suffers seriously. Details are given of the kinds of treatment to be given to patients after air-raids, etc.

See *Shell Shock.* Cttee. Rep.; 1922 Non-Parl. War Office.

Medical Personnel (Priority)

Cttee. 1st, 2nd, Interim Reps., app. pp. 12, 1942

1942 *Non-Parl. Min. of Health apptd. —. sgd. Feb.,* 1942

G. Shakespeare (*Ch.*), Ball, Blackham, Bramwell, Brown, Knox, Nicholls, Picken, Richardson, Smith, Souttar, Webb-Johnson.

'*To investigate in the light of the recommendations made in January* 1941 *by the Committee of Enquiry on Medical Personnel, what further steps can usefully be taken to secure the utmost economy in the employment of medical personnel in H.M. Forces, the Civil Defence Services, the Emergency Hospital Scheme and all other medical services, including general practice. . . .*'

In view of the shortage of doctors, their distribution must be reviewed continuously. Committees in each Civil Defence Region should meet continually to ensure co-operation in meeting civil and Service needs, to eliminate under-employment and overlapping. The age of recruitment for military service for doctors should be raised and powers taken to transfer them from one hospital to another. The Air Force, Army and Navy reduced their original demand by 37 per cent, 40 per cent and 30 per cent respectively. To meet Service demands in the first quarter of 1942, reductions of whole-time staff in civilian hospitals and mental hospitals were recommended. The Report of the Robinson Committee on the same subject was not published. See the recommendations given in Commons Debates 371 H.C. Deb. 5s. 24th April, 1941, col. 264.

Mass Miniature Radiography in the Detection of Pulmonary Tuberculosis among Recruits for H.M. Forces

Medical Advisory Cttee. Rep., app. pp. 6. 1942

1941–42 *Cmd.* 6353, *ix*, 155 *apptd. May,* 1940. *pres. April,* 1942

It was not practicable at present to introduce mass radiography as a normal part of the medical examination of men and women before entry into the Forces or Auxiliary Services at the 200 centres where recruits are examined. It should be used to the greatest extent possible after entry.

Voluntary Aid Detachments

Cttee. Rep., apps. pp. 23. 1943

1942–43 *Cmd.* 6448, *vi*, 683 *apptd. July,* 1942. *sgd. —*

W. E. Elliot (*Ch.*), Coates, Dudley, Hood, Limerick (Lady Angela), Mountbatten (Lady Edwina), Smieton (Miss M. G.), Stocks (Mrs. M.), Watt (Miss K. C.).

'*To consider the scope and method of employment of mobile V.A.D.'s by, and their relationship to, the Services.*'

The V.A.D. was a creation of the 1914–18 war, when a group of women, under no compulsion at all, undertook voluntarily to serve in naval, military, and air force medical units. As the older body they enjoy privileges not enjoyed by comparable groups in the women's auxiliary services. The situation has been altered by the expansion of the A.T.S., which provides a new framework for all women's auxiliary units and is closely integrated with the organisation and discipline of the service, and by the conscription of women for national service. The Army Council thought that a merger of the two would make for a better use of man and women power. Recommended: the status and range of duties of the V.A.D. nursing members be the same as for an A.T.S. nursing orderly; the V.A.D.'s retain their separate identity; V.A.D. personnel be subject to military law in the same degree and the same manner as members of the A.T.S. and be enrolled into the women's forces; for the V.A.D. Council be substituted a standing committee representing the voluntary bodies concerned, including the Council of Territorial Associations. The supersession of the V.A.D. Council will make it necessary for the voluntary bodies to reconsider county machinery and the position of county controllers.

Duties of Local Authorities in Relation to (I) The Casualty Services and (II) Public Health in Time of War

Memo. pp. 15. 1951

1951 *Non-Parl. Min. of Health*

Casualty Services.—The realisable expansion of the hospital services would be finally limited by the number of available doctors and must be planned to make the best use of them. Hospitals would be in three operational groups: casualty transit centres, in closed hospital buildings in central big areas; cushion hospitals, existing or improvised, in fringe areas; base hospitals. A reserve of plasma for blood transfusion is being built up. The static first-aid posts and mobile first-aid units of World War II immobilised too many doctors and nurses. In future, the first-

aid service will be integrated with the hospital service, so that staff can be used for normal work. There will be mobile units, based on selected hospitals, for every 15,000 population. A National Hospital Service Reserve of trained nurses and auxiliaries has been constituted. The chain of command is detailed.

Evacuation and Care of the Homeless.—Guidance is given on the medical inspection and care of children and expectant mothers, and the formation and sanitation of rest centres and transit camps.

See *Evacuation*. Circular 37/50 and Memo. Ev. 1 (1950). *Care of the Homeless*. Circular 38/50; 1950 Min. of Health.

(ii) Health Services

Post-War Hospital Problems in Scotland

Cttee. Rep., apps. pp. 44. 1943

1942–43 *Cmd.* 6472, *iv*, 609

apptd. Jan., 1942. *sgd. Aug.*, 1943

H. J. W. Hetherington (*Ch.*), Anderson, Cook, Erskine, Fraser, Gunn, Murdoch, Robertson, Rose (Miss B. M.), Shaw (Mrs. C. McN.), Vallance.

'*To consider and make recommendations within a policy aimed at the post-war development of a comprehensive and co-ordinated hospital service in Scotland on a regional basis. . . .*'

The policy of the Government was to ensure that by means of a comprehensive hospital service, treatment should be available to every person in need of it. Local authorities were asked to co-operate with voluntary agencies to make this possible. The Health Services Committee, 1936 (*Breviate 1917–39*, p. 405), had already reached the conclusion that with the ever-mounting costs of running hospitals, the prospects of substantial expansion of voluntary hospitals was diminishing, and that the necessities of the case would fall on the local authorities. Local authorities were experienced in administering hospitals for infectious diseases, tuberculosis, mental diseases and maternity. As it was now assumed that they would continue to do so, the problem was one of securing co-operation between voluntary hospitals and local authorities.

Co-operation will be more readily achieved if in the remuneration of the doctors, as for other staff, conditions throughout the whole system are more uniform. The government of a local authority hospital by the Public Health Committee, with the medical superintendent working under the Medical Officer of Health, should move towards the full clinical responsibility being assigned to the several clinical units; and the senior medical staff should have independent corporate access to the Public Health Committee. Local health authorities should be given powers to provide outpatients' departments, clinics and ambulances for general hospital purposes. There should be an advisory regional council for five hospital regions, which should prepare comprehensive regional schemes; but in view of geography and population, the South-Western Region should form sub-regional organisations. Regional appointments committees should advise hospitals on senior medical appointments. Real partnership between local authorities and voluntary hospitals cannot be secured without some uniformity in the financial relationship between all general hospitals and their patients. Methods of payment involving assessment—charging patients at or near the time of treatment—and voluntary contributory schemes are both rejected. There should be a compulsory contributory scheme co-extensive with the social security scheme, and an exchequer subsidy, and from the fund so created payments should be made to hospitals on the basis of services rendered, hospitals being graded into three categories for this purpose. If the necessary subvention to voluntary hospitals is to come from local authorities, it should be a uniform rate based on rateable value or population, the amount being determined by a standard rate of hospital expenditures. A proportion of strictly charitable or voluntary income should be left for development.

A National Health Service

Statement, apps. pp. 85. 1944

1943–44 *Cmd. 6502, viii,* 315

In spite of substantial progress in building up health services by public, voluntary and private effort, not everyone can get all the kinds of medical services he requires. There is no guaranteed link between the doctor and other medical services, and many services are not related to one another. The object is to provide for everybody a comprehensive service (with the temporary exception of dental and mental health treatment), irrespective of means, age, sex or occupation, and to divorce it from questions of personal means by giving it, with a few exceptions, free of charge. People and doctors will be free to choose whether to use or enter the service or not, the doctor will be professionally free and the patient-doctor relationship will be preserved.

The new service will weld together and expand existing services; it will be democratically controlled, and special provision will be made for professional and expert guidance. Central responsibility will be with the Minister, local responsibility with the county and county borough councils individually for some services or acting jointly over large areas for others. The Minister will be aided by an independent, statutory and primarily professional Central Health Services Council, and the local organisation by Local Health Service Councils. To bring together the activities of the various separate and independent hospitals will require areas of population and financial resources large enough to enable adequate and economical specialised services to be provided and to blend the needs of town and country. The new joint authority for these areas will also have the task, in consultation with the local professional body, of preparing for the area plans for the Health Service as a whole. The voluntary hospitals should continue side by side with the publicly provided hospitals; they will be able if they wish to participate in the national health service without loss of identity or autonomy by maintaining services approved under the plan, and by complying with the national conditions for all hospitals as to the pay of nurses and the appointment and salaries of senior medical posts. They will be paid for specified services at a figure less than cost. To ensure that the services of consultants are available to all, there must be more of them and they must be better distributed. The payment of consultants and creation of posts will help to achieve both these ends.

The right of the whole population to the services of a general medical practitioner in conditions of free choice raises difficult problems. The creation of a system in which all doctors would be salaried employees is a matter on which opinion inside and outside the profession is sharply divided, but it is not necessary for an efficient service. An extension of the National Insurance Panel system, under which a doctor could set up anywhere he wished, and which has meant that some areas are over- and some under-supplied with doctors, would be inconsistent with the obligation to provide a medical service for all. Further, the practice of medicine now requires modern facilities for diagnosis, etc., which cannot be provided by a private surgery. The scheme will try to provide for doctors to collaborate in group practice, especially in areas of high density, in which the surgery, equipment, secretarial help, etc., will be in health centres which the local authorities will equip and maintain. The scheme will also retain separate private practice. But to ensure a proper distribution of doctors, unrestricted entry into new practice, whether by purchase or by 'squatting', cannot be permitted. Doctors wishing to set up in a new public service practice will require the consent of a Central Medical Board, which may refuse sanction. Since these restrictions may destroy the value of some existing private practices, which have often been bought, compensation will be paid to any doctor transferring his public service practice to a health centre, or when a vacant public service practice is not allowed to be filled. Doctors in separate practices will be remunerated on a capitation basis; limits will be set to a number of patients a doctor may take. The individual doctor's contract will be with a professional Central Medical Board, which will be set up to watch over the distribution of public medical practice generally. The existing local insurance committees will be abolished. The joint authority will plan the clinics and other necessary services, but these will be administered by the county and county borough authorities. The education authorities will continue medical inspection in schools, but the children will be referred to the health service for treatment.

The individual members of the public will obtain medical treatment without payment of any kind except for the cost of certain appliances. The cost of the service will be paid for partly by a social insurance contribution, partly by taxes and rates. The hospitals may receive bed-unit payments from central funds, while the joint authorities will receive the bed-unit payments and raise money by precept on the constituent local authorities. The latter will be aided by Exchequer grants.

The general principles of the Health Service will apply equally in Scotland, but there will be some differences in organisation, arising partly out of the concentration of 80 per cent of the population in the industrial 'waist' of the country, with the rest in sparsely populated areas.

Appendix E gives a rough estimate of the cost of the service to the public funds. For England and Wales this is £132 mn., of which £70 mn. would be the expenditure of the new joint authorities, and £32 mn. the payments to doctors and chemists. Of this total £48 mn. would come from rates and £84 mn. from taxes. If certain assumptions are made, the cost would be divided between social insurance contributions, taxes and rates in the proportions of 27 per cent, 36·6 per cent and 36·4 per cent respectively.

See *National Health Service Bill.* Summaries; 1945–46 Cmd. 6761, Cmd. 6946, xx, 511. *Report of the Chief Medical Officer for 1917–18;* 1918 Cd. 9169, xi, 309. *Future Provision of Medical and Allied Services;* 1920 Cmd. 693, xvii, 1001. *Breviate, 1917–39*, pp. 395–7.

Central Health Services Council

[1st Ann.] Rep. and Statement, apps. pp. viii, 33. 1950

1950 (84) *xi*, 661
F. Messer (*Ch.*).

The Central Health Services Council is constituted by section 2 (1) of the National Health Service Act, 1946, and is required by section 2 (5) to make an annual report to the Minister. It acts as a confidential body of advisers to the Minister and those members appointed 'after consultation with representative organisations', serve as individuals, and not as delegates. The Report covers the proceedings of the following Standing Advisory Committees constituted under section 2 (3) of the Act: Medical, Dental, Pharmaceutical, Ophthalmic, Nursing, Maternity and Midwifery, Mental Health, Tuberculosis, Cancer and Radiography and Child Health. To prevent wasteful prescribing in the general practitioner service advice was given to the Minister on the classification of border-line substances as foods or drugs, and on the restrictions to be imposed on the use of expensive drugs and medicines still in the experimental stage, or of doubtful value, or unnecessarily expensive. Owing to the pressure on hospitals and the difficulty of securing admissions, recommendations were made on the priorities and methods to be observed in dealing with acute emergency, early

malignant and various types of non-urgent cases.

See succeeding annual reports. *Scottish Health Services Council.* First Report; 1950 Cmd. 7921, xi, 703, and succeeding Ann. Reps.

Dentistry

Inter-Dept. Cttee. Interim Rep., apps. pp. 25. 1944

1943–44 *Cmd.* 6565, *iii,* 169
apptd. April, 1943. *sgd. Oct.,* 1944

Lord Teviot (*Ch.*), Attkins, Ballard, Bearn, Bradlaw, Brocklehurst, Douglas, Fry, Helliwell, Henderson, Hutchinson, McKeag, Rankin, Raynes, Shearer, Stewart, Trubshaw (Dame G.), Weaver, Wood, Woodward.

'*To consider and report upon:* (a) *the progressive stages by which, having regard to the number of practising dentists, provision for an adequate and satisfactory dental service should be made available for the population:* (b) *the measures to be taken to secure an adequate number of entrants to the dental profession:* (c) *existing legislation dealing with the practice of dentistry and the government of the dental profession:* (d) *measures for the encouragement and co-ordination of research into the causation, prevention and treatment of dental disease.*'

Dentists have formed themselves into three professional bodies: the British Dental Association, the Incorporated Dental Association and the Incorporated Dental Society. The General Medical Council is responsible for securing proper standards of examination, and for controlling matters of discipline, and the Dental Board is responsible for regulations and registration, etc., which it must submit to the Council for confirmation. The Board's chief source of revenue is the fee paid annually by registered dentists, much of which is used for subsidising dental schools. There are five schools in London, seven in provincial cities, one in Belfast and four in Eire, with a total student capacity of 2000–2500. Most schools are staffed, apart from perhaps one professor and two or three whole-time teachers, on a part-time or voluntary basis. Some dental schools are closely associated with hospitals, others with universities or with both. The dental hospital was established to give treatment to the poor and to provide clinical training for students. Contributions from patients account for the bulk of the hospital revenue.

Before 1939 about 400 students entered annually, of whom about 10 per cent were women. The total cost of training was about £800. The wartime entry of students fell so low that if their numbers rose to 400 in 1945–52 and to 425 thereafter, it would be about 30 years before the effective total of the profession would be increased. The majority of dentists have surgery assistants, but there is no training available. There are also some 8000 dental mechanics in the country, but there is no systematic training and formal apprenticeship has lapsed.

In the School Dental Service in 1928 there was one dentist to every 11,300 children; 70 per cent of the children were examined; 50 per cent needed treatment, and 65 per cent of those needing treatment received it. Dental treatment in the Maternity and Child Welfare Services is extremely meagre, though the younger mothers are beginning to appreciate the value of conservative dentistry. Roughly two-thirds of the insured population are entitled to dental benefit under National Health Insurance, but on the average, only 7 per cent claim. The broad picture is, therefore, of a number of uncorrelated services, each with shortcomings, an apathetic public affected more by lack of education than by the costs which treatment entails, and a bad state of dental health for the population.

The recommendations include a comprehensive dental service as an integral part of the national health service. The dental practitioner service should be analogous to the general medical practitioner service; dental health centres should be developed in conjunction with health centres; there should be freedom for both dentist and patient to participate in the service; full use should be made of expert service; the appropriate authorities should encourage and provide dental service for expectant mothers.

—— Final Report, apps. pp. 60.   1946
1945–46 Cmd. 6727, xi, 339
sgd. Oct., 1945
add Mahony, del. Bearn.

The Committee reaffirms its recommendation that there should be a comprehensive dental service as part of the National Health Service. To achieve a total of 20,000 dentists in active practice, the target should be an annual entry to the dental schools of 900 students. Dental schools should be integral parts of Universities, and the standard of entry the same as for other subjects. State and local authority grants should be available to assist students to whatever extent may be necessary. Priority should be given to building new and rebuilding existing dental schools and there should be a national scale of remuneration for all teachers in dental schools. The Government should provide £1,250,000 towards capital expenditure and annual grants of £150,000 rising to £300,000 in five or six years. The profession should be governed by a separate Dental Council, the Dentists Act, 1921 amended to prohibit the practice of dentistry by unregistered persons. Recommendations are also made for recruiting and training dental mechanics, for postponing any scheme for dental operative assistants until a shortage of dentists for a comprehensive service is proved, and for promoting and aiding research. In a reservation Helliwell objected to a separate Dental Council, as dentistry in its preventive and surgical sense is no way different from other specialist branches of medicine or surgery. The combination in the same person of dental surgery or preventive dentistry with the sale of artificial teeth means that 88 per cent of a dentist's income is derived from the sale of artificial teeth. In view of the shortage of dentists and the need for operative dentistry, the law should be amended to permit the provision of dentures being carried out by specially trained technicians and prosthetists.

Health and Industrial Efficiency: Scottish Experiments in Social Medicine

Pp. 56. 1943

1943 *Non-Parl. Dept. of Health, Scot.*

The availability of accommodation in emergency hospitals built and administered by the Department of Health for Scotland made possible experiments in the early ascertainment of disease and disability; in rehabilitation and in the training and resettlement of disabled men. Work had already been done on similar lines by the Department of Health, which had launched an investigation in 1937 on what could be done to minimise the amount of long-continued incapacity for work. By 1939 some 50,000 cases had been reviewed and a sample of 1000 cases from this number was analysed. The tables include figures on the types, duration and incidence of incapacitating sickness, and confirm the value of a periodic review of incapacitated persons and the need for the co-operation of the various branches of the medical service. There is a description of the Clyde Basin Experiment in the investigation and treatment of young industrial workers, and of the health and working experience of 1000 men invalided out of the Forces as unfit for further service.

Industrial Health Services

Cttee. Rep., apps. pp. iv, 35. 1951

1950–51 *Cmd.* 8170, *xv,* 57
apptd. June, 1949. *sgd. Nov.,* 1950

E. T. Dale (*Ch.*), Byrne, Davies, Edwards (Miss M. M.), Gosling (Miss E. M.), Hyde, Jope, Julian, Loughlin (Dame A.), Pheazey, Roberts, Rogers, Vickers.

'To *examine the relationship (including any possibility of overlapping) between the preventive and curative health services provided for the population at large and the industrial health services which make a call on medical manpower (doctors, nurses and auxiliary medical personnel). . . .'*

In announcing the enquiry, the Prime Minister asked industry to postpone any substantial development of industrial health services until the Committee's recommendations were available.

The National Health Service employs the equivalent of the whole-time service of 14,500 doctors in the hospital and specialist services, 21,000 general practitioners, 60,000 trained nurses, 15,000 enrolled assistant nurses, and 54,000 student nurses. The industrial medical services are much smaller, and include 15 Medical Factory Inspectors, 1800 Appointed Factory Doctors, mostly also in active general practice, some 250 full-time Industrial Medical Officers appointed voluntarily by employers, as well as a number of part-time officers and about 2600 State Registered Nurses and 1200 other nurses. There are also 26 whole-time doctors employed by the National Coal Board and seven by the National Dock Labour Board. There is no evidence that medical manpower was less well employed in the industrial than in the other health services.

There was a possibility of some overlapping and a need for co-operation between the School Medical Officer and the Appointed Factory Doctor. In many cases the Industrial Medical Officer is made the Appointed Factory Doctor, but where this is not so, there is overlapping and a young person will get two examinations. In some smaller factories the State Registered Nurse is required because there is no full-time medical officer, but owing to the great variation of risks it was not possible to say what was the minimum size of a factory requiring a State Registered Nurse.

The industrial health services were complementary to the health service, they should be encouraged and expanded, but they must be co-ordinated with the National Health and Public Health Services. Voluntary provision by employers should be encouraged. Eventually there should be some comprehensive provision for occupational health covering not only industrial establishments, both large and small, but also non-industrial occupations. Claims for more doctors and nurses for industrial health can, at present, only come from employers initiating or increasing their own services at their own expense; guidance of a restraining kind can only take the form of advice, which should be effective. The ban imposed on substantial further development of industrial health services should be lifted at once. Surveys and experiments are needed, particularly in group service for small factories, but there will have to be an increase in medical manpower before there can be further great extensions of the service. Postgraduate and research facilities are needed.

See *Application of Scientific Methods to Industrial and Service Medicine.* Conference. Proc.; 1951 Non-Parl. Medical Research Council.

Child Health

Scottish Health Services Council. Cttee.
Rep. pp. 21. 1953
1953 *Non-Parl. Dept. of Health, Scot.*

A. Cunningham (*Ch.*).

'*To inquire into matters raised by Prof. Fleming's paper.*'

There were a large number of detailed recommendations on the administration and integration of the services, antenatal, neo-natal, those dealing with the child 1 to 12 months, the pre-school and the school child.

(iii) Hospitals

Hospital Surveys

1945, 1946 *Non-Parl. Min. of Health*
1946 *Non-Parl. Dept. of Health, Scot.*

England and Wales. Separate Reports were published for the following ten areas: Berks., Bucks., and Oxon.; Eastern; London and Surrounding Area; North-Western; Sheffield and East Midlands; West Midlands; Yorkshire; North-Eastern; South Western; South Wales and Monmouthshire.

Scotland. A General Introduction and separate Reports were published for the following five regions: Eastern; North-Eastern; Northern; South-Eastern; Western.

The purpose of the surveys was to obtain information about the hospitals and hospital services in each region, together with the surveyors' opinions on the adequacy and quality of both buildings and services. In England and Wales the total number of beds needed varied from 7·1 per 1000 population in the Eastern area to 8·25 beds per 1000 population in London and 9·9 per 1000 in Berks., Bucks. and Oxon. In Scotland the needs were assessed at 4–5 general beds per 1000 in rural districts to 8 per 1000 in industrial districts.

See *Min. of Health.* [Ann.] Rep. p. 63; 1946–47 Cmd. 7119, xii, 1.

National Health Service. Development of Consultant Services

Memo., apps. pp. 39. 1950
1950 *Non-Parl. Min. of Health*

'The object of this memorandum is to assist Regional Hospital Boards in the planning and future development of the consultant services. The immediate result of the introduction of the National Health Service was the payment of consultants for their work within the Service, thus providing a means of securing additional staff where it is most needed. The attempt has been made to examine the scope and content of the different consultant services; to consider how they might best be organised on a regional basis, bearing in mind the part to be played by the Teaching Hospital.' For the various specialist services, e.g. general medicine, general surgery, obstetrics, anaesthetics, cardiology, etc., estimates are made of the number of beds for a town of 100,000 to 120,000 or per million population and the number of whole-time consultants or their equivalent, and of clinical hours of work required.

The General Practitioner and the Hospital Service

Scottish Health Services Council. Jt. Sub-Cttee. Rep., app. pp. 39. 1952

1952 Non-Parl. Dept. of Health, Scot. apptd. Jan., 1950. sgd. Aug., 1951

H. B. Lindsay (*Ch.*), Baird, Cappell, Dundas, Esslemont (Dr. Mary), Grant, Ireland, Kerr, Millar, Reid, Small, Stewart (Miss Eleanor).

'To consider and advise on the relationship between the general practitioner and the hospital and specialist services.'

Whilst it has long been the custom in the hospitals for infectious diseases and tuberculosis to appoint full-time clinical officers who work in association with the Medical Officer of Health, the voluntary hospitals looked largely to the part-time services of selected practitioners, often acting in the role of specialists; even in the teaching hospitals there were numbers of general practitioners with clinical responsibilities. But specialisation has led to full-time appointments, and active participation in general practice was increasingly regarded as inconsistent with specialist work. The general practitioner's place in midwifery practice has narrowed, since institutional midwifery is now responsible for some two-thirds of all confinements. If this present tendency is not reversed, there will be a decline in domiciliary midwifery. The difficulties of arranging for general practitioners to use beds for the treatment of their own patients under the scheme include: distance of practice from the hospital; not every practitioner by restricting his practice could carry out clinical work in hospital; there is a shortage of beds, and successive ward rounds by practitioners would disorganise the nursing staffs. Cottage hospitals, traditionally staffed by the local general practitioners, have important bearing on the standard of practice in the areas which they serve, and should be retained as general practitioner hospitals. There is dissatisfaction over the difficulties of access to ancillary facilities, especially X-ray and laboratory services, for aid in diagnosis and treatment. At present some of these are due to shortages of accommodation, equipment and staff, but policy ought to be governed by the principle that ancillary facilities are available for the health services as a whole. Other questions concern a more close working between hospitals and practitioners on admission and discharge of patients, out-patients, attendance on ward rounds and out-patient departments, clinical meetings, refresher courses.

The interest of the general practitioner must be represented at the policy-making level in relation to hospital and specialist services. The new establishment structure should include suitably qualified and experienced doctors engaged part-time as specialists and practitioners as members of the hospital team. A practitioner undertaking part-time hospital work must be able to limit his practice, and his remuneration for hospital work should be such that his total income is fully maintained. If normal midwifery is accepted as part of general practice, the practitioner should supervise confinement whether at home or in an institution. General practitioner wards and hospitals should be envisaged as part of long-term policy. He should have direct access to ancillary facilities and the right of entry into the hospital, where he can meet colleagues on terms of equality.

Co-operation between Hospitals, Local Authority and General Practitioner Services

Central Health Services Council. Standing Advisory Cttee. Sub-Cttee. Rep., app. pp. 34. 1952

1952 Non-Parl. Min. of Health apptd. March, 1950. sgd. —

F. Messer (*Ch.*), Cohen, Daley, Howard, Howells, Lloyd (Prof. Hilda), Oakes, Carling, Yorke.

'To consider and make a report on (a) existing forms of co-operation between (i) Regional Hospital Boards, Hospital Management Committees, Boards of Governors; and (ii) local authorities; and (iii) Executive Councils; and (b) whether it is possible to formulate any general principles on which co-operation might be promoted between these authorities.'

The Service is administered through three separate statutory branches; the hospital service through the Regional Hospital Boards, Hospital Management Committees, and Board of Governors; the general practitioner service through Executive Councils; and the local health services through local health authorities. These branches are co-ordinated at the national level, but below the national level there is no executive, and only isolated instances of advisory co-ordination. Only in the local authority field is there a single authority to be considered; as some delegate work to area sub-committees and others do not, complications are created. Secondly, there are special relations not created by the Act; e.g. between the universities and the hospital service, the local health authorities services and the local education services, etc. Thirdly, while local health authorities and executive councils have the same areas, the regional boards are superimposed on the local government areas, some of which are divided between two or three Boards' areas.

The problems of the relationship between each pair of statutory agencies are detailed. Co-operation between local health authorities and the hospital service is needed in the maternity and child welfare services in the use of clinical facilities, the interchange of patients' facilities, records, grounds for admission to hospital confinements, the use of the flying squad, of domiciliary specialists, post-natal care, etc. For tuberculosis, the local health authorities are responsible for preventive and social

work, the Regional Hospital Boards for institutional treatment, and the general practitioners and tuberculosis officers for domiciliary treatment. Co-operation is needed in the use of radiography for early diagnosis, admission and discharge from hospital, after-care and domiciliary treatment, in cases of the chronic sick, elderly sick and the mentally defectives, etc. Local authorities and general practitioners want their views on the use of hospitals and the provision of new beds to be considered by the hospital boards; they resent the making of decisions of which they are not even informed. To improve co-operation, in the Act and subsequent arrangements, use has been made of interlocking membership, exchange of papers, Ministry circulars, ad hoc meetings, co-operation between officers, and finally of standing joint committees, which is the only method capable of effective wide development.

Recommended that local joint health consultative committees should be set up for convenient groupings of local health authorities, executive councils and hospital committees; the Minister should invite each Regional Hospital Board to take what it deems to be the most suitable steps to further co-operation of the health services within its region. In a supplementary memo. A. Howard said that it is not the creation of additional committees, compulsions, or sanctions which are needed, but the willing co-operation of a host of individuals acting with mutual confidence and loyalty. The Minister might examine the possibility of using his wide powers to secure greater flexibility in the allocation of functions.

Reception and Welfare of In-Patients at Hospitals

Scottish Health Services Council. Standing Advisory Cttee. Sub-Cttee. Rep. pp. 19. 1951. Central Health Services Council. Rep., apps. pp. 24. 1953

1951 *Non-Parl. Dept. of Health, Scot.*
1953 *Non-Parl. Min. of Health*

Scottish Report: J. Steel (*Ch.*).

These two reports, with slight variations cover the same ground, many passages being common to both. Hospitals have a responsibility to patients as people in addition to that of dealing with a bodily ailment. This question is acute because the National Health Service has altered the relations between staff and patients, and while medical theory increasingly recognises the influence of non-medical factors on the patient's medical condition, increased specialisation requires that the patient should come into contact with experts each concerned with his own line.

The recommendations include: that members of the hospital staff should show utmost consideration and understanding; before entry patients should be sent a letter telling them what to bring, and giving other information; after entry they should be given a brochure describing hospital routine, etc.; reception arrangements should ensure quick and sympathetic treatment; relatives should be told when to make enquiries, visiting periods should be frequent and short. Long stay patients should be given facilities to entertain or employ themselves; bed curtains should be used for privacy in large wards; ear-phones should replace loud speakers; meal-times should be spaced so that patients have no long fasts; patients should not be wakened before 6 a.m.—later, if possible; noise in hospital should be reduced. Hospitals should ensure that a patient's doctor is notified of his discharge, and that there are suitable arrangements at his home for his reception.

Internal Administration of Hospitals

Central Health Services Council. Cttee.
Rep., apps. pp. iv, 87. 1954
1954 *Non-Parl. Min. of Health*
apptd. March, 1950. *sgd. Aug.,* 1954

A. F. Bradbeer (*Ch.*), Stancliffe, Ball, Bird, Cable, Carling, Constable, Cunningham, Dain, Douglas (Miss K. G.), Evans (Miss L. A. D.), Feldon, Gibson, Kitchen, Lesser, Linstead, Masefield, Murray, Trusson, Watt.

'*To consider and report on the existing methods of administration in individual hospitals,* and within Hospital Management Committee groups, *with particular reference to (i) matter of finance, staff and supplies; (ii) the extent to which differences in the work undertaken at different hospitals call for differences in their administrative organisation; (iii) the extent to which administrative duties should be undertaken by medical and nursing staff.*'

The National Health Service took over 1143 voluntary hospitals with some 90,000 beds and 1545 local authority hospitals with about 390,000 beds. The voluntary hospitals were administered by a tripartite organisation of governing body, Medical Committee advising the governing body, and matron representing the nursing staff. In the local authority hospitals there was no common administrative model, though there was a number of distinctive features. The governing body was, under the Council, the public health committee, but it did not control finance and building, and sometimes not the purchase of stores. The status of chairman of the governing body never approached that of the chairman in a voluntary hospital. Each hospital had a medical superintendent responsible to the Medical Officer of Health for lay and nursing administration. From an analysis of the two systems it emerged that hospital administration should be subdivided into medical, nursing, and lay or business administration, with a chief administrative officer, and that partnership between the three parts was fundamental.

The recommendations include that every hospital should have a medical staff committee to advise on all questions within the content of medical administration. An alternative for the larger hospitals would be to appoint as medical administrator a consultant combining clinical with administrative duties. The introduction of group medical superintendents is not recommended. At group level there should be a medical advisory committee. The matron should be head of the nursing services, including the training school for student nurses, and directly responsible to the governing body of the group. In her non-professional functions she should be responsible to the administrative officer in the first instance. In the nurse-training school there should be a nursing education committee to assist the matron. The matron should be consulted about, but not normally control the laundry and catering services. Control of the domestic staff may be vested either in the matron or a lay administrator. There should be group nursing advisory committees, and hospital nursing staff committees. For lay administration all principal specialist officers at group level should be responsible to the governing body through the chief administrative officer. The unit hospital administrator should be regarded as the senior lay officer of his hospital and responsible for its lay administration. The duties of various individual officers are specified in the recommendations. The special circumstances of sanatoria and mental hospitals demand wider medical control in the hands of a medical superintendent.

Proposals for a Scottish Medical Research Fund

Hospital Endowments Com.   Memo.
pp. 8.   1952

1951–52 *Cmd.* 8615, *xxv*, 793
sgd. Feb., 1952

The Hospital Endowments Commission is empowered to frame schemes for the management and if necessary, transfer of endowments from one Regional Board to another, but cannot transfer to any other body. The total funds amounted to £13 mn., and these should be redistributed between the Boards. A considerable proportion should be available to finance medical research without prejudicing other reasonable requirements. Some Boards with small numbers of beds have large endowments, while others with wide scope for research cannot finance it.

This should not continue. The Secretary of State should promote legislation to establish a central Scottish Medical Research Fund, with a steady income of £120,000 per annum. Hospital Boards would still be able to draw for research on their own funds held under the Commission Schemes.

See *Hospital Endowments (Scotland) Act, 1953;* 1 & 2 Eliz. 2. c. 41. *Scottish Hospital Endowments Research Trust.* 1st Rep.; 1956–57 (37) xiv, 429, and succeeding Ann. Reps.

Clinical Research in Relation to the National Health Service

Jt. Sub-Cttee. Rep., app. pp. 23.   1953

1953 *Non-Parl. Medical Research Council, Min. of Health, Dept. of Health, Scot. apptd. June,* 1951. *sgd.* —

H. Cohen (*Ch.*), Carling, Gaddum, Harington, Himsworth, Learmonth, McMichael, Paterson, Spence, Thomson.

'*To consider what arrangements should be made for the further encouragement and development of clinical research in relation to the National Health Service.*'

Before the introduction of the National Health Service Acts the responsibilities of the Health Departments in research were confined to public health; they did not touch medical research concerned with sick individuals and requiring access to hospitals and general practice, which was done by the university medical departments and the Medical Research Council acting either directly or indirectly in supporting members of hospital staffs, or by independent general practitioners. Under the Acts all clinical facilities passed to the charge of the Health Departments and the medical personnel serving them were brought within one unified service. The recommendations provide that a central Clinical Research Board should be appointed by the Medical Research Council to work in close liaison with Health Departments and the clinical departments of the universities; funds should be made available to the Board, rising to £250,000 in three or four years' time. Decentralised research would be related to medical practice and should be financed either by the Ministry of Health from National Health Service Funds, or by local bodies from their own funds. Careers in clinical research should carry the same status, salary, etc., as careers in the Health Service.

2. MEDICAL PROFESSIONS

(i) Medical Practitioners, Dentists, etc.

Remuneration of General Practitioners

Inter-Dept. Cttee. Rep., apps. pp. 31. [1946]

1945–46 *Cmd.* 6810, *xii*, 419
apptd. Feb., 1945. *sgd. April,* 1946

W. Spens (*Ch.*), Brown, Carter, Davies, Knox, Lister, Smyth, Winstanley, Fass.

'*To consider, after obtaining whatever information and evidence it thinks fit, what ought to be the range of total professional income of a registered medical practitioner in any publicly organised service of general medical practice; to consider this with due regard to what have been the normal financial expectations of general medical practice in the past, and to the desirability of maintaining in the future the proper social and economic status of general medical practice and its power to attract a suitable type of recruit to the profession.*'

Professor Bradford Hill's figures show that in the years 1936–38, between the ages of 40 and 49 almost 20 per cent of urban practitioners had a net income of under £700 a year and over 40 per cent had a net income of under £1000. These levels of remuneration, as well as the proportion able to reach a net income of £1300 or over, were too low. Unless general practice were made more attractive, it would recruit only the less able young doctors, whilst the abler men would seek to become specialists with an equal outlet for their interests

in medicine, a contact with the hospitals and a less arduous life. The Committee recommended a spread of incomes such that on the 1939 basis only 7 per cent would be below £700, 27 per cent below £1000 and a half above £1300. If recruitment were to be maintained, men must be able to feel that more than ordinary ability and effort would receive an adequate reward, and a single salary scale would not provide this. Capitation affords the method of differentiation which is acceptable to the majority of the profession. Additional remuneration should be given in unattractive areas, in practices involving an abnormal number of old persons and chronic invalids, and the difference between urban and rural incomes should be reduced.

The Committee did not feel qualified to form an opinion on what adjustment of the 1939 incomes was necessary to produce corresponding incomes in 1946, but observed that such adjustment should have regard not only to the change in the value of money, but to the increases which have taken place since 1939 in other professions.

In a Rider to the Report H. E. Fass suggested a higher scale of payment, bearing in mind the salaries of medical officers of health and the scales at the Middlesex County Hospital in November 1945.

Remuneration of Consultants and Specialists

Inter-Dept. Cttee. Rep., apps. pp. 30. 1948

1947–48 *Cmd.* 7420, *xi*, 289
apptd. May, 1947. *sgd. May,* 1948

W. Spens (*Ch.*), Dale, Hamilton, Lister, Looker (Miss E.), Lyon, L. Moran, Peppiatt, Platt, Shanks, Turton.

'*To consider, after obtaining whatever information and evidence we thought fit, what ought to be the range of total professional remuneration of registered medical practitioners engaged in the different branches of consultant or specialist practice in any*' *publicly organised hospital and specialist service. . . .'*

The term 'specialist' was interpreted to include the whole group of practitioners who after registration and completion of junior house appointments are appointed to hospital posts in training for a special branch of medicine. In the past the remuneration for junior hospital posts bore little relation to the responsibilities, the standard of living required and the need to be free from financial worry. Many potential specialists get diverted to general practice as the income is not sufficient to support a home. For example hospital registrars in 1939 received £300 to £400 or less, even in non-resident posts. No substantial income was derived from staff appointments in voluntary hospitals and a specialist had to face the risks, etc., of building up a private practice. All varieties of specialists should be remunerated within the same range of income, the place of the individual within this range being dependent upon his responsibilities, experience and skill. Thus the highest remuneration would be open to specialists in all fields. In the future there should be a more uniform level of hospital efficiency throughout the country, a better distribution of specialists and permeation by the influence of a university centre.

The chief recommendations were that medical practitioners in training for special branches of medicine should receive a salary of £600 in the first year, rising to £1200 in the fourth year. A specialist appointed to the staff of a hospital at the age of 30 should be receiving a starting salary of £1250. This should be increased each year by £125 until £2500 is reached. Details are given for starting salaries at other ages. A committee should be set up to select, for higher awards, specialists of outstanding distinction. The recommendations were framed in terms of 1939 money values, the adjustments to post-war money values being left to others.

Medical Partnerships

Legal Cttee. Rep., apps. pp. 21.   1948
1948–49 Cmd. 7565, xvii, 787
apptd. April, sgd. Nov., 1948
G. O. Slade (*Ch.*), Radcliffe, Philip, Pearson, Stamp.

'To consider whether, in the application of the principles set out below to partnerships existing at the appointed day, it is desirable, in order to secure an equitable result as between partners, to amend Sections 35 and 36 of the National Health Service Act, 1946. . . .'

The principles referred to in the terms of reference concern the general prohibition of the sale or purchase of the goodwill of a medical practice; method of compensation; the encouragement of partnerships; exceptions within the general prohibition of sale and purchase of goodwill; the possibility of legislation to provide a sum additional to £66 mn. in relation to buying goodwill if it is necessary to secure an equitable distribution. There are a number of detailed recommendations on the modifications of obligations and options, apportionment of compensation, their application to various types of service and mixed partnerships, etc.

Distribution of Remuneration among General Practitioners

Working Party. Rep. pp. 8.   1952
1952 *Non-Parl. Min. of Health, Dept. of Health, Scot.*
apptd. — 1951. *sgd.* —

'To secure an equitable distribution of the Central Pool based upon the recommendations of the Spens Committee, the object being to enable the best possible medical service to be available to the public, and to safeguard the standard of medical service by discouraging unduly large lists; at the same time, to bring about a relative improvement in the position of those practitioners least favourably placed under the present plan of distribution, to make it easier for new doctors to enter practice, and to stimulate group practice.'

The maximum number of patients a general practitioner may accept under the service should be reduced from 4000 to 3500 for a single-handed practitioner, from 5000 to 4500 for a member of a partnership, provided the average of the partnership is not above 3500, and from 2400 to 2000 for a permanent assistant. The reduction in the maxima would lead to a redistribution of patients between doctors already in practice and those wishing to join the service; 'practice areas' should be classified in three categories, 'restricted', 'doubtful' and 'designated'. Those wishing to set up in the latter should be entitled to initial practice allowances. The uniform capitation fee should be changed to a basic rate of 17s. od., plus a loading of 10s. od. per head for patients within the range 501 and 1500. The income from 3500 patients would be £3475.

For the Danckwerts Award on the size of the Central Pool, see *Min. of Health*. [Ann.] Rep. p. 37; 1952–53 Cmd. 8933, xiii, 39.

General Practice within the National Health Service

Central Health Services Council. Cttee. Rep., apps. pp. iv, 67. 1954

1954 Non-Parl. Min. of Health apptd. Dec., 1950. sgd. Feb., 1954

H. Cohen (*Ch.*), and 21 others.

'*To consider . . . the existing arrangements for engaging in general practice under the National Health Service . . . in particular to advise upon—(i) the range of work and standards of practice which should be expected from the general practitioner by the public and the medical profession; (ii) types of general practice; (iii) mode of entry into general practice; (iv) non-medical help; (v) equipment and environment; (vi) method of remuneration; (vii) liaison with hospital and specialist services; (viii) liaison with local authority services.*'

General practice makes for continuity of treatment and allows the doctor to link together preventive, social and curative medicine. The range of his work includes (a) continuing responsibility for the health of his patients, (b) diagnosis of illness which can be properly treated at home, (c) reference to hospital for special diagnosis at the same time forwarding the relevant clinical details, (d) emergency treatment, (e) supervision of convalescence, (f) practice for his patients of preventive medicine and health education and (g) giving certificates and other legal and administrative requirements.

The total number of practitioners providing unrestricted general medical services in 1952 was 17204 of which 7459 were single-handed and 9745 were in partnership. The structure of general practice varies according to the type of area, prevailing local conditions and the availability of other medical services, particularly hospitals: all practitioners are affected by specialisation, which influences them when making a decision to refer patients to hospital. The present method of administering the medical services through Executive Councils and Local Medical Practice Committees should be retained.

About 65 per cent of the persons on practitioners' lists are seen during the year, with an average of 4·8 consultations per person. The limitation of doctors' lists to 3000 for a principal, plus 2000 if there is an assistant, is satisfactory. Many single-handed practitioners would be assisted if there were ancillary help, e.g. a secretary receptionist, and routine appointments systems should be tried. A low standard of surgery and waiting-room accommodation costing much less than the 38·7 per cent practice expenses allowance cannot be justified. Group practice properly organised has many of the advantages of and is more immediately practicable than the establishment of health centres. A period of assistantship is usually the best introduction to practice, subject to arrangements to prevent abuse. Suggestions are made regarding advertising vacancies, exchange of partnerships, etc. There should be an inquiry into future medical man-power and entry

z

into practice. The present method of remuneration by capitation fees, with initial practice allowances and inducement payments, is preferable to alternative methods.

Other recommendations concern the relations between practitioners and the hospitals, including availability of beds for practitioners' own patients, access to diagnostic facilities, co-operation with medical officers, etc. As prescribing is an integral part of the service, private patients should not be allowed to obtain medicines under the Health Service, especially as many doctors would not accept the limitations imposed by the Health Service.

Medical Certificates

Inter-Dept. Cttee. Rep., apps. pp. 102. 1949

1949 *Non-Parl. Min. of Health, Dept. of Health, Scot.*
apptd. —. sgd. Oct., 1949

A. Safford (*Ch.*), Arthur, Hancock (Miss F.), Jope, MacGregor.

'*To consider . . . how far it would be practicable to reduce the number of certificates to be signed by medical practitioners and to improve and simplify the forms of certificate and the rules governing their issue.*'

The National Health Service Act, 1946, Section 1 (1), requires provision 'for the issue to patients of . . . certificates reasonably required by them under or for the purposes of any enactment', which may include Regulations, Rules, etc. Many of the documents examined by the Committee were not medical certificates, but were medical reports, attestations or statements, or certificates with reports. The increasing demand for these documents, some of which are of great complexity, detracts from the doctors' true function and acts to the disadvantage of both doctors and patients. The doctors' function in signing certificates should be confined to the giving of medical facts.

Forms should be simplified and standardised under expert advice. The number of certificates could be reduced if the Ministry of National Insurance provided, at the request of insured persons, extracts of certificates of incapacity which could be used for more general purposes than at present. Amendments to the Acts should be made to provide for the free issue only of such certificates as may be prescribed, being certificates reasonably required, etc.

Part II of the Report reviews the kinds of forms, etc., issued by the departments, local authorities and other bodies.

Definition of Drugs

Jt. Sub-Cttee. 1st Rep. pp. 7. 1950. 2nd Rep. pp. 4. 1950. 3rd Rep. pp. 3. 1951

1950, 1951 *Non-Parl. Min. of Health, Dept. of Health, Scot.*
apptd. —. sgd. —.

H. Cohen (*Ch.*).

'*To formulate principles for determining whether preparations should properly be regarded as drugs or foods or cosmetics, and to give guidance on the application of these principles.*'

Regulations of the National Health Service provide that where a practitioner prescribes preparations not drugs or medicines, their cost may be recovered from him, but no guidance was given him as to whether borderline preparations were drugs or were foods or cosmetics. The three reports give specific recommendations on the preparations to be regarded as drugs, foods or toilet preparations and when disinfectants were to be regarded as drugs.

Prescribing

Jt. Cttee. 2nd Interim Rep. pp. 7. 1950. Rep. pp. 6. 1954. (1st Interim Rep. not published.)

1950, 1954 *Non-Parl. Min. of Health, Dept. of Health, Scot.*
apptd. July, 1949. sgd. —, Nov., 1953

H. Cohen (*Ch.*).

'*To consider and report from time to time whether it is desirable and practicable to restrict or discourage the prescribing by practitioners giving general medical services under the National Health Service Acts of 1946 and 1947 of (1) drugs and medicines of doubtful value or of unethical character; (2) unnecessarily expensive brands of standard drugs.*'

The Committee agreed that there should be no absolute restriction on the prescribing by a practitioner of any drug which in his opinion was necessary for the treatment of his patients; any recommendation made that certain drugs should not be prescribed or not be approved would still leave the practitioner free to use them, though he might be asked to justify his action to the Local Medical Committee. 5000 proprietary preparations were classified by the date of the Report. Standard drugs in the British Pharmacopoeia, etc., and proprietary drugs of proved value not yet standard should be freely prescribable. Three other categories of proprietary preparations should be prescribable, subject to their not being advertised direct to the public, not being designated as foods, toilet preparations, etc., and to satisfactory arrangements for prices being made between the Health Departments and the manufacturers.

Differences in Dispensing Practice between England and Wales and Scotland

Working Party. Rep., apps. pp. 46. 1948

1948 *Non-Parl. Min. of Health, Dept. of Health, Scot.*
apptd. *Sept.,* 1947. sgd. *April,* 1948

W. Penman (*Ch.*), Bryan, Graham, Meldrum, Shields.

'*To investigate the differences in the work of pharmacists in England and Scotland in dispensing and supplying medicines and appliances, with particular reference to the position likely to arise under the National*

Health Service. . . . To advise how far there are likely to be differences of practice in the new Service which would justify the continuance of differences in remuneration.'

Eighty-three per cent of the dispensing in England and Wales was based on formularies. This showed a greater degree of standardisation than in Scotland, where it was 3·5 per cent. In Scotland the medicine bottle is a 6-ounce one with dessertspoon doses, in England a 10-ounce bottle with tablespoon doses. There are fewer ingredients in the Scottish mixtures, etc.; stock mixtures are used more in England and Wales than in Scotland. In England 80 per cent of the doctors dispense their own medicines for their private patients as against 12 per cent in Scotland, which will mean a larger increase in National Health dispensing in England.

The Committee concluded that the differences in prescribing and dispensing will continue; that when mixtures are priced on a dosage basis the average cost differs very little; that over the whole range of dispensing medicines the existing tariffs meet the varying conditions in England and Wales and Scotland and measure out comparative justice to each as a unit. But this result has been arrived at by unnecessarily diverse routes and it is possible to devise a single tariff of a flexible character.

Dentistry

Reps.

1943–44 *Cmd.* 6565
1945–46 *Cmd.* 6727. See *Health Services.* p. 309.

Remuneration of General Dental Practitioners

Inter-Dept. Cttee. Rep., app. pp. 13. 1948

1947–48 *Cmd.* 7402, xi, 501
apptd. *Sept.,* 1946. sgd. *May,* 1

W. Spens (*Ch.*), Attkins, Cocker, Dale, Flitcroft, Hamilton, Lister, McFarlane, Peppiatt.

'To consider, after obtaining whatever information and evidence we thought fit, what ought to be the range of total professional income of a registered dental practitioner in any publicly organised service of general dental practice; to consider this with due regard to what have been the normal financial expectations of general dental practice in the past, and to the desirability of maintaining in the future the proper social and economic status of general dental practice and its power to attract a suitable type of recruit to the profession; and to make recommendations.'

A questionnaire regarding the incomes in 1936–38 of dentists between the ages of 35–54 in large towns showed that very few dentists make large incomes, that most were making net incomes of less than enough to meet minimum middle-class expenditure, and that a quarter of the profession lived below this standard. For example 25 per cent have incomes under £450 a year, 50 per cent under £700 and 75 per cent have incomes under £1100. The practice of dentistry is very arduous, involving the performance by a dentist of intricate manual work at the chairside for 33 hours a week for 46 weeks, some 1500 hours in the year: employment in excess of this impairs efficiency and recruitment to the profession has been unsatisfactory for a long period. The recommendations of the Committee on *Dentistry* (see p. 309) were endorsed.

Recommendations were made to scale up the incomes of dentists equivalent to an increase in general of £400 a year on incomes below £800 in 1938, and an increase on incomes above this figure of one-third of the amount by which the 1938 income falls short of £2000. Until there are sufficient dentists to secure a spread of incomes compared with that of 1938, a single-handed dentist making full use of appropriate assistance and working efficiently for 1500 hours a year should receive in terms of the 1939 value of money a net annual income of £1600. Additional remuneration could be earned under partnership agreements, by working more hours and by working in consultant and specialist capacity, etc. Special payments should be made for work in sparsely populated or unattractive areas. These incomes would have to be adjusted to changes in the value of money.

Chairside Times taken in carrying out treatment by General Dental Practitioners

Working Party. Rep., apps. pp. 77. 1949

1949 *Non-Parl. Min. of Health, Dept. of Health, Scot.*
apptd. Feb., sgd. Aug., 1949

W. Penman (*Ch.*), Bishop, Condry, Lauer, Macgregor.

'To ascertain the average chairside time taken by general dental practitioners in England, Wales and Scotland (1) in the National Health Service and (2) in private practice to complete each of the types of dental treatment. . . .'

The Spens Report (p. 321) decided that 33 hours a week for 46 weeks in a year, together with the hours spent outside the surgery, represented full employment, and that hours in excess of these tended to impair efficiency. This sample enquiry showed that the excess over this time is 9 per cent, and as owing to age, etc., a number of dentists are doing less, 64 per cent of them are working 25 per cent in excess. On an average earnings were 19 per cent in excess of the Spens' standard, 14 per cent being on account of National Health Service, 5 per cent on account of private work. The excess earnings are due as to 11 per cent to excess hours and 8 per cent to greater speed of work than was assumed in 1948. A small minority are working too long and too quickly and have excessive earnings. These should be the subject of investigation.

Statutory Registration of Opticians

Inter-Dept. Cttee. Rep., apps. pp. iv, 35. 1952

1951–52 *Cmd.* 8531, *xv*, 37
apptd. Sept., 1949. *sgd. March,* 1952

Lord Crook (*Ch.*), Black, Champness, Corlett, Critchley, Evans, Gerrie, Giles, Keeler, Marshall, Martin, Morgan, Shanks, Turville.

'*To advise, on the assumption that it would be to the public interest that provision should be made by legislation for the registration of opticians, how registration could best be carried out and what qualifications should be required as a condition of registration.*'

When the National Health Service was introduced the diplomas of five bodies were recognised as entitling a holder to take part in it. During 1939–45 there was created the Joint Emergency Committee (Optical Profession) which put forward a common 3-year training syllabus, instead of a 2-year one which had generally been accepted by the professional bodies. An alternative 5-year course was also drawn up. There are about 6835 ophthalmic opticians and 755 dispensing opticians taking part in the National Health Service.

In 1927 the Merriman Committee (see *Breviate 191/–39*, p. 363) rejected the registration of opticians because they were not regarded as sufficiently qualified to diagnose disease, and registration would retard the work of the specialist oculist. They hoped that the medical profession would be able to provide the service for insured persons. Subsequently the National Ophthalmic Treatment Board was formed and ophthalmic and medical practitioners and dispensing opticians provided facilities for insured persons. Since there is no control by special statute, there is a certain number of both ophthalmic and dispensing opticians who are not diplomates of any examining body. Certain of the optical diplomas, judged by scholarly standards, were cursory and inadequate.

The professional examining bodies should review critically the procedure under which the diplomas are conferred. Legislation should provide for the establishment of a General Optical Council, which should maintain at the outset three registers: one for opticians who test sight and supply glasses, one for dispensing opticians and one for opticians engaged solely in sight testing. The closure of the first register should take place when the danger of hardship to individuals had passed. Opticians should be qualified to register if they have already been approved by the Central Professional Committees for Opticians to take part in the National Health Services; applicants not so approved should be required to obtain the qualification of one of the examining bodies. New applicants should be required to possess qualifications which accord broadly with the recommendations of the Joint Advisory Board. Further recommendations cover inspection, discipline and supervision, etc.

See *Opticians Act, 1958;* 6 & 7 Eliz. 2. c. 32

Average Time taken to Test Sight by Ophthalmic Medical Practitioners

Working party. Rep., app. pp. 31. 1950

Average Time taken to Test Sight by Ophthalmic Opticians and . . . by Ophthalmic Opticians and by Dispensing Opticians in Fitting and Supplying Glasses

Working Party. Rep., Pt. I, app. pp. 39. 1950. Rep., Pt. II, apps. pp. iv, 36. 1950

1950 *Non-Parl. Min. of Health, Dept. of Health, Scot.*

W. Penman (*Ch.*).

The three Reports give the result of the statistical investigations made in order to arrive at the average time taken by ophthalmic medical practitioners, ophthalmic opticians and dispensing opticians, in testing sight and in fitting and supplying glasses under the Supplementary Ophthalmic Services.

(ii) Nurses

Nurses' Salaries

Cttee. 1st Rep., *Salaries and Emoluments of Female Nurses in Hospitals*, app. pp. 42. 1943

1942–43 *Cmd.* 6424, v, 715
apptd. Nov., 1941. sgd. Feb., 1943

Lord Rushcliffe (*Ch.*), and 39 other members.

The appointment of the Committee followed the recommendation of the Athlone Committee on *Nursing Services*, 1939, that a committee analogous to the Burnham Committees for the teaching profession should be appointed to draw up scales of salaries and emoluments for the nursing profession. Consideration was given to what was a fair and appropriate remuneration for the nurse, having regard to her proper status, the nature of her work and responsibilities; to the importance of attracting the right type of entrant and to a uniform rate, so as to prevent competition between hospitals. The various categories of nurse had to be defined—matron, assistant matron, qualified sister tutor, departmental sister, ward sister, staff nurse, etc. Details are given on the various categories, scales of wages, emoluments, transfers and promotions and conditions of service.

The recommendations of this Committee set in motion investigations covering the whole nursing profession, including midwives, and as a result a number of separate reports were published setting out detailed salary scales:

See 1942–43 Cmd. 6424, Cmd. 6425, Cmd. 6439, Cmd. 6460, v; 1943–44 Cmd. 6487, Cmd. 6488, Cmd. 6505, Cmd. 6542, iv; 1944–45 Cmd. 6603, v; 1945–46 Cmd. 6684, xiv; 1947–48 Cmd. 7238, Cmd. 7239, xvi.

Mental Nursing and the Nursing of the Mentally Defective

Inter-Dept. Cttee. on Nursing Services. Sub-Cttee. Rep., app. pp. vi, 57. 1945
1945 *Non-Parl. Min. of Health, Min. of Education*

apptd. *April,* 1938. sgd. *Oct.,* 1945

W. Rees-Thomas (*Ch.*), Cowlin (Miss G.), Feldon, Gibson, Masefield, Walton.

'*To consider the arrangements at present in operation with regard to the recruitment, training, registration, and terms and conditions of service of persons engaged in nursing the sick or mentally defective. . . .*'

Mental nursing and nursing of the mentally deficient employ approximately 16,400 women and 12,600 men: the very large proportion of male nurses distinguishes it from other branches of nursing and raises special problems of conditions of service, training and relationship to the General Nursing Council. The shortage of female nurses is not new, but has been aggravated by the increased demands of general hospitals, by the expansion of mental hospitals and competition from other occupations. As a result there has been a general lowering in the standard of selection, some hospitals having to accept any girls who apply. The main source of recruits must continue to be girls who do not go through a full secondary education, but who from 14 to 16 have been in industry or commerce. The wastage rate is extremely high. Mental nursing is very arduous, has many unpleasant duties and is sometimes dangerous. The advances in mental treatment demand highly skilled nursing. There is little opportunity to transfer to other branches of nursing, many of the institutions are gloomy and barrack-like and their physical isolation restricts the opportunities for outside social intercourse which are more necessary for mental than general nurses. Through ignorance mental nursing is still regarded as inferior work. Every step must be taken to improve its status and attractiveness as a profession. Improvement was hindered by the fact that there are two competing examinations, one the supplementary part of the State Register, under the General Nursing Council, while the great majority of mental nurses held the qualifications of the

Royal Medico-Psychological Association.

All qualified mental nurses should be registered by a statutory body and there should be only one qualification. Attempts to secure a compromise between the two examining bodies having failed, the Royal Medico-Psychological Association examinations should be discontinued, subject to some indispensable conditions, including complete protection for nurses already holding the Association's Certificate and of training schools which the Association had recognised. Mental and mental deficiency nurses should be adequately represented on the General Nursing Council and be in a majority on any of its committees dealing primarily with mental matters. Modifications should be made in Part II of the Preliminary State Examination to make it more suitable, and the State Register should provide Part I for General Nursing, Part II for mental nursing and Part III for special branches.

Conditions of service must make the profession attractive. The salary of a mental nurse should be somewhat above that of a trained nurse, there should be interchangeability of pensions, and freedom of female nurses to retire at 50. Mental nurses off duty should have the personal liberty of private persons, trained nurses should be allowed to live off the curtilage of the hospital, should not require late passes, etc., and should be helped to establish outside interests. Accommodation and cooking need improvement. The standard of staffing is inadequate and the ratio of staff to patients should be raised above 1 to 11. In opposition to the views of the Departmental Committee on Nursing in County and County Borough Mental Hospitals (1924) and of the Royal Commission on Lunacy and Mental Disorder (1926), the sub-committee was strongly against the introduction of a recognised grade of assistant mental nurse.

Training of Nurses for the Colonies

Cttee. Rep., apps. pp. 65. 1945

1945–46 Cmd. 6672, xiv, 39
apptd. Nov., 1943. pres. Aug., 1945

Lord Rushcliffe (Ch.), Lloyd, Bagot (Miss R. A.), Bennett (Mrs. B. A.), Blacklock (Mary G.), Bourdillon (Lady), Dreyer (Miss R.), Fenoulhet (Miss R.), Kauntze, Macaulay, Moody, Parsons (Miss H. C.), Smith (Miss D. M.), Taylor (Miss M. G.), Walker, Watt (Miss K. C.).

'To examine the question of training, both in this country and overseas, for nurses who are to serve in Colonial territories. . . .'

(i) Originally nurses were recruited from this country and local male recruits were trained: female recruits came forward as their education advanced and prejudices were broken down. It is the aim of Colonial policy to staff the growing nursing services with a locally recruited personnel, especially since the general shortage after the war has made recruitment difficult from the United Kingdom and the Dominions. The recommendations are concerned with the creation of Nursing and Midwives Councils in each separate colony; a four years' course of training which would render a Colonial certificate acceptable to a General Nursing Council of England and Wales for State Registration; the establishment of efficiently equipped and staffed training schools, and of pre-vocational training and employment for girls wishing to take up nursing. (ii) Candidates in this country for the Colonial Nursing Service should be on the general part of the State Register, should normally be State Certified Midwives, have had one year's hospital experience and be given a special course of instruction for Colonial service. Conditions of service for such appointments should be at least as favourable, taking local purchasing power and taxation into account, as the Rushcliffe salaries and conditions in this country.

Recruitment and Training of Nurses

Working Party. Rep., apps., index. pp. v, 122. 1947

1947 *Non-Parl. Min. of Health, Dept. of Health, Scot., Min. of Labour and N.S. apptd. Jan., 1946. sgd. July, 1947*

R. Wood (*Ch.*), Bridges (Miss D. C.), Cockayne (Miss E.), Cohen, Inch.

'*To review the position of the nursing profession.*'

In view of the impending establishment of the National Health Service the Working Party was appointed to survey the whole field of recruitment and training of nurses, and to assess the needs of a national health service.

The nursing world is in a crisis, wards being closed through shortage of nurses while the demand for hospital beds is increasing. The total number of trained nurses and midwives in 1938 was 79,000 or 1·7 per 1000 population, and of all nurses, including student nurses, pupil midwives and assistant nurses, 158,000 or 3·4 per 1000 of the population. The increase by 1945 of nurses other than trained nurses by 15,000 still fell short of the greatly increased demand. The wastage of trained nurses meant that their average working life was only nine to ten years, and that 9000 were needed for the annual replacement before there could be any expansion. The present system breaks down primarily by the 50 per cent wastage of student nurses during training.

Nearly half the nurses had received full-time education up to the age of 14 or 15, another 30 per cent further education without reaching School Certificate standard and only 4 per cent reached Higher School Certificate level and above. In intelligence some 40 per cent of nurses fall in the top 30 per cent, while 24 per cent fall into the lowest 30 per cent of the population. But one in five of the assistant nurses in hospitals— about 6000—have an intellectual capacity not inferior to the best student or trained nurses. No uniform system of training can be devised for such diverse levels of previous education and ability. A course requiring average ability would mean that 30 per cent of the present students were unsuitable. The selection of candidates (in which intelligence tests must be used) must have regard to ability to meet requirements. Apart from marriage, the chief cause of wastage during training was the traditional code of discipline and control over personal life unsuited to a generation nurtured in modern ideas of freedom and relations between the sexes. Nurses in training must be accorded full student status and not subjected to an outworn system of discipline. The training day should be reduced to approximate to the normal working day, and this involves the introduction of a 3-shift system.

The 2200 student hours necessary to give essential training could be given in a 2-year course, if domestic work and nursing duties were eliminated, training hours adjusted to the needs of the student, and the 3-shift system adopted. There should be provisional registration at the end of two years, subject to confirmation at the end of another year, and a uniform qualification and title for all nurses. Student nurses should be responsible to the training authority, and not to the hospital. The Departments of Health should be responsible for securing the necessary recruitment, and for approving and inspecting training units. Without the assistant nurses, most of whom were appointed on the basis of nursing experience without necessarily any formal training, the nursing services would long ago have broken down. Their services will be needed for some time to come, but after a given date there should be no more admissions, and their duties should be transferred partly to trained staff and partly to the nursing orderlies who will replace them.

In each Hospital Region, selected hospitals and public health agencies should be grouped to form composite training units, a Regional Nurses Training Board should plan and co-ordinate training and there should be a General Council of Nurses and Midwives of Great Britain, which should include governmental, university and other educational representatives, together with nurses and midwives elected regionally. The additional staffs required to give effect to these changes would be approximately 24,000 trained and 14,000 untrained nursing orderlies. Apart from the staff needed for expansion, the requirements would be met theoretically in five years if reduction in wastage came about as a result of the changes recommended.

Chairman's note.—Although the personnel needed for the nursing services could not be secured without the radical changes outlined in the Report, as it was estimated that by 1951 there would be a drop of over 350,000 women and girls in the working population, it might be felt impracticable to make the changes other than slowly.

—— Minority Report, apps. pp. vi, 78. 1948

1948 *Non-Parl.*

J. Cohen.

Cohen dissents from the majority report on the ground that useful conclusions on staffing needs cannot emerge from the material presented. Many conclusions and recommendations of various bodies are conflicting, being based on opinion rather than scientific research. A nursing service cannot be planned until the hospital service is planned and the correct proportion of national effort to be devoted to health known and decided upon. Using patient's duration of stay as a criterion of nursing effectiveness, the Report argues that there is a *prima facie* case for increasing the number of trained nurses in general hospitals.

Position of the Enrolled Assistant Nurse within the National Health Service

Central Health Services Council. Standing Advisory Cttee. Rep. pp. 10. 1954. *The State Enrolled Assistant Nurse in the National Health Service.* Scottish Health Services Council. Standing Advisory Cttee. Sub-Cttee. Rep. pp. 12. 1955

1954, 1955 *Non-Parl. Min. of Health, Dept. of Health, Scot.*

Miss K. G. Douglas (*Ch.*), and 22 others, England and Wales. Miss E. G. Manners (*Ch.*), and six others, Scotland.

After the war there were not enough registered nurses to fill the available posts and large numbers of assistant nurses were employed. There is work to be done which does not require the full training of a registered nurse, of which there are still not enough, and there is a permanent place for them. Both reports recommend that additional training schools should be established, that the standards of admission should be maintained or selection improved. The report on England and Wales discusses the nursing unit in which the trained nurse with assistants can look after a specified group of patients, and examines the Assessment test; the Scottish report proposes a new grade of senior assistant nurse to encourage recruitment.

Function, Status and Training of Nurse Tutors

Cttee. Rep., apps. pp. 26. 1954

1954 *Non-Parl. Min. of Health, Dept. of Health, Scot.* *apptd.* — 1951. *sgd. May,* 1953

Miss J. K. Aitken (*Ch.*), and 20 other members.

The Committee was set up following the recommendation of the Working Party on *Recruitment and Training of Nurses* (see p. 325) that 'measures should be taken to provide adequate teaching staff trained in modern educational methods'. The profession in the past used experienced nurses who were doing practical work in the wards of hospitals to teach probationers, but with the increasing complexity of modern methods of treatment and the widening field of preventive care it became obvious that more teachers were required, and that the training given by a ward sister, whose primary duty was the nursing care of patients, had to be supplemented. Since the inception of the National Health Service the shortage of teachers has been alleviated to some extent by the tendency to group hospitals to form a single nursing training unit. But inquiries amongst the nurse tutors showed that there was much dissatisfaction over their lack of contact with the patient, and the frustration felt because of the misunderstanding and lack of appreciation in hospitals of their function and status.

A nurse tutor should be encouraged to stay in her profession by recognition of her status, giving her adequate scope and an avenue of promotion. In many nursing schools the tutor is regarded as an instrument for getting a nurse through the State examination instead of being an educator in the widest sense. A principal nurse tutor should be able to co-operate with the matron of her hospital with regard to the allocation of student nurses to wards and departments for the purpose of their training, and be recognised by the hospital authorities as the expert in nursing education.

Hospital authorities should consider the introduction of the principle of a 'school of nursing' both from a point of view of the student, and as a medium of promotion for a nurse tutor. There are 62,000 student and pupil assistant nurses, and by group schools it would be possible to plan a ratio of one tutor to 40–50 students. Qualified nurses should not be employed on pre-nursing courses. Ward sisters employed in nursing schools should have some preparation in teaching methods. Methods of selection of students should be considered, so as to relieve the tutor of having to cope, in the same course, with students of different educational standards. The Nurse Tutor Diploma, open to a registered nurse who has practised for three years, is provided by the London and Edinburgh Universities. In London this has been extended to two years but in view of the shortage of teachers the Committee recommended that the University of London should

be asked to reduce the time to five terms. The general principles of 'schools of nursing' applied also to mental hospitals. In a Note Dr. Fleming and Professor Wilson stated that they could not agree to a shortened university course from six to five terms.

Midwives

Working Party. Rep., apps., index. pp. viii, 132. 1949

1949 *Non-Parl. Min. of Health, Dept. of Health, Scot., Min. of Labour and N.S. apptd. April, 1947. sgd. Nov., 1948*

Mrs. M. D. Stocks (*Ch.*), Ferlie (Miss J. P.), Shand (Miss V. R.), Titmuss, Winner (Miss A. L.).

'To enquire into the reasons for the shortage of midwives.'

The National Health Service Act, 1946, transfers midwives, health visitors and domiciliary nurses to the local health authorities. The Committee of 1929 found that the service was faced not with a shortage of qualified midwives, but with some maldistribution as between town and country. In 1949, though there were several thousand more midwives, there was an absolute shortage because the birthrate was higher in 1946 and 1947, and because the standard of work and complexity of requirements were rising; a midwife now makes up to a dozen or more antenatal visits. The numerical deficiency of the midwifery service must therefore be measured by actual case-loads in relation to current ideas of what is to be required of her and what constitutes an optimum case-load, etc. The Departmental Committee, 1929, accepted a case-load of 100 deliveries a year, in 1949 the Royal College of Midwives 50, and the Rushcliffe Committee 66. A case-load of 55 in urban areas is recommended.

There is an annual loss of practising midwives on account of retirement, marriage, etc., of 1300, and a post-training loss of newly-qualified midwives who did not practise of 29 per cent, so that of the 1725 who qualified in 1946, only 1200 actually took up practice and remained in it for one year. Some loss to health visiting, etc., is unavoidable. Balancing these wastages, the probable trend of the birth rate, and the proposed reduction of case-load to 55, the annual recruitment should be raised from about 1790 to 2100. But for some time there will be a decreasing number of women in the age groups from which not only midwives, but teachers, health visitors, nurses, etc., which are also to be increased in number, must be drawn.

The many recommendations include: provision of cars, houses, off-duty times, salary adequate to provide domestic help; attraction of women aged 30 to 45 by special arrangements for their needs; a common basic training for both nurses and midwives, followed by specialist midwifery courses; until the new course is provided, only S.R.N.'s should be trained as midwives. Schools of Midwifery should be separate from Schools of Nursing. Midwives should be represented on a Maternity Services Committee for each hospital region.

The Medical Research Council should be asked urgently to set up a Committee to find a safer analgesic agent which midwives working alone can use. The working of the maternity services should be reviewed in three to five years to ensure that the partnership of doctors and midwives is maintained. But in a postscript on p. viii, the Committee says that while the Report was being printed there were many complaints that general practitioners were tending to take over the whole of antenatal care, as well as relegating midwives to the status of maternity nurses. It hoped that prompt administrative action would be taken to stop this new and unwelcome trend.

See *Use of Trilene by Midwives.* Cttee. on Analgesia in Midwifery. Rep.; 1954 Non-Parl. Medical Research Council.

Preventive Dental Services

Standing Advisory Cttee. (Scotland). Sub-Cttee. Rep., apps. pp. 33. 1952

1952 Non-Parl. *Dept. of Health, Scot. apptd. March,* 1949. sgd. —.
R. C. S. Dow (*Ch.*), Logan, Campbell, Aitchison, Henderson, Rodger, Shiach.

'To consider the development of preventive dental services, with special reference to orthodontic services.'

The existing preventive services are for expectant and nursing mothers and pre-school children at the local authority clinics under the National Health Service and the school dental service under the Education Act. None of these services has developed substantially, and effective prevention has not been possible. Until 1948 there was a steady rise in the numbers of school dentists and in the numbers of children who received routine treatment, but just when clinics and equipment, etc., were being strengthened there commenced a drift of professional staffs to the new general dental service where remuneration was much higher. In some areas the school dental service closed down. Children's teeth are getting worse through lack of treatment and the position will soon be such that the school dentist will be giving only emergency treatment to children in pain. Only a small number of pre-school children receive systematic dental care from any source. In the year 1950 only 227,776 out of 785,380 children on the school registers were inspected, and without inspection there can be no routine treatment. The Penman Report (see p. 322) showed that dental practitioners in Scotland devoted only one in every 300 hours to the 'conservation of deciduous teeth'. The fall in the numbers of nursing mothers seeking treatment under the local authority, is due partly to their having been treated under the general dental service. An efficient dental service for children and expectant and nursing mothers would require 500 dentists (1500 children per dentist), a number which cannot be attained in the near future.

Until the shortage of dental personnel can be remedied, the services should concentrate on the nursing mothers and the younger children, dental ancillaries on the line of the New Zealand Scheme should be used. There should be routine inspection and mothers should be instructed regarding diet, regularity of meals and hygiene, and the importance of breast feeding. Static or mobile clinics should be provided. Orthodontic treatment should be carried out by a dental officer under the guidance of a consultant; the difficult cases to be referred to a central specialist clinic. Post-graduate courses should be provided and dental research and propaganda intensified.

New Zealand School Dental Nurses

United Kingdom Mission. Rep., apps. pp. iv, 43.   1950

1950 Non-Parl. Min. of Health, Dept. of Health, Scot., Min. of Education apptd. —. sgd. Aug., 1950

R. Bradlaw (*Ch.*), Douglas, Roper-Hall, Senior, Wynne.

'To obtain first-hand information as to the work and training of New Zealand School Dental Nurses.'

In 1920, in view of the high degree of dental caries amongst the people of New Zealand and the shortage of dentists, the Chief Dental Officer advised a radical departure from accepted methods—the selection and training of young women of School Certificate standard to care for the dental health of school children. The scheme was eventually approved by the dental profession. The responsibility of the school dental nurse, working under the supervision of a Principal Dental Officer, is the routine inspection and treatment, within prescribed clinical limits, and instruction in oral hygiene of pre-school and school children up to the age of 12. The School Dental Nurse is a dental auxiliary, her training was deliberately divorced from that of the dentist in an undergraduate dental school, and was given in the Department's training school; the clinical standards of the final year students were remarkably high. The scheme, which has the full support of the dental profession and the public meets an urgent need in New Zealand. Essential features of the scheme are central control of and training of the auxiliaries, of their employment and supervision, and a strict limitation of the number of children for whom an auxiliary is responsible. A like system of dental auxiliaries for this country would have to take into account necessary modifications and the fullest co-operation of the dental profession would be important.

(iii) Other Services

Laboratory Services

Medical Advisory Cttee. Rep. pp. 11. 1947

1947 Non-Parl. Dept. of Health, Scot. apptd. April, 1944. sgd. Sept., 1946

J. Fraser (*Ch.*), and 13 others.

'To advise on technical matters involved in the development of laboratory services in Scotland having regard to the existing facilities and to the range and quality of service that ought to be available as part of a comprehensive medical service.'

In England and Wales there is practically complete separation of the public health and the other laboratory services, and integration is not considered feasible. In Scotland there has been successful integration in many centres, but this should include university teaching departments, public health, hospital and other laboratories. The participating laboratories primarily responsible for the training of recruits, mainly university departments, will be the central laboratories. A period of five years post-graduate training should be required before recognition as a specialist in laboratory medicine. The service should be under central administration, with regional grouping of laboratories centred round the four university medical schools. There would be inter-regional co-operation, and the professional and technical staffs would be interchangeable.

Medical Auxiliaries

Cttees. Reps., apps., index. pp. xii, 227.
[1951]

1950–51 *Cmd.* 8188, *xv*, 97
apptd. May, 1949

Members of all Committees: V. Z. Cope (*Ch.*), Clark (*Ministry of Health*), Taylor (*Dept. of Health for Scotland*).

'*To consider the supply and demand, training and qualifications of certain medical auxiliaries employed in the National Health Service and to make recommendations.*'

Medical auxiliaries are persons who assist medical practitioners (otherwise than as nurses) in the investigation and treatment of disease by virtue of some special skill acquired through a recognised course of training. Those specified in the Reports are almoners, chiropodists, dieticians, medical laboratory technicians, occupational therapists, physiotherapists, radiographers, and speech therapists. Part II of the Report consists of reports from eight committees each dealing with one auxiliary service; Part I, signed by three members common to all committees, deals with problems of recognition, registration and co-ordination.

It is not possible to give any precise estimate of demand and supply. In some of the auxiliary services demand exceeds supply, but since there is a limited pool from which recruits can be drawn, attempts by professional bodies to expand individually may defeat their own end. A balanced programme of recruitment is required. For some auxiliaries some common basic training might be possible. Advances in medical practice may affect the content, standard and scope of any auxiliary service or require a new type. To ensure that the patient under the National Health Service is properly treated, the Minister has power to prescribe the qualifications of persons employed in them. It is not appropriate that professional associations should have final and undivided responsibility for the registration or recognition of schools and examinations. The Board of Registration of

Medical Auxiliaries is handicapped by being a voluntary body. There should be set up under the aegis of the Privy Council a statutory Council for the Medical Auxiliaries Services in the National Health Service, to maintain registers of qualified persons, recognise schools, courses, and any additional types of auxiliary services required, and to promote co-ordination of training. It should be advised by professional committees for the several auxiliary services, with medical auxiliary members in a majority.

The reports from each sub-committee deal with the questions of recruitment, training and registration of members of the several services. There are three minority reports, one of which objects that the proposed Council could not effectively direct a number of distinct professions, each of which should have the full responsibility for establishing and maintaining its own standards. There should be separate registration boards, with a central advisory council.

See *Professions Supplementary to Medicine Act, 1960;* 8 & 9 Eliz. 2. c. 66.

Social Workers in the Mental Health Services

Cttee. Rep., apps., index. pp. 58. 1951

1950–51 *Cmd.* 8260, *xv*, 779
apptd. July, 1948. *sgd. Jan.*, 1951

J. M. Mackintosh (*Ch.*), Bates, Brown (Miss S. C.), Lewis, McDougall (Mrs. K. F.), Mackenzie (Miss J. M.), Parry, Roberts, Roxburgh (Miss M. J.), Soddy, Younghusband (Miss E. L.).

'*To consider and make recommendations upon questions arising in regard to the supply and demand, training and qualifications of social workers in the mental health service. The Committee to present an interim report on these questions in relation to psychiatric social workers.*'

The Committee was asked as a matter of urgency to study means of relieving the acute shortage of psychiatric social workers. It presented an interim report in April 1949, which was not published because some of the recommendations would have involved fresh expenditure and because another committee was examining services likely to draw on the same source of recruitment. P. 7 gives a summary of the recommendations. Those accepted by the Minister were that fuller use should be made of married psychiatric social workers by part-time appointments, the recruitment of men should be encouraged, the term psychiatric social worker should be restricted to persons holding a university mental health certificate, and efforts made to economise in the use of fully qualified workers.

The mental health services in England and Wales are responsible for the social care of some 150,000 persons who are under treatment for mental illness in hospitals; 51,000 mental defectives in institutions; 76,000 on licence and under guardianship, and large numbers of persons receiving treatment at psychiatric and child guidance clinics. Some 1500 trained social workers are needed as against the 331 who are in active service. There are many others working in this field, some untrained and unlikely to take a full course of training, and some with other forms of training. For the years 1945–46 to 1949–50 there were 231 students who qualified in a mental health course. There are 70 places available in the three Universities providing such courses. Nineteen University Social Science Departments in England and Wales offer training in social science of which practical work forms part.

The further recommendations were that the universities' social science courses should give general training designed to meet the needs of workers engaged in case work, to include academic and practical work. Psychology should be taught in its application to the living situations which a candidate is likely to meet in her daily work; mental health courses, on the lines of those already established, should be provided in other universities. For those persons already working who have experience and no qualifica-

tion, there should be training concurrent with work under the supervision of a psychiatric social worker or mental welfare officer with experience. In order to attract recruits to meet the immediate needs, a trainee scheme should be organised by regional hospital boards by which candidates, who should be paid maintenance grants, will be trained under the supervision of experienced psychiatric social workers for two years.

Recruitment, Training and Qualification of Sanitary Inspectors

Working Party. Rep., apps. pp. vi, 145.
1953
1953 Non-Parl. Min of Health
apptd. June, 1951. sgd. —

N J. Maude (Ch.), Beattie, Burnett, Lewis, White, Williams.

'To enquire into the work at present being done by sanitary inspectors, and the functioning of the present arrangements for their recruitment, training and qualification.'

Councils of metropolitan boroughs are obliged to appoint an adequate number of sanitary inspectors, who must be qualified; councils of county boroughs must also appoint inspectors, but there is no provision as to numbers or qualifications. Councils of non-county boroughs, and of urban and rural districts must appoint inspectors, as a condition of grant they must be qualified, but there is no requirement as to numbers. The sanitary inspector's functions are nowhere exhaustively defined: the Ministry's regulations give a list of some of his duties and provide for an approved qualification, while in practice much of his work is the part of the employing authority's duty which it has decided to assign to him. Table 24 shows the average proportion of their time spent by sanitary inspectors on their various duties. In 1951 there were 4680 established posts in England and Wales, a ratio of one inspector to 9000 inhabitants, though this average conceals large variations not accounted for by difference of work, e.g. as between an area with much slum property and a rural area, but by under-staffing in some areas.

Three-quarters of the recruits have come from young men with School Certificate or with Matriculation, who had just left school or had served as clerks to the local authority; up to one-quarter from older men, mainly in the building and plumbing trades, and a small proportion of men from the Merchant Navy, mainly attracted to port health work. To maintain the 4680 established posts in 1951, there would have to be an annual intake of 250 students. Recruitment has dropped off.

Examinations are conducted by the Royal Sanitary Institute and Sanitary Inspectors Examination Joint Board and by the Royal Sanitary Institute, which are legally distinct bodies sharing a common staff. The existing arrangements are criticised by the technical institutions and by the sanitary inspectors, who said that the training and examination were not thorough and were out of date, that standards were too low and that there was no single body considering the whole field of training and the new developments which arise from time to time. There is a high rate of failure of 50 per cent.

Sanitary inspectors should in future be called public health inspectors. Passing a qualifying examination should be made obligatory for all new appointments. The Minister's recognition of the existing certificates should be withdrawn and a new, independent Public Health Inspectors' examination board established to examine, award diplomas, approve training courses, etc. There should be one standard of entry to the course, based on the General Certificate of Education and to meet the requirements of recruits from other trades, the Navy, etc., equivalent professional or semi-professional examinations and a test suitable for older men who reach the standard after leaving school. The theoretical training should be a 4-year course, practical work being taken concurrently in the service of local authorities approved for the purpose.

3. PARTICULAR PROBLEMS AND DISEASES

Accidents in the Home

Standing Inter-Dept. Cttee. Rep., apps. pp. 11. 1953

1953 *Non-Parl. Home Office*

'*To co-ordinate departmental action in connexion with the prevention of accidents in the home. . . .*'

During the ten years from 1940 to 1949 over 60,000 people died from accidents in their home, and each year since 1943 there have been well over 1000 more fatal casualties in the home than on the roads. More than 25 per cent of the victims are under 15 and more than 50 per cent over 65. The commonest kinds of fatal accidents are falls, burns and scalds, suffocation and coal gas poisoning. Whilst there is some connection between falls and faulty building design, the majority are due to the risk inherent in ordinary domestic activities, especially during busy periods.

The Children and Young Persons Act, 1933, prohibited children under seven years of age being in a room with an inadequately protected open fire. This has been amended by raising the age to 12 and including any heating appliance likely to cause injury by contact. The Heating Appliances (Fireguards) Act, 1952, prescribes the standards of design for heating appliances. Under the Fire Services Act, 1947, the fire authorities give advice on fire prevention, fire escapes, etc., and the Home Office and Scottish Home Department conduct educational campaigns, etc. The Committee stressed the need for more publicity and propaganda and emphasised the work being done by the voluntary bodies.

The Ageing Population

Standing Medical Advisory Cttee. (Scotland). Sub-Cttee. Rep. pp. 13. 1953

1953 *Non-Parl. Dept. of Health, Scot. apptd.* Oct., 1949. *sgd.* Dec., 1952

W. G. Clark (*Ch.*), Briggs, Esslemont (Miss M.), Hill.

'*To investigate and report what the health services can do to meet the medical needs arising from an increase in the older age groups of the population.*'

The problems of medical care of the elderly are more domiciliary than institutional and stress should be laid not on hospital geriatrics, but what can be done to stimulate *eugeria*—the condition of ageing serenely, slowly and painlessly. Persons of pensionable age have increased from 1 in 13 of the population in 1921 to about 1 in 8, and they are still increasing. The small size of families means fewer children to look after parents and smaller houses make it more difficult to house the older members. There is a general waiting list for hospitals, but the elderly should not be sent there unless they need medical care beyond the scope of the general practitioner and nursing care beyond the scope of the district nurse or a long-term convalescent home. The number of hospital beds needed for them would be 1000 per 1 mn. population. Services should aim at keeping healthy persons in their own homes as long as possible, but when they become too frail to manage their own lives even with assistance, they should be given hostel accommodation. It is estimated that 35 old people can be looked after in a hostel with a staff of 7 or 8; in a hospital they would require a staff of 20; in a long-stay annex, a staff of 13 or 14; and in their own homes 12 full-time home helps. Scotland needs accommodation for 17,000 persons, but has only 10,000 places.

Artificial Limbs

Dept. Cttee. Rep., apps. pp. 23.   1945
    (Interim Rep. App. II)

1945 *Non-Parl. Min. of Pensions apptd. —. sgd. June,* 1945

B. Cohen (*Ch.*), Atkinson, Bain, Hall, McMurray, Parker, Perkins.

'*To consider the design, development and use of artificial limbs and appliances connected therewith.*'

An interim report, printed as App. I, recommends the establishment of an experimental department at Roehampton, and a small standing committee to develop research.

The concentration of the artificial limb industry in the last 25 years was recognised to be the result of the recommendations of the Collins Committee on Metal Artificial Limbs (1925 Non-Parl. Min. of Pensions). Some witnesses felt that this had had the effect of discouraging design and manufacture. The Government should not take over the existing firms and make its own limbs nor should a pensioner have the option of having a limb supplied by the Government, or choosing his own manufacturer and receiving part or whole payment from the Government. The present artificial leg contract gives the Ministry full power to ensure that a satisfactory limb is supplied at a fair price, and the newly appointed Standing Advisory Committee should ensure that new ideas are tried out and new methods adopted, etc.

The existing arrangements for the provision and maintenance of limbs should continue; any firm proposing a better limb should receive fair payment; any firm which submits and can supply an improved limb should be offered a contract; firms not supplying the Government should not be forced out of business. There are a number of recommendations on fitting, the training of limb fitting surgeons, and training the patients in the correct use, etc., of the artificial limbs.

See *Artificial Limbs.* Standing Advisory Cttee. Reps.; 1947, 1948, 1950, 1951 Non-Parl.

Monocular Blindness

Scientific Advisory Cttee.   Sub-Cttee.
        Rep. pp. 23.   1950

1950 *Non-Parl. Dept. of Health, Scot. apptd. Dec.,* 1946. *sgd. July,* 1950

T. Ferguson (*Ch.*), Dickson, Mackenzie (Miss J. S.), Marshall, Seiler, McKinlay, Robertson.

'To survey all possible sources of information on monocular blindness and to analyse and report on any data which could be obtained.'

The incidence of monocular blindness (visual acuity—6/24 or less in the blind eye, 6/12 or better in the other eye) in school children is 7 per 1000, varying from 1·4 in entrants to 7·3 in intermediate and 10·4 in leavers. The survey of a number of industries showed too much variation to give a reliable average figure for the adult population. The important causes are untreated squint and amblyopia in childhood, and to a lesser extent injury. Apart from excess of injuries in Wales, there is no significant sex variation. It is not seriously incapacitating, but common enough to call for the early treatment of squint and for measures to prevent industrial eye injury.

The Causes of Blindness in England and Wales Rep. 1950

The Causes of Blindness in England 1948–1950. Rep., apps. pp. iv, 41. 1953
The Causes of Blindness in England 1951–1954. Rep., apps. pp. vi, 53. 1956
1950 *Non-Parl. Medical Research Council.*
1953, 1956 *Non-Parl. Min. of Health*

A. Sorsby.

The reports show that from 1935–1953 the blind population has risen from 67,000 to 94,000, the increase being largely accounted for by the increase in the numbers and proportion of elderly blind as a result of increase in numbers and proportion of elderly persons in the population. In the next 20 years an increase of double this dimension is to be expected, raising the blind population to about 140,000. There has been some increase in blindness amongst children under 1 year, and from 1–4 years. There is an excess of female blindness in age groups over 65. Blindness due to infectious diseases

has been largely eliminated, and there is no reason, unless effective and purposive action is taken, to anticipate any considerable change in the major blinding affections. Blindness from cataract could be reduced if available measures were used.

Congenital Deaf-Mutism in Scotland

Rep., apps. pp. 13. 1945
1945 *Non-Parl. Dept. of Health, Scot.*

J. A. G. Keddie.

As there is no complete register of deaf-mute cases, information was collected from the various residential and day schools at which deaf children are taught. The average number of congenital deaf-mutes born was 3·88 per 10,000 live births. There was no significant difference in incidence between males and females. Data relating to 402 cases from 372 families showed an incidence of the hereditary type in 19 per cent of the cases. The incidence of deaf-mutism is high in the north and north-east and the extreme south-west. The areas presenting a low relative incidence are either in the south-east or the eastern part of the central belt. No attempt was made to give reasons for these variations, but in the Preface to the Report the Ministry of Health refers to investigations which suggested that there is a high incidence in areas in which the iodine content of the water supply is low.

Special Welfare Needs of Deaf-Blind Persons

Cttees. Rep., app. pp. 11. 1951
1951 *Non-Parl. Min. of Health*
sgd. Feb., 1951

G. Robinson (*Ch.*), and 6 other members, Welfare of the Blind. Miss M. O'Conor (*Ch.*), and 2 other members, Welfare of the Deaf.

The small numbers (2500 deaf-blind) conceal a great deal of loneliness and frustration. The blind person who becomes deaf has no knowledge of the deaf world, and the deaf person who becomes blind is unable to use his skills at lip reading, sign language, etc. There should be close consultation with those arranging for the welfare of deaf persons, to ensure that the welfare of the deaf-blind person is promoted. Home teachers of the blind should continue to deal with deaf-blind persons in general, but should be helped by refresher courses and in other ways to improve their experience in dealing with the deaf-blind. The aims of the home-teacher in dealing with the deaf-blind are set out in detail, and include welfare assistance to deaf-blind children where there are no educational facilities. The deaf-blind in need of residential accommodation require careful classi-fication to ensure that those with some useful degree of hearing are likely to be dealt with in a home for the blind and those with a fair/good intelligence and those with poor intelligence are dealt with in Homes especially established for these classes. There is need for hostel accommodation for deaf-blind workers near to workshops for the blind. The provision of gated stairways and roped walks, single bed sitting rooms, type-writers, etc., is recommended.

Mortality and Morbidity during the London Fog of December 1952

Cttee. Rep., apps. pp. iv, 61.   1954

1954 *Non-Parl. Min. of Health*

A dense fog covered the Greater London area during the 5th–8th December, 1952, and was accompanied by 3500 to 4000 more deaths than were normally expected during the first three weeks of December. Analysis of all the deaths during this period showed no evidence of an epidemic of infectious origin or of a new type of disease. There were apparently no deaths attributable to fog amongst normally healthy people, the increased morbidity occurring main-ly among people with pre-existing res-piratory or cardiac disorders, mainly of a chronic nature. Between 80 and 90 per cent of the increase in deaths was due to respiratory and cardiovascular

diseases. Over 90 per cent of the increase in deaths were of people over the age of 45 and between 60 and 70 per cent over the age of 65. Infant deaths were approximately doubled. The conclusion was that substances in the fog caused irritation of the bronchi and bronchioles and so accelerated death in those already suffering from the diseases named. Oxides of sulphur were the main irritants, but it was im-possible to state that any one pollutant was the cause of death.

See *Air Pollution*. p. 381.

Industrial Diseases

1948–49 *Cmd.* 7557.   See *Workmen's Compensation*. p. 300.

Infant Mortality in Scotland

Scientific Advisory Cttee.   Sub-Cttee. Rep. pp. 84.   1943

1943 *Non-Parl. Dept. of Health, Scot. apptd. —. sgd. Aug.,* 1943

J. B. Orr (*Ch.*), Baird, Douglas (Char-lotte A.), Ferlie (Jane P.), Graham, Hendry, Leitch (Isabella), Macgregor, Mackintosh (Jean M.), McKinlay, McNeil, Scott-Dickson (Margaret), Simpson (Elenora J.), Wattie (Nora I.).

'*To consider the high infantile mortality experience in Scotland, with a view to estimating its principal causal factors and suggesting lines of action to ensure its reduction.*'

Scotland has the highest infant mortality rate of 17 countries, including the Dominions, the United States of America and all the countries of West-ern Europe, except Spain and Portugal. The adverse conditions contributing to this are worst in the West Central (urban) and the North East (rural) areas. Congenital debility is mainly responsible for the excess mortality in the first month, and therefore the causes are mainly operative before birth, but some reduction could be effected by improving nurseries and nursery staffing in maternity hospitals, so that premature and sick babies could be isolated and neo-natal infection brought under control. The excess mortality between one and twelve months is due chiefly to infectious disease resulting from poverty, faulty feeding and poor housing. In Scotland, as compared with England and Wales, the percentage of unemployment is higher, the proportion living in poverty twice as high and the percentage of over-crowding twice as great.

The excess of still-births is as great as the excess of neo-natal deaths. Two-thirds are due to poor physique and poor health of the mothers and one-third to the hazards of birth. Working-class mothers are often underfed and their diets of poor quality, deficient in materials for bone and blood formation. There may be a high proportion of unsatisfactory and short lactations. Scotland has lagged behind in the provision of welfare services and the clinic premises are often poor, ill-equipped and over-crowded, health visitors' districts are too large, and the powers to supply food and domestic help are not sufficiently used by local authorities.

Recommendations are made for temporary housing schemes, the provision of more food for mothers and infants, improved welfare services, and unified administration in connection with the supervision of illegitimate and boarded-out infants.

See *Neo-Natal Deaths due to Infection*. Rep.; 1947 Non-Parl. Dept. of Health, Scot.

Scottish Lunacy and Mental Deficiency Laws

Cttee. Rep., app., index. pp. 131. 1946
1945–46 *Cmd.* 6834, *xiii*, 657
apptd. Feb., 1938. *sgd.* —

Lord Russell (*Ch.*), Andrew, Hamilton (Mrs. L.), Henderson, Leonard, Neven-Spence, Patrick, Phin, Robertson (Violet M. C.), Thomson.

To enquire into the existing law of Scotland relating to the certification, detention and supervision of persons who are, or are alleged to be, of unsound mind; of persons not certified but suffering from mental illness; dangerous lunatics; mental defectives.

An historical review of Scottish lunacy and mental deficiency laws is followed by a very detailed examination of existing law and practice. In general, they have not kept pace with changes in public sentiment and the developments in mental science. Continuing the use of the convenient local administrative agency of the Inspectors of Poor (now Public Assistance and Social Welfare Officers), has perpetuated an association with the Poor Law which has long been the source of criticism. Delay in seeking treatment for mentally ill persons has at times been due to the reluctance of relatives to accept poor relief. Even where the assistance has been refunded, the case is retained on the registers as one of pauper lunacy. No such stigma attaches to the person who requires such assistance on account of physical illness.

A very large number of recommendations were made which, while retaining much of the Scottish Acts, on the whole show the Committee's acceptance of the Mental Treatment Act, 1930. The term mental patient, instead of lunatic, should be applied to a person certified by two medical men as requiring to be detained for the purpose of care and treatment; idiots should be placed under the Mental Deficiency Acts. There should be three categories (1) the voluntary patient, (2) the patient undergoing temporary detention without a Statutory Order; and (3) the patient detained by Order of the Sheriff or the sanction of the Board. There should be opportunities for early treatment for a limited period, but prolonged treatment under compulsory detention should be covered by Judicial Order. The right to submit objections and the consent of next-of-kin should be provided for in any case of compulsory deprivation of liberty. Lunatic wards in poor houses should be discontinued; the placing of lunatics under private care should require the support of two medical certificates. Medical certification and hospital care should be with a branch of the local health authority. There should be a special branch of the Central Health Authority to deal with all branches of mental health, and local authorities should have an advisory and rehabilitation department, with psychiatric and social workers. Recommendations are made on the procedure for temporary and permanent release. For voluntary patients who have not been certified, there should be arrangements for temporary treatment, properly equipped observation wards attached to general hospitals, as well as more mental clinics for out-patients. There is insufficient accommodation for dangerous lunatics; there should be one central institution, managed as part of the State Asylum for criminal lunatics and financed by national funds. Control should pass from the Prisons Division to the General Board of Control.

The 1914–18 war and the subsequent retrenchment stopped the development of the possibilities of the Mental Deficiency Act, 1913, and with one or two exceptions, local authorities failed to provide the necessary institutional accommodation for mental defectives. At a low figure of 2 per 1000, institutional care is needed for 10,000 persons, though there are only 4548 beds. The definitions in the Mental Deficiency Act, 1927, are satisfactory, but should be subject to modifications. The three grades described as feebleminded, imbecile and idiot, should be superseded by the terms Grade A, Grade B, and Grade C respectively. Education and training of those under 16 should pass from the Public Assistance Committee to the Education Authority; training needed from 16 to 18 should be given under the Disabled Persons (Employment) Act, 1944, in co-operation with the Education Act. Care and training of mental defectives over the age of 18 should no longer rest with the Public Assistance Committee, but should become the duty of a composite Mental Health Committee. There should be power to compel local authorities to carry out their statutory duties under the Mental Deficiency Acts. There is a deplorable lack of accommodation for mental defectives of dangerous or violent propensities. A central state institution should be provided for mental defectives.

In Reservations Professor Henderson argued that the procedure under the 1930 Act in relation to the granting of a Judicial Order was more formidable than had previously been the case; that the Judicial procedure under the 1862 Act had worked well and that it would be a retrograde step to supersede it; that although the White Paper on the National Health Service had been published after the Committee had heard evidence, it should have been considered by them; that the procedure for the provision of treatment for the voluntary patient was better under the 1866 Act than the 1930 Act; and that defective children 5–18 who were educable should be supervised by Directors of Education, that otherwise the children should be under the jurisdiction of the Health Authority, and that a Mental Health Committee would be the most suitable body to deal with them. The last reservation was signed also by John Phin.

Treatment and Rehabilitation of Miners in the Wales Region Suffering from Pneumokoniosis

Advisory Cttee.   Rep., apps. pp. 18.
1944

1944 *Non-Parl. Min. of Fuel and Power apptd. May,* 1943. *sgd. May,* 1944

W. Jones (*Ch.*), Alban, Aslett, Bevan, Evans, Finch, Jenkins, Keating, Perry, Wade, Williams.

'*To advise as to the measures which should be taken to provide for the medical treatment and rehabilitation by institutional treatment or otherwise, of coal miners in the Wales Region suffering from Pneumokoniosis. . . .*'

The comprehensive term 'pneumokoniosis of coal workers' is used for all pulmonary conditions described as due to all forms of dust arising from coal getting. The one immediate measure likely to reduce the incidence is the reduction in the amount of air-borne dust, but observations over a number of years may be necessary to assess what constitutes a dust hazard. Not enough is yet known to allow recommendations to be made for large-scale measures of treatment including rehabilitation.

Recommendations include: a centre with beds for 30 in-patients, with equipment and facilities for clinical study and research, periodical clinical and X-ray examinations of miners, correlated with scientific assessment of dust concentration and dust constitution; a bureau to co-ordinate all aspects of the work.

See *Medical Research Council*. Rep. for 1939–45. pp. 156–8; 1947–48 Cmd. 7335, xiii, 87. Special Reports, Nos. 243, 244, 250 of the Medical Research Council; 1942, 1943, 1945 Non-Parl. *Employment in South Wales for Persons suspended from the Mining Industry on account of Silicosis and Pneumoconiosis.* p. 261.

Poliomyelitis. Survey of the Outbreak in Scotland in 1947

Rep., apps. pp. 80. 1950

1950 *Non-Parl. Dept. of Health, Scot.*

I. N. Sutherland.

Poliomyelitis has been a notifiable disease in Scotland since 1924, but there had been no epidemic until 1947. A statistical analysis is made of the information collected about the 2002 cases which occurred in 1947. Poliomyelitis is somewhat different in its epidemiology from most of our common infectious diseases. It seems to occur in countries where the standard of living is high, and is associated with better housing, as is the severity of the resulting paralysis. It seems to attack small family groups rather than large families which are more likely to be overcrowded, and there is no evidence of correlation with definable degrees of insanitation. The 27 tables in an appendix show that the 1947 outbreak had somewhat different features from previous outbreaks in Scotland. Comparison with others should help to establish the common features of the infection and the development of techniques of confirmation and control.

Work of Psychologists and Psychiatrists in the Services

Expert Cttee. Rep., apps. pp. 95. 1947

1947 *Non-Parl. Privy Council Office apptd.* — 1942. *sgd. Jan.*, 1945

F. R. Fraser (*Ch.*), Dudley, Whittingham, Hood, L. Moran, Bartlett, Henderson, Lewis, Wolters.

'(1) *To examine and correlate the facts and the results of the psychiatric and psychological work in the three Services.* (2) *To make suggestions in the field of further co-ordination or development or improvement of this work.* (3) *To study the application of these methods with a view to their post-war application.*'

Service psychiatry grew out of the cumulative experience of the wars of 1914–18 and 1939–45 and the need for proper selection procedures and the detection of mental deviations, etc. With the introduction of conscription it was to be expected that the various forms of psychiatric disorders occurring in the civilian population would also be found in comparable proportions among the men and women in the Services. The sphere of psychological work in the Services should be extended. During their training all officers should be instructed in the psychological aspects of their future duties; psychologists should be represented on the principal scientific and advisory committees, etc.; there should be an inter-service body of the senior Service psychologists to continue discussions and research. To prevent undue wastage of manpower, psychiatrists should continue to make their contribution to selection, classification, training, mental hygiene and morale in the Services; they should collaborate as closely as possible with Service psychologists. A central co-ordinating and statistical section should be established to improve contacts with the emergency civilian Neuroses Centres and with Service Departments. There are 70 pages of appendices relating to conditions and information available at the end of 1944.

See *Re-adjustment in Civil Life of Soldiers Discharged from the Army on account of Neurosis*. E. Guttman. E. L. Thomas. Rep.; 1946 Non-Parl. Min. of Health.

Rehabilitation

Medical Advisory Cttee. (Scotland). Sub-Cttee. Rep., apps. pp. 35. 1946

1946 Non-Parl. Dept. of Health, Scot. apptd. May, 1944. sgd. Nov., 1945

E. P. Cathcart (*Ch.*), Logan, Aitken, Duthie, Illingworth, McNiven, Stirling.

'To consider the types of condition for which rehabilitation facilities should be provided in a comprehensive medical service in Scotland and the nature and extent of the further facilities required.'

'Medical rehabilitation' is concerned with accessory treatment aimed at restoring physical and mental functions which suffer incidentally as a result of disease or local injury. Physiotherapy, electro-therapy, occupational therapy and remedial exercises are methods used, but a better evaluation of their results should be made. They should form part of a balanced daily programme carried out under medical supervision, and should include, for various types of patients, the teaching of good posture and sound body mechanics, speech therapy, the use of artificial limbs, hearing aids, lip reading, training for the blind, and schooling for children. Attention should be paid to diet, meal-times and hours of work for patients with alimentary disorders, etc., supervised convalescence for cardiac cases, etc. Rehabilitation is unnecessary for patients suffering from short-term illnesses and for most general surgical cases, but is of value for injuries, diseases of the central and peripheral nervous systems, articular rheumatism,

and a quarter of the cases in general medical wards. There should be close liaison between the medical service and the industrial medical service concerning employment and resettlement.

The extent to which hospitals undertake rehabilitation varies widely, the shortage of beds requires a rapid turnover, and there is insufficient medical and auxiliary staff. The facilities required include continuity of provision during the whole process of primary treatment and rehabilitation, and a planned programme of increasing activity through convalescence until employment is resumed. Additional facilities should include non-residential rehabilitation centres, better equipped and better organised convalescent hospitals. The needs for an independent residential rehabilitation centre could not be assessed; but one large centre should be provided, which would cater for all patients from all sections of the community. Rehabilitation centres should be under one medical officer in charge; the physician or surgeon who refers the patient should discuss treatment with this officer; the auxiliary staff must work together as a team; and the programmes of individual patients should be reviewed at weekly meetings. Other administrative details are outlined.

Chronic Rheumatic Diseases

Medical Advisory Cttee. (Scotland). Sub-Cttee. Rep., apps. pp. 27. 1945

1945 Non-Parl. Dept. of Health, Scot. apptd. —. sgd. Sept., 1944

J. Fraser (*Ch.*), Macgregor, Patrick, Logan, Miller.

'To consider what action can be devised for the treatment of chronic rheumatism among the general population.'

The social and economic implications of rheumatism came into prominence through several investigations made in connection with the National Health or Social Insurance Services. In England and Wales in 1922 rheumatic diseases accounted for one-sixth of the industrial invalidity; half the loss was due to chronic joint diseases. A similar picture is disclosed for Scotland. So little is known about the nature and cause of the disease that treatment is largely empirical. Co-ordinated research was needed.

The existing facilities in Scotland for diagnosis and treatment were inadequate, most patients depending on the general practitioner, whose treatment at present was necessarily limited to symptomatic relief and general or local medication. There should be central clinics of 20–40 beds in at least one hospital affiliated to each of the four universities, long-term accommodation being reserved for those with a reasonable prospect of alleviation or cure. These should be linked with peripheral clinics associated with the orthopaedic service and mainly for physiotherapy. Stress should be laid on active therapy; and medical students instructed in the methods of physical medicine.

Prevalence and Control of Scabies

Pp. 4. 1942

1941–42 *Cmd. 6355, ix, 161 sgd. May, 1942*

Since 1936, for reasons unknown, scabies (The Itch) was increasing. In view of the probability that war conditions would favour a further increase a Memo. on *Scabies and how to deal with it* (1940 Non-Parl. Min. of Health) was issued to Medical Officers. Under the Defence Regulations, where scabies or any other disease associated with verminous conditions prejudiced the efficient conduct of the war, the Minister made an Order providing for inspection, examination and treatment. Research shows that infection is spread by direct contact with the infected person, though not much is known about the spread from infected clothes. Details are given on the methods of treatment.

Tuberculosis

Cttee. Rep., apps. pp. 63. 1951

1951 *Non-Parl. Dept. of Health, Scot. apptd. July, 1948. sgd. Dec., 1950*

J. P. Younger (*Ch.*), Cameron, Crew, Elder, Fyfe, Laidlaw, Langmuir, Maclean.

'*A review of the available information . . . on the incidence of respiratory tuberculosis, with special reference to social conditions and nature of employment as affecting the increased incidence of the disease in recent years. . . .*'

In many countries, during the war (1939–1945) there was a rise in the incidence of tuberculosis, but whereas elsewhere improvement set in rapidly after the war, in Scotland the heavy rates persisted. The report reviews exhaustively the statistical and other evidence on the trend, age, occupation, class and geographical incidence, the influence of nutritional and housing conditions, etc. The majority of people have been infected by middle life and only a small minority develop active disease, the resistance of the individual is paramount, and since information on associated biological and social factors is incomplete, control must aim at prevention and raising the level of resistance. There is unequivocal evidence that the nutritive level in Scotland has fallen so much as to become a contributory factor in the rise of incidence. Early diagnosis and care of the adolescent and young adults, the provision of at least three beds per annual death, B.C.G. vaccination for tubercle-negative nurses, and a detailed programme of research are recommended.

Vaccination against Smallpox

Memo. pp. 8. 1952

1952 *Non-Parl. Min. of Health*

When the National Health Service Act, 1946, came into operation the Vaccination Acts, providing for compulsory vaccination against smallpox, ceased to have effect. The Memo. is designed to assist medical practitioners. Infant vaccination at four months is recommended as it not only provides immunity until school-age, but it makes any later emergency vaccination less severe in its reactions.

See *Historical Note on the Prevention of Smallpox in England and the Foundation of the Government Lymph Establishment.* J. R. Hutchinson. Min. of Health [Ann.] Rep. App. A; 1946–47 Cmd. 7119, xii, 1.

Venereal Diseases (Scotland)

Medical Advisory Cttee. Scotland. Sub-Cttee. Rep., app. pp. 28. 1944

1943–44 *Cmd.* 6518, *iv*, 611
apptd. —. sgd. Dec., 1943

S. A. Smith (*Ch.*), Fyfe, Harrower (Dr. Catherine).

'*To consider* (a) *what further measures, if any, are necessary for the education of the public with regard to the dangers of venereal diseases and the need for early diagnosis and treatment, and* (b) *what improvements, if any, are required with regard to the arrangements for diagnosis, supervision, treatment and control of venereal diseases.*'

An actual increase of venereal disease has occurred, though owing to statistical difficulties the incidence could not be assessed precisely. Between 1939 and 1942 58,000 persons were exposed to the risk of acquiring infection and 29,000 contracted a major venereal disease. The increase is more marked in ports and large towns and the data suggest that it is due to the temporary influx of Service personnel and seamen; although a decline will probably occur with the return of normal conditions, the situation warrants energetic action.

A definite step forward was made by the introduction of Regulation 33B of the Defence (General) Regulations, 1939, whereby under due safeguards, compulsory treatment of promiscuous persons who spread infection is made a statutory obligation, but under the Regulation action is limited to the case where the person is the probable source of infection common to at least two known patients and has been unres-

ponsive to persuasion. There should be some form of legal power to require the intractable defaulter who transmits the infection to others to follow continued treatment. Legislation should be devised to require notification of every established case; there should be strict anonymity for the patient who co-operates, but intractable defaulters should be liable to public prosecution. Private practitioners should be required to notify the Medical Officer of Health in code, indicating how he is treating or disposing of a case, etc. Parents of infected children who also have been deemed to be infected and required to submit to examination and treatment, should be allowed a right of appeal.

Control of Midges

Scientific Advisory Cttee. Sub-Cttee. Interim Rep., app. pp. 11. 1946. 2nd Rep. pp. 11. 1948

1946, 1948 *Non-Parl. Dept. of Health, Scot.*
apptd. — 1944. *sgd. Sept.,* 1946, *Jan.,* 1948

F. A. E. Crew (*Ch.*), and 4 other members, Interim Rep. A. S. M. Macgregor (*Ch.*), and 5 other members, 2nd Rep.

'*To advise* (1) *whether there are repellents which would act as safeguards against midge bites and if so, how they should be used, and* (2) *whether midges can be destroyed in their breeding grounds and elsewhere and, if so, what preparations and methods can safely be used and how they should be used.*'

The midge in Scotland may not be a carrier of infection but its biting propensities make it a serious source of irritation to the Scottish workers, domestic animals and to tourists. A preliminary survey showed that of the 15 species recorded, one, *C. impunctatus*, was more frequent than all the others taken together. It breeds on damp soil, decaying vegetation, etc., and in some areas 50,000 midges per acre are active simultaneously at the peak periods. Before control measures can be directed against the larvae or pupae, more precise information is needed about the breeding grounds of the different species. Successful experiments were made with repellent creams, impregnated gauntlets, over-socks and head veils. The reported slight smarting produced by the cream, and the negligible impairment of vision associated with the veil, are far out-weighed by the efficiency of midge-repellents. An anti-midge cream must have a D.M.P. content of not less than 40 per cent, by volume, and the product should be stable.

Synthetic Detergents

Cttee. Interim Rep. pp. 7. 1954. Rep., apps. pp. iv, 60. 1956

1954, 1956 *Non-Parl. Min. of Housing and Local Gov.*
apptd. May, 1953. sgd. Feb., 1954, Dec., 1955

H. Jephcott (*Ch.*), and 14 others.

'*To examine and report on the effects of the increasing use of synthetic detergents with particular reference to the functioning of the public health services.*'

The usefulness and popularity of detergents as cleansing agents is accompanied by fears that they may cause dermatitis, etc., that they corrode domestic equipment and plumbing and that excessive foaming reduces operational efficiency at sewage works and causes concern over the purity of the rivers. There is no cause for alarm amongst household users, though care should be taken to rinse the hands and the crockery, etc., after using detergents. A nuisance may be caused at sewage works, where foam occurs which could in some cases endanger health, or the purification processes may be retarded. At virtually all works the effluent discharged into rivers contains some residual surface-active materials, and there are risks to fish and plant life and that the water supply for a quarter of the population, which is taken below effluents, will contain traces of it. 'Our environmental health services are functioning without any large margin of safety, and can be kept safe only by continuous action' to minimise dangers.

The recommendations include: improvements in the methods of determining small concentrations of surface-active material in sewage effluents and water; regular determinations of the concentrations in effluents, and by water undertakers using such rivers as sources of supply; the effect on health of detergents in drinking water and on crockery should be kept under medical review; manufacturers should investigate the feasibility of producing a detergent which does not foam. An advisory body of the interests concerned should be set up to facilitate research. Four members of the committee did not think that any special safeguards of the public were needed whilst the research was being carried out, but the majority thought a worsening of the situation not inconceivable, and pointed out there were no powers for controlling the composition of such detergents.

See *Synthetic Detergents*. Standing Technical Cttee. [1st], 2nd., 3rd Progress Reps.; 1958, 1959, 1960 Non-Parl.

Treatment and Disposal of Sewage Sludge

Informal Working Party. Rep. pp. iii, 64. 1954

1954 *Non-Parl. Min. of Housing and Local Gov.*
apptd. Oct., 1951. sgd. —

F. G. Hill (*Ch.*), Brown, Davies, Edmondson, Elliott, Jenkins, Jepson, Key, Lawrence, Miller, Orchard, Pettet, Townend.

'*To study and report on all aspects of the sludge disposal problem.*'

In 1918 a Committee of the National Salvage Council regarded it as profitable to recover grease from sludge if it contained 15 per cent on a dry basis, provided that there were 100 tons of wet sludge available daily and that the selling price of the grease was not less than £15 per ton. There was sufficient nitrogen in fresh sewage sludge to give it a definite fertilising value.

During World War II and thereafter there was difficulty in obtaining fertilising material and the costs of sewage disposal increased. Of the population of 43 mn. in England and Wales, the sewage of 6 mn. is drained to the sea and estuaries without appreciable arrest of suspended solids, while that from 4–5 mn., chiefly in rural areas, does not enter sewers. The sewage from the remaining 32–33 mn. drains into works at which sludge is separated and disposed of. Some 16 mn. tons of wet sludge or 800,000 tons of dry solids have to be disposed of each year, as well as 11 mn. tons of house and trade refuse, of which 8 mn. tons are got rid of by controlled tipping, 2 mn. by separate incinerator and 1 mn. in other ways.

The problem is the final disposal of this complex of waste material at reasonable cost and without risk to health and amenity. In many cases it is possible to produce certain by-products of local or national importance, provided the cost is economic and is justified by demand. About one-third of the sewage sludge is disposed of as manure or fertiliser base. The report reviews, in technical detail, each stage of the process from the arrest of the sludge, its conditioning, dehydration to reduce bulk and transport, to final disposal, together with examples of experiments in recovery. Costs vary widely. At costs of 1949–50 and ignoring income from sales of by-products, costs of disposing of liquid sludge to a permanent tip were about 15s. od. a ton, crude sludge could be dried to a 50 per cent moisture content for 40s. od. a dry ton, while costs rose to £7 a ton for digested primary sludge. Sales of by-products depend on good marketing.

A standard form should be drawn up for recording all important data of sludge treatment and disposal, of costs incurred, and sewage disposal authorities should keep records, an annual summary of the results being published by the Ministry. Research should be continued jointly by the Water Pollution Board and the Universities.

4. DRUGS, FOOD PURITY

The Labelling and Advertising of Foods

app. pp. 4. 1943

1942–43 *Cmd.* 6482, *xi*, 113

sgd. Nov., 1943

As a result of the recommendations of the Committee of 1934 (*Breviate 1917–39*, p. 431) provisions for the determination of standards of food were made in the Food and Drugs Act, 1938. But as this Act did not come into force until October 1939, when the Ministry of Food had come into existence, the Minister of Health had not exercised the power conferred upon him by the Act. The need for standards was accentuated by war-time shortage of supplies and the consequent danger of a reduction of the quality of certain foodstuffs. The Minister of Food was therefore made responsible for exercising existing statutory powers to make regulations stipulating the manner in which foods are to be labelled, and regulating the composition of food and requiring pre-packed foods to be labelled with indication of their weight and measure. Additional powers under the Defence Regulations enable him to make it an offence to give a label or publish an advertisement which misleads as to the nutritional or dietary value of food, etc., and to create standards for particular foods as the necessity arises. An advisory committee was set up to give technical assistance in fixing appropriate food standards.

See *Advertising, Labelling and Composition of Food*. Rep. (App. A is a reprint of Cmd. 6482); 1949 Non-Parl. Min. of Food.

Manufactured Meat Products

Working Party. Rep., apps. pp. 48. 1950

1950 *Non-Parl. Min. of Food*
apptd. May, 1949. sgd. Aug., 1950

S. W. Hood (*Ch.*), Battersby, Dence, Gale, Howat, Lamont, Lethem, Marritt, Marsh, Martine, Menzies, Moore, Neal, Priestley, Pyatt, Stewart, Sutherland, Taylor (Mrs. A.), Vigor, Ward.

'*To review present trade practice and legal requirements for securing that conditions in the meat manufacturing trades are clean and sanitary, and that the products, and the materials from which they are prepared, are wholesome in all respects. . . .*'

To secure conditions and practices necessary to public health the provisions of the Food and Drugs Act, 1938, should be amended and extended to require that premises and rooms used for meat preparation should be registered; domestic kitchens, sculleries, and rooms with direct access to living rooms and bedrooms should not be used; regulations should specify impervious floor and wall coverings, equipment, constant hot water, etc. Legislation should be supplemented by a voluntary code of specified practices which are highly desirable, but which not all manufacturers could achieve with the facilities available. Six members propose that the manufacturer as well as the premises should be registered.

Food Standards

Cttee. Preservatives Sub-Cttee. Revised Rep., *Antioxidants*, app. pp. 11. 1954
1954 *Non-Parl. Min. of Food*
apptd. Jan., 1951. sgd. Aug., 1954

C. Dodds (*Ch.*).

Antioxidants are substances which retard or prevent oxidative deterioration of food (rancidity). Hitherto their main use has been for addition to edible oils and fats, but proposals have been made for their use in fat-containing foods such as pork, bacon, fish, milk powder, synthetic cream, mayonnaise, edible nuts, fruit juices, cut and pared fruits and vegetables and essential oils. Recommended that antioxidants should not be added to any foods other than edible oils and fats and to essential oils, and compounded foods should not contain more than the amount of antioxidant necessarily introduced by the use of oils, etc., as ingredients. Details of the kinds and amounts to be permitted are outlined.

—— Metallic Contamination Sub-Cttee. Revised Rep., *Lead*. pp. 11 1954
1954 *Non-Parl.*
apptd. Oct., 1948. sgd. July, 1954

G. G. Barnes (*Ch.*).

Lead is one of the most widespread and serious of the metallic contaminants of food and drink. The principal sources are lead compounds in food processing plant, in piping by which water and other liquids are conveyed, and in agricultural insecticides. Shellfish may ingest and absorb lead compounds, and it may be inhaled from the air. Some of these sources are uncontrollable, but others attributable to human agency can be regulated.

Recommended that the limits suggested for beverages, sugar, edible oils and fats, etc., should be made statutory, and that its use in lead piping for conveying beer, etc., in packing materials, or in domestic culinary equipment, should be controlled; that shellfish and crustacea, where lead is naturally present in varying amounts, should be the subject of a general reservation.

Freezing Point (Hortvet) Test of Milk
Rep.
1945 *Non-Parl.* See *Agriculture*. p. 95.

Hygiene in Catering Establishments
Working Party. Rep., apps. pp. 50.
1951
1951 *Non-Parl. Min. of Food*
apptd. Nov., 1948. sgd. Nov., 1950

W. G. Savage (*Ch.*), and 20 others.

'*To make recommendations to the Ministers of Food and Health and the Secretary of State for Scotland as to the precautions con-*

sidered practicable and desirable with a view to securing the observance of sanitary and cleanly conditions in the catering trade.'

There are 236,000 catering establishments, exclusive of many public houses and numerous small boarding houses not registered for rationed food. These very diverse establishments are classified into 11 groups having different hygiene requirements, from the larger units of hotels, boarding houses, holiday camps, etc., to the smallest unit of mobile van, coffee stall, marquee, etc. Community feeding has greatly extended during the war, establishments have often been opened or extended without due consideration of hygienic requirements, and there has been a shortage of essential equipment, and experienced staff. During 1942–48 there were 20 outbreaks of food poisoning associated with communal feeding, but whilst the number is small compared with the numbers of meals supplied, unsatisfactory conditions are common to certain types of premises.

Improvement can be achieved by the adoption of codes of practice, and two were drawn up for this purpose. The Standard Code is short and simple and contains essential requirements only, no structural requirement being included unless it has direct bearing on the prevention of infection. It should be required of every catering establishment. The application of this code should take account of the special requirements of some of these groups of establishments; for mobile vans and coffee stalls it should be legally enforceable. The Target Code sets out the best practical conditions for serving food which all establishments should aim at. All catering establishments should be required to register with the appropriate local authority. The Food and Drugs Act, 1938, should be extended, e.g. to passenger-carrying vessels, places where meals are supplied free, etc. App. III is a report of a sub-committee on the use of detergents in the catering industry.

Toxic Chemicals in Agriculture

Rep., *Residues in Food*

1954 *Non-Parl.* See *Agriculture.* p. 88.

XIII A.   HOUSING

1. Housing
2. Rents

3. House Management, Housing Estates

1.   HOUSING

Temporary Accommodation

Memo., apps. pp. 31. 1944

1944 *Non-Parl. Min. of Health, Min. of Works*

Temporary accommodation should not be considered in isolation, but in relation to the whole housing programme, e.g. in the selection of sites not likely to be required in the early stages of permanent building. The use of temporary factory-made types of houses will make it possible to provide double the number of dwellings with the limited amount of skilled labour available in the first year after building can be resumed. The local authorities will provide the sites and services, the Ministry of Works the sub-structures and the houses. This will involve the Ministry in a cost of £68 11s. 0d. per house for ten years and the local authorities, assuming exclusive rents of 10s. 0d., will pay the Ministry £23 10s. 0d. per house. The local authorities will let and manage the houses. If when occupied they show a loss of more than £8 per house, they can ask for an adjustment. The tenants should be those without a home, particularly men and women who have been on war service and cannot find a home.

See separate Memo. for Scotland; 1944 Non-Parl. Dept. of Health, Scot., Min. of Works. See also *Housing (Temporary Accommodation) Act, 1944*; 7 & 8 Geo. 6. c. 36.

Temporary Housing Programme
Pp. 7. 1945
1945–46 *Cmd. 6686, xix, 653*

Owing to difficulties of supply of materials, labour and productive capacity, the estimated costs of aluminium houses had risen from £914 to £1,365 and of other types by an average of £268. An analysis of the increase is given. The cost of the programme will rise to nearly £185 mn.

See *Temporary Housing Programme;* 1947–48 Cmd. 7304, xxii, 3.

Distribution of New Houses in Scotland
Housing Advisory Cttee. Sub-Cttee. Rep., apps., index. pp. 127. 1944

1943–44 *Cmd. 6552, iv, 1*
apptd. Oct., 1942. sgd. —

G. P. Laidlaw (*Ch.*), Drysdale (Miss G.), Gordon, Imrie, Jamieson, Lindsay, Lockie, MacGregor, Mann (Mrs. J.), Stirling, Watson, Cunnison, Mears, Wilson.

'To consider and advise on the measures required to secure the most appropriate distribution of the houses to be erected in Scotland in the immediate post-war years.'

Between 1919 and 1939, in relation to population, Scotland built one-third less houses than England and Wales, 70 per cent having been erected by local authorities and 30 per cent by private enterprise, whereas in England and Wales the proportions were reversed. Although the gross population may decline after 1971, there will be an increased proportion of older persons wanting to continue in their own homes. The estimated need for 500,000 houses in the post-war years is confirmed.

The defects in the existing distribution of houses are due to congested areas, 'pepper-pot' development, derelict central sites, ribbon development, suburban sprawl, houses at excessive distances from work places, lags between new industrial development and housing, and insufficient grouping in rural areas. Ample land is available, though unnecessary obstacles to its acquisition should be removed. As population would be stationary, unless mechanisation provides a solution, there cannot be more industry in country areas, small or medium sized towns or in new towns, without drawing population from existing large urban areas.

Housing will be required for 'static' families needing homes in the areas of their own local authority and for 'transferee' families needing homes outside it. The need is so great that participation by local authorities, private enterprise and housing associations will be required. Local authorities should receive subsidies for building houses for general needs. Whilst the shortage of houses lasts the problem of distribution will be aggravated by the immediate demands; the main recommendations are therefore divided into short-term and long-term phases.

Short-Term Phase.—The decisions on distribution of houses will fall on the Central Department, whose responsibility will be to balance the needs of families requiring houses in the national interest, e.g. families transferred to a new industry of national importance, rural workers, and those rendered homeless by enemy action. The Central Department should make a general allocation to all authorities and a special one where special needs occur. Temporary houses should be allocated and let in the same way as if they had been permanent. The Scottish Special Housing Association should build for 'transferee' families, when the local authority does not wish to do so.

Long-Term Phase.—A house-to-house survey should be made of families in unfit houses, families living in overcrowded conditions, families without houses, families living in temporary houses and those living at unreasonable distances from work. A system of consultation with industry should be maintained in order to take account of the needs of transferee families. 'Static' families in areas of heavy unemployment before the war should be provided for if there is a reasonable prospect of employment and the area is suitable for industrial expansion from a planning point of view. Strong arguments were put in favour of the neighbourhood unit consisting of 5000 to 10,000 persons or, on an average of four persons per house, of between 1250 to 2500 houses. A special enquiry should be made into the question of densities in redevelopment areas, the standards of shopping facilities for different types of neighbourhood units, and the question of siting shops. Re-development and modernisation in urban areas should improve and strengthen existing communities and the replacement of small congested factories by flatted factories to let, in order to keep place of work in proper relation to houses, should provide more open space. Decentralisation is likely to be inevitable in nearly all towns for a period after 1945, if for no other reason than that little redevelopment beyond the planning stage will be practicable at this time. Dispersal should first take the form of the expansion of small towns. There is a case for a small number of new towns. They should be sited by the local authorities concerned and, where not satellite towns, be developed by a public Board financed by the Exchequer. Congestion, rather than mere population, is the criterion for the optimum size of towns, but new and expanding small towns should be zoned for populations of 15,000 to 50,000. An interim decision on the optimum size of each town should be taken.

Planning our New Homes

Scottish Housing Advisory Cttee. Sub-Cttees. Rep., apps., index. pp. 96, xliv. 1944

1944 *Non-Parl. Dept. of Health, Scot. apptd.* — 1942. *sgd. Nov.,* 1943

R. Adam (*Ch.*), and 19 other members, Housing Design. J. Welsh (*Ch.*), and 12 other members, Furniture.

'*To make recommendations as to the design, interior planning, layout, and standard of construction of new houses in Scotland.*'

'*To consider how best local authorities can exercise their powers under the Housing (Scotland) Acts to provide furnishings, fittings, and conveniences in houses provided by them, and to advise on what additional powers, if any, should be available to local authorities for this purpose.*'

The cottage type of house is widely preferred and should form the largest proportion to be built in the future; flatted houses should be well insulated; flats (tenements) should be insulated and should not exceed three storeys unless lifts are provided. Programmes should include houses for the ageing and for single persons and provide for special needs, such as accommodation for nets in a fishing community. Detailed recommendations are made on standards of space, services, construction, equipment, design and lay-out. Standards of persons per room should count all children as persons and bedrooms be not less than 120 sq. ft. for two persons; bedrooms only should be counted, so that the living room is not used as a bedroom. This would prevent the over-building of undersized houses which is the radical defect of Scottish housing. Local authorities should be prepared to use their powers to ensure provision of essential furniture and furnishings for those who have insufficient means, but not for other categories of their tenants. House Management service should be widely extended. New housing estates should be planned as communities, with open spaces, communal buildings, and grouping into neighbourhood units. The post-war need was 500,000 houses, and immediate post-war need 166,000 houses.

There were four reservations dealing with flats; who should live in them, lifts in flats, the importance of architectural design and the need for an independent committee to investigate the differences in local costs, etc.

See *Housing of Special Groups*. Cttee. Rep.; 1952 Non-Parl. Dept. of Health, Scot.

Design of Dwellings

Central Housing Advisory Cttee. Sub-Cttee. Rep., apps. etc. pp. 75. 1944

1944 Non-Parl. Min. of Health apptd. March, 1942. sgd. Feb., 1944

Lord Dudley (*Ch.*), Adburgham (Miss J. F.), Bellman, Burt, Cook (Mrs. C.), Coppock, De Soissons, Dollar (Mrs. M. M.), Gooch (Mrs. E.), Haworth (Miss M. E.), Keay, Lloyd George (Miss M.), Mitchell, Monks, Scott, Sanderson (Lady), Watson, Williams, Wilson.

'*To make recommendations as to the design, planning, layout, standards of construction and equipment of dwellings for the people throughout the country.*'

The Committee contemplated that local authorities would have to build 2 mn. houses in the first ten years after the war, and recognised that there had been a general rise in standards regarding house room, domestic convenience and labour-saving fittings, together with a changed attitude regarding the functions of the living room and scullery. A minimum over-all floor area of 900 sq. ft. was necessary to remedy the defects of the inter-war house and to give effect to the detailed recommendations on standards of space, design and equipment. The rise of building costs (100 per cent) was out of all proportion to the rise in the cost of living (30 per cent) and the building programme would never be completed unless they were brought into reasonable relationship. The Committee assumed that steps would be taken to ensure this and that building costs would eventually stabilise at about 30 per cent above those of 1939. The cost of these improvements would mean

that while a pre-war house could be let at a minimum rent of 8s. 1d. plus rates, the rent of the suggested house could be 13s. 0d. plus rates. Of the increase of 5s. 0d., 2s. 7d. would be due to improved standards and 2s. 5d. to increased building costs. Part II of the report deals with technical notes on the recommendations, and App. II gives the estimated costs of the various improvements separately.

The Committee's Report is followed by the Report of a study group of the Ministry of Town and Country Planning on Site Planning and Lay-out in Relation to Housing, which sets out the principles of re-development, the extension of large and small towns and of the creation of new towns. It advocates the planning of residential neighbourhoods for groups of population up to 10,000 persons, in which every house has easy access to a neighbourhood centre.

Rural Housing

Central Housing Advisory Cttee. Sub-Cttee. 3rd Rep., apps. pp. 67. 1944

1944 Non-Parl. Min. of Health apptd. April, 1942. sgd. Dec., 1943

A. Hobhouse (*Ch.*), Cook (Mrs. C.), L. Crawford, Dilnot, Dollar (Mrs. M. M.), Lloyd George (Miss M.), Gooch (Mrs. E.), Hort (Miss I. E.), Methuen (Mrs. G.), Molson, Monks, Pole, Scott, Schomberg, Williams.

'*To review the subject of rural housing, especially in relation to changes caused by the war and the policy to be pursued after the war.*'

As a result of war shortages further deterioration of rural housing can be expected. Proposals to transfer house building from rural district councils to a national body or to county councils are rejected. While some rural district councils have been active, others have been backward in building, in inspection, staffing and standards. Joint Committees of county and rural district councils should be established, and default powers used. Recommendations include a comprehensive survey of rural housing, active reconditioning and a 5-year building programme, the use of architects and small builders. On the basis of a minimum agricultural wage of 65s. 0d., rents should not exceed 7s. 6d. to 8s. 0d. plus rates, and the preferential subsidy for agricultural houses should be continued.

For 1st and 2nd Reports, see *Breviate 1917–39*, p. 446.

—— Fourth Report, *Reconditioning in Rural Areas*, apps. pp. 48. 1947

1947 *Non-Parl.*
apptd. Sept., 1945. sgd. Sept., 1946

A. Hobhouse (*Ch.*), Allerton, Cook (Mrs. C.), Dilnot, Lloyd George (Lady), Gooch (Mrs. E.), Macgregor, Methuen (Mrs. G.), Molson, Monks, Reading (Lady), Lee (Miss J.).

'*To advise generally on the reconditioning of rural cottages, with special reference to the supply of labour available without diversion from new building, and to consider what improvements could be made in the Housing (Rural Workers') Acts.*' And '*to recommend what steps should be taken to encourage reconditioning by local authorities, and also how to adapt any future reconditioning scheme to preserve cottages, groups of cottages and village streets of special architectural and historic merit.*'

The sharp contrast between the old rural cottage which lacks amenity and which has deteriorated because it has been impossible to have repairs, etc., done, and the new houses with their additional comfort has lead to a growing demand for improved conditions, especially amongst men and women returning from the Services. Reconditioning could be carried out by the small country builder who has immobile labour, and who is not equipped to undertake new housing contracts.

As the powers to make grants under the Housing (Rural Workers) Act expired in September 1945, new legislation should make available a grant in respect of houses occupied or to be occupied by any person living in a rural area, provided that his income is such that he would not ordinarily pay a rent in excess of that paid by rural workers in the district. The grant should be two-thirds of the estimated cost, or a maximum of £300 whichever is less. In a Minority Report Miss Lee objected to grants being given to private persons except for houses of historical interest.

Private Enterprise Housing

Central Housing Advisory Cttee. Sub-Cttee. Rep., apps. pp. 56. 1944

1944 *Non-Parl. Min. of Health*
apptd. Oct., 1942. sgd. April, 1944

F. J. C. Pole (*Ch.*), Ager, Bellman, Burt, Gooch (Mrs. E.), Newman, Smith, Townroe, Watson.

'*To consider the part that private enterprise can best play in post-war housing, the conditions in which it can most effectively operate, and the methods of finance and organisation required.*'

The pre-war output of private houses by private enterprise showed that given favourable conditions, the housing needs of large sections of the people can be met without subsidy. If private enterprise is to maintain its position, it must produce a larger proportion of houses for letting, an essential condition of which is that building costs, now out of scale with living costs, should be brought into relation with them. To bring it into a state of readiness for the long-term building programme, it should participate in the short-term programme, receiving the same subsidies as local authorities where it meets the same needs, subject to control of selling price, rents, size and standards of construction. The subsidy should be periodically reviewed in relation to building costs and withdrawn when practicable. There should be a permanent body to review the prices of building materials.

Housing

Statement of Government Policy. pp. 8.
1945

1944–45 *Cmd.* 6609, *x*, 247

In the years 1934–39 the total output of houses exceeded 300,000 a year. By 1939 the number of houses was approximately equal to the number of separate families, 30 per cent of the population were living in new houses built since 1919 and the proportion of the population living in unfit and overcrowded houses had been reduced to some 6 per cent. Between 1939 and 1945 enemy action destroyed about 200,000, made uninhabitable some 250,000 and severely damaged a much larger number.

The Government's final objective is to provide a separate dwelling for every family which desires to have one. For this purpose it is estimated that 750,000 will be needed. The second objective is to complete slum clearance, and the third, long-term objective is to procure improvement in standards of housing and equipment. It was hoped to raise the labour force from 337,000 to 800,000 in 1946 and then to increase it beyond the 1939 figure of 1 mn. The maximum target would be 300,000 permanent houses built or building at the end of the second year. To check any rise of building costs owing to demand exceeding the industry's capacity, the Government will control the volume of local authorities' and private building and repair contracts, and the prices of materials and components. There will be other claims on the building force, but first-aid repair and the building of houses will have the highest priority. There will be a subsidy for privately built houses of approximately the same size as that for local authorities. The Housing (Temporary Accommodation) Act, 1944, authorised the spending of £150 mn. The temporary house will be produced and erected by the Government on sites acquired and prepared by the local authorities.

See *Housing Programme;* 1946–47 Cmd. 7021, xix, 567. Circular 90/49, *Housing Act, 1949;* 1949 Non-Parl. Min. of Health.

BB

Housing Manual, 1944, 1949

Pp. 103. 1944. Technical Apps., C–L. 1944. pp. 150. 1949. Technical Apps. 1951

1944 *Non-Parl. Min. of Health, Min. of Works.* 1949 *Non-Parl. Min. of Health,* 1951 *Non-Parl. Min. of Local Gov. and Planning, Min. of Works*

Gives guidance to local authorities as to the lines on which their proposals for permanent houses should be framed: lay-out of sites, density, house types, sizes of rooms, flats, efficiency in building, new methods and materials, heat, insulation, etc. In view of the immediate post-war needs of younger families, the 1944 edition emphasised the provision of two-bedroomed temporary and three-bedroomed permanent houses. The long-term housing programme called for a greater variety of types, some larger, some smaller, illustrated in the 1949 edition. Its designs are based on 900–950 feet super for a 3-bedroomed house instead of the 800–900 in the 1944 Manual, and special attention is given to lay-out, grouping, etc.

See 1st Supplement, *Housing for Special Purposes.* Sub-Cttee. Rep.; 1951 Non-Parl. Min. of Local Gov. and Planning. 2nd, 3rd Supplements; 1952, 1953 Non-Parl. Min. of Housing and Local Gov. *Scottish Housing Handbook.* Pts. 1–7; 1950–1958 Non-Parl. Dept. of Health, Scot.

Provision of Houses for Owner-occupation in Scotland

Scottish Housing Advisory Cttee. Sub-Cttee. Rep., apps., index. pp. iv, 74. [1945]

1945–46 *Cmd.* 6741, *xii*, 517 *apptd. March,* 1944. *sgd. Aug.,* 1945

H. B. Lindsay (*Ch.*), Laidlaw, Allison, Brown, Cessford, Gordon, Imrie, Jamieson, MacGregor, McIntosh, Russell, McKinna, McPhail, Tweedie.

'*To consider and advise on the measures required to encourage the provision of houses for owner-occupation in Scotland.*'

While the building of houses for owner-occupation appears to have been carried on to some extent in most areas, there existed an exceptionally strong tradition of home ownership in particular localities and particular occupations. A large proportion were owned by miners and railway workers, and ownership was common in the crofting and fishing communities. Before 1939 the working-class home ownership was financed by benefit building societies which raised funds by issuing shares or taking deposits from their members, built a group of houses, and sold them to their members.

The psychological inducements to owner-occupation are important not only from a point of view of investment, but because of the strong instinct of possession. A man will work hard to pay for his house and his efforts serve as an example to his family. The advantage to the local authority is that it creates a spirit of independence which not only relieves the local authority from responsibility, but adds a rate-producing subject to the Valuation Roll. The State also benefits from this form of durable capital investment. It is thought that owner-occupation may affect the mobility of labour to a slight degree, but this danger can be overcome.

In order to encourage and facilitate owner-occupation planning authorities should include land suitable for owner-occupation in their plans, and they should advise local builders on appropriate procedure, etc. Local authorities and Dean of Guild Courts should use their powers freely to acquire land, contribute to the cost of street construction, services, and general amenities, and prospective owners should be encouraged to consult the technical staffs. The Treasury should consider releasing post-war credits for house purchase, and consider whether stamp duty could be suspended. Advances under the Small Dwellings Acquisition (Scotland) Act should be revised to take account of building costs. Building societies, local authorities, etc., should lend on mortgage up to 90 per cent. of the valuation or selling price of the house. There should be a subsidy at not less than two-thirds of the capitalised value of contributions payable for assisted local authority housing.

In a Minority Report Jamieson, Miss Jobson, McTaggart, Paterson and Robertson objected to the encouragement of house-ownership on the grounds that houses should be provided to the community as a public service. Such a service will in time provide the necessary income to meet current liabilities without recourse to either rates or taxes. In a further Minority Report Cessford and McPhail recommended that home owners should be able to borrow, to have subsidies, and to buy land as cheaply and at the same rate, etc., as the local authority.

Conversion of Existing Houses

Central Housing Advisory Cttee. Sub-Cttee. Rep., apps. pp. 52. 1945

1946 Non-Parl. Min. of Health apptd. Jan., sgd. Aug., 1945

L. Silkin (Ch.), Bellman, Brooke, Burt, Calverley, Coppock, De Soissons, Groser, Keay, Key, Townroe, Watson, Wilson (Mrs. B.).

'To advise on the possible scope for, and difficulties in the way of, the conversion and adaptation of existing houses on the assumption that requisitioning powers will shortly come to an end.'

From the results of a sample survey to discover the numbers of houses (a) empty, but in sound condition; (b) empty, but damaged or dilapidated; (c) not fully occupied; (d) occupied by three or more families but not properly sub-divided, it was estimated that conversions and adaptations might make available 970,000 rooms in categories (a) to (c) and 75,000 in category (d). In view of the shortage of accommodation, it was essential to use conversion of some properties as a long-term policy and adaptation of others for a limited period. Although expensive in terms of money, conversions use less material than new houses and where the cost does not exceed £500, less skilled labour. Where the local authority does the work it should contribute a fixed sum, leaving the Exchequer to bear the rest. Private owners should receive cheap loans or a subsidy based on a percentage of costs, subject to the observance of prescribed standards, reasonable rents, etc. When a private owner is unwilling and the house would remain unoccupied, the local authority should have powers to intervene by compulsory acquisition, etc.

Selling Price of Houses

Inter-Dept. Cttee. Rep., app. pp. 31.
1945
1945–46 Cmd. 6670, xii, 485
apptd. March, pres., Aug., 1945

J. W. Morris (Ch.), Allison, Butcher, Lewis, Raymond, Silkin.

'To consider, and report, whether it is practicable to control effectively the selling price of houses with or without vacant possession and to prevent undue financial advantage being taken of the present housing shortage. . . .'

The housing shortage was due to the large increase in the number of separate families, the virtual cessation of building during the war and to enemy action, which destroyed 200,000 houses and made 250,000 uninhabitable. The average increase of price above the figure at which the same houses were previously sold pre-war varied from 60 per cent in London to 127 per cent in Wales; those sold without vacant possession rose by 30 per cent. Price control would not increase the number of houses, but would remove the feeling that in competition the bidder with the longest purse would obtain a house against one whose needs were more pressing. Fixing the maximum price by applying a multiplier to rateable or Schedule A value, or at value without vacant possession, or at 1939 value plus a percentage for increased cost of building, and taxation of excess prices were all rejected.

Recommended that the maximum permitted sale price should be the value of the house with vacant possession, as certified by the District Valuer on 31st March, 1939, plus a percentage to be prescribed. This percentage should yield a figure which would not unduly limit sales and should have regard to the probable level of building costs when control ends.

Modernising our Homes

Scottish Housing Advisory Cttee. Sub-Cttee. Rep., apps., index. pp. 59, xxix.
1947
1947 Non-Parl. Dept. of Health, Scot. apptd. March, 1944. sgd. April, 1946

A. McTaggart (Ch.), Adam, Burgess, Gardner, Jobson (Miss B.), Macgregor, Millar (Mrs. E. M.), Preston, Weekes, Dallas, Gilzean, Lappin (Mrs. I.), MacNiven, Menzies, Purdie, Scott, Smith.

'To consider what standards of habitability and convenience can be laid down for the modernisation of existing houses, and what measures might be adopted to facilitate such modernisation.'

By modernisation was meant not only making a house fit for human habitation as understood by the Housing (Scotland) Acts, but doing so in such a way as to provide the sanitary and kitchen, heating and lighting equipment and labour-saving devices of a modern house. Nearly one-third of the houses in Scotland, although not classed as unfit, are seriously deficient in sanitary facilities and modern conveniences. The most frequent defect is the sharing of W.C.'s, and large numbers are without baths or separate kitchens. Many are of sound stone construction, and are sited in areas where accommodation will be required for many years to come.

Jobbing building labour will be available without diversion from the new building programme. Though not economic for landlords, modernisation may be an advantage to the State by postponing replacement of old houses and maintaining the use of old streets, etc. Where the life of the property is not less than 20 years there should be full modernisation, where not less than five years, improvement aided by grants or loans to owners, local authorities and housing associations. In reservations some members oppose financing the repair, etc., of private property, some say that the permitted rise of rent would be inadequate, and others point to the dangers that modernisation may hamper redevelopment, etc.

Standards of Fitness for Habitation

Central Housing Advisory Cttee. Sub-
    Cttee. Rep. pp. 10. 1946

1947 *Non-Parl. Min. of Health*
apptd. Jan., 1945. *sgd. Oct.*, 1946

M. E. Mitchell (*Ch.*), Allerton, Burt, Calverley, Campbell, Dilnot, Hobhouse, Lee (Miss J.), Lloyd George (Miss M.), Molson, Monks, Reading (Lady), Smith, Wilson.

'*To consider whether further guidance as to standards of fitness for habitation can be given within the terms of the existing Housing Acts; and if so what form the guidance should take.*'

While the first objective of post-war housing policy must be to build new houses rather than raise the standards of existing ones, further guidance on standards should now be given, even though improvement may not be fully attainable for some time. The Housing Act, 1936, gives local authorities guidance on standards for determining whether a house is fit for human habitation, but it does not prescribe one. The Minister of Health in the *Manual of Unfit Houses*, 1919, suggested a standard for a fit house, but this was never made enforceable at law.

The Act should be amended to include the 1919 definition that a house shall be regarded as unfit for human habitation unless it is free from serious dampness, is satisfactorily lighted and ventilated, properly drained and has adequate sanitary conveniences, etc., is in good repair, has a satisfactory water

supply, has adequate washing accommodation, adequate facilities for preparing and cooking food and has a well ventilated food store. This revised standard should take effect as from a day to be appointed by the Minister.

Building Studies

For reports and memos. on questions affecting costs, etc., of house-building, see *Trade and Industry*. p. 132.

Cost of House-building

Cttee. 1st Rep., apps. pp. vi, 65. 1948.
2nd Rep., apps. pp. iv, 35. 1950.
3rd Rep., apps. pp. vi, 25. 1952

1948, 1950, 1952 *Non-Parl. Min. of Health, Min. of Housing and Local Gov. apptd. June*, 1947. *sgd. June*, 1948, *Feb.*, 1950, *May*, 1952

J. G. Girdwood (*Ch.*), and four other members.

'*To consider and keep under review the costs of House-building and to make recommendations.*'

The typical local authority 3-bedroom house in 1938–39 cost £380 and the size was 800 sq. ft. In 1947 the cost was £1242 and the size was 934 sq. ft. plus an outbuilding of some 95 sq. ft. An analysis of the increased costs showed that extra size accounted for £201; the various improvements in construction, finish and equipment £127; cost of labour £297 (£96 wages and other emoluments, £75 improvement in housing standards, and £126 to the decline in productivity since 1939); increased price of materials £284; extra materials £188; extra overheads and profit £77. That is, a 1947 house cost three-and-a-quarter times as much as a pre-war counterpart, required twice as much labour, and one-third more material to build. There had been no official check on the upward trend in sizes, and it was thought to have been accelerated by the Ministry of Health's practice in examining tender prices by reference to the price per sq. foot rather than to total price. The increase of size and the elaborate equipment provided had created additional demands for scarce materials and labour. The main contributory causes of the loss of productivity were: shortages of materials and labour, quality of labour, and war-time systems of 'cost-plus' contracting and payment by results, lack of individual effort, and bad weather in 1947.

Open competitive tendering was generally most satisfactory. No saving was obtained by building with direct labour, and there was no evidence that private enterprise was able to build more economically than local authorities or their contractors. Hourly rates of wages were not considered excessive and there was no evidence of excessive profits having been made on contracts.

By the end of March 1948 the total amount of subsidy was £7½ mn. for a period of 60 years. If houses continue to be completed at the 1948 rate, the cost of subsidies will increase cumulatively by about £3·3 mn. per annum for so long as subsidies remain at the 1947 level. Recommended that policy regarding the standards of accommodation and equipment of new houses should be reviewed in the light of present conditions, and the need for a larger proportion of 2-bedroom houses studied.

The Second and Third reports review the changes in costs, etc.

See *Distribution of Building Materials and Components.* p. 133. *Quicker Completion of House Interiors.* Cttee. Rep.; 1953 Non-Parl. Min. of Housing and Local Gov.

Scottish Building Costs

Cttee. Rep., apps. pp. iv, 66. 1948

1948 *Non-Parl. Dept. of Health, Scot. apptd. June,* 1947. *sgd. July,* 1948

G. P. Laidlaw (*Ch.*), Adam, Hutson, McInnes, McKellar, Maxwell, Paterson.

'*To consider and keep under review the cost of house building in Scotland, and to make recommendations.*'

The finished cost of a 4-apartment local authority house, which was £480 in 1939, had risen in 1947 by two and two-thirds to £1280. Cost of materials rose from £264 to £614, of labour from £173 to £449 and of management from £43 to £124. An additional £93 represented the cost of the increased size of house and improvements in construction and equipment. The rise in labour costs were accounted for by an additional cost of £40 for overtime, travelling, subsistence allowances and guaranteed time, 52½ per cent increase in wages, and 50 per cent additional man-hours. The housing programme has run ahead of available resources of labour and materials.

The average output per man has fallen by one-third, so that the time spent in building a house has increased by one-half; it therefore takes three men to do what before the war was two men's work. Some of the causes for the reduction in output were inadequate and irregular supply of materials, shortage of labour, delays and the fear of unemployment, which have a psychological effect on workmen by slowing the tempo of the work.

The payment by results targets initiated by the Ministry of Works in 1941, which gave a quasi-official sanction to such standards as the laying of 320 bricks a day, etc., has created the generally recognised impression amongst operatives of what constitutes a reasonable day's work. Whilst a well-conceived scheme of incentives can provide a stimulus towards increased output, it does not go to the root of the matter, each separate factor contributing to the decline must be dealt with, including a greater use of suitable mechanised methods. Management costs have increased proportionately more than labour and materials, but there was no evidence of 'rings' affecting tender prices, no excessive profit and no lowering of managerial efficiency. The most serious defect of management appeared to be inadequate co-ordination between the separate trades. Departmental control provided a useful check on tender prices but it could not control the general rise in building costs.

Productivity in House-building

Rep., apps. pp. iv, 28. 1950

1951 Non-Parl. Min. of Works

During 1949 the Ministry of Works, with the active collaboration of the sections of the building industry concerned, carried out an investigation of changes in productivity occurring on 160 contracts covering 3000 local authority houses in six areas in the South, East and West of England and in South Wales between August 1947 and October 1948. The findings were based mainly on direct observation, and the method used was new to studies of productivity in the building industry. The three main factors affecting productivity revealed by the survey were incentive payments, which reduced man-hours by 60 and total cost by £5 net for every £5 paid in bonus, the general rise in productivity resulting from an easing of post-war difficulties and the number of houses in the contract. The reduction of total costs per house was £12 10s. od. with every additional ten houses on the site.

—— Second Report, apps. pp. iv, 37. 1953

1953 Non-Parl. D.S.I.R.

In this survey, covering 177 housing contracts, attention was given not only to the total man-hours expended per house, but also to the man-hours expended in each trade by both main contractor and sub-contractor. It was thus possible to determine the factors affecting productivity in the separate trades and to compare productivity where work was done by the main contractor's labour with that where the work was done by a sub-contractor.

Although there were some contracts of high productivity, the average level was low when compared with estimates of pre-war performance published in the Girdwood Report (p. 354). There were great variations in the labour required on different contracts for the same work. Productivity was high compared with the average on contracts directly supervised by the main contractor, where there were incentive schemes, and where the contractor was experienced in house building and the organisation of work on the site was adequate.

Design and Workmanship of Non-traditional Houses

Scottish Housing Advisory Cttee. Sub-Cttee. Rep., apps. pp. 35. 1951

1951 Non-Parl. Dept. of Health, Scot. apptd. May, 1950. sgd. Jan., 1951

T. Paterson (*Ch.*), Baird, Brownlie, Daly, Lawrence, Lindsay, Maxton (Miss A.), Walker.

'*To examine, in the light of the experience gained by housing authorities and the Scottish Special Housing Association, the present arrangements for securing a satisfactory standard of design and workmanship in non-traditional houses, and to make recommendations.*'

The origin of the remit was the 'shortcomings which had been met in several types of non-traditional house which had been designed and built since the war'. Whilst no defect appeared serious enough to render any house permanently unfit for habitation, they were serious enough to create a prospect of heavy maintenance expenditure to keep them in good condition: e.g. the unsatisfactory laying and jointing of large pre-cast concrete walling-slabs, which led to damp penetration. Many of the defects reported occur in the traditional as well as the non-traditional houses. The desire for speedy erection was in some measure responsible for defects not being detected earlier. A system of safeguards was recommended to produce more satisfactory results. The distinction between non-traditional and traditional housing should be replaced by a distinction between standard and locally-designed houses, either of which may yield types with unorthodox features. Both types of houses should be subject to the same safeguards.

Care and Maintenance of Fittings and Equipment in the Modern House

Central Housing Advisory Cttee. Sub-Cttee. Rep., apps. pp. 57. 1950

1950 Non-Parl. Min. of Health
apptd. May, 1948. sgd. April, 1950

R. Coppock (*Ch.*), Calverley, Keay, Mackintosh, Marr-Johnson, Murray (Miss E.), Swift.

'To consider what advice could be given to local authorities on the care and maintenance of new types of internal fittings and equipment.'

The more lavish scale of equipment in modern houses represents one of the chief differences between them and their pre-1939 counterparts, and more maintenance is required as more equipment is installed. Assuming that design and manufacture is correct, the maintenance problems arise from faulty installation, harsh and careless handling by tenants resulting in distortion, denting, scratching, erosion and corrosion. Advice is given to local authorities, to transmit to their tenants, and on charging part costs to seriously negligent tenants.

Increase in Cost of Maintaining Houses

Scottish Building Costs. Cttee. Sub-Cttee. Rep., apps. pp. 20. 1953

1953 Non-Parl. Dept. of Health, Scot.
apptd. Oct., sgd. Dec., 1952

L. W. Hutson (*Ch.*), Barr, McGregor.

'To enquire into and to report on the extent of the increase between 1939 and 1952, in the cost of maintaining houses.'

Although property owners are spending more money on repairs, they are carrying out a smaller volume. To maintain the same volume as in 1939 a privately-owned house built before 1914 would require an increase of

expenditure of 81 per cent, and take 94 per cent of income instead of 52 per cent. For inter-war council houses the increase of expenditure would be 98 per cent and would take 85 per cent, instead of 43 per cent of income. In both cases the increase is the equivalent of a 42 per cent increase of net income.

Cost of House Maintenance

Cttee. Rep., app. pp. 23. 1953

1953 Non-Parl. Min. of Housing and Local Gov.
apptd. Dec., 1952. sgd. April, 1953

J. G. Girdwood (*Ch.*), Carter, Daines, Slimmings.

'To consider and report on the relationship of the present annual cost with that ruling in 1939 of maintaining house property in good tenantable repair, having regard to the relative cost of wages, materials, overheads and rates of profit.'

Taking 1939 as 100, the cost of keeping a house in good tenantable repair and doing the same amount of maintenance work as was done in 1939, is 316. This takes no account of the increasing age of houses and the need for more repairs, any change in the incidence of expenditure to make good war-time deterioration, or changes in the frequency or extent of painting and decoration, which has declined. The index of labour costs is 318. Productivity is difficult to measure, but is definitely lower.

Living in Flats

Central Housing Advisory Cttee. Sub-Cttee. Rep., apps. pp. iv, 39. 1952

1952 Non-Parl. Min. of Housing and Local Gov.
apptd. July, 1950. sgd. Dec., 1951

H. Brooke (*Ch.*), Eddie, Gibson, Keay, Laing, Leigh-Breese, Mackintosh, Murray (Miss E.), Wilson (Mrs. B.).

'To examine the social needs and problems of families living in large blocks of flats.'

Families living in blocks of flats experience many problems not shared by families living in separate houses. The 34 recommendations are concerned chiefly with planning and design to give space round the flats, light, and a personal atmosphere which develops community life, facilities for children, privacy in access, and other amenities. Research was recommended on planning and equipping restricted playgrounds, improving and cheapening insulation against noise and the removal of certain disadvantages connected with refuse chutes. Other suggestions were that as the costs of extra amenities affect rents, misdirected expenditure should be avoided; families with several children should be accommodated in houses or maisonettes rather than flats; there has been excessive concentration of flats in some large towns, but experience has shown that the inclusion of houses and maisonettes is practicable in areas of high density.

Requisitioned Properties in Use for Housing

Working Party. Interim Rep., app. pp. 8. 1952. 2nd Interim Rep. pp. 12. 1953. 3rd and Final Rep. pp. 7. 1954 1952, 1953, 1954 *Non-Parl. Min. of Housing and Local Gov.* apptd. *April*, 1952. sgd. *Aug.*, 1952, *May, Nov.*, 1953

S. F. Wilkinson (*Ch.*), and 13 others.

'*To review the arrangements for emergency accommodation which have been continued in England and Wales since the end of the war, and to report on the measures necessary for relieving the central government from financial responsibility for the housing of families in requisitioned premises at an early date.*'

In the financial year 1951–52 the net charge to the Exchequer in respect of emergency housing was £6,900,312 in respect of 131,964 families housed in 86,136 requisitioned properties and a further 31,169 families housed in 1385 ex-service camps. The three Reports contain recommendations on ways of reducing the financial burden by releasing properties from requisition by

stages as alternative accommodation is found. The Final Report recommends the closing of all camps, in order of priority on public health and social grounds; tenancies should not be encouraged by over-easy rent conditions, rent defaulters should be evicted and persons entering without authority proceeded against for trespass.

Houses—The Next Step

apps. pp. 20. 1953
1953–54 *Cmd.* 8996, *xxvi*, 1

As the 1951 target of 300,000 new houses a year had been reached, it was possible to deal with old houses. Of the $7\frac{1}{2}$ mn. privately-owned houses, over half are more than 75 years old. 1. *Sound Houses.*—These could be kept in good repair given a reasonable rent, but many rents are insufficient to cover these costs. A general percentage increase of rents would accentuate existing anomalies and rent tribunals for this purpose would have too heavy a task. The Government propose to permit an increase of rent in respect of cost of repairs of twice the statutory deductions, subject to a maximum and on condition that the landlord has spent a specified multiple of this during a period. 2. *Slum Houses.*—The 140,000 slum houses left outstanding from the pre-war programme have now greatly increased by large numbers which have become slums since then. Local authorities will be required to submit clearance programmes, but where an authority cannot demolish and replace within about five years, as an interim measure local authorities should buy and patch up for a limited life. 3. *Dilapidated Houses.*—Where a landlord is unable or unwilling to repair houses up to standard, the local authority may do the work and charge him the cost. No rent increase will be given on account of such repairs. 4. *Improvements and Conversions.*—The provisions of the Housing Act, 1949, have not been effective, only 3000 houses having been improved with grant-aid and 700 new houses created by conversion. The limit of 30 years expected life and of £800 in cost will be abolished (though the grant will not be increased), and the rate of return raised to 8 per cent.

Private enterprise has been encouraged to build for owner-occupation and for letting by the grant of licences and the removal of the development charge. Building societies and local authorities are being consulted with a view to improving facilities for advances to those wishing to build or buy a house.

See *Housing Repairs and Rents Bill.* Financial Resolution; 1953–54 Cmd. 9038, xxvi, 149. *Housing Repairs and Rents Act, 1954;* 2 & 3 Eliz. 2 c. 53.

Housing Policy, Scotland

Pp. 10. 1953

1953–54 Cmd. 8997, xxvi, 151

A total of 204,112 new dwellings have now been built in Scotland and building is proceeding at a record rate, but so long as there are large numbers of families with no separate homes of their own the Government proposes to go on building additional houses. But they consider that the time has come when the bad condition of older houses—two-fifths of the houses are over 70 years old—should be dealt with. The proportion of gross rent of controlled houses required in 1939 for repair averaged 20 per cent; by 1953 this had risen to three-fifths, an increase of 40 per cent. Where owners put their property into good repair they should be authorised to increase the rent by this proportion; but steps will be taken to see that this amount is not decreased by a consequential increase in owner's rates. Exchequer grants are already available to private owners and local authorities for improvements and conversions and to make houses fit for habitation, etc., though their use has been disappointing. To encourage private building restrictions on building have been relaxed, the issue of licences made automatic and development charges have been abolished. The rents of houses belonging to Housing

Associations and Development Corporations should cease to be controlled.

See *Housing (Repairs and Rents) (Scotland) Bill.* Money Resolution; 1953–54 Cmd. 9032, xxvi, 257. *Housing (Repairs and Rents) (Scotland) Act, 1954;* 2 & 3 Eliz. 2. c. 50. *Scottish Valuation and Rating.* p. 51.

Houses of Outstanding Historic or Architectural Interest

Cttee. Rep., apps. pp. iii, 80.   1950

1950 Non-Parl. Treasury apptd. Dec., 1948. sgd. March, 1950

E. A. Gowers (*Ch.*), Anderson (Lady), Ansell, Blunt, Fox, Imrie, Little.

'*To consider and report what general arrangements might be made by the Government for the preservation, maintenance and use of houses of outstanding historic architectural interest which might otherwise not be preserved, including, where desirable, the preservation of a house and its contents as a unity.*'

Houses of the sort described in the terms of reference may be large or small, in the country or the town, inhabited or uninhabited, yet in practice it is mainly the big country mansion of historical, educational and cultural value that sets the problem. Some take from £6000 to £10,000 to maintain them, but no taxpayer, however much his gross income, has more than £5000 to spend, and that sum represents a gross income of £100,000.

The main recommendations were, 'that new statutory bodies should be appointed with functions partly advisory and partly administrative, in order to integrate such powers and duties as the central Government already possess to preserve historic houses, and to exercise certain new ones; that these bodies (like the Arts Council) should be appointed by and responsible to the Chancellor of the Exchequer; that they should compile, besides the statutory list required by the Town and Country Planning Acts, a list of houses of outstanding architectural or historic importance for the preservation of which they should assume a general responsibility; that taxpayers owning houses on that list should be granted certain reliefs from income tax (including surtax) and death duties; and that funds should be placed at the Councils' disposal out of which they could make grants or loans for the repair or upkeep of the houses so listed, or, in case of need, purchase them.'

See *Historic Buildings Councils. England, Scotland, Wales.* 1st Ann. Reps.; 1953–54 (169) (170) (171) xv, 1023, and succeeding Ann. Reps.

2. RENTS

Rent Control

Inter-Dept. Cttee. Rep., apps. pp. 63. 1945

1944–45 *Cmd.* 6621, *v*, 499
apptd. Nov., 1943. *sgd. Feb.,* 1945

Lord Ridley (*Ch.*), Buchanan, Davidson, Davies, Endicott, Falconer, Hudson, Hunter, Key, Kimpton, MacCalman, Mitchell, Owen, Raikes, Spencer.

'*To review the question of rent control, including the working of the Rent Restrictions Acts, and to advise whether any, and if so what, changes are necessary.*'

The Rent and Mortgage Interest Restrictions Act, 1939, brought under control all houses, whether previously controlled or not, where the rateable value did not exceed £100 in the Metropolitan District, £90 in Scotland and £75 elsewhere, thus embracing the great majority of houses in the country. Whilst after 1914 it was possible to restrict rent increases to a uniform percentage, in 1939 there were widely differing standard rents for precisely similar houses, according to the period at which the houses were let.

New legislation should be based on the expectations of control for ten years, the existing rateable value limits should remain unchanged, houses built after the war and those built by the local authority should remain uncontrolled, but those of housing associations re-main controlled. The incidence of the Acts is so uneven that no simple formula can be applied to produce fair rents. Local authorities should keep a register of the rents of all controlled houses, and rent tribunals should be established to fix fair rents, on application by tenants or landlords. There should be no general increase of rents on account of repairs, but a technical committee should report on costs when conditions have stabilised. Furnished lettings should be controlled as in Scotland. There were two reservations, by Buchanan and Key, and by MacCalman, both of which disagreed with the proposal that houses built after the war should be decontrolled.

See *Rent Control in England and Wales.* Memo.; 1946 Non-Parl. Min. of Health. *Landlord and Tenant (Rent Control) Act, 1949;* 12 & 13 Geo. 6. c. 40.

3. HOUSE MANAGEMENT, HOUSING ESTATES

Community Centres

Rep., apps. pp. 40. 1944
1944 *Non-Parl. Min. of Education*

The Government regarded centres for athletic, social and educational objects as part of the education service, and made provision for them in Section 53 of the Education Act, 1944. The report deals with the aims, functions, activities, and organisation of such centres. The recommendations include: there should be a large-scale development of centres, particularly on new housing estates, and a village hall in all villages with a population exceeding 400. Local education authorities should be responsible for meeting the cost of the building and its maintenance, and the Warden's salary.

Housing Management

Central Housing Advisory Cttee. Sub-Cttee. 2nd Rep., *Management of Municipal Housing Estates,* apps. pp. 31. 1945

1945 *Non-Parl. Min. of Health apptd. Jan., 1944. sgd. July,* 1945

Lord Balfour of Burleigh (*Ch.*), Ager, Bellman, Campbell, Dilnot, L. Dudley, Gooch (Mrs. E.), Keay, Limerick (Lady), Reading (Lady), Watson, Wilson (Mrs. B.), Wilson (J. G.).

'*To consider whether any further advice ought to be given to local authorities regarding the management of municipal housing estates in the light of special conditions likely to arise in the immediate post-war period, with particular reference to any special steps which ought to be taken in connection with the various types of temporary accommodation to be provided under the Housing (Temporary Accommodation) Act.*'

Owing to the length of the war, the destruction of houses by bombing, and the settlement of people in new areas, the public provision of houses has to be extended to cover a wider and more representative section of the population. The circumstances of the individual district affect the nature of the arrangements for the selection of tenants: for example some districts select on the basis of 'need' as assessed by a trained officer, some according to the number of children, and others partly by a weighting under a point system which takes account of factors relative to housing conditions, family circumstances, etc. The point system is reviewed, and the recommendations state that where it is used it should be a sieve for sorting applications into priority groups, and that the final order should be determined on merits after a full individual investigation of each case. But whatever the method of selection used, local authorities should make known the general principles on which selection will proceed. Owing to changed family circumstances over a period of years some houses are under-occupied, while others are over-crowded. Transfers can often be arranged or alternatively during the period of shortage the taking of lodgers or sub-letting in under-occupied houses should be encouraged. Local authori-

ties should apply the recommendations of the First Report, 1939 (*Breviate 1917–39*, p. 447), and make provision in their housing department for trainees to do practical work, under competent officers, and to pay these students when their work becomes of value to the Department.

—— Third Report, *Selection of Tenants and Transfers and Exchanges*, apps. pp. 28. 1949

1949 *Non-Parl.*

apptd. May, 1948. *sgd. Jan.,* 1949

C. W. Gibson (*Ch.*), Allerton, Campbell, Dilnot, Mitchell, Monks, Reading (Lady), Wilson (Mrs. B.), Wilson (J. G.).

'*To consider what further advice should be given to local authorities on the allocation and re-allocation of tenancies and on the facilitation of exchanges within their areas and between one area and another.*'

The evidence received shows that there is still the same variety in the qualifications required of applicants before they are admitted to a waiting list. Local authorities should revise their methods to ensure that their houses are let to applicants with the 'greatest housing need'; restrictions on admission to waiting lists should be reduced to a uniform level; applications should be accepted from any person who has lived in the district for one year or more, or is employed or to be employed there; overcrowding should be measured in terms of bedroom deficiency; length of residence, date of application and war service should only be used to discriminate between applicants having an equal claim on grounds of housing need. Point systems should give 'basic points' to factors related to housing conditions, and 'balancing points' to length of residence, date of application, war service, etc. Balancing points should be used to distinguish between applicants who have the highest number of basic points. Local authorities should give preference to agricultural workers, miners, midwives, nurses, etc. During the period of shortage permission should be given to take lodgers and sub-let. App. III gives a sample points scheme.

—— Fourth Report, *Transfers, Exchanges and Rents*, apps., index. pp. iv, 40. 1953

1953 *Non-Parl. Min. of Housing and Local Gov.*

apptd. Oct., 1952. sgd. Aug., 1953

H. Brooke (*Ch.*), Atkinson, Bellman, Gibbs (Mrs. B. F.), Leigh-Breese, Lloyd George (Lady), Marr-Johnson, McIntire, Miskin (Miss D. E.), Stamp.

'To examine local authorities' existing practice and experience with regard to (a) *the exchange of tenancies and* (b) *the fixing and review of rents and the granting of rent rebates in respect of their houses and flats; to consider in the light of the results of that examination what more could be done towards securing the best use of existing housing accommodation whether in local authority ownership or otherwise. . . .'*

Transferring or authorising exchanges between tenants secures for each household a house better suited to them in size, location and rent, and local authorities can be more certain what sizes of new houses are really needed. Most housing authorities keep a list of their tenants who want to transfer into houses which are larger or smaller or nearer work or with less rent, etc. Under powers of supervision and management the local authority can contribute to the cost of removal, or where a tenant persists in staying in a house too large for his needs and refuses alternative accommodation, he can be charged an unsubsidised rent. Exchanges, where there are no vacancies, under the same or different authorities, are more difficult to bring about, but are more successful when the tenants take the initiative. Some authorities keep lists which can be consulted—the L.C.C. runs a mutual Exchange Bureau—and much has been done, but there are still councils which refuse to permit exchanges.

On rent and maintenance costs there is much variation in policies and opinions. In the north of England and in Wales the tenant is responsible for internal decorations; in the south-east it is done by the authority, elsewhere responsibility is divided. The statutory minimum of £8 a year for maintenance adds 3s. 0d. a week to the rent. The L.C.C. fixes it at £18, whilst the fund of some metropolitan boroughs goes up to £30 which is equal to 11s. 6d. on the rent. It is possible that some tenants would accept the responsibility for some internal decoration for themselves rather than pay the extra rent. Fluctuations in building costs have resulted in widely different rents which do not reflect the three differences of size, location and amenities of the house or flat, but by relating rent to accommodation the subsidies would be available for the houses which cost the most to build.

The basic purpose of the subsidies is to enable local authorities to let their houses at rents within the means of those for whom they were provided. In 1946 this was approximately 8s. 6d. per house per week; in 1952 it was 13s. 8d., and for flats on high-cost land it can amount to £2. The advice of 20 years ago to local authorities to give rent relief to 'those who need it and only so long as they need it' and 'that subsidies . . . do not benefit persons who do not require them' has not been withdrawn, and in 1949 was added the power to consider 'the housing conditions and housing needs of all members of the community'. Housing authorities now find they have applicants on their lists with incomes which enable them to pay decidedly higher than the fully subsidised rent of a council dwelling; even the rebate schemes fixed at a time of slum clearance and unemployment have lost their former importance in these days of full employment. In this dilemma a variety of methods are being used. Some authorities have graded their estates into rent categories, some pool low rent accommodation for applicants unable to pay the high rent for a post-wa house. The alternative is to adapt rent according to the tenant's capacity to pay, which can take the form of 'an additional earner' or lodger charge; a rent surcharge when the tenant's income exceeds a certain figure; a differential rent scheme, where the actual rent paid may vary above or below the former basic rent of the dwelling, according to the tenant's income. The recommendations are concerned with an active policy in arranging transfers and exchanges: all owners, public and private, should keep themselves continuously informed as to the numerical occupation of their property. The division of responsibility between council and tenants for internal decorations should be decided. Rents should be related to size, location and amenity. The 'additional earner charge' can be operated with little extra work. Differential rents require those who 'can well afford it to pay more; this has nothing in common with the purpose of the old and much criticised means tests', which inquired into personal expenditure and children's earnings. Local authorities should discuss their differential rent schemes with the local officers of the National Assistance Board.

Housing Management in Scotland

Scottish Housing Advisory Cttee. Sub-Cttee. Rep., apps., index. pp. iv, 43. 1946

1945–46 Cmd. 6901, xii, 595
apptd. Dec., 1945. sgd. July, 1946

T. Paterson (Ch.), Gordon, Gratton (Mrs. N. F.), Imrie, Lang (Mrs. J. R.), Maclean, Maxton (Miss A. D.), Mitchell, Moffat, Maxwell (Miss J.), Mill (Mrs. N.), Walker.

'To consider and advise on the general question of the management of dwelling-houses provided by local authorities, with special reference to the employment of trained managers.'

The new function of owning and managing houses is probably the largest and most important one which local authorities have received in the twentieth century. From 1919 to 1929 houses were built mostly for those who could afford to pay the rents, which resulted in the management of property presenting few difficulties, but this altered after 1930 when subsidies were restricted to slum clearance, and local authorities had to educate the worst tenants to live in the new houses. The position changed again in 1944, when the needs of Service and ex-Service men, and of families who had lost their homes as a result of war damage and families with no homes of their own, had to be provided for—families representing a great variety of income groups. Management is therefore of a comprehensive nature and includes such functions as letting, rent collection, maintenance, and general administration, welfare and social education having received insufficient attention.

The functional system of management whereby responsibility is distributed amongst the various departments is the one generally used in Scotland, and not the centralised system (Octavia Hill) where one person is responsible for 300–350 tenancies. But there is a shortage of trained staff for both systems.

Local authorities should review their management arrangements; pay more regard to welfare and social education; consider the centralised system on an experimental basis; give preference to trained managers; grant facilities to students in training. Previsitation of prospective tenants should be universally adopted; tenants with unsocial conduct should be under supervision and the co-operation of tenants should be sought to bring gardens back to the pre-war condition, etc. The Board of Trade should be asked to consider making 'Utility' furniture available to local authorities for supply to tenants unable to purchase direct.

Choosing Council Tenants

Scottish Housing Advisory Cttee. Sub-Cttee. Rep., apps. index. pp. 52. 1950

1950 Non-Parl. Dept. of Health, Scot. apptd. Jan., sgd Dec., 1949

A. Maclean (*Ch.*), Daly, Gratton (Mrs. N. F.), Laidlaw, Lawrence, McGowan (Mrs. M.), Maltman, Maxton (Miss A. D.), Ritchie, Pollock (Miss J. B.), Morton, Munro.

'*To survey local authorities' existing methods of allocating tenancies and to make recommendations.*'

In the first decades of this century lack of dwellings, food and fuel was confined to the lowest income groups and they alone had a claim on the assistance of the State. As standards and prices rose, more and more income groups were affected, but though the restriction to 'working classes' disappeared, the 1932 Committee (*Breviate, 1917–39,* p. 442) recommended that State-aided houses should be occupied only by those whose financial circumstances justified it. Scarcity and the control of distribution since the war have increased the numbers of people who rely on the State to meet their needs, and the relationship between means and the extent of this dependence is far less direct. Since the Housing (Scotland) Act, 1949, a local authority may allot one of their houses to any member of the community, whatever his vocation and means, without exceeding their powers and without affecting their claim to Exchequer subsidy. Whilst laying on the local authority the obligation of providing houses for large families occupying insanitary and overcrowded houses or who are otherwise living under unsatisfactory housing conditions, the Act also makes provisions 'to enable account to be taken of the housing conditions and housing needs of all members of the community'. The Committee took the view that it is the duty of a local authority in allocating houses to place the interests of the community before the compassionate claims of the individual family, e.g. a schoolteacher should be allocated a house to enable him to take a post.

Investigations showed that the 'allocation schemes' could be divided into five main categories; date of application, merit, points, group and dual schemes. Date of application and dual schemes were regarded as taking little account of the communities' interest and merit schemes are bound to be influenced by local sentiment and personalities. Group schemes which divide eligible applicants into groups and allot a percentage of vacant houses to each group and point schemes which assign comparative values to different considerations are the most efficient means of allotting houses to meet the varying needs of the community. The recommendations are concerned with making efficient the group-plus-point, and the points schemes. For example, in the former the waiting list should be divided into the four groups: health, homeless, badly housed and emergency, and a percentage of vacancies allotted to each group after an analysis of their waiting list. Employment grounds, length of residence, and war service, etc., should come under consideration. Periodic reports should be published to show how the houses have been allocated.

Appearance of Housing Estates

Central Housing Advisory Cttee. Sub-Cttee. Rep., apps. pp. 27. 1948.
    Supplement, *Our Gardens.* 1948

1948 Non-Parl. Min. of Health apptd. Oct., 1946. sgd Oct., 1947

Lord Faringdon (*Ch.*), Campbell, De Soissons, Groser, Jenkinson, Murray (Miss E.), Reading (Lady), Wilson (Mrs. B.).

'*To consider means of improving the appearance of local authority housing estates, particularly by enlisting the help of tenants, and to make proposals.*'

Many estates are well laid out and attractive and show great improvement over earlier ones. But in other individuality has been lost by monotony of design and lay-out and neglect of underlying landscape features, and many back gardens are desolate. Some tenants take little pride in their houses or the neighbourhood, but some of the fundamental defects are due to economies forced on local authorities, and in part to their errors of judgment. There are recommendations on planting of forest and roadside trees. Local authorities should make available advice on garden lay-out, cheap plants and trees from municipal nurseries, and should encourage communal activity in these matters; should take over neglected gardens and charge the tenants the cost, and when materials are available should provide garden sheds, etc. The cost of the amenities should be excluded from the bare cost of new houses for approval purposes, and should be allowed as additional expenditure.

Estate Development and Management in War-damaged Areas

Central Advisory Cttee. Rep., app. pp. 48. 1947

1947 Non-Parl. Min. of T. and C. Planning

apptd. June, 1945. sgd. Feb., 1946

L. Neal (Ch.), Wells, Bigwood, Gillett, Goodbody, Lawrance, Marr-Johnson, Robinson, Saunders.

'To advise the Minister on any question relating to estate management and estate development of land acquired or appropriated for the purposes of the Town and Country Planning Acts, 1932, and 1944, which may be referred by the Minister to the Advisory Committee.'

1. The general problem of war-damaged areas.—The re-development plan of the central areas should define the size and boundaries of the central area, and there should be a well-balanced distribution of intensity of use and thus of values throughout each use zone. Bus routes, etc., should be distributed in relation to shopping areas. Shops should have continuous frontages, with secondary access at the rear. Cinemas, etc., attracting queues should not be in the centres of main shopping streets. War damage has destroyed the pre-war pattern of land use and values in the central areas; temporary development should therefore fit in with the long-term distribution of use and values which the plan aims at. 2. Temporary shopping accommodation should be provided for in 'very short life' temporary buildings and ground floors of multi-storeyed buildings. 3. A well-administered leasehold system has substantial merits, as it divides the function between the landlord who lays out and develops the estate and the lessees who build. In the past the landlord was able to secure development with a high standard of lay-out, architectural design, etc., but the break-up of urban estates has led to deterioration. Legislation has enabled local authorities to re-introduce a system of guidance. Leases should be governed by the length of the useful life of the proposed developments as a whole, and for commercial and industrial buildings should be for 75 years or less, instead of 99. In view of the uncertainty of the rental value of land at the time when disposals are made, ground rents should be reviewed between the 10th and 20th year from the first grant of the lease. Existing buildings in conflict with the re-development plan should be given a short life and let at rack rents. No old building should have a lease longer than for a new building. Land should be disposed of by means of building agreements, followed by ground leases when the buildings have been erected.

XIII B. TOWN AND COUNTRY PLANNING

Town and Country Planning

In the eight years 1943–1951 five major Acts were passed: Town and Country Planning (Interim Development) Act, 1943, which extended planning control to all land and made it effective in the 'interim development' period before schemes became operative; the Town and Country Planning Act, 1944, which enabled local authorities to tackle their war damage; the New Towns Act, 1946, which provided for the creation of New Towns by means of Development Corporations; the Town and Country Planning Act, 1947, which established a new and comprehensive planning system; and the National Parks and Access to the Countryside Act, 1949.

In addition to the reports dealt with below, the papers include the following. (1) *Town and Country Planning, 1943–51; 1950–51* Cmd. 8204, xx, 133, which reviews some planning problems of national importance, e.g. competition for the use of land, mineral working, new towns, amenities, national parks, etc., and gives in Apps. a list of publications up to 1951. (2) Memos. on Acts, Bills, etc., e.g. those on Town and Country Planning Act, 1944, Town and Country Planning (Scotland) Act, 1945, Town and Country Planning (General Interim Development) Order, 1945, (Non-Parl.). (3) Publications, Non-Parl., giving guidance on principles and practice on certain problems, e.g. *Design and Lay-out of Roads in Built-up Areas;* 1946. *Re-development of Central Areas;* 1948. *Control of Mineral Working;* 1951. *Siting of Houses in Country Districts;* 1950. *Design in Town and Village;* 1953. (4) Regulations made under the Acts. See annual *Consolidated List of Government Publications.*

The Distribution of the Industrial Population
Rep.

1939–40 *Cmd.* 6153. See *Trade and Industry.* p. 121.

Compensation and Betterment

Expert Cttee.   Interim Rep. pp. 18.
1941

1940–41 *Cmd.* 6291, *iv,* 205
apptd. —. sgd. April, 1941

A. A. Uthwatt (*Ch.*), Barr, Eve, Evershed.

'*To make an objective analysis of the subject of the payment of compensation and recovery of betterment in respect of public control of the use of land: To advise, as a matter of urgency, what steps should be taken now or before the end of the war to prevent the work of reconstruction thereafter being prejudiced . . . to consider* (a) *possible means of stabilising the value of land required for development or re-development, and* (b) *any extension or modification of powers to enable such land to be acquired by the public on an equitable basis; to examine the merits and demerits of the methods considered. . . .*'

In accordance with a Ministerial statement the Committee proceeded on the assumptions that the principle of planning would be accepted as national policy and that a central planning authority would be established to proceed on a positive policy. To prevent any inflation of property values which would increase the cost of reconstruction to the public purse, the Government should announce immediately as a general principle that compensation ultimately payable in respect of any public acquisition or control of land will not exceed values at 31st March, 1939. This basis should continue for such period as will enable long-period planning policy to be determined. The Central Planning Authority should have power forthwith to control building and development throughout the country with a view to preventing work being undertaken prejudicial to a satisfactory reconstruction plan. Areas which ought to be considered for development as a whole, e.g. areas of extensive damage, should be defined as soon as practicable by a competent authority and no reconstruction or development in them permitted without licences, until detailed reconstruction plans are finally determined.

—— Final Report, apps. pp. vi, 180.
1942
1941–42 *Cmd.* 6386, *iv*, 15
sgd. Aug., 1942

The planning of rural, undeveloped land and of urban, built-up land falls into two distinct problems. In the former it is necessary to prevent a repetition of past errors, in the latter the removal of unsatisfactory buildings and adequate control of re-development is required. In the case of undeveloped land, the difficulties of compensation which have hindered planning arise from floating value and shifting value. The potential value of a piece of fringe land outside a town depends on the probability of its being built on, but it is impossible to predict with certainty on which piece of land and when this floating value might settle as sites are required. When development of a particular piece is prohibited, its owner is compensated for the loss of probability that floating value will settle upon it. If, when land belongs to a number of different owners, this process of valuation is repeated, the aggregate loss and so the compensation when individual pieces are separately assessed, greatly exceeds the loss of all of them when taken together, for the 'float', limited to actual demands, can settle only on a portion of the area. In addition, if by prohibition of development land is taken out of the building market, potential value is not destroyed, but merely shifted on to other land. Compensation then has to be paid in excess to the real loss and for land values that have not been destroyed, but merely shifted. In theory, compensation to owners who lose could be paid out of betterment levies on owners who have gained, and if land were in one ownership, the two would balance and no adjustment would be required. But betterment cannot be collected in any substantial degree, because it is impossible to say with certainty whether a given piece of land value is due to a given cause.

In the case of developed, built-on land, if cities are to be re-built, there must be restrictions on rights, and these do not decrease the total demand for land, but merely divert it to the perimeter or other areas. But the compensation payable has to be determined by reference to the most profitable use of the land, and land values in the centre are very high.

The solution of the problem must lie in such measure of unification of existing rights in land as will enable the shift in values to operate within the same ownership, thus removing the conflict between public and private interest. Unification by private pooling schemes is rejected, because it would have to be nation-wide, and become indistinguishable from nationalisation. The rights of development in all land outside built-up areas should be vested in the State immediately, on payment of compensation, by a prohibition of development without consent. The compensation to owners should be on the basis of a fixed sum representing a fair value to owners of the development rights taken as a whole, divided amongst them in proportion to the development value of their various holdings. The State should purchase the land itself if and when required for approved public or private development; if for private development, the land should not be re-sold, but leased to the developer.

For developed built-up areas, the authorities should have wide and simplified powers of purchasing areas as a whole at prices not exceeding values of the land at 31st March, 1939. This will involve compensation. If planning is to be effective, no legal right to preferential treatment should be conferred on dispossessed owners, though in administration due regard should be paid to their claims. Local authorities should be empowered to buy, compulsorily, for the purpose of recoupment, land adjoining public improvements. But increased values may still accrue in part to land which for the time being remains in full private ownership. The system of the Town and Country Planning Act, 1932, of recovery of betterment by direct charge has failed and should be abandoned in favour of a periodic levy of 75 per cent of the increase of annual site value.

The Report gives many detailed recommendations on the legal and administrative questions which would arise from the implementation of these principles. There is a Note of reservations by Barr.

See *Town and Country Planning Act, 1947;* 10 & 11 Geo. 6. c. 51. *Town and Country Planning (Scotland) Act, 1947;* 10 & 11 Geo. 6. c. 53, and the amending Acts: *Town and Country Planning Act, 1953;* 1 & 2 Eliz. 2. c. 16. *Town and Country Planning Act, 1954;* 2 & 3 Eliz. 2. c. 72. *Town and Country Planning (Scotland) Act, 1954;* 2 & 3 Eliz. 2. c. 73.

Land Utilisation in Rural Areas

Cttee. Rep., app., index. pp. vi, 138. 1942

1941–42 *Cmd.* 6378, *iv,* 421
apptd. Oct., 1941. *sgd. July,* 1942

L. Scott (*Ch.*), Stamp, Cobb, Cooper, Deman (Lady G.), Hichens (Mrs. H.), Monks, L. Radnor, Roberts, Robinson, Ward, Dennison.

'*To consider the conditions which should govern building and other constructional development in country areas consistently with the maintenance of agriculture, and in particular the factors affecting the location of industry, having regard to economic operation, part-time and seasonal employment, the well-being of rural communities and the preservation of rural amenities.*'

As a result of the diversity of types and quality of land, there are 17 different types of British farming, five based on permanent pasture, six on arable land used for crops and garden produce, the rest being types of mixed farming. Besides geographical and climatic factors, land ownership, traditional methods, industrialisation and the growth of urban populations and other economic forces have played an important part in determining the use of agricultural land. The report reviews the history of agriculture, agricultural wages, the lack of amenities in rural areas and the loss of agricultural population. In 1927–31 the area of agricultural land lost to urban and various constructional uses was 794,400 acres, with an average annual net loss of 60,000 acres. This was due to motor transport, which made the country accessible, to the housing programme, and to growth of light industries, sports grounds and aerodromes. Uncontrolled development did great harm, cheap land was bought up regardless of its nature and economically balanced farming units were broken up. The results of attempts to control development of rural land through the Town and Country Planning Act, 1932, and the Restriction of Ribbon Development Act, 1935, were disappointing because of the difficulties caused by possible claims against the planning authorities for compensation. Although during the war there was an extension of agriculture and a rise of agricultural wages, land was still being lost to Service Departments, aerodromes, etc.

After the war, the countryside may be in a stronger position to resist the invasion of the town, but it will still not be strong enough to hold its own unless suitable conditions are created and suitable machinery and powers provided to enable it to fight its battle on terms of greater equality. One of the basic assumptions the Committee had to make was the maintenance of prosperous agriculture after the war. The well-being of rural communities and the preservation of rural amenities were dependent on this, and no conditions imposed on constructional development in the countryside would be effective unless agriculture itself were in a healthy condition. And this meant 'the continuance and revival of the traditional mixed character of British farming'. The matters dealt with in the many recommendations included rural housing programmes, the provision of gas, water and electricity, and of social amenities such as institutes, playing fields, etc., and restoration of sites by extractive industries. Linked industries should be confined to trading estates; mobile industries when brought into rural areas should be linked with small towns rather than villages; industries should be encouraged to go first to vacant or derelict town sites, though carefully regulated industry in towns in country areas would be beneficial.

There should be a central planning authority to formulate general principles, including those necessary to secure the best use of agricultural land, and to guide and approve the plans of local authorities, which should be freed from the restrictions on zoning agricultural land arising from liability for compensation. Instead of fixed national zoning, there should be a national delimitation of land areas, e.g. National Forest Zones, National Parks. Land included in the main categories of good land and indifferent land an essential part of a well-balanced farming unit, should not be alienated from its existing use unless this could be definitely shown to be in the national interest. Land nationalisation was not necessary if control is adequate, but the State should exercise its powers of compulsory acquisition of any agricultural land when required by planning or for the permanent efficiency of agriculture. There should be a five-year plan for carrying out the recommendations, based on a five-year plan for agriculture.

Minority Report. S. R. Dennison.— The Majority regard it as essential, if the amenities of the countryside are to be preserved, that agriculture must be maintained at its existing size and land farmed in the traditional way, i.e. that acreage and employment should be maintained. But the ultimate prosperity of agriculture depends on efficiency: more mechanisation, a decrease of tillage and an increase of pasture, and more specialisation might maintain acreage, but decrease employment. Our ability to maintain standards by importing cheap food in return for exports is more than ever important as our overseas investments have been depleted. The wage of the agricultural worker could not be raised to the level of that of the industrial worker by a large or prosperous agriculture without costly subsidies at the expense of the rest of the community. The rural community ought not to be protected from the impact of higher standards. His recommendations include: (1) All land in the countryside should be included in planning schemes, and no interests of national importance should be excluded from the aims of planning. (2) While particular planning schemes will certainly involve preservation of much land in agricultural use, it should not be accepted as a *necessary principle* that construction in the countryside must be prevented in order to maintain agriculture, to preserve rural communities, or to preserve amenities. (3) The introduction of industry into the countryside, under effective planning control, could be of considerable benefit to rural communities; rather than preventing such development, some measure of it should be encouraged as part of the dispersal of existing concentrations. (4) The needs of agriculture (including the protection of good quality land) should be met through the normal machinery of planning schemes, and not given any prior rights.

See *Utilisation of Land in Rural Areas, Scotland;* 1942–43 Cmd. 6440, v, 31. This Report states that the recommendations of the Scott Committee are being referred to the appropriate Scottish committees, departments, etc.

The Control of Land Use

Statement. pp. 15. 1944
1943–44 *Cmd. 6537, viii, 273*

While the Government accepts the analysis of the Uthwatt Report, there would be practical difficulties in carrying out its particular proposals, especially those relating to compensation and betterment. The Committee proposed substantially different treatment for undeveloped land outside and undeveloped land inside town areas, and for developed land, and that all development rights in undeveloped land outside town areas should be vested in the State. The Government propose a universal restriction on development rights on all land so that, although they remain vested in the owner, they cannot be exercised without consent. The Committee proposed that where consent had been given, the State should purchase the land and lease it to the applicant. The Government proposes that control should be by licensing and that this should rest with the local authorities.

The Committee proposed a betterment levy of 75 per cent on increases in the annual site values of developed land. This would be complicated to administer, especially as the levy was proposed even on increases of value which have not been received by the owner in cash and in certain cases when he may have paid for it. Increases of value arise mainly from changes of use. If by planning control, e.g. a green belt is established, development will be diverted to land beyond it, and the State should collect such shifted value. It is proposed to collect a betterment charge of 80 per cent at the time when permission to develop is granted, the remaining 20 per cent being left to owners as an incentive.

The Uthwatt Committee proposed that a global sum should be fixed for compensation. The Government are not prepared to recommend this, since it is doubtful whether any reasonably accurate estimate can yet be made of floating value. Instead, owners of land who are refused consent to develop will be paid in respect of the loss of development value existing on 31st March, 1939, but not for further development value accruing after that date. This will avoid any excess over true development value due to an element of floating value. The actual level of compensation will not be determined until the expiration of five years, when more information will be available. In the meantime, land will be divided into rural land which had no development value at March 1939 ('green' land), other unbuilt-on land ('white' land), of which individual valuations will be made of development value on 31st March, 1939, and built-on land, which will be valued only if the owner establishes a claim that it possessed re-development value. It is expected that in so far as refusal of consent to develop is matched by consent to develop elsewhere, the payments in respect of betterment will provide a fund which will be adequate to pay compensation. As schemes of reconstruction and thinning-out of towns and for a balanced distribution of industry will involve a diversion of development values for some areas to others, the finance of compensation and betterment will be centralised in a new authority, a Central Land Commission.

The Government accepts the recommendation that local authorities should be given power to acquire compulsorily areas where large-scale re-development of severely war-damaged or obsolescent urban areas is required, or where a landowner is unwilling to sell land required in the interests of good planning.

Town and Country Planning Bill, 1947

Memo. pp. 22. 1947

1946–47 *Cmd.* 7006, *xix*, 1463

The Town and Country Planning Act, 1932, enabled local authorities to prepare planning schemes, and the Town and Country Planning (Interim Development) Act, 1943, extended interim development control throughout the country. Two other measures were directed to the problems of particular localities: the Town and Country Planning Act, 1944, which gave positive powers to re-plan and rebuild areas of extensive war damage or obsolescence and the New Towns Act, 1946. The defects of this system are: it is static, planning schemes having the force of law and being difficult to alter; it is localised; local authorities are not obliged to prepare plans; and it is negative.

The Bill replaces the planning scheme with a more flexible development plan. Plans must be prepared by county and county borough councils within three years, and they must be reviewed every five years. In order to give positive powers for executing plans by making land available, local authorities will be given wider powers to buy land compulsorily for leasing to the private developer, and will be able to designate as subject to compulsory purchase land likely to be required within ten years for development by government departments, local authorities and private enterprise.

So far planning has been governed by short-term financial considerations. The Uthwatt Committee argued that over-valuation due to floating value produces an aggregate value two or three times greater than the value based on actual possibilities. The burden of compensation falls on the individual authority, which may not be able to bear it, so that local authorities have tried to keep shifting values in their own areas and have had to allow building in too haphazard a manner. Under the Bill, no development may take place without consent and where permission to develop is refused, there is no right to compensation. But if no compensation were paid hardship might be caused, and £300 mn. will be set aside out of which payments will be made to owners. Where development is permitted, any resulting increase in land values will be collected in the form of a development charge to be paid before development is carried out. These financial transactions will be the responsibility of a Central Land Board.

To obtain the land necessary to re-plan and redevelop congested central areas local authorities may have to pay high prices, but will not be able to recoup themselves because of the less intensive use to which the land is put, nor be able

to collect the betterment in overspill areas because it cannot be identified. The total cost of buying and clearing land in areas of extensive damage may be £600 mn. spread over 25 years and of dealing with obsolete areas £15 mn. per annum. Grants of 90 per cent for war-damaged areas and of 80 per cent for obsolete areas will be made for varying periods. The total will be £3 mn. per annum at the end of five years, ultimately rising to two or three times that amount.

See *Town and Country Planning Act, 1947*. Memo. Pts. I, II; 1947, 1948 Non-Parl. Min. of T. & C. Planning. *Town and Country Planning (Scotland) Bill, 1947;* 1946–47 Cmd. 7034, Cmd. 7075, xix, 1485. *Town and Country Planning (Scotland) Act, 1947.* Memo.; 1948 Non-Parl. Dept. of Health, Scot. For regulations under the Acts, see annual *Consolidated List of Government Publications.*

Regional Plans

The following reports on regional plans prepared at the request of the Minister, and related papers, were published by H.M.S.O.:

Greater London Plan 1944. P. Abercrombie. Rep.; 1945 Non-Parl. Min. of T. & C. Planning. *London Regional Planning.* Advisory Cttee. Rep.; 1946 Non-Parl. *Greater London Plan.* Memo.; 1947 Non-Parl. *Merseyside Plan 1944.* F. L. Thompson. Rep. Illus.; 1945 Non-Parl. *South Wales Outline Plan.* T. A. Lloyd, H. Jackson. Rep.; 1949 Non-Parl. *Clyde Valley Regional Plan 1946.* P. Abercrombie, R. H. Matthew. Rep.; 1949 Non-Parl. Dept. of Health, Scot.

For a list of plans for other areas see *Town and Country Planning 1943–1951.* Progress Rep. p. 23 and App. II; 1950–51 Cmd. 8204, xx, 133.

New Towns

Cttee. Interim Rep., apps. pp. 21. [1946]. 2nd Interim Rep., app. pp. 25.

[1946]. Final Rep., apps., index. pp. 83.
1946

1945–46 *Cmd. 6759, Cmd. 6794, Cmd. 6876, xiv, 679*
apptd. Oct., 1945. sgd. Jan., April, July, 1946

Lord Reith (*Ch.*), Brown, Bunbury, Cadbury, Felton (Mrs. M.), Gaunt, Morgan, Osborn, Shaw, Stewart, Thomas, Watson, Younger.

'*To consider the general questions of the establishment, development, organisation and administration that will arise in the promotion of New Towns in furtherance of a policy of planned decentralisation from congested urban areas; and in accordance therewith to suggest guiding principles on which such Towns should be established and developed as self-contained and balanced communities for work and living.*'

Interim Report.—The New Towns are to provide for the overspill of population and industry as the congested areas of cities are rebuilt at lower densities. They will not be dormitory or satellite towns, but self-contained, balanced communities which provide industrial, shopping and other amenities. There may be two types: those built in an area of scattered rural population, and major extensions of existing small towns. Their optimum size is between 20,000 and 60,000 population. Situation and boundaries must be decided by the Government, which will need compulsory powers of purchasing land for a whole town on behalf of the agency appointed to develop it. The land should include all built-up land and a surrounding belt of appropriate depth.

For each town one agency should be responsible for planning and development, but it should have no other responsibilities. Neither ordinary commercial enterprise nor a housing association would be an appropriate agency. It should be a Government-sponsored public corporation financed by the Exchequer, though in some cases it could be sponsored by the interested local authorities and in certain circum-

stances an authorised association might be appropriate. Subject to direction on major questions of policy, the agency should have the same freedom of action as a commercial undertaking. The freehold or feu of the site should be held by the corporation. A Central Advisory Commission should be established to advise the individual agencies. Housing and factory construction can be financed on the normal basis, but as the initial expenditure on roads, sewers, etc., will not produce a return for some years, where the agency is sponsored by the Government funds should be provided by the Public Works Loan Board or the Exchequer, and interest deferred until the income of the new town can meet it. Legislation will be required to enable the Government to acquire a complete town site.

Second Interim Report.—This deals with questions of land acquisition and disposal, speed of development, and the local government status of the new town. The agency should purchase at the onset the whole land required for the authorised population, which should not be exceeded unless unforeseeable new factors emerge; its powers of development should be as wide as those of any landowner; when the corporation holds the freehold it should not dispose of land save in exceptional circumstances, but should grant leases. The agency should retain and let at rack rents shop premises and some factories. New towns should provide not only for dispersal, but for other movements of industry and population. The construction of new towns might require $7\frac{1}{2}$ per cent to 10 per cent out of the building programme of 4 mn. houses in 8 to 10 years. For each town the rate of construction should not exceed 1000 to 1250 houses nor the growth of population 3500 to 4250 per year: 20,000 is the maximum population which could be absorbed in a balanced way in 6 to 8 years. The large capital investment is in the main an alternative to expenditure elsewhere. Finance should be found by the State by way of loan, interest should be deferred till the town can meet it, and any surplus over interest and amortisation should be used for public benefit. Dispersing authorities should pay a rate contribution. The area should be created a separate civil parish, and urban district powers should be granted in due course. The agency should not exercise the functions of a local authority, but should not be precluded from providing works and services.

Final Report.—This discusses the principles of planning, and the preparation and execution of the plan. The size of towns recommended was adjusted to 30,000 to 50,000, rising in certain cases to 80,000, requiring 5500 acres of land for a 30,000 town, with proportionately more for other sizes. The diverse preferences of different people should be expressed to prevent architectural monotony; to avoid making a one-class town, not only factories but offices, shops, administrative offices, etc., should be included. The main centre will require ten acres for each 10,000 maximum population, and standards in relation to population are recommended for the number of shops, hospital beds, libraries, acres of recreation ground, etc. Shops should be provided by the agency and let at rack rents to different economic types of traders on leases which specify the trade to be carried on. There should be shops within half a mile of all residents. The capital cost of a 50,000 town would be £27 mn. to £36 mn. Other recommendations deal with zoning, densities, control of design and landscaping.

See *New Towns Bill.* Memo.; 1945–46 Cmd. 6801, xx, 347. *New Towns Bill.* Scotland. Memos.; 1945–46 Cmd. 6804, Cmd. 6850, Cmd. 6867, Cmd. 6874, xx, 387.

Qualifications of Planners

Cttee. Rep., apps. pp. vi, 85. 1950
1950 *Cmd.* 8059, *xiv*, 45
apptd. May, 1948. *sgd. Sept.,* 1950
G. Schuster (*Ch.*), Gray, Hart, Jackson, Kenrick, Paterson, Sharp (Dame E.), Wood.

'*To take account of the present and prospective scope of Town and Country Planning and to consider and report what qualifications are necessary or desirable for persons engaged in it and to make any recommendations affecting those persons which appear to the Committee to be relevant.*'

The early steps in planning were restrictive, designed to prevent serious evils, but the conception generally widened until it was seen that the negative idea of restraining what is undesirable must be accompanied by positive conceptions of what is desirable. The private initiative of industrialists and landowners in laying out model towns and villages contributed to this positive conception and showed that fruitful work in planning was not limited to those in government employment. The town planning profession was founded when the conception of planning was local and restrictive and when the main skills required were those of the architect, engineer and surveyor. The work in depressed areas, and the Barlow Commission, the Uthwatt and Scott Committees made it clear that planning should be extended to the whole country and that there should be a national policy on the location of industry and distribution of population. The process now involves the economist, the geographer, geologist, etc. Since the primary aim of planning is now to ensure that land is so utilised as to provide the best environment for living, it is a social and economic activity limited, but not determined, by the technical possibilities of design. It is thus a task requiring the contributions of specialised skills and unified direction. There are now ten universities, colleges and schools whose examinations are recognised. The main types of employment are with local planning authorities, new town corporations, central departments and private practice.

In local planning the chief officer should be responsible for handling the whole planning function, he must be able to organise the use of specialists, to arrange the carrying-out of surveys and to advise on the interpretation of information and the broad solutions of policy. He need not possess technical skill in design, but he needs to be creative and imaginative and must have an expert qualification which enables him to appreciate good design. For the 'basic educational discipline' a degree may be in any subject, but a post-graduate course should provide 'specialist education in planning'. The post-graduate course should be two years, or one year for an architect. The present qualification of membership of the Town Planning Institute should be improved until it indicates the standard of a university graduate with two years of post-graduate training.

An authoritative national institute is needed to watch the whole field of planning studies and to promote liaison between field workers and to evolve a system for granting recognition to persons qualified in accordance with the suggestions. The Town Planning Institute is an obvious foundation on which to build, but its membership should be widened, there should be more university representation, and it should co-opt persons representative of the economic and social sciences.

In a reservation Paterson stated that the planning authorities should be represented on the council.

National Parks. Scottish Survey

Cttee. Rep., apps. pp. 27. 1945

1944–45 *Cmd.* 6631, *v*, 341
apptd. Jan., sgd. Oct., 1944

J. D. Ramsay (*Ch.*), Darling, Moir.

'*To advise upon the areas in Scotland which might be suitable for National Parks, and to supervise an actual survey of potential areas by one of the Planning Officers of the Department of Health for Scotland.*'

It is necessary to distinguish between national parks and national forest parks projected or established by the Forestry Commission. The forest parks make a valuable contribution to free access facilities, and should be regarded as additional rather than alternatives to national parks. Where convenient, tentative boundaries of the proposed national parks are drawn to march with areas already controlled by the Commission. The national park should be large enough for the nation to enjoy and important enough to justify State intervention, whilst 'green belts', playing fields, etc., should be the concern of local planning authorities. Five areas amounting to 1870 square miles should become national parks and three areas amounting to 730 square miles should be on a reserve list. These are chiefly mountainous country in the west of Scotland, but include the Cairngorms as a Park and St. Mary's Loch as a reserve area. Within these areas certain parts should be designated nature reserves. Areas such as the Pentland Hills should be dealt with as regional parks. The characteristics, etc., of each area are given in the appendices.

National Parks in England and Wales

Rep. pp. 57. 1945

1944–45 *Cmd.* 6628, *v*, 283
sgd. April, 1945

J. Dower.

'*To study the problems relating to the establishment of National Parks in England and Wales.*'

In Great Britain a national park means an extensive area of beautiful and relatively wild country in which, for the nation's benefit and by appropriate national decision and action, natural beauty is preserved and progressively enriched, access made possible, wild life and historic buildings protected and established farming maintained. The relatively wild country of England is about one-fifth and Scotland two-thirds of the total land area, but the whole of this is either not required or is not suitable, e.g. the industrial section of the Pennines, or the isolated patches of the Malvern Hills and Cannock Chase which are of critical local importance for open spaces or green belt schemes. Out of the 12,000 square miles of wild country, 8000 are potential national park areas. This is far more than is required initially, or may ever be required, but while national parks are being established, the remainder should be reserved for possible future parks, where no substantial development other than farming and forestry should take place.

A preliminary list in three divisions is suggested. (*a*) Ten areas of the most desirable parks to be established in the next five years, e.g. the Lake District, Snowdonia, Dartmoor, the Roman Wall, etc. (*b*) Twelve areas to be reserved for the future, e.g. The Broads, Berkshire and Marlborough Downs, Swaledale Pennines, Merioneth coast and mountains including the Berwyns. (*c*) Other amenity areas. They should be given some county or regional status as 'Parks', 'Reserves', 'National Forest Park' or 'Nature Reserves'. These include the North, South, Hampshire and Dorset Downs and the New Forest.

The purpose of designation is to preserve the landscape and to give the public ample access and facilities for open-air recreation. Recommendations are made for the negative and positive methods for securing these ends, on maintaining farming use, on suitable and unsuitable facilities, the rights of access, rambling, footpaths, the conservation of wild life in special habitat reserves. It is not essential to acquire the land in national parks, since the cost of doing so would severely limit the number of parks established and the main purposes can be secured without it, except in special cases where control alone would be inadequate. There should be a National Parks Commission under the general responsibility of the Minister of Town and Country Planning. Some special arrangements for appropriate use of the general powers will be required, the most important being that each national park should form a single planning area, and a planning committee should be composed partly of persons nominated by the national parks authority and partly of representatives of the county and district authorities concerned.

National Parks (England and Wales)

Cttee. Rep., apps., index. pp. v, 134.
1947
1946–47 Cmd. 7121, *xiii*, 303
apptd. July, 1945. *sgd. March*, 1947

A. Hobhouse (*Ch.*), Buxton, L. Chorley, Dower, Elmhirst, Gavin, Graham, Haythornthwaite (Mrs. E. B.), Huxley, Williams-Ellis.

'To consider the proposals in the Report on National Parks in England and Wales (Cmd. 6628) of May 1945, (a) as to the areas which should be selected as National Parks; and to make recommendations in regard to the special requirements and appropriate boundaries of those areas which should be first selected. (b) As to the measures necessary to secure the objects of National Parks . . . and (c) on such other matters affecting the establishment of National Parks and the Conservation of Wild Life as may be referred by the Minister to the Committee.'

The multiplicity of public and private interests affected and the complexity of town and country planning law which forms the legislative setting for the proposals made are given detailed explanation. A comparison with the proposals in the three Divisions in the Dower Report shows the alterations which the committee have made for the proposed areas for national parks. Except for some alterations of names and size all ten areas of the A Division are selected, except the Cornish coastline. Its long narrow shape from Ilfracombe to Land's End would give rise to serious administrative difficulties. The Broads and the North York Moors are selected from the B Division because of their intrinsic beauty and unspoilt country and wealth of architectural interest, and the South Downs from the C Division because of their intrinsic merits and accessibility from London.

Omitting smaller areas which should be protected by local planning, 52 areas were selected as Conservation Areas. These areas, such as the Malvern Hills and the Cotswolds, do not call for the degree of positive management required in National Parks, but special measures should be taken to preserve their natural beauty and interest. Any future increase of national parks would be sought from among the conservation areas. The selection was made in close co-operation with the Wild Life Conservation Special Committee.

The recommendations include the following: twelve National Parks should be declared by annual instalments of four over a period of three years immediately following legislation. A National Parks Commission should be established as a body corporate, with a chairman and eight members appointed by the Minister of Town and Country Planning, and local park committees for each national park. All proposals to develop land in a national park will be subject to the permission from the park committees; the activities of public corporations, Government departments, etc., affecting national park policy should be considered by the Commission. Within 12 months of the passage of the necessary legislation, local planning authorities should submit detailed boundaries of Conservation Areas for the approval of the Minister of Town and Country Planning. A coastal planning advisory committee should be set up to consider the overall co-ordinated planning of the coast of England and Wales. The Commission must have full responsibility for the conservation of nature in national parks. Capital grants should be provided from the National Land Fund for a 10-year programme amounting to £9,250,000; for initial recurrent expenditure £170,000, and £750,000 in the fully operative stages. Many other recommendations are concerned with the details of management, legal procedure, finance, etc. Appreciations of the proposed national parks are in App. A and a general history of National Parks in Chapter II.

See *National Parks*. Com. 1st Rep.;

1950–51 (26) xvii, 499, and succeeding Ann. Reps.

Conservation of Nature in England and Wales. Wild Life Conservation

Special Cttee. Rep., apps., indexes. pp. v, 139. 1947

1946–47 *Cmd.* 7122, *xiv*, 535 *apptd. Aug.*, 1945. *sgd.* —

J. S. Huxley (*Ch.*), Tansley, Buxton, Diver, Elton, Ford, Gilmour, Nicholson, Steers, Trueman.

'(a) *To consider the proposals set out in paragraphs 60–68 of the Report on National Parks in England and Wales (Cmd. 6628) as to the Conservation of Wild Life, and to advise the National Parks Committee in regard to any modifications in these proposals, or any additional measures which, in the view of the Special Committee, may be necessary or desirable.* (b) *To consider such other matters relating to Wild Life Conservation as may be referred by the Minister of Town and Country Planning to the National Parks Committee and delegated by them to the Special Committee.*'

(*a*) The conservation of nature includes not only the preservation of selected areas of natural beauty, but also the advancement of scientific knowledge on how to control nature in order to maintain a series of varied and balanced conditions. This is fundamental to agriculture, forestry, horticulture and other kinds of 'farming' of living resources. Changes in nature are slow, not easily detectable and often irreversible, so that conservation cannot be achieved merely on the principles of good estate management: a sanctuary left to itself may become the focus of weeds and destructive animals. Increased facilities are needed for effective field research. The Government should now take a general responsibility for the preservation of flora and fauna and the protection of geological features by dedicating and managing certain areas of scientific value with the aid of a body of scientists.

While the National Parks Commission should be responsible for the conservation of nature within all National Parks and for reserving areas of scientific value within them for the benefit of the public, for scientific purposes there should be established quite distinct National Natural Reserves of 70,000 acres, made up of 73 small sites scattered throughout the country (13 covering 11,000 acres already protected by various bodies). They should be managed by a Biological Service, which should acquire all shooting rights. In addition, 35 areas of outstanding scientific value should be 'Conservation Areas', i.e. tracts of country the existing character of which should be preserved, and 41 geological monuments, averaging one acre a site, should be preserved. Lists of all sites of special scientific importance should be made for use in planning schemes or proposed for local reserves. The Biological Service should be equipped for survey and research, and a Nature Conservation Board appointed to supervise its work. Local authorities should be empowered to establish local reserves and given grant aid. A Coastal Planning Advisory Committee should be set up. The costs of acquisition of sites might be £500,000 and of the Service £250,000 per annum when fully developed.

(b) The human actions adverse to conservation—killing, biological control, artificial introduction and collection—are pursued by a limited number of persons by known methods at known seasons. The categories most exposed to danger should be given general protection by developing licensing systems. A committee should be appointed to make recommendations for a comprehensive Wild Life Protection Bill.

See *Nature Conservancy.* Reps.; 1953–54 (16) xvii, 49, and succeeding Ann. Reps. *Protection of Birds Act, 1954;* 2 & 3 Eliz. 2. c. 30.

National Parks and the Conservation of Nature in Scotland. National Parks

Cttee. Rep., app. pp. 1–56. 1947

1947–48 *Cmd.* 7235, *xiv,* 1 *apptd. Jan.,* 1946. *sgd. July,* 1947

J. D. Ramsay (*Ch.*), Bannerman, Campbell, Cruickshank, Darling, Grieve, Howat, Macintosh, Moir, Murchison, Ritchie, Roberts (Mrs. J.).

'(a) *To consider and report on the administrative, financial and other measures necessary for the provision, on the lines recommended in the Report of the Scottish National Parks Survey Committee, of National Parks in Scotland.* (b) *To consider and make recommendations on such other matters relating to National Parks and on the conservation of wild life as may be referred to the Committee by the Secretary of State for Scotland.*'

Those national parks capable of productive use should be fully utilised for the maintenance of thriving rural communities, an end to which the creation of park facilities and the income to be derived from a flourishing tourist industry would contribute. Preservation of scenic and recreational facilities should accompany the rehabilitation which in parts will be necessary. A National Parks Commission should be established. It should appoint a local committee for each park. A scheme for planning the parks should fit in with the least disturbance with the proposed pattern of Town and Country Planning. For each park the local planning authority should appoint a Park Planning Committee, two-thirds being representatives of the authority and one-third nominated by the National Park Commission. The first development plan should show all proposed development in the area. In dealing with development applications from private developers, the local park planning committee should consult the Commission and it is assumed that government departments proposing development will consult the local committee and the Commission. Other recommendations outline in detail the proposed set-up of the administrative machinery, etc. The Committee endorse the findings of the Wild Life Conservation Committee, which is printed as Part II of this Report. It has been assumed that the five areas on the priority list of the Scottish National Parks Survey Committee will be established as parks as soon as possible. The estimated all-in price of 25s. to 35s. an acre in these areas would require a sum not exceeding £1,300,000 and £1,950,000 for compensation, development, etc. The annual expenditure might be about £150,000. The capital costs should be met from the National Land Fund of £50 mn.

—— *Conservation of Nature in Scotland*
Scottish Wild Life Conservation Cttee.
Rep., app. pp. 57–72. 1947
apptd. Feb., 1946. sgd. June, 1947

J. Ritchie (*Ch.*), Matthews, Berry, Darling, MacGregor, Ramsay.

'*To consider and to advise the Scottish National Parks Committee as to the steps which it is desirable and practicable to take to conserve wild life in Scotland.*'

The progressive increase in the numbers of people deriving pleasure from natural beauty is an important reason for nature protection, but this is reinforced by the urgent scientific need for a policy of wild life conservation. There was agreement with the English Committee that such a policy would prove to be a good business proposition. The need was urgent because of changing conditions which endanger or upset any established balance of wild life. Land taken for war purposes, factories built in the country, afforestation, drainage, hydro-electrical development, have taken their toll, while the growing demands of the market have led to the sales of eggs and the killing of birds and animals, including some legally protected all the year round.

To safeguard wild life the requirements are: a Biological and Wildlife Service; nature reserves, encouragement by educational methods of an active interest in nature conservation; and the enforcement of effective legislation to ensure the conservation of wild life. The recommendations give the administrative details of such a scheme. Many proposed areas are already owned by State departments, others are privately owned. Total cost of acquisition is unlikely to exceed the proposed English figure of £500,000 although the gross annual sum of £250,000 is likely to be required, as in England.

—— —— Final Report, *Nature Reserves in Scotland*. pp. 34. 1949
1948–49 *Cmd.* 7814, *xviii*, 653
sgd. Nov., 1948

A Nature Reserve is created for the express purpose of safeguarding and perpetuating the natural assemblages of plants and animals and preserving features of geological interest. Four types are required: the National Park Reserves, where the larger mammals and birds may breed in safety and rarer plants survive; National Nature Reserves for the conservation of plant and animal communities under constant and close scientific scrutiny, access by the public being subject to the permission of the Biological Service; Nature Conservation Areas for the preservation of the existing beauty and scientific value, essentially observational areas for the Biological Service; and Local Nature Reserves, under the local authority, for the preservation of relatively small areas of local interest and available for nature study in the schools. The Report gives details of 51 areas chosen as being fully representative of the wild life of Scotland.

Footpaths and Access to the Countryside
Special Cttee. Rep., apps., index. pp. iv, 64. 1947
1946–47 *Cmd.* 7207, *x*, 1
apptd. July, 1946. sgd. July, 1947

A. Hobhouse (*Ch.*), Elmhirst, Buxton, Dower, Jones, L. Merthyr, Ritchie, Stamp, Stephenson, Wheatley.

'*To consider, with due regard to agriculture, forestry and other essential interests, the measures necessary for:* (a) *The preservation and maintenance of existing rights of way; the provisions where required of new rights of way (rights of way to include rights of way over both land and water but not to include rights of way enjoyable by vehicular traffic); and the provision of long-distance and coastal footpaths;* (b) *the provision of access for the public to mountain, moor, heath, down, cliff and common land, and uncultivated land generally, with particular reference to the recreational use of the countryside by the public.'*

The obscurity in which the origins of the great majority of footpaths are shrouded has given rise to innumerable disputes involving great expense in time and money. When brought before the Courts, these have been decided on the basis of the interpretation of property rights, but public opinion is now insistent upon the practical needs and reasonable claims of those seeking to make use of footpaths. The right of the public on a footpath, if not created by Statute, is assumed in law to have been 'dedicated', that is, consent has been given by the owner. Dedication may have been made expressly or it may be inferred from the conduct of the owners and use by the public for 20 years or other periods according to circumstances. The Report reviews the law relating to the determination of rights of way, their maintenance and repair, closures, diversions, and the convenience of the public, various amendments being suggested. The Access to Mountains Act, 1939, was defective in the categories of land included, the limitation of access to the hours of daylight, the cumbrous legal steps to be taken by an application for an Order, while in the case of certain land an owner's common law right of redress for trespass by civil action for damages was replaced by provision making it a criminal offence, so that barren land might be more protected than first-class agricultural land; and there were no provisions for compensating owners adversely affected. A new Act is required providing simple

machinery and relating it to the planning machinery. County and county boroughs should make and complete a survey of all rights of way (footpaths, bridlepaths, driftways and towpaths) within four years; a right of way used for 20 years should be deemed dedicated. Disputes and applications for closure or diversion should be determined by Quarter Session. Highway authorities should be required to maintain and repair rights of way, and to prosecute any one obstructing a right. The planning authority should have the duty of designating access land, which should include all uncultivated land, whether mountains, heath, moor, down, cliff, beach or shore, and have power to include inland water. The proposals of the Committee on National Parks and Conservation Areas on long-distance and coastal footpaths should be carried out. Compensation should be paid to owners, etc., where after five years it is shown that financial loss occurs by reason of designation. A Country Code should be published.

See *National Parks and Access to the Countryside Act, 1949;* 12, 13 & 14 Geo. 6. c. 97. *Country Code for Visitors to the Countryside;* 1951 Non-Parl. Nat. Parks Com. *Survey of Rights of Way.* Memo. prepared by the Commons, Open Spaces and Footpaths Preservation Society in collaboration with the Ramblers Assoc. and issued by the Ministry for the use of local authorities. Jan., 1950.

Restoration Problem in the Ironstone Industry in the Midlands

Rep. Summary of Findings and Recommendations. pp. 17. 1946

1945–46 *Cmd.* 6906, *xiii,* 537
apptd. —. *sgd.* Sept., 1946

A. H. S. Waters.

By 1944 iron ore had been extracted from some 20,000 acres, the remaining areas of possible reserves totalling approximately 116,500 acres. Of the total of some 18,500 acres which had been worked out, 12,000 had been restored to agriculture, 2900 had been afforested or used for industrial purposes and 3600 were derelict and incapable of being restored to agriculture. With the new mechanical excavator, the 'walking dragline', it was possible to make the operation of restoration concurrent with that of excavation. In order to ensure the most efficient and economic use of machinery, restoration of the surface must be considered as part of the operation of extracting the ironstone. If a legal obligation stated the degree of restoration to be imposed on the ironstone producer, progress in operational technique and restoration methods would soon be considerable. Estimates are made of the costs of restoration for agriculture and afforestation. The industry proposed the setting up of a statutory authority, financed from a levy on ironstone producers and royalty owners. Mr. Waters' recommendations comprised a simplification of the scheme.

Sand and Gravel

Advisory Cttee. Rep., Pts. I, II, app., index. pp. 139. 1948

1948 *Non-Parl. Min. of T. & C. Planning apptd. June, 1946. sgd. Jan., 1948*

A. H. S. Waters (*Ch.*), Beaver, Brewis, Collier, Collins, Duke, Gillie, Kear, Lowe, Smith, Wassell, Wooldridge.

'*To make recommendations on future policy for the control under the Town and Country Planning Acts of the extraction of sand and gravel. . . .*'

Part I.—Before 1919 gravel was used mainly for road metal and the yearly output was 2 mn. cubic yards. New uses and improved methods of extraction resulted in an increase in output to 22 mn. cubic yards in 1938 and 27 mn. cubic yards in 1943. In 1945 output was 22 mn. cubic yards. Estimated future demand for the whole country is about 30 mn. cubic yards.

In the quantity produced sand and gravel are second only to coal in the country's mineral output, but it has a low intrinsic value and being very bulky, is affected more than any other mineral by transport costs. Reserves of good gravel conveniently placed for the markets in general are so small as to require most careful management. Whilst the working of some areas should be postponed indefinitely, no step should be taken which will irrevocably sterilise any gravel deposit without the importance of the mineral being considered. Some damage to the land surface and amenity is inevitable. There is public hostility to gravel working because of its effect on amenities of a neighbourhood, temporary nuisance because of noise, traffic on quiet country roads, lasting damage from the alteration of the landscape, derelict areas or algae-covered sheets of water, lowering the water table, etc. Much of the damage to agriculture is due to the fact that the best areas for gravel working and for market gardening may coincide. The damage, though serious, is not necessarily complete destruction, as most wet and dry pits can be dealt with so as to be capable of subsequent agricultural production, though with some reduction of former productivity. The planning powers exist to implement the recommendations both for preservation from disturbance by gravel workings of those parts of the gravel field which comprise agricultural land of the finest quality, and for the due and timely restoration of beneficial use of those parts of the gravel field where mineral working is allowed.

Part II.—The Greater London's demand for gravel exceeds present output and will rise to an average of 10 mn. cubic yards a year. The assumption of the *Greater London Plan* that gravel reserves were abundant was unfounded and drawing largely from centres further afield would be very costly. This output will require the working of 6000 acres every 15 years, and since it is uneconomical for a firm with modern equipment to work a site for less than 15 years, planned working should be on the basis of three 15-year cycles, requiring 18,000 acres, which is the net workable field of the four main producing areas. If left to market forces, the working of the areas would be disproportionate to the reserves, but detailed control of output would present serious difficulties in this industry. Planning should be co-ordinated, 10,000 acres reserved indefinitely for agriculture, 20,000 acres allocated for working and 9200 already earmarked for other projects allocated for prior working if possible. The allocated area should be worked in phases.

—— Report, Pt. 18, apps., index. pp. vi, 38. 1953

1953 *Non-Parl. Min. of Housing & Local Gov.*
sgd. Dec., 1952

add Brockie, Quick, Schaffer. del. Gillie, Kear, Lowe.

Is concerned mostly with the after-treatment of gravel pits and prospecting for sand and gravel. Suggestions for a centralised body or a local planning authority, which should be responsible for organising and paying for special surveys, were rejected in favour of allowing site surveys by gravel operators with guidance from the local planning authority and the central government.

See (Regional) Reports, Pts. 3–17; 1950, 1952, 1954, 1955 Non-Parl.

Air Pollution

Cttee. Interim Rep., apps. pp. 31. 1953. Rep., apps. pp. 80. 1954

1953–54 *Cmd.* 9011, *Cmd.* 9322, *viii,* 629 *apptd. July, sgd. Nov.,* 1953, *Nov.,* 1954

H. Beaver (*Ch.*), Boyd (Miss A. D.), Burn, Dennison, Duncalfe, Ferguson, Foxwell, Lessing, Nonhebel, Regan, Sutton. Interim Rep. add Charles, Rep.

'*To examine the nature, causes and effects of air pollution and the efficacy of present preventive measures; to consider what further preventive measures are practicable; and to make recommendations.*'

Interim Report.—The main source of air pollution is smoke, i.e. solid particles of soot, fine dust, and minute liquid droplets of tar and oil. With few exceptions no industrial chimney need emit more than a light haze of smoke, but this involves capital expenditure. The complete prevention of domestic smoke at the present state of knowledge rests with the use of smokeless fuels; it should be possible to provide enough of this within a few years for use in the worst areas. Much of the smoke from railway engines, ships and the exhausts of motor vehicles is preventable. For immediate action it was recommended that meteorological warnings should be given when serious fog is expected; industry, shops, offices, hotels, etc., should bring smoke control measures to the peak of efficiency at the beginning of the winter. Testing devices are quite simple. The householder should store smokeless fuel against the fog. Ordinary fires should not be banked at night.

Part II is a more detailed technical survey into the conditions producing smog, the sources of pollution by smoke, sulphur dioxide and carbon monoxide. The cost of pollution to the community may be £100 mn. per year, apart from the cost of wasted fuel.

Report.—The emission of dark smoke from any chimney should be prohibited by law and the use of efficient grit and arresting plant made obligatory in new industrial installations. Local authorities should have power to establish smokeless zones and smoke control areas in which the use of bituminous coal for domestic purposes would be restricted. There should be a progressive extension of smokeless zones as smokeless fuels become available. Financial assistance should be given to houseowners to convert their appliances. The 50 per cent purchase tax on gas and electric room and water heaters should be removed. Other recommendations deal with training stokers, railway electrification, smoke control staffs for local authorities, a Clean Air Council, etc.

See *Clean Air Act, 1956;* 4 & 5 Eliz. 2. c. 52. *Mortality and Morbidity during the London Fog of December 1952.* p. 336.

XIV. EDUCATION

1. General Policy, Schools
2. (a) Handicapped Children,
       Curriculum, Examinations
   (b) Particular Vocations

3. Teachers, Youth Leaders:
       Supply, Training, Salaries
4. (a) Universities
   (b) Scientific and Social Research
5. Museums, Libraries

1. GENERAL POLICY, SCHOOLS

Education 1900-1950

Ministry of Education. [Ann.] Rep.,
   apps., etc. pp. xii, 250. 1951

1950-51 *Cmd.* 8244, *xi*, 261

Reviews the events and developments since 1900.

Adjusting between Authorities the Expenditure Incurred by them in Respect of Evacuated School Children

Rep., app. pp. 18. 1940. 2nd Rep.
        pp. 10. 1941

1940, 1941 *Non-Parl. Bd. of Education
apptd. Nov.,* 1939. *sgd. Jan.,* 1940, *July,*
1941

D. Du B. Davidson (*Ch.*), and 13 other
members, Rep.   15 other members,
2nd Rep.

'*To consider the problems of adjusting
expenditure between Authorities in respect
of evacuated school children.*'

In November 1939 the Board issued
Circular 1481 outlining the general
principles applicable to expenditure on
children moved to reception areas under
the Government evacuation scheme.
Adjustments were proposed by the
Committee over a wide field of elementary and secondary education. For
example all expenditure by the receiving
authorities due to evacuation, air-raid
precautions, supplementary school accommodation, conveyance of evacuated
school children, etc., should be met by
a direct charge on the Exchequer. The
expense of children from evacuation
areas where their parents still had
homes, should be met by the evacuation

authority and children coming from
neutral zones should be the responsibility of the receiving authority; apportionment to be based on the school
roll at the end of each week. Additional
expenditure for extra teachers, books
and stationery, medical inspection, upkeep of buildings and grounds, etc.,
should be met by mutual arrangements
between evacuating and receiving authorities.

Educational Reconstruction

Paper, apps. pp. 36. 1943

1942-43 *Cmd.* 6458, *xi*, 21

The Government propose to recast
the national education service on the
principle that education is a continuous
process conducted at successive stages.
At present children take an examination
at age 11 and about 9·5 per cent go on
to secondary schools, less than half the
remainder going on to separate senior
schools and departments for children of
that age staffed for the purpose, more
than half remaining in all-age schools.
Little new accommodation has been
provided for junior children aged 7-11,
and the classes are too large. Only 25
per cent of the admissions to secondary
schools are independent of the ability
of the child's parents to pay fees, and as
these are only one-third of the cost, a
parent can buy his child a place to the
exclusion of an abler child whose
parents cannot pay.

   The school-leaving age will be raised
to 15 without exemptions, and to 16 at
a later stage. The division into elementary and higher education will be
replaced by organisation into primary,
secondary and further education. The
local authorities will be required to

survey their areas, and prepare development plans which, if approved, will be embodied in an Order applying to the area concerned. Local authorities will have a duty to provide or aid the supply of nursery schools. There will be separately built primary schools for ages 5–11 and secondary schools 11–15. Large primary school classes will be eliminated. The competition list at age 11 will be replaced by classification on the basis of individual aptitudes, school records, intelligence tests, parents' wishes, etc. To provide for different aptitudes the present grammar, senior and junior technical schools will be organised into three types of secondary schools, grammar, modern and technical. To ensure that accommodation, size of classes, etc., are brought up to the level of the best grammar schools, all secondary schools will be conducted under a single code of regulations, and no fees will be charged in any such school maintained by a local authority. Provision will be made in all primary and secondary schools for the school day to begin with a corporate act of worship, and for religious instruction on the basis of a syllabus agreed between the churches, teachers and the authority. Parents may withdraw children from the act of worship or from religious instruction and may ask for separate denominational instruction in the school or elsewhere.

A solution for the problem of the voluntary school is proposed. In 1938 there were 10,363 council schools and 10,553 non-provided, mainly denominational schools, but only 30 per cent of the children were in the non-provided schools, which were therefore smaller. The churches will be unable to finance senior or modern schools of the new equal standard proposed, or to modernise the infant and junior departments. There is general agreement that they should not be abolished, but aided to take part in the re-organisation. But the dual system implies denominational religious tests for teachers and as appointments are in the hands of church managers, no teacher can serve in or be

promoted to headship in any of the 12,500 Church of England or R.C. school departments unless he is a practising member of the faith concerned. The local authority will be empowered within a time limit to make local agreements with voluntary schools for capital grants, the religious instruction being in accordance with the trust deed of the school, and provision made for agreed syllabus instruction for such parents as desire it. Voluntary schools unable to meet half the cost of the necessary alterations will be able to become controlled schools, in which case the local authority will take over the financial responsibility, and the power of appointing teachers, but the managers will be consulted on the appointment of the head teacher and of reserved teachers who will give denominational instruction for not more than two periods of the week. Other religious instruction will be on the basis of the agreed syllabus. If they are able to meet half the cost of alterations, etc., they will become Aided Schools, the other half being received directly from the Exchequer. In Local Agreement and Aided Schools, one-third of the managers will be appointed by the local authority, and in Controlled Schools, two-thirds.

Independent schools catering for children of compulsory school age will be registered and inspected. All children from 15–18 not already at school or some suitable part-time instruction will be compelled to attend in the hours of employment for part-time instruction, and 'young people's' colleges will be established for the purpose. The facilities for technical, art and adult education will be co-ordinated and extended, more university awards made.

The existing balance of local educational administration will have to be revised, the present division of duties between Part II and Part III authorities being unsatisfactory, and based partly on a population figure in 1901. The education authority will be the county boroughs and counties; counties will be required to prepare schemes for country district education authorities, each having a minimum of 60,000 population or a minimum of 7000 children, to which powers may be delegated.

See the Hadow and Spens' Reports, etc., on the proposed re-organisation of the educational system (*Breviate 1917–39*, pp. 466–84). *Education Bill*. Explanatory Memos.; 1943–44 Cmd. 6492, viii, 83. 1944–45 Cmd. 6602, x, 105. *Education Act, 1944*; 7 & 8 Geo. 6. c. 31. *Public Education in Scotland*. Rev. ed.; 1955 Non-Parl. Scottish Education Dept. See also Educational Pamphlets 1–3; 1945 Non-Parl. Min. of Education.

Primary Education

Advisory Council. Scotland.   Rep.,
    apps. pp. vii, 140.   1946

1946–47 *Cmd. 6973, xi, 25*
referred Feb., 1943. sgd. Sept., 1946

W. H. Fyfe (*Ch.*), and 21 others.

'*To review the educational provision in Scotland for children from the time of entry into the nursery school until the completion of primary education, and the arrangements for promoting them from primary to secondary education, and to make recommendations.*'

The Report sets out the purposes of primary education, discusses the physical background and appropriateness of buildings and site, co-operation between home and school, the curriculum and methods of teaching in various subjects, the qualities and functions of head teachers and staff and the purpose and methods of religious instruction, on all of which principles are enumerated and suggestions made. Since Scotland, with the exception of the Highlands and Western Islands are part of the native home of English, the children should be taught to speak and write it well, but they should have a weekly period for Scottish tradition and language, should learn Scottish folk songs and something of Gaelic life.

Amongst the recommendations are: no school with less than ten children is

satisfactory; 450 is a reasonable maximum size for a primary school, normal classes should be reduced to 30, those for the backward and retarded to 25. The maximum size of a one-teacher school with ages 5–12 should be 25. There should be no compulsory homework, and the approved school should be co-ordinated as part of the system. The normal age of transfer to a secondary school should be 12, and the selection of the type of school needed should be based on the school's views and an average of an intelligence test, an attainments test and the teacher's scaled estimate.

Abolition of Tuition Fees in Grant-Aided Secondary Schools

Cttee. on Public Schools and the General Educational System.   Special Rep.,
    apps. pp. 43.   1943

1943 *Non-Parl. Bd. of Education*
apptd. July, 1942. sgd. April, 1943

D. P. Fleming (*Ch.*), and 17 others.

'*To consider means whereby the association between the Public Schools and the general education system of the country could be developed and extended; also to consider how far any measures recommended . . . could be applied to comparable schools for girls.*' Extended terms: to consider '*The question of the abolition of tuition fees in Grant-Aided Schools.*'

The Committee was set up in response to a request made jointly by the Governing Bodies Association and the Headmasters' Conference, both of which had been considering by what means the schools which they represented could be of service to a wider range of pupils. It was asked to deal with the extended terms first.

Majority Report.   Aitken, Binns, Birley, Brock (Dr. M. Dorothy), Clay, Cole, Gruffydd, Jacks, Nichols, Pennington, Tanner (Miss E. M.).   As a result of historial development, three categories of secondary schools had emerged: those provided and fully maintained by the local authority; those aided by the local authority on condition that they offered 25 per cent of Special Places, and Direct Grant Schools (232 in number) receiving a direct grant from the Board of Education on condition that they were part of the local provision and offered not less than 25 per cent free or special places.

The proposal to replace fees by grants as the chief source of income for some schools raised the problems of the independence of the schools, in particular (1) defining and safeguarding the functions and duties of the governors and teachers in the internal organisation of secondary schools of all types and (2) preserving within the grant-aided system an autonomy compatible with the local authorities' responsibilities for the needs of their areas. (1) The first can never be easy to solve, but 40 years of secondary education administered by local authorities happily proves that this risk can be taken. Instruments or Articles should be drawn up providing for a separate Governing Body for every secondary school (including those maintained or aided) giving it power, in consultation with the local education authority, to appoint headmasters or headmistresses, and giving the latter right of access to the Governing Body, control over assistant staff, etc. (2) Direct Grant Schools. Where these are part of the local provision, they should be assimilated with the local system. But there are old-established foundations, mostly for boys, and the recent foundations, for girls. A few have large endowments, and some of them have boarders—sometimes recruited from all over the country. Some of these schools should continue to receive their grant from the Board and to exist under their own governing bodies, provided they contribute to local needs and can be responsible for their own future capital development. The selection of schools for direct grant should be made by the Board after considering (i) their claim to non-local character, (ii) special characteristics, (iii) financial position, (iv) observations by the local authorities on the circumstances of the area. A proportion of the places should

be reserved for the Governors to award at their discretion, provided the selection arrangements were generally approved by the Board.

The retention of fees would be a serious obstacle to securing secondary education as a right to every child; they should be abolished in grant-aided Schools as a whole. The loss of income should be made up by liberal grants to ensure that standards are maintained.

Minority Report. D. P. Fleming (*Ch.*), Crowe, Bishop of London, Macdiarmid, Pickard-Cambridge, Pooley, Reynolds. The Minority regretted that it was found necessary to ask the Committee's opinion on the abolition of tuition fees in isolation, before the taking of evidence had been completed. They agreed with the Majority on the 'rights' of a child and on the independence of the schools, but to assist in preserving that independence, a third of the governors in the maintained schools should not be appointed by the Authority. To preserve the traditional connections and clientele the governors of the direct grant schools should, subject to safeguards, be able to allocate 50 per cent of the places; and this system should apply to the governors of secondary schools, though the percentage need not necessarily be as much as 50 per cent. If there were sufficient free places to satisfy the requirements of the local authorities, as there should be, fees graduated to the financial circumstances of the parent could be charged for the other places. If there is a shortage of places, the remedy is to provide more. Shortage at first will be in grammar schools, but under present conditions a parent who wishes to send his child to a grammar school should not be compelled to send him to a modern school with the sole alternative of an independent school. The Minority did not recommend the abolition of fees in grant-aided Schools.

—— Report, *Public Schools and the General Educational System*, apps. pp. iv, 132. 1944

1944 *Non-Parl. Bd. of Education*

sgd. June, 1944

add Barrington-Ward.   del. Cole,
Macdiarmid.

Public Schools are generally thought of as the independent boarding schools which receive no government grant. The public schools defined in the terms of reference consist of 89 independent schools and 99 schools which are aided by local and/or central grants. Thus about half already receive aid, and about half are entirely or mainly day schools. At some of the latter, the cost, quality and kind of education is similar to that of aided and maintained schools. There were two problems: (1) associating the wholly independent schools (mainly but not entirely boarding schools), with the general system of grant-aided and public controlled schools and (2) extending and developing the association between a number of grant-aided day and boarding schools and the general system of schools which are in administrative relation with the local authorities. As these schools have only 9000 vacancies annually for boys and girls, no substantial provision of boarding school places can be made without building many new boarding schools. Witnesses hostile to the continued existence of the independent public schools wanted the endowments and premises appropriated by public authorities; but this would destroy schools doing good work, would require a repugnant degree of compulsion, and would require a ban on all independent schools. Others advocated that the public schools should be brought wholly under the control of the local authorities, but this would not suit the circumstances of those schools drawing pupils from all over the country and from abroad. A third suggestion was that these schools do not possess qualities worth securing for the general system and they should be left to work out their own future, and given no financial aid. But while rejecting proposals to abolish or absorb public schools, it was equally agreed that they could not be left entirely outside the public system of education. A national scheme of association ought to offer scope for spontaneous agreements between these schools and the local authorities.

Opportunities of education in the schools included in the terms of reference should be made available to boys and girls capable of profiting thereby, irrespective of the income of their parents. The Board of Education should compile a list and the terms of admission of schools to such a list. There should be two schemes. Scheme A should be open to those schools recognised as efficient and not conducted for private profit; the local authority or authorities should have the right to reserve a number of day or boarding places, and the number of such local places should be settled between the Governors and the local authorities with reference to the Board, if necessary. In boarding schools the Board should nominate as many pupils as agreed upon by the Board and the governing bodies. The schools would be required to abolish tuition fees, or if they are retained, to grade them according to an approved income scale. Scheme B should apply to such boarding schools, or schools taking a substantial number of boarders, which are recognised as being efficient and not being conducted for private profit and in which the system of private profits in the management of boarding hostels has been or will be abolished. The Board should grant bursaries to qualified pupils who have spent five years in a grant-aided primary school. The schools admitted should offer in the first instance up to 25 per cent of their annual admissions to pupils from grant-aided primary schools. Applications for bursaries at ages 11 and 13 should be made by parents or guardians through the local authorities to the Board. There should be no competitive examination for bursaries tenable under the schemes. The Board should have the assistance of a central advisory committee. Local authorities should be encouraged to provide boarding schools and boarding hostels.

Principles of Government in Maintained Secondary Schools

Pp. 10. 1944

1943–44 *Cmd.* 6523, *viii*, 109

Under the Education Bill every county and auxiliary secondary school is to have an instrument of government which shall determine the functions to be exercised in relation to the school by the local education authority, the body of governors and the head teacher. Hitherto for pupils over 11 years of age there has been a distinction between secondary schools for higher education, and senior and central schools for elementary education. In recasting the system the term 'secondary' includes all schools for senior pupils.

There has been general agreement between the President (Minister) and the main interests concerned relating to: governing bodies, appointment and dismissal of staff in County, Controlled, Special Agreement and Aided Schools; the relation of head teacher to the governing body, finance, curriculum. The abolition of fees means that methods of admission must be re-examined. The local authority alone has all the information on which to decide the broad type of secondary education the child should follow, but head teacher's view, parents' wishes, etc., should be taken into account.

Secondary Education

Advisory Council. Scotland. Rep., apps. pp. vi, 198. 1947

1946–47 *Cmd.* 7005, *xi*, 173
referred Feb., 1943. *sgd. Sept.*, 1946

W. H. Fyfe (*Ch.*), and 21 others.

'*To review the educational provision in Scotland for young people who have completed their primary education and have not attained the age of 18 years or discontinued full-time attendance at school, whichever is the later, the examinations for which they may be presented, and the certificates which may be awarded. . . .*'

After the Education Act, 1918, in centres of small population the secondary school was expanded until it became an 'omnibus' comprehensive school of post-primary education. In larger centres of population the established secondary school with a five or six years' course was continued, and other centres with a three years' course of less academic type (junior secondary schools) developed for those who did not attain the required standard for admission to the senior secondary school. The English tripartite system of grammar, modern and technical is unsuited to Scottish conditions, because it is difficult to assess ability and still more difficult to determine aptitudes and bents at age 12, and because the poor parent cannot get round the verdict at age 12 as a better-off parent can. The choice is between the system of senior and junior secondary schools and the omnibus school. The latter is most in accord with the ideals of the age, but large multilateral schools of 2000 favoured by America and London are rejected in favour of omnibus schools of not more than 600, since such schools would secure the personal knowledge of the head teacher and have organic as distinct from administrative unity. Junior secondary schools would be improved by raising the age, by encouraging them to grow a IVth or Vth year, by larger bursaries and by prohibiting senior secondary schools from having in the first three years practical courses which properly belong to junior secondary schools. Where the authority is convinced that the omnibus school is not in the best interests of its area, the system of senior and junior secondary schools should be given a longer trial in more favourable circumstances. Rural secondary education should have 'rural colour', but not agricultural bias. In rural areas there are too many tiny ill-equipped schools: none should be recognised unless it is a combined primary and secondary unit with five, or a secondary unit with four full-time teachers. There should be more generous provision of specialists and equipment and joint senior secondary schools of technical type, with hostels, should be established.

The case against the external examination is proved. The schools' assessment of children would be right as to order of merit, but not as to standard and spread of marks. Exact statistical methods, with a scaling procedure, which is given in detail, should be used to standardise severity and spread. There should be no external examination for children leaving at 15, but they should be supplied with a school record. At 16 there should be a School Certificate awarded on the basis of an internal examination standardised as suggested, and an external Higher Certificate on a subject basis. There should be an Advisory Examination Council.

There is much failure in secondary education because of rigid, ineffective methods. Scotland has lagged behind England in experiment. In England almost all pioneer schools are private, the heads are free to choose staff willing to experiment and to select pupils whose parents are hospitable to new ideas. The report discusses teaching methods in general and in relation to the various subjects in the curriculum. There are recommendations on homework, libraries, the inspectorate, etc.

See the booklets on the various subjects of the curriculum in Scottish Secondary Schools; 1950–1952 Non-Parl. Scottish Education Dept.

The Future of Secondary Education in Wales

Central Advisory Council. Wales. Rep., apps. pp. viii, 160. 1949

1949 Non-Parl. Min. of Education referred —. sgd. Dec., 1947

R. I. Aaron (Ch.), and 18 others.

'To consider the content and development of Secondary Education in Wales under the Education Act, 1944, and its relation to Primary Education on the one hand and to Further Education on the other.'

The people of Wales have strongly supported the policy of providing grammar schools rather than technical schools, which they have regarded as inferior. In the industrial areas labour representatives have tended to reject the central school, and have aimed boldly at free compulsory education for all up to the age of 16. Secondary technical education was not popular when most pupils refused to consider occupations which threatened to end in the 'dole' and frustration.

If education is to be according to age, ability and aptitude, the common characteristics of early adolescence are not the only factors which should be taken into account. Each individual has the right not to the *same* education as his neighbour, but to that kind of education which will enable him to develop his gifts and potentialities. Surveys in England, Scotland and the U.S.A., and based on intelligence tests, show that if differentiation of provision for secondary education were to be effected according to the factor of general intelligence, there would need to be nearly three times as many places for the children in the lower range (71 to 110) as for children in the higher range (111 to above 140). But there are special aptitudes to be considered and this does not necessarily correlate with general ability, though they make for success in certain studies and occupations. There is much evidence to show that special technical aptitudes, as distinguished from general ability, appear in the majority of children *during* and not at the beginning of the secondary stage. What is needed is a variety of opportunity which will develop special interests and aptitudes and a progressive differentiation in the curriculum as these aptitudes emerge.

The psychological evidence appears to be consistent with two schemes: (*a*) multilateral schools for pupils of a wide range of ability and (*b*) two kinds of secondary schools, grammar-technical for the more highly intelligent pupils (I.Q. above 110) and modern-technical (for those with I.Q. 70–110), both types to be adequately staffed and equipped for progressive differentiation of the curriculum.

The basic curriculum is then reviewed. There seems to be practically no difference in average native ability or general intelligence of boys and girls of the same chronological age and an artificial limitation of choice by a mistaken convention of a sex type might hinder the development of individuals of both sexes.

There has been little progress in the teaching of the Welsh language since the Committee of 1925, partly through lack of coherence and co-ordination, but language is only one aspect of the relation between Welsh schools and the Welsh community. The schools are not sufficiently in touch with Welsh life and tradition. Suggestions are made for the effective use of Welsh material in history and geography, and for a course on 'contemporary Wales'. In both grammar-technical and modern-technical schools, the medium of instruction should be English in the predominantly English-speaking areas, Welsh in the predominantly Welsh-speaking areas, and the language of the contributory primary schools in the linguistically mixed areas: in each area there should be proper provision for the other tongue. The same principles are suggested for modern-technical schools, except that as many pupils will not be able to take a second language, the language of the other tongue should be taken to a basic level, for the purposes of ordinary life.

See *Curriculum and the Community in Wales*. Pamphlet No. 6; 1952 Non-Parl. Min. of Education.

Educational Administration in Wales

Working Party. Rep. pp. vi, 54. 1948

1948 *Non-Parl. Min. of Education apptd. Dec., 1946. sgd. Oct., 1947*

D. R. Hardman (*Ch.*), Jones (D. T.), Jones (J.), Longhurst, Lush, Roberts, Thomas (B. B.), Thomas (H. R.), Thomas (T. G.), Thomas (W.), Thomas (W. D.), Weston.

'*To investigate in consultation with representatives of Welsh Local Education Authorities, the Central Welsh Board and other interested bodies . . . whether it is generally agreed that it is expedient that Welsh Local Education Authorities should combine to establish a national body in the form of a Joint Education Committee under paragraph 3 of Part II of the First Schedule to the Education Act, 1944. . . .*'

The Central Welsh Board, established in 1896, through examinations and inspection exercised a considerable influence on the Intermediate schools in their early years, but the local education authorities have since come into being, with powers and duties extended over the whole field of education, including Intermediate schools. As a result, the Federation of Education Committees (Wales and Monmouthshire), and the Advisory Councils for Technical Education for South Wales and North Wales were established. Intermediate schools are now to be absorbed into the new comprehensive system.

A Joint Education Committee should take over the powers of the Federation and Advisory Councils. It should not inspect authorities' schools nor concern itself with the provision of schools for normal day pupils. It should manage secondary school examinations, be able to establish boarding schools, take over teachers' training colleges, the South Wales College of Domestic Arts, establish a National College of Art, plan provision for handicapped children, ensure the services of specialists in music, drama and the visual arts. Its general expenditure should be met by a levy on authorities based 50 per cent on population and 50 per cent on rateable value, special services to authorities being paid for by capitation fees. It should consist of 112 members, a somewhat undesirable size arising from the insistence of smaller authorities on a representation of three members.

Early Leaving

Central Advisory Council. England. Rep., apps. pp. vii, 99. 1954

1954 *Non-Parl. Min. of Education referred* — 1952. *sgd. Aug.,* 1954

S. Gurney-Dixon (*Ch.*), and 19 others.

'To consider what factors influence the age at which boys and girls leave secondary schools which provide courses beyond the minimum school-leaving age; to what extent it is desirable to increase the proportion of those who remain at school, in particular the proportion of those who remain at school roughly to the age of 18 . . .'

School records of children in different social groups show that from the children of parents in professional or managerial occupations at one extreme, to the children of unskilled workers at the other, there is a steady and marked decline in performance at the grammar school, in the length of school life and in academic promise at the time of leaving. Two important considerations are, adverse home conditions which falsify many predictions made in the process of selection, and the different social assumptions of the child's parents. On the whole boys stay longer and do better academically than girls; parents attach more importance to their sons' education than to their daughters'. Though shortage of money is a less common reason for leaving than some others, a fair number of boys and girls do leave for this reason, especially the children of unskilled and semi-skilled workers. But boys normally leave grammar school at 16 if they are not thought suitable for an advanced course. Many trades and professions do nothing to encourage a longer school life and craft apprenticeship schemes encourage boys to leave at that age.

The value of extending school life beyond 16 depends on the character and intellectual ability of the particular child. The 1946 grammar school intake showed that in addition to the 10,000 boys and 7000 girls who took advanced sixth form courses, there were about 5000 boys and 5000 girls who had the capacity to do so if they had stayed longer. Of these 2900 boys and 1300 girls would have been suited for courses

in mathematics and science. A good many of the remaining 5800 start careers too early because of the conditions of entry in a wide range of professions, posts and apprenticeships. But the schools could not envisage more than half the intake staying on into the sixth form in the most favourable circumstances. These may amount to 7000 boys and 9000 girls, and though a fair number may be 'misfits' and some are 'premature leavers' who are right to leave when they do, several thousand boys and rather more girls would have done well to stay on two or three terms to complete their fifth year, even though their academic prospects were not promising.

The Committee rejected proposals to charge fees for a proportion of grammar school places, the general adoption of school-life agreements, a differential leaving age for grammar schools, and sixth form scholarships. Amongst the proposals were: family allowances for children still at school up to any age; building more grammar school places; more transfers from modern schools; provision of facilities for work after school hours by keeping schools open; later closing of public libraries; increases in maintenance allowances, including a drastic revision of the less generous scales, higher grants for older children; more science facilities for girls; comparable courses for pupils of similar ability in grammar and modern schools; reduction of length of craft apprenticeships for secondary school boys, etc.

Appendix II contains statistical tables relating to the Grammar School sample enquiry.

Compulsory Day Continuation Classes

Advisory Council. Scotland.   Rep.,
        apps. pp. 41.   1943

1943 *Non-Parl. Scottish Education Dept. referred May, sgd. Oct.,* 1943

W. H. Fyfe (*Ch.*), and 24 others.

'To review the educational provision in

Scotland for young people who have completed their primary education and have not attained the age of 18 years or discontinued full-time attendance at school.'

The Education Act, 1918, made provision for compulsory day continuation classes, but in spite of long continued efforts only 25 to 30 per cent can be induced to attend them voluntarily and many of those for brief periods only. Rugby is the only area in England where a scheme of compulsory attendance has been carried on continuously since 1921; it has received sympathetic co-operation of employers.

The Report proposes compulsory, part-time education in day continuation classes up to the age of 18, beginning three years after the raising of the school age to 15. Attendance inside normal working hours should be obligatory for 320 hours a year. For those engaged in agriculture the most suitable period for attendance would be between November and February. The main considerations should be the non-academic interests of the children, their outlook towards employment and wages. A variety of schemes will be necessary for different areas, including sparsely populated ones.

Further Education

Advisory Council. Scotland.   Rep.,
        apps. pp. 176. 1952

1951–52 Cmd. 8454, x, 579
referred Jan., 1947. *sgd. June,* 1951

W. McClelland (*Ch.*), and 21 others.

'*To review the provision made in Scotland for further education within the meaning of Section 1 (5) (b) and (c) of the Education (Scotland) Act, 1946, and to make recommendations.'*

Industry needs the services of the craftsman, the technician and the technologist. The system of apprenticeship needs an overhaul; attendance at pre-apprenticeship courses should count towards a boys' apprenticeship; pending the setting up of junior colleges, educational authorities should take an interest in works schools; steps are suggested for arresting the decline in continuation class attendance towards the end of the session. No fees should be charged for students up to 18 or for any organised course in evening continuation schools. Each Regional Advisory Council on Technical Education should report on the establishment of technical colleges. Education authorities should provide facilities for students who wish to qualify late in life for university entrance or award them bursaries to private institutions, should have discretion to make grants for professional correspondence courses, and provide intensive commercial courses. There is ample scope for technical colleges, whose status should be improved by the creation of institutions of high rank with degree-granting powers.

Liberal studies must be available for the majority of people; the Workers' Educational Association has pioneered with a restricted, more able minority, but it should now cast its net more widely. Liberal studies should be an essential part of all day-release courses. With the aid of voluntary organisation, authorities must make a determined effort to increase the number who attend courses. Newbattle Abbey, the only residential institution for adult education in Scotland, should become a national institution linked with the four universities. Recommendations are made for promoting music, drama, and arts and crafts. Youth clubs should be provided with instructors on individual subjects without fee, with full-time paid wardens for clubs of not less than 300. Swimming baths and playing fields should be provided.

There should be a single short code of regulations for further education; the maximum number in practical classes should be 20, in theoretical classes 40 and in cultural tutorial classes 25. Four specified types of training courses for teachers in further education should be provided by the Institutes of Education.

Greenhill dissents from the recommendation regarding Newbattle Abbey and regrets the failure to provide certain types of direct grant to voluntary bodies concerned with adult education.

County Colleges in Wales

Central Advisory Council. Wales. Rep., apps. pp. vii, 126. 1951

1951 Non-Parl. Min. of Education referred Dec., 1947. sgd. Sept., 1949

R. I. Aaron (*Ch.*), and 17 others.

'*The County College in Wales in relation to Sections 43–46 of the Education Act, 1944.*'

Under the Education Act, 1944, persons over compulsory school age and under 18 are required to attend county colleges for one whole day (or its equivalent) in each of 44 weeks in the year. In an urban area with a population of 250,000 the number of young persons between 15 and 18 years of age requiring part-time education may be approximately 10,000, or 2000 on each of five days in a week. If 300 students a day in each college is regarded as a convenient size, a city such as Cardiff may require six or seven colleges. In thinly populated rural areas, residential wings of day colleges, or predominantly residential colleges may be necessary. The curriculum should allow freedom of choice, but Welsh and English, social studies, physical education and practical subjects should be compulsory for all. Recommendations are made on language policy in bi-lingual and Welsh-speaking areas, on continuity between secondary school, the county college and adult education; on vocational guidance, and on intensive training courses for the teachers.

Minority Report (four members).— The consolidation of the recently expanded secondary system of education, which will necessitate extensive building programmes, should be accomplished before county colleges are founded. A county college curriculum should take account of special aptitudes and interests, and should not be a repetition of the basic secondary school curriculum.

School and Life

Central Advisory Council. England. Rep., app. pp. 115. 1947

1947 Non-Parl. Min. of Education referred —. sgd. Dec., 1946

F. Clarke (*Ch.*), and 19 others.

'*Enquiry into the transition from school to independent life.*'

A great many unhealthy and obsolete school buildings have to be replaced. More attention should be paid to primary schools, and the authorisation of classes larger than those for seniors discontinued. More secondary schools are needed. Methods of co-operation between parents and school, and of promoting local studies of the school's neighbourhood are suggested. Schools should not attempt to prepare the pupils for particular types of employment, but can serve industry by helping to develop personal qualities and the general rudimentary skills, and by using local knowledge as teaching material. Courses at county colleges should not be devoted to any specific employment; the work of the juvenile employment service should, where possible, be carried out at the technical colleges. Youth clubs, etc., must be voluntary and their members given as much responsibility as possible for carrying out their activities, mixed clubs should be established. There should be more comprehensive supervision of the health of school children, the School Medical Service made a more satisfactory career for doctors, the work of the school nurse and health visitor should be amalgamated, full health records should be at the disposal of the school medical service and health supervised during the early years of employment; health should be taught at the schools, the numbers of handicapped children ascertained, and provision made for them.

Youth Service after the War

Youth Advisory Council. Rep., apps. pp. 32. 1943

1943 Non-Parl. Bd. of Education referred Aug., 1942. sgd. June, 1943

J. F. Wolfenden (*Ch.*), and 20 others.

'*To consider the position of the Youth Service as an element in the educational system after the war.*'

Leaving school at 14 forces a sharp break, and it is not surprising that young people, earning wages under the same conditions as adults, should think themselves adults, claiming similar rights and recreations. The transition from school to work should be more prolonged and more regulated and the curriculum in schools for the higher age groups should be more closely related to need. A wide choice in recreation is necessary to develop personality. The cinema, dancing and reading are the three greatest leisure activities, and in spite of imperfections all three activities have great potentialities for healthy recreation.

The recommendations included: partnership between all organisations, voluntary, statutory and pre Service; raising the school age accompanied by maintenance grants to 16, a measure of educational supervision of all children until they are 18; choice of employment powers should be made a statutory obligation of the local education authority; in peace-time the permitted maximum hours of work should be 44, inclusive of part-time school and there should be an annual holiday of 24 days; substantial grants to voluntary bodies and statutory authorities who provide holiday facilities; national provision for educational, social and physical recreation; increased aid to voluntary organisations, accompanied by inspection of their accounts.

—— Second Report, *Purpose and Content of the Youth Service*. pp. 16. 1945

1945 *Non-Parl. Min. of Education sgd. April*, 1945

J. F. Wolfenden (*Ch.*), and 13 others.

Existing voluntary societies catering for youths fall into two main groups, those with fairly specific activities like the Boy Scouts and those catering for more general needs, but as a whole they are preoccupied with filling the gaps left by an inadequate national system of full-time education. The purpose of the Youth Service as part of the education system should be to promote and provide the opportunity for participating in activities which are carried on in a community different in its nature from school or work, which are voluntarily undertaken, which are complementary to other activities; and to which the approach is from the standpoint of recreation. This requires the provision of buildings and equipment not only to established groups but also to comparatively unorganised groups of young people who have a genuine need, more facilities for drama, camp sites, hostels, and travel. The Service will need more youth leaders who possess those qualities which closely identify them as members of the community.

Needs of Youth in these Times

Scottish Youth Advisory Cttee. Rep. pp. 97. 1945

1945 *Non-Parl. Scottish Education Dept. referred March*, 1943. *sgd. March*, 1945

J. Keith (*Ch.*), and 27 others.

'*To inquire into and make recommendations regarding the needs of youth and how far they are met by existing agencies . . . the influences leading to a sound development of character and to the prevention of anti-social conduct and juvenile delinquency.*'

There are certain fairly well-defined phases through which every adolescent passes and each phase gives rise to a different set of needs. In the first stage, from approximately 10 to 14, a child is highly charged with physical energy and seeks boisterous outlets, his psychological development produces a need for the society and support of his contemporaries. In the next stage, somewhere between 14 and 16, turbulences are slowing down, he sees himself more clearly as a member of his family, his school, etc., although developing individuality and desire for recognition may still bring him into conflict with his family. He will derive a new satisfaction in things of his own making or doing. In the third stage, beginning somewhere round 16, most young people are at work. If the child is given reasonable facilities in these earlier stages he should know in what direction his abilities lie. As a result, this third stage brings a widening of cultural and social interests. The final stage is the transition from childhood to adulthood, though it is impossible to say whether 18, 19 or 21 is the age when physical adolescence with its psychological concomitants is really over.

In the first stage there should be ample provision of playing space, courses for the 12 to 14 stage should aim at educating young people through their questing curiosity; a team approach to learning should be encouraged. In the 14 to 16 stage, when a young person is beginning to know the direction of his own abilities, he should be given the option of courses with vocational trends; in secondary schools psychological and manipulation tests should be used to supplement a young person's preferences. The omnibus type of secondary school was favoured for young people up to the age of 16. Up to the age of 18 he should be regarded as a learner and not an earner and the education authorities should be responsible for providing facilities for his continued education, not only in vocational courses, but over a wider field of education including preparation for family life, social and community living, sex education and religious instruction.

For leisure time young people should be given the opportunity of engaging in all kinds of hobbies, and pursuing lines of study, etc., and between school-leaving age and 18 should have 28 days' holiday a year. Voluntary organisations have generally aimed at enabling their members to become acquainted with things which are not included in the school curriculum; they should have no fear that the State-aided or rate-aided authority will compete with them on the same plane. All populous areas should be equipped with play centres, recreation halls, swimming baths, reading rooms, hobbies rooms, dancing halls, restaurants, etc., adequate facilities for out-door recreation, and cultural entertainment. Young people should be prohibited from entering public billiard rooms, breaches of the licensing laws should be guarded against, and proprietors and managers of cinemas and dancehalls should be consulted nationally and locally regarding the education and welfare of children and young persons.

Post-War Youth Service in Wales

Welsh Youth Cttee. Rep. pp. 20. 1945
1945 *Non-Parl. Min. of Education referred March*, 1943. *sgd. Feb.*, 1945
J. Griffiths (*Ch.*), and 18 others.

'To consider what should be the position of the Youth Service after the war.'

Local authorities are the executive bodies of the Youth Service, but as some are more progressive than others the service has developed unevenly; in some areas they assist voluntary agencies whilst in others they have made their own experiments. Until there is complete provision, existing machinery must be used to supplement the resources of the local authorities. This has been done by making available, since 1939, a direct grant to existing national organisations, but local authorities are not informed about the extent of expenditure from such grants in their areas. Under present conditions every church and every chapel, every unit of voluntary organisation can establish its recreational club and seek State aid.

The provision of facilities and opportunities should be made part of the statutory functions of the education authorities. During the transition period this provision should be made both inside and outside organised groups, and the direct financial assistance should be adjusted on a gradually decreasing scale as indirect assistance increases. Special care should be exercised before giving direct grants to new organisations, and grant-aid to clubs whose membership is confined to those professing particular religious creeds.

Out of School

Central Advisory Council. England. 2nd Rep., apps. pp. 39. 1948

1948 *Non-Parl. Min. of Education* referred June, 1947. *sgd. Feb.*, 1948

F. Clarke (*Ch.*), and 18 others.

'*To consider and report on the natural interests and pursuits of school children out of school hours; the provision made for these outside their homes; the value of such provision and the desirability of further or different provision; and the extent to which school work and activities can and should be related to and develop these interests.*'

The different needs of the various age groups show the complex nature of an out - of - school activity programme. From 5 to 7 years the child is full of curiosity, must have space to explore, make, experiment with water, sand, etc. Some children have no space to play in or depend on a dusty patch of public playground with a few swings and see-saws at one end. Between 7 and 11 domestic duties make claims, free time becomes more precious, there is an overwhelming urge for physical activity requiring space and equipment, in reading and crafts. Between 11 and 15 physical energy grows, the child begins to operate as a member of a gang, and if without lawful means of expending his energies and satisfying his urges, may become anti-social. Between 13 and 15 they begin to choose friends more carefully, to realise that art or music may have a special appeal and to be interested in the opposite sex.

The predominant place is the home, but the majority of children will need some provision outside it, though there must be freedom to make much or little use of what is offered. The Minister should ask all local education authorities to increase the facilities for play and recreation outside school, and to appoint 'Out-of-School Committees' to plan them. Grants should be paid to voluntary organisations. There should be training courses for workers, more equipment, library facilities within reach of children. The Arts Council should be invited to help to provide concerts, exhibitions, etc., in out-of-school hours.

Adult Education Grants

Advisory Council. Scotland. Rep., apps. pp. 20. 1944

1944–45 *Cmd.* 6574, *iv*, 1 referred, Feb., 1943. *sgd. July*, 1944

W. H. Fyfe (*Ch.*), and 24 others.

'*To consider whether grants from the Education (Scotland) Fund should be made to voluntary organisations making provision in Scotland for the education of adults of* 18 *years of age and over, and if so, under what conditions, and to make recommendations.*' Extended terms: '*The general question of the conditions under which grants in aid of adult education should be made.*'

In 1934 provision for adult education was made in separate regulations. Although there was a steady growth of numbers attending classes, these represented but a small fraction of the field, the distribution over the country was uneven, and there were few advanced classes. The effect of the block grant system is disadvantageous in that it is related to the number of pupils and teachers, whatever the stage, irrespective of the fact that some items of provision are expensive. The established residential college at Newbattle Abbey is important, but its financial position is precarious.

It should be the duty of the local education authorities to provide facilities for adult education in consultation with universities and voluntary bodies: they should be the only bodies receiving direct grants in their areas for the purpose; grants should be a percentage of approved net expenditure. Four regional Councils based on the universities should be established, and a fifth council for the Highlands and Islands considered. A small Scottish

Adult Education Council should be set up.

Organisation and Finance of Adult Education in England and Wales

Cttee. Rep., apps. pp. iv, 67. 1954

1954 *Non-Parl. Min. of Education apptd. June*, 1953. *sgd.* — 1954

E. Ashby (*Ch.*), Bullock, Burn, Jones, Martineau, Skinner, Thorneycroft.

'*To review the present system by which the extra-mural departments of universities, the Workers' Educational Association and the other responsible bodies provide local facilities for adult education, with special reference to the conditions under which the facilities are organised and are aided by grant from public funds. . . .*'

The Education Act, 1944, makes it a statutory duty of the local education authority to provide adequate facilities for further education, including leisure time occupation. By the 1946 Regulations they must take into account the work of three kinds of 'responsible bodies' which may provide facilities— the universities, voluntary associations and joint bodies. The Ministry makes grants up to three-quarters of the approved costs of teachers' remuneration. In 1951–52 there were 150,000 students in 8000 classes diffused all over the country. The high cost of organisation and administration (36 per cent of the total) was due to this diffusion, 44 per cent of the W.E.A. class centres being in places with population from 1000 to 10,000. The total cost was £699,000, or £4 13s. 2d. per student, of which £3 6s. 3d. came from the Exchequer, 8s. od. from the rates and 18s. 11d. from voluntary funds.

The W.E.A. maintained that the existing pattern of highly diffused responsibility provided the flexibility and diversity needed to recruit mature and experienced students, to maintain independence and ensure the right to discuss controversial subjects; it objected to any transfer of financial responsibility to local education authorities. Amongst the universities there was a great diversity of opinion: one group was satisfied with the present pattern, another held that universities had a responsibility to a much wider public than could be recruited by voluntary bodies traditionally aiming at manual workers who had left school at 15, and that they should be free in the kinds of classes they provide. But both agreed that universities should continue to take a large share of the work in adult education and should not surrender it to local authorities, and that full-time tutors should be assimilated in status and salary to university staffs. Municipal corporations and county councils were on the whole satisfied with the present machinery, but disliked the high pay of the teachers compared with that of technical teachers doing work of equivalent difficulty, and because the class fees were much lower than those of their own classes. The universities and W.E.A. held that class fees should be determined locally.

The recommendations included: the present partnership between the voluntary bodies, local education authorities and Ministry should continue, but be reviewed every five years; voluntaryism should be encouraged, the W.E.A's districts' status and work as responsible bodies should be preserved; the local authorities should be encouraged to contribute to the administrative costs of responsible bodies, and provide free accommodation; the limits on salaries of full-time tutors should be removed, subject to approval of new appointments; students' fees should be determined locally, but the Ministry and local authorities in determining grants should take into account the total financial contribution made by students; 'teaching' costs should include pioneer lecturing, etc. The grants should be altered to a maximum allocation made after consideration of quality and standards of work, proposed programme, and needs of the region.

Education Authority Bursaries

Advisory Council. Scotland. Rep., apps. pp. 23. 1944

1944–45 *Cmd.* 6573, *v*, 27
referred Feb., 1943. *sgd. Sept.,* 1944

W. H. Fyfe (*Ch.*), and 24 others.

'*To inquire into the system of bursaries and other forms of assistance which has developed under Section* 4 *of the Education (Scotland) Act,* 1918, *as amended.*'

Section 4 of the Education (Scotland) Act, 1918, gives powers to local authorities to award bursaries to those debarred from education 'by reason of the expense involved' and the Department had interfered as little as possible with schemes submitted for approval. The inadequacy of the bursaries was such as to deter many parents from applying for them, and there was a great diversity in the awards made to students in similar financial circumstances and as between different authorities. The Education Act, 1944, gives powers to the Minister to make regulations to award bursaries 'to enable pupils to take advantage without hardship to themselves or their parents of any educational facilities available to them.' The standard of need is therefore more favourable under the English than the Scottish Act. The local authorities should continue to award bursaries, but should be more closely controlled by the Secretary of State. Statutory provision on the lines of the English Act should replace Section 4 of the Act of 1918 and an expert committee should frame regulations regarding the assessment of need, etc. To enable university students to take part in corporate life residence in a hostel could be made a condition. No restrictive condition should be attached to bursaries to training colleges.

Educational Endowments in Scotland

Cttee. Rep., apps. pp. 68. 1950

1951 *Non-Parl. Scottish Education Dept. apptd. Jan.,* 1948. *sgd. July,* 1950

T. M. Taylor (*Ch.*), Allan, Greenhill, Lawson (Miss J. M.), Marshall, Peddie, L. Selkirk, Wilson.

'*To consider the present arrangements for the reorganisation, administration and application of educational endowments in Scotland. . . .*'

As each form of new educational activity has become the subject of public provision, endowments have had to move to other spheres of usefulness. In 1927 the Mackenzie Committee came to the conclusions that 'the purpose of an educational endowment is to confer on its recipients an educational benefit which they would not otherwise obtain.' But it was not possible, as it had been previously, to devise a hard and fast rule that educational endowments shall not be applied to purposes which the statutes direct shall or may be met out of the rates, for the educational purposes to which rates may *not* be applied are now almost non-existent. Powers which are now invested in the Secretary of State by Part IV of the Education (Scotland) Act, 1946, 'for altering the purposes to which endowments are applied or applicable' provide a workable and flexible framework within which further reorganisation can proceed to meet new demands.

Some purposes have become unsuitable for endowment expenditure, e.g. school meals, nursery schools, hostels for school children. Although education authorities are using their powers to give bursaries at school age and university awards generously, there are still fields in which local authorities could reasonably exercise their powers, and where help could be given: postgraduate awards; help for students wishing to study outside Scotland; late starters; student-apprentices; parents requiring assistance to send their children to fee-paying schools; Scottish parents abroad sending children home for education; students afflicted by family hardship, and circumstances in which an authority cannot reasonably exercise their powers, etc. Further recommendations concern other forms of endowments and the administrative machinery of Governing bodies, etc.

See *Educational Endowments in Scotland.*

Dept. Cttee. Rep.; 1927 Non-Parl. Scottish Education Dept.

2. (a) HANDICAPPED CHILDREN, CURRICULUM, EXAMINATIONS

Handicapped Children

Advisory Council on Education. Scotland. Reports

referred Jan., 1947

W. McClelland (*Ch.*), and 22 others.

'*To review the provision made in Scotland for the primary and secondary education of pupils who suffer from disability of mind or body or from maladjustment due to social handicaps, and to make recommendations.*'

Seven reports as below.

Pupils who are Defective in Hearing. Rep., app. pp. 72. 1950

1950 *Cmd.* 7866, *ix*, 341
sgd. Aug., 1949

No physical condition is more highly correlated with educational retardation than deafness, children with extreme forms being retarded by at least four years in linguistic ability. In order to plan for their education, it is necessary to ascertain, by the use of audiometers, etc., the frequency of the types and grades of deafness, but for educational purposes the degree of hearing loss is only one criterion: account must be taken of intelligence, age of onset of deafness, skill in lip-reading, ability to profit by a hearing aid.

Using the classification adopted in the report on *Children with Defective Hearing* (*Breviate*, *1917–39*, p. 472), in Scotland there would be 37,500–60,000 in Grade I (those needing no special arrangements), 1500–6750 in II A (those needing a favourable position in class, individual hearing aids and lip-reading instruction), 375–750 in II B (those who cannot make progress in ordinary schools, but should not be educated with the 525 in Grade III, whose hearing is so defective that they must be taught by special methods).

Schools for Grade II B need not be residential, but since they should be big enough for a minimum of five classes of not more than 15, three residential schools will be needed. There should be three residential schools for those Grade III children who cannot be educated in local schools of not less than five classes of not more than 10. There should be an audiometric survey of Scottish children, one audiometrist to every 15,000–25,000 children, grading should be done by a medical officer, an educational psychologist and a teacher of the deaf. A centre of research and training should be established at Donaldson's School.

Pupils who are Defective in Vision. Rep., app. pp. 68. 1950

1950 *Cmd.* 7885, *ix*, 413
sgd. Sept., 1949

Children with defective vision include those who with correction can be placed in the same category as pupils with normal vision; those who while having some perception of light are so lacking in visual discrimination that they will require to be educated by methods appropriate to the blind, and those who while not being so deficient in vision as to require methods appropriate to the blind, have not sufficient sight to enable them to profit by ordinary schooling, or whose vision would deteriorate if subject to the visual strains of ordinary education. The main problems centre in the blind who belong to the world of the blind and the partially sighted who belong to the world of the sighted.

Blind pupils, defined as those with no sight or insufficient sight to enable them to be educated by methods requiring vision may be expected to number 0·25 per 1000 on the school roll. All blind children in Scotland should be given residential education in the Royal Blind School, Edinburgh. The maximum number in any class should be 15, and in any nursery school, infant or secondary school class 10. Selection for admission to a blind school should be made by a team including a medical officer, a psychologist and a specialist teacher, with the co-operation of an ophthalmic surgeon.

Partially-sighted children are likely to number 0·75 per 1000 of the school roll. Their education should approximate to that of normally sighted children as closely as their visual handicap permits and they should mix freely with their sighted contemporaries. Consideration of the conflict of opinion as to whether since they have to live in a sighted world, it is best to segregate them or associate them with the sighted, leads to the conclusion that they should be segregated from the blind, not segregated from the sighted, but associated for appropriate subjects and activities. There should be one residential school for the partially-sighted in Edinburgh, for those children from sparsely populated areas or small burghs where the facilities cannot be provided. Many recommendations are made regarding the curriculum, equipment, etc., required for both the blind and the partially-sighted.

See *Breviate, 1917–39*, p. 472.

Pupils with Physical Disabilities. Rep.,
app. pp. 73. 1951
1950–51 *Cmd.* 8211, *xi*, 815
sgd. Sept., 1950

In relation to educational needs, children with physical disabilities include: (1) children of lowered vitality; (2) physically handicapped children who are unable to attend ordinary classes in ordinary schools; (3) epileptic children with severe or frequent seizures. Rough approximations of the incidence for the three categories was 20·0, 5·0 to 9·0 and 0·3 per 1000 of the school population. Thus 20,000 to 23,000 children of school age are in need of special treatment because of bodily ailments. Many of these children are receiving special educational treatment, but some have inadequate care and some are entirely neglected. Provision should be made for early ascertainment; children in hospitals and home-bound children should be reported to the education

EE

authority, which should maintain a register showing the category of disability and what instruction the child is receiving if any. Appropriate forms of education should be provided for all physically disabled children, including special day and residential schools, full-time teachers in hospitals with 15 or more children, a school to meet the need for secondary education, and arrangements made for those with heart disorders, cerebral palsy and for the home-bound.

Pupils with Mental or Educational Disabilities. Rep., apps. pp. 59.   1951
1951–52 *Cmd.* 8401, *x*, 755
sgd. April, 1951

Slow learners—children with intelligence quotients ranging from 70 to 85—probably form 12 to 16 per cent of the population. They have difficulty in keeping pace in the primary schools and are found to be following modified courses in the secondary schools, but these should not be regarded as suffering from 'disability of the mind'. The education of the slow learners should be the subject of a remit to the Advisory Council.

Children with mental and educational disabilities cannot be successfully treated by assuming that the cause of their difficulties appear when their I.Q. has been determined. Their problems and the underlying causes are invariably complex. They form the following wide categories for the purpose of planning their primary and secondary education: (*a*) pupils requiring special education because of absence, frequent change of school, faulty teaching and other similar causes, not more than 5·0 per cent of the primary school roll; (*b*) pupils with special disabilities in reading, arithmetic, spelling and other school subjects, 1·0 per cent of the primary school roll; (*c*) pupils who are retarded, but who are capable of making some progress in the school arts, normally with intelligence quotients ranging from 55 to 70, 1·5 per cent of the primary school roll; (d) pupils who are unable to make much progress, if any, in the school arts, but who are capable of being trained, normally with intelligence quotients from approximately 40 to 55; (e) psychotic pupils. No estimate can be made of the incidence of (d) and (e).

There should be early ascertainment by trained personnel with adequate observation by teachers, working in a team based on the child guidance clinic. Forty per cent of the mentally retarded pupils are not receiving the educational treatment they require. They should be taught in their own schools in small communities or form an all-age group attached to an ordinary school. The maximum size of class should be 20 pupils and the maximum size school should be 200. They should not attend schools for the physically disabled. Ineducable children, category (d), should be taught the common warnings and signs in printed word and visual symbol, and encouraged in music, crafts, dancing, etc. Day centres should be established in all areas where at least ten ineducable children can be brought together. Other recommendations concern the training of teachers and specialists, etc.

Pupils Handicapped by Speech Disorders. Rep., apps. pp. 46. 1951
1951–52 *Cmd.* 8426, x, 815
sgd. April, 1951

Speech disorders are classified as defects of articulation (dyslalia), stuttering (stammering), mutism and retarded speech, disorders of the voice and perceptual disorders of speech (aphasia, dysphasia). Of the pupils under treatment, 60 per cent suffered from dyslalia, 2·7 per cent were stutterers, 3 per cent had cleft palate speech, and 3 per cent had vocal defect. The numbers receiving treatment in May 1950 were 3803, but the estimate of the Ministry of Education of a frequency of 3 per cent speech disability amongst school children, would mean that there would be over 20,000 in Scotland needing treatment. The

causes of speech disorders may be organic, defective hearing, the child's physical and emotional condition, etc., home and school environment.

Most speech disorders arise in early childhood, and uncorrected may cause educational retardation and social maladjustment. Speech therapy should be made available as early as possible for the defective speaker, either in the school or near at hand. One speech therapist should be appointed for every 8000 of the school population and his weekly case load should not exceed 80. The difficult cases should have accommodation provided in central clinics where consultation with other specialists can be arranged. Speech training and speech therapy should be regarded as separate services. Nursery, infant and primary teachers should have sufficient skill to help the normal child to overcome minor defects. The two schools of training for speech therapists, one in Glasgow and one in Edinburgh should be placed under a board of management, including representatives of education authorities and of the hospitals and should receive grant-aid.

Pupils who are Maladjusted because of Social Handicaps. Rep., apps. pp. 87. 1952
1951–52 *Cmd.* 8428, x, 861
sgd. April, 1951

One of the most disturbing factors in childhood is the incidence of neglect and cruelty. The Royal Scottish Society for the Prevention of Cruelty to Children have brought to its notice something like 23,000 children per annum. Almost 90 per cent of the cases are neglect, 10 per cent are classified as ill-treatment and assault, abandonment, exposure, begging, singing and selling, indecent and criminal assaults, immoral surroundings and other wrongs. Many parents who fail in their duty are themselves emotionally unstable, or are mentally retarded. A child suffering from strains at home may deteriorate rapidly at school if a teacher fails to understand his background. Incidence of any form of mental or physical mal-adjustment cannot be accurately ascer-tained until a diagnostic service has been in operation on a considerable scale, meanwhile the planning of educa-tion and treatment should be based on Cyril Burt's figure of 5 per cent of pupils of school age. From 3 per cent to 5 per cent of school children need the help of the child guidance service.

Since maladjustment is the product of many social causes, prevention would require wide-scale social recon-struction. The many recommendations include: provision of more nursery schools; more child guidance services; four residential child guidance clinics for 40 pupils each; training teachers to recognise the common signs of develop-ing maladjustment; placement of child-ren deprived of family life in foster homes, small cottage homes and institu-tions according to age and other con-ditions; small institutions should have 12–15 pupils; two additional homes for maladjusted boys and one for girls; an experimental approved school for 20 to 30 boys or girls conducted on the family pattern; schools for junior retarded boys; a classifying and guid-ance centre to classify all boys com-mitted to approved schools; arrange-ments for psychiatric guidance for each girls' approved school. Pupils in approved schools should not be differen-tiated according to the condition of their committal except for sexual offences; psychopaths and certifiable pupils should be dealt with separately.

Administration of Education for Handi-capped Pupils. Rep. pp. 9. 1952

1951–52 *Cmd.* 8432, x, 949

sgd. May, 1951

The existing powers of the education authorities and of the Secretary of State are adequate to secure effective educa-tion for handicapped pupils. A proposal for a national organisation to administer the education of handicapped children was rejected because it would create a dual system and might lead to segrega-tion, but a central planning and advisory body should be established as a special committee of the Advisory Council on Education in Scotland. Arrangements should be made for the transfer of pupils to schools in England where they are not sufficient in numbers to warrant special schools. Fresh con-sideration should be given to the raising of the school age beyond 16, or some means of continuing the education of handicapped school-leavers. Grant aid should be based on the system normally applied to education.

Curriculum and Examinations in Secondary Schools

Examinations Council. Cttee. Rep., apps., index. pp. ix, 151. 1943

1943 *Non-Parl. Bd. of Education apptd. Oct.,* 1941. *sgd. June,* 1943

C. Norwood (*Ch.*), Clarke (Miss M. G.), Hastings (Miss O. M.), Hutchings, Innes, Jones, Myers, Naisbitt, Sharp, Shurrock, Thomas, Williams.

'To consider suggested changes in the Secondary School curriculum and the question of School Examinations in relation thereto.'

Part I. The term 'secondary educa-tion' refers to any type of education following primary education, and is a stage in the child's growth, in which special interests and aptitudes develop. Three rough groups can be made of children, according to whether these aptitudes will take them into (i) the learned professions and high adminis-trative posts; (ii) into applied science and art; or whether (iii) they are more interested in concrete things than in ideas. The discipline of the grammar school for some pupils, was over-weighted on the intellectual side, but the Secondary Schools have had to adapt themselves to the varied interests of the children entering them; but too much has been asked of the schools and in trying to do justice to all their pupils, they have had to compromise, so that the curriculum and methods, though suitable to some, are unsuitable to others. There should be three types of secondary education corresponding to the three broad groups of pupils: grammar, modern and technical; each type should have parity of amenities and conditions. Parity of esteem can be won only by the school itself. There should be ease of transfer from one type of school to another. At 11+ all pupils should pass to one of the three types of school, selection being based on the judgment of the primary school teachers, supplemented by intelligence, performance and other tests, consideration being given to the pupils' and parents' choice. The 'lower school' in each type should be 11+ to 13+, at which age the selection of the type of school should be reviewed. Up to 18+ all pupils should receive full-time or part-time education.

Parts II and III discuss the examinations and curricula in existing secondary schools. Part II. When secondary schools were expanding, the external School Certificate examination gave standards and a sense of direction, but is now cramping students and teachers. It should become an entirely internal examination conducted by the teachers, and for an interim period it should be a 'subject' examination, pupils taking whatever subject they wish, and a certificate granted, together with the school record. The Higher Certificate examination often leads to an unduly specialised course, it is used also for university awards, and a written examination only is not the best method of selecting university students. It should be abolished and replaced by awards based on university scholarships. For the awards of State and local education authority scholarships there should be an examination in March by university examining bodies. The State should pay the cost of State scholarships. The local authority should be able to make awards, the Exchequer paying half the cost.

Part III discusses the principles of the curriculum and the aims and methods of teaching the various subjects.

Examinations in Secondary Schools

Examinations Council. Rep. pp. 8. 1947. 2nd Rep. pp. 4. 1952

1947, 1952 Non-Parl. Min. of Education apptd. June, 1946. sgd. Aug., 1947, April, 1952

P. R. Morris (Acting Ch.), and 30 other members, Rep. J. F. Wolfenden (Ch.), and 29 other members, 2nd Rep.

'To advise on the future of examinations in secondary schools.'

Throughout all secondary schools, and other forms of education for the age groups between 11 and 18 years, the courses should consist of a variety of subjects and treatments to suit ages, abilities and aptitudes. In the latter years future careers should be considered, but the degree of specialisation should be adjusted to the individual and should not be premature or excessive. Full-time education beyond 16 should be encouraged, the conceptions of 'Sixth Form work' maintained, and the highest possible intellectual standards and discipline should be achieved. Cumulative records should be kept to assist in fitting the course of study to the aptitudes and abilities of individual students.

Every school-leaver should receive a comprehensive school report. Records of objective tests should assist in guiding pupils to suitable employment. Individual schools should have systematic internal examinations. Experiments in these examinations should be assisted by the central and local authorities. An external examination at Ordinary, Advanced and Scholarship levels should be available each year to candidates who are 16 on September 1st. All subjects should be optional, so that pupils and schools have the greatest freedom. A General Certificate of Education should be awarded at each level, and results should be available by August 1st. The new exams should be introduced in 1950. The Second Report states that a head of a school should have full discretion to enter pupil below the stated age if he certifie that the pupil has the necessary degree of competence; and that a Distinction at Advanced Level should be awarded to candidates whose performance merits it. It is hoped that candidates will offer only those subjects in which they are reasonably likely to succeed and that the number of subjects offered will be limited so that a significant proportion of every pupil's time will be concerned with work which will not be externally examined.

Art Examinations

Cttee. Rep., apps. pp. 27. 1948

1948 Non-Parl. Min. of Education apptd. March, 1947. sgd. —

F. Bray (*Ch.*), Butler, Belle, Cooper, Freeman, Hancock, Holmes, Milner, Moffett, Read, Russell, Walton, Wedgwood, Woodhead, Shelley, Dickey.

'*To examine the present system of Art Examinations for the Award of the Intermediate Certificate in Art and Crafts and the National Diploma in Design of the Ministry and to consider the possibility of replacing them by a system of internal examinations with external assessment.*'

In 1946 the Ministry of Education reorganised numerous Art examinations into two, an Intermediate, designed to provide a broad foundation, and a National Diploma of uniformly high standard. But it was still possible to take the Diploma without having first obtained the Intermediate.

The main fields of employment for art students were (*a*) painting and sculpture, (*b*) design for illustration and advertising, (*c*) design for industry, and (*d*) teaching. Students entering employments (*a*) and (*b*) often do not take the examinations, but more would do so if employers recognised these qualifications. Many of those recruited to advertising rely on evening classes; most designers and craftsmen obtain their training within industry and a few have attended junior art schools. The two main careers are therefore teaching and design in industry and commerce, but all students should have a broad basic art education up to the age of 16, and there is no need to introduce different courses in the intermediate for would-be teachers and would-be designers. All full-time Intermediate students should take a common two-year course. Passing the Intermediate should be a condition of admission to the Diploma, except for part-time students with industrial experience who have reached an acceptable standard.

Schools desiring to enter candidates should submit schemes of study for approval. Art school teachers should participate in the examination of their students; the work and marking in certain specified subjects should have national assessors and marks should be awarded in respect of work during the course. A National Committee should be established to advise the Minister.

See *Art Examinations.* National Advisory Cttee. Rep.; 1952 Non-Parl.

Provision made for Religious Instruction in the Schools in Scotland

Memo. pp. 16. 1943

1942–43 Cmd. 6426, xi, 97

Religious freedom for the managers of Scottish schools and for parents of the children attending these schools, is the principle adopted in legislation. In 1872 the School Boards were empowered to continue use and wont in providing for religious instruction. Parents have the right to withdraw children from religious instruction. This was further strengthened in 1930, when the county councils and town councils succeeded the *ad hoc* education authorities, by the requirement that religious instruction might not be discontinued until a resolution, passed by the council, had been approved by a majority of local government electors. The rights of the Church of Scotland to approve teachers, and supervise teaching disappeared when the schools were transferred to the School Boards, which however had invited ministers to inspect the religious instruction. The Church of Scotland are now wishing to appoint local ministers as honorary members of the school staffs. The Roman Catholic and Episcopal Churches, whose schools were transferred to the education authorities after 1919, have this right of approval and supervision.

The systematic training of teachers was first begun by the Church of Scotland, whose example was soon followed by the other churches. In the training centres there are Directors of Religious Instruction appointed by the Church of Scotland, but representatives of other churches are given access to students belonging to their church. There is a long-established practice whereby the Secretary of State refrains from intervening on questions of religious instruction. This is based not on any failure to appreciate its importance, but upon a desire to honour the principle of religious freedom.

Training for Citizenship

Advisory Council. Scotland.   Rep., apps. pp. 27.   1944

1943–44 *Cmd.* 6495, *iii*, 91
referred, Feb., sgd. Nov., 1943

W. H. Fyfe (*Ch.*), and 24 others.

'*To consider how the educational system of Scotland can most effectively contribute to training in the duties, rights and practice of citizenship. . . .*'

All the witnesses agreed with the importance of training for citizenship, but few of them could suggest any plan for it. The principal recommendation was that the next five years should be set apart as a period of experiment and of deliberate striving towards a theory and practice in training for citizenship. The Scottish Education Department should each year publish a report on the experiments entitled 'Scottish Book of Citizenship'. A change of emphasis in the work of schools may involve the revision or re-writing of many school books.

See *Young Citizens at School.* Rep.; 1950 Non-Parl.   Scottish Education Dept.

Visual and Aural Aids

Advisory Council. Scotland.   Rep., apps. pp. 55.   1950

1950–51 *Cmd.* 8102, *xi*, 909
referred Jan., 1947. *sgd. Aug.,* 1950

W. McClelland (*Ch.*), and 21 others.

'*To consider the use of visual and aural aids in primary and secondary schools and in further education in Scotland.*'

The advantages and potentialities of sound recording apparatus, radio and television are set out, and recommendations made on the provision of apparatus, formation of film and record collections, television experiments, etc.

The Place of Welsh and English in the Schools of Wales

Central Advisory Council. Wales. Rep. apps. pp. xii, 111.   1953 (Summary Rep., pp. vi, 69; 1953 Non-Parl.)

1953 *Non-Parl. Min. of Education*
referred — 1949. *sgd. Nov.,* 1951

R. I. Aaron (*Ch.*), and 18 others.

'*To review the place of Welsh and English in the Schools of Wales and problem of bilingualism in Wales generally.*'

The distinct culture of Wales was closely and ultimately bound up with the language.   Welsh and English should be taught in the schools, due regard being paid to the abilities and aptitudes of the pupils and to the varied linguistic patterns in which they live. Out of the total numbers of pupils between 5–15, 21 per cent spoke Welsh either as the mother tongue or could understand simple lessons or conduct elementary conversations in it as a second language, 70 per cent spoke Welsh first where both parents spoke Welsh, 6 per cent where the father alone spoke Welsh and 10·5 per cent where the mother alone spoke Welsh. The proportion of children with both parents Welsh-speaking who spoke Welsh fell from 75·5 per cent at age 5 to 67·7 at age 10. A child growing beyond the influence of the home and the anglicising process is more rapid in already anglicised areas. For Wales as a whole only 4 per cent of English-speaking children become thoroughly bilingual at age 11, but in anglicised areas such as Glamorgan, only 3 per cent have an active control of Welsh as a second language and 4 per cent a comfortable understanding of it. Four kinds of language policy were in operation. First, teaching is determined by the linguistic character of the area; secondly, only those children who express a desire to be taught Welsh are provided for; thirdly, provision is made for teaching Welsh to all pupils, except those who say they do not wish to be taught the language, and fourthly the provision for teaching English and Welsh as equal and parallel activities.

The problem of bilingualism is not to teach two languages in the void and much depends on how much the two languages are spoken in the homes, and in the influential institutions such as the chapel or church, youth clubs, newspapers, etc., the age at which a child is brought into contact with the second language, etc. Opinions differ over the possible effects of bilingualism upon the intellectual and emotional development of the child. Some contend that in vocabulary a bilingual child is seldom advanced by age six in either of the two languages to be as ready for school instruction as the average monolingual child, others argue that any vocabulary handicap does not function after the age of 12. But the cultural significance of the bilingual problem is important because the Welsh tradition is preponderantly literary and linguistic, and the preservation of the language is the most effective means of maintaining cultural integrity and 'rootedness'.

Welsh and English should be taught in all the schools of Wales including Monmouthshire, according to the children's ability to profit from the instruction; there should be a sufficient number of Welsh speaking teachers trained in bilingual education; and an all-Welsh training college. Some local authorities set aside a fairly large sum to be spent on buying Welsh books: difficulties of shortages would disappear if other authorities did the same.

The Council is not satisfied that the universities are sufficiently progressive towards the use of Welsh in teaching, and welcomes the enquiry into the possibility of a Welsh University College.

Welsh Language Publishing

Cttee. Rep., apps. pp. 30. 1952
1951–52 *Cmd.* 8661, *xviii*, 1095
apptd. Oct., 1951. *sgd. June*, 1952

A. W. Ready (*Ch.*), Roberts.

'To examine the present arrangements for the publication of books, magazines and periodicals in the Welsh language and to report as to any measures which are desirable and practicable to meet the needs of Welsh schools and colleges and the Welsh-speaking population of Wales.'

The occasion for setting up the present Committee was a memorandum submitted in June 1951 to the Council for Wales and Monmouthshire by the Welsh Publishers' and Booksellers' Union, and forwarded by it to the then Home Secretary. Of the major Welsh publishers, only one, the University Press Board, is not also a printer. None could live on publishing alone. The average size of a Welsh edition is about 2500 and its average sale about 1200 copies in two years: there is rarely a second and never a third edition. The effect on retail prices per copy of a junior reader of 30,000 words is shown from estimates from an English printer: edition of 1000 copies 2s. 11d.; 3000 copies 1s. 5d.; 5000 copies 1s. 2d. If the Welsh publisher could double his sales he could halve his costs. The cultural situation causes deep concern, 'a bookless people is a rootless people'. During 1951, about 13,000 new titles were published in Great Britain in English; in Welsh, only about 50, and the position regarding periodicals is the same. The Welsh local education authorities spent £126,475 on books for schools, only a small proportion of which was spent on Welsh books.

The main recommendation was that

a Welsh book foundation should be set up to supply books to schools at ordinary trade terms. The income for the first five years should be £40,000 a year, derived from local authorities (rates), up to £16,000, government grant, and Welsh tithe money. Each authority would spend up to its contribution plus the corresponding grant.

The Arts in Education

Central Advisory Council. Wales. Reps. 1953, 1954, 1956 *Non-Parl.   Min. of Education*

A. Oldfield-Davies (*Ch.*).

Music in the Schools of Wales, apps. pp. viii, 53. 1953. *Drama in the Schools of Wales*, apps. pp. vii, 89. 1956. *Arts and Crafts in the Schools of Wales*, apps. pp. vii, 89, 1956

The Reports discuss the educational value of music, drama and the arts and crafts, and reviews experiments and progress made, the standards of achievements possible at each stage, training and supply of teachers, etc. App. III to that on Arts and Crafts gives an account of the characteristic changes in the drawing and painting of the child as he grows up.

2. (b) PARTICULAR VOCATIONS

Post-War Agricultural Education in England and Wales

Cttee. Rep., app. pp. 92. 1943

1942–43 *Cmd.* 6433, *iv*, 1
apptd. July, 1941. *sgd. Jan.*, 1943

F. Luxmoore (*Ch.*), Beaumont, Cumber, Evans, Goodenough, Loveday, McClean, Youard (Mrs. R. J.).

'*To examine the present system of Agricultural Education in England and Wales, and to make recommendations for improving and developing it after the war.*'

The teaching of science in modern and secondary schools as a cultural background and as the basis of subsequent agricultural education and the training of teachers to give instruction related to the life and work of the countryside both need improvement. Many students entering farm institutes have a low standard of general education. The agricultural colleges have no uniformity of aim or method, some competing with farm institutes, others with university agricultural departments. Students in university departments do not get enough practical experience. There is a lack of co-ordination between provincial and county advisory services, and in the arrangements for instruction classes, demonstrations, etc. The main defects arise from the absence of any one authority having the duty of providing agricultural education, the number of authorities, the lack of co-ordination, and the diversity of sources of finance.

The school age should be raised to 15 as soon as possible, educational re-organisation completed, and part-time continued education for one day a week till the age of 18 made compulsory. A statutory National Council for Agricultural Education should be given the duty of providing a comprehensive system of agricultural education, should take over existing and create new farm institutes; it should provide a national advisory service, which should be organised into six provinces, the counties, each with its organiser, being units. The grants to university departments of agriculture and agricultural colleges should be adequate to ensure stability. The capital and annual expenditure required should be met by the Government.

In a minority report Mrs. Youard objects to the separation of agricultural from other forms of technical education provided by the local authorities and the segregation to which it will lead. The local education authorities and Board of Education should be responsible for all education, including agricultural education. The true distinction is between the giving of advice to the entrepreneur and giving instruction to all those engaged in the industry. For the former a statutory National Advisory Council for Agriculture should be established to be responsible for the National advisory service.

See *Agriculture (Miscellaneous Provisions) Act, 1944;* 7 & 8 Geo. 6. c. 28.

Provision in Secondary Schools of Courses Preparatory to Agricultural Employment

Jt. Advisory Cttee. Rep. pp. 13. 1945
1945 *Non-Parl. Min. of Agric. & Fish., Min. of Education*
apptd. July, 1944. sgd. —

T. Loveday (*Ch.*), and 10 others.

'To *advise on all aspects of agricultural education to be provided by local education authorities and particularly on the educational policy and methods of training to be adopted at farm institutes.*'

Agriculture and its allied industries should get a fair share of the abler secondary school pupils, but the grammar school with its tradition of training for the professions often tends to draw them away from the land. Up to a point the need would be met by a rural bias in country secondary schools. Whilst condemning vocational training before the age of 15, the Committee thought a more advanced course of training, similar in character to, but differing in scope from the more academic education, could be provided as an alternative for the abler boys and girls of a practical bent who aspire to more responsible posts than that of an ordinary farm worker. The course should be planned as a coherent whole—half should be in subjects of the more general cultural value only slightly coloured by vocational aim, and half by such subjects as mathematics, science and practical work, in which the selection of material for study is largely governed by vocational aim. A course essentially similar to that for boys would be suitable for girls. The Committee reviews the advantages and disadvantages of agricultural technical schools, junior rural polytechnics, the addition of agricultural sides to rural grammar schools, urban technical schools, pre-agricultural courses for the 'A' stream in rural modern schools.

Higher Agricultural Education in England and Wales

Cttee. Rep., apps. pp. 86. 1946
1945–46 *Cmd.* 6728, x, 49
apptd. July, 1944. sgd. Dec., 1945
T. Loveday (*Ch.*), Beloe, Brown (D. G.), Brown (G. A.), Crowther, Engledow, Jones, Neame, Salisbury, Sutherland, Tomkinson (Miss D. S.), Troup, Turner.

'To *consider the character and extent of the need for higher agricultural education in England and Wales and to make recommendations as to the facilities which should be provided to meet the need.*'

As the distinctive function of higher agricultural education is to train persons capable of advancing either the theory or practice of agriculture and of providing the industry with leadership, it should give greater attention to general intellectual development and the understanding of fundamental principles than to purely technical efficiency. The range of occupations to be provided for include practical farmers, those concerned with estate management, scientific, agricultural and horticultural advisers, researchers, economists, engineers and the commercial group. The requirements for these occupations and the various degree and other courses are reviewed and their deficiences noted. The degree courses should be raised in standard, planned in accordance with the principles specified, and the instruction in science and husbandry combined into a coherent whole. The courses in estate management give undue attention to surveying, exemption from professional examinations, etc. In horticulture the grower has no confidence in the graduates performing the simplest tasks, the courses having failed to turn out men well-grounded in principles or skilled in practice. The main need is for highly skilled growers and managers. The provision for agricultural economists is deficient; in America every important university has a Professor of Agricultural Economics, while in England there are only two. Two-year courses in agriculture, horticulture and estate management should be provided for potential farmers, etc., who wish for something more than the farm institutes provide, but do not go to the university. Agricultural engineers should start with a degree course in engineering, farm mechanisation experts with a degree course in agriculture.

In addition to first degree courses, 18 different graduate courses for graduates in science, engineering, economics, agriculture and horticulture are needed. The average numbers required to complete these courses in any year were: degree courses in agriculture and horticulture, 359; in the 18 graduate courses, 163. Taking the length of course into account, this would require some 1250 university places, of which 960 exist in the university departments, and the rest can be supplied by the three agricultural colleges in process of acquiring university status. The two-year courses should be provided by the independent colleges, other colleges, and by farm institutes. The various national diplomas except that in horticulture, which is defective, have outlived their usefulness. Grants to universities should rise to £150,000, and a capital expenditure of not more than £500,000 is needed.

Agricultural Education in Scotland

Cttee. Rep., apps. pp. 42. 1945

1945–46 Cmd. 6704, x, 135
apptd. Feb., 1944. sgd. Dec., 1945

Lord Alness (Ch.), Allardyce, Ballantine (Miss H. S. D.), Cameron, Duncan, L. Forbes, Howie, McCallum, Mackie.

'To enquire into the organisation, staffing, curricula and external services of Agricultural Colleges in Scotland, and the relationship of the Colleges to the Universities and to the Research Institutes, and to make recommendations.'

There are Colleges of Agriculture in Aberdeen, Edinburgh and Glasgow; the neighbouring universities give degrees in Agriculture, but delegate to the Colleges certain teaching in degree courses. A conference between representatives of the institutions agreed in principle that universities should be solely responsible for degree work, which should be designed for research workers, advisory officers and county organisers, while the Colleges should provide diploma and shorter, more practical courses for farmers and farm workers.

The total number of degree students at the three universities before the war was 80, and even a 50 per cent increase would mean a total annual output not exceeding 40. As the small size of the University departments and division of financial resources means that all three are inadequately equipped and staffed, the teaching of degree students should be concentrated in one university. The regional system based on the three colleges should not be disturbed; the county organisers and specialist advisory officers should continue to be attached to and directed from them. Recommendations are made on the colleges' governing bodies, buildings, curriculum, staffing and collaboration with research institutes, and on a common standard national diploma. Three new farm institutes should be set up under the control of the respective Colleges. The Scottish Agricultural Advisory Council should advise on the financial requirements of the colleges.

Alness, Forbes and McCallum strongly dissented from the proposal to centralise university agricultural education. Duncan argued that since the total number of college diploma students would not exceed 215 a year, the arguments in favour of centralisation applied also to the colleges.

See *The General Organisation and Finance of Agricultural Education and Research in Scotland*. Dept. Cttee. (Lord Constable, *Ch.*), Rep. pp. 54; 1924 Non-Parl. Dept. of Agric., Scot.

Agricultural and Horticultural Institutes

Interim Rep., apps. pp. vi, 50. 1947

1947 *Non-Parl. Min. of Agric. & Fish., Min. of Education*
sgd. Nov., 1946

T. Loveday (*Ch.*), and 11 others.

With the impact of science on agriculture and horticulture the argument that experience on a well-managed holding is sufficient preparatory training for responsible work has lost its validity. These institutes, which are essentially residential and located on farms of 250–300 acres, provide full-time one-year (some two-year) courses of instruction designed to meet the requirements of the first stages of a practical career for those students aiming at work of special responsibility. They also provide shorter courses for older people.

The entry qualification is one year's practical experience, or its equivalent, for students of 18 years of age. The success or failure of teaching hinges on synchronising the whole of theoretical with the practical work of the farm so that all students learn the manual efficiency of the skilled operative and the technical efficiency of the competent farmer or grower.

Almost every county should aim at a separate institute with a minimum annual intake of 40 students. There are 18 institutes in England and Wales and 7 centres will ultimately become available.

Calculated on the basis of 10 per cent of the annual intake of 24,000 persons into the industry, there would be 2400 students, but staffing difficulties make it impossible to establish more than an additional 16, or at most 17 institutes in the interim period. The student capacity of the agricultural institutes should be 40–80, of horticultural institutes 40–100. The Report shows existing and proposed geographical distribution of the institutes, etc., and recommends the courses to be provided, and an entry age of 18.

Provision of Part-Time Instruction by Local Education Authorities for Agriculturists, Horticulturists and Domestic Producers

Interim Rep., apps. pp. vi, 54. 1949

1949 *Non-Parl. Min. of Agric. & Fish., Min. of Education*
sgd. March, 1949

T. Loveday (*Ch.*), and 15 others.

The Government's agricultural expansion programme aims at increasing agricultural net output by 50 per cent above the pre-war figure and 15 per cent above the war-time peak. There is a certain amount of discussion and instruction through voluntary bodies such as Young Farmers' Clubs, the National Allotments and Gardens Society, etc., but systematic part-time instruction is provided by the local education authorities. The present problem is to provide instruction (1) in the more specialised traditional skills, such as thatching, hedging, spraying, etc., and in the new skills relating to farm machinery, silage making, etc.; (2) in general principles; (3) in the specialised branches, and (4) for adults. In relation to the expansion programme the priorities are instruction in the practical skills, including the use and care of farm machinery and specialised courses in livestock production. Local education authorities should review their programmes accordingly and suggestions are made as to the types of courses. Certificates of proficiency should be awarded to apprentices. All counties should have an organiser of part-time instruction, together with a minimum of the equivalent of three full-time teachers: for such teachers there should be a uniform scale in all counties. Institutes should aim at a generous complement of junior posts.

Agricultural Education

Working Party. Rep., apps. pp. 19. 1953

1954 *Non-Parl. Min. of Agric. & Fish.*
apptd. Nov., 1952. sgd. Oct., 1953

Lord Carrington (*Ch.*), Bray, Browne, Gibson, Loveday, Oxspring, Roberts, Rollinson, Simmons, Wakeman, Watson, Wilcox.

'*To review the relations between the agricultural education service of Local Authorities and the National Agricultural Advisory Service, and to make proposals for their more effective co-operation; to examine the need for an inspectorate of agricultural education; and to consider the future of the Joint Advisory Committee on Agricultural Education.*'

After its establishment in 1946, the staff of the National Agricultural Advisory Service grew to 1500 by 1951; the total teaching and organising staff of the local education authorities is between 400 and 500. Circular 3/123, which demarcates the responsibilities of the two bodies and asks for co-operation between them, does not place upon any one organisation or person in each area the responsibility for making friendly approaches, with the result that co-operation has depended on the personalities of those concerned. As the tasks of the two services are interlocked, much is to be gained from team-work. The chief officers of the two services should have regular meetings twice a year, the arrangements for which should be reported to the Ministries. Other suggestions for co-operation include the giving of lectures by advisory officers, common meetings of the two staffs, etc. The work grant-aided by the Ministry of Agriculture needs supervision by field officers: suitably qualified inspectors should be members of the Ministry of Education Inspectorate. The Joint Advisory Committee in its present form should lapse, but should be reconstituted for specific purposes.

Technical Education

Advisory Council. Scotland. Special Cttee. Interim Rep., app. pp. 13. 1945
1944–45 *Cmd.* 6593, *v*, 563
apptd. *Nov.*, 1943. sgd. *Oct.*, 1944

J. C. Smail (*Ch.*), Fyfe, Wilson, Ayre, Ball, Douglas, Erskine, Hampton, Howie, Kelly (Annette G.), McGee, Mair, Munro, Penman, Walton.

'*Having regard to the prospective requirements of Trade and Industry and to the provision made for technical education in the Universities, to enquire into the provision, administration and finance of technical education outwith the Universities.*'

The three existing main groups of institutions are: the central institutions, the technical schools and the continuation classes, but the lines of demarcation between them are by no means clear. There should be national planning for technical education: central institutions should serve a region or in some cases the whole country and should provide day and evening courses of an advanced type; technical colleges serving local requirements should provide day and evening courses of a less-advanced type, colleges for compulsory further education for young persons should include technical education in their curriculum. Where the establishment of a technical college is impracticable, voluntary day and evening classes should include courses in technical subjects. There should be a National Advisory Council for Technical Education to survey national requirements and to make recommendations on the capital needs of central institutions, and four or five regional councils.

See *Education (Scotland) Act, 1945;* 8 & 9 Geo. 6. c. 37.

—— Report, apps. pp. vi, 118. 1946
1945–46 *Cmd.* 6786, *xi*, 515
sgd. *April*, 1946

del. Erskine, McGee.

The report reviews the technical education required by various trades and industries and makes a number of recommendations in each case, e.g. a system of national certificates in agriculture, a special technical college for aeronautics near Prestwick, courses of training for foremen, courses in preparation for workshop management, and a staff college for Scottish industry as a department in one of the central institutions. Steps should be taken to control the multiplication of examinations by professional bodies. For craftsmen there should be courses with a national hall-mark as alternatives to the National Certificate, entry to which should be restricted to students with the Junior Leaving Certificate. There should be State bursaries enabling evening class students to proceed to centres for more advanced training, five regional advisory councils for technical education, a higher technical college established at Inverness, with local technical colleges at such places as Stornoway, Wick, Oban, Fort William, and mobile workshops and classrooms with itinerant teachers for short courses at local centres. Selected institutions should conduct as one of their activities a national school for work of the highest grade in a particular branch of technology.

See *Technical Education in Scotland;* 1953 Non-Parl. Scottish Education Dept.

Higher Technological Education

Special Cttee. Rep., app. pp. 31. 1945
1945 Non-Parl. Min. of Education apptd. April, 1944. sgd. July, 1945

Lord Percy (*Ch.*), Anderson, Bragg, Chance, Darwin, Evans, Jones, Laws, Lowery, Magnay, Nelson, Rees, Southwell, Wright.

'*Having regard to the requirements of Industry, to consider the needs of higher technological education in England and Wales and the respective contributions to be made thereto by Universities and Technical Colleges; and to make recommendations, among other things, as to the means for maintaining appropriate collaboration between Universities and Technical Colleges in this field.*'

The failure to secure the fullest possible application of science to industry is partly due to deficiencies in education. The annual intake from the universities is insufficient in quantity and quality, particularly of scientists and technologists who can administer and apply the results of research to development. The supply of engineer scientists and development engineers should come from the universities, of engineer managers from both universities and technical colleges. The total annual output required was 3000 mechanical, electrical and civil engineers (2700 in England and Wales); of which 45 per cent would come from the universities and 55 per cent from technical colleges. Though susceptible of improvement, the output from the universities and technical colleges is reasonably satisfactory, but industry needs another class of entrant, with a training comparable in standard with university degree courses, but planned on different lines. About a third, 500, of the engineers from the technical colleges need this more advanced course, approximating in total length to that of the university degree course, but with planned courses of works practice. To meet this need six colleges outside London should be selected; they should be partly residential, should conduct their own examinations, receive Exchequer grants, and staff salaries should be comparable with those of universities. There should be eight regional advisory councils, with academic boards, representative of universities, the college of technology and technical colleges, with a central National Council of Technology. Transference from the colleges to the university should be made possible, especially at the postgraduate stage. Opinion on the Committee was divided on whether the qualification to be awarded by the selected colleges should be a B.Tech. corresponding to a university first degree, or a diploma which would soon win national reputation, while the Chairman proposed associateships and fellowships of the new 'Royal Colleges of Technology'. They should award research qualifications. All students of technology should be introduced to management studies, and there should be one selected centre for post-graduate study of industrial administration.

Future Development of Higher Technological Education

National Advisory Council. Rep., apps. pp. 28. 1950

1950 *Non-Parl. Min. of Education referred* —. *sgd. Oct.*, 1950

R. M. Weeks (*Ch.*), and 72 others.

'*How best higher technological education should be developed in this country, with particular reference to the technical colleges.*'

'Advanced' technological education means instruction which at a minimum is of a standard comparable with a university first degree or that accepted by the major professional institutions for corporate membership. The universities and the technical colleges provide not identical, but complementary technological education. The University Grants Committee stated that the work of the universities should be much more closely related to fundamental science than that of the technical colleges, and that their courses should contain a smaller amount of training related to immediate or special work in industry. A technological university is not an alternative to developing advanced work in technical colleges, since the latter have a unique tradition in meeting the educational needs of the worker in industry and already undertake work of a university degree standard and beyond. Advanced courses are required at first award and post-graduate level, conducted in an atmosphere of experiment and freedom, but with conditions of entry and of a length comparable to those of universities. A suitable award is needed, but an extension of the London external degree system is rejected because this is limited to a few technologies and does not give the colleges flexibility.

New courses of advanced technology should be developed in technical colleges in close association with industry and with the co-operation of the regional academic boards; increased financial aid should be considered; a royal college of technologists should be established to concern itself with the educational problems of technology, approving courses and awards, and for improving the general conditions for the conduct of examinations, and external examiners appointed. The title of the awards to be made should be Associate-ship for the first award, membership for the second award, and fellowships and honorary fellowships for those who further distinguish themselves in the field of technological education and research.

See *A Note on Technology in Universities*; 1950 Non-Parl. Treasury.

Higher Technological Education

Statement. pp. 4. 1951

1950–51 *Cmd. 8357, xxvii*, 173

The University Grants Committee have provided funds for increasing staffs, new buildings and equipment and post-graduate study in particular fields, for example, civil, mechanical, electrical, chemical engineering and metallurgy, mining and textiles. Proposals to create a new technological university for 2000 to 3000 students at the cost of £6 mn. was thought not to be in the national interest whilst the expansion of existing institutions is taking place. The Government accept the view that more educational provision, under which higher technological education similar in age-range, length and standard, and serving the same professions, should be provided both in universities and a number of selected technical colleges. A college of technologists with the responsibility for granting awards of associate-ships, etc., approval of courses, will be set up.

Training for Business Administration

Cttee. Rep., apps. pp. 15. 1945

1945–46 *Cmd. 6673, x*, 261

apptd. Feb., sgd. June, 1945

F. Newson-Smith(*Ch.*), Anson, Beevers, Carruthers, Hann, Hooper, MacEwen

(Mrs. M.), McLean, Mathias, Palmer, Parker, Piper, Ramsbotton, Schuster, Southwell, Tennyson, Tewson, Thomas.

'To consider how far the absorption into industry and commerce of young men and women released from war service who desire to begin or resume a business career would be facilitated by the provision of training in business administration and salesmanship. . . .'

The main problem concerns those who went into the Services either straight from school or college or after only a short period as learners in industry, etc., who will be returning to civil life at ages between 20–30, with no or too short business experience to give them a right to reinstatement, whose educational standards and character are such as to qualify them for employment which will lead to administrative and executive posts, and who desire immediate employment. From their employer's point of view it involves placing men well over 20 in occupations where recruitment normally takes place well under 20.

A basic training, general in character and lasting approximately three months, should be provided. The Report outlines a suggested syllabus. Provisional acceptance by an employer is desirable. Training should be given in technical and commercial colleges and financial assistance should be available. Employees should assist where special training is needed. An individual of proved capacity should be appointed by the Minister of Labour to direct planning, etc., and to work with an inter-departmental committee of representatives of the Ministers of Labour and Education, and the Service Departments.

National Advisory Council on Education for Industry and Commerce

Working Party. Rep., app. pp. 8. 1947
1947 *Non-Parl. Min. of Education apptd. Sept., sgd. Dec.,* 1947

D. R. Hardman (*Ch.*), Tennyson, Gallie, Schofield, Holbein, Wheeler, Trueman, Lawe, Owen, Magnay, Myers, Hirst, Bray, Shelley.

'To advise on the question of setting up a National Council of Technology and on the principal steps necessary to that end.'

The ten regional councils and boards recommended in the Percy Report had been set up. The Percy Committee was concerned with advanced technology, but a national body, to be called the National Council on Education for Industry and Commerce, is required to advise the Minister on all questions bearing on education for industry and commerce, including training for the professions, management and design in relation to industry and commerce.

Education for Management.
Management Subjects in Technical and Commercial Colleges

Special Cttee. Rep., apps. pp. 32. 1947
1947 *Non-Parl. Min. of Education apptd. Oct.,* 1945. *sgd. Aug.,* 1946

L. Urwick (*Ch.*), Berger, Farr, Jones, Montgomrey, Northcott, Perkins.

'To advise the Minister of Education on educational facilities required for management in industry and commerce . . . bearing in mind requirements of professional organisations and the need for their co-ordination.'

Before 1939 some technical and commercial colleges were finding difficulty in providing classes to cover the varying requirements of professional bodies for the instruction of their students in management subjects, and by 1945 they could not make the necessary provision. Adequate instruction could be given if the professional bodies accepted a syllabus covering a large area of common management content and confining the specialised fields to the essential minimum. Courses leading to qualifications should be limited to intermediate and final. The intermediate course should consist of three parts: introduction to management, 'background' subjects and 'tool' subjects. There should be two types of final course, one for those who wish to qualify in some specialised field and one for those who wish to qualify in general management. An advisory council on education for management should be associated with the proposed institute of management. A commission of enquiry should be sent to the United States of America to investigate and report on the facilities for education in management in that country as compared with those provided in Great Britain.

Education for Commerce

Special Cttee. Rep., apps. pp. vi, 80.
1949
*1949 Non-Parl. Min. of Education
apptd. June, 1946. sgd. —*

A. M. Carr-Saunders (*Ch.*), Anderson (Dr. Kitty), Austin, Crick, Deakin (Miss P.), De Paula, Geddes, Godwin (Miss B. A.), Hirst, Jones (B. M.), Jones (J. C.), Plant, Raynes, Rees, Smith, Terry.

'*To consider the provision which should be made for education for commerce and for the professions relating to it, and the respective contributions to be made thereto by universities and by colleges and departments of commerce in England and Wales.*'

Education for commerce is regarded as embracing educational facilities for those preparing for, or engaged in business occupations of every kind, professional or otherwise, from office routine, such as shorthand and typewriting, to positions of high responsibility.

To meet all requirements there should be educational facilities for three distinct groups (*a*) persons engaged in minor routine operations and who usually enter employment at 15 or 16; (*b*) persons, also recruited at an early age, who aspire to more responsible positions, and (*c*) those whose ultimate requirements are for professional training or advanced education in special techniques and processes.

A fully satisfactory pre-employment secondary commercial education can be devised and an examination should be provided through the medium of the General Certificate of Education. Professional associations should be invited to consider including only general commercial subjects at the intermediate stage, and to advise recruits to the professions under the age of 18 to take national certificate courses. Courses for the professional examinations should be extensively developed in technical colleges. A higher national certificate should provide a series of schemes of vocational education and specialised vocational training, and professional bodies should be invited to consider the extent to which exemptions could be granted to holders of these certificates. Technical colleges should provide both vocational education and vocational training, but ultimately should not include courses for university degrees. Courses for a new qualification of first degree standard having national recognition, occupying not less than three years, and normally full-time on the sandwich basis, should be set up in selected technical colleges. The National Advisory Council on Education for Industry and Commerce should advise on administration, etc. Education for management should be provided in the major technical colleges.

Miss Godwin and Dr. Anderson wished to see shorthand and typewriting included in the final year of the school curriculum. Professor Plant and Professor Smith discussed the danger of pushing the distinction between education and training too far as 'all training may be education, and much education can be training'.

Cadet Entry into the Royal Navy

Cttee. Rep., apps. pp. viii, 114. [1953]
*1952–53 Cmd. 8845, xvi, 1
apptd. July, 1952. sgd. April, 1953*

E. E. S. Montagu (*Ch.*).

'*To review the scope of the present methods of officer recruitment in the*

Executive, Engineering and Supply branches and . . . whether some alternative methods of entry should be introduced. . . .'

Since 1948 there have been two main methods of training as officers: entry to the Naval College at Dartmouth at 16 and Special Entry at 18. The aim has been to obtain roughly equal numbers from each source. There is also Direct Entry at 18 from the Nautical College at Pangbourne and from the training ships Worcester and Conway, and by selection from artificer apprentices. These methods had not produced the required numbers and the general standard of candidates for both the main entries had been disappointing.

The educational witnesses regarded 18 as the ideal age for entry, since the boy had completed his normal school life and both boys and headmasters are clearer about the correctness of the choice of profession. But only 5000 leave grant-aided grammar schools at 17 and 3000 at 18, and there were competing opportunities, such as entry to the university, other professions and business. Entry at 16 was not well regarded by educationalists, on the ground that if boys were to spend two further years at school, this should not be interrupted by transfer at that age, and because it was difficult to be certain of a boy's potentialities as an officer at that age. But the arrangements could be improved and for many boys two years at Dartmouth would be a valuable asset.

The present special examinations caused difficulties to boys and to schools, and exemptions from the written examinations should be given on the basis of passes in the G.C.E. As an order of merit was required for selection, the Civil Service Commission should be asked to correlate marks and group candidates into categories of merit.

The interview procedure had been criticised as resulting in an undue pro-portion of boys from independent schools and too few from grant-aided grammar schools being selected, though this was partly because few of the grammar schools had any tradition of sending boys into the service and the boys did not know the opportunities. Educationalists who had watched the interviews agreed that they were fair and that there was no bias. There were difficulties in selecting boys from widely different backgrounds. Headmasters should continue to serve on the boards, and should be from grant-aided grammar schools. All boys should be tested by a qualified psychologist.

Direct entry should be discontinued, but a place reserved for one candidate each from Pangbourne, the Worcester and the Conway. A detriment to applications for the engineering branch was the early retirement of the naval officer as compared with posts in industry. Recruitment from the secondary technical school at 16 and from technical colleges at 18 from boys taking the national certificate course should be encouraged.

Six members held that even with the suggested improvements these sources would not provide the required number and they proposed a new entry to Dartmouth at 13, liberal financial arrangements as in grant-aided boarding schools, and an examination adapted to grammar school boys, for whom 65 per cent of the places should be reserved. But these and boys entering at 16 should not be committed to a naval career; commitment should be postponed till Special Entry age. The Headmaster at Dartmouth should be in direct charge of the school, which should also have civilian housemasters as well as naval officers.

Barraclough thought that the new early entry scheme would not produce the additional officers required, that the improved arrangements would do so, and that the Admiralty should aim at making the minimum age of entry 18.

3. TEACHERS, YOUTH LEADERS: SUPPLY, TRAINING, SALARIES

Teachers. Supply, Recruitment and Training in the Period immediately following the War

Advisory Council. Scotland.   Reps., apps. pp. 56. 1944

1943–44 *Cmd. 6501, iv, 555*
referred Feb., sgd. Nov., 1943

W. H. Fyfe (*Ch.*), and 24 others.

'*To consider whether the existing arrangements for the recruitment and supply of teachers in Scotland are adequate, and to make recommendations.*'

I. After the war teachers will be needed to fill vacancies due to undersupply and casualties, to cope with the rising school population, and to provide for developments such as raising the leaving age, compulsory continuation classes, reduction in size of classes, new types of secondary schools, etc. The maximum deficit of teachers, which would have to be made good by exceptional means, would be 4090, and this would occur if the school leaving age were raised to 15 in the post-war years and if compulsory day continuation classes were instituted in the second year and brought into full operation in the fourth year. On the other hand, the deficit would be at its minimum of 1220, if the developments were not introduced until the seventh and eighth years respectively. This was assuming that some 2500 married women and retired teachers would be employed.

II. Recruitment and training. The attractiveness of the profession should be increased by better salaries and conditions of service, by the creation of more posts of responsibility, and development of research. Normal training arrangements should be improved by better staffs in the training institutions, more liberal bursaries, etc. To get recruits from new sources— mainly ex-service men and women—it will be necessary to break with accepted practice. The flexible conditions of entry, selection, length of course necessary are set out in detail.

Training of Teachers

Advisory Council. Scotland.   Rep., apps. pp. 97. 1946

1945–46 *Cmd. 6723, xi,* 417
referred Nov., 1943. *sgd. Dec.,* 1945

W. H. Fyfe (*Ch.*), and 21 others.

'*To enquire into the provision made for the training of teachers in Scotland . . . and the administration and finance of the said services. . . .*'

The emphasis in the training of teachers was first upon classroom techniques and practical skills, then upon the increasing importance of general education. The new setting is one of changing educational values. Experimental or venture schools of a pioneer type, such as Bedales and Dartington Hall, embodying new ideals and employing new methods have furnished suggestions which are being adopted in greater or lesser degree in the State schools. Emphasis should be on the individual child, on his interests, needs and rate of progress. The new teacher requires a complete recasting of educational ideas, and will also have to be trained in the new techniques relating to the training of the mind, the scientific testing of intelligence, school attainment, methods of teaching various subjects, etc. The special professional preparation, as distinct from academic studies, required by the modern primary teacher of general subjects cannot be adequately covered in less than two years' full-time study. The Committee preferred professional training to be taken concurrently with the course for general education, decided that graduation should not be required of all teachers and rejected proposals for a degree in education.

Courses are suggested for women teachers of general subjects in primary schools, for teachers of younger classes in secondary schools, for specialist teachers, teachers of handicapped children, teachers in junior colleges, etc.

Amongst many recommendations are: instruction of the younger classes in secondary schools should be largely in the hands of teachers able to teach three subjects; with the exception of mature men entering from other walks of life, men teaching younger classes in secondary schools should have a five years' course, including the degree. Courses in preparation for work with younger classes in secondary schools should include a study of the problems of adolescence. There should be improvements in the salaries and conditions of service for teachers of handicapped children, who should not normally be admitted for this training until they are 40; classes in the study of religion should be provided for those who wish to attend them.

Special courses should be planned for persons entering from other walks of life. Experiments in the use of intelligence tests to be applied to candidates for training should be considered.

Institutes of Education should be established at each of the four universities to serve as a focal point for teachers and the educational activities of the area and as a centre of research and higher study. Each should have two constituent colleges. The Institutes should be managed by a council representative of the universities, educational authorities, constituent colleges. There should be a Scottish Council of Institutes to manage the finances, control the supply of teachers, etc. The opportunity afforded by the changes should be taken to reconsider the finance of teachers' training.

Teachers and Youth Leaders

Cttee. Rep., apps. pp. 176. 1944

1944 *Non-Parl. Bd. of Education apptd. March,* 1942. *sgd. April,* 1944

A. D. McNair (*Ch.*), Clarke, Fleming, Hichens (Mrs. H.), Mander, Morris, Ross (Miss A. H.), Stocks (Mrs. M.), Thomas, Wood.

'*To investigate the present sources of supply and the methods of recruitment and training of teachers and youth leaders and to report what principles should guide the Board in these matters in the future.*'

I. Primary and secondary schools. The annual wastage in 1938 was 6 per cent or 12,000, but output from the colleges and training departments 7000–8000. The difference was made up partly by the use of untrained teachers in all types of school and alleviated by the fall in the child population. Though the Board fixed the quota of students in training colleges and departments each year, it could not relate this strictly to demand, as it did not know how many untrained teachers would be appointed, or the output of training colleges not recognised. An enlarged staff of 250,000 would require an annual recruitment of 15,000, but the numbers of boys and girls between 17 and 18 is 21,000, from which other professions and callings, e.g. engineers, architects, lawyers, etc., also draw their recruits. The field of recruitment must be widened. Maintenance allowances should be paid to encourage early leavers to stay on at school, and to men and women of mature years who wish to train. Teachers should not have to resign on marriage, deterrent conditions of service should be altered, e.g. the 'Pledge' abolished, the undue limitations on the participation of teachers in public affairs relaxed. On the test of personal need for an appropriate standard, the market test of securing the right numbers, the professional test of not giving rise to anomalies, and the educational test of not adversely affecting any type of school or area, basic salaries should be raised substantially, and special responsibility allowances should be substantial and more widely distributed. There should be a central training council to advise on the form of the area training services, on which the Committee was divided. Five members wanted university schools of education, consisting of an organic federation of approved training institutions, to be responsible for the training and assessment of all students in training. Five members wanted re-constituted joint boards in which university departments and the colleges would preserve their identity, a common professional examination, etc. In either form the area training authority would be responsible for curricula, etc., and final assessment. The normal period of training should be three years, or one year for graduates.

The present rate of replacement for training college staff of 30–40 will have to be greatly increased. Many of the colleges are too small to provide the necessary variety of courses, they are badly distributed geographically and need a substantial amount of building. Salaries should be on a higher level than in schools and should approximate to university salaries.

II. The Youth Service. The contribution of the voluntary worker is fundamental, but a fully developed service would require 5000–6000 full-time leaders involving, on account of the shorter working life, an annual recruitment of 300. Courses of training should be for one or three years, according to previous experience, and salaries should be comparable with those of teachers. Young People's Colleges, when fully established, will require an annual replacement of 1000. The training should be undertaken by the area training authorities.

III. Technical Colleges. The number of full-time teachers will have to be doubled and the annual replenishment rate will be 400–500, but the problem of supply is critical. There is no recognised method of entry, and it will not be possible at present to ensure that they all possess the ideal qualifications. Salaries should be related to those obtainable by persons of similar qualifications in industry, commerce, etc. There should be more than one grade of department, and the heads of important ones should be paid on a professorial level. The load of teaching should not be such as to debar them from undertaking research.

IV. The University of Wales should assume the responsibility for the education and training of teachers in Wales.

See *Challenge and Response: an Account of the Emergency Scheme for the Training of Teachers.* Pamphlet No. 17; 1950 Non-Parl. Min. of Education. *Training and Supply of Teachers.* See p. 420.

Recruitment and Training of Youth Leaders and Organisers

Scottish Youth Advisory Cttee. Rep., apps. pp. 39. 1946

1946 *Non-Parl. Scottish Education Dept. referred March,* 1943. *sgd. June,* 1946

J. Keith (*Ch.*), and 25 others.

'To inquire into . . . the recruitment and training of youth leaders and youth organisers.'

The Education (Scotland) Act, 1945, should extend the field of full-time employment under both statutory and voluntary bodies, should produce posts in which the workers will be concerned with the needs and possibilities of a locality or district and will call for workers who possess a working acquaintance with both youth and adult needs, interests and techniques. But it would not be sound policy to fill all the posts by full-time workers, for a major role should be played by the voluntary worker, and to ensure that adequate voluntary leadership was forthcoming, education authorities should keep local youth panel registers which would record the needs of the district and the resources in leadership. Every effort should be made to bring out from the local churches, employers' associations, trade unions, etc., the people with the appropriate ability and skill. Part-time paid workers may be needed in clubs which open three or more nights a week, or in those where there is no full-time worker. Three types of full-time workers are required: the administrative and organising personnel employed by education authorities; the same kind of personnel employed by the voluntary bodies, and those employed by education authorities and voluntary bodies as workers and leaders in local youth centres, clubs and units of youth organisations. Their training should be such as would give equal status with that of the teachers' training colleges and the university departments of social study. It would include basic training in Social Studies and a specialised training. Three streams of entry should be encouraged: the social service stream, the educational stream and those from other callings. The training of the third group should be the responsibility of a new national supervising and organising body. Dr. Boyd dissented from the setting up of a special body and considered that the obvious course was to extend the functions and membership of the present National and Provincial Committees for the Training of Teachers.

Recruitment, Training and Conditions of Service of Youth Leaders and Community Centre Wardens

Cttee. Rep., apps. pp. iv, 16. 1949

1949 Non-Parl. Min. of Education apptd. Jan., 1947. sgd. —

E. J. W. Jackson (*Ch.*), Butler, Cowper (Miss C. L. H.), Fox, Mee (Mrs. E. C.), Browne, Davies, Rhodes, Richardson, Williams.

'To consider . . . the recruitment, training and conditions of service of youth leaders and community centre wardens.'

Youth and community centre service will require full-time qualified leaders and wardens on a professional basis, but as club leadership is only a temporary form of service it should be integrated with the education service as a whole, so as to offer a career in which club leadership will be a part. New entrants not under 23 with university degrees, social science qualifications and approved teaching experience should be required to have a three months' course in youth and community centre work. More mature men and women not under 25 without these qualifications should be admitted in limited numbers, but be required to take a one-year's course. The length of service in the youth service should not exceed ten years. Full-time community centre wardens should not enter under

28. Salaries should be comparable with those for teachers.

See *Training and Supply of Teachers. National Advisory Council. 2nd Rep., Recruitment and Training of Youth Leaders and Community Centre Wardens;* 1951 Non-Parl. Min. of Education.

Supply of Women Teachers

Working Party. Rep., apps. pp. iv, 19. 1949

1949 Non-Parl. Min. of Education apptd. April, 1948. sgd. —

M. P. Roseveare (*Ch.*), Barrow, Beloe, Bishop (Miss M. J.), Browne, Carter (Miss D. E.), Consitt, Heaton, Hoyle (Miss R.), Hurford (Miss M. E.), Moffett, Parker (Miss H.), Richardson, Tann (Miss F. M.).

'To advise on the steps necessary to secure enough suitable women candidates for normal training as teachers.'

By 1952 11,000 women recruits will be needed, apart from those required for building up teaching staffs for County Colleges, yet in 1948 there were only 14,000 girls of 17 to 18 in secondary schools other than independent schools. As many other occupations are open to women, the number of girls staying at school till 18 should be increased to 20,000. Suitable women who have left school before 18 and married teachers must be attracted back to teaching. Recommendations are made for making the profession more attractive by improved physical surroundings, more prospects of headships and other posts of special responsibility, etc.

Supply of Teachers. Scotland

Dept. Cttee. 1st Rep. pp. 20. 1951

1950–51 Cmd. 8123, xi, 889 apptd. May, 1950. sgd. —

T. G. Stewart (*Ch.*), Belford, Frizell, McClelland, Rodger, Young.

'. . . to ascertain the existing and to estimate the prospective vacancies for teachers

in schools and other educational establish-
ments, and . . . to estimate the number of
recruits likely to be obtained; and to report
from time to time.'

The Emergency Scheme recommended in the 1943 Report was successful in providing the estimated numbers
of teachers needed. The present requirements arise out of factors not taken into
account or not foreseen at that date,
such as the higher standards for staffing
primary schools, new school buildings
on new housing estates, the claims of
National Service, the resumption of
developments interrupted by the war,
e.g. the appointment of specialist
teachers in art, etc., classes for retarded
children, and increased numbers of
pupils after the school leaving age.

On 1st October, 1949, there was a
staff shortage of 2300 needed to fill
vacancies and to replace uncertificated
and retired teachers and married women
wishing immediate replacement. In
addition, the annual demand arising
from wastage, new school building,
increased school population and the
development of further education would
increase from 1625 in 1949–50 to 2205
in 1955–56. But the total annual supply
in the same period from all sources
would fall from 2270 in 1949–50 to
1630 in 1955–56. The total deficiency
in the latter year would be 3241. But
no account had been taken of any
reduction in the size of classes, there was
a shortage of teachers of science and
mathematics, and the fall in the ratio of
graduate to non-graduate women
teachers would jeopardise the staffing
of junior secondary school classes.

—— Second Report, app. pp. 25. 1953
1952–53 Cmd. 8721, ix, 675
sgd. Sept., 1952
add Campbell. del. Belford.

On 1st October, 1951, the staffing
deficiency was 2300 and will probably
rise to 3000 by 1957. The wastage rates
used in the First Report, which differen-
tiated only between the sexes, have
been recalculated for the separate

categories of teachers, some of whom
have exceptionally high wastage rates.
Those qualifying are not distributed
between the subjects in accordance with
requirements, too few taking mathematics and science, and too many history and geography. The question is
whether 4000 per year taking the
Scottish Leaving Certificate well enough
to gain entrance to universities or
training colleges will produce 1600
teachers in competition with other
professions and callings. If conscription
were abolished 1000 possible teachers
would be available.

Training and Supply of Teachers

National Advisory Council. Reports
1951, 1953, 1954 *Non-Parl. Min. of
Education*
apptd. — 1949
P. R. Morris *(Ch.)*.

*'To keep under review national policy on
the training and conditions of qualifications of
teachers and on their recruitment and distribution in ways best calculated to meet the
needs of the schools and other educational
establishments.'*

Training and Supply of Teachers. pp. vi,
24. 1951. *Recruitment and Training of
Youth Leaders and Community Centre
Wardens.* pp. 14. 1951. *Graduate
Teachers of Mathematics and Science.* pp.
iv, 11. 1953. *Training and Supply of
Teachers of Handicapped Pupils.* pp. vi, 45.
1954.

Amongst the recommendations in the
reports were: a minimum recruitment
and training programme for an additional 10,000 graduate teachers (1st
rep.); the average annual requirement
of graduate teachers of science and
mathematics in 1955–60 would be 1020
instead of 580, but there was an insufficient number to meet this and the
competing demands of industry and the
universities (3rd rep.); special courses
of training for teachers of the various
types of handicapped children (4th
rep.).

Teachers' Salaries

A series of reports on the periodic reviews and recommendations on the salaries of various categories of teachers and lecturers, made in the case of teachers by the Burnham Committee, was issued by the Ministry of Education as follows: in 1947, one on the salaries of teachers in farm institutes and teachers of agricultural subjects; in 1948, 1951, 1954, 1956, 1959, four separate reports on the salaries of teachers in primary and secondary schools, of teachers in further education, of the staff of training colleges, and of those in farm institutes, etc. The maximum basic salary, without special allowances, etc., of qualified male assistant teachers in schools, assistants in institutions for further education, and in farm institutes, etc., recommended in 1948 was £555, in 1951 £630 and in 1954 £725, in 1956 £900 and in 1959 £1000, while that of lecturers in training colleges was £725, £850, £915, £1200, £1370. The range of allowances for special responsibility, work of an advanced character, etc., was related to a unit system which reflected the size of school or department, etc., the age of the children, or in the case of special schools and classes, the character of the children's disability. In 1961 the pay of men and women teachers are to be equal, the Report of 1956 setting out the stages by which this was to be achieved.

4. (a) UNIVERSITIES

University Development

University Grants Cttee. Reps.

1948 *Non-Parl. Treasury.* 1951–52 *Cmd.* 8473, *xviii*, 985. 1952–53 *Cmd.* 8875, *xvii*, 931. 1956–57 *Cmnd.* 79, *xix*, 595. 1957–58 *Cmnd.* 534, *xviii*, 605.

The reports review the growth of Universities, the numbers and distribution of students, capital grants, etc., and also discuss general questions, such as the need for libraries, the place of extra-mural education in University activities, the place of science, the provision and function of halls of residence, and the quality of students, etc.

See *Methods used by Universities of Contracting and of Recording and Controlling Expenditure.* U.G.C. Cttee. (G. H. Gater, *Ch.*). Rep.; 1956–57 Cmnd. 9, xix, 621.

Application by the University Courts of the Universities of Scotland for an Increased Grant from the Education (Scotland) Fund

Special Cttee. Rep. pp. 12. 1946

1945–46 Cmd. 6853, xi, 639
apptd. March, sgd. June, 1946

T. M. Cooper (*Ch.*), Greig, Taylor.

'*To inquire into the application under Section 16 (1) (b) of the Education (Scotland) Act, 1908 . . . made by the University Courts of the Universities of Scotland for the payment from the Education (Scotland) Fund of increased sums in respect of yearly maintenance expenditure. . . .*'

As private resources are insufficient to meet university expenditure, the difference has to be made up from central grants and local rates. Whilst the Education (Scotland) Acts, 1908, 1918, contemplate that the Scottish ratepayer might co-operate with the British taxpayer in shouldering the burden, neither Act indicated a basis for computing a ratio which local contributions from rates should bear to central grants. The view has been taken that there should be parity between the local contributions in England and Scotland. When in 1938 the Alness Committee recommended a grant of £43,000 it was assumed that the so-called local contribution made by Scotland to the Scottish universities was less than the local contributions made in England. Alternative methods of analysis show that on the contrary Scottish local authorities were paying more than their share. Financing university education from a fund which has grown out of statutory provisions and administrative expedients and not out of a co-ordinated scheme is defective and should be subject to investigation. Recommended that a grant of £60,000 should be paid from the Education (Scotland) Fund to be reviewed in three years.

Scientific Man-Power

Cttee. Rep. pp. 26. 1946
1945–46 Cmd. 6824, xiv, 629
apptd. Dec., 1945. sgd. April, 1946
J. A. Barlow (*Ch.*), Appleton, Blackett, Crowther, Egerton, Nelson, Zuckerman.

'*To consider the policies which should govern the use and development of our scientific man-power and resources during the next ten years and to submit a report on very broad lines at an early date so as to facilitate forward planning in those fields which are dependent upon the use of scientific man-power.*'

The immediate task was to facilitate, through demobilisation, the release of scientists to peace-time occupations and to re-habilitate the universities and research establishments. The long-term policy was to provide qualified scientists for future requirements, especially as the demand as a whole and in each major branch of science is likely to exceed the supply.

Taking into account the average working life of a scientist as 30 years, wastage through retirement, death, etc., the maximum potential number of scientists in 1946 would be 60,000. The assessment of future demand was problematical, but it was estimated that the minimum number required by 1950 would be 70,000 (though this might be a serious under-estimate). With the raising of the school leaving age and the demand for scientists in central and local government, the number required by 1955 would be 90,000.

Before 1939 the British Universities were turning out 2500 scientists each year or 12,500 in five years. Oxford and Cambridge estimated that, ignoring costs, they could not expand above pre-war level, while the other universities

thought they might expand up to 85 per cent above the pre-war level in ten years or some 18,000 in five years. If to this figure is added the 45,000 registered scientists and the figure of 3000 deducted for death and retirement, there would possibly be a trained man-power of 60,000 in 1950 and 64,000 in 1955. The aim should be to double the output from the universities. There was every reason to believe that there is available a large reserve of innate intelligence, for whilst rather less than 2 per cent reach the university, 5 per cent of the whole population show on test an intelligence as great as the upper half of university students. Amongst university entrants elementary school pupils are only half the number to be expected; increased financial assistance is necessary. Each university should be asked to assess its possible contribution to the expansion, the needs of individual sciences should be assessed and related to the existing capacity of the universities. Regard should be paid to the expansion of the humanities, etc., to prevent a 'lack of balance'. A university building programme will have to be drawn up. Expansion should be regarded as a duty by Oxford and Cambridge, there is scope for it in London University, though it may mean some decentralisation, but in the civic universities it depends on how far they can compete with Oxford and Cambridge and London for the limited supply of talented students. To this end they must improve their amenities and local authorities must revise their scholarship system. A completely new university must be considered as soon as possible. Strong research schools are needed in all university science departments.

The priorities should be (i) teaching and fundamental research, (ii) Civil Science, both government and industrial, (iii) Defence Science. Any increase in Exchequer grants should not infringe on the independence of the universities.

See *University Development, 1935 to 1947.* U.G.C. Rep. p. 29; 1948 Non-

Parl. Treasury. *University Development, 1947 to 1952.* U.G.C. Rep.; 1952–53 Cmd. 8875, xvii, 931. *Scientific Policy.* Advisory Council. 1st Ann. Rep. p. 12; 1947–48 Cmd. 7465, xvi, 47, and succeeding Ann. Reps.

Scientific Policy

Advisory Council. 5th Ann. Rep. *Scientific Manpower.* Standing Cttee. Rep., apps. pp. iv, 12. 1952

1951–52 *Cmd.* 8561, *xviii,* 507 *sgd, March,* 1952

S. Zuckerman (*Ch.*), and ten others.

There is a pressing need to increase absolutely and relatively the number of scientists in our industries; we are producing a smaller proportion relatively than either America or Switzerland. In the long run there is likely to be a shortage of scientists of all kinds, particularly of chemists, chemical engineers, electrical and mechanical engineers. Many students with ability to reach a University standard leave school at 17 and should be persuaded to stay. A further expansion of facilities for science in the Universities is needed, and the output from technical colleges can be increased fairly rapidly if employers will encourage the flow of students. The scientific attainments of science graduates are adequate but their education frequently too narrow. As the number of men possessing the highest qualities of intellect and leadership is limited, a substantial increase in the number of them taking up science can only be at the expense of other disciplines and this will not happen without a change in the climate of opinion about the prestige of science. Special measures may have to be taken to increase the supply of science teachers at the expense of the more immediate demands.

University Awards

Working Party. Rep. pp. iv, 26. 1948

1948 *Non-Parl. Min. of Education apptd. April,* 1948. *sgd.* —

G. G. Williams (*Ch.*), Adams (Miss M. F.), Alexander, Arculus, Barrow, Brown, Duff, Duke, Grave, Hickman, Hutchings, Mann (Miss J. de L.), Pearson, Roseveare, Stephens, Stephenson.

'*On the basis of the present system of state scholarships and major awards to advise on any administrative or other changes that may be desirable, particularly having regard to (a) the increased numbers at universities, (b) the termination of the Further Education and Training Scheme and (c) the probable abolition of four-year grants for intending teachers.*'

Since the war (1945) the improvements have been such that reasonable opportunity exists for the ablest students to reach the university irrespective of means. In ten years the number of full-time university students has increased from 40,000 to 60,000 and the annual admissions have risen from 12,000 to 18,000. A considerable increase in the number of awards is needed and no qualified student should be prevented from entering the university by lack of means. The new examination for the General Certificate of Education is likely to become the normal method for admission to the university. State scholarships, for which the Ministry of Education should be responsible, should be given to assist students of high academic promise (as indicated by two subjects in the G.C.E. at scholarship level and satisfactory evidence of general education). Local scholarships awarded by the local education authorities should be available to all eligible candidates accepted by universities and qualified by reaching advanced standard in two subjects and showing satisfactory evidence of general education. Local authorities should also work out suitable methods of making awards for students of technology, art, music, drama. State scholars were free to choose their own university, and nine out of ten chose Oxford, Cambridge or London. The system of allocation between universities adopted when their numbers increased should be terminated and scholars left free to make their own choice. The four-year grants to intending teachers based on a signed undertaking should be abolished. The figures for maintenance should include allowances for vacations as well as term time; and the income scale for assessment should begin at £500 and rise to £2000. The Ministry should be responsible for 4000 awards, the local authorities for 7000.

Medical Schools

Inter-Dept. Cttee. Rep., apps. pp. 313. 1944

1944 *Non-Parl. Min. of Health, Dept. of Health, Scot.*

apptd. March, 1942. *sgd. May,* 1944

W. M. Goodenough (*Ch.*), Stopford, Elliott, Gray, Hendry, Hill, Jameson, Learmonth, Pooley, Vaughan (Dr. Janet).

'Having regard to the statement made by the Minister of Health in the House of Commons on 9th October, 1941, *indicating the Government's post-war hospital policy, to enquire into the organisation of Medical Schools, particularly in regard to facilities for clinical teaching and research, and to make recommendations.'*

A letter of 7th April, 1942, directed the Committee's attention to the general and specific problems they were asked to consider. The Committee also took account of the later proposals for a National Health Service. To meet the claims a National Health Service would make upon the medical practitioner, it was anticipated that there would have to be some radical re-orientation in his training and practice. The necessary reforms would be slow in maturing because of the need for a changed outlook of teachers and examiners, and because of the dearth of teachers, but in order to shorten the time lag, early action would be needed for building up the supply of teachers, the granting of financial help and other assistance (including priorities in building materials and labour) to the medical schools and the provision of post-graduate courses to existing practitioners.

The unit of organisation for the national system of under-graduate medical education should be a medical teaching centre, consisting of a university medical school, a group of teaching hospitals (parent and associated) in as close proximity as possible to the medical schools, and such clinics of the health service of the district as should be used for teaching purposes. Each institution should be self-governing, but so interrelated that the institutions function as one in the field of medical education and research. Every medical school should be a university medical school. In the teaching hospitals care of patients and furtherance of teaching and research should receive equal emphasis. For every 100 students a year, there should be access to 950 to 1000 hospital beds, excluding beds for tuberculosis, acute infectious diseases, mental diseases, and any highly specialised service. Educational associations should be developed between the teaching centre and the major hospitals in the centre's 'zone of influence', and the Medical Schools should take part in the administration of the National Health Service through representation on Central Health Councils in England, Scotland and Wales.

The first objective should be to expand those schools below an economical size to an entry of 80 to 100 a year. Too many students were being trained in Scotland and there was an over-concentration in London. As a long-term policy, Glasgow, Edinburgh and Aberdeen should aim at reducing numbers; in London, Charing Cross Hospital should remove to a site in Middlesex, St. George's Hospital to South London. Oxford should develop its proposed special clinical school. Cambridge should not provide clinical undergraduate teaching until the hospital services had been raised in standard. New medical schools should not be established at present, but existing schools expanded.

For the general advancement of the pre-clinical departments the professorial heads should receive higher salaries, there should be more readerships and more junior staff. In clinical departments only a small minority of the senior staff and whole-time appointments should replace the part-time work of teachers in private practice and each clinical division should have an academic head, with senior, intermediate and junior members for his staff. Medical Schools should have whole-time professorial heads in general medicine, general surgery, obstetrics and gynaecology. Selection and appointment to university chairs and senior posts should follow the usual university plan. There should be suitable advisory machinery for selecting other staff. To secure an adequate supply of teachers, a national range of salaries, family allowances and pensions, etc., should be set up. The ratio of students to staff should be about 6 to 1 to 8 to 1. All appointments should be advertised.

Unsuitability for a medical career should be the sole barrier to admission to a medical school. Exchequer grants to medical schools should be conditional upon co-education. Awards to students should be adequate to cover the whole training and simplified selection machinery should be set up. As there should be a central source from which medical schools should obtain advice and guidance, the General Medical Council should be empowered to inspect courses of study, staffing, equipment and arrangements for undergraduate education; reports and comments should be communicated to the University Grants Committee. Every medical school should provide a single, organised course of training for undergraduate students based on the requirements of the medical degree of the university of which the medical school is a part. The medical curriculum should be drastically overhauled, the General Medical Council taking the initiative. Post-graduate training and experience for intending specialists should cover four to five years after

registration; qualifications, status and standards should be determined by some suitable central machinery. The exceptional resources of London for post-graduate education are not properly used: the nucleus for such a centre is the British Post-Graduate Medical School, which should be part of a post-graduate hospital centre. Refresher courses should be organised by the Medical Faculties at hospitals other than those used for undergraduate teaching. The Medical Research Council should have funds placed at its disposal by Parliament for the promotion and development of its work.

To remedy the present defects and to create an adequate national service the increased expenditure over a period of ten years was estimated at £5 mn. for capital expenditure and £3 mn. to £3,700,000 in annual grants, both at pre-war costs. The money should be distributed by the University Grants Committee. This amount was a reasonable price for the community to pay for the promotion of national health.

University Education in Dundee and its Relationship with St. Andrews University

Inquiry. Rep., apps. pp. 37. 1949

1949 Non-Parl. Scottish Education Dept. apptd. Feb., sgd. June, 1949

T. M. Cooper.

'*To review the organisation of university education in Dundee and its relationship with St. Andrews University: and to report.*'

In the Universities (Scotland) Act, 1889, Parliament gave anticipatory approval to a union between St. Andrews (founded in the early 15th century, and developing a collegiate structure as in Oxford and Cambridge) and University College, Dundee (founded in 1881). This Act and the subordinate legislation which followed, was so indeterminate as to cause much dissension and bitterness, and for 50 years there has been a 'co-existence of incompatibility'. The war 1914–18 put an end to contemplated litigation. The inter-war years of depression affected Dundee severely, and the absence of any policy of parallel development permitted great expansion at St. Andrews and relative stagnation at Dundee. Since the war Dundee has experienced a civic and industrial renaissance and has demanded a separate university.

The extreme expedient of severance would be damaging to both centres and is regarded generally as a counsel of despair; it also rests on the assumption that University College Dundee would automatically receive university status. The best hope for the future is a re-orientation of academic policy leading to a unified and integrated university. Teaching facilities should be re-organised so as to secure free interchange. The Governors, Council and Education Board of University College Dundee should be abolished and the whole University brought under the control of a single University Court. The collegiate system has become a dangerous source of separation, and should be abolished. The administrative headship of the University should be a separate appointment; the three offices of principal of the separate colleges should be abolished. Dundee should have an administrative head subordinate to the Principal of the University.

University Education in Dundee

R. Com. Rep., app. pp. 75. 1952

1951–52 *Cmd.* 8514, x, 959
apptd. May, 1951. *sgd. April*, 1952

Lord Tedder, L. Greenhill, Keir, Muirhead, Baird, Evans, Finlayson (Isabel), Melville, Robertson.

'*To inquire into the organisation of University education in Dundee, and its relationship with St. Andrews University, and to recommend what changes, if any, should be made in the constitution, functions and powers of the University of St. Andrews, of University College, Dundee, or of any other body or institution concerned.*'

The recommendations of the Cooper Report were not implemented and the hope of a negotiated settlement had grown less. St. Andrews and Dundee now looked to the Commission to end the uncertainties, which were affecting the academic reputation of St. Andrews and particularly of its departments in Dundee. Problems of organisation, academic policy and finance so divided university education in Dundee and St. Andrews that the open breach was inevitable. The trend of student numbers in St. Andrews and Dundee differed so markedly from what had been assumed by witnesses in 1949, that a fresh examination of this aspect of the problem was essential. The Commission agreed with the main proposals of the Cooper Report that there should be no separate university in Dundee and that there should be a 'single integrated and unified academic structure'. An integrated structure should not, as recommended in the Cooper Report, involve the abolition of the collegiate system, but be based upon it. The University College Trust should be terminated and the old common law incorporations of the St. Andrews Colleges should be abolished. The colleges should be unincorporated societies of teachers and students, all professors and lecturers should be appointed by the University, but each should be a member of a college. The teachers and students in Dundee University College and the Medical and Dental Schools are one society.

The recommendations included that there should be a University Court and Senate based on a remodelled collegiate system; the office of the Principal of the University should be separated from the headship of any college; there should be two colleges—the new College in Dundee and the United College in St. Andrews, both with a Council and a Provost. The Councils should initiate proposals for academic policy, frame budgetary proposals and make to the Court recommendations for filling vacancies. So as not to encroach on the teaching facilities in either college, Dundee should develop the social sciences and St. Andrews the literary and linguistic studies. Education, law and economics (involving the incorporation of the Dundee School of Economics and the appointment of three new professors) should be taught in the new College, and the teaching of pure science should be on complementary lines in both colleges. Certain branches of medical studies should be concentrated in Dundee and engineering should be developed there, but students should be allowed to choose to do their preliminary studies at St. Andrews.

See *University of St. Andrews Act, 1953;* 1 & 2 Eliz. 2. c. 40.

Veterinary Education in Great Britain
Rep.
1943–44 *Cmd.* 6517. See *Professions.* p. 281.

4. (b) SCIENTIFIC AND SOCIAL RESEARCH

Scientific Research and Development
Paper. pp. 12. 1944
1943–44 *Cmd.* 6514, *viii*, 451

A description of the Government machinery for research provides a background for the discussion on the part to be played by the Government in this field after the war (1945).
1. The Development Commission funds were made available through the Development and Road Improvement Funds Act, 1909, for 'aiding and developing agricultural and rural industries by promoting scientific research' and for 'the development and improvement of fisheries'. 2. The Committee of the Privy Council and the Department of Scientific and Industrial Research.—A number of research establishments are maintained, some 27 autonomous research associations are helped and independent research assisted by grants and postgraduate awards. 3. The Committee of

the Privy Council for Medical Research and the Medical Research Council (formerly the Medical Research Committee).—The Council has full liberty to pursue an independent scientific policy. It is financed by an annual grant-in-aid under the vote for Scientific Investigation in the Civil Estimates. The Council provides research through its own institutes, including the National Institute for Medical Research, some through its staff working in other institutions and through grants to individuals, etc. 4. The Committee of Privy Council for Agricultural Research and the Agricultural Research Council, established in 1930, 1931 respectively.— The Council is responsible for the scientific oversight of all agricultural research, advises the Development Commission and is free to spend, at its own discretion, its grants-in-aid and to undertake its own research. The services of all these bodies are at the disposal of all departments, but many departments have their own research sections and scientific advisors. The responsibility for 'fundamental' and 'pure' research rests with the universities, for which grants-in-aid are made. All research is co-ordinated through inter-departmental consultation, advisory committees, etc. Since 1940 the main body has been the Scientific Advisory Committee of the War Cabinet.

See *Dept. of Scientific and Industrial Research.* Rep. for 1947–48, with a review of the years 1938–48; 1948–49 Cmd. 7761, xxi, 49. *Medical Research in War.* Report of the Medical Research Council for the years 1939–45; 1947–48 Cmd. 7335, xiii, 87. *Government Scientific Organisation in the Civilian Field;* 1951 Non-Parl. Treasury.

Provision for Social and Economic Research
Cttee. Rep., apps. pp. 15. 1946
1945–46 *Cmd.* 6868, *xiv*, 655
apptd. —. *sgd. June,* 1946

J. Clapham (*Ch.*), Barlow, Carr-Saunders, Clay, Hetherington, Moberly, Robbins, Tawney.

'To consider, without any formal or public enquiry, "whether additional provision is necessary for research into social and economic questions".'

Modern industrial communities rest on the knowledge and subject matter of the natural sciences and for their smooth running and balance depend on a knowledge of the subject matter of the social sciences. Much research can be satisfactorily performed only by governments, e.g. the census, the compilation of statistics of global profits, etc., but it is important that government departments, which collect and analyse material relevant to social and economic research, should be in continuous contact with outside experts who can keep them aware of the needs arising in the speculative branches of the field and who can assist in assessing the value and possible uses of material which is already being collected.

Universities are under-staffed and under-endowed. The provision for libraries, calculating machines, computors and research assistants is as important as provision for laboratories and experimental stations. The social sciences do not need expensive laboratory facilities, but research is seriously hampered by lack of adequate finances, the few research institutes or divisions having limited but precarious funds. In the past the finance for such purposes had depended on private enterprise (Booth, Rowntree, Webb) and on scientific and educational foundations. But it is not satisfactory that the work in important branches of knowledge should receive little in routine allocations and have to depend on appeals to outside foundations, some of which get their funds from abroad.

There should be an increase of resources on a permanent and routine basis, more chairs and readerships, and necessary equipment and assistance. The sum needed would be £250,000–£300,000 a year. There should be a standing inter-departmental economic

and social research committee to survey and advise upon research work in government departments, favourable consideration should be given for increased university grants for these purposes, and the University Grants Committee should consider the establishment of a sub-committee to advise on matters relating to the social sciences.

See *University Development from 1935 to 1947*. U.G.C. Rep. pp. 72, 73; 1948 Non-Parl. Treasury.

Social and Economic Research

Inter-Dept. Cttee. Rep., app. pp. 15. 1948

1948 *Cmd.* 7537, *ii*, 145 *apptd.* Jan., 1947. *sgd.* —

G. North (*Ch.*), Blackwell, Campion, Carr-Saunders, Chester, Clark, Davies, Fenelon, Hall, Hutton, Kirk, Kyd, Maddex, Reeder, Simey, Stafford, Stone.

'To survey and advise upon research work in Government Departments, and in particular (a) to bring to the notice of Departments the potential value for research purposes of the material which they collect and to suggest new methods and areas of collection; (b) to advise on how there could be made available to research workers information gathered for their own purposes by the Departments. . . .'

The administrator within the Departments is becoming increasingly dependent on the knowledge which social and economic research supplies and the research worker outside the departments has to depend more and more upon the factual raw material which departments collect for their own purposes. Many members of university staffs were employed in government departments during the war where they built up contacts with departmental officers; formal and informal forms of collaboration should continue. Sub-committees were set up to survey the work of departments, to suggest what material could be made available to research workers and whether the collection and treatment of it could be made more useful. Suggestions are made about the preservation of war-time records and those of industries now nationalised. The conditions which should govern whether material should remain confidential or be released from this restriction include that the requirements of statutes and of security and public policy must be observed, the practical administration of the departments must not be hampered, the cost of making it available should not be out of proportion to the subject matter. The obligation that individuals and firms should not be identified must be honoured. Departments should give sympathetic consideration to research schemes involving information of a personal nature, some time limit to inaccessibility might be put on certain classes of information which departments obtain for administrative purposes from various bodies, e.g. copies of detailed information not confidential could be distributed under safeguard to various specialised institutions.

See succeeding Reports; 1950–51 Cmd. 8091, xix, 117. 1956 Non-Parl. Lord President's Office, H.M. Treasury.

Arrangements for the Expenditure of Counterpart Funds derived from United States Economic Aid

Pp. 9. 1953

1952–53 Cmd. 8776, xxx, 1087

The effect of the Benton and Moody Amendments to the United States Economic Co-operation Act, 1948, and the Mutual Security Act, 1951, 1952, is that 100 mn. dollars of the funds appropriated by Congress may be spent only on condition that countries receiving a share of it undertake to spend the counterpart in local currencies on a number of purposes intended to encourage a healthy and expanding economy by promoting the productivity of industry. The British share was 9 mn. dollars.

The programme in Britain aims at the spread of knowledge throughout British industry of the best and most modern techniques and practices, and includes the employment of technical advisers by research associations, the promotion of technological studies, research into social and economic factors affecting efficiency, and short-term loans to industry and agriculture.

Programme of Expenditure of Counterpart Funds derived from United States Economic Aid. pp. 8. 1953. 1952–53 Cmd. 8918, xxiv, 867, sets out in detail the projects supported.

5. MUSEUMS, LIBRARIES

Functions of National Gallery and Tate Gallery and, in respect of Paintings, of the Victoria and Albert Museum

Cttee. Rep., app. and Standing Com. on Museums and Galleries. Memo. pp. 36. 1946

1945–46 Cmd. 6827, xiii, 855 apptd. April, sgd. Dec., 1944

V. Massey (*Ch.*), Ashton, Clark, Maclagan, Ridley, Rothenstein.

'To examine the functions of the National Gallery and Tate Gallery, and in respect of paintings, of the Victoria and Albert Museum, with special reference to their relations with one another and to the fuller representation of British art; and to consider the working of the Chantrey Bequest.'

The recommendations of the Curzon Committee in 1913 were either not carried out or had given rise to inadequate measures, and there is still confusion of purpose and practice in the organisation of the national art collections. Although they were, in all cases, founded with a specific intention, they have long outgrown their original function, and the general position is now one of distinguished individual achievement without adequate co-ordination. The Tate, though named the National Gallery of British Art, has not effected an assemblage of national painting to justify the title, and the gaps in the department of modern foreign art and of sculpture are equally flagrant.

Of the 200 pictures purchased by the Chantrey Bequest up to 1922 only a few are of sufficient merit to be hung on the walls of the gallery. The representatives of the Tate on the Recommending Committee for the Chantrey Bequest are in a minority and, for the sake of unanimity, have agreed with the Academy representatives on certain pictures which would not have been their first choice. The Victoria and Albert Museum was founded primarily as a museum of applied art but it has acquired, by legacy, collections of pictures. The title 'national' is applied to certain collections of paintings at the Victoria and Albert Museum as well as to the National Gallery of British Art. Many paintings, recommended for transfer as early as 1908, should go to the National and Tate Galleries, whilst the Stephen collections of decorative sculpture, architectural designs and academy studies, as well as certain examples of William Blake as an illustrator, should be removed from the Millbank to South Kensington. There are collections of British water colours at the British Museum, South Kensington and Millbank, but the confusion in administration prevents the Tate from having a proper representative collection of the national watercolour school.

The Tate should be divided into two distinct departments—The National Gallery of British Art of all periods and the National Gallery of Modern Art. A keeper should be appointed for each department. The Gallery of Modern Art should 'feed' the other galleries. Every 25 years pictures of outstanding merit, which have been confirmed by time, should be transferred to the National Gallery, Trafalgar Square, and sculpture of similar merit should go to South Kensington. The Tate Trustees should be independent and not subordinate to the National Gallery. The income derived from the Chantrey Bequest should be vested in the Tate Board. If this is impracticable, there should be a new recommending committee, and the academicians appointed should be members of the Tate Board

appointed in the ordinary way; and the Tate should be given the power of refusing Chantrey Bequests. In the absence of a Government fund for the acquisition of examples of British and modern art, an annual purchase grant of £5000 should be allotted to the Tate, but if the Tate has control of the Chantrey Bequest income of £2100 the Grant could be reduced to £3000. Loans from national collections should be increased in quality and quantity. To increase administrative efficiency, and to give scope to individual ability, the staffs of the national art galleries should be interchangeable.

In the Memorandum of the Standing Commission there is general agreement on the main recommendations, with suggestions on points of detail.

See *Museums and Galleries*. Standing Cttee. 1st–4th Reps.; 1933, 1938, 1948, 1954 Non-Parl.

Wellington Museum Bill [Lords]

Sel. Cttee. Special Rep., proc., mins. of ev. pp. iv, 5. 1947

1946–47 (128) *ix*, 987
apptd. June, o.p. July, 1947

G. Benson (*Ch.*), Beswick, L. Hinchingbrooke, Keeling, Lee, Willey.

The Bill to transfer to the Crown Apsley House, etc., and certain chattels formerly belonging to the first Duke of Wellington, was felt by the Committee to need certain alteration in details to meet future needs. Recommended that the Crown and the Duke of Wellington should further discuss the matter.

Libraries, Museums and Art Galleries

Advisory Council. Scotland. Rep., apps. pp. 145. 1951

1950–51 Cmd. 8229, *xi*, 669
referred Jan., 1947. *sgd. Dec.*, 1950

W. McClelland (*Ch.*), and 21 others.

'*To Review*—(a) *the libraries and museums conducted under the Public Libraries (Scotland) Acts*, 1887 *to* 1920, *and other libraries and museums providing similar services; (b) school libraries; and (c) the arrangements for the provision of books by the education authorities of counties under section 12 of the Education (Scotland) Act, 1946. . . .'*

Scottish library legislation, beginning in 1850, was vague and cumbersome, and expenditure was limited to the product of a penny rate until it was raised to threepence in 1920. All the Scottish county education authorities, with the financial encouragement of the Carnegie Trust, used the fifth section of the Education (Scotland) Act, 1918, to set up county libraries outwith the burghs who had adopted the Libraries Acts. They had a privileged position because there was no limitation of expenditure on the provision of books. Much of the development of libraries in Scotland has been due to the generosity of Andrew Carnegie and the activities of the Carnegie Trusts.

A survey carried out in the northern counties, for the Scottish Library Association, showed that only a few of the dozen burgh libraries or more could be classed as reasonably efficient. It is impossible to provide a reasonable independent library service in a 'typical Scottish burgh with a small population'. On the whole the larger libraries are more efficient, though some may be out of date, whilst some smaller ones are strikingly efficient.

As far as it is geographically possible, equal and full provision should be made throughout Scotland of a library service suited to all ages, capacities and interests; children should be encouraged to make personal libraries; in primary schools book provision should be associated with the class teacher and the classroom; school libraries should be established in all secondary schools; there should be co-operation between the school and the public library; a trained librarian should assist the school with a system of classification; every public library should have a trained librarian; as a proper service cannot be provided for a population of less than 30,000, burgh and county library systems should be amalgamated; rate limitation should be abolished and grants-in-aid given. The education authority should be the library authority, and should submit for approval a scheme for the provision of library facilities in its area. A grant-aided national library service should be established, for which the Central Lending Library in Edinburgh should be a clearing house for the whole lending library system. A Library Council for Scotland should act as an advisory body to the Secretary of State and education authorities; it would have no concern with the administration of university libraries, professional and institutional libraries, nor with the National Library for Scotland.

In Scotland a library, a museum and an art gallery may be found in the same building. The Library Acts of the last 100 years have associated them together as agencies of public culture, but have not defined the terms nor specified the distinction between them. A museum service should be accepted as an integral part of education and provision should be made in the Education Acts enabling education authorities to provide museums and art galleries. There should be a national loan service, and a national council for school museum services; a national folk museum and a national folk lore commission. Schemes for an advisory service and grant-aid are outlined. Art galleries are specialised museums and they should continue to be associated with museums with similar administrative and financial arrangements. A survey should be made of all art galleries in the hope that out of this may come a plan for having an art centre or gallery in every town of considerable size. A gallery of modern art is much needed.

National Museum of Antiquities of Scotland

Cttee. Rep., apps. pp. 28. 1952
1951–52 Cmd. 8604, *xvii*, 229
apptd. April, 1951. *sgd. July*, 1952

J. R. Philip (*Ch.*), Kendrick, Rose.

'To *inquire into the scope and functions of the National Museum of Antiquities of Scotland and its relations with other institutions.* . . .'

The National Museum of Antiquities came into existence in 1780, under the auspices of the Society of Antiquaries and its collections came to include objects of antiquarian and archaelogical interest. In 1851 the Society transferred its collection to the Board of Trustees for Manufactures in Scotland, on behalf of the nation, and in a Treasury Minute, 1851, the Government undertook to house the collection and provide the staff. The intention was that the Society should be as 'unfettered in the charge and management of the Museum' as the controls over public expenditure would allow. In 1906 under the National Galleries of Scotland Act (6 Edw. 7. c. 50) the National Galleries and Museums were placed under the new Board of Trustees for Scotland. Thus arose the present dual system in which this Board, primarily responsible for art collections and the promotion of fine arts, is also the owner and chief controller of the Museum of Antiquities, whilst the Society of Antiquaries retains the day-to-day supervision, and is the source of the yearly accessions.

The National Museum of Antiquities should be placed under the single control of a new and separate Board of Trustees and that, when conditions permit, it should have a building of its own. The Folk Museum should be physically separate, but should be administered by the same Board.

Export of Works of Art, etc.

Cttee. Rep., apps. pp. iii, 90.   1952

1952 *Non-Parl. Treasury*
apptd. Oct., 1950. *sgd. Sept.,* 1952

Lord Waverley (*Ch.*), Blunt, L. Crawford, Dalton (Mrs. R.), Galbraith, Hussey, Robbins.

'To *consider and advise on the policy to be adopted by His Majesty's Government in* controlling the export of works of art books, manuscripts, armour and antiques. . . .'

With the exception of modest duties on certain classes of imports, both exports and imports of works of art, etc., were entirely free before 1939. Export control was a war-time measure to safeguard the nation's resources in foreign exchange and to prevent the flight of capital, and was not instituted in order to safeguard our national treasures, though gradually attention was given to the use of it for that purpose. Nevertheless it has, in spite of many defects, set some limits to the export of the more important and more valuable treasures, and has to some extent eased the anxieties which, as far back as 1903 had led to the formation of the National Art-Collections Fund. In 1949 a Reviewing Committee was established to consider appeals against refusal of a licence. Export controls had been severely criticised, especially for the way in which they prevented an owner from getting the market price for his property, etc., but even if alternative safeguards could be devised, export licensing, designed for exchange controls, would continue to affect art treasures. It is only when these controls are lifted that alternative methods will have to be thought out.

The State must retain the right to prevent the export of important objects and licensing should continue, but in every case where export is prohibited the owner must be assured of an offer to purchase at a fair price. Everything possible should be done to secure *desiderata* before they come into the market. Control should be limited to objects of national importance, for which the criteria should be the closeness of its association with our history and national life, whether it is outstanding in aesthetic importance or in significance for the study of some particular branch of art, learning or history. Except with permission to the contrary, the originals of manuscripts, etc., should never be exported without copies being made and appropriately deposited. Grants to assist purchase by grant-aided collections should be made on recommendation by the Reviewing Committee, and the amounts made available should be increased substantially. Only in exceptional cases should applicants for export licences be kept waiting for as much as two or three months. Advisers should bear in mind the needs of institutions outside London and Commonwealth institutions should be able to appoint London representatives.

Prof. Galbraith protested against any relaxation of the control of manuscripts, documents in archives.

See *Export of Works of Art*. Reviewing Cttee. 1st Rep.; 1953–54 Cmd. 9292, xiii, 53, and succeeding Ann. Reps.

Departmental Records

Cttee. Rep., apps. pp. 88. [1954]

1953–54 *Cmd.* 9163, *xi*, 457
apptd. June, 1952. *sgd.* May., 1954

P. J. Grigg (*Ch.*), Buckley, Chambers, Creswick, Edwards, Gowing (Mrs. M. M.), Habakkuk.

'*To review the arrangements for the preservation of the records of Government Departments (other than the records of Scottish Departments and records transmissible to the Keeper of the Records of Scotland) in the light of the rate at which they are accumulating and of the purposes which they are intended to serve. . . .*'

The Public Record Office was established 1838 to provide proper accommodation for the public records and to facilitate the free use of them by the public; and to prevent the Office being encumbered with documents of insufficient value to justify preservation, an Act of 1877 prescribed a procedure for the destruction of those without value. The arrangements for the preservation of the records of Government departments are governed by the Act of 1838 which was not meant to apply to them, while that of 1877 makes selection very complicated, and an agreement of 1845–46 removed oversight from those responsible for their ultimate preservation. Useless material has been unnecessarily retained, while papers which ought to be in the Record Office are still in the hands of the departments. The records already transferred, which go back to the Conquest and beyond, occupy 40 miles of shelving, while those at present in the departments and liable to transfer will occupy 120 miles of shelving; and eight miles will be needed each year. The amount of preservable records can be reduced, but the expansion of Government business, typewriting, etc., have increased the number of records created each year and the situation will soon become unmanageable.

Records should be selected for preservation either because they are needed for departmental purposes or because of their potential value for historical, economic or sociological reasons. The Destruction Schedule is prepared in the Department, but even an experienced officer may take account only of his own department's administrative needs. Some departments have standardised periods of retention, others have different periods for different classes of documents. The major onus of exercising the 'historical' criterion falls on junior recording officers not qualified to do it. The opening towards the end of the war of a repository at Hayes (commonly called the Limbo), where departments should employ their own staffs to review, select, destroy or strip and transfer, has encouraged postponement.

Many recommendations are made to ensure that records worthy of preservation are transferred regularly to the Record Office and made available for use, that the Office is not swamped with valueless material and that the methods of selection are administratively workable. The responsibility for preservation should rest with the Departments, the Record Office should appoint a Records Administration Officer to co-ordinate and supervise the work on behalf of the Government as a whole. Previous legislation should be repealed; fresh legislation should provide for the transfer of headship of the Public Records Department from the Master of the Rolls to a Minister of the Crown, and should authorise destruction. Departments should review records not later than five years after they have passed out of active use and destroy those they do not need, those remaining being again reviewed when they are 25 years old. Those still in use should be retained by the department, the rest to be transferred to the Record Office. A Committee under the chairmanship of the Records Administration Officer should take a census of departments' Particular Instances papers and decide which should be preserved. The records should be open to public inspection after 50 years, but special access should be granted to individuals under the 50 years where this was considered unobjectionable. Some classes of records might be opened to public inspection before the lapse of 50 years. The responsibility for the Department's arrangements should, under the Head of the Department, be vested in the Director of Establishments or an officer of similar status, and a departmental record officer should be responsible to him for the care of papers from the time they are created until they are either destroyed or handed over to the Record Office. Under the Minister there should be established a new post of official head of the Department, with the title of Keeper of the Records. Inspecting officers should be appointed under the Records Administration Officer to keep in touch with the departments and act as liaison officers, each being responsible for dealing with a group of departments. Accommodation should be provided first at Chancery Lane and then at Ashridge Park and Hayes. Microphotography could not at present play any great part in arrangements for preservation, since it does not permit easy cross-reference from one document to another and the costs of reproducing a varied assortment of papers is high. Other recommendations concern the preservation of films, photographs and sound recordings.

Imperial Institute

Cttee. Rep., apps. pp. vi, 39.   1952
1952 Non-Parl. Min. of Education apptd. Oct., 1950. *sgd.* —

Lord Tweedsmuir (*Ch.*), Adams (Miss M. F.), Beloe, Graham, Molesworth, Read (Margaret), Sargent, Spry (Mrs. I. M.).

'*To advise on (i) the aims and constitution of the Institute, and the extent to which they are in line with present-day conditions in the British Commonwealth, (ii) how far the activities of the Institute are satisfactory having regard to the new responsibilities of the Minister of Education and (iii) to what extent the present financial arrangements and premises are satisfactory.*'

The recommendations of the Ormsby-Gore Committee, 1923 (*Breviate, 1917–39*, p. 497) was followed by the Imperial Institute Act, 1925, which gave control of the Institute to the Department of Overseas Trade. In 1949 the control of the Institute was transferred to the Minister of Education, the scientific and technical work to the Colonial Office, and the purposes of the Institute were re-defined, mainly on an educational basis. This re-definition indicates that the aims have ceased to be primarily economic and should become social and cultural in the widest sense. The Institute should be called the 'Commonwealth Institute', should serve as a Commonwealth forum, providing facilities for the presentation and exchange of ideas and information. It should provide facilities for exhibitions, cinema, lectures, social amenities, social club for students, meetings and discussions for outside organisations. Other recommendations concern management, the office of Director, staff, building, finance, etc.

XV A. POPULATION

Population

R. Com. Rep., apps. pp. xii, 259. [1949]
Papers, Vols. I–V. 1950. Vol. VI. 1954
1948–49 *Cmd.* 7695, *xix*, 635. *Papers;*
1950, 1955 *Non-Parl.*

apptd. March, 1944. *sgd. March,* 1949

H. D. Henderson (*Ch.*), Carr-Saunders,
Cassie (Ethel), L. Cranbrook, Ellis,
Ensor, Hobhouse, Jay (Margaret C.),
Longmoor (Gwen), Morris, Ogilvie
(Mary), Pawson (Helen H.), Roberts,
Robieson.

*'To examine the facts relating to the
present population trends in Great Britain;
to investigate the causes of these trends and to
consider their probable consequences; to consider what measures, if any, should be taken
in the national interest to influence the future
trend of population; and to make recommendations.'*

In addition to the Commission three
specialist committees—Statistics, Economics and Biological, and Medical—
were appointed to investigate and
advise on scientific problems. On their
advice, special investigations were
undertaken, including the Family Census and a Fertility Inquiry.

In the mid-Victorian era married
couples produced on the average $5\frac{1}{2}$ to
6 live-born children, while those married in 1925–29 produced 2·2. This
reduction of 60 per cent has been
achieved by the virtual disappearance of
families of more than 6 and by the
substitution of one or two child
families for those of 5, 6 or 7. The
decline has been most rapid in the
higher occupational categories. There
is no evidence of a decrease in repro-
ductive capacity and even if there had
been, it would have accounted for only
a small part of any fall of births, for
powerful economic, social and cultural
forces told against the continued acceptance of any uncontrolled birth rate.
The great majority now of married
persons limit the size of their families.

In 1935–38 the Net Reproduction
Rate, an index developed in the 1930's
to remove the distorting influence of
age-distribution on the rate of natural
increase, was about 0·81, which suggested that the birth-rate was one-fifth
below the level needed for replacement.
But its rise above unity for several years
after the war was misleading, for it was
unduly influenced by the temporary
factors of earlier marriages and of the
occurrence of births which had been
postponed. The notion of a replacement rate can be most appropriately
attached not to fertility rates, but to the
size of the completed family. Family-
building habits were arrived at by com-
paring the average number of births to
'cohorts' of married women having
similar durations of marriage at the end
of 1938 and 1948. This shows that the
size of the completed family has remained steady at 2·2 for many years and
is about 6 per cent below the replacement rate. If married couples continue
to have families of the same average
size as in the immediate post-war years
there will ultimately be a slow decline
in the trend of births, though a small
increase would fill the gap. If existing
tendencies continued total numbers
would reach a maximum in 1977; there
would be a substantial increase in the
proportions of the higher age groups,
though this is largely due to a fall in
mortality. A continued moderate net
emigration rate would accelerate the
ultimate decline in numbers. There
would be an increase in the proportion
of men to women.

Some of the consequences of these
movements are inescapable, since they
arise out of changes which have already
occurred or are in progress. An increasing population would have to be
provided with capital equipment of all
sorts and would have the effect of decreasing the amount of land per head of
population, whilst it is possible that
food and raw materials may be obtainable only on worsened terms of trade.

On the other hand, it would facilitate production on a larger scale, while the increase of numbers entering the working ages would make it easier to change the relative size of industries by the diversion of recruits, thus making the system more flexible. By contrast, a falling population would reduce flexibility. The community might lose something of the initiative and enterprise associated with youth. Though the improved health and fitness of older people will make it possible to use their productive capacity, the dependence on pensions on their retirement operates against their being employed. Even making no allowance for any further lengthening of life, the cost of pensions will double between 1948 and 1978. Two undesirable consequences of a family size below replacement level are first, that the sources of suitable immigrants to make up any deficiency, as well as our capacity to absorb those who are alien in race and religion, are limited, and secondly, that a diminishing flow of British emigrants will have serious consequences in other parts of the Commonwealth, since they are likely to form no more than a third or a quarter of the number needed by these countries if they are to maintain their pre-1930 rates of growth. And as the rate of growth of oriental peoples has by contrast been accelerated, military strength will be affected, though more important are the maintenance and extension of Western values, which depend on the vitality and population of the constituent peoples. Family size could continue below replacement level for a long period and finally become stabilised at a lower level, but since it depends on habits and tradition–which spread slowly, raising it afterwards to replacement level might not be easy. 'We have no hesitation in concluding that replacement size of families is desirable in Great Britain at the present time.' How far special measures are required to achieve this end is a complex question, but public policy conducted without any deliberate intention of affecting the birth rate has in fact in a number of ways had the incidental effect of discouraging parenthood.

Proposals.—(1) In all classes except the wealthiest, married couples with young children to support are at an economic disadvantage compared with childless ones, and the non-monetary handicaps fall on the mothers, who have shared little in the modern growth of leisure. Public policy should seek to encourage voluntary parenthood and make it easier for women to combine motherhood and the care of the home with outside interests. Free grants should be made to parents on the principle of equal assistance to parents of all income levels; the deterrence to parenthood in the upper and medium ranges of income by unfair taxation should be removed. Family allowances should be increased to 7s. od. and for children over 11 to 10s. od. per week, and when circumstances permit the exclusion of the first child should be ended; until then a moderate lump sum should be paid for the first birth. The deductions from income chargeable to tax for each dependent child should be not less than £60 and should rise to one-tenth of earned income in excess of £1000, subject to a maximum of £150. (2) Family services should be developed to give help to mothers with young children through home helps, sitters-in, day nurseries, nursery schools, etc., not only in emergencies, but in the normal running of the household. Recommendations are made on washing and laundry facilities, family holidays, rest homes, etc. (3) Health Services. Facilities should be provided by the National Health Service for investigating and treating infecundity and giving advice to parents on contraception. Anaesthetics or analgesia should be available to all mothers who want them, the period of attendance of midwife and health visitor should be increased, the appointments system at hospitals and clinics developed. The recommendations of the Biological and Medical Committee for continued nutritional policies, better obstetric practice, health education, etc., are endorsed.

(4) Housing. There is an undue concentration on the five-roomed house, more larger ones being required. Priorities should be given to families with three or more children. There is a case for rent rebates related to the number of dependent children. Re-conditioning and improved sanitation and equipment of old houses, the provision of parks and open spaces in town planning schemes are recommended. (5) Public Opinion. The public should be made aware of the broad features of population trend and policy; preparation for family life should be given a more prominent place in the educational curriculum in the widest sense. (6) Research. The problem of differential fertility and its possible effects on the level of intelligence should be investigated; family census questions should be included in the census, the statistical division of the General Registry Office strengthened and improved; the possibilities of a general scheme of rent rebates should be examined.

In a reservation Margaret Jay argues that the only way to ease the pressure to restrict births in the middle and professional classes is to remove from them the burden of privately financed education by levelling of educational standards to those of the best public schools.

App. 3 is a Memo. on the statistical methods of measuring reproductivity.

Papers: Vol. I. *Family Limitation and its Influence on Human Fertility during the past Fifty Years* by E. Lewis-Faning; 1950. Vol. II. Statistics Committee. Reports and Papers; 1950. Vol. III. Economics Committee Report; 1950. Vol. IV. Biological and Medical Committee Reports, 1950. Vol. V. Memoranda; 1950. Vol. VI. Pts. I, II, *The Trend and Pattern of Fertility in Great Britain. A Report on the Family Census of 1946*, by D. V. Glass and E. Grebenik; 1955 Non-Parl.

See *Current Trend of Population in Great Britain*. Memo.; 1941–42 Cmd. 6358, ix, 139. *Population*. R. Com. Statement by the Chairman; 1945 Non-Parl.

XV B. SOCIAL PROBLEMS

1. Evacuation of Women and Children
2. Child Care, Homeless Children, Adoption, the Cinema
3. Charities
4. Betting

1. EVACUATION OF WOMEN AND CHILDREN

Reception of Children Overseas

Inter-Dept. Cttee. Rep. pp. 8. 1940 1939–40 *Cmd*. 6213, v, 467 apptd. —. pres. June, 1940

G. Shakespeare (*Ch.*).

'*To consider offers from overseas to house and care for children, whether accompanied or unaccompanied, from the European war zone residing in Great Britain, including children orphaned by the war, and to make recommendations thereon.*'

The Children's Overseas Reception Scheme was worked out to take advantage of the tentative offers from Canada, Australia, New Zealand, South Africa, other parts of the Empire and America to receive children from Great Britain for the duration of the war. The scheme should be administered by the Children's Overseas Reception Board, presided over by a Minister responsible to Parliament. The scheme should at first be confined to children between 5 and 16 years of age. Detailed recommendations were made regarding the machinery for the selection and medical examination of children, shipping facilities, the cost to the Government and the financial liabilities of parents whose children were sent overseas.

Conditions in Reception Areas

Cttee. Rep. pp. 18. 1941

1941 *Non-Parl. Min. of Health apptd. Nov., 1940. sgd. Jan., 1941*

G. Shakespeare (*Ch.*), Johnston (Miss A. C.), Darlow.

'*To inquire into the welfare of evacuated and homeless persons in the reception areas and examining the provision made for their comfort and contentment and for easing the burden on the householders receiving them.*'

The influx in reception areas in 17 counties was: 1. Organised evacuation: unaccompanied children 290,000, teachers, helpers, A.R. personnel, civil servants, etc., 75,000 (approx.), mothers and children 123,000. 2. Unorganised evacuation: 1,078,000, of which 600,000 made their own arrangements and no billeting allowances were paid. The total represented a 25 per cent increase of population in the reception areas. This mixing of urban with rural populations was not achieved without friction. The country housewife who is a better cook and whose interests are more centred on the home, found it difficult to understand the gregarious London woman, who is more partial to tinned food and who readily resorts to the fish and chip shops. The evacuated woman may arrive in the country in a state of mental distress, from bombing and full of anxieties for her husband and her home, and if an unfriendly atmosphere is suspected the urge to return to the town becomes overwhelming. The fact that she stays, and that migration is succeeding, is witness to the tremendous efforts of local authorities, voluntary bodies and warmhearted householders.

Features essential to the continued success of the scheme include the following: adequate reception arrangements, and re-fitting evacuees before suitable billeting; continuous surveys and close co-ordination in billeting arrangements; welfare facilities and more welfare officers; more drastic use made of powers of requisitioning premises for the various needs; e.g. for large families, unbilletable cases, difficult children, maternity cases, etc. The influx of evacuees to a district should cease when saturation point—one per habitable room—was reached. Rest shelters should not be used as permanent billets. Attention was also called to questions of the supply of clothing for unaccompanied children, Assistance Board scales and allowances, contributions from absent husbands, rent of evacuated homes and the establishment of the Advice Bureau, etc.

See *Care of the Homeless;* 1942 Non-Parl. Min. of Health. Rev. ed.; 1944 Non-Parl.

Hostels for 'Difficult' Children

A Survey of Experience under the Evacuation Scheme. pp. 23. 1944

1944 *Non-Parl. Min. of Health*

Under the pressure of evacuation in 1940–41 many unaccompanied children were settled in hostels, which were brought into being for children who, through difficulties of behaviour or temperament, could not suitably be billeted, but needed a period of special care or supervision. The differences between the work of these hostels and Homes administered by public authorities is that they are called upon to provide a suitable environment for a considerable number of difficult and maladjusted children who are separated from their homes and parents, but for most of whom a home exists to which they will eventually return. It was some time before a proper classification of hostels and a sorting out of children could be done. This process was helped in many areas by the pooling of hostel resources between different authorities, etc.

A sample survey was made of 48 of the 215 hostels. Mixed hostels and those for older boys alone amounted to 75 per cent of the total, the number taking children of a restricted age group, and those taking only girls, being comparatively small. Children can be handled successfully in small hostels taking about 25 boys and girls of mixed ages, where there can be a family atmosphere and a feeling of responsibility for the younger children. Hostels do not specialise, most of them containing children with a variety of problems, but differences show themselves in the particular gifts of the matrons, e.g. some can manage adolescent girls, others can deal with anxious and insecure children, etc. But those children needing psychiatric treatment go where facilities are available.

The ratio of staff of all kinds to children was on an average one full-time member to every five children. Success in running a hostel depended only to a small extent on the initial possession of any particular kind of knowledge; the essentials are sympathy, understanding and ability to win the confidence of the children. The staffs possessed a variety of other qualifications and have been teachers, nurses, social workers, wardens in institutions, etc. Voluntary workers played their part in relieving the full-time staff or in taking over special duties. The usual educational arrangements were for hostel children to be attached to an evacuated school party, and only where local conditions made it necessary were the children educated separately. The survey gives an account of the daily activities in some hostels, some typical case studies and statistical analyses of problems of behaviour, etc.

2. CHILD CARE, HOMELESS CHILDREN, ADOPTION, THE CINEMA

The Boarding Out of Dennis and Terence O'Neill at Bank Farm, Minsterley and the Steps taken to Supervise their Welfare

Rep., app. pp. 21. 1945

1944–45 *Cmd.* 6636, *iv*, 185

apptd. March, sgd. May, 1945

W. Monckton.

'*To inquire into and report upon the circumstances which led to the boarding out of Dennis and Terence O'Neill at Bank Farm, Minsterley, and the steps taken to supervise their welfare.*'

The circumstances leading to the enquiry were that the two boys, aged 8 and 11, were committed by the Newport Juvenile Court in 1940 to the care or protection of the Newport Borough Council, who had finally boarded them out in 1944 with Mr. and Mrs. Gough, Bank Farm, Minsterley, Shropshire. Six months later Dennis died and Terence was removed to a place of safety. The verdict given was that Dennis' death was due to acute cardiac failure following ill-treatment and under-nourishment. The rider stated that there had been serious lack of supervision by the local authority. Making due allowance for the fact that the local authorities were understaffed and overworked in wartime, especially with the placing of evacuated children in homes, and that there had been a number of unfortunate slips in the way letters had been handled in the filing systems of the local authorities, there had been too great a readiness to assume that all was well, without sufficient realisation of the direct and personal nature of the relationship between the supervising authority and the boarded-out children.

The Goughs had been selected without adequate inquiry having been made as to their suitability; during the six months that the children were at Bank Farm they had never been medically examined; they were not visited in the first month of their stay and what visits were made were inadequate. The last visit, on 20th December before Dennis died on 9th January, was made by a clerk of the Newport authority concerned with administrative duties in connection with boarding-out, who was in Shropshire to discuss administrative problems with the Shropshire authority and who, though not experienced in visiting, was selected to go to the home. She reported in favour of immediate removal and advised calling a doctor, but did not follow up the visit and was not able to impress her authority with a sense of urgency. There were delays both by the Newport and Shropshire authorities in acting on her report.

Making allowance for difficulties of staffing, the Newport authority must accept the primary responsibility for the failure to discharge their obligation; they failed in the selection and supervision of the foster home, and assumed without making sure that the Shropshire authority was supervising for them, and even after Shropshire had refused to supervise, they did not make an adequate visit. Shropshire cannot escape some measure of blame for deficiencies arising out of its system of delegation, and for declining to supervise before the question of rates of allowance had been settled. There was a lamentable failure of co-ordination between the two authorities. It is undesirable for children to be boarded out in another authority's area without its knowledge and approval.

No changes in the principles of the 1933 Act for boarding out were necessary, but the administrative machinery should be improved and informed by a more anxious and responsible spirit. There should be a more careful selection of foster homes: the personal relationship between the local authority and the child should be more clearly recognised. Medical attention and skilled supervision should be insisted upon.

Care of Children

Cttee. Interim Rep., *Training in Child Care*, app. pp. 17. [1946]

1945–46 *Cmd.* 6760, *x*, 539
apptd. March, 1945. *sgd. Jan.*, 1946

Miss M. Curtis (*Ch.*), Brown (Miss S. C.), Evans, Fildes (Miss L. G.), Harford (Miss M. L.), Hastings, Jones (Miss K.), Litten, Moss, Murtagh (Miss H.), Nichol (Miss M. E.), Salt, Spence, Temple (Mrs. F. G. A.), Walmsley, White.

'To inquire into existing methods of providing for children who from loss of parents or from any cause whatever are deprived of a *normal home life with their own parents or relatives; and to consider what further measures should be taken to ensure that these children are brought up under conditions best calculated to compensate them for the lack of parental care.*'

On account of their key position and the lack of training facilities, the Report confines itself to the training of the residential staff of the House Mother type in charge of small groups of children in small and independent scattered homes. Large sections of these staffs are without any special training and mistaken handling of children in homes is likely. A Central Council for Training in Child Care should be set up to draw up a curriculum and administer a scheme of training. A candidate for a post of House Mother or Assistant Matron should be suitable to take charge of a 'family' group of up to 12 children. She must play the part of mother to the children and be able to create for them the atmosphere of affection and security necessary for their happiness; must understand the domestic, household and health side of her work, and be business-like and orderly in keeping simple records and in making necessary reports. A two-year course leading to a Certificate Part I is recommended. This should include theoretical training in household management, care of health and the prevention of disease, child development, playing with children, etc., and practical work in the Homes. Grants should be provided for theoretical training in teachers' training colleges, polytechnics and technical colleges, etc. A Certificate Part II should lead to senior posts. The Appendix sets out the different types of training courses for social work, e.g. child care organisers, boarding out visitors, probation officers, etc.

—— Report, apps., index. pp. 195. [1946]

1945–46 *Cmd.* 6922, *x*, 559
sgd. Aug., 1946

Section I. Existing Arrangements.——

Responsibility for providing or supervising the substitute home for the deprived child may be taken by the State, by local authorities, by voluntary organisations or by private persons. Of the 124,900 deprived children now provided for, the Ministry of Health and Home Office are responsible for 57,600 destitute; the Ministry of Health for 5200 homeless evacuees, 10,700 children maintained for reward, and 2400 pending adoption; the Home Office for 23,400 removed by Order of Court; the Board of Control for 7500 mentally disordered and defective; the Ministry of Education for 14,500 handicapped and the Ministry of Pensions for 3600 war orphans. There are possibly another 200,000 who do not come under any public care. Of the 124,000, some 40,000 are in local authorities' institutions, 11,200 in approved schools, 1500 in remand homes and 700 in approved probation homes and hostels, 40,100 in voluntary hospitals and homes, and 27,800 in foster homes. There are often historical and other reasons for these differences, which may correspond to genuine differences of circumstances, but often children similar in type and circumstances receive quite different treatment because they have been dealt with by different departments under different statutes. Thus, if voluntary organisations receive no public subscriptions, and do not take in Poor Law children their Homes may, if they take children under nine years of age 'for reward', be visited by the welfare authority's child protection visitors; otherwise, they may come under no public supervision at all. Children under nine years of age 'fostered' for reward, or placed by private persons (not the parents or guardians) for adoption, are supervised by local authorities under the direction of the Minister of Health through the child life protection service. Those over nine received for reward and those for whose maintenance no reward is given are not the care of any public authority.

Section II. How children are cared for.—The Committee was far from satisfied with the immediate provision by the local authorities for children who have to be placed in a permanent home. In far too many areas they are put into the unsatisfactory conditions of a workhouse ward, where they may have to stay for months before a place is found for them. In long-term provision, more has been done for infants than for older children, where both aim and achievement is on a lower level. The public anxiety concerning out-of-date, harsh and repressive methods is justified and there is much that calls for reform, but there is also much that is good and highly creditable to those responsible. In Homes for children there was very little evidence of seriously bad conditions involving neglect or hard usage. When establishments fell below a satisfactory standard, the defects were not of harshness, but of dirt, dreariness, drabness and over-regimentation. In many places the standards were no better than they were 30 years ago, and there was a deplorable lack of the right kind of staff. In many Homes there was a shocking lack of personal interest and affection for the children. Apart from the absence of this essential element in a child's well-being, there was much to criticise in accommodation and equipment in which, in spite of war shortages, a higher standard should be set. The most outstanding fact was that the happiness of the children depended primarily on the personality and skill of the good matron, or house-mother. On the whole, foster homes made a good impression, there were few where a child was not a member of the family or did not appear to be finding happiness and affection. The Committee was impressed, however, with the need for a greater sense of personal interest and responsibility for the boarded-out children at the local authority's headquarters. While there may be a greater risk of acute unhappiness in a foster home, a happy foster home is happier than life as generally lived in a large community.

Section III. Conclusions.—The problem of providing for children deprived of home life has not hitherto been regarded as a single one and therefore a large part of the task consisted of devising means of simplifying and unifying the exercise of public responsibility. Public care should be extended to cover children over 9 and not over 16 years of age taken into the care of foster parents for reward, children of all ages up to 16 taken by foster parents without reward (including children placed for adoption), and children in unregistered voluntary Homes. Local authorities should be under an obligation to undertake the care of children whom the Courts wish to commit to their care. The local authority should be notified in all cases where a child's pension, etc., is paid to a person other than its mother, close relative or legal guardian. Every orphan or deserted child maintained or supervised by the local authority should have a legal guardian. There should be concentrated in one central department all relevant statutory powers, and it should be responsible for defining and maintaining standards by inspection, advice and direction. It should make rules, binding on both voluntary organisations and local authorities, and on boarding out and maintenance in institutions, and should register and inspect all voluntary homes. Local authorities, i.e. county and county borough councils, or Joint Boards where the numbers of children are small, should have the immediate responsibility for the care of children. They should appoint Children's committees, with an executive officer who is a specialist in child care. Subject to the needs of the individual child, adoption, boarding out and institutional care are to be preferred in that order. The changes recommended in the law relating to adoption increase the supervisory powers, etc., of the local authority. The investigation and approval of foster homes should be the duty of the local authority's children's officer. Other authorities should not board out in an authority's area except

through its children's officer. A family group system in grouped cottage homes, with from 8 to 12 children in a group, should be developed. Other detailed recommendations make more specific the functions of the various types of Homes, reception centres, approved schools, remand homes, and the development of After Care, etc. There are Notes on safeguarding adequate religious care, signed by six members of the Committee. Appendix I deals with training in child care.

See *Children Bill*. Summary of the Main Provisions; 1947-48 Cmd. 7306, xxii, 717. *Children Act, 1948*. 11 & 12 Geo. 6. c. 43. *Conduct of Children's Homes*. Memo.; 1951 Non-Parl. Home Office. *Work of the Children's Dept.* 6th, 7th Reps.; 1951, 1955 Non-Parl. Home Office. *Children in the Care of Local Authorities in England and Wales;* 1952-53 Cmd. 8910, xxiv, 305, and succeeding Anns.

Homeless Children

Cttee. Rep., apps. pp. 41. 1946
1945-46 *Cmd. 6911, x, 755*
apptd. April, 1945. sgd. July, 1946

J. L. Clyde (*Ch.*), Baird (Mrs. M. D.), Curr, Forsyth, Gordon, Kerr (Lady M.), Jobson (Miss M. F.), Lamb, McJerrow (Mrs. E. H.), Mitchison (Mrs. N.), Paterson (Mrs. J. C.), Roberts (Mrs. J.), Strachan, Taylor, Wattie (Miss N. I.).

'To enquire into existing methods of providing for children who, from loss of parents or from any other cause whatever, are deprived of a normal life with their own parents or relatives; and to consider what further measures should be taken to ensure that these children are brought up under conditions best calculated to compensate them for the lack of parental care.'

The main solutions adopted in Scotland to meet the problem are boarding-out homeless children with foster parents, sending them to voluntary Homes or to Homes maintained by the local authorities. Approximately 14,329 children were dealt with in 1945.

Originally homeless children found their way into the hands of foster-parents or Homes without any recognised system of inspection or departmental supervision, and their treatment depended on the wisdom and humanity of the person or body to whom the child was entrusted. While the introduction of orphan's pensions has tended to encourage relatives to take unwanted children, social tendencies have increased the problem of a child who, through neglect, may be below standard. At the same time the rise in standards of living and in wages has tended to make the assumption or responsibility for bringing up a homeless child less attractive to many who might otherwise have undertaken it. The public appreciation of the growth of this problem has led to a series of attempts by the Legislature to meet it, but the piecemeal way in which it has been built up has led to the regulation and supervision of homeless children becoming dissipated among a series of bodies and departments with inevitably different outlooks and guided by different considerations. Fusion of departmental control would be an important starting point, but it will not solve the problem; something more is needed to weld together the existing system. Undoubtedly the solution of the problem is the finding of a good foster-parent. Meanwhile, the number of children in large institutions, which sometimes have as many as 40, 50 or even 60 children sleeping in one dormitory, should be reduced.

The principal recommendations included the transfer of all functions regarding the care of homeless children to one department, with a uniform set of regulations and a single staff of inspectors. Local Authorities should set up one committee exercising uniform jurisdiction over such children. An improved foster-parent system, with greater care in selection and supervision of foster-parents, should be set up with trained officials; standard rates of payment to foster-parents should be fixed for all authorities; responsibility must rest with the boarding-out authority, which should notify the authority of the area of residence; generally prior to boarding-out, a child should be temporarily placed in a Home for medical and other inspection. Other recommendations concern the tightening up of a systematic and unified system of periodic inspection for each child placed in a foster home. Large institutions should be divided up, no more than 12 to 15 children should sleep in one dormitory; no Home should be housed in a Poorhouse, children should attend church and school outside the Home. Training schemes and examinations should be prepared for the staffs of homes and for persons engaged in child care work.

Reservation I (five members). Since the Local Government Act (Scotland), 1929, made a big step in the direction of reducing the too numerous authorities, it would be retrogressive to introduce another administrative body to deal exclusively with a small group of children, representing only a fraction of the children in Scotland, who at present come under the Health and Education authorities. The Health and Education authorities within their respective fields of administration should be responsible for providing for homeless children. The central control of voluntary Homes should be transferred from the Home Department to these two Departments. Reservation II (three members). If a good foster-parent could be had, that would no doubt be the easiest solution to the problem of the unwanted child. Whilst recognising the supreme importance of the family, the fact must be faced that not only the theoretical educationalist, but the practical school teacher and social worker is often up against the average parent's influence in holding back the child both educationally and socially. Recommended, a combination of hostel or boarding school with part-time foster-parents as possibly the best method of treating the deprived child, so that he will become a good citizen.

See *Child Care*. Scottish Advisory Council (J. E. Hamilton, *Ch.*). *After-Care* Cttee. (H. C. Whitley, *Ch.*). Rep. pp. 12. 1950. *Boarding-Out* Cttee. (Mrs. J. Roberts, *Ch.*). Rep., app. pp. 22. 1950. *Homes*. Cttee. (Miss M. Jobson, *Ch.*). Rep., app. pp. 30. 1950; 1950 Non-Parl. Scottish Home Dept.

Boarding out of Children and Young Persons

Memo., app. pp. 18. 1946

1946 *Non-Parl. Home Office, Min. of Health*
sgd. Dec., 1946

Local authorities are empowered to board out any child or young person committed to their care. The memorandum explains the functions and qualifications of the visitor or boarding out officer, the requirements of a foster home and duties of foster-parents; placing children in a suitable receiving home in preparation for placement in a foster home; supervision of the foster home and medical care, etc. Full records should be kept of every foster child in or from another area and it may be useful to set up a central index for all foster homes of all departments of the local authority. The Appendix gives the changes made in the 1933 Rules.

Adoption of Children

Dept. Cttee. Rep., apps., index. pp. iv, 88. 1954

1953–54 *Cmd.* 9248, *viii*, 1
apptd. Jan., 1953. sgd. April, 1954

G. Hurst (*Ch.*), Edwards (Mrs. M. E.), Harris, Hopkin (Mrs. L.), Kermack, Odlum (Dr. D.), Prestige, Robinson (Mrs. M. J.), Rowe.

'*To consider the present law relating to the adoption of children and to report whether any and, if so, what changes in policy or procedure are desirable in the interests of the welfare of children.*'

The report reviews the history of legislation about adoption.

During the last 30 years legal adop-

tion has become important in our social life. In 1927 the number adopted was 3000, in 1946 21,000 and now the average is about 14,000 annually. This is very different from what was expected in 1925, when the Tomlin Committee reported that they believed that the number of people wishing to get rid of children by way of adoption was greater than the number of people wishing to adopt. The primary object, however, at which all should aim in the arrangement of adoptions is finding the right home for a child rather than satisfying would-be adopters. In the interests of the child the aim should be to protect the three parties concerned—children, natural parents, adopters—from risks which may lead to unhappiness. There are risks inherent in 'third party' and 'direct' adoptions and there is more chance of success where the arrangements are made by persons of special experience and training. It is acknowledged that it is in the child's interest that he should grow up knowing that he has been adopted, thereby safeguarding him from any emotional shock, especially in adolescence, which might occur when he finds out or is told suddenly. The Committee was satisfied that in spite of various shortcomings in the law and administration, legalised adoption had increased immeasurably the well-being of probably over a million members of the community. Far-reaching changes in the law could, however, not be advocated until more systematic records had been kept, and more research on them had been done. The recommendations are mainly concerned with defects in the law, practice and procedure, etc.

Local authorities should be empowered to arrange for the adoption of any child, be required to work through a case committee and to notify any other authority in whose area it wishes to place a child. Of the 60–70 adoption societies, some are only introducing societies, some run homes and others are moral welfare societies concerned with the unmarried mother. Those societies which inspect the prospective home are to be preferred; many societies which do not employ trained workers would have to close if this were required. One-third of the adoptions are through third parties and by direct placing; while some of these are prompted by affection, others are to be deprecated, but prohibition would be evaded. Third parties should be made to feel their responsibility, should be made respondents in the application, and be present at the hearing. All children who are to be legally adopted or are adopted *de facto* should be brought within the 'Child Life Protection' provisions. The supervising authority's report should in every case be submitted to the Court. An application for adoption should not be lodged until two months after the child has come into the adoptor's home, and no period before the child is six weeks old should count towards the probationary period. A suitably qualified person, unconnected with the arrangements for placing a child, should be appointed guardian *ad litem*, by the Court. Clerks to Justices should be able to appoint the guardian *ad litem* and the applicants and the child should attend the hearing. The recommendations make more specific what information should be required on the form of consent and from whom consent should be obtained. Applicants should be required to undertake to bring up a child in the knowledge that he is adopted. After a specified future date, an adopted child should be treated as a child of the family for the purpose of succession to property. The licensing system should be maintained in order to provide for the transfer of children to destinations outside 'the British Islands'.

Children and the Cinema

Dept. Cttee. Rep., apps. pp. v, 109. [1950]

1950 *Cmd.* 7945, *vii*, 169
apptd. Dec., 1947. *sgd. March*, 1950

K. C. Wheare (*Ch.*), Barnard, Bartlett, Booth, Bower (Mrs. H.), Brutton, Campbell, Earl (Mrs. H.), Emmet (Mrs. E.), Heycock, Hyde (Mrs. M.), Jackson, Milson, Roberts, Stark, Towne (Miss M. M.), Turnbull, Vardy, Wall (Miss J. I.), Wilson.

'*To consider and report upon—(a) the effects of attendance at the cinema on children under the age of* 16, *with special reference to attendance at children's cinema clubs;* (b) *whether, in the light of these effects, any modification is desirable in the existing system of film classification, the existing position with regard to the admission of children to cinemas, or in the organisation, conduct and management of children's cinema clubs.*'

Anxiety as to the effect of cinema attendance on the happiness and welfare of children is reflected in the large number of enquiries made by public and private bodies during the last 30 years. Investigation showed that 31 per cent of the children in Great Britain go to the cinema once a week and a further 21 per cent go twice a week. Only a little over half of these went with their parents as part of 'family entertainment' and they were usually under 10; only a minority of those aged 14 went with their parents. The increase in children's clubs and matinees raises the question as to whether they encourage an additional visit or are a substitute for the ordinary cinema. In 1948 some 896,000 were attending cinema exhibitions, chiefly on Saturday mornings, attendance at an individual cinema being up to 2000.

The attempt to control the films children see at the ordinary cinema (though not in Scotland) by the classification of 'U' for universal exhibition, 'A' for adult audiences and 'H' for horrific, is successful only in the case of the prohibition of children from 'H' films, which are in any case few in number. One of the reasons why children see 'A' films is because programmes consisting only of 'U' films have been comparatively rare since it became customary to show two full-length feature films in every programme: the production tends to be three 'A's to one 'U' film.

At the children's exhibitions only 'U' films are shown, but many conscientious managers were disturbed at the total inadequacy of suitable films, and some went as far as to say that they thought the standard of films obtainable for children was deteriorating. The Committee examined critically the various types of films shown—serials, feature or story films, cartoons and general interest films on travel, sport, nature, etc.

There was a strong representation from the local authorities and educational bodies against the development of cinema clubs where other indoor and outdoor activities are catered for. Teachers and social workers disliked the clubs because they could not have the true characteristics of a club: they were too big and monitors could not exercise supervision over a large audience; a cinema manager was not trained in youth service, and there may be a clash with the loyalties of school or youth organisations. Children would be better occupied on Saturday mornings playing outdoor games or helping at home. In any case it was undesirable to have children's leisure time organised by commercial enterprise.

The influence of the film is bound to have considerable effect on the child. There was agreement about the immediate effects of the films on the child, but less agreement about the more remote and lasting psychological or physical effects. It is, however, these more deep-seated influences with which the serious social problems of juvenile misdemeanour have been linked in the public mind, which constituted the main field of the committee's reference.

There were no established conclusions that cinema attendance had physical ill-effects—not even on eyesight, though the L.C.C. lay down requirements as regards the angle of vision. Late performances did produce disturbing effects on children and several licensing authorities prohibit attendance. Evidence was conflicting on the deeper and more enduring nervous and emotional effects of films,

even 'gangster films' were thought to do less harm than was supposed. But a constant harping on brutality was another matter, and no sadistic film should be seen by a child. More concern was shown in evidence about the effects of the low standards of sexual morality, in many films, on adolescent boys and girls and to the false values of riches, power, luxury and public adulation. This is more persuasive and dangerous than the depiction of crime and impropriety. The result of an enquiry into the effects on delinquency summarised in the reply of the London Juvenile Court Magistrates 'The panel sees no evidence . . . of any connection between the cinema and juvenile delinquency or moral laxity.'

The recommendations were concerned with raising and making uniform the prescribed minimum standards to safeguard the welfare of children; prescribing the minimum age of entry of seven for unaccompanied children, and five for accompanied children. No unaccompanied child under 12 should be allowed to stay after 8 p.m. The practice of issuing cheap tickets for early performances for children was commended. Seats should be reserved for unaccompanied children. The maximum number of children who may attend a children's performance and the minimum number of adults in attendance should be prescribed. A number of seats should be reserved for the general public. Greater attention should be given by adult attendants to children's behaviour and general needs. Performances should not last longer than 1½ hours. Films for children should be classified by experts and consultations between the industry and voluntary bodies encouraged. The classification of the 'A' films should be discontinued because it is unworkable. The new categories should be 'X' including the horrific, to which there is absolute prohibition, 'C' which can be shown at children's exhibitions and 'Advisory "U"' for family entertainment and 'Advisory "A"' preferably for adults. Cinema clubs should seek the advice and have co-operation of the local youth service. A central committee on children and the cinema should be appointed by the government departments now concerned with cinema questions. Educating children to view films with discrimination should be encouraged. There should be research into some of the effects of the cinema on children.

In a memorandum Mrs. Bower thought the Report understated the power exercised by the cinema on children. The 550,000 children who attend the cinemas three times a week in the ten years between ages 5 and 15 have been to 1560 performances. Such weight of impact is either absorbed, resisted or adjusted by the mind of the child. Recommended that all juvenile courts should keep records of the number of cinema performances a juvenile delinquent attends. Mrs. Bower appealed to the industry and the trade unions to produce children's films at the lowest possible costs.

See *Children and the Cinema*. An inquiry made by the Social Survey for the Dept. Cttee. J. C. Ward. Report. Central Office of Information, 1949.

3. CHARITIES

Law and Practice relating to Charitable Trusts

Cttee. Rep., apps., index. pp. iv, 251.
1952

1952–53 *Cmd.* 8710, *viii*, 5
apptd. Jan., 1950. *sgd. May*, 1952

Lord Nathan (*Ch.*), Allen, Astbury, Brockington, Corrin, Jones-Roberts (Mrs. K. W.), Kemball (Mrs. M. M. C.), Maude, Ruck, Whitley-Jones, Salt, Younghusband (Miss E. L.).

'*To consider and report on the changes in the law and practice (except as regards taxation) relating to charitable trusts in England and Wales which would be necessary to enable the maximum benefit to the community to be derived from them.*')

The enquiry arose out of public discussion on the importance of voluntary action which is not directed or controlled by the State, but is, in the main, financed by private funds. The best possible use should be made of the country's voluntary agencies, including charities, but difficulties were caused by the rise in costs and drying up of the sources of financial support, including charitable trusts. Additional finance should be provided from private, as opposed to public, funds by the re-allocation of charitable trusts thought to be moribund and dormant. There was no legislation to secure the due and honest administration of trusts till the middle of last century, and while this has been of great benefit, circumstances require some changes.

Charitable trusts enjoy both the privileges of holding property in perpetuity exempt from the rule against the rendering of property inalienable for a longer period than the lives in being and for 21 years, and a limited right to acquire new purposes. But it is impossible to change the purposes of a trust unless the original ones were initially or became impracticable of execution, and then only to new purposes as near as possible (*cy-près*) to the old.

There are thought to be some 110,000 charitable trusts in existence. Of these 30,000 are educational, and practically all are subject to the wider scheme-making powers of the Act of 1869, but the remaining 80,000 are still subject to the strict *cy-près* doctrine. It is thought that well over half of these are trusts appropriated to the poor or the sick in doles of money, gifts in kind, almshouse hospitals, etc., all being affected by the rise in the standard of life in the last hundred and by the social legislation of the last fifty years. Hundreds, perhaps thousands, need revision. A vast number of 'social welfare trusts' are not serving the community as they might do if the *cy-près* doctrine were relaxed. Trustees should be required to submit details of their trusts to the Commissioners or Ministry.

The definition of 'charity' goes back to the statute of 1601 and is archaic.

HH

Attempts to define it by an enumeration of all charitable objects would be impracticable and wrong in principle. There should be a new definition based on the four groups suggested by Lord MacNaghten: those for the relief of poverty, those for the advancement of education, those for the advancement of religion, and others benefiting the community. It should leave the existing case law unchanged.

Charitable trusts should cease to be subject to the law of mortmain. The doctrine of *cy-près*, which was broken into in the case of educational trusts, still applies to all other trusts. It should be relaxed, even though the carrying out of the trust objects has not become impracticable. Authorities with powers to make schemes should have special regard to the founders' intentions, the interest of the locality and to economy by merging endowments: this should safeguard religious bodies. Alterations of trusts under the widened powers should not be made within 35 years of the foundation of the trust without the consent of the trustees and of the founder, if living.

Proposals for schemes to alter trust objects should normally be put forward by the trustees, or by the county or county borough council in relation to any trust in its area, to the scheme-making authorities, which should be the Charity Commissioners and the Ministry of Education. Mixed charities, i.e. those with income from endowments or from subscriptions, universities, cathedrals, British Museum, etc., should be exempt from jurisdiction. The Board of Charity Commissioners is not well constituted to exercise the new powers proposed, into which questions of policy will enter, and is understaffed. It should be reconstituted with 5-9 members. A non-Departmental Minister with limited powers should be responsible for representing their views in Parliament.

By legal decisions in the Oxford Group and Ellis cases, whenever a trust includes certain kinds of secondary non-charitable objects, it is null and void:

and this decision affects thousands of trusts, e.g. for maintenance of church halls, which have been operating as valid. The property therefore belongs to the persons, e.g. next of kin or donors, to whom it would have belonged had the trust not been created. To save these funds for charity, all trusts which had been in existence for six or more years on 31st December, 1950, should be declared valid by Act, and the funds remain in the hands of the existing trustees.

Great advantages could be gained from a judicious merging of trusts, e.g. by a reduction in the number of the 35,000 trusts with less than £25 annual income, and in the holdings of endowments of trusts with less than £100 annual income by county unified trust funds and by merging non-ecclesiastical parochial trusts. Local and national common good trusts to help voluntary experiments should be encouraged.

In a Minority Report Mr. Salt discusses the differences between endowed, mixed, and plain charities, and the rights of 'Third Parties'. Doubts are expressed about the exact scheme-making powers of the various authorities concerned with the relaxation of *cy-près*, and how far these divided powers may cause confusion to trustees, their advisors and the public. A peripatetic Charity Referee emanating from the Chancery Judges should be available for hearing differences upon strict and relaxed *cy-près* schemes and pooling schemes where the income from the trust concerned does not exceed £100 per annum. In the few cases where agreement was not reached, reference to the Court or its Referee would be suitable. Her Majesty's Judges, who command a high degree of public confidence, would be less bound by policy and more able to consider each individual case on its merits and so make for diversity in unity in the whole range of trusts. The Commissioners should re-unite the Commission's existing functions and additional functions and those of the Minister of Education qua Charity Commission in educational and quasi-educational trusts, and it should be disembarrassed of judicial or quasi-judicial functions in respect of strict and proposed relaxed and pooling *cy-près* schemes.

See *Government Policy of Charitable Trusts;* 1955–56 Cmd. 9538, xxxvi, 463, which sets out which of the Committee's proposals the Government accept and which it rejects. *Charities Act, 1960;* 8 & 9 Eliz. 2. c. 58.

4. BETTING

Betting, Lotteries and Gaming

R. Com. Rep., apps., index. pp. vi, 190. [1951] Mins. of ev., 25 days, statements, index. 1949–51

1950–51 *Cmd.* 8190, *viii,* 625. *Mins. of ev., etc.;* 1949–51 *Non-Parl.*
apptd. *April,* 1949. sgd. *March,* 1951

H. Willink (*Ch.*), Mieville, Canny, Gore-Browne, Jewkes, Wolstencroft, Hunter, Campbell, Hodges, Jones, Kidd (Miss M. H.), Sutcliffe.

'To *inquire into the existing law and practice thereunder relating to lotteries, betting and gaming, with particular reference to the developments which have taken place since the report of the Royal Commission on Lotteries and Betting in* 1933, *and to report what changes, if any, are desirable and practicable.*'

The law relating to betting, lotteries and gaming, except for modern legislation covering only a small part of the field, is obscure, illogical and difficult to enforce. There is therefore a pressing need for simplification and clarification of a code. By various Acts it is illegal to keep any place for the purpose of betting with persons resorting to it, to frequent streets to sell or make bets, to advertise ready money football betting, etc. The general effect is that the only form of betting off the course (other than private betting between individuals) which is legal is credit betting by post, telegram or telephone. Though gaming—playing a game for money hazarded by the players—is not in itself illegal, the law is complicated and difficult to understand; and there is a risk of illegality where chance plays a part.

The place of gambling in the national economy is indicated by the numbers of people taking part and the amount of money spent in the three important types of gambling. During the season 1949–50, about 14 mn. persons or 1 in 3 of the adult population took part in football pool betting; 500,000 persons are regular attenders at dog-racing; 2½ mn. bet on the horse-racecourse and 4 mn. bet regularly off the course. The amounts staked in 1950 were £25 mn. on horse-racecourse totalisators, £70 mn. on dog-track totalisators and £52 mn. (estimated) on football pools. The amounts deducted before payment of winnings were £2·6 mn., £11 mn. and £26 mn. respectively, a total of £39·8 mn. To this must be added £22·5 mn. net expenditure in on- and off-course betting with bookmakers and £5 mn. for other forms of gambling, making the total about £70 mn. This is about 1 per cent of total personal expenditure and ½ per cent to 1 per cent of total national resources. It represents about £2 a year per head of the population, but since not all families take part in it, the burden on the standard of living must be heavier on those who do, especially as winnings normally tend to be used for luxury spending which would not otherwise be made.

The report reviews the various forms of betting and gambling, and the business organisation involved.

The prohibition of cash betting off the course is unenforceable and undesirable, but if it were unrestricted it would lead to loitering, continuous betting and solicitation. The alternatives of legalising cash betting by post or by the deposit of cash bets in bookmakers' offices, and the repeal of the Street Betting Act, 1906, are all rejected in favour of legalising the establishment of betting offices to which persons may resort, under strict conditions of licensing and control. At the time of the Royal Commission on Lotteries and

Betting, 1933 (*Breviate, 1917–39*, p. 504), betting on football was more frequently at fixed odds than on the pool principle. The Royal Commission unanimously recommended that all forms of off-the-course betting on the totalisator or pool principle, including betting on football, should be prohibited. But between the publication of the recommendations and the passage of the bills through Parliament there was a rapid growth in football pools and the attempts to prohibit them were defeated, the Bill of 1934 being rejected on a free vote on Second Reading by 287 votes to 24. There should be restrictions on football pool betting because those who participate have no contractual rights, and because large prizes are 'created' as an inducement to bet by unloading commission and expenses of one pool on to another. In view of the large sums of money accepted from the public, detailed accounts should be published.

It is extremely difficult to establish by abstract arguments that all gambling is inherently immoral without adopting views as to the nature of good and evil which would not find general acceptance amongst moralists. Apart from isolated cases, no support was found for the belief that gambling, within 'reasonable bounds', does serious harm either to the character of those who take part in it, or to their family circle or to the community generally. As expenditure on gambling represented not more than 1 per cent of total personal expenditure and absorbs about ½ per cent of the national resources, and the 100,000 persons engaged in the industry represented considerably less than 1 per cent of the total number of employed persons, the economic effects were unimportant. There was no conclusive evidence that gambling interferes with production, the widespread gambling in industry being due to the absence of legal facilities for cash betting off the course. It had no significance as a direct cause of serious crime and was of little importance as a direct cause of minor offences of dishonesty.

Legislation should interfere as little as possible with individual liberty to take part in the various forms of gambling, but should impose restrictions to discourage and prevent excess. Legislation designed only to prohibit or restrict participation in particular forms of gambling is likely to fail because it is difficult to enforce, frequently becomes out of date, leads to class distinctions and is ineffective as a method of checking gambling generally. But certain basic principles should be observed. There should be strict control over the provision on a commercial basis of all major forms of gambling facility, the law should apply fairly to all sections of the community and the public should be well-informed as to the extent and the conduct of various forms of gambling. The provision of betting facilities by the State is rejected, because it would be strongly opposed, and the Commission's proposals made would deal with most of the evils.

All bookmakers should require a certificate of eligibility from the licensing authority, and their offices should be registered with the police. Each office in which a bookmaker conducts business with people resorting to it must be registered, and should be subject to strict conditions about hours of opening, loitering and continuous betting, and restrictions on use by young persons. In pool betting, any commission, expenses, etc., must be charged proportionately against the total stakes in each pool, the total winnings in each pool must equal total stakes in that pool less the deductions for commission and expenses, etc., and any prizes should not exceed an amount fixed by statute. Full accounts for each competition must be sent to the licensing authority. The licensing authority should be judicial, should consider applications for registration, appoint accountants to supervise pool betting, and arrange for the hearing of objections to applications for licensed betting offices. Amongst other recommendations were that gaming should be permitted, provided that the proceeds derived from any charges made are devoted to purposes other than private gain, that only one charge not exceeding 5s. is made to each player, only one distribution of prizes takes place and that the total value of prizes does not exceed £20. Fun-fairs should be licensed and stakes should not exceed 1s. and prizes 5s. Coin-actuated machines which deliver a prize automatically should be prohibited.

See *Pool Betting Act, 1954;* 2 & 3 Eliz. 2. c. 33. *Small Lotteries and Gaming Act, 1956;* 4 & 5 Eliz. 2. c. 45. *Betting and Gaming Act, 1960;* 8 & 9 Eliz. 2. c. 60.

XVI. LEGAL ADMINISTRATION, POLICE, LAW

1. Legal Administration, Procedure, Legal Aid
2. Police
3. Prisons, Prisoners, Punishment, Probation
4. Legal Problems arising out of

War, War Damage
5. Law of Property, Succession
6. Nationality, International Law
7. Law Revision and Reform
8. Marriage and Divorce
9. Miscellaneous Regulatory Powers

1. LEGAL ADMINISTRATION, PROCEDURE, LEGAL AID

Law Reporting

Cttee. Rep. pp. 30. 1940

1940 *Non-Parl. Ld. Chancellor's Dept. apptd. —,* 1939. *sgd. Feb.,* 1940

G. T. Simonds (*Ch.*), Wrottesley, Holmes, Hunter, le Quesne, Macaskie, Roxburgh, Stamp, Winfield, Woodthorpe, Goodhart.

The law of this country consists substantially of legislative enactments and judicial decisions. The former are printed at the public expense and preserved under conditions which ensure that they shall be permanently and authentically recorded whilst the latter are in the hands of private enterprise. Because of the binding force of precedent and the need for judicial consistency, accurate reports of judicial decisions are of permanent importance. Reports should contain all that is material and nothing else, should deal with all cases introducing a new principle or rule, should be accurate and speedy. Between 1535 and 1765, more than 100 persons were responsible for volumes of reports, some of ill repute. A higher standard of reporting developed after 1765, but its success provoked further competition until in 1863 members of the Bar commenced an agitation which led to the establishment by the Incorporated Council of Law Reporting of the Law Reports, for which the Judges approve their reports before publication. It was hoped that they would drive competitors out of the field, but this has not been achieved. The criticism and complaints of the present state of affairs are of the cost of the various series of reports, the difficulty of accommodation, the repetition of cases in the competing series, the difficulty of tracing cases in the multiplicity of reports, that the Law Reports, whilst accurate, omit cases that should be reported; that reports from other series are not always accurate, and that far too many cases are reported.

The Committee opposed the establishment of a monopoly of a single series under official control and any licensing of particular reporters, as there was always a possibility of error by a reporter or editor. It also rejected a proposal that to deal with oral judgments an official shorthand writer should take a note of every judgment, which should be passed by the Judge before publication and filed in the Records of the Court. There could be no large measure of reform. Where a case has been reported in the Law Reports, the practice of exclusive citation should be rigidly enforced. Publication of Law Reports should be speeded up. Law Reports should take a more generous view of cases to be included.

In a Dissentient Report Prof. Goodhart argued that the fallacy of the majority report was the emphasis placed on the semi-official Law Reports when they covered only 250 cases a year, whilst the unofficial reports taken together covered an additional 1000. Many cases which could be properly cited were unreported or reported inaccurately in out of the way places. He supported the proposal, rejected by the majority, for the publication of the reports of all judgments by an official shorthand writer as passed by the Judge, as this would reduce inaccuracy, allow for deletion of unconsidered phrases, would make it necessary to consult only one source, and improve the choice of cases. The system should be commenced in the various Appellate Courts.

Cases of Defective Court Procedure

Hereford Juvenile Court Inquiry. 1942–43 Cmd. 6485, iv, 653 (R. Goddard). On January 26 W. J. Payne, aged 13, and D. H. Craddock, aged 11, were sentenced to receive 4 strokes with a birch rod on the charge of malicious damage, and on the charges of larceny. They were committed to the care of the local Education Authority till they were 18, the parents of Payne were ordered to pay 7s. 6d. a week and those of Craddock 10s. od. a week towards their maintenance. Leave to apply for an Order of Certiorari to quash the conviction was supported by an affidavit sworn by the father that there had been a number of irregularities in the proceedings. The Divisional Court found that there had been a number of irregularities and quashed the convictions, but their findings on some of these depended on the assumption that

the boys had pleaded guilty to one charge only. In matters relating to certiorari the Court proceeds on affidavit evidence. Owing to a long lapse of time between the hearing of the case and the application to the High Court it was difficult for persons to recall details and there was a serious failure to observe the Rule that notice should be served on the Clerk or Registrar of the Court and on other parties, including the police in this case, from whom there was therefore no affidavit. The affidavits filed on behalf of the applicant and the Justices were such as to give the Divisional Court an incomplete and wholly wrong picture of what took place and in particular, that there had been an admission of guilt on two charges. There had been no miscarriage of justice.

Procedure at a Case heard before two Justices at Longton, Stoke-on-Trent. 1945 Non-Parl. Home Office (Lord Goddard). Cecil Basil Whelan, a Roman Catholic priest, was charged with indecent assault on a male person under 16 years of age and was admitted to bail in his own recognisance and that of the surety of the Rev. W. Walsh, the rector of a local Roman Catholic Church and he was to appear at the Longton Police Court on June 4th. The Chief Constable decided that the case should be heard by the Stipendiary sitting at Tunstall on the same day. On the day following the arrest Mr. Walsh called on Mr. Hawley, clerk of the Longton Court, who is also a Roman Catholic and is also Mr. Walsh's private solicitor, to ascertain his obligations as bailor, and for information as to the nature of the charge and the possible penalty. Mr. Hawley obtained details of the case irregularly from a Superintendent Edge; arranged a sitting of the court, and without informing the magistrates on the rota telephoned two magistrates of some three years' standing, one of whom is also a Roman Catholic, and arranged for them to hear the case fifty minutes before the three justices on rota for that day were to sit. The police had no knowledge of the proceeding, and the persons who did attend the hearing could have known only from Mr. Hawley. The inexperienced magistrates, who relied entirely on Mr. Hawley, heard him read the police reports, heard the doctor's evidence and some remarks of the solicitor for the defence and then bound the prisoner over upon certain conditions for 12 months. This order was correct, but the proceedings had been arranged by Mr. Hawley, who had resolved to get the case disposed of in secret. This could only be attributable to the fact that the accused was a priest of his Church. That such a thing could happen was in part due to the fact that in the city of Stoke there is a lack of a satisfactory system for allocating cases to the Stipendiary. As there are three justices' clerks to the city magistrates besides the Stipendiary's clerk, the idea is fostered that there are separate jurisdictions within the city based on the previous unamalgamated boroughs, whereas there is but one court sitting in separate places.

Proceedings at the Hearing of Two Informations before Justices of the Aberayron Division of the County of Cardigan on 24th April, 1946. 1946–47 Cmd. 7061, xiii, 51 (F. J. Tucker). The informations were brought against Mr. Lewis, solicitor and Clerk to the Justices. The decision of the Justices to dismiss the summons was a bad one, but was not due to dishonesty or conscious bias in favour of Mr. Lewis. The Justices needed some guidance on the issues involved, and this was not forthcoming because the Chairman, who was well advanced in years, had not the assistance he was accustomed to have from his Clerk. Suggestions are made about points of procedure in which Justices and their clerks need guidance.

Case heard by Justices of the Gilling East Division North Riding of Yorkshire

Inquiry. Rep. pp. 10. 1946

1945–46 *Cmd.* 6783, *xii*, 325
apptd. Feb., sgd. March, 1946

F. J. Tucker.

'*To enquire into and report on the circumstances leading up to the hearing of an application for recovery of possession under the Small Tenements Recovery Act, 1838 . . . at an occasional Court-house at Darlington on 26th November, 1945, and into the proceedings at the hearing.*'

Mr. Hinks, solicitor, who practices before the Gilling East Bench 'prompted by a sense of duty and jealous regard for proper administration of justice' reported the matter to the Home Office and this brought about the Inquiry. Mr. Steavenson of Stapleton Manor wished to take possession of his cottage occupied by Mr. Currie, who had obtained employment as groom with Mr. Steavenson by misrepresentation. Mr. Steavenson as J.P. for 20 years and Chairman of the Bench for 10 years had used his position to have summoned a Special Court purely for his own convenience to get an eviction order at a time when he required it. 'In my view a Magistrate, so far from using his position to further his own private convenience, should be prepared to put up with a greater degree of inconvenience than an ordinary litigant if there is any danger of conflict between his rights as an ordinary citizen and his position as a Justice of the Peace.'

Justices' Clerks

Dept. Cttee. Rep., app. pp. 70. 1944
1943–44 *Cmd.* 6507, *iv*, 189
apptd. April, 1938. *sgd. Jan.,* 1944

Lord Roche (*Ch.*), Burrows, Buxton (Lady), Foyster, Fry (Miss M.), Harris, Oakes, Page, Schuster, Webster.

'*To enquire into the conditions of service of Clerks to Justices and their assistants, including qualifications, appointment, remuneration, superannuation and duties. . . .*'

The office of clerk to the justices grew up to meet the needs of a lay magistracy. The basis of the system is the

Justices' Clerks Act, 1877, which required that clerks should be either lawyers or men who had worked as assistants to clerks and that they should be salaried. Each bench appoints its own clerk, whole-time or part-time, to hold office at the pleasure of the justices. The clerk is left to engage his own assistants and to pay them out of his own inclusive salary. The extension of jurisdiction, the addition of new classes of work and new methods of treating offenders means that he must be not only an expert in law, procedure and the laws of evidence, but in the courses open to the justices if they find a charge proved. Originally a servant of the justices, his office has now assumed a public character, though decisions and judicial acts are those of the justices and not of their clerks. He is legal adviser to the justices on matters of law and the admissibility of evidence, but his advice on admissibility should not be binding on the justices; in many cases law and fact are so mixed that common sense may be a more valuable guide than legal advice, and the responsibility for decisions should remain with the justices. In cases of summary jurisdiction the parties may be ignorant of the law and without professional assistance; in such cases, in some areas clerks conduct almost all the examinations, though this is not in accordance with the law and is undesirable. Clerks should do as little of the examination of witnesses as possible. There is a temptation for clerks 'to run the court'. The retirement of the clerk with the justices at the end of a hearing is a matter for the discretion of the justices.

There are 90 whole-time and 722 part-time clerks in England and Wales, excluding those of the Metropolitan Police Courts. But 395 divisions have less than 500 cases a year, 439 have over 1000, while in large cities the number of cases reaches 50,000. While some urge that part-time clerks who are solicitors in good private practice are well qualified for the work, the weight of evidence, including difficulties arising from a conflict of interest, was that

where the work was sufficient for a whole-time clerk there should be one.

The system of whole-time clerks should be extended, adjacent divisions and boroughs being combined where necessary, separate commissions of the peace for boroughs with less than 25,000 population being abolished and those with over 75,000 remaining exempt from grouping. In each administrative county a Magistrate's Court Committee should be established to make all new appointments and to whom all existing whole-time clerks and whole-time assistant clerks should be transferred. Clerks should not be appointed below the age of 30 or over that of 50 and should have professional qualifications. Persons without professional legal qualifications should no longer be eligible for appointment by virtue of services as assistant, though existing qualifications by service should not be affected; special examinations not leading to accepted professional qualifications were rejected. Assistants doing responsible professional work should have professional qualifications.

The salaries of clerks should cover all their own duties, but should not include those of their assistants which, owing to the inclusive system, are much too low. As there will be part-time clerks for some years, in all new appointments there should be restrictions on certain classes of private and public work which may be undertaken.

To maintain the courts, all fees and fines should be paid to the Exchequer and distributed amongst the various authorities to meet approved expenditure, any deficiencies being shared between the local authorities and the Exchequer. There should be compulsory audit of clerks' accounts. Courts of Summary Jurisdiction should be known as Magistrates Courts; benches should be composed of 3 to 5 and not more than 7 justices. The rules of procedure should be consolidated and simplified.

In a Memo. Schuster, while agreeing with the general plan of reform, argued that the grouping could be accomplished only if the initiative rested with the central authority, and that the audit should be central.

Justices of the Peace

R. Com. Rep., apps. pp. viii, 111. [1948] Mins. of ev., 22 days, apps. 1–4, index. 1946–48

1947–48 *Cmd. 7463, xii, 733. Mins. of ev., etc., 1946–1948 Non-Parl.*

apptd. June, 1946. sgd. May, 1948

Lord Du Parcq (*Ch.*), L. Exeter, L. Rosebery, L. Calverley, Cadogan, Maxwell, Oakes, Jones (Miss M. L. K.), Evans, Cotton, Denholm (Thelma), Foot, Watson, Welsh, L. Merthyr.

'To review the present arrangements for the selection and removal of Justices of the Peace in Great Britain . . . the selection and appointment of chairmen of Magisterial Benches, of Justices to form panels for Juvenile Courts; and on the appointment of Stipendiary Magistrates. . . .'

There are 19,000 justices in England and Wales, about 1100 being appointed annually by the Lord Chancellor, assisted by a Secretary of Commissions and, in accordance with the R. Com. of 1910 (*Breviate, 1900–1916*, p. 357), the advice of local committees appointed by him.

The Secretary of the Commission should have improved status and a more adequate staff. Separate Commissions of the Peace for areas of small population are detrimental to the selection of justices and organisation of their work. The Advisory Committees were intended to be in touch with and represent the various views and currents of public opinion, but this has been interpreted to mean political opinion. The dominance of members of political parties has meant that justices have been drawn too narrowly from certain sections of the community, recommendations for appointment being made on the ground of good political party record. While there is no reason to think that political partisanship has affected the decisions of benches, 'political' appointments are to be condemned

because they are not true selections on merit. The proportions of members of committees appointed for their political affiliations should be restricted and enquiries of party political headquarters should cease. The committees should be small and their membership and proceedings secret, but the secretaries should be publicly known. Membership of a political party should be no bar to appointment and no party should be unduly favoured. Clear directions should be given to committees on the criteria, including that of political balance, they are to use in making recommendations.

The paramount consideration for appointment should be personal fitness, and not reward of political or other forms of public service. All sections of the community should be represented, including those with a knowledge of working people. A third of the justices are also members of local authorities, but it is undesirable that local authorities who often have to bring proceedings should be too strongly represented and the proportions could be reduced. The administrative bars to appointment of certain categories of persons should be as few as possible, and recommendations are made on desirable practice as regards M.P.s, party agents, ministers of religion, persons in the licensed trade, etc. One-third of the justices are between the ages of 65 and 75 and 11 per cent are 75 and over. While justices are under an obligation to do a fair share of the work, a substantial number fail to attend court. Justices may be placed by the Lord Chancellor on a supplementary list by reason of age or unfitness, but the arrangements for providing him with reliable information are not adequate. There should be a retiring age of 75, the Lord Chancellor having discretion for five years to continue appointments beyond that age. Owing to the need of preserving the independence of the justices, removal for neglect of duty or unfitness should be only for substantial, indisputable causes. After an annual review, the Advisory Committee should consider whether each justice is fully effective and inform the Lord Chancellor accordingly. Steps should be taken to instruct justices before they commence their duties. The total number of justices should be based on court work and not on the duties of 'signing papers', which can be undertaken by persons on the approved lists duly extended. The chairman of county and district councils should cease to be justices *ex officio*, mayors should continue to be so during their year of office, but their powers of presiding curtailed.

The system of lay justices should continue, as it would be impossible to find a sufficient body of qualified persons to act as stipendiaries, but the Lord Chancellor should have power to appoint a stipendiary without the initiative of the local authority. Efforts should be made to obtain as chairmen of quarter sessions legally qualified persons who will give voluntary service; failing this, they should be paid.

Juvenile courts should be organised to provide a good selection of justices, a good chairman and an adequate volume of work. No first appointment should be made after the age of 50 and retirement at 65 should be compulsory.

In London, in addition to stipendiary magistrates, there are 582 justices in petty divisions. The advisory committee is made up on party lines, and there is bargaining over the allotment of justices to each party. This should discontinue, the advisory committee should be reconstructed as in other areas, nominations from political parties should not be received and the proportion of political party members reduced.

Recommendations are made to apply the similar principles to Scotland.

In a memo. of dissent Lord Merthyr, A. F. Stapleton and J. A. F. Watson argued that political appointments on the bench were undesirable, and that they were largely the result of political appointments to the advisory committees. The present system by which

regard is paid to the political affiliations of a proportion of members should be discontinued. The committees should be composed of persons drawn from every social class whose qualifications are confined to character, intelligence and local knowledge. In a separate Report Lord Merthyr recommended that Lancashire should not be allowed to increase the cost of administration by continuing the system of the appointment of the justice by the Chancellor of the Duchy; there should be no justices *ex officio;* over a period of years lay justices should be replaced by professional justices, paid out of national funds, and the City of London should be served by the metropolitan magistrates. There should be no justices in Scotland, as Scottish figures show that a system of sheriff or professional justices sitting alone is practicable in town and country alike.

Evidence includes a memo. by the Lord Chamberlain's Department, mins. of ev., App. 1 and statement of evidence by Leo Page, mins. of ev., App. 3.

Inquiries into Convictions for Murder

Confession made by David John Ware of the Murder of Olive Balchin in respect of which murder Walter Graham Rowland was convicted . . . 16th Dec., 1946; 1946–47 Cmd. 7049, xiv, 515 (J. C. Jolly). Ware had made a false statement; had been in a mental hospital. There was no miscarriage of justice.

Conviction at Liverpool Assizes on 27th February, 1952, of Edward Francis Devlin and Alfred Burns of the Murder of Beatrice Alice Rimmer; 1951–52 Cmd. 8522, xxv, 387 (A. D. Gerrard). There had been no miscarriage of justice.

Deaths of Mrs. Beryl Evans and of Geraldine Evans and . . . the Conviction of Timothy John Evans of the Murder of Geraldine Evans; 1952–53 Cmd. 8896, Cmd. 8946, ix, 65 (J. S. Henderson). The findings were that (1) The case for the prosecution against Evans as presented to the jury at his trial was an overwhelming one (para. 28). (2) 'Having considered all the material now available relating to the deaths of Mrs. Evans and Geraldine Evans, I am satisfied that there can be no doubt that Evans was responsible for both' (para. 41); (3) Christie's statements that he was responsible for the death of Mrs. Evans were not only unreliable, but were untrue (para. 48).

Witnesses Allowances Order

Dept. Cttee. Rep., apps. pp. 16. 1947

1947 *Non-Parl. Home Office*
apptd. April, 1939. *sgd. Dec.,* 1946

F. C. Johnson(*Ch.*), Cordes, des Forges, Mathew, Morrison, Nops, Oakes.

In view of the changes in the standards of wages and of the cost of living the Committee recommended increases. They provided for professional, expert and ordinary witnesses, interpreters and seamen. They are set out in the form of revised draft Regulations in Appendix III.

Depositions

Dept. Cttee. Rep., apps. pp. 35. 1949

1948–49 *Cmd.* 7639, *xiv,* 309
apptd. March, sgd. Dec., 1948

L. A. Byrne (*Ch.*), Allen, Artemus-Jones (Lady), Cotton, Curtis-Bennett, Halsall, Hawke, Johnson, Lane (Mrs. E.), Martin, Mathew, Morrison.

'*To inquire into the existing practice with regard to the taking of depositions in criminal cases and to report whether any, and if so what, alterations in the law are necessary or desirable with a view to securing the more effective despatch of the business of the courts while retaining public confidence in the administration of justice.*'

Depositions are the written record in a criminal case of the preliminary examination of witnesses prior to their giving evidence at the trial of an accused person. They have played an important part in the administration of English justice for 400 years, but it is now suggested that taking them is an anachronism and a waste of time of the justices and the clerk. They still form an essential part of the system at each stage. They ensure that evidence is recorded while it is fresh in the minds of witnesses, and that the accused knows precisely the case he has to meet. Committal proceedings are not a formality, but are a safeguard to the accused and against speculative prosecutions. Various suggestions for dispensing with them wholly or in part are rejected.

Amongst the criticisms are that much inconvenience and expense is caused to the accused, prosecution and witnesses by the practice of taking depositions in a case at short weekly or fortnightly intervals, by recording in longhand, by the number and complexity of forms to be prepared by the clerk on committal, and the elaborate procedure for binding over witnesses. The recommendations include: Magistrates Courts should set aside a sitting to ensure that all indictable cases are dealt with regularly and promptly; court lists should be staggered. Depositions should contain a full and accurate record in narrative form of all the evidence given by the witnesses; as soon as recorded they should be read over to the witness, be signed and he should be released forthwith. Provided these conditions are satisfied the court should use the method of recording they find most convenient. Where several indictable offences are charged against the same accused based on the same facts, one set of depositions should be taken. Forms for committal proceedings should be simplified, notices to attend substituted for formal binding of witnesses, statutory declarations and draft depositions used subject to safeguards.

County Court Procedure

Cttee. 1st Interim Rep. pp. 13. 1948

1947–48 *Cmd.* 7466, *xi,* 321
apptd. April, 1947. *sgd. July,* 1948

A. E. L. Jones (*Ch.*), Davies, Pugh,

Barrow, Coldstream, Dodd, Elborne, Evans, Fawcett, Hale, Haynes, Hicks, Holland, Hollis, Marshall.

'*To enquire into the present practice and procedure of the county court, and to consider what reforms might be introduced with a view to reducing the cost of litigation and securing greater efficiency in the despatch of business.*'

The main criticism of county court procedure is that litigants who are kept waiting at the Court for their cases to be heard often find that they are not needed or that their cases are not completed on the day fixed for the hearing and therefore suffer waste of time, additional costs where Counsel are employed, etc. The returns from all county courts show that in 1946, 1227 cases and in 1947, 1335 cases were adjourned for 'want of time'.

Evidence submitted to the Committee suggested that all defended cases in registrar's courts should be heard after the disposal of the undefended cases, and more days should be set apart exclusively for the hearing of defended 'possession' cases.

The problem is how to arrange the judge's list so that no case shall go over to another day unless one of the parties desires an adjournment. Recommended that the judge should stress the great importance of preventing adjournment and should supervise the arrangement of the list. The chief clerk should be responsible to the registrar and the registrar to the judge for its arrangement. Cases should be grouped for hearing according to their nature, etc., an excessive number should not be assigned to a single hearing day, some days should be kept free for cases of exceptional length. About a week before the hearing day the list should be reviewed or revised if overloaded. Full use should be made of the registrar's powers to relieve the judge's list. Modifications in the recommendations will be necessary in the case of country courts. If arrears begin to accumulate the Lord Chancellor should be informed and it should be made lawful to appoint a deputy judge whenever a judge certifies it necessary.

—— Final Report, apps. pp. 111 [1949] 1948–49 *Cmd.* 7668, xiii, 805 sgd. *April,* 1949

The County Court Act, 1934, and the Administration of Justice (Miscellaneous Powers) Act, 1938, conferred considerable powers upon the Registrar by Rules. An extension of these powers, subject to the consent of the parties and leave of the judge, would enable the judge to devote more time to substantial cases and would reduce the risk of adjournments through want of time. Where necessary the registrar should have additional subordinate and clerical staff. Recommendations are made for enabling more than one deputy judge to sit at the same time as the judge, and for increasing the number of judges, where this proves to be necessary. Service of ordinary summonses by A.R. registered post would enable bailiffs to execute the judgments and orders of the Court more promptly. The recovery of debts should be expedited: judgment should be entered by the officers of the Court immediately a plaintiff notifies his acceptance of the defendant's offer and the judge should be empowered to cause a judgment debtor who neglects to attend the hearing of a judgment summons to be apprehended and brought before the Court. Recommendations were made for improving and simplifying the county court forms and for reducing expense in contested and non-contested cases, and for abolishing or reducing certain fees. Witnesses' allowances should be raised to a maximum of £2 for professional persons; other employed persons £1; police officers 15s. 0d.; other persons 10s. 0d.

See *County Courts Act, 1955*; 4 Eliz. 2. c. 8. *County Court Manual.* R. C. Gregory; 1951 Non-Parl. Home Office.

Supreme Court Practice and Procedure

Cttee. Rep. apps. pp. 59. 1949

1948–49 *Cmd.* 7764, *xiv*, 1
apprd. April, 1947. *sgd. Aug.,* 1949

R. Evershed (*Ch.*), Lynskey, Willmer, Barnes, Coldstream, Crowther, Driver, Fletcher, Gallie, Gardiner, Geddes, Gibbon, Goodhart, Gridley, Hanbury-Williams, Herbert, Marshall, Moseley, Newton, Norton, Upjohn, Wells, Willmott, Yeabsley.

'(1) *To enquire into the present practice and procedure of the Supreme Court (excluding the practice and procedure in actions for the infringement of patents and under the Patents and Designs Acts,* 1907 *to* 1946, *and in matrimonial proceedings in the Probate, Divorce and Admiralty Division of the High Court, but including the practice and procedure on appeals from that Division), and to consider what reforms . . . should now be introduced . . . for the purpose of reducing the cost of litigation and securing greater efficiency and expedition in the despatch of business. . . .'*

If the cost of litigation is to be successfully tackled, it must be approached and judged as a whole rather than piecemeal, and decisions—possibly far-reaching in effect—made upon matters of general principle. On extended jurisdiction and other matters related to county courts, the Committee's views may be regarded as complementary to the Report of the Committee on County Court Procedure. Increase in jurisdiction in the county courts is desirable, but it must not destroy or imperil the value of the county court as a 'poor men's court'. The pecuniary jurisdiction of the County court in contract and tort should be increased to a sum of £300. But as there is a reluctance to have cases tried in the County court, partly because costs allowed are not sufficiently remunerative to solicitors, scales of costs should be remunerative. In certain classes of cases plaintiffs should not in general be entitled to any more costs in the High Courts than in the County courts. Unless there is sufficient reason for certain classes of action to remain in the High Court, the Court or the judge should be able to have it transferred to the county court. The jurisdiction in the county court for claims for damage, towage, seamen's wages, etc., should be raised to £1000, and in contentious probate matters where the real personal estate is under £1000. In the London area it may be necessary to appoint one or two more judges.

Fixed Dates.—The difficulties encountered by this Committee and all other Commissions and Committees since the Judicature Commission, 1869, in arranging for efficient despatch of business and the remedies suggested have, in spite of the passage of time, varied very little; there is widespread demand for dates to be fixed for the hearing of cases both in London and at the Assizes. The real basis of the loss occasioned by the absence of such a system is that once it is known that a case may appear in the lists for trial some day about a month ahead, no party or ordinary or expert witness can safely make any engagement on any day within that period. In a period of manpower shortage such loss and inconvenience cannot be justified where a system of fixing dates is at all practicable. England is the only civilised country in the world where litigants are *not* told, as a matter of course, the date on which their action will be heard.

Fixed dates are not at present practicable at Assizes; they already apply for commercial cases and (for practical purposes) in probate and admiralty cases; they should apply in all other witness actions. In the King's Bench Division the scheme detailed should be adopted, on condition of an increase in the number of judges. Whatever scheme is adopted a case once started should be finished, even if it cannot be completed in the allotted time. Long vacation should last 8 weeks and the Christmas vacation should be shortened by one week. There should be 2 additional judges, but if the recommendations are accepted a total of 4 should be authorised by Parliament.

—— Second Interim Report, apps. pp. 68 [1951]

1950–51 *Cmd.* 8176, *xvi*, 661
sgd. Feb., 1951

The Report is confined to cases of a highly technical nature which are not dependent upon conclusions having been first reached on matters of general principle. Detailed recommendations are made for re-writing the procedural code for Admiralty cases; miscellaneous matters of procedure in the Chancery Division and the Court of Protection, and before Official Referees. There should be a complete revision, long overdue, of the Rules of the Supreme Court, which should be published officially on the loose-leaf principle. Practice Notes and Directions should be issued separately. The Lord Chancellor, in consultation, should be the Rule-making authority.

—— Third Interim Rep. *Durham Palatine Court.* Working Party. Rep., apps. pp. 22. 1952

1951–52 *Cmd.* 8617, *xvi*, 409
sgd. July, 1952

Romer, Upjohn, Willmott.

'*To consider whether, having regard to the existing state of business, the Chancery Court of the County Palatine of Durham should continue to exist. . . .*'

The Committee was asked to consider these additional terms of reference, but as they involved matters purely local, they appointed the Working Party, and approved and adopted its Report and recommendations.

There was strong local feeling in favour of its retention. The presence of a local court saves expense to persons engaged in litigation and is far more convenient than a hearing in London, especially as the date of hearing can be more easily fixed to suit all concerned. And the Court already exists.

The Durham 'Palatine' Court rests on custom and immemorial tradition. But its geographical boundaries are anomalous, litigation initiated in the Durham Court cannot be transferred to the High Court and although the jurisdiction of the Court is wholly Chancery, no purely Chancery practitioner has been appointed since 1846, so that the volume of work coming before the Court has been meagre.

The Durham Palatine Court should be retained, future Chancellors should have practised in the field of Chancery litigation. A map shows the territorial jurisdiction recommended. Substantive jurisdiction should be the same as that of the Chancery Division of the High Court of Justice, there should be powers of transfer of a case from Durham to London and vice-versa, all the Rules of the Supreme Court should be substituted for the Rules of the Palatine Court.

—— Final Rep., apps. pp. 380. 1953

1952–53 *Cmd.* 8878, *xiv*, 601
sgd. May, 1953

del. Moseley.

The Hanworth Committee and Peel Commission concentrated on the efficiency and despatch of business, this Committee on the problem of costs. If by reason of high costs or fear of them any citizen is deterred from making a just claim or defence or is induced to accept a settlement which he feels unjust, the administration of justice has fallen short of its proper function. And if commercial disputes are for reasons of cheapness taken to arbitration tribunals rather than to the courts, the natural development of law is retarded. The 'average litigant' constitutes a large class not helped by great corporations nor poor enough to be helped at public expense. Most of the costs are incurred in preparation for or at the trial, and the amount increases substantially with its length. The most effective way of reducing them is to limit at an early stage the issues to be tried and to reduce the number of operations to be performed. There was a general failure to make adequate use of existing opportunities to save costs already provided in the Rules.

Civil procedure must consist of four stages: a claim made by a person that his rights have been infringed by another person; an answer by that other; a trial of the issues raised, and a decision and the giving of any necessary remedy. The purpose of rules of procedure is to guide those concerned in these essential stages. In the course of 440 meetings of committees and sub-committees the Rules were examined at each stage, the questions being 'Is this step necessary' and 'Is there a reasonable cause of grievance by the litigant?', 229 detailed recommendations being made.

A new approach to the problem could be made in two ways. The originating summons procedure used in Chancery is less formal than a writ. It should be generally available in any case in which the sole or principal question is one of law or the construction of a document, where there is no substantial issue of fact and where such evidence of fact as is necessary can be given by affidavit. This would help to limit the issues to be tried and to substitute means of proof more economical than formal ones. Queen's Bench cases are different in character, since there is a greater emphasis on fact, and the extension to them of the originating summons would be ineffective. There should be an analogous new procedure by writ by which a plaintiff after appropriate notice should be able to apply to the Master on summons for an order to proceed without pleadings. The defendant would be required to set out his defence in an affidavit and the Master of the Supreme Court on that information would then decide whether the action should proceed without formal pleadings. This new procedure would be commenced by writ, with statement of claim. The fact that the claim and defence had to be on oath would compel each party to disclose before the hearing, the true nature of his case, and discourage the raising of formal issues having no substantial basis of fact. Certain forms of action, such as libel actions and

actions where fraud was alleged should at least to start with be excluded from its scope and also, in general, actions for personal injuries.

In cases not suitable for the extended originating summons procedure or the new analogous procedure by writ, the same results of reduction in costs can be obtained by strengthening the summons for direction, and by postponing it until after discovery has been completed, this having become under the recommendations a matter normally carried out by the parties without the intervention of the Court. This should help to strip the case down to essentials. When it is heard, both parties should be in possession of all the material, and the issues could then become precise and closely confined. It must not, however, become a dress rehearsal for the trial, and in straightforward cases counsel should not attend; if they do, costs should not be allowed.

For an ordinary citizen an alarming prospect is the risk of a double appeal, to the Court of Appeal and to the House of Lords. In certain cases, e.g. when the construction of a statute has been fully argued in the High Court and is essential to the determination of the case, the appeal should leap-frog the Court of Appeal and go to the House of Lords. Forty per cent of the Queen's Bench cases concern personal injuries. As their main characteristic is a sharp conflict over fact, recommendations are made to bring them to trial at the earliest moment, together with proposals designed to limit expenditure on plans and drawings; to limit conflicts of experts—each side would be compelled to disclose to the other before the trial the medical report of any doctor called for witness—and to have police evidence available at an earlier stage.

The broad principle is that the winner of an action is entitled to recover his costs, subject to the condition that the loser cannot be made to pay costs unreasonably incurred through extravagance, etc. In addition to these party and party costs, there are costs as between solicitor and own client, and in lengthy cases there may be a gap between the latter and what is recovered from the loser. This and the unrestricted freedom of bargaining between a solicitor and his client tends to drive both parties to extravagance. The legal profession was not personally overpaid, but some alterations in charges could be made. Refresher fees should, in default of express agreement, be related to brief fees by means of fixed and descending scale, with an overall maximum for every day after the first. The rule that a junior's fee should be two-thirds that of the senior should operate only if the senior's fee does not exceed 50 guineas; after that it should be on a descending fractional basis.

Other recommendations were:—there is no sufficient case for introducing Continental rule and practice in regard to evidence, but there should be more liberal acceptance of documents as evidence, in order to save the cost of calling oral witnesses. In a case involving a point of law of public interest the Attorney General should have power to subsidise the parties to prosecute the case in accordance with ordinary appeal procedure.

New Trials in Criminal Cases

Dept. Cttee. Rep., apps. pp. 37. 1954
1953–54 *Cmd.* 9150, xi, 237
apptd. Dec., 1952. *sgd. April,* 1954

Lord Tucker (*Ch.*), Bass, Coldstream, Graham-Harrison, Humphreys, Levy, Mathew, Taylor.

'*To consider and report whether the Court of Criminal Appeal and the House of Lords should be empowered to order a new trial of a convicted person who has appealed to the Court of Criminal Appeal, or whose case has been referred to the Court by the Secretary of State. . . .*'

When the Criminal Appeal Bill was introduced in 1907 it was decided not to give a right of appeal by way of re-hearing, but to give a right of appeal on specific grounds and to give the Court of Criminal Appeal powers of quashing a conviction or passing a different sentence, etc. It seemed at the time that powers had been given virtually to re-try a case, but the Court of Criminal Appeal have never considered it a part of their duty to substitute their verdict for that of the jury or to bring about any such drastic change in a matter fundamental to criminal practice in indictable cases. The Court therefore had no alternative, where there had been some irregularity or misdirection at the trial, but to quash the conviction and enter a verdict of acquittal, even where there was little doubt of the appellant's guilt, and although in some cases it could be truly said that the appellant had never been properly tried. Successive Lord Chief Justices have expressed regret that there was no power to order a new trial in order to make the Court 'a still more perfect instrument in the attainment of justice', but there is a considerable divergence of opinion both among the Judges and the two branches of the legal profession.

The arguments for the change are that because of some serious irregularity or misdirection at a trial a dangerous criminal may have to be acquitted. Further, the possession of the power would tend to diminish the number of cases in which the Home Secretary finds it necessary to order extra-judicial enquiries in cases where the appeal has been unsuccessful. Against the change it was argued that it would be contrary to the fundamental principle that no man should be put in peril a second time on the same charge, particularly because of some mistake of the judge, the jury or the prosecutor, etc.; that it would be difficult to ensure a fair trial if the second jury had read the accounts in the paper of previous convictions and any adverse comments by the judge: it might infer that the Court would not have directed a new trial unless they had considered the accused probably guilty.

Recommended that the Court of

Criminal Appeal should not be empowered to order a re-trial where the appellant has been acquitted; there should be power to order a new trial of a convicted person where the appeal is based on grounds of fresh evidence, no particular offence should be excluded from the exercise of this power. By a majority (5 to 3) the Committee recommended that the Court should not be empowered to order a new trial of a convicted person *except* in cases where the appeal is based on grounds of new evidence. There should be power to order a re-trial in cases referred by the Secretary of State. If the Court is given unlimited power to order a re-trial, it should not be exercised more than once in a particular case. The Court should have the power to direct that the costs incurred by the accused in the first or second trial should be paid out of public funds. The House of Lords should be given the same power to order a new trial as may be given to the Court of Criminal Appeal.

Court of Record for the Hundred of Salford

Dept. Cttee. Rep., apps. pp. 21. 1951
1950–51 *Cmd. 8364, xi*, 55
apptd. Sept., 1950. *sgd. Aug.*, 1951

G. R. Upjohn (*Ch.*), Vick, Parkinson, Boyce, Farrington

'*To enquire into the practice and procedure of the Court of Record for the Hundred of Salford and to report how far the Court is now of benefit to the parties for whose use it is intended. . . .*'

Evidence showed that the court forms a popular and speedy remedy for a large number of litigants in the locality, and that in comparison with the county court its procedure is preferred, is speedier, more convenient and no more costly. The monetary jurisdiction of the court should be increased and made automatically coterminous with that of the county courts.

See *Breviate 1900–1916*. p. 358.

Central Criminal Court in South Lancashire

Dept. Cttee. Rep., apps. pp. 32. 1953
1952–3 *Cmd. 8955, xiv*, 997
apptd. Dec., 1952. *sgd. Aug.*, 1953

A. Maxwell (*Ch.*), Allen, Holmes, Jalland, Jones, Moss, Nield, Shennan, Somerville, Thesiger.

'*To enquire into the need, in order to relieve pressure on Courts of Assize and Quarter Sessions, for the establishment in South Lancashire of a court on the lines of the Central Criminal Court. . . .*'

The increase in the criminal cases at the assizes for South Lancashire, held at Liverpool and at Manchester, in the three years 1950–1952 has been 44 per cent and in the time spent by the judges 56 per cent. This was almost entirely due to the increase in serious crime and not to any general tendency to remit for trial cases which would at one time have been dealt with summarily. Civil work also has increased, and falls into arrears when all criminal and civil cases cannot be dealt during an assize. The establishment of a central criminal court in South Lancashire would relieve the assize judges and could take all the work of the City sessions at Liverpool and Manchester, but the abolition of the City courts was open to strong objection and it was recommended that in the place of part-time Recorderships at Liverpool and Manchester, there should be two full-time judicial posts. The holders of these posts should have the double duty of trying criminal cases as commissioners of assize and of performing Recorder's functions. They would relieve the judges by taking criminal cases, except those of special gravity, which would be reserved for trial by a Queen's Bench Judge.

Legal Aid and Legal Advice in England and Wales

Cttee. Rep., apps. pp. iv, 48. 1945
1944–45 *Cmd. 6641, v*, 187
apptd. May, 1944. *sgd. May*, 1945

Lord Rushcliffe (*Ch.*), Aitken, Bickford-Smith, Burnand, Crout (Miss M.), Crowder, Gillett, Haynes, Hodson, Hughes, Lewis, Littlewood, Manningham-Buller, Mathew, Napier, L. Schuster, Smith, L. Southwood, Watson.

'*To enquire what facilities at present exist in England and Wales for giving legal advice and assistance to Poor Persons, and to make such recommendations as appear to be desirable. . . .*'

By the end of the war it was impossible to find enough solicitors to do the gratuitous work on Poor Persons cases, as the number in the profession had fallen from 17,000 in 1939 to 7000 in 1944. The report reviews the existing facilities of legal aid and defence certificates, the work of the Legal Aid sections, the Law Society's Poor Persons Civilian Department and of various voluntary bodies offering legal aid and advice, but taken together the existing free facilities were inadequate to meet the increasing demand and the legal profession could not be expected to provide a voluntary service for an increasing section of the community.

Legal aid should be available in all courts for persons in need, should not be limited to the 'poor', but should include a wider income group. It should be free to persons unable to pay anything, but be based on a scale of contributions from those who can. Barristers and solicitors should receive adequate remuneration. The State should bear the cost of the scheme, which should be administered neither by the State nor local authorities, as they are often parties to litigation, but by the Law Society. The Law Society should be requested to frame a scheme which should provide for the establishment of legal aid centres, of area committees and of local committees with solicitors as full time secretaries and panels of solicitors and barristers. The Society should be answerable to the Lord Chancellor, a Central Advisory Committee being established to advise him on policy. Legal aid should be

granted in criminal courts where it is desirable in the interest of justice and in civil cases to those who have a *prima facie* case and are within the section of the community for whom legal aid is intended. The proposed rules for assessing income and capital are set out and provide for free aid where the income of a married man is under £4 a week and for graded contributions according to means, until the income reaches a maximum of £420.

The cost of Poor Persons Schemes administered by the Law Society was £42,339, of which £30,789 was expended on the Services Divorce Department. The cost of maintaining the administrative machinery proposed would be slightly under £200,000.

See *Legal Aid and Advice Bill, 1948.* Summary of the Proposed New Service; 1948–49 Cmd. 7563, xxix, 891. *Legal Aid and Advice Act, 1949*; 12 and 13 Geo. 6. c. 51. *Legal Aid Scheme 1950.* Law Society; 1950 Non-Parl. Ld. Chancellor's Dept. *Operation and Finance of Part I of the Legal Aid and Advice Act, 1949.* Law Society. 1st Rep.; 1951 Non-Parl. See succeeding Ann. Reps.

Legal Aid and Legal Advice in Scotland

Cttee. Rep., apps. pp. 31. 1946
1945–46 Cmd. 6925, *xiii*, 555
apptd. Nov., 1945. sgd. May, 1946

J. Cameron (*Ch.*), Balfour, Henderson, Inglis, MacBean, Stephen.

'*To consider the detailed recommendations providing for the establishment of Legal Aid Centres contained in the Report of the Committee on Legal Aid and Legal Advice in England and Wales (Cmd. 6641) and to frame a corresponding scheme for Scotland, with the necessary modifications; and to include a statement of the estimated cost of the scheme.*'

The evidence showed a general measure of agreement as to the organisation necessary to implement the main purposes of the Rushcliffe proposals, but the differences in legal organisation and tradition called for some modifications. The General Council of Solicitors should be responsible for the administration of the scheme under the joint supervision of the Lord President and Lord Advocate. There should be five areas with panels of solicitors and counsel, and whole-time appointments for giving advice. As the tradition in Scotland is that no person should be prejudiced in his defence to a criminal charge by lack of means to pay solicitor or counsel, the right to receive assistance should be applicable to all courts at all stages, on a certificate granted after declaration of means. The Rushcliffe formula for the ascertainment of means and the inclusion of so much of capital assets might in Scotland render the scheme valueless for persons of moderate means. The Muir Society's scheme for compulsory universal contributions, on the analogy of health insurance contributions has much to commend it, but is outside the Remit. Within the framework of the Rushcliffe proposals, the assessment of contributions should take account of the applicant's actual and prospective earning capacity.

See *Legal Aid and Solicitors (Scotland) Bill*, Memo. on Legal Aid and Legal Advice; 1948–49 Cmd. 7562, xxix, 903. *Legal Aid (Scotland) Scheme* 1950, Law Society of Scotland; 1950 Non-Parl. Scottish Home Dept. *Legal Aid Scheme*. Law Society of Scotland. 1st Rep.; 1951 Non-Parl. See succeeding Ann. Reps.

2. POLICE

Income Tax on Rent Allowances. Police Council. Sub-Cttee. Rep., apps. pp. 20. 1945. 1945 Non-Parl. Home Office (S. J. Baker, Ch.). *Police Rent and Supplementary Allowances*. Police Council. Cttee. Rep., apps. pp. 33. 1948. 1948 Non-Parl. Home Office (J. H. Burrell, Ch.)

The 1945 report deals with the difficulty that a police officer who is provided with quarters does not pay income tax on their value, while an officer who receives a rent allowance in lieu of quarters is assessable on the allowance. The 1948 report states that many men joining the forces have to live in houses not controlled by the Rent Restriction Acts or to purchase them at inflated prices: a policeman must live within easy reach of his place of duty. The rent allowances are too low and new maximum limits are suggested.

Police Post-War

Government Statement and Cttee. 1st Rep., *Higher Training for the Police Service in England and Wales*, apps. pp. 22. 1947

1946–47 Cmd. 7070, xiii, 629 *apptd. May, 1944. sgd. June, 1946*

F. A. Newsam (*Ch.*).

'*To consider and report on the principles to be followed in the post-war police service.*'

The aim of the police service must be to ensure that every post is filled by the person best qualified, but, other things being equal, positions of responsibility should be filled by men with police experience. In the absence of a college course, the influence of long service in a subordinate capacity may hamper the growth of a broad outlook, quality of leadership and the independent habits of mind essential to a senior officer. The Committee aimed at a long term plan by which the police would produce its own leaders without promoting young untried men. The recommendations outline a scheme of training at a residential college open to the forces in England and Wales, and in certain cases, to members of other police forces. The junior courses, intended to prepare for promotion to inspector, should last 6 months, have an annual output of 100, the average annual number of promotions. The senior course of 3 months should prepare for higher ranks. The capital cost would be £20,000, and the average annual cost £50,000 shared between the Exchequer and the local authorities. When sufficient college-trained students are available and suitable, no man should be appointed inspector until he has completed the course. The responsibility lies on police authorities and Chief Officers of Police to promote to sergeant and send to the college a proportion of outstanding young officers, as well as men of 35 or so who will form the bulk of the students.

—— Second Report, *Police Organisation, etc.* pp. 53. 1949

1949 Non-Parl. Home Office, Scottish Home Dept.

sgd. Nov., 1946

The present system is essentially sound and no radical alteration in the present organisation was suggested, though the justification for any wide differences in methods is progressively decreasing. The various types of beat and patrol systems are examined. In principle, some beats should remain wholly on foot in view of the foot man's special value in maintaining public confidence and obtaining information. Recommendations are made on the use of cycles, cars and mobile patrols for different types of work and districts.

Policewomen. In Nov. 1946 there were 679 regular policewomen and 66 Class A auxiliaries employed in England and Wales. In Scotland there were 37 and in 1946 there were 102. The Police Federation has always opposed both the employment of women, on the grounds that the work can be done better by men or by voluntary organisations, and the exercise of their right to membership of the Federation. If the present attitude persists it will be necessary to give women separate facilities for collective action. Apart from patrol duty and some classes of detective work, the duties of a policewoman are mainly concerned with women and children, including sexual offences, though there should be no rule that they *must* be employed in all such cases. Policewomen should not, apart from training, be employed in clerical and typing duties. Quasi-police work, such as interviewing the public at the police station, should be performed as a relief from ordinary police duties. Except in special circumstances women should be appointed in all forces and they should receive the same training as men at the training schools.

Police Prosecutions. The revised Regulations under the Prosecution of Offences Acts 1879 and 1884, enable the Director to advise in any type of case, and it would be an advantage if Chief Constables consulted him more freely. It is of concern to the police that prosecutions should be properly conducted, as their work can so easily be rendered ineffective through the faulty conduct of cases in court. A very small proportion of police prosecutions in magistrates' courts are conducted by a solicitor, but the wide variations between forces is in some part due to the type of legal representation available. A prosecuting solicitor may be a member of the Town Clerk's staff; in country districts geographical difficulties may hinder the employment of legal representatives and there is reluctance to employ a solicitor who may be appearing against the police in other cases on the same day.

Recommended that a solicitor should appear where the cases 'require the exercise of the skill and proper art of the professional advocate'. Where satisfactory legal representation is not attainable, the arrangements should be reviewed to secure either the appointment of a full-time or part-time prosecuting solicitor as a member of the police organisation or, if the legal staff of the Clerk to the police authority takes prosecution work, that the more difficult cases are handled by an experienced officer or, the concentration of all legal work of one or more forces in one or more firms. In cases conducted by the police officers the questioning of witnesses should be carried out, and the cases opened, where the court permits, by the officer who decided on the prosecution.

Recruitment, training and promotion. There should be a standard educational test for entry, the normal seven stages of training should extend over the two years' probationary period, and a Central Board should be established to regulate promotion examinations.

—— Third Report, *Buildings, Welfare and the Incidence of Sickness*, apps. pp. 40. 1949

1949 *Non-Parl.*
sgd. Dec., 1946

The Report gives a detailed account of the requirements of the police force for buildings and welfare services. The incidence of sickness is small, but exposure to weather changes, unsatisfactory and irregular meals, changes of duty and meal times, and standing or walking for long periods cause illnesses for which remedies are proposed, e.g. altered tours of duty, free chiropodist service, etc.

—— Fourth Report, *Standardisation of responsibilities in the Higher Ranks of the Police Service and . . . Post-War Organisation of the Special Constabulary*, apps. pp. 56. 1949

1949 *Non-Parl.*
sgd. May, 1947

The Desborough Committee (*Breviate, 1917–1939*, p. 527) found that there was little uniformity in the duties performed in different forces by officers of the same nominal rank and recommended the assimilation of the various ranks in the provincial forces, so that similar work was performed by corresponding ranks, and on this assumption they classified the several higher ranks in the police service for pay according to the size of the force. Partly because assimilation was not carried out and partly because the premise that responsibility varies with the size of the force was true only in a general way striking anomalies have arisen, e.g. a superintendent might command from 20 to 270

men. The responsibilities of officers in divisional posts should be measured by the authorised establishment of the unit, and the responsibilities of officers attached to headquarters should be assessed on the basis of strength of the force as a whole; there are detailed recommendations on numbers, grades of posts, etc. Recommendations deal with the Special Constabulary on the basis that it should be in every police force a reserve against special contingencies, but it should not be employed to effect economies in the regular establishment.

See *New Promotion System*. Com. of Police for the Metropolis. Rep. for 1947. App.; 1947-48 Cmd. 7406, xiv, 235.

Local Conditions of Service for the Police

Police Council. Cttee. Rep., apps. pp. 16. 1947

1947 *Non-Parl. Home Office*
apptd. Dec., 1946. sgd. July, 1947
S. J. Baker (*Ch.*).

'*To review local rules or conditions of service for the police forces in England and Wales, with special reference . . . to those which impose restrictions on the liberty of members of the police service and their families, and to report thereon.*'

The police service is a disciplined service, and its efficiency and reputation depend in a large measure on the maintenance of rules of conduct which are such as to ensure public respect. Constables may be under the critical eye of the public even when they are off duty and in plain clothes. Nevertheless restrictions on the private conduct of members of the service should be kept to the minimum. There should be no restriction whatsoever on the freedom of a member of the police force to marry. He should be free to enjoy leisure on his weekly rest day, but should leave his address if he intends to be away for the night; should not frequent licensed premises *in uniform*, or smoke in streets or public places and in cases where the public have reason to think that he is on duty; should be allowed to join a club, but would be expected to exercise reasonable judgment as to its reputation. To keep complete impartiality unimpaired, he should not take any active part in politics. Wives should be allowed to follow gainful occupations. There should be published a book of advice designed to give all members of the service an appreciation of the position of the service in the public life of the country, and the standard of conduct expected of members of the service.

See *Police Conditions of Service*. Police Council. Sub-Cttee. Rep.; 1925 Non-Parl. Home Office.

Police Conditions of Service

Cttee. Rep., Pt. I, apps. index. pp. iv, 123. 1949. Pt. II, apps., index. pp. iv, 124. 1949. Memo. of ev. 1949

1948–49 *Cmd.* 7674, *Cmd.* 7831, *xix*, 251. *Evidence;* 1949 Non-Parl.
apptd. *May,* 1948. *sgd. April, Oct.,* 1949

Lord Oaksey (*Ch.*), Freeman (Miss Z.), Davies, Gallie, Parkes, Sullivan.

'*To consider in the light of the need for the recruitment and retention of an adequate number of suitable men and women for the police forces of England, Wales and Scotland, and to report on pay, emoluments, allowances, pensions, promotion, methods of representation and negotiation and other conditions of service.*'

The undermanning of the police forces owing to the cessation of recruitment and enlistment in the Armed Forces during the War and the withdrawal of the bans on resignation had been partly made up by the end of 1948. The rate of recruitment was $2\frac{1}{2}$ times the normal and the deficiency, nearly 12,000 in England and Wales, was due mainly to wastage by resignation, particularly during the middle years of service. If this could be reduced to pre-war level, establishments would be built up reasonably soon. The causes

of the wastage were said to arise from pay and housing.

Legislation and the better technique of criminals have increased the responsibilities of the police. Comparisons with other employments show that the police have fallen behind relatively in pay, and particularly in hours of work, while full employment and social security have diminished any advantage in security of tenure. The value of the 'concealed emoluments' in free accommodation, clothing, pension, etc. is under-estimated by the men and by potential recruits. The scales of pay for all ranks should be substantially increased, policewomen's rates being raised in the same proportion as men's. The system of standardisation and of provincial differentiation should remain. Too large a proportion of expenditure on pay is on retirement pensions, but it would be impracticable to alter the scheme. The recommendations give details of basic pay and the varieties of allowances, etc., appropriate to the conditions of work of the police.

App. II to the report is a statistical survey of police recruitment, promotion and wastage.

The Memos. of evidence contain historical and factual material and the Apps. include reprints of three previously unpublished reports: *A General Purposes Fund and a Claims Department* (1931), *Pay of Superintendents in County and Borough Police Forces in England and Wales* (1948), *Pay of Chief Constables in England and Wales* (1947).

Report, Pt. II.—The police authorities decide on matters of local, as distinct from national importance, fix the establishments of the forces and numbers in the various ranks, provide houses, cells, etc., and although these matters require the approval of the Secretary of State, he has exercised his powers with regard to the views of the authorities. There is a measure of uniformity and of variation and experiment. In the counties of England and Wales the police authorities appoint the chief constable, but have no powers over the appointment, promotion and discipline of the ranks under his command, but one-third of the police are in boroughs where, as a legacy of the Municipal Corporations Act, 1835, the Watch Committee has these powers, although there is wide delegation to the chief constables. The chief constable should not have to share his full responsibility for internal administration with an elected body subject to local pressures and prejudices, especially as he and other members of the forces are not the servants of the police authority in any ordinary sense of the term. In the exercise of their duty they are held in law to be 'ministerial officers of the central power, though subject in some respects to local supervision and local regulation.' The legal powers in the boroughs should be transferred to the chief constables, as in the counties; but there should be a right of appeal to the Secretary of State in case of a finding of guilt, and an improvement and standardisation of disciplinary procedure.

Other recommendations include arrangements to enable good men to be promoted earlier, a central examination board, a progressive reduction in the age of entry to police colleges, the building of more police houses and special tenancies for married police. It had yet to be seen if the health service would be able to look after the special features of police health as well as the old system based on police surgeons. The basis of all police work is the traditional beat system, and as one-half of a man's service in the lower ranks is spent on evening and night duty, and most of it on his own, the work may be lonely and tedious. The Aberdeen system (App. V.) where individual beats are absorbed into districts policed by a team, should be considered.

Both the statutory Police Federations (for England and Wales and for Scotland) are organised on the basis of the election in each force by the three ranks of constable, sergeant and inspector, of separate branch boards.

These may make representations to the chief constable, the authority and the Secretary of State, elect representatives to a Central Conference for each rank. Each conference elects a central committee. All members of the forces are members of the Federation. Meetings and attendances at conferences are occasions of duty, so that in practice the expense of running the Federation is met out of public funds. Meetings outside duty hours should be permitted, but held in camera. No member of a force may join an outside trade union which has as an object the influencing of police matters. The restriction on political activities must remain, but police individually and collectively should have the right to approach M.P.s on police conditions of service as such, so long as confidential information is not disclosed and there is no breach of discipline. The general arrangements are appropriate for a disciplined, impartial force and the claim for permission to form a free association of all ranks was rejected. It was also rejected by two of the ranks. The representative organisations of superintendents and chief constables should be given statutory recognition, subject to the usual restrictions. Public funds should finance basic activities only, but other activities could be undertaken out of members' additional voluntary subscriptions. In future, there should be a Police Council for Great Britain, with two Advisory Boards for England and Wales and for Scotland. For 'negotiable' subjects, e.g. pay, hours and allowances, the council should be organised like a Whitley Council into an official and a staff side, with three independent members appointed by the Lord Chancellor, and the agreements it reaches should be binding on all parties, subject to the overriding authority of Parliament.

See *Pay and Conditions of Service of Police*. Statement; 1948–49 Cmd. 7707, xxix, 1095. *Standardisation of Promotion Examinations*. Police Council. Cttee. Rep.; 1951 Non-Parl. Home Office.

Police Representative Organisations and Negotiating Machinery

Police Council. Cttee. Rep., apps. pp. 36. 1952. Scottish Police Council. Cttee. Rep., apps. pp. 26. 1952

1952 Non-Parl. Home Office, Scottish Home Dept.
apptd. July, 1950. sgd. June, 1952, Nov., 1951

S. J. Baker (*Ch.*), England and Wales. F. O. Stewart (*Ch.*), Scotland.

'To examine and report upon the detailed measures arising out of the recommendations as to representative organisations and negotiating machinery contained in Part II of the Report of the Committee on Police Conditions of Service.'

The function of the Committee was to review and if necessary clarify the detailed arrangements which would be needed to implement the Oaksey Committee's recommendations though some members were not in agreement with them. Appendix I reproduces the suggested constitution of the Police Federation, and the report sets out the proposed changes in representation and negotiating procedure. There is some divergence from the Oaksey recommendations on matters of detail, and a number of reservations by members of the Committee.

Police Extraneous Duties

Cttee. Rep., app. pp. 16. 1953
1953 Non-Parl. Home Office
apptd. Aug., 1950. sgd. April, 1953

J. H. Burrell (*Ch.*), Brutton, Dodd, Lyon, Lythgoe, Neate, Peel, Simpson, Smith, Tarry, Templeman, Waterhouse, West.

'To examine, in the light of the recommendations contained in Part I of the Report of the Committee on Police Conditions of Service, the extraneous duties at present performed by the police and to report thereon.'

The Oaksey Committee recommended that members of the police should not be employed on extraneous duties without the consent of the Secretary of State, that these duties should be reviewed and only those relevant to police functions should be permitted; such duties should be done as police duty and attract police remuneration only.

In England and Wales as a whole, the equivalent of 500 men or 1 per cent of the police strength was employed on these duties. If every duty which the police were qualified to undertake were placed upon them, there would be no limit to their extraneous duties. Their primary duty is prevention and suppression of crime and enforcement of law, their training is costly and they should not have duties which take them off this or bring them into conflict with the public on other matters. They should not be asked to collect money, e.g. affiliation payments, to perform duties requiring technical knowledge, issue licences, or execute distress warrants. As there cannot be complete uniformity between areas, there should be a statutory prohibition of extraneous duties except those approved by the police authority and not prohibited by the Secretary of State in regulations. The appendix gives a list of duties which should be prohibited, except with the special consent of the Secretary of State.

—— Scottish Police Council. Rep., app. pp. 10. 1953
1953 Non-Parl. Scottish Home Dept.
apptd. Nov., 1950. sgd. May, 1953

R. D. M. Bell (*Ch.*).

Police authorities should be given as much scope for discretion as possible; but statutory provision should preclude the employment of the police on any extraneous duty apart from those which the police authority may approve, not being duties specifically prohibited by Regulations; duties which should be prohibited are set out in the Appendix. The police should not be employed on the collection of money, or duties which could be performed by civilians or which call for specialised knowledge.

For example Road Safety Propaganda should not be a police duty, though members of the police forces will be willing to co-operate with local authorities in this respect.

Police Pensions

Police Widows' Pensions. 1940–41 Cmd. 6312, iv, 395 (Lord Snell, *Ch.*). This deals with the anomalies in comparative benefits because the police were exempted from the Contributory Pensions Act and had a scheme of their own. The basic rates and allowances were too low; most of the cost of the increases would be met by the men by a 2 per cent addition to deductions.

Special Pensions. Police Council; 1948 Non-Parl. Home Office (P. Allen, *Ch.*). In order to give the officers a sense of security, the police pensions code distinguished between injuries intentionally inflicted or incurred during the performance of duty, and accidental injury, but the needs of the widow were the same in both cases. The distinction should be abolished and a single modified scale paid for all injuries on duty.

Police Pensions. Police Council. Working Party; 1952 Non-Parl. Home Office (F. C. Johnson, *Ch.*), and Scottish Police Council; 1953 Non-Parl. Scottish Home Dept. Both reports recommend that police officers should be allowed after 25 years' service to allocate part of their pay to increase pensions for their widows, etc., but commutation in whole or part for a lump sum is rejected. A contributory scheme for additional widows' benefits was desirable, but no agreement could be reached on their level or on the incidence of costs.

See *Police Pensions Bill, 1948.* Summary of main provisions; 1947–48 Cmd. 7312, xxii, 1011.

Police (Scotland) Bill 1955

Memo., apps. pp. 26. 1955
1954–55 *Cmd.* 9435, *xiii,* 403

In their third rep. the Scottish Local Government Law Consolidation Committee submitted a draft bill consolidating with amendments the main statutes relating to police forces in Scotland (1953–54 Cmd. 8993, xvi, 1953–54 Cmd. 8992, xxvi). The memo. sets out the differences between their draft and the Bill presented to Parliament, the chief being that this retains 50,000 population as the minimum for a new separate police force as against 75,000 proposed by the Committee. In accordance with the Oaksey Committee's recommendation, the police authority becomes the disciplinary authority for the chief, assistant chief and deputy chief constables.

3. PRISONS, PRISONERS, PUNISHMENT, PROBATION

Psychological Treatment of Crime

Psychological Treatment of Crime. W. N. East and W. G. de B. Hubert. Rep.; 1939 Non-Parl. Home Office. *Society and the Criminal.* W. N. East; 1949 Non-Parl. Home Office. *Psychological Treatment at Wormwood Scrubs Prison.* Rep. *Prisons.* Com. [Ann.] Rep. p. 72; 1950–51 Cmd. 8088, xvii, 379.

Alleged Ill-treatment of Individual Prisoners

The Case of Arthur Alfred Clatworthy. 1945–46 Cmd. 6736, xiv, 461 (T. Eastham). The report reviews the events, and concludes that there had been no act of violence against Clatworthy, though one officer had dealt tactlessly with the boy, and there was no connection between anything which occurred in March and his subsequent illness and death. Mrs. Clatworthy had called at the office of the Prison Commissioners without appointment, refused to write out a statement, and Clatworthy's file could not be located because it was 'in action'. She should have been offered more assistance, but she had not been treated with any discourtesy.

The Case of John Elliott. 1945–46 Cmd. 6933, xiv, 477 (J. C. Jolly). After reviewing the circumstances, the report concludes that there had been no act of violence committed against Elliott and no more force had been used than was found necessary to restrain him.

Treatment and Rehabilitation of Offenders

Scottish Advisory Council

apptd. Sept., 1944

C. W. G. Taylor (*Ch.*).

'*To advise the Secretary of State on any matter connected with the treatment and rehabilitation of offenders which he may refer to the Council or which the Council may consider it expedient to bring to his notice.*'

—— *Police Warnings.* Rep., app. pp. 8. 1945

1945 *Non-Parl. Scottish Home Dept. sgd. Feb.,* 1945

'*To consider the arrangements in operation in certain police areas under which certain young offenders who admit their guilt are brought before a senior police officer and warned as an alternative to prosecution; and to advise as to the desirability of extending this system.*'

The practice of senior police officers administering warnings to certain young offenders was operated 30 years ago and has now spread to many county and county boroughs. In some cases the warnings are administered by the police after consultation with the prosecutor, in others by the police on their own initiative, or by the officer who is himself the prosecutor in the juvenile court. A high proportion of the children warned do not again get into trouble. The system had been commended by previous committees and by all the present witnesses, but it had been criticised as not having statutory authority and therefore had no statutory safeguards; it lacks knowledge of the offender's previous history

and as it is 'off the record' it cannot be referred to in any subsequent charge.

Whilst the essence of the system is its informality, guidance should be set out for the police authorities. The word 'court' should not be used; there should be adequate evidence that guilt will be admitted; the procedure should be used only for first offenders; the offender and his parents should be *invited* to attend before a senior officer; there should be no contact with the formal business of the charge room. Records of warnings should be kept, but they should not appear in the criminal statistics.

—— *Remand Homes.* Rep., apps. pp. 20. 1946

1947 *Non-Parl. sgd. Feb.,* 1946

'(a) *To consider the existing provision and organisation of Remand Homes in Scotland . . . To consider* (b) *whether . . . there is a need for some form of institution providing residential treatment for a period of a few months to about a year, e.g. a short-term Approved School.*'

The provision of remand home accommodation is inadequate and in many respects unsatisfactory. The Remand Home has to cater for six different types of children. Persons against whom no charge has been brought, and if alternative arrangements can be made, those awaiting a vacancy in an approved school, should not go to Remand Homes. A considerable degree of segregation is necessary: there should be separate accommodation for the sexes, separate sleeping, recreational and schoolroom facilities for those under and those over 13, and those who have committed no offence should not mix with offenders. Outside Edinburgh and Glasgow the numbers are so small that Remand Homes of efficient size can be maintained only by having small local remand homes near the Court for children needing care, not found guilty of an offence, and offenders who stay not more than four nights. Regional Remand Homes are needed for all other cases. There are recommendations on control and administration, inspection staffs, and contact with specialists and child guidance clinics.

—— Probation with a Condition of Residence (as it affects Children and Young Persons). Rep., app. pp. 7. 1946
1946 *Non-Parl.*
sgd. March, 1946

When probation is ordered by the Court it is desirable that wherever possible the offender should live at home. A condition of residence should be imposed only where it is necessary in the probationer's interest. Even in such cases he should not be sent to a probation home for the full period, but for a short period of training (not normally exceeding six months) as a prelude to a hostel, lodgings or return home. To prevent too much segregation homes or hostels should cater for other classes as well as probationers: they should be adequately staffed with trained people. There should be close co-operation between the Court, the probation officer and the education authority.

See *Probation Service in Scotland*; 1947, 1955 Non-Parl. Scottish Home Dept.

—— Approved Schools. Rep., app. pp. 27. 1947
1947 *Non-Parl. Scottish Education Dept.*
sgd. Sept., 1946

Witnesses were concerned with the difficulties in those schools where there was a large proportion of backward and mentally defective children. At present schools are classified in terms of age, sex and religion; junior schools for children under 12, intermediate schools for those aged 12–14 or 15 and senior schools for those between 14 or 15 and 17. Some witnesses favoured the segregation of offenders, care or protection cases, and truants; others took the view that classification should be according to different physical,

intellectual and emotional types. In Scotland there are 8 senior, 6 intermediate and 12 junior approved schools, but this number is too small to allow for the various classifications in age groups. Classification cannot be laid down at this stage with any finality, though there is an immediate necessity for one senior school for those girls who may be a moral danger to other girls and one for boys who require special treatment.

Recommended that no mentally defective child should be sent to an approved school. Courts should have full reports on a child before deciding that an approved school is the appropriate method of treatment. Children who are fit for licence should be dealt with at the earliest possible moment. Intermediate schools should be discontinued, and schools classified into junior for those under 13 and senior, for those over 13. There should be separate Roman Catholic Schools, separate senior schools, one for boys, one for girls, needing special treatment, and a classifying school for boys and for girls.

The rest of the Report is concerned with the qualifications and conditions of service of the staffs, education and vocational training, privileges, discipline and welfare of the children and the equipment in the school buildings.

—— Scottish Borstal System. Rep., app. pp. 23. 1947
1947 *Non-Parl. Scottish Home Dept.*
sgd. April, 1947

In order to emphasise the new developments in remedial training and education of young offenders, the name Borstal shall be replaced by 'Approved Training Institute', with a separate name for each institution. The law should be amended to make the Borstal training a uniform one of three years, to include the period in a classifying centre, in a training institution, and a period of supervision under licence. Accommodation should be for groups of fifty completely disassociated from prison, and should be of the open type.

The staff should be appropriately qualified, should include trade instructors and should be given Borstal training. Psychoanalysis should be undertaken where necessary. Hostel life, technical instruction, outside work, together with the contact of the After-Care Committee should form the final stages of the approved training.

—— *Psycho-Therapeutic Treatment of Certain Offenders.* Rep., apps. pp. 15. 1948

1948 *Non-Parl.*
sgd. Dec., 1947

'*To give consideration to the psychotherapeutic treatment of certain offenders with special reference to the case of persons convicted of sexual and unnatural offences.*'

During 1941–46, 2,066 persons were convicted of sexual offences, 50 per cent being imprisoned and sentenced to penal servitude. In selected cases repeated imprisonment had had no apparent remedial or deterrent effect, though it could not be inferred that in such cases imprisonment has no value; and the public must be protected. Cases fell into three groups. (1) Cases where the offence is a mere episode in adolescence should be medically examined and required to accept treatment, proceedings being taken if this is refused. In all other cases the Court should have a report from a psychiatrist before making an order. (2) Cases which might respond to long term psycho-therapeutic and other medical treatment, but could not be successfully treated in prison, should be placed on probation on condition of treatment; where restraint is necessary, the prison sentence should be long enough to enable treatment to be completed before release. They should be sent to a special centre in the prison. (3) Cases where there is no chance of success should be sentenced to a period of preventive detention or be detained in a state mental hospital on the certificate of two medical psychiatrists, with a periodic review.

—— *Scottish Prison System.* Rep., apps. pp. 46. 1949

1949 *Non-Parl.*
sgd. July, 1949

There are ten prisons in Scotland, the total accommodation available being 2975 and the average daily population in 1945 was 1548. 50·37 per cent received sentence of not more than 1 month; 29·35 per cent over one and not more than 3 months; 12·07 per cent over 3 and not more than 6 months. Convicted male prisoners are classified as (1) Young prisoners under 17 years of age; (2) juvenile adults of 17 and under 21 years of age, other than short-term prisoners; (3) first offenders of 21 years and over undergoing their first term; (4) non-recidivists 21 and over, who are not first offenders; (5) young recidivists under 30; (6) older recidivists. Civil prisoners, untried prisoners, certain other groups, e.g. certain old recidivists and short term prisoners are not classified. Young prisoners are segregated from recidivists. Women are not classified. The Report describes the staffing and the prison régime.

Imprisonment is imposed for common law crime (short of murder), a statutory contravention for which a sentence of imprisonment is expressly authorised, and the non-payment of taxes, fees or penalties due to His Majesty, etc. In the case of non-payment of fines, etc. imprisonment should be imposed only where a person refuses to pay when he has the means to do so.

There are four possible views on the purpose of imprisonment; punitive and deterrent, safe custody (warehousing theory), means for rehabilitation and a combination of these purposes designed to fit individual cases. Experience has shown that punitive methods neither reduce the number of people who return to prison nor reduce the number of offences which lead to a sentence of imprisonment. Punishment lies in being sent to prison; when in prison the aim should not be to increase it.

Punitive measures tend to aggravate the state they are attempting to cure. Safe-custody, or warehousing is a negative policy as 70 per cent of prisoners are of dull intellect and unable to stand on their own feet in the world; in prison such people cause no trouble and can be trusted. Two out of every 5 persons return to prison. The difficulties lie with, for example, the habitual drunkards, recidivists and 'hardened' criminals. The main difficulty appears to be to combine an effective reformative policy with a punitive system. The study of human behaviour has a long way to go before it can prescribe for all forms of anti-social conduct, and it may be necessary to 'warehouse' those offenders who cannot at present be expected to respond to remedial treatment, but no prisoner should be allocated to a 'warehouse' régime until experience has shown that other methods have proved fruitless.

Reformative treatment should be the first consideration. Short sentences of less than 6 months are harmful to the offender, allow no time for reformatory treatment, and should be imposed only if there is no other method of dealing with the case in the interests of the community and of the offender. Convicted prisoners whose sentences are over 6 months should be classified in two groups—low intelligence and mentally agile; classification should be carried out in one central prison by a trained staff. Those of low intelligence should go to 'open' prisons and be put on work of public utility, and those of 'high' intelligence should be housed in open establishments and put on work giving scope to their abilities. There should be a special establishment for those prisoners who may respond to psychiatric treatment.

The vicious and depraved prisoners will require to be kept 'warehoused' under strict discipline, but it should not be assumed that all are incapable of being reformed. Closed prisons would also be used for those who do not respond to 'open' prisons; habitual drunkards should receive special treat-ment for not less than 6 months. Other recommendations cover training, wage payments to prisoners, clothing, amenities, etc., and prison staff promotions. The Scottish Central After-Care Council should be reconstituted and it should direct all after-care work.

See *Prisons in Scotland, 1939–48*. Rep.; 1948–49 Cmd. 7747, xx, 635.

London County Council Remand Homes

Cttee. Rep. pp. 29. 1945
1944–45 Cmd. 6594, v, 253
apptd. Nov., 1944. sgd. Jan., 1945

G. R. Vick (*Ch.*), Curtis (Miss M.).

'*To consider and report on the provision of Remand Homes made by the London County Council and on the administration by the Council of such Remand Homes.*'

The enquiry was made following criticism made by John Watson, Chairman of a Juvenile Court, and reinforced by Henriques of the Toynbee Hall Juvenile Court. They complained of the inadequate and unsuitable provision for the mixed group of children sent to Marlesford Lodge Remand Home. Investigation showed the difficult conditions under which the London County Council had been labouring, the evacuation of the children which emptied the Homes and the return, which flooded them to capacity, the damage done by flying bombs, and the difficulties of rehousing some of the children.

There were seven possible classes of children in Remand Homes, varying from small children under 8 to children committed to approved schools and girls with V.D. The complaints of the Magistrates really turned on the desirability of segregating the classes, in particular the separation of girls who had and who had not had sexual experience. This was not a matter on which there was agreement and the L.C.C. had not failed in its duty because it adopted a particular policy. Despite the evidence of some experienced witnesses, the Committee did not regard the segregation of adolescent girls according to any particular formula as desirable. Four classes should be removed or segregated: children under 8, girls suffering from V.D., children and young persons committed to an approved school or under preventive detention. There was no easy means of communication between the parties interested in the Homes, and the Home Office should be responsible for setting up and operating the machinery.

Approved Schools and Remand Homes. Remuneration and Conditions of Service.

Cttee. Rep. pp. 42. 1946

1946 *Non-Parl. Home Office*
apptd. June, 1945. *sgd. April,* 1946

B. J. Reynolds (*Ch.*), Anderson (Miss D. G.), Cliff, Gilbey, Green, Gregory (Mrs. E.), Holmes, Johnstone, Magnay, Marshall, Owens, Seal (Miss A. M.)

'*To enquire into the remuneration and conditions of service, including superannuation, of the staffs of approved schools and remand homes and to suggest such changes as may be considered desirable.*'

The greater number and complexity of problems presented by boys and girls during the war, and the increasing tendency to reserve the approved school for the more difficult cases has put too great a strain on the staffs, especially the new recruits. Work in a remand home is comparable with work in an approved school, though it cannot build up the loyalties necessary in longer term work, but it can do much to help a child in a crisis. For both institutions officers with special qualities are required, and professional qualifications are desirable. The remuneration and conditions of service should not only compensate for the specialised service, residential employment, etc., but should be calculated to attract recruits well equipped by experience, training and personal qualities. The general approach to the problem was to raise the increments beyond the maximum Burnham Scales.

Recommendations cover the salaries and conditions of service of the various teaching and domestic staffs. The cost of the proposed increases in pay and additions to staff would be about £180,000 per annum.

Conduct of Standon Farm Approved School

Cttee. Rep., apps. pp. 39. 1947

1946–47 *Cmd.* 7150, *xiv,* 461
apptd. April, sgd. May, 1947

J. C. Maude, J. Corlett

'*To investigate and report on the state of discipline prevailing at Standon Farm School before the crime of 15th February was committed by some of the boys. . . .*'

The crime referred to was the murder of William Peter Fieldhouse, assistant gardening instructor. One of the boys stated that 'We didn't intend to kill Mr. Peter, but were determined to kill the Headmaster, because he was always stopping our money and our licences'. The school is owned by the Church of England Children's Society. The causes of the crime were the physical isolation of the school, the prolonged bad weather and lack of suitable means of recreation, the inadequacy of religious guidance, the prohibition of smoking and the cumulative effect of a long-standing régime of limited freedom, collective punishments and the threats of collective fines, the inadequate system of distributing pocket money, the lack of understanding on the part of the Headmaster and the boys' belief in his unfairness, his gross carelessness in the safe custody of firearms and ammunition, and the presence of a boy of strong personality and sense of grievance.

The school should be closed and the services of Mr. Dawson dispensed with as Headmaster. Various general recommendations are made: all applications for the post of Headmaster should be considered in consultation with the Home Office, and appointments should be subject to a 6 months' probation; no ammunition should be kept in an approved school; there should be more inspection by the Home Office. The system of awards and privileges should be subject to approval.

Punishments in Prisons, Borstal Institutions, Approved Schools and Remand Homes

Cttee. Rep. Pts. I.–II. *Prisons and Borstal Institutions*, apps. pp. 122. [1951]

1950–51 *Cmd.* 8256, *xviii*, 713 *apptd. Nov.*, 1948. *sgd. Dec.*, 1950

H. W. F. Franklin (*Ch.*), Bates (Mrs. D. M.), Curran, Page, Watering.

'*To review the existing methods of punishment in prisons, Borstal Institutions, Approved Schools and Remand Homes (other than corporal punishment in prisons and Borstal Institutions), to consider the procedure adopted in enquiries into breaches of discipline. . . .*'

I. Prisons.

Offences against prison discipline today have to be considered in the light of overcrowding and understaffing in buildings which are by any standard ludicrously inadequate, though some advance has come through the treatment of prisoners in open conditions. In 1938 there were 31 prisons with a daily average population of 8926 and a staff of 1779. In 1948 there were 40 prisons, 16,659 daily average population and 2610 staff. Some 2500 prisoners are still sleeping 3 in a cell. An increase of staff and an extension of accommodation necessary to fulfil modern requirements should be secured as speedily as possible.

Prison life is monotonous, lack of accommodation restricts the number of prisoners who can enjoy the privileges of 'association', etc., and boredom and frustration may lead to outbreaks of indiscipline. The greatest source of trouble is trafficking in tobacco. As the vast majority spend their earnings on it, these should be related to its price: prisoners should be allowed to earn 2s. 6d. a week. The severe staff shortage and undue proportion of young, in-experienced officers, whose training has had to be limited, imposes severe restrictions on classes, etc. Whilst alternatives to the staple prison mailbag and coir mat industries are difficult to devise, the introduction of vocational training classes and new trades should make the maintenance of discipline easier.

In spite of overcrowding and under-staffing the increase of offences is less than might be expected, 0·13 per cent of the daily average population being punished. But there is a fairly sharp rise in the attacks on officers and fellow-prisoners, partly owing to the greater number committed to prison for crimes of violence. The Committee reviews the various authorised forms of punishment, rejecting a number of proposals for abolition or modification. Restricted diet No. 2 should be replaced as soon as an alternative punitive diet adequate for health can be devised. It is un-desirable for a prisoner to be deprived of a substantial part of his remission in the early stage of a sentence. Care is needed in determining what specific privileges should be forfeited. The Committee declined to recommend that entitlement to letters and visits should not be affected. Ten per cent of the prisoners are mentally abnormal and five per cent should be accepted as medical responsibilities; the principle of their transference to a special institution has been approved. Prisoners who engage in wholesale trafficking or gangster activities should be transferred to a special establishment. The safe-guards against injustice were adequate. No prisoner should remain in ignorance of the charge made against him until he is actually brought before the Governor; the Governor should not be closeted with the committee while it is delibera-ting the finding or sentence. Even where corporal punishment is con-cerned, prisoners charged with offences against discipline should not have legal representation.

II. Borstals

Despite some early experiments, little

constructive work was done in the nineteenth century in the treatment of prisoners aged 16–21 which was comparable to the creation of reformatory and industrial schools for those under 16. The Gladstone Committee of 1894 reported that these were the ages when the majority of criminals were made. After the establishment of the Borstal in 1900 and the statutory recognition of the system of training in the Prevention of Crime Act 1908, the system constantly developed on the basis of men of good quality in the service and the treatment of each lad as a human problem. At the outbreak of the war the whole system disintegrated.

Punishments are given for offences and offences are related to discipline. While many of the lads have been led to criminal associations by lack of self-control and anything like military discipline would be undesirable, their unsatisfactory bearing and appearance did not tend to improve their self-respect. A higher standard should be aimed at. There is a substantial difference of view between the governing and the subordinate grades on the kind of discipline necessary and the means by which it should be maintained: witnesses from officers serving in Borstal staffs said that discipline had deteriorated since the war, though this was not accepted by the Prison Commissioners. There is a danger in putting the young and comparatively inexperienced recruits since the war in charge, under a policy of leniency, of lads with criminal tendencies. Bearing in mind that the success rate has decreased, and that absconding has increased and is increasing, discipline should be tightened even at the cost of some increase of punishments. Senior officers should not give subordinate officers the impression that they wish reports to be suppressed; and reporting officers should not be excluded from the adjudicating room.

The various punishments are reviewed. Removal from the House should include complete segregation, useful hard work, and loss of all normal amenities. Restricted diet No. 2 should be abolished and the power of awarding restricted diet No. 1 should be restored. The 2 to 3 per cent who by persistent misconduct or subversive activities interfere with the training of others should be sent to a special 'closed' corrective institution. Absconding is a serious offence, and should be dealt with not by the Governor, but by the superior disciplinary tribunal, the Board of Visitors; persistent absconders should be sent to the closed corrective institution. Disciplinary proceedings should follow the normal judicial pattern.

—— Report. Pts. III, IV. *Approved Schools and Remand Homes*, apps. pp. 72.
1951
1951–52 *Cmd.* 8429, *xviii*, 39
sgd. May, 1951

add Brown.

III. Approved Schools.

On 31st Dec., 1948 the school populations were 7689 boys and 1500 girls. The children are first sent to 'classifying schools' and then to the school most likely to fit their needs. In approved schools 60–70 per cent of the children have an I.Q. below 95, as compared with 30 per cent in ordinary schools. While the Children's Department thought it preferable to deal with the very backward or unstable or maladjusted children in the same school, the very wide variety of types now in the same school is neither educationally desirable nor economical. There should be further classification and there would be less strain and difficulty if the very dull and emotionally unstable were removed to schools adapted to their needs. The establishment of psychiatric observation centres for selected children should be considered. The Ministries of Education and Health, and the Home Office should establish an interdepartmental committee to investigate the ways of dealing with the educationally sub-normal, the mentally abnormal and the maladjusted. The problems of discipline in senior girls' schools are severe and impose great strain on the staff. The request of headmistresses for a voluntary retiring age of 55 is reasonable. Senior girls' schools should be allowed wider discretion in the methods of punishment they use to maintain discipline and their request for separate punishment blocks should be considered.

The various punishments, loss of marks and concomitant privileges, temporary loss of recreation, alteration of meals, and use of separation and detention rooms are reviewed in turn, and various amendments suggested. Powers of punishment given to boys ('prefects') should be withdrawn, and children should not in School Councils take part in any decision on punishment. Though it is infrequently used and in some schools not at all, the power to give corporal punishment should be retained, and the safeguards and restrictions on its use are adequate. The mental state of boys needing repeated corporal punishment should be most carefully investigated. There were 1407 absconders in 1950, an undue proportion being from senior schools. It should be regarded as a serious offence, especially as it is frequently accompanied by offences, and in the case of girls, by maintaining themselves by immoral means. The experiment of a closed school or block for persistent offenders should be tried as soon as possible.

IV. Remand Homes.

Remand Homes contain a wide variety of children aged 8 to 17, the length of stay may vary from a few days to a month or more; special disciplinary problems are bound to occur. Pay, service conditions and training of the staff should be improved. The various punishments are reviewed. The amount of corporal punishments in boys' schools is not excessive. Some of the strongest advocates that the power to use it should be retained are amongst those who use it least. It should not be administered in the presence of other boys and the prohibition of various forms of striking, cuffing, etc., should be maintained.

Capital Punishment

R. Com. Rep., apps., index. pp. 506. 1953. Mins. of ev., 31 days, memos. I–III. 1949–53.

1952–53 *Cmd. 8932, vii, 677. Mins. of ev., etc.; 1949–53 Non-Parl. apptd. May, 1949. sgd. Sept., 1953*

E. Gowers (*Ch.*), Maxwell, Jones, Cameron (Elizabeth D. C.), Fox-Andrews, Macdonald, Slater, Mann, Montgomery, Hancock (Florence M.), Radzinowicz.

'*To consider and report whether liability under the criminal law in Great Britain to suffer capital punishment for murder should be limited or modified, and if so, to what extent and by what means, for how long and under what conditions persons who would otherwise have been liable to suffer capital punishment should be detained, and what changes in the existing law and the prison system would be required; and to inquire into and take account of the position in those countries whose experience and practice may throw light on these questions.*'

Part I. The Liability to Capital Punishment.

In the period 1900–1949 1800 men and 130 women were sentenced to death in England and Wales, and 54 men and 5 women in Scotland. There is no single class of offence which varies so widely in character and culpability; the motives may spring from weakness, wickedness, lust, revenge, duty; it may occur in the heat of passion or be brutal and callous to an unbelievable degree. The view is therefore widely held that capital punishment should be reserved for the most heinous cases, but in England the concept is that a murderer forfeits his life because he takes that of another. This rigidity, which is the chief defect of English law, is mitigated by the Royal Prerogative of Mercy—45 per cent of condemned persons have been reprieved—and by the large number of recommendations to mercy made by the juries. Some criticised the free use of the prerogative as interference with the Judiciary, or regarded it as undesirable that the solemn formula of the death sentence should be followed by its cancellation.

Of the three purposes of punishment, retribution, deterrence and reformation, in this case reformation can mean only repentance; capital punishment is an emphatic denunciation by the community of a crime, and though the continued public demand for retribution cannot be ignored, deterrence is the most important. On this the statistical evidence is not convincing, but distinguished judicial witnesses agreed with the police and prison officials, who were virtually unanimous that it had a deterrent effect on professional criminals. But as there are many offenders on which the deterrent effect is limited or negligible, this should not be exaggerated.

Suggestions for limiting the liability to suffer death for murder: (a) Abolition of the doctrine of constructive malice. If a person engaged in committing a felony or resisting an officer of justice kills another person, he may be guilty of murder, although otherwise the offence might amount only to manslaughter. The doctrine infringes the principle that persons ought not to be punished for consequences of their acts they did not intend or foresee, and should be abolished. There was strong judicial support for the change. The police exaggerated the possible dangerous consequences. Principals in the second degree and accessories before the fact should remain liable to conviction of murder if the principal in the first degree is liable. (b) The Commission rejected the suggestion of some witnesses that the sole test of provocation should be whether the accused was in fact deprived of self-control and not whether a 'reasonable' man would have been so deprived, but agreed that provocation by words alone should be recognised equally with other forms of provocation. (c) Special categories of murder. No satisfactory definition of 'mercy killings' can be framed which would allow mercy killers to be convicted of any offence other than murder. Unless the survivor has killed the other party, aiding and abetting suicide should not be treated as murder, but be punishable with imprisonment for life. (d) Special categories of offenders. There are no rational grounds for exempting women from capital punishment whilst it still applies to men. A 6 to 5 majority of the Commission recommended raising the age limit for capital punishment from 18 to 21.

Insanity and Mental Abnormality.— (a) Criminal responsibility.—Where crime is committed by a person so mentally disordered that he could be certified as insane, or suffered from the grosser forms of mental deficiency or certain types of epilepsy, there is an overwhelming presumption that the crime was wholly or largely caused by the condition. The McNaghten rules state that to establish a defence on the grounds of insanity it must be proved that the accused was suffering from such defect of reason, disease of the mind that he did not know the quality of the act, or if he did, did not know that it was wrong. Medical opinion was that they are based on an incomplete conception of insanity, which affects not only the cognition faculties, but the whole personality and emotions, so that the accused might know the quality and wrongfulness of the act yet commit it as a result of emotional disorder. Other witnesses felt that juries applied the rules with commonsense. The McNaghten rules are so defective that the law should be changed either by extending their scope by adding 'or was incapable of preventing himself from committing it' or by abrogating the rules and leaving the jury to decide. (b) The doctrine of 'diminished responsibility' on account of mental abnormality or psychopathic personality applies to a much wider range of offences and could not be restricted to these offences only.

General Amendment of the Law of Murder.—(*a*) It is impracticable to limit the scope of capital punishment by re-defining murder more narrowly without over-riding disadvantages. The existing definition is in substance satisfactory. (*b*) Dividing murder into two degrees, one only of which would be capital. There is no clear criterion for distinguishing between them: a sudden killing may express a vicious nature, while a premeditated murder by wife of brutal husband may be more excusable. (*c*) Maintaining the definition of murder, but giving judges or jury power to decide in each case whether a lesser sentence should be imposed. This is too heavy a responsibility to place on one individual. Alternatively, the jury could be asked, if they decide on a verdict of guilty, to find if there were extenuating circumstances; if there were, the sentence would be life imprisonment. This would not be too heavy a burden for a jury, though there might be some diversity of verdicts. This is the only way of limiting the effects of the existing law. If it is not acceptable, the real issue becomes whether capital punishment is retained at all or abolished.

Part II. The Alternative to Capital Punishment.

The recommendations would lead to a decrease in the number of executions and an increase in the number of persons serving life imprisonment sentences, including those who are mentally abnormal although not insane. Those not mentally abnormal should be detained in the conditions in force in long term prisons. Two institutions, one in England and one in Scotland, should be established for the detention and treatment of psychopaths and other mentally abnormal patients.

Part III. Methods of Execution.

Neither electrocution nor the gas chamber have a balance of advantages over hanging. The method of lethal injections has too many difficulties but should be re-examined in the light of progress in anaesthetics.

See *Capital Punishment*. Statement. pp. 20. 1948; 1947–48 Cmd. 7419, xxi, 189.

Broadmoor

Cttee. Rep., apps. pp. 14. 1952
1951–52 Cmd. 8594, xviii, 25
apptd. May, sgd. June, 1952

J. S. Henderson (*Ch.*), McCowan, Waterhouse, Younger.

'To inquire into the adequacy of the security arrangements at Broadmoor, and to make recommendations.'

The Committee was appointed following an escape in April 1952. Whereas there had been no escape from Broadmoor between the years 1932–1940, there had been 13 since 1941. Some carelessness and lapses in supervision were established, but this had been due to deficiencies of staff not only in numbers but in qualities which the needs of Broadmoor make imperative. The security rules for the guidance of the staff were last printed in 1908, and are now out of print. Many of the locks in the institution were installed years ago, and were not as effective as the modern locks: a key to an old lock had been made and used effectively by a patient.

Amongst the recommendations were that salaries and conditions should be improved to attract the right kind of staff; the Medical and Deputy Medical Superintendents should have prison experience. Every officer should have a copy of the security rules, there should be a distinctive siren or audible warning automatically connected with the police station; schools should be warned.

Discharged Prisoners' Aid Societies

Cttee. Rep., apps. pp. iv, 50. 1953
1952–53 Cmd. 8879, ix, 325
apptd. March, 1951. sgd. March, 1953

A. Maxwell(*Ch.*), Ackroyd, Allen, Cape, Lees-Jones, Mellanby(Miss M.), Pinker.

'To review the functions and finance of the Discharged Prisoners' Aid Societies, and

of the National Association of Discharged Prisoners' Aid Societies in so far as it acts in the capacity of an Aid Society. . . .'

A National Association of Discharged Prisoners' Aid Societies was incorporated in 1932, the 38 local societies being affiliated to it. A society cannot work in prisons unless it holds a certificate, renewable every 5 years, from the Secretary of State.

Recent social legislation has confronted the Aid Societies with a fundamentally new situation, since the Assistance Board may at once assume responsibility for the discharged prisoner's maintenance, the Ministry of Labour will assist him in finding work and the Ministry of Health will look after him if he is sick. Though the help from official sources is extensive, a large proportion of the prisoners discharged need after-care help, and Aid Societies should shift their emphasis to this activity. The existing case committees held in prison cannot do this work effectively. Prison Welfare Officers should be appointed to local prisons, and the weight of evidence was that they should be employed by an outside body, the National Association. Salaries should be the same as those of probation officers. The Aid Societies' welfare officers, released from duties inside prisons, should act as the field workers and after-care agents of the societies. The funds of the societies have come in varying volumes and proportions from private and public sources and these arrangements, while explicable by historical analysis, cannot be recommended as simple or convenient. Societies should receive a grant of half their approved expenditure on administration and on clothing for prisoners on discharge. Subsistence needs on discharge should be met by a grant to the National Association.

Policy and Practice

Explanatory Papers: *Prisons and Borstals;* 1945 (rev. eds.; 1950, 1957, 1960). Non-Parl. Home Office. *Proposals for the Development of the Prison System for Adults. Prisons.* Com. [Ann.] Rep. p. 64; 1946–47 Cmd. 7146, xiv. *The Probation Service;* 1938 (rev. ed.; 1952). *Probation Service in Scotland;* 1947 (rev. ed. 1955). *Juvenile Delinquency;* 1949. *Making Citizens;* 1946. *Approved School Boys;* 1952. Non-Parl. Home Office. Scottish Home Dept.

4. LEGAL PROBLEMS ARISING OUT OF WAR, WAR DAMAGE

Requisitioning and Compensation

Rep. pp. 26. 1941

1940–41 Cmd. 6313, iv, 447

sgd. Aug., 1941

J. W. Morris.

There had been a number of complaints about the requisitioning of land and buildings and about the operation of the Compensation (Defence) Act, 1939, in regard to properties requisitioned. The scale on which requisitioning has taken place has inevitably led to hardship, embarrassment and inconvenience. Some of the complaints, e.g. that there is no compensation for loss of profit or goodwill, resolve themselves into criticisms of the general policy of the Compensation Act, and others, concerned with delays, are being met by administrative action. In order to relieve tenants of dwelling houses or in full occupation of business premises who have been dispossessed from having to pay more net rent in the new accommodation than compensation rent, they might be given the option in certain circumstances to disclaim their lease and compensation officers might be instructed to consider existing rents when assessing compensation rents. Machinery might be devised whereby a depossessed tenant, paying inclusive rents, did not have to pay more than net rent to his new landlord. Many hardships would be averted by faithful observance of the Prime Minister's Memorandum.

Equal Compensation

Sel. Cttee. Rep. pp. 14. 1943. Proc.,
   mins. of ev., apps. index. 1943

1942–43 (53) *iii*, 41.   *Mins. of ev., etc.;*
1942–43 (53) *iii*, 55
apptd. Dec., 1942. o.p. Feb., 1943

H. U. Willink (*Ch.*), Bartlett, Burgin,
Lloyd George (Miss), Grenfell, Hardie
(Mrs.), Hely-Hutchinson, Kier (Mrs.
Cazalet), MacAndrew, McGovern, Mor-
gan, Ridley, Summerskill (Dr.), Tate
(Mrs.), Ward.

'*To examine and report on the effect of
the proposal that civilian women should be
compensated equally with civilian men for
war injuries on the general principles of
compensation, and on levels of remuneration.*'

The Personal Injuries (Emergency
Provision) Act, 1939, introduced a
national code of compensation for those
amongst the civilian population who
might be injured as a result of enemy
action.   The scheme which at first
covered only those 'gainfully occupied',
was framed partly on rates paid under
War Pensions, Workmen's Compensation and National Insurance, though it
maintained the principle of sex differentiation and made a distinction between
the gainfully occupied and the housewife.   Neither in theory nor public
opinion is there any necessary connection between remuneration for work
and flat rate compensation for all classes
unrelated to value of service.   The
distinction between gainfully and non-
gainfully occupied persons should be
abolished and flat rates of compensation
adopted for all adults irrespective of
sex or occupation.

Government Compensation Scheme.
   ### Principles of Assessment of Damage.

Cttee. 1st Rep. pp. 9. 1939. Final Rep.
         pp. 7. 1940

1939–40 *Cmd.* 6136, *Cmd.* 6197, *v*, 543
*apptd. Sept., 1939.   sgd. Nov., 1939,
March,* 1940

A. A. Uthwatt (*Ch.*), Canny, Firth,

Gladstone, Hall, Healing, Lewis,
Linney.

'*To advise as to the general principles on
which physical damage to property real or
personal within Great Britain or Northern
Ireland, arising from enemy action such as
bombardment from the air or from the sea,
or from counter-action taken against such
attacks, should be assessed. . . .*'

1st Rep.—The scheme applies to real
and personal property other than that
insurable under the War Risks Insurance
Act, 1939.   The Government has undertaken to pay the highest compensation
possible after the end of the war in the
light of the country's financial circumstances and the total damage.   The
damage is physical damage and does not
include consequential trading loss, etc.
As it will occur at different points of
time and there will be fluctuations in
the cost and availability of materials,
the damage should be assessed as at a
fixed date, March 1939.   The basis of
assessment for the various categories
should be as follows: for immovable
property, cost of reasonable reinstatement less value of old materials or
diminution of market value, whichever
is less; for furniture, value as between
a willing seller and willing buyer who
wishes to use it for the same purpose,
less, if partly damaged, any value
remaining or, cost of reasonable repairs;
for plant and machinery, diminution of
going concern value or reasonable
reinstatement, whichever is less; for
motor cars, market value at date of
damage or cost of repair, whichever is
less. For consumer goods and personal
clothing, cost of replacement, taking
condition into account.

Final Rep.—Floating livestock, value
in the open market at time of damage;
permanent stock, going concern value
or cost of reasonable replacement on
the farm at the time of damage.   For
growing crops, according to stage of
growth, expenditure on cultivation and
seeds, or harvested values if they are
established enough for yield to be
estimated.

See *War Damage to Public Utility*

Undertakings; 1941–42 Cmd. 6403, ix, 535. Public utility undertakings were excluded from the Act, because neither the contribution nor the payment structure were appropriate. The Memo. explains the proposals relating to them.

War Damaged Licensed Premises and Reconstructions

Cttee. Rep., apps. pp. 56.   1944

1943–44 *Cmd.* 6504, *iv,* 259
apptd. Aug., 1942. *sgd. Jan.,* 1944

J. W. Morris (*Ch.*), Bryson, Dyer, Edwards, Gillie, Griffiths, Hayward, Jones, Malone (Mrs. L. L'E.), Nevile, Wall (Miss J. I.), Hunt, Mitchell.

'To consider what will be the best means of ensuring when rebuilding is practicable that the provision of licensed houses in place of those destroyed or damaged by enemy action shall be planned with due regard to local requirements and in harmony with proposals for redevelopment and reconstruction. . . .'

The congestion and density of public houses, which are commonly found in the old quarters of our towns, are associated with old-fashioned structure, fittings and decoration, primitive sanitary provision and inadequate size by any standard of amenity. The Home Secretary should have power to declare areas of extensive, as distinct from isolated, war damage as 'designated' areas, and overspill areas as 'associated areas', and to constitute licensing Planning Committees, composed of equal numbers of the licensing justices and the local authorities, to survey and replan the number and distribution of licences when the area is re-planned. There would be some modification of the powers of the licensing justices.

Hunt, supported by Mitchell, points out that licensed premises, like all other properties, are subject to town planning control; they are in a special position only in respect of licensing. The powers of the justices should be entrusted to a small committee of three to collaborate with the Reconstruction Authority

by exercising their normal and independent judicial functions in considering the licensing needs.

War Damage

Com. Rep. under Section II of the War Damage Act 1943 regarding the amount of value payments. pp. 8. 1947

1947 *Non-Parl. Treasury*
sgd. Jan., 1947

M. T. Eve (*Ch.*) and 7 others.

Since 1939 there have been increases of building costs and substantial increases in market values. In general, had a claimant to a value payment received it at the date of the bomb he could have re-invested in real property with great advantage compared with his existing position. Value payments are inadequate and cannot be divided into categories according to location, etc. Original value payments should be increased by 45 per cent, converted value payments by 60 per cent.

Limitation of Actions and Bills of Exchange

Cttee. Rep., app. pp. 14.   1945

1944–45 *Cmd.* 6591, *v,* 239
apptd. — sgd. Oct., 1944

W. L. McNair (*Ch.*), Branson, Bridges, Speed.

'To consider and report—Whether any amendment of the law relating to the limitation of actions is desirable in order to afford relief to any party who has been prevented or hindered from enforcing any cause of action by reason of the fact that he or any person against whom a cause of action has accrued has at any time since 3rd September, 1939 been an enemy at common law or under the Trading with the Enemy Legislation or is or has at any such time been in enemy or enemy occupied territory. . . .'

At the end of the 1914–18 war, the periods of limitation suspended during the war began to run three months after the coming into force of the Versailles Treaty. This problem was aggravated during the 1939–45 war because such great territories had been occupied by Germany and Japan, and large numbers of British and Allied nationals had become enemies at common law or by statute. The statutory periods should be suspended until 12 months after a person had ceased to be an enemy for the purpose of the Trading with the Enemy Act, 1939 or to be detained as a prisoner or as a civilian internee in enemy country. Enemy territory is defined as that to which the *Trading with the Enemy Act, 1939*, applies. No amendment should be made to the *Bills of Exchange Act, 1882*.

Limitation of Actions

Cttee. Rep., app. pp. 16. 1949
1948–49 *Cmd. 7740, xvii*, 727
apptd. Jan., 1948. *sgd. June*, 1949

F. J. Tucker (*Ch.*), Fox-Andrews, Mac-Calman, Napier, Parker, Phillips, Pollard, Roberts, Wade, Walker, Willey.

Under the existing law the period of limitation is one year for a local authority, three years for the National Coal Board; one year for the claimant under the Fatal Accidents Act, 1846, and six years for a claimant making a claim in respect of his personal injuries against a living tort-feasor. This makes it difficult for an employee of one body to appreciate why he has six years in which to bring an action, whilst if employed by another body he has only one year. A plaintiff who brings an action against a body not protected by the Public Authorities Protection Act has only to consider who is responsible but in the case of bodies protected by the Act has also to prove that the injury was caused in the performance of a public duty.

The period of limitation for actions in respect of personal injuries should be two years and for actions founded upon contract or tort (other than actions for personal injuries) should remain at six years. The periods of limitation in the case of bodies set up by Nationalisation Acts should be the same as for other public bodies and private individuals.

Distribution of German Enemy Property

Advisory Cttee. Rep., app. pp. 29. 1951
1951 *Non-Parl. Bd. of Trade apptd. — sgd. March*, 1951

J. Morison (*Ch.*), Lever, Oppenheim, Pollen, Reid, Gregory, McKenzie.

'To advise, as regards the distribution of German enemy property under the Distribution of German Enemy Property Act, 1949, on the classes of claims to be admitted to, or excluded from, the scheme of distribution . . . the scheme, or schemes, of distribution between the classes and the priorities, if any, to be established. . . .'

The whole volume of debt which could be brought within the scheme of distribution was not likely to be less than £100 mn. The sum expected to be available for distribution was about £15 mn. Certain claims should be excluded: e.g. claims by companies incorporated in but doing all their business outside U.K.; claims expressed in Reichmarks, except trade debts, royalties, certain rents and dividends, etc. The Committee was dealing with an *ex-gratia* distribution, not with settlement of debts between debtors and creditors.

The five groups of claims under the Distribution of the Enemy Property Act were: long and medium term debts; debts arising from banking transactions; debts arising from insurance transactions; debts arising out of the sale of goods and the rendering of services (including shipping services); and miscellaneous. The schemes of distribution suggested took into consideration equity of treatment between different groups of creditors, and equitable distribution between individual creditors within the group.

See *Distribution of German Enemy Property Act, 1952*; 15 & 16 Geo. 6. & 1 Eliz. 2. c. 30.

5. LAW OF PROPERTY, SUCCESSION

Compensation and Betterment

Reps.

1940–41 *Cmd.* 6291
1941–42 *Cmd.* 6386

See *Town and Country Planning*, p. 366.

Land Transfer

Cttee. Rep., app. pp. 9. 1943
1942–43 *Cmd.* 6467, *v*, 21
apptd. — sgd. July, 1943

Lord Rushcliffe (*Ch.*), Grey, Pott, Schuster, Smith, Stamp, Withers, Yeaman.

'*To consider one of the recommendations made by the Committee on Land Utilisation in Rural Areas . . . viz:* 238. Registration of Title.—*We recommend that registration of title should be made compulsory over the whole of England and Wales. . . .*'

Universal compulsory registration of title irrespective of sale, etc., is neither economical nor practicable at a moment of time. To institute compulsory registration on all sales throughout England and Wales simultaneously would be also so impracticable that it may be called impossible. The proper method of procedure would be to apply it to those areas where post-war development first takes place; where there is choice, the areas selected should have a population density sufficient to provide enough business to cover the cost of registration in those areas. The experience of Land Registry as far as the Act of 1925 is concerned, has been to enable them to relax the stringent examination of title, and the Chief Registrar should consider whether any further relaxation is possible and desirable. Land acquired by the State should be registered on acquisition. In areas where compulsory registration is not in force, voluntary registration should be of greatest assistance to those concerned with the development of building sites, and would provide a useful way of accustoming solicitors

and the public generally to a system of transfer by registration. Dudley Stamp, in a memorandum, suggested that branch offices of the Central Registry should be set up in areas which coincide with those used for planning purposes.

See *Advisability of Extending Compulsory Registration of Title on Sale to the County of Surrey*. J. N. Gray. Rep.; 1951 *Non-Parl.* Ld. Chancellor's Dept.

Local Land Charges

Cttee. Rep., apps. pp. iv, 72. 1952
1951–52 *Cmd.* 8440, *xvi*, 287
apptd. March, 1949. *sgd. Dec.,* 1951

J. Stainton (*Ch.*), Abbey, Bentley, Collins, Cowlishaw, Curtis, Enever, Goulding, Marshall, Martin, Poole, Weston, Wheway.

'(1) *To review the present system whereunder prohibitions of or restrictions on the user of land imposed by a local authority or by a Government Department under certain statutes are registrable in the Registers of Local Land Charges; . . . (2) To consider whether . . . legislation should be introduced for the purpose of making registrable . . . any like matters as to which there is at present no statutory provision for such registration. . . .*'

Registration of local land charges formed part of the extensive land reforms (1926) with a view to simplifying conveyancing. The local charges which the reformers presumably had primarily in mind were those imposed on the land under health legislation for securing money recoverable by local authorities from successive owners and occupiers of land. The immense growth of local authorities' powers to control the use of land (culminating in the Town and Country Planning Act, 1947) by prohibition or restriction and a series of enactments requiring the registration of matters outside the scope of the Charges Act has put a load on the structure it was not intended it should bear. The load is increasing every year with the passing of fresh legislation, but improvements suggested in the recommendations should be made before any breakdown occurs. Amongst the recommendations were: the practice of making supplementary enquiries should continue on a voluntary basis; legislation making a number of additional matters registrable should, so far as is possible, take the form of a general formula rather than an itemised schedule, but there should be powers to make exceptions from the formula to remove anomalies and obscurities. Outside London the county registries should be absorbed into district registries. The same government department should be responsible for making and for administering local Land Charges Rules. Responsibility for keeping the register should be placed on the local authority and not on its clerk.

Land Registration in Scotland

Cttee. 1st Rep., apps. pp. 22. 1948

1947–48 Cmd. 7451, *xiii,* 1
apptd. March, sgd. June, 1948

Lord MacMillan (*Ch.*), Cruickshank, Henderson, Masson, Nicol.

'(a) *To review further the processes of the registration of writs in the Sasines Office and to report; and* (b) *to consider the case for introducing registration of title to land in Scotland. . . .'*

The 'Key to unlock Records' was provided by the Acts of 1672 and 1693, which directed that on the presentation of a deed to be registered a brief minute should be drawn up to form an abstract or abridgement of its contents, setting out the names and designations of the parties, or description of the lands affected and the day and hour of its presentment for registration. These Minutes, printed and indexed, constituted for some 200 years the sole aid for searching records and today they are the only aid available of right to the public. The proposal of the Bill before Parliament is that the Index should be superseded by the Search Sheet. The Search Sheet arranged in subject order was started in the 1870's and acted as a

supplement to the Minutes, which are arranged in chronological order. The Search Sheet is of great value and should be continued as complementary to the Minute Book and not as a substitute for it. The preparation of a new form of Search Sheet would present many technical difficulties and would be impracticable until the arrears under the existing system had been worked off.

See *Public Registers and Records (Scotland) Act, 1948;* 11 & 12 Geo. 6. c. 57.

Tenure of Shop Premises. Scotland

Cttee. Rep., app. pp. iv, 10. 1947

1947–48 Cmd. 7285, *xvi,* 257
apptd. March, sgd. Nov., 1947

T. M. Taylor (*Ch.*), Collyer, Dryer, McDonald, MacGregor, Roberts (Mrs. J.), Shinwell, Taylor.

'*To investigate the present position in Scotland in which tenants of shops are placed at the termination of their tenancies, and to consider and advise* (1) *whether tenants should be given a right to renewal of their tenancies and . . .* (2) *whether provision should be made for giving to tenants a right to compensation for improvements and goodwill. . . .'*

Out of all the shops in Scotland only 1 per cent were affected by a notice of 'Buy or quit' and 'Eviction without option of Purchase', and of these there were only 50 cases of proven hardship. There was no widespread grievance such as to support a recommendation for immediate legislation and no evidence was found to support the need for legislation on the question of compensation for improvements and goodwill. The situation should be watched in case deterioration takes place. It was suggested that where landlords and tenants cannot settle their differences by agreement the matter should be settled by summary proceedings, which are both cheap and expeditious. In the event of legislation being thought necessary, tenants should be allowed first options on re-let or sale and the Sheriff should decide, where there is disagreement, on what is 'reasonable' on both sides. Any legislation should be made applicable for a period not exceeding 5 years.

Tenure of Shops and Business Premises in Scotland

Cttee. Interim Rep. pp. 11. 1949

1948–49 *Cmd. 7603, xiii, 513*
apptd. Nov., sgd. Dec., 1948

H. W. Guthrie (*Ch.*), Collyer, Dryer, McDonald, MacGregor, Roberts (Mrs. J.), Taylor.

'(a) *To consider and report whether, in the light of recent experiences, any modification of the conclusions recorded in their previous Report with regard to shop premises in Scotland (Cmd. 7285) is called for; and* (b) *to investigate the position at the termination of their tenancies of tenants of premises in Scotland used for business, trade or professional purposes. . . .*'

The Committee was re-convened because it became evident that the situation had deteriorated. The majority of leases of shops are annual and are terminable by 40 days' notice, and as the 1948 May term approached it was found that an increasing number of shopkeepers were being given notice to quit without alternative or were being asked to buy with the alternative of eviction. There were 450 cases of threatened eviction as against 150 cases considered in the original enquiry. Recommended that temporary protection to tenants should be given by putting into operation forthwith the original recommendations, with suitable modifications; e.g. the Sheriff could renew the tenancy for not more than one year.

See *Tenancy of Shops (Scotland) Act, 1949*; 12 and 13 Geo. 6. c. 25.

—— Final Rep., app. pp. 19. 1950

1950 *Cmd. 7903, xiv, 19*
sgd. Nov., 1949

add Chalmers.

The Tenancy of Shops (Scotland) Act provides that a tenant of shop premises may apply to the Sheriff for a renewal of his tenancy within a period of 21 days after the service of the notice to remove and the Sheriff may renew the term for a period of one year. The revival of business activity since the war coupled with a slight decrease in accommodation has resulted in there being some 2000 fewer shops in the four counties of cities than there were in 1938–39, a decrease of some 6 per cent. The tenancy Act had afforded a measure of protection to shop tenants against arbitrary ejection or extortionate increase in rents. Evidence suggested that disinflationary tendencies were not sufficient to allow the tenure of shop premises to be solved in accordance with the laws of supply and demand and that some form of protection which would not affect the value of property was required. The Tenancy of Shops (Scotland) Act, 1949, should be continued in operation until 1955. There was not sufficient evidence to prove the need for the extension of the Act to other business premises. In a Minority Report J. Taylor and Mrs. Roberts stated that the existing system provided the same potentialities for hardship to tenants of other business premises, in spite of the lack of evidence on the matter. It was logical to extend the Act to all business premises.

Leasehold

Cttee. Interim Rep., *Tenure and Rents of Business Premises*, app. pp. 42. 1949

1948–49 *Cmd. 7706, xii, 471*
apptd. Feb., 1948. *sgd. March,* 1949

Lord Uthwatt (*Ch.*), Alford (Miss H.), Bowean, Hale, Harfield, Lloyd, Reddaway, Ungoed-Thomas.

'*To consider and report on the following questions, in so far as they affect England and Wales:* (1) *Whether . . . an occupying tenant of residential or other premises should be given the right to purchase compulsorily the freehold and any other prior interests in the premises, and . . .* (2) *Whether . . . an occupying tenant of business premises . . . should be given security of tenure . . .*

(3) Whether it is desirable and practicable to control rents charged for business premises . . . (4) Whether the rights of a landlord to impose and enforce covenants to repair should be further restricted . . . (5) Whether further provision should be made for giving to tenants a right to compensation for improvements on the termination of their tenancies. . . .'

Majority Rep.—While there has been no general abuse, the shortage of business accommodation owing to increased demand, bombing and the virtual cessation of building for ten years, has given landlords a superiority of bargaining power which a number of individual landlords are exploiting unfairly. The committee rejects permanent rent control of all business premises as unnecessary; but temporary protection of sitting tenants is needed. Sitting tenants should have a *prima facie* right to renewal, obtainable by the Order of a tribunal, unless the landlord can prove that the tenant is undesirable and the premises are required for demolition or re-building. In fixing rents the tribunal should have regard to the general level of rents in the neighbourhood, etc., and should not take into account increase in the goodwill attached to the premises by the activity of the tenant. Contracting-out should be prohibited.

Minority Rep.—E. S. Herbert. The scheme would create a new class of vested interests, the sitting tenants. The scarcity value of business premises cannot be dealt with by legislation. As the sitting tenant could not be saddled with a lease if he wished to dispose of or discontinue his business, he must be given power to assign it. Speculators could buy up leases and sell at a premium or sub-let to a newcomer who would have no protection. The scheme would also maintain the status quo, since the sitting tenant would have the right to remain. The needs of new entrants were not provided for.

—— Final Report, app. pp. 162 [1950].

1950 *Cmd.* 7982, *xii*, 703

sgd. *June*, 1950

add D. Jenkins (*Ch.*), del. Lord Uthwatt (*Ch.*).

The aim of the Report was to consider and state conclusions as to the desirability of permanent changes in the law of landlord and tenant. (There are no recommendations of a temporary character). This relationship of landlord and tenant still depends mainly on the common law, though for the protection of tenants the effects of free bargaining have been limited by the legislation of the last 30 years.

Leasehold enfranchisement has been a serious political demand since the 1880's, when there was extensive urban development under the leasehold system. The demand grew for easier facilities for workers to build their own houses and for the right of leaseholders to become freeholders by compulsory purchase of the fee simple of their holdings. The current arguments for and against are still substantially the same, and the majority view, which is against, maintains that injustices and inconveniences have been mitigated by legislation, that the leasehold system has financed, controlled and unified development and that it has maintained standards and amenities. Leasehold enfranchisement involves compulsory purchase for private purposes, and lettings might be discouraged. Leasehold enfranchisement is not desirable. The occupying tenant should have the first refusal, but it is not practicable to create an enforceable right of first refusal by legislation.

Security of tenure for business premises, such as is enjoyed by tenants of premises which are subject to the Rent Restriction Acts would freeze existing rents so that they became unreal in relation to the fair market level; it would introduce unfair rigidity inappropriate to business tenancies. But there should be greater security than is afforded under the Landlord and Tenant Act, 1927. A tenant should be able to make a direct claim for renewal in the first instance, without first establishing a claim to compensation. He should be entitled to renewal of his tenancy at a fair market rental if he can establish that his business will be diminished if he is not granted it.

The extent and incidence as between landlord and tenant of liability for repairs depends primarily on the terms of the particular lease or tenancy. The Leasehold Property (Repairs) Act, 1938, does protect the small residential lessee from enforcement of repairing covenants before the last five years of a 21 year term, except in cases where it was reasonable and proper that repairs in question should be done at once. Similar protection should be extended to all types of premises irrespective of their rateable value. Compensation for improvements, available to tenants of business premises, should be available also to tenants of residential and other property. Covenants against subletting or change of user without consent should be construed to mean that consent should not be unreasonably withheld. There should be a standard form of weekly tenancy agreement and a code of covenants was suggested to apply to lettings of various types in the absence of specific agreement on the relevant matter. Such a code is summarised at the end of the report.

In a Minority Report Mr. Ungoed-Thomas and Mr. Hale recommended a scheme of leasehold enfranchisement for dwelling houses. Selwyn Lloyd was in favour of introducing a temporary scheme for security of tenure for business tenants before deciding on the lines of permanent legislation. A Supplementary Report, signed by half the committee, proposed a modified form of security for tenants of residential premises outside the limits of the rateable value prescribed in the Rent Restriction Acts (£100 per annum in London and £75 per annum elsewhere in England and Wales).

Leasehold Property in England and Wales

Government Policy. pp. 17. 1953

1952–53 *Cmd.* 8713, *xxiv*, 627

As the Leasehold Committee was not unanimous on a number of questions, instead of permanent legislation being introduced, the Leasehold Property (Temporary Provisions) Act, 1951, was passed. It extended on existing terms long leases due to expire and gave tenants of shops the right to apply to the County Court for renewal. The Majority rejected leasehold enfranchisement. The market value of the landlord's interests includes the capital value both of the ground rent and of his right to the reversion of the property, landlords' and leaseholders' interests are bought and sold every day, and in the case of a long lease the existing landlord is often not the original one, but has bought it in the market at a price reflecting the fact that the property will revert to the landlord. The values have often been the basis of investment by trustees, of mortgages, etc. The leaseholder who occupies the property as his home has a greater claim than the leaseholder concerned with it only as an investment. The amenities of large estates are often protected by amenity covenants and public-owned estates would have to be excluded. In view of these complexities, the Government has decided that it is better to give security of tenure by right of occupation than to give a new right of ownership. Security of tenure is to be given to a tenant at the expiration of a 21-year tenancy, even though the rent under that tenancy is less than two-thirds of the rateable value. An occupying sub-tenant, on the expiry of the mesne-tenancy, should become a direct statutory tenant of the head landlord. Security of tenure should be made available to all business (including professional) tenants: landlords of business premises should have the right to resume possession for their own business, or for a scheme of development, and failing this, the sitting tenant should be able to resume tenancy at a fair contemporary market rent. The enactment of a standard model code of covenants as regarding repairs, etc., was being considered.

See *Landlord and Tenant Act, 1954*; 2 & 3 Eliz. 2. c. 56.

Scottish Leases

Cttee. Rep., apps. pp. 54. 1952
1951–52 *Cmd.* 8656, *xvi,* 433
apptd. Feb., 1951. *sgd. July,* 1952

Lord Guthrie (*Ch.*), Hutchison, Mc-Kellar, McLaren, Monteath, Muirhead, Pinkerton, Ross.

With certain exceptions all land in Scotland is held on feudal tenure, the services having been commuted to an annual money payment, feu-duty. The various prohibitions of sub-feuing which impeded many owners who wished to make their lands available to others for building, were surmounted by the grant of long leases for building purposes. (i) In ground leases, the land reverts to the owner, and the erections on it become the property of the landowner and pass to him without payment of compensation. Very lengthy ones, e.g. for 999 years, raise no social problems, but many of those for 99 years, granted during the period of Scotland's maximum industrial expansion, have expired or are expiring at a time of inflated property values and housing shortages. Whilst there were cases where the landowners have demanded a price at an enhanced value, Scottish landowners on the whole have granted feu titles without regard to their full legal rights in premises built on the land. Ground leases are still being entered into as commercial transactions, and there are advantages for planning and development in the grant by Government Departments and local authorities of leases in preference to feus. The Committee declines to recommend that in all cases lessees should be entitled to have their rights converted to a feu: the right to compel conversion should be limited to residential property occupied by the lessee: for five years after the passing of an enabling act a lessee or sub-lessee whose permanent home is built on land under a ground lease for at least 50 years granted before the passing of the Entail (Scotland) Act, 1914, should be entitled to have his temporary right converted to a feu on the financial terms specified.

(ii) Occupation leases, by which the landlord lets land with its buildings, whether residential or business.—Many are let on yearly missives. No statutory right should be given to a tenant of residential premises nor, since he makes improvements for his own enjoyment, any right of compensation for them. Owing to the high costs of business development, trading companies have increasingly obtained working capital by selling their premises to an insurance or investment company, which lets to the sellers at a rent on an 'investment lease'. These are freely entered into by both parties, and such tenants should not be given the option to purchase or any statutory rights to compensation for improvements. Occupation tenants of shops and business premises should not have a statutory right of purchase, and the Committee does not recommend that the protection given to tenants of shops should be extended to business premises.

See *Leases in Scotland*; 1952–53 Cmd. 8714, *xxiv,* 645. A Government statement accepting the report.

Law of Succession in Scotland

Cttee. Rep., app. pp. 29. 1951
1950–51 *Cmd.* 8144, *xvi,* 731
aaptd. July, 1949. *sgd. Dec.,* 1950

Lord Mackintosh (*Ch.*), Brydon, Cunningham, NcNeill, Primrose, Stewart, Tudhope (Mrs. C. J.), Wedderburn.

'*To inquire into the law of Scotland in regard to* (a) *intestate succession,* (b) *the legal rights of spouses and children, and* (c) *the law of succession in relation to adopted persons and adopters, and to recommend what alterations are necessary or desirable.*'

The amendment of the Law of

Intestate Succession had been under discussion since 1924 when the Law of Property Act, 1922, made radical reforms to the law of Succession in England. The occasion of the present enquiry was the passing of the Adoption of Children Act, 1949, which gave adopted children status and rights of children born in wedlock. This could not be applied to Scotland, particularly because of the rules of primogeniture and the preference for males over females. The majority of witnesses were in favour of changes suggested by various law societies since 1924, but the landed interests maintained that it would disrupt the Scottish familial system. But rules suitable in a period of large landownership are not suitable when the number of small proprietors has enormously increased. An attempt to meet this criticism was made by special proposals which safeguarded agricultural interests. The chief recommendations were that, subject to certain exceptions, the law of primogeniture should be abolished, all differentiation between the sexes in succession should be abolished and all property, whether heritable or movable should devolve according to the same rules. The exceptions concerned owner-occupied farms, the succession of which should be governed by a system of options designed to preserve the farm as a single unit; the succession of agricultural leases should continue to be regulated by the Agricultural Holdings Act, 1949, and succession to hereditary titles, coats of arms and similar rights continue as heretofore. The surviving spouse should get furniture and plenishings, a preferential claim up to £5000 free of death duties, and legal rights on the remainder of the estate.

Legal rights should continue to be exigible from heritable and movable estate as at present, except that a right corresponding to the widow's terce should be substituted for the husband's courtesy. The doctrine of equitable compensation should be abolished; the present rule of legal rights being exigible

on divorce should be abolished and the Courts given power to adjust the provision made for the innocent spouse. The principle of representation should apply throughout the whole course of the succession and to legitim.

Law of Intestate Succession

Cttee. Rep. pp. iii, 19. 1951

1950–51 *Cmd.* 8310, xvi, 637

apptd. Oct., 1950. sgd. June, 1951

Lord Morton (*Ch.*), Albery, Astbury, Brown, Chance, Fletcher, Foster, L. Kershaw, Rees (Mrs. D.).

'(a) *To consider the rights under Section 46 of the Administration of Estates Act, 1925, of a surviving spouse in the residuary estate of an intestate.* (b) *To consider whether, and if so to what extent and in what manner, the provisions of the Inheritance (Family Provision) Act, 1938, ought to be made applicable to intestacies. . . .*'

The Administration of Estates Act, 1925, allows to the widow all personal chattels, a statutory legacy of £1000, and an interest in the remainder of the estate. Through inflation this has become inadequate and has led to conditions of great hardship, especially where the spouse is forced to leave the matrimonial home, which may be valued at more than £1000, so that it can be sold to satisfy the claims of the children. Recommendations are made for raising the statutory legacy to £5000; giving the spouse an option to purchase deceased's interests in the matrimonial home at a fixed price; a life interest in half the remaining estate, with power to redeem for a capital sum, if there are issue; if there are no issue, increasing the spouse's charge on the estate where there are parents, brothers and sisters and giving the spouse the residual capital where there are none. There are also recommendations on the shares of the next of kin.

The question as to whether the Inheritance (Family Provision) Act, 1938, applies to cases of partial intestacy is one of grave doubt and difficulty. It would be better that the Court, when making provision out of a testator's estate, should be entitled to regard the estate as a whole, and not be arbitrarily limited to such part thereof as he may have chanced to dispose of by Will. The needs of a dependent under the Act remain just the same whether the testator's estate devolves under his will or under his intestacy, or partly under both. Recommended that the Inheritance (Family Provision) Act, 1938, should be applicable to partial and total intestacy.

See *Intestates' Estates Act, 1952*; 15 & 16 Geo. 6 & 1 Eliz. 2. c. 64.

6. NATIONALITY, INTER-NATIONAL LAW

British Nationality Bill, 1948
Summary of Main Provisions, app. pp. 10. 1948

1947-48 *Cmd.* 7326, *xxii*, 673

This Bill provides a new method of giving effect to the principle that the people of each of the self-governing countries within the British Commonwealth of Nations have both a particular status as citizens of their own country and a common status as members of the wider association of peoples comprising the Commonwealth, including that a woman citizen of the United Kingdom and Colonies will not lose her citizenship by marrying an alien and a woman who had lost British nationality by marriage will regain it.

See *British Nationality Act, 1948;* 11 & 12 Geo. 6. c. 56.

Private International Law
Cttee.

apptd. Sept., 1952

'To consider what alterations may be desirable in such rules of private international law as the Lord Chancellor may from time to time refer to the Committee....'

—— 1st Report, apps. pp. 16 [1954]

1953-54 *Cmd.* 9068, *xvi*, 517

sgd. Jan., 1954

H. W. Parry (*Ch.*), Beevor, Cheshire, Cross, Dobson, Druitt, Fitzmaurice, Innes, Mann, Speed, Wilberforce, Wortley.

'To consider what amendments are desirable in the law relating to domicile, in view especially of the decisions in Winans v. Attorney General [1904] A.C. 287 and Ramsay v. Liverpool Royal Infirmary [1930] A.C. 588 and whether, in the light of any alterations which the Committee may recommend in that law, it appears desirable that Her Majesty's Government should become a party to the draft Convention to regulate conflicts between the law of nationality and the law of the domicile.'

The draft convention deals with the difficulties which arise in private international law from the differences in the various countries of the world as to whether domicile or nationality should determine personal law. This country, the Commonwealth and the U.S. rely upon the law of the domicile, while many Continental countries look to the law of the country of nationality. Difficulties arise when excessive importance is attached to the domicile of origin and in establishing proof of intention to change a domicile; or when a judge decides that the case before him is governed by foreign law and is then required to decide whether foreign law means the whole of that country's law. The law of domicile in England and Wales should conform to a Code: every person shall have a domicile of origin assigned to him at birth or a domicile of choice. No person shall have more than one domicile. The domicile of choice of a person shall be in the country in which he has his home and intends to live permanently. The domicile of a married woman shall be that of her husband, but if she is separated by order of a competent court, she shall be treated as a single woman. The changes should not be made without prior consultation with other members of the Commonwealth.

State Immunities

Inter-Dept. Cttee. Rep., *Diplomatic Immunity*. pp. 7. 1952

1951–52 *Cmd*. 8460, *xxx*, 197
apptd. Nov., 1949. *sgd. July*, 1951

D. Somervell (*Ch.*), Barnes, Lauterpacht, Hamson, Beckett, Dobson, Murrie, Roberts-Wray, Innes, Speed.

'*To consider whether the law of the United Kingdom in regard to diplomatic immunity is, having regard to the principles of public international law, in any respects wider than is necessary or desirable.*'

No question arises as to the secrecy and inviolability of an embassy's official papers, its rights of secret correspondence, etc. The practice of the Foreign Office is that diplomatic immunity is accorded for the benefit not of the individual, but of the State in whose service he is, in order that he may fulfil his diplomatic duties with the necessary independence. The immunity is from legal process and the person possessing it is still subject to the law of the land, civil and criminal. Most countries grant immunity to clerical and similar staffs, who may perform duties of a secret nature. The Foreign Office has usually imposed the condition that while local nationals employed by a foreign embassy on diplomatic or clerical duties should have immunity in respect of official acts, they should have no personal immunity. In future, the Foreign Office should impose a like condition on domestic servants. Consideration should be given to the question of legislation empowering H.M. Government to reduce the immunities accorded to the embassy or mission of a foreign country so that they correspond with those granted by that country to our own embassies and missions.

7. LAW REVISION AND REFORM

Law of Defamation

Cttee. Rep. pp. 52. 1948

1948 *Cmd*. 7536, *i*, 559
apptd. March, 1939. *sgd. September*, 1948

Lord Porter (*Ch.*), Birkett, Bowen, Burnand, Crocker, Forster, Holmes, O'Sullivan, Slade, Taylor, Wade, Christian.

'*To consider the Law of Defamation and to report on the changes in the existing law, practice and procedure relating to the matter which are desirable.*'

The general criticism of the law of defamation is that it is unnecessarily complicated, unduly costly, it is difficult to forecast the result of an action both as to liability and as to the measure of damages; it is likely to stifle discussion on matters of public interest and concern, is too severe on a defendant who is innocent of any intention to defame and is too favourable to 'gold-digging' plaintiffs. An attempt to codify the law would not simplify or shorten proceedings or enable practitioners or the public more easily to understand the law and calculate the chances of success or failure or lessen the expense of litigation, and flexibility gives a wider scope to judges and juries.

Proposals to extend the scope of the law to include invasions of privacy, defamation of the dead and defamation of racial or other groups are rejected; the first because it is a matter of taste, the second because there is no ground for giving the relatives of the deceased a right of action for defamation of the deceased alone and because historians would be unduly hampered, the third because no alteration suggested would avoid prohibiting proper criticism of groups and classes and because the law of seditious libel gives as much protection as is possible.

All libels (i.e. in written or other permanent form) are actionable without proof of special damage (pecuniary loss); slanders (in transitory spoken or visible form) which do not fall within limited classes of statements are not actionable unless special damage is proved. Owing to the difficulty of proving special damage as defined, actions for slander usually fall in one of the limited number of classes, e.g. imputing crime, infectious disease, unchastity in a female or injuring professional reputation. The assimilation of slander to libel and making all defamatory statements actionable without proof of special damage is rejected as opening out a field of litigation on trivial matters. All defamatory broadcasts, whether from written script or spoken extempore, should be treated as libel and the party responsible for broadcasting should be responsible.

Proposals that in case of unintentional defamation, lack of intention coupled with absence of negligence should be a complete defence, would leave an innocent victim without any reparation or means of clearing his name publicly. The plaintiff's remedy should be restricted to requiring the defendant to publish a correction and apology; if so published, no damages should be recoverable. Justification that words are true in substance and fact is a good defence, but this does not prevent the resuscitation of a past lapse. Requiring in addition to justification that publication was in the public interest would make the task of an author or journalist impracticable. To succeed in the defence of justification it should not be necessary to prove that the substance of the libel is true in respect of each separate charge contained in it, but only in so substantial a part of the defamatory statement that the part remaining unproved does not substantially add to the plaintiff's injury. The defence of 'fair comment on a matter of public interest' is an important safeguard of free speech, but the law has become unduly rigid. This defence should succeed if so much of the defamatory facts is true that the remainder not proved does not substantially add to the plaintiff's injury and that the comment was honestly made and based on matters of public interest. The defence of qualified privilege, i.e. that the person publishing the statement had a duty or interest in publishing it and those to whom it was published a duty or interest in receiving it, should be extended by widening the definition of newspapers to cover monthly journals as well as those published at shorter intervals and to include the reports of the proceedings of meetings of more bodies, which are specified. The person defamed should have the right to require the newspaper to publish correction and explanation. Agreements to indemnify a publisher against libels which exist without his knowledge should be made legal. The right to mitigation of damages when the plaintiff has recovered damages against other persons, now limited to newspapers, should be extended to all defendants.

The rules of pleading should be improved to give greater precision and to prevent either party from being taken by surprise in the cases of innuendo, express malice, where fair comment or qualified privilege is pleaded and in 'rolled up' pleas. Discovery of documents should be granted, the use of interrogatories abolished and the Court of Appeal should be given wider discretion to review the amount of damages awarded by a jury.

See *Defamation Act, 1952*; 15 & 16 Geo. 6 and 1 Eliz. 2. c. 66.

Law of Civil Liability for Damage done by Animals

Cttee. Rep. pp. 11. 1953

1952–53 Cmd. 8746, xiv, 981 apptd. — sgd. Nov., 1952

Lord Goddard (*Ch.*), L. Tucker, Devlin, Davies, Goodhart, Archibald, Croom-Johnson, Williams, Winn.

'*To consider the law of civil liability for damage done by animals and to make recommendations.*'

Hitherto the law of England has regarded animals as falling into one of two classes, wild and domesticated. With the former, absolute liability was imposed on their keeper for any injury they might cause; with the latter, apart from negligence, the owner or keeper was liable if it could be proved that he knew that the particular animal which caused the damage was vicious. The development of this distinction has made the law complicated; it should be abolished and liability for the acts of every class of animal should be based on negligence. Similar considerations would logically lead to the abolition of the doctrine of absolute liability for cattle trespass, which is based on the duty of the owner to keep his cattle on his own land and to prevent them from straying. But as the general incidence of liability is well understood by farmers, and small cases are generally settled amicably, no change was suggested beyond limiting the liability to damage done to land and to the crops whether growing or gathered. Damage outside those limits may be recoverable by means of an action based on negligence.

Common Law imposes no duty on the owner or occupier of land to prevent animals escaping on to the highway. A farmer who allows his cow to escape and eat a few of the neighbour's cauliflowers is liable in damages, but if it escapes and causes an accident, the farmer is not liable. Liability here should depend on negligence and the occupier should be under a duty to take reasonable care that cattle and poultry do not escape on to the highway. The same general duty to take reasonable care or to prevent animals causing damage should apply, e.g. to dogs not under proper control on the highways. The right to shoot a dog attacking animals should be extended to the right to shoot a dog who is trespassing, where it is reasonably believed that cattle would thereby be injured.

Distress damage feasant is obsolete, and should be abolished. A person finding an animal trespassing on his land, should be entitled to keep it until it is claimed by the owner and costs of keep are paid, less benefits derived. It should be treated with reasonable care and if unclaimed after 14 days may be sold, the proceeds being paid into the County Court, or paid to the owner, less costs of keep, etc.

Professor Goodhart disagreed with the abolition of the strict liability on owners of wild animals (e.g. tigers); they should be liable in all circumstances even though there is no negligence. Damage recoverable for trespassing animals should be extended to cover e.g. injury to another animal or infection of a pedigree herd. Professor Glanville Williams would abolish cattle trespass and substitute action of negligence.

Law Reform

Cttee. 1st Rep., *Statute of Frauds and Section 4 of the Sale of Goods Act*, 1893.
pp. 4. [1953]

1952–53 *Cmd.* 8809, *xiv*, 993
apptd. June, 1952. *sgd. March*, 1953

D. Jenkins (*Ch.*), L. Goddard, L. Asquith, Devlin, Parker, Burrows, Diplock, Gardiner, Goodhart, Gray, Megarry, Outen, Parry, Wade.

The Law Revision Committee, reporting in 1937, recommended that section 4 of the Statute of Frauds, section 3 of the Mercantile Law Amendment Act, 1856, and section 4 of the Sale of Goods Act, 1893, should be repealed (*Breviate, 1917–39*, p. 554) because they had outlived the conditions which generated and in some degree justified them, that they operate in an illogical and often one-sided and haphazard fashion arbitrarily chosen, and that on the whole they promote rather than restrain dishonesty. Except on contracts of guarantee, the Committee agreed with the recommendations.

In order to avoid the danger of inexperienced people being led into undertakings they did not understand, the Minority of the Law Revision Committee had recommended that a contract of guarantee should be void unless it is embodied in the document. The balance of convenience lies with leaving the law as it is. The circumstances in which it is permissible to spell the contract out of a series of documents are now well established and it is rare to find injustice caused by the fact that the absence of writing renders the contract unenforceable by action but not void.

—— Second Report, *Innkeepers' Liability for Property of Travellers, Guests and Residents*. pp. 8. [1954]

1953–54 Cmd. 9161, *xvi*, 465
sgd. April, 1954

The custom of the realm, subject to modifications in the Innkeepers Liability Act, 1863, is that the innkeeper is liable for the goods which travellers bring with them to the inn. The historical origins of the custom were that travellers were exposed to the dangers of highwaymen in league with innkeepers. As the liability depended on custom, the innkeeper could not escape liability by warning guests to take precautions, or by contract, but only by proving Act of God, the Queen's enemies or the guests' own negligence. It was argued that the historical origins have disappeared and that as there are now residential hotels not inns in which guests do not have the special protection, innkeepers should now be in the same position as residential hotels, and be liable for negligence only. A traveller today was exposed to the risk of loss through neglect of the innkeeper or his servants, but it would be difficult for him to prove negligence. An innkeeper who undertakes to provide for all comers and has a lien for his charges should be under a special obligation and be expected to insure. Recommended that strict liability should be retained for goods other than motor cars, and the statutory limits for goods not deposited for safe keeping should be increased from £30 to £100 and not more than £50 for any one article. Strict liability covers a 'traveller' who stays one night at an inn or by or for whom a bedroom is engaged. New legislation should define an inn.

—— Third Report, *Occupiers' Liability to Invitees, Licensees, and Trespassers*. pp. 44. 1954

1953–54 Cmd. 9305, *xvi*, 473
sgd. Oct., 1954

del. L. Goddard, L. Asquith.

The occupier of premises owes some duty of care in regard to the safety of those premises to persons lawfully coming upon them, and he has a negative duty of care towards trespassers, but in assessing the standard of care distinctions, not always easy to define, are made between persons who enter premises under contract and those who enter by invitation or permission. A person entering by invitation is entitled to a higher standard of care than one coming for a purpose not of material interest to the occupier.

The recommendations define an occupier's liability towards contractual visitors; the duties of landlords remaining in occupation of the means of access to premises let; trespassers and injury to third parties through breach of landlord's obligations to repair. In the case of lawful but non-contractual visitors, the distinction between invitees and licensees should be abolished and occupiers should have a duty to take reasonable care that the premises are reasonably safe for use for the purpose to which the invitation or permission relates.

Minority report.—K. Diplock did not agree with the suggested codification of 'rights and obligations which arise in multitudinous circumstances'. However imperfect in theory, the practical compromise which the common law has evolved of dividing persons who enter on land into two categories of invitees and licensees gives substantial justice except in the case of persons lawfully on land or premises where the public have access and persons using means of access which remain in the occupation of the landlord. These should be in the category of 'invitees'.

8. MARRIAGE AND DIVORCE

Matrimonial Causes (Trial in the Provinces)

Cttee. Rep., app. pp. 18. 1943

1942–43 *Cmd.* 6480, *v*, 659
apptd. — sgd. Oct., 1943

R. L. Wedgwood (*Ch.*), L. Drogheda, Finnemore, Gillett, Hodson, Holmes, Lewis, Lowe, Schuster, Trapnell.

'*To consider the existing facilities in England and Wales for the instituting and trial of matrimonial causes outside London, and to report whether it is desirable to increase the facilities, and, if so, what rearrangements of the present system are desirable.*'

The procedure of the old Court for Matrimonial Causes established by the Matrimonial Causes Act, 1857, was of a highly specialised type, but it affected only the small class of persons who brought their matrimonial troubles to court. Under Poor Persons' procedure new Rules were made in 1920 enabling Poor Person's cases to be instituted and prosecuted up to trial in a limited number of District Registries, and as no substantial inconvenience had arisen, the Registries to which jurisdiction was committed had increased to 44 out of 115. The problem now was whether any reason exists for refusing to include not only Poor Person's cases, but cases of such other persons as may desire that their matrimonial suits should be commenced locally.

Facilities should be given for the institution of divorce proceedings in the selected Registries, but interlocutory proceedings after trial, which concern custody of the children and financial arrangements, and had some technical difficulties, should be retained in the Principal Registry in London.

The trial of divorce cases in the provinces should be extended to include defended cases. The Committee rejects a scheme of independent Divorce Assizes in favour of extending the hearings to all Assize towns now authorised to deal with divorce matters as part of the normal Assize work. Two additional Judges will be necessary.

Procedure in Matrimonial Causes

Cttee. 1st Interim Rep. pp. 6. [1946]

1945–46 *Cmd.* 6881, *xiii*, 789
apptd. June, pres. July, 1946

A. T. Denning (*Ch.*), L. Bridgeman, Calver (Grace), Collingwood, Cresall (Mrs. N.), Davies, Donovan, Foster, Herbert, Lane (Mrs. E. L.), L. Rusholme, Smith (Mrs. J.).

'*To examine the present system governing the administration of the law of divorce and nullity of marriage in England and Wales and to report on what procedural reforms ought to be introduced in the general interests of litigants.*'

The purpose of the six months interval between the decree nisi and the decree absolute was to enable the King's Proctor or any member of the public to show cause why the decree should not be made absolute, but the period has been unnecessary in plain cases where further investigation is superfluous and even causes hardship, e.g. in the case of a serviceman who on returning from the war finds his wife living with another man and who wishes to marry again. The King's Proctor has difficulties because of the great increase in the number of cases; if the time were reduced he would be investigating the more doubtful cases. The period between decree nisi and decree absolute should be reduced to six weeks; solicitors should not have to search at the Divorce Registry before applying for decree nisi to be made absolute.

—— Second Interim Report. pp. 31. 1946

1945–46 *Cmd.* 6945, *xiii*, 795
sgd. Oct., 1946

The report discusses in what courts matrimonial suits ought to proceed. Cases have been determined in the Superior Courts, assisted by the attendance of the bar, because of the gravity of divorce and other matrimonial cases which affect the family and the status of its members. Careful and dignified proceedings create a more respectful view of the marriage tie and marriage status. But the present difficulty was to maintain the principle when there was such a large increase in the number of cases. Trial of divorce cases as part of the assize system is a failure; trial by Judges of the Divorce Division has kept the judges in the provinces too long, and the London lists have mounted to as many as 7284 cases in a term. The 59 High Court Registries in the provinces, where petitions are filed and all interlocutory proceedings are transacted, dealt satisfactorily with 9000 in 1945. The costs are too high: an ordinary undefended divorce case costs £70.

Conclusions were that undefended divorce cases should no longer be tried by King's Bench Judges as part of the work of the Assizes; that County Judges should be appointed as Commissioners for matrimonial causes; that High Court procedure should be so reformed as to effect a reduction in costs. The rest of the report makes detailed recommendations for procedural reforms.

—— Final Report, app. pp. 37. 1947
1946–47 *Cmd.* 7024, *xiii*, 187
sgd. Jan., 1947

The preservation of the marriage tie is of the highest importance in the interests of society. Where there is estrangement, reconciliation should be attempted in every case where there is prospect of success. Sometimes the causes are personal to the parties, sometimes the marriage is strained by external difficulties. The prospects of reconciliation are more favourable in the early stage of marriage, but are usually small by the time the conflict has reached the divorce court, and any form of compulsion is detrimental. Each party must have full confidence that nothing he says will be disclosed without his permission, will not affect his legal rights or be used in court

against him. Any machinery must be quite separate from judicial officers and judicial proceedings. There should be a Marriage Welfare Service, sponsored by the State, but not a State institution, evolved gradually from existing voluntary agencies, to whom financial assistance should be given. Welfare officers should be appointed to give advice and guidance.

Parents who have been or are about to be divorced have no absolute right to determine the future of their children, since they have created a situation in which the interests of the children need consideration apart from those of their parents. But children are rarely separately represented in court, and the judge is never in possession of a report by an independent person as to their welfare. Court welfare officers should report on the welfare of the children and represent their interests before the Court.

Decisions on financial questions, maintenance, alimony, etc., are dealt with at the hearing, and there is often intolerable delay. Decisions on these questions and on variation of marriage settlements should normally be made by the Judge at the hearing or immediately after it.

Further reforms in procedure are suggested, including the abolition of the rule in *Russell* v. *Russell*.

Grants for the Development of Marriage Guidance

Dept. Cttee. Rep., apps. pp. 18. 1948
1948–49 *Cmd.* 7566, *xvii*, 769
apptd. Feb., sgd. Oct., 1948

S. W. Harris (*Ch.*), Barlas (Mrs. E. G. M.), Goode (Miss W. M.), Haynes, Herbert, Larkin.

'*To consider on what lines marriage guidance as a form of social service can be most advantageously developed in England and Wales if assisted by Exchequer grants, and to advise on what basis Exchequer grants could properly be made to this service.*'

The experimental work in marriage

guidance of the National Marriage Guidance Council, the Catholic Marriage Advisory Council and the Family Welfare Association should be given help from public funds and the experiment should be given some measure of official supervision. The 3 bodies should together devise schemes for selection and training of marriage counsellors as part of a unified policy rather than in isolation and a representative body should be set up for this purpose. Ministers of religion might be given facilities to take advantage of the training schemes. A grant of £5000 a year should be given to the Headquarters of the National Marriage Guidance Council and £1500 each to the Catholic Marriage Advisory Council and the Family Welfare Association respectively. Local centres should approach the local authorities; where the work is approved by the Home Office, one-half of the expenditure should be met by a Government grant.

9. MISCELLANEOUS REGULATORY POWERS

Disaster at the Bolton Wanderers' Football Ground

Enquiry. Rep. pp. 12

1945–46 *Cmd.* 6846, *x*, 1
apptd. March, sgd. May, 1946

R. M. Hughes.

'*To enquire into the circumstances of the disaster at the Bolton Wanderers' football ground on the 9th March, 1946, and to report.*'

The disaster of the 9th March, 1946, causing 33 deaths and injuries to hundreds, occurred at Burnden Park, Bolton, on the occasion of the Cup-Tie between the Bolton Wanderers and Stoke City. The circumstances are reviewed in detail.

Upon their information and judgment the Club and the police had taken proper steps; the spirit of co-operation between them was good, but the machinery was lacking. The real trouble lay in the fact that there had been no scientific ascertainment of the ground's capacity, there were no means of knowing when the maximum capacity was or was about to be reached, nor facilities for immediate closing of the turnstiles, and in the grounds there was no system to allow for a free in and out movement of a crowd. Burnden Park, like so many similar grounds, had grown from small beginnings. The Home Secretary should be given powers to make regulations for different kinds of ground covering the broad conditions necessary for safety. Grounds of any considerable size should be licensed.

Cremation

Inter-Dept. Cttee. Rep., apps. pp. 27.
1950

1950 *Cmd.* 8009, *viii*, 635
apptd. May, 1947. *sgd. July*, 1950

H. A. Strutt (*Ch.*), Howat, Ross, Summers, Wall (Miss J. I.).

'*To review the Regulations made under section 7 of the Cremation Act,* 1902, *and to make recommendations.*'

The Cremation Committee of 1903 concentrated on the danger that cremation might be used to destroy evidence of crime and framed regulations to prevent this. The total number of cremations had risen from 1796 in 1920 to 79,607 in 1949. The siting, establishment and plans of crematoria should require prior approval, they should be open to inspection and regulations should provide that the staff should be suitable and technically proficient. The regulations should prohibit cremation where the deceased was known to have held views or beliefs inconsistent with it. To prevent theft, each coffin should be cremated separately, there should be no interference with the coffin at the crematorium or during incineration, and no person should be allowed to enter the committal room without express sanction of the superintendent. There was a conflict of evidence on whether the confirmatory certificate of an independent practitioner need be retained: the committee decided that it should, but it should also serve the purpose of authorising cremation.

Celluloid Storage

Cttee. Rep., apps. pp. 33. 1950

1950 *Cmd.* 7929, *vii*, 1.
apptd. June, 1948. *sgd. Jan.*, 1950

J. I. Wall (*Ch.*), Eccles, Farnsworth, Gayton, Hodges, Jessup, Skillern, Studd, Watts.

To inquire 'upon the suitability of, or the need for amendment of, the regulations under the Factories Acts and the Celluloid and Cinematograph Film Act, 1922, which govern the storage of celluloid.'

A fire at Richmond resulting in the deaths of 6 persons living in houses close to a factory, involved scrap celluloid stored pending re-sale. Celluloid in all forms is highly inflammable, scrap being the most dangerous. The existing controls are applied by two general and three Local Acts, and three sets of regulations. All celluloid storage should be subject to common standards, whether stored in factory or non-factory premises. All celluloid in excess of minimum quantities should be controlled, but the standards should vary with its type—raw celluloid, manufactured celluloid, photographic film, and scrap and waste celluloid.

As these suggested standards of storage are not to be found in the majority of store rooms, in view of existing building difficulties the new regulations should apply as soon as is practicable.

APPENDIX I

MEMORANDA ON THE PROCEDURE AND PRIVILEGES OF THE HOUSE BY OFFICERS OF THE HOUSE AND OTHERS

1. *Offices of Profit*, by Sir Gilbert Campion, in *Offices or Places of Profit under the Crown*. Sel. Cttee. Rep. App. 2; 1940–41 (120) iii.
2. *Offices of Profit*, by Sir Gilbert Campion, in *Elections*. Sel. Cttee. Rep. App. I; 1945–46 (3–1) vi.
3. *Lobby Journalists*, by G. Eden, Hon. Sec. of the Parliamentary Lobby Journalists, in *Budget Disclosure*. Sel. Cttee. Rep. App. III; 1947–48 (20) vi.
4. *Petitions*, by Sir Gilbert Campion, in *Public Petitions*. Sel. Cttee. Special Rep. App.; 1943–44 (80) ii.
5. *Government Proposals for the Acceleration of Legislation*, by the Speaker (D. Clifton Brown), Sir Gilbert Campion and P. F. Cole, Editor of the Official Report, in *Procedure*. Sel. Cttee. 1st Rep., mins. of ev.; 1945–46 (9–1) ix.
6. *Questions*, by E. Fellowes, Second Clerk Assistant and the Speaker (D. Clifton Brown), in *Procedure*. Sel. Cttee. 2nd Rep., mins. of ev.; 1945–46 (58–1) ix.
7. *Possible Methods of Reducing the Time taken for Divisions in the House of Commons*, by Clerks of the Public Bill Office, in *Procedure*. Sel. Cttee. 2nd Rep., mins. of ev.; 1945–46 (58–1) ix.
8. *Proposed Public Expenditure Committee*, by the Clerk of Financial Committees, in *Procedure*. Sel. Cttee. 3rd Rep., mins. of ev.; 1945–46 (189–1) ix.
9. *Suggestions for Reform in Procedure*, by Sir Gilbert Campion, in *Procedure*. Sel. Cttee. 3rd. Rep., mins. of ev.; 1945–46 (189–1) ix.
10. *Statutory Instruments*, by Sir Cecil Carr, C. K. Allen and E. C. S. Wade, in *Procedure*. Sel. Cttee. 3rd Rep., mins. of ev.; 1945–46 (189–1) ix.
11. *Standing Orders*, by Sir Gilbert Campion, in *Standing Orders (Revision)*. Sel. Cttee. Rep., app.; 1947–48 (192) ix.
12. *Nationalised Industries*, by Sir Frederic Metcalfe, Clerk of the House, in *Nationalised Industries*. Sel. Cttee. Rep., apps.; 1951–52 (332–1) vii.
13. *Actions calculated improperly to influence a Member in the Exercise of his Parliamentary Duties*, by Sir Gilbert Campion, in *Privileges*. Cttee. Rep. App. 4; 1946–47 (118) ix.
14. *Adverse Reflections on the House*, by Sir Gilbert Campion, in *Privileges*. Cttee. Rep. App. 5; 1946–47 (138) ix.
15. *Reflections on Unnamed Members*, by Sir Gilbert Campion, in *Privileges*. Cttee. Rep. App. 1; 1947–48 (112) ix.
16. *Procedure on Private Bills without a Preamble*, by L. A. Abraham, Clerk of Private Bills, in *Trafalgar Estates Bill*. Sel. Cttee. Mins of ev.; 1947–48 (7) ix.

APPENDIX II

SELECT LIST OF ANNUAL REPORTS 1940–54

THE annual reports of Departments and other statutory bodies, and the memoranda and statistics they contain, are invaluable sources of information. Reference numbers to those issued in the sessional papers are given in the General Alphabetical Index, 1900–1949, and in the sessional indexes thereafter. For working convenience the list below gives the paper and volume numbers of the principal series bearing on the major subjects covered by the Breviate and most frequently required by researchers.

This list, that in the *Select List, 1833–1899*, and in the *Breviate, 1900–16*, which continues the series from 1900–1939, together give the chief relevant annuals from 1833–1954.

Omissions.—Certain annuals, formerly issued as sessional papers, in this period have either become non-parliamentary publications, for which H.M.S.O. Consolidated Lists or Annual Catalogues should be consulted, or have been discontinued, merged with or replaced by other annuals differently titled.

The reports have been tabulated according to their substantial contents, and not under the precise name of the issuing body, which may have changed during the period.

The titles of the reports in each series are as follows:

1. Finance. Finance Accounts of the U.K.
2. Inland Revenue. Reports of Commissioners.
3. Customs. Customs and Excise. Reports of Commissioners.
4. Economic Survey.

5. National Income. An Analysis of the Sources of War Finance and an Estimate of the National Income and Expenditure. 1945–46: National Income and Expenditure of the U.K. 1951–52: Preliminary National Income and Expenditure Estimates.
6. Balance of Payments. U.K. Balance of Payments.
7. Bank of England. Reports.
8. Coal. National Coal Board. Annual Reports and Statements of Accounts.

9. Gas. Gas Council. Reports and Statements of Accounts.
10. Electricity. British Electricity Authority. Reports and Statements of Accounts.
11. Transport. British Transport Commission. Annual Reports, Statements of Accounts and Statistics. 1953–54: Vol. I, Report. Vol. II, Financial and Statistical Accounts.
12. Labour. Ministry of Labour and National Service. Reports.

13. Factories. Chief Inspector of Factories. Annual Reports.
14. Assistance Board. Reports. 1948–49: National Assistance Board. Reports.
15. Pensions. Ministry of Pensions. Reports. (Ministry of Pensions amalgamated with Ministry of National Insurance in 1953.)
16. National Insurance. Ministry of National Insurance. Reports. 1953–54: Ministry of Pensions and National Insurance. Reports.

17. Health. Ministry of Health. Summary Reports. 1946–47: Reports.
18. Health, Chief M.O. Ministry of Health. Report of the Chief M.O. on the State of the Public Health (1946–47 to 1950 included in Reports of Ministry of Health).
19. Health (Scotland). Department of Health for Scotland. Summary Reports. 1946–47: Reports. 1950: Reports of the Department of Health for Scotland and of the Scottish Health Services Council.
20. Education. Ministry of Education. Reports and Statistics of Public Education for England and Wales.

21. Education (Scotland). Scottish Education Department. Summary Reports. 1948: Reports.
22. Civil Judicial Statistics, England and Wales.
23. Civil Judicial Stats. (Scot.). Civil Judicial Statistics, Scotland.
24. Criminal Statistics. England and Wales. Statistics relating to Crime and Criminal Proceedings.

25. Criminal Statistics (Scot.).
26. Prisons. Commissioners of Prisons and the Directors of Convict Prisons. Reports. 1950–51: Commissioners of Prisons. Reports.
27. Prisons (Scot.). Prisons in Scotland. Reports.
28. Statistical Abstract for the U.K.

1—4

Session	Finance		Inland Revenue		Customs		Economic Survey	
1939-40	(134)	vi						
1940-41	(92)	v						
1941-42	(91)	v						
1942-43	(94)	vii						
1943-44	(85)	v						
1944-45	(99)	vii						
1945-46	(145)	xv	Cmd. 6769	xiii	Cmd. 6703	xi		
			Cmd. 6770	xiii	Cmd. 6951	xi		
			Cmd. 6771	xiii				
			Cmd. 6772	xiii				
			Cmd. 6773	xiii				
			Cmd. 6774	xiii				
1946-47	(109)	xv	Cmd. 7067	xii			Cmd. 7046	xix
1947-48	(180)	xvii	Cmd. 7362	xii	Cmd. 7252	xi	Cmd. 7344	xxii
1948					Cmd. 7547	i		
1948-49	(189)	xxii	Cmd. 7738	xvii	Cmd. 7834	xiv	Cmd. 7647	xxix
1950	(79)	xv	Cmd. 8052	xii			Cmd. 7915	xix
1950-51	(201)	xxi	Cmd. 8103	xvi	Cmd. 8120	xi	Cmd. 8195	xxvii
1951-52	(203)	xix	Cmd. 8436	xv	Cmd. 8449	x	Cmd. 8509	xxv
1952-53	(191)	xviii	Cmd. 8726	xiii	Cmd. 8727	ix	Cmd. 8800	xxiv
1953-54	(197)	xx	Cmd. 9030	xvi	Cmd. 9031	xi	Cmd. 9108	xxvi
1954-55			Cmd. 9351	vi	Cmd. 9358	iv	Cmd. 9412	xiii

5—8

Session	National Income		Balance of Payments		Bank of England		Coal	
1940-41	Cmd. 6261	viii						
1941-42	Cmd. 6347	ix						
1942-43	Cmd. 6438	xi						
1943-44	Cmd. 6520	viii						
1944-45	Cmd. 6623	x						
1945-46	Cmd. 6784	xv						
1946-47	Cmd. 7099	xv			Cmd. 7115	x		
1947-48	Cmd. 7371	xvii	Cmd. 7324	xvii	Cmd. 7411	x	(174)	x
							(175)	x
1948			Cmd. 7520	ii				
1948-49	Cmd. 7649	xxii	Cmd. 7648	xxii	Cmd. 7759	xi	(187)	xiii
			Cmd. 7793	xxii				
1950	Cmd. 7933	xv	Cmd. 7928	xv	Cmd. 8002	vi	(82)	vii
			Cmd. 8065	xv				
1950-51	Cmd. 8203	xxi	Cmd. 8201	xxi	Cmd. 8317	viii	(188)	x
			Cmd. 8379	xxi				
1951-52	Cmd. 8486	xix	Cmd. 8505	xix	Cmd. 8625	viii	(190)	viii
			Cmd. 8666	xix				
1952-53	Cmd. 8803	xviii	Cmd. 8808	xviii	Cmd. 8911	vii	(157)	viii
			Cmd. 8976	xviii				
1953-54	Cmd. 9118	xx	Cmd. 9119	xx	Cmd. 9226	viii	(160)	x
			Cmd. 9291	xx				
1954-55	Cmd. 9423	viii	Cmd. 9430	viii				

9—12

Session	Gas		Electricity		Transport		Labour	
1946-47							Cmd. 7225	xii
1947-48								
1948								
1948-49			(336)	xiv	(235)	xii	Cmd. 7559	xvii
							Cmd. 7822	xvii
1950			(149)	ix	(139)	xiv	Cmd. 8017	xii
1950-51	(69)	xiii	(267)	xii	(210)	xx	Cmd. 8338	xvi
1951-52	(20)	xiii	(262)	xi	(218)	xviii	Cmd. 8640	xvi
	(309)	xiv						
1952-53	(249)	xii	(251)	x	(190)	xvii	Cmd. 8893	xiv
1953-54	(262)	xiv	(234)	xii	(268-1)	xix	Cmd. 9207	xvi
					(268-11)	xix		

13—16

Session	Factories		Assistance Board		Pensions		National Insurance	
1940–41	Cmd. 6251	iv						
	Cmd. 6316	iv						
1941–42	Cmd. 6397	iv						
1942–43	Cmd. 6471	iv						
1943–44	Cmd. 6563	iii						
1944–45								
1945–46	Cmd. 6698	xii	Cmd. 6700	x				
			Cmd. 6883	x				
1946–47	Cmd. 6992	xi	Cmd. 7184	x				
1947–48	Cmd. 7299	xii	Cmd. 7502	x				
1948					(10)	ii		
1948–49	Cmd. 7621	xvi	Cmd. 7767	xi	(260)	xix		
	Cmd. 7839	xvi						
1950			Cmd. 8030	vi	(145)	xiii	Cmd. 7955	xii
1950–51	Cmd. 8155	xiii	Cmd. 8276	viii	(288)	xviii		
1951–52	Cmd. 8445	xii	Cmd. 8632	viii	(290)	xvii	Cmd. 8412	xv
							Cmd. 8635	xv
1952–53	Cmd. 8772	xi	Cmd. 8900	vii	(271)	xvi	Cmd. 8882	xiv
1953–54	Cmd. 9154	xiii	Cmd. 9210	viii			Cmd. 9159	xviii
1954–55	Cmd. 9330	v						

17—20

Session	Health		Health Chief M.O.		Health (Scotland)		Education	
1940–41					Cmd. 6308	iv		
1941–42	Cmd. 6340	iv			Cmd. 6372	iv		
	Cmd. 6394	iv						
1942–43	Cmd. 6468	iv			Cmd. 6462	iv		
1943–44	Cmd. 6562	iii			Cmd. 6545	iii		
1944–45								
1945–46	Cmd. 6710	xii	1922–46 Non-Parl.		Cmd. 6661	xii		
1946–47	Cmd. 7119	xii	Cmd. 7119	xii	Cmd. 7188	xii		
1947–48	Cmd. 7441	xii	Cmd. 7441	xii	Cmd. 7453	xii	Cmd. 7426	xi
1948								
1948–49	Cmd. 7734	xvi	Cmd. 7734	xvi	Cmd. 7659	xvii	Cmd. 7724	xiv
1950	Cmd. 7910	xi	Cmd. 7910	xi	Cmd. 7921	xi	Cmd. 7957	ix
1950–51	Cmd. 8342	xv	Cmd. 8343	xv	Cmd. 8184	xv	Cmd. 8244	xi
1951–52	Cmd. 8655	xv	Cmd. 8582	xv	Cmd. 8496	xv	Cmd. 8554	x
1952–53	Cmd. 8933	xiii	Cmd. 8787	xiii	Cmd. 8799	xiii	Cmd. 8835	ix
1953–54	Cmd. 9321	xv	Cmd. 9009	xv	Cmd. 9107	xv	Cmd. 9155	xi
			Cmd. 9307	xv				
1954–55					Cmd. 9417	v		

21—24

Session	Education (Scotland)		Civil Judicial Statistics		Civil Judicial Stats. (Scot.)		Criminal Statistics	
1940–41	Cmd. 6317	iv						
1941–42	Cmd. 6370	iv						
1942–43	Cmd. 6452	iv						
1943–44	Cmd. 6540	iii						
1944–45								
1945–46	Cmd. 6667	xi						
	Cmd. 6887	xx						
1946–47	Cmd. 7089	xi					Cmd. 7227	xv
1947–48							Cmd. 7428	xxi
1948							Cmd. 7528	ii
1948–49	Cmd. 7519	i			Cmd. 7821	xxviii	Cmd. 7733	xxviii
	Cmd. 7656	xiv						
1950	Cmd. 7914	ix					Cmd. 7993	xix
1950–51	Cmd. 8200	xi	Cmd. 8186	xxvi	Cmd. 8106	xxvi	Cmd. 8301	xxvi
					Cmd. 8373	xxvi		
1951–52	Cmd. 8515	x	Cmd. 8404	xxiv	Cmd. 8637	xxiv	Cmd. 8616	xxiv
			Cmd. 8567	xxiv				
1952–53	Cmd. 8813	ix	Cmd. 8867	xxiii	Cmd. 8868	xxiii	Cmd. 8941	xxiii
1953–54	Cmd. 9141	xi	Cmd. 9164	xxv	Cmd. 9187	xxv	Cmd. 9199	xxv
1954–55	Cmd. 9428	iv						

25—28

Session	Criminal Statistics (Scot.)	Prisons	Prisons (Scot.)	Statistical Abstract
1939–40		Cmd. 6137 v		Cmd. 6232 x Continuing Non-Parl.
1940–41				
1941–42				
1942–43				
1943–44				
1944–45				
1945–46		Cmd. 6820 xiv		
1946–47		Cmd. 7010 xiv		
		Cmd. 7146 xiv		
1947–48	Cmd. 7505 xxi	Cmd. 7271 xv		
		Cmd. 7475 xv		
1948				
1948–49	Cmd. 7554 xxviii	Cmd. 7777 xx	Cmd. 7747 xx	
	Cmd. 7595 xxviii			
	Cmd. 7708 xxviii			
1950	Cmd. 7980 xix		Cmd. 7966 xiii	
1950–51	Cmd. 8330 xxvi	Cmd. 8088 xviii	Cmd. 8261 xix	
		Cmd. 8356 xviii		
1951–52	Cmd. 8583 xxiv		Cmd. 8543 xviii	
1952–53	Cmd. 8818 xxiii	Cmd. 8692 xvi	Cmd. 8817 xvi	
		Cmd. 8948 xvi		
1953–54	Cmd. 9134 xxv	Cmd. 9259 xviii	Cmd. 9144 xviii	
1954–55	Cmd. 9441 xiii		Cmd. 9448 vii	

ALPHABETICAL INDEX

This brief index is designed to assist readers to find individual documents in cases where their location is not sufficiently indicated by the Table of Contents. It is based on the key word or words of the title. Where this is identical with the main subject heading, no separate entry has been made. Where there is a series of reports under the same title, the page number of the first only is given.

Accidents, aircraft, 212
    home, 333
    paper mills, 271
    road, 204
Accounts, Government, 60
    public, 72
Adoption, 444
Aged, medical care, 333
Agricultural education, 406-10
Agricultural Survey, Scotland, 79
Agriculture and Fisheries, Ministry of, 29
Air pollution, 381
Air-Raid Precautions, finance, 39
Air-Raid shelters, conditions, 304
Air transport, 210-16
Alderney, 2
Allotments, 84
Animals, damage by, 495
Antioxidants, food, 345
Apples, marketing, 101
Apprenticeship, building, 250
    coal face workers, 175
Approved schools, 473, 476, 478, 482
Approved societies, 291
Art, examinations, 403
    works of, export, 432
Artificial limbs, 334
Arts and crafts, Welsh schools, 406
Atomic energy, 189-90
Availability rule and insurance, 295
Aviation, 210-16
Awards, university, 423

Ball-clay industry, 137
Bank of England, 75
Banking, manpower, 231
Berkeley Hotel Ltd., 167
Betterment, 366
Betting, 449
Bilateral trade negotiations, 125
Bills, hybrid, 12
    of exchange, 484
    private, 12, 13
Birds, in London, 58
Blasting, regulations, 273
Blind, blindness, 261, 334-5, 398
Bolton, football ground, 500
Boots and shoes, 153
Borstals, 473, 477, 482
Boundary Commissions, 5
Bread, post war, 91
Bretton Woods, 73
Brick industry, 131, 132, 249
Bristol Rovers Football Club, 166
British Electricity Authority, 187
British Film Institute, 142
British Industries Fair, 128
British Institute of Management, 127
British Standards Institution, 128
British Transport Commission, 195
Broadcasting, 219-23
Broadmoor, 481
Budget disclosure, 9
Building industry, 131-6, 250-1, 354-6

Burns, A., conviction, 456
Bursaries, 396
Business administration, training, 412
Business premises, tenure, 488-90

Cable and Wireless Ltd., 218
Calico printing, 159
Canals, 194, 198
Capital investment, 74
Capital issues, 73
Capital punishment, 479
Car parks, 205
    London, 56
Carpets, 153
Catering establishments, hygiene, 345
Catering Wages Commission, 244-49
Cathode ray tubes, 163
Celluloid storage, 501
Cement, 135
Census, of Distribution, 130
    of Production, 129, 130
Central areas, redevelopment, 366
Cereals, decontrol, 93
Chairman of Ways and Means, 10
Channel Islands, 2-3
Charities, 447
Chemical engineering research, 146
Child care, 439-44
Children, 439-47
    boarding out, 439, 444
    evacuation, 382, 437-9
    handicapped, 398-401, 420
    health, 312
    migration, 279
    out of school, 395
    theatrical work, 267
China clay, 137, 153
Cinema, children and, 445
Cinematograph films, 141-6
Citizenship, training, 404
Civil Aviation, Ministry of, 30
Civil Defence, 45
Civil engineering, 251
Civil List, 1
Civil Service, 32-9, 230
    political activities, 35, 37
    security, 37
Clatworthy, A. A., 471
Clergy, disqualification, 708
Clinical research, 316
Clothing, 129, 153
Clyde, 194, 207
    planning, 371
Coal industry, 172-83
Coastal flooding, 115
Collective discrimination, 156
Colonial Service, 25
Commerce, education for, 414
Commonwealth Economic Conference, 125
Community centres, 360
    wardens, 419
Company law, 164
Compensation, and betterment, 366
    equal, 483

Compensation, requisitioned property, 482
    war damage, 483
Consultants, 312, 317
Consumption, civilian, during war, 120
Continuation classes, 390
Co-operative marketing, horticulture, 100
Copper, semi-manufactures of, 160
Copyright, 228
Cost of living, 236
Cotton industry, 137-41, 153, 251-5, 269
Counterpart funds, 429
Country districts, houses, 366
Countryside, access to, 378
County colleges, Wales, 392
Courts, 452-63
Cremation, 500
Crichel Down, 31
Crime, criminals, 471-82
Criminal cases, new trials, 462
Crofts, 82, 85, 124
Crown, offices of profit under, 6
Curriculum, secondary schools, 401
    Wales, 389
Customs and excise, 61
Cutlery trade, 153, 255

Deaf-blind, 335
Deaf children, 398
Deaf-mutism, 335
Dedham Vale, 192
Deer, 107, 108
Defamation, law of, 494
Defence, 26, 73, 232
Delegated legislation, 14
Dental goods, 157
Dental nurses, 330
Dental services, 329
Dentists, 309, 321, 322
Depositions, 457
Design in industry, 129
Detergents, 343, 346
Determination of needs, 281, 296, 302
Devlin, E. F., conviction, 456
Diet, working-class, 238
Diplomatic immunity, 494
Disabled children, 399
Disabled, rehabilitation, 260-2
Disablement, assessment, 300
Discharged prisoners aid societies, 481
Diseases, industrial, 300
Dispensing practice, 321
Disputes, industrial, 238-9
Distribution, census of, 130
    of industry, 123
District heating, 133
Dividends, control, 74
Divorce, 498-9
Dock labour, 257-9
Domestic employment, 265
Domestic food production, 84
Drainage, land, 113, 114
    trade premises, 113
Drama, Welsh schools, 406
Drop forging industry, 274
Drugs, definition, 320
Dundee, University College, 425-6
Durham Palatine Court, 460
Dust, card rooms, 269
    steel foundries, 273
    tile making, 272
Dwellings, design, 349
    heating, 170

Early leaving, school children, 389

Elections, 7
Electoral reform, 3-5
Electric lamps, 157
Electric wires and cables, 158
Electrical machinery, 164
Electricity, 184-7, 189
    in mines, 182
Electrification, railways, 199
Electronic valves, 163
Elliott, J., 472
Emigration, 279
Employers and workers, relations, 234
Employment, control, 229
    policy, 233
Endowments, educational, 397
Enemy property, distribution, 485
English language, Welsh schools, 404
Entertainment industry, insurance, 294
Equal compensation, 483
Equal pay, 263
Estate duty, 61
Estate expenditure and rent, 82
European Payments Union, 73
Evacuation, 382, 437-9
Evans, T. J., conviction, 456
Examinations, art, 403
    secondary schools, 401-2
Exchange, control, 74
    saving of, 80
Exchequer equalisation grants, 50, 52
Exhibitions, trade, 127, 128
Expenditure, national, 72
Explosions, explosives, mines, 183

Factories, lighting, 268
Fairs, trade, 127, 128
Family allowances, 290
Fares, passenger, 197
Farm prices, 80
Farm rents, 82
Farm Survey, 79
Feeding stuffs, decontrol, 93
Ferries, 200
Fertilisers, chemical, 164
Festival Gardens Ltd., 57
Festival of Britain, 127
Film industry, 141-6
Financial statistics, Scotland, 72
Fire Brigades, 45
Fire in ships, 209
Fish, fishing, 88, 115-17, 255
Fishermen, insurance, 292
Flats, 357
Flooding, coastal, 115
Flying boat base, 211
Fog, mortality, 336
Food and Agriculture Organisation, 73
Food, consumption, 89, 238
    decontrol, 93
    labelling, 344
    purity, 344-6
    shortage, 90
    standards, 345
    toxic chemicals in, 88
Foot-and-mouth disease, 107
Football ground disaster, 500
Footpaths, 378
Foreign Office officials, disappearance, 38
Foreign Service, reform, 25
Forestry, 88, 109-11, 151
Freezing point test, milk, 95
Full employment, 235
Furniture, 153
Further education, 391

G.A.T.T., 73
Galleries, 429–31
Gaming, 449
Gas, 188–9, 192
Gases, industrial and medical, 162
Gathering grounds, 192
Gatwick airport, 215
General practitioners, 313, 317, 318, 319
German enemy property, 485
Glassware, 153
Government scientific organisation, 427
Grain, drying, storage, 102
    world position, 90
Groundnuts, 90
Guardian's allowances, 292
Guild churches, London, 57

Handicapped children, 398–401, 420
Hard fibre cordage, 161
Hearing, defective, 398
Helicopter, 215
Hereford juvenile court, 452
Herring industry, 115
Higher appointments, 279
Highlands, 85, 124, 185
Hill farms, 77
Historic houses, 359
Holidays, staggering of, 248
Home information services, 28
Homeless, care of, 438
Hops, 99
Horses, export, 103
    slaughter, 103
Horticultural produce, marketing, 100
Hortvet test, milk, 95
Hosiery, 153
Hospital patients, insurance, 294
Hospitals, 306, 312–17
Hostels, 'difficult' children, 438
Hotel industry, 246
House of Commons, accommodation, 23
    Library, 22
    rebuilding, 22
Household expenditure, 238
Housing estates, 360, 364, 365
Housing management, 360–5
Hybrid Bills, 12
Hydrocarbon oil duties, 59
Hydro-electricity, 47, 184

Imperial Institute, 434
Income tax, 66–72
    police, 465
Incomes, costs and prices, 235
    small, and national insurance, 295
Index of retail prices, 237
Industrial catering, 244, 246
    design, 129
    diseases, 300
    disputes, 238–9
    health, 311
    injuries, 289, 297–302
    population, distribution of, 121
    relations, 238
Industry and commerce, education for, 413
Infant mortality, 336
Information services, 28
Inland waterways, 194, 198
Insulin, 158
Insurance, manpower, 231
    national, 290–6
    social, 283–9
    time limits, 294, 301
    unemployment, 281–3

Intermediaries, 30
International Clearing Union, 73
International law, 493–4
Inventors, awards, 227
Investment, control, 74
Iron and steel industry, 147–9
    lung diseases, 274
Iron pipes, deterioration, 150
Ironfoundries, conditions, 273
Ironstone industry, 379

Jewellery and silverware, 129, 153
Justices, clerks, 453
    of the peace, 455
Jute industry, 153, 270
Juvenile court, 452
Juveniles, coal industry, 174
    delinquency, 482
    employment, 266–8
    hours, 275, 278

Laboratory services, 330
Lace, 153
Lancashire, criminal court, 463
Land, drainage, 113, 114
    local charges, 486
    needs of Forces, 80
    registration, 486, 487
    settlement, 82
    transfer, 486
    utilisation, 368, 369
Law, reporting, 451
    revision, reform, 494–7
    Scottish local government, 42
Lead, in food, 345
Leasehold property, 488–91
Legal aid, 463–4
Lend-Lease, 73
Liability, innkeepers', occupiers', 495, 497
Libraries, 22, 430
Licensed premises, reconstruction, 484
Licensing, road passenger services, 205
Lighting, factories, 268
Limitation of actions, 484–5
Linoleum, 153, 162
Loaf, post-war, 91
Local authorities, bursaries, 396
    catering, 246
    members' expenses, 43
    wartime services, 306
Local government, 39–47
    Boundary Commission, 40
    manpower, 44
Local taxation, 47–53
London, 53–8
    airports, 215
    buildings, 160
    planning, 54, 371
    remand homes, 475
Lotteries, 449
Lunacy law, 337
Lung diseases, industrial, 274

Machinery, duty-free import, 125
MacManaway, Rev. J. G., 7–8
Management, British Institute of, 127
    education, 413
Manpower, 229–32
    scientific, 422–3
Marginal farms, 81
Marketing, agricultural, 92, 93
    horticultural, 100
Marriage guidance, 499
Marshall Aid, 73

Matches, 158
Matchwood, 151
Materials, Ministry of, 29
Maternity benefits, 293
Matrimonial causes, 498–9
Meat, inspection, 104
    products, 344
Medical auxiliaries, 331
Medical certificates, 320
Medical personnel, 305
Medical professions, 317–33
Medical research, 316, 427
Medical schools, 424
Members of Parliament, conduct, 9
    election, 6–8
    expenses, 8
    Members' Fund, 8
Mental deficiency, 337
Mental health services, 331
Mental nursing, 324
Merseyside, planning, 371
Metals, economy in use, 150
Midges, control, 342
Midwives, 328
Migration, 279
Milk, 94–8
Milling machines, safeguards, 274
Minerals, development, 149
    overseas, and taxation, 60
    working, control, 366
Miners, pneumoconiosis, 261, 338
    wages, 172
Mines, 172–83
Ministers, official conduct, 24
Monopolies, 141, 153–64
Motor industry, 150
Murder, convictions for, 456
Museums, 430–2
Music, Welsh schools, 406
Mutual Aid, 73
Myxomatosis, 109

National assistance, 296–7
National Coal Board, 179
National expenditure, 72
National Farm Survey, 79
National Fire Service, 45
National Food Survey, 90
National Gallery, 429
National Health Service, 307
National insurance, 290–6
National Museum of Antiquities of Scotland, 431
National parks, 374–8
National Service, 232
Nationalisation, coal industry, 178–9
    electricity, 187
    gas, 189
    iron and steel, 147
    transport, 194–5
Nationalised industries, 15
Nationality, British, 493
Natural resources, 89
Nature Conservancy, 377
Nature reserves, 376, 378
Neuroses, 304, 340
New Forest, 110
New towns, 371
Newcastle-upon-Tyne inquiry, 46
Night baking, 278
Non-industrial employment, 277
Nuclear power, 189–90
Nursing, 305, 324–330

Offenders, treatment of, 471–82

Oil, sea pollution, 117
Old age pensions, 302–4
Older persons, employment, 262
O'Neill, Dennis and Terence, 439
Opticians, 322, 323
Ordnance Survey, 28
Overseas Food Corporation, 91
Overseas information services, 28

P.A.Y.E., 58, 59
Palace of Westminster, 23
Paper mills, accidents, 271
Parliament, 3–24
    Bill, 1947, 3
    Square, 57
Partnerships, medical, 318
Patents, 226
Payment by results, 251
Peat, 183
Pensions, 302–4
    Civil Service, 34
    Ministry of, 30
    Police, 471
Petitions, 10
Petrol rationing, 184
Petrol stations, 205
Pigs, 102
Planners, qualifications, 373
Pneumoconiosis, 261, 301, 338
Police, 465–471, 472
Poliomyelitis, 339
Pollution, air, 336, 381
    rivers, 111, 112
    sea, 117
Population, 435
    industrial, distribution of, 121
Port transport industry, 257–9
Ports, 199, 208–10
Post Office, 217
Postal voting, 4
Pottery, 129, 153, 272
Power presses, safety, 272
Power stations, 187
Prescribing, 320
Press, the, 223
Prices, personal incomes and, 235
    stabilisation, 232
Primary education, 384
Prisoners, prisons, 471–2, 474, 477, 481, 482
Private Bills, 12, 13
Private flying, 211
Privileges, 16
Probation, 473, 482
Procedure, Parliamentary, 11–13
Production, Census of, 129, 130
    concentration of, 118
    Minister of, 24
Productivity, house-building, 356
    industrial, 126
Professions, medical, 317–33
Profit, offices of, under Crown, 6
Property, law of, 486–91
Psychiatrists, psychologists, in Services, 339
Psychological treatment, crime, 471
Public accounts, 72
Public offices, site, 57
Public schools, 384
Publications and debates, 21
Purchase tax, 62–3

Queen's Hall, 58
Queensland-British Food Corporation, 91

Rabbits, myxomatosis, 109

Radio valves, 153
Radiography, 305
Rag flock, 270
Railways, 193, 197, 199
    London, 53, 54
    rating, 49
Rainwater goods, 157
Rates and rating, 47–53
Rationing, fuel, 169
    petrol, 184
Raw Cotton Commission, 140
Raynaud's Phenomenon, 302
Re-armament, 73
Reception areas, conditions, 438
Reception centres, 297
Reconstruction, Wales, 124
Records, Departmental, 433
Redistribution of seats, 4
Regent's Park Terraces, 56, 57
Regional boards, 119
Regional plans, 371
Registration of title, 486, 487
Rehabilitation, disabled, 260–2, 340
Religious instruction, schools, 403
Remand homes, 472, 475, 476, 479
Rents, 359, 360, 362
    business premises, 488
    farm, 82
    police allowances, 465
Requisitioned property, 358, 482
Resale price maintenance, 154, 156
Research, agricultural, 75, 408
    building, 132
    chemical engineering, 146
    medical, 316, 427
    scientific, 427
    social, 427, 428
Restrictive practices, 141, 153–64
Retail prices, index, 237
Retail trade, 118
    wages in, 240–4
Retention moneys, building contracts, 135
Retirement, reasons for, 302
Rheumatism, 340
Rights of way, 379
River boards, 190
River pollution, 111, 112
Road Haulage Disposal Board, 198
Road safety, 201–3
Roads, road traffic, 198, 201–6, 366
Roosevelt Memorial, 57
Rowland, W. G., conviction, 456
Royal Navy, cadet entry, 414
Rubber footwear, 162
Rubber proofed clothing, 153
Rural areas, land utilisation, 368, 369
    housing, 349, 350
    Wales, 86

Salford Hundred, Court of Record, 463
Salmon, poaching, 117
Sand and gravel, 161, 380
Sanitary inspectors, 332
Savoy Hotel Ltd., 167
Scabies, 341
Schools, 384–90, 392
    dental nurses, 330
Scientific Civil Service, 33
Scientific manpower, 422–3
Scientific policy, 423
Scottish affairs, 26
Scottish Land Court, 84
Seamen, welfare, 256, 269
Seasonal workers, insurance, 293

Secondary education, 387, 388
Seeds, qualitative control, 87
Services, skilled men, 229
Severn Barrage, 185
Sewage, 89, 113, 343
Shares of no par value, 165
Sheep, 77
Shell shock, 305
Shift-working, 275
Shipping, 200, 206–10
Shops, 276
    tenancy, 487–8
Silicosis, 261
Site values, rating, 49
Slate industry, 136
Slaughterhouses, 105
Smallholdings, 83
Smallpox, 341
Social insurance (Beveridge), 283
Social workers, mental health services, 331
Sovereign, title of, 1
Speaker's Conference, 4
Specialists, remuneration, 317
Speech disorders, 400
Standardisation, engineering, 128
Standing Orders, 12, 13
State immunities, 494
Statutory Instruments, 13
Statutory Rules and Orders, 13
Steel foundries, dust, 273
Steel industry, 147–9
Stocks, tax-paid, 64
Subsidence, mining, 182
Succession, law of, 491–3
Sugar industry, 94
Supervisors, training, 239
Surveys, agricultural, 79
    staffs, 28

Tate Gallery, 429
Taxation, 58–9, 60, 62–72
    local, 47–53
Taxicab service, 56
Tea, 163
Teachers, 416–21
Technical education, 410–12
Technological education, 410–12
Telegraphy, 218
Television, 219, 223
Temporary housing, 346, 347
Tenants, selection, 361, 363
    transfer, 361, 362
Tendring Hundred, 192
Textile machinery, cotton industry, 139
Tile dust, 272
Timber, imported, 159
    supply, 151
Tomatoes, marketing, 101
Towns' wastes, agricultural use, 89
Toxic chemicals, agriculture, 87
Trade fairs, 127, 128
Trade harbours, 199
Trade premises, drainage, 113
Trade statistics, Scotland, 72
Trading profits, taxation, 65
Trafalgar Estates, 57
Traffic, London, 55
    signs, 204
Transport, Ministry of, 30
Trawlers, crews, 255
Trilene, 329
Tuberculosis, 301, 305, 341
Tudor aircraft, 211
Tyres, pneumatic, 160

U.N.R.R.A., 73
Unemployment insurance, 281–3
Universities, 421–7
  technology in, 412
Utility schemes, purchase tax, 62

Vaccination, 341
Valuation, agricultural, 80
  for rates, 48, 49, 51, 52
Venereal diseases, 342
Veterinary education, 281
Veterinary practice, 280
Victoria and Albert Museum, 429
Visual aids, 404
Voluntary Aid Detachments, 305

Wages, catering trades, 244–9
  Councils, 241–4
  miners, 172
  retail trades, 240–4
Wales, and Monmouthshire, 87, 124
  ports, 210
  slate industry, 136
  South, planning, 371
War:
  Air Raid Precautions, finance, 39
  Air raid shelters, conditions, 304
  Civil Servants, call-up, 230
  civilian consumption, 120
  coal industry, 172
  equal compensation, 483
  evacuation, 382, 437–8
  food consumption levels, 89
  homeless, care of, 438
  housing, temporary, 346–7
  industrial policy, 118–20
  labour supply, 229–31
  Lend Lease, 73
  limitation of actions, 484
  manpower, 229–32
  medical personnel, 305
  milk, 95
  Mutual Aid, 73
  neuroses, 304
  Production, concentration of, 118
    Minister of, 24

radiography, 305
rationing, fuel, 169
reception areas, 438
requisitioning, 482
retail trade, 118
shipping, 206–7
sugar industry, 94
temporary housing, 346–7
U.N.R.R.A., 73
Voluntary Aid Detachments, 305
war damage, 483–4
war effort, statistics, 73, 120, 231
welfare work, outside factories, 269
women, hours of work, 275
Ware, D. J., confession, 456
Water, 190–3
  London, 53
  rates, 49
Weights and measures, 167
Welders, health, 274
Welfare work, outside factories, 269
Wellington Museum, 430
Welsh language, publishing, 405
  schools, 404
White Fish Authority, 117
Wild animals, cruelty, 106
Wild life, conservation, 376, 378
Wimpey, Geo., & Co. Ltd., 30
Windows, metal, 163
Wireless telegraphy, 218
Witnesses allowances, 457
Women, employment, 263–6
  equal pay, 263
  hours of work, 275
Wool, 129, 153
  marketing, 98
  textile industry, 271
Working-class diet, 90
Working Party Reports, 152
Workmen's compensation, 289, 297–302

X-ray, 305

Youth Employment Service, 266
Youth leaders, 417–19
Youth service, 392–5

INDEX TO CHAIRMEN AND AUTHORS

This index is intended as a guide to finding documents by the name of the chairman or author as printed on the document. It does not necessarily identify persons, since there may be change of surname, elevation to the peerage under a different name, or change of individual's practice in signature respecting initials and hyphens. Sometimes individuals may be popularly known by both Christian and surname together: readers should then consult the index under both.

Aaron, R. I., 388, 392, 404
Abercrombie, P., 371
Abraham, L. A., 57, 502
Adam, R., 348
Aitken, Miss J. K., 327
Allen, C. K., 12, 502
Allen, G. C., 135
Allen, P., 471
Alness, Lord, 408
Anderson, J., 4
Appleton, E. V., 183
Aronson, V. R., 244, 273
Ashby, E., 396
Asquith, C., 263
Assheton, R., 15, 32
Atkinson, E. H. T., 154
Attlee, C. R., 16, 17
Ayre, A. L., 59

Baillieu, C., 127
Baker, H. T., 110
Baker, S. J., 465, 467, 470
Balfour, G., 135
Balfour, Lord, 26
Balfour of Burleigh, Lord, 77, 361
Bamford, E. St. J., 60
Barlow, J. A., 33, 34, 422
Barlow, M., 121
Barnes, G. G., 345
Barnett, G. P., 269, 274
Barrington-Ward, V. M., 54
Bateson, D. L., 267
Beaton, N. S., 200
Beaver, H., 187, 381
Bell, R. D. M., 470
Bellenger, F. J., 7
Benson, G., 12, 22, 57, 75, 218, 430
Beveridge, W. H. (Lord), 169, 220, 229, 283
Blenkinsop, A., 44
Brabazon, Lord, 214
Bradbeer, A. F., 315
Braddock, T., 57
Bradlaw, R., 330
Braithwaite, J. G., 202
Bramley-Harker, R., 274
Bray, F., 403
Breslin, J. J., 151
Brierly, J. L., 275
Brooke, H., 357, 362
Brown, D. C., 4, 11, 502
Brown, G., 28, 83, 84
Browne, J. N., 52
Bryan, A. M., 183
Burrell, J. H., 465, 470
Burrows, R., 46
Byrne, L. A., 457

Cadbury, E., 197
Cairns, D., 156
Callaghan, J., 202

Cameron, J., 258, 464
Campbell, C., 216
Campbell, E., 10
Campion, G., 6, 7, 10, 11, 12, 18, 19, 20, 502
Carr, C., 12, 502
Carr, C. T., 5
Carr-Saunders, A. M., 414
Carrington, Lord, 109, 410
Cathcart, E. P., 340
Catto, Lord, 72
Chancellor of the Exchequer, 1, 290
Chancellor, J. R., 280
Chasteney, H. E., 273
Chelmsford, Lord, 267
Chorley, Lord, 34
Citrine, W., 120
Clapham, J., 427
Clark, A., 31
Clark, W. G., 334
Clarke, F., 392, 395
Clifton Brown, D., 4, 11, 502
Clow, A. G., 186
Clyde, J. L., 30, 442
Cohen, B., 334
Cohen, H., 316, 319, 320, 321
Cohen, J., 327
Cohen, L. L., 164, 227
Cole, P. F., 11, 502
Constable, Lord, 408
Cook, C. M., 199
Cook, F. C., 204
Cooper, T. M., 184, 207, 421, 425
Cope, V. Z., 331
Copeland, M. A., 120
Coppock, R., 357
Corlett, J., 476
Courtney, C. L., 211
Cremer, H. W., 146
Crew, F. A. E., 342
Cribbett, G., 215
Crick, W. F., 60
Crook, Lord, 323
Crookshank, H. F. C., 21
Cunliffe, G., 128
Cunningham, A., 312
Cunningham, C. C., 52
Curtis, M., 440

Dale, E. T., 300, 311
Danckwerts, H. O., 319
Daniel, C., 223
Davidson, D. Du B., 382
Davies, C., 8, 14, 20, 54
Davies, W. T., 229
De La Warr, Lord, 77, 105
Delevingne, M., 183
Denning, A. T., 498
Devonshire, Duke of, 25
Dodds, C., 345
Doig, A. T., 274

Donkin, S. B., 185
Douglas, J. B., 82
Douglas, Miss K. G., 327
Douglas, W. S., 62
Dow, R. C. S., 329
Dower, J., 374
Drogheda, Lord, 13, 28, 146
Du Parcq, Lord, 455
Dudley, Lord, 349
Duguid, L. N., 274
Duncan, J. F., 113

Earle, L., 58
East, W. N., 471
Eastham, T., 471
Ede, J. C., 2, 20
Eden, G., 10, 502
Edwards, F. L., 50
Edwards, L. J., 44
Egerton, A. C., 170
Elliot, W. E., 43, 99, 115, 305
Eve, M. T., 40, 250, 484
Evershed, R., 139, 251, 257, 459

Faringdon, Lord, 364
Faulkner, P., 117
Fellowes, E., 11, 502
Ferguson, T., 335
Fergusson, D., 76
Fforde, A., 135
Fisher, M. G., 43
Fitzgerald, M., 48
Fleck, A., 179
Fleming, D. P., 384
Fletcher, E., 57
Forster, J., 174, 257
Foster, W., 175
Franklin, H. W. F., 477
Franklin, H., 98, 102
Fraser, F. R., 339
Fraser, J., 330, 340
French, H. L., 28, 91
Fry, R., 129
Furse, R., 26
Fyfe, W. H., 384, 387, 390, 395, 397, 404, 416

Gardiner, T. R., 35
Garrett, A. W., 249, 272, 301
Gater, G. H., 143, 251, 421
Gedge, M. L., 165
Gerrard, A. D., 456
Gibson, C. W., 361
Girdwood, J. G., 354, 357
Glass, D. V., 437
Goddard, R. (Lord), 452, 495
Goodale, E. W., 128
Goodenough, W. M., 424
Gorell, Lord, 56, 129
Gould, R. M., 186, 236, 237
Gowers, E. A., 107, 276, 359, 479

Grant, F., 63
Gray, A., 256
Gray, J. N., 486
Grebenik, E., 437
Greene, Lord, 173
Greenwood, A., 18, 19
Gregory, H. S., 228
Gregory, R. C., 458
Grenfell, D. R., 7, 261
Gretton, J., 9
Griffiths, J., 394
Grigg, P. J., 433
Guillebaud, C. W., 239
Gurney-Dixon, S., 390
Guthrie, H. W. (Lord), 488, 491
Guttman, E., 340

Halcrow, W. T., 185
Halifax, Lord, 57
Hall, G., 13
Hamilton, J. E., 444
Hancock, E., 300
Hancock, Miss F., 265
Handford, J. J. W., 105
Hankey, Lord, 219, 279
Hardman, D. R., 389, 413
Harris, P., 22
Harris, S. W., 499
Harvey, P. N., 291
Helmore, W., 213
Henderson, H. D., 435
Henderson, J. S., 106, 456, 481
Henderson, W. C., 118
Heneage, A. P., 114, 192
Hepburn, H. A., 271, 273, 274
Herbert, D., 6, 22
Herbert, E. S., 30
Herbert, R., 105
Hetherington, H. J. W., 259, 265, 297, 306
Heyworth, G., 188
Hill, F. G., 150, 343
Hilleary, E. L., 185
Hindley, H. O. R., 140
Hobday, S. R., 111
Hobhouse, A., 349, 350, 375, 378
Hodgson, E. H., 167
Holland, E. M., 167
Honeyman, G. G., 241
Hood, S. W., 345
Hopkins, R. V. N., 130, 140
Horder, Lord, 304
Horne, F. R., 87
Howitt, H. G., 35
Hubert, W. G. de B., 471
Hughes, R. M., 53, 249, 253, 500
Hunt, F. W., 270
Hurcomb, C., 54, 58
Hurst, G., 444
Hutchinson, A. S., 45
Hutchinson, J. R., 342
Hutson, L. W., 132, 357
Hutton, M., 64
Huxley, J. S., 376

Ince, G. H., 266
Inglis, C. E., 53
Isaacs, G. A., 234
Izard, G. G., 291

Jackson, E. J. W., 419

Jackson, H., 371
Jacob, G. H. L., 154
Jeffrey, J., 43
Jenkins, D., 489, 496
Jephcott, H., 343
Jobson, Miss M., 444
Johnson, F. C., 457, 471
Jolly, J. C., 456, 472
Jones, A. E. L., 457
Jones, J. H., 204
Jones, N. H., 271
Jones, W., 338
Jones, W. R., 137

Keddie, J. A. G., 335
Keith, J., 393, 418
Kennet, Lord, 61, 230, 231
Keynes, J. M. (Lord), 73
Kirkaldy, H. S., 243

Laidlaw, G. P., 347, 355
Law, R. K., 8
Lawson, J. J., 9
Lee, A. G., 291
Lemon, E., 128
Lewis-Faning, E., 437
Lindon, J. B., 167
Lindsay, H. B., 112, 313, 351
Lindsay, Lord, 43
Linstead, H. N., 58
Llewellin, Lord, 209
Lloyd, T. A., 371
Lloyd Jacob, G. H., 154
Loveday, T., 281, 407, 409
Lucas, Lord, 92
Luxmoore, F., 406
Lynskey, G. J., 24

Mabane, W., 45
McClelland, W., 391, 398, 404, 430
Macgregor, A. S. M., 95, 342
McIntyre, J. G. (Lord Sorn), 47, 51
Mackeson, H. R., 125
Mackintosh, C. (Lord), 491
Mackintosh, J. M., 331
Maclean, A., 364
MacMillan, Lord, 487
McNair, A. D., 417
McNair, W. L., 484
Maconochie, R. H., 108, 117
McTaggart, A., 353
Mance, H. O., 194
Manners, Miss E. G., 327
Markham, Miss V., 265
Massey, V., 429
Masterman, J. C., 35
Matthew, R. H., 371
Maude, H. J., 332
Maude, J. C., 476
Maxton, J. P., 88
Maxwell, A., 463, 481
Mersey, Lord, 12
Merthyr, Lord, 270
Messer, F., 309, 314
Metcalfe, F., 15, 502
Millbourn, P. E., 208
Milne, D., 44
Milne, Lord, 190
Milner, J., 12
Mitchell, M. E., 354
Molson, H., 203
Monckton, W., 298, 439

Montagu, E. E. S., 414
Morison, J., 485
Morris, J. W., 353, 482, 484
Morris, P. R., 402, 420
Morris, R. H., 57
Morrison, H., 17, 18, 20
Morton, Lord, 492
Moss, J., 279
Moyne, Lord, 142
Murrant, E. H., 209
Murray, D. K., 175

Nathan, Lord, 447
Neal, L., 365
Nelson, G. H., 129
Newsam, F. A., 465
Newson-Smith, F., 412
Newton, C. M., 212
Noel-Baker, P., 201
North, G., 428
Northumberland, Duke of, 104
Norwood, C., 401
Nugent, G. R. H., 203

Oake, G. R., 104
Oaksey, Lord, 468
O'Conor, Miss M., 335
Oldfield-Davies, A., 406
Oliver, D. A., 150
Oliver, G. H., 5
O'Neill, D., 209
Orr, J. B., 336

Pakenham, Lord, 211
Palache, A., 141
Parry, H. W., 493
Paterson, T., 356, 363
Penman, W., 321, 322, 323
Percy, Lord, 411
Perry, Lord, 94
Philip, J. R., 97, 432
Phillips, T. W., 134, 303
Pick, F., 129
Piercy, Lord, 99
Plant, A., 144
Platt, F., 137
Playfair, E. W., 44
Pole, F. J. C., 350
Porter, Lord, 494
Price, K., 151
Priestley, R. E., 38
Proctor, P. D., 44

Radcliffe, C. J. (Lord), 66, 142
Ramsay, J. D., 374, 377
Ramsden, Lord, 127
Ready, A. W., 405
Rees, J. F., 124, 136, 278
Rees-Thomas, W., 324
Reid, C. C., 176
Reid, T., 49
Reith, Lord, 372
Reynolds, B. J., 476
Ridley, Lord, 170, 360
Ritchie, J., 378
Robbins, L., 58
Roberts, Mrs. J., 444
Robinson, Mr., 305
Robinson, G., 335
Robinson, J. F., 78
Robinson, R. L., 109
Roche, Lord, 453
Rogers, H. R., 272, 273
Rosebery, Lord, 103

Roseveare, M. P., 419
Ross, W. D., 223
Runciman, Lord, 56
Rushcliffe, Lord, 324, 325, 464, 486
Rusholme, Lord, 198
Russell, Lord, 337
Ryan, J., 29

Sachs, E., 272
Safford, A., 320
St. Aldwyn, Lord, 109
Samuels, A., 55, 56
Savage, W. G., 345
Schuster, G., 373
Scott, L., 368
Seal, E. A., 135
Shakespeare, G., 305, 437, 438
Shawcross, H., 244
Shimmin, A. N., 255
Silkin, L., 352
Simes, E., 49
Simmonds, O., 131
Simon, E. D. (Lord), 133, 169, 250
Simonds, G. T., 451
Slade, G. O., 318
Smail, J. C., 410
Smith, H. W., 34, 125
Smith, S. A., 342
Smith, T., 8
Smith, W. R. V., 130
Snell, Lord, 471
Somervell, D., 494
Sorn, Lord, 47, 51
Sorsby, A., 335
Spens, P., 61
Spens, W., 292, 317, 321
Stainton, J., 486
Stanhope, Lord, 23
Steel, J., 314
Stewart, A. B., 88

Stewart, F. O., 470
Stewart, T. G., 419
Stocks, Mrs. M. D., 328
Stokes, R. R., 23
Straight, W., 211
Strauss, G. R., 201
Streat, E. R., 138
Strutt, H. A., 500
Sutherland, I. N., 339
Swan, K. R., 226

Taylor, C. W. G., 472
Taylor, T. M., 85, 397, 487
Taylor, W., 111, 261
Terrington, Lord, 217
Teviot, Lord, 309
Thesiger, G. A., 205
Thomas, B., 196
Thomas, E. L., 340
Thompson, F. L., 371
Thornton, W. M., 182
Threlkeld, T. P., 269
Tizard, H., 126
Tomlinson, G., 260
Topham, H., 271
Tucker, F. J. (Lord), 453, 462, 485
Tucker, J. M., 65, 71
Turner, G. W., 150
Turner, T., 182
Tweedsmuir, Lord, 434

Upjohn, G. R., 463
Urwick, L., 413
Uthwatt, A. A. (Lord), 366, 483, 488

Vandepeer, D., 76
Vaughan-Lee, A. G., 185
Viant, S. P., 8
Vick, G. R., 184, 475
Vivian, S. P., 3

Wade, E. C. S., 12, 502
Waleran, Lord, 205
Walkden, Lord, 193
Walker, R. B., 49
Wall, J. I., 501
Ward, A. F., 166
Ward, J. C., 447
Ward, L., 94
Ware, R. R., 80
Waters, A. H. S., 379, 380
Watkinson, H., 262
Watson, L. H., 113
Waverley, Lord, 115, 190, 432
Wedgwood, R. L., 498
Weeks, R. M., 412
Welsh, J., 348
Weston, W. G., 207, 208
Westwood, J., 10
Westwood, Lord, 149
Wethered, E. H. C., 167
Wheare, K. C., 445
White, H. G., 256
Whitley, H. C., 444
Wilcock, C. A. B., 214
Wilkinson, S. F., 358
Williams, G. G., 423
Williams, W. D. A., 96
Willink, H. U., 449, 483
Wilson, D. R., 268
Wilson, P. H. St. J., 239
Winterton, Lord, 22
Wolfenden, J. F., 393, 402
Wood, R., 326
Woods, C. R., 205
Woodward, F. N., 88

Young, R., 11
Younger, J. P., 341

Zuckerman, S., 87, 89, 423